1911 · PROCL··· · 986

PROCLAMER LA PAROLE DE DIEU

The Gideons International in Canada take pleasure in presenting this special edition of Scripture to you in celebration of our 75th anniversary. Since 1911, Canadian Gideons have placed over 25 million Scriptures throughout Canada and in other lands.

1911 - 1986

"Righteousness exalts a nation,
but sin is a disgrace to any people."
—*Proverbs 14:34*

*P*resented to

Laura Douglas
NAME

1441 Terrace AVE
ADDRESS

North Vancouver

B.C. V7R 1B5

980-1606 or 980-2150
~~DATE~~

August 86 (Expo 86

By

THE GIDEONS INTERNATIONAL
IN CANADA

501 IMPERIAL ROAD
GUELPH, ONTARIO N1H 7A2

> "THIS BOOK of the law shall not depart from your mouth, but you shall meditate on it day and night, so that you may be careful to do according to all that is written in it; for then you will make your way prosperous, and then you will have success."
>
> Joshua 1:8

THE GIDEONS INTERNATIONAL is an Association of Christian Business and Professional men, banded together in more than 130 countries for fellowship and the promotion of the Gospel of Jesus Christ to all races and creeds, to the end that all might come to a knowledge of the Lord Jesus Christ as their personal Saviour.

We have placed and distributed over 370 million Bibles or New Testaments in hotels, hospitals, penal institutions, public schools, and to school students and those in the nursing profession.

We are pleased to present to you this copy of the New Testament with Psalms and Proverbs and various helps, and trust you will find joy and satisfaction in reading this sacred Book.

THE GIDEONS INTERNATIONAL
IN CANADA

i

The Ten Commandments

    I. You shall have no other gods before Me.

   II. You shall not make for yourself an idol, or any likeness of what is in heaven above or on the earth beneath or in the water under the earth.

  III. You shall not take the name of the LORD your God in vain, for the LORD will not leave him unpunished who takes His name in vain.

  IV. Remember the sabbath day, to keep it holy.

   V. Honor your father and your mother, that your days may be prolonged in the land which the LORD your God gives you.

  VI. You shall not murder.

 VII. You shall not commit adultery.

VIII. You shall not steal.

  IX. You shall not bear false witness against your neighbor.

   X. You shall not covet your neighbor's house; you shall not covet your neighbor's wife or his male servant or his female servant or his ox or his donkey or anything that belongs to your neighbor.

Exodus 20:3–17

THIS BOOK

This book reveals the mind of God, the state of man, the way of salvation, the doom of sinners, and the happiness of believers.

Its doctrines are holy, its precepts are binding, its histories are true, and its decisions are immutable.

Read it to be wise: believe it to be safe, and practise it to be holy. It contains light to direct you, food to support you, and comfort to cheer you.

It is the traveller's map, the pilgrim's staff, the pilot's compass, the soldier's sword, and the Christian's charter. Here, too, heaven is opened, and the gates of hell disclosed.

Christ is its grand subject, our good its design, and the glory of God its end.

It should fill the memory, rule the heart, and guide the feet. Read it slowly, frequently, prayerfully. It is a mine of wealth, a paradise of glory, and a river of pleasure.

It is given you in life, will be opened at the judgment, and be remembered forever. It involves highest responsibility; will reward the greatest labour; and condemn all who trifle with its sacred contents.

Owned, it is riches; studied, it is wisdom; trusted, it is salvation; loved, it is character; and obeyed, it is power.

"Children, obey your parents in the Lord, for this is right. Honor your father and mother (which is the first commandment with a promise), that it may be well with you, and that you may live long on the earth."

Ephesians 6:1–3

"Seek the LORD while He may be found; Call upon Him while He is near. Let the wicked forsake his way, And the unrighteous man his thoughts; And let him return to the LORD, And He will have compassion on him; And to our God, For He will abundantly pardon."

Isaiah 55:6, 7

"I have set before you life and death . . . So choose life."

Deuteronomy 30:19

"Jesus said to him, 'I am the way, and the truth, and the life; no one comes to the Father, but through Me.'"

John 14:6

"Submit therefore to God. Resist the devil and he will flee from you."

James 4:7

"For I confess my iniquity; I am full of anxiety because of my sin."

Psalm 38:18

"If we confess our sins, He is faithful and righteous to forgive us our sins and to cleanse us from all unrighteousness."

1 John 1:9

"No temptation has overtaken you but such as is common to man; and God is faithful, who will not allow you to be tempted beyond what you are able, but with the temptation will provide the way of escape also, that you may be able to endure it."

1 Corinthians 10:13

"My son, if sinners entice you, Do not consent."

Proverbs 1:10

"The things impossible with men are possible with God."

Luke 18:27

"But if any of you lacks wisdom, let him ask of God, who gives to all men generously and without reproach, and it will be given to him."

James 1:5

"Trust in the LORD with all your heart, And do not lean on your own understanding. In all your ways acknowledge Him, And He will make your paths straight."

Proverbs 3:5, 6

"Yet those who wait for the LORD will gain new strength."

Isaiah 40:31

"All Scripture is inspired by God and profitable for teaching, for reproof, for correction, for training in righteousness."

2 Timothy 3:16

This Book is given to you with only one request—that you read it every day.

The boy who promised

Many years ago, John Nicholson, a boy aged 13, promised his mother, who gave him her Bible, that he would read a portion of it every day of his life. John kept that promise—for 73 years.

God's blessing followed

And God blessed John Nicholson greatly throughout his life, for God has promised to honour and bless those who read His Word. It was through John's faithfulness in reading his Bible when he had to share a hotel bedroom with another traveller that they decided to form the Gideon Association, resulting in the placing or distributing of over 150 million Bibles or Testaments.

Will you promise?

It is because John kept his promise many years ago that you have been given this New Testament. So will *you* read it, too? Will you promise to read a portion of God's Word every day of *your* life? If you will, God will bless you as He blessed John Nicholson.

The daily readings provided on the next few pages will guide you in systematically reading this entire Book. It is designed as a two-year program of approximately one page each day. If you wish to read this Book in one year, use the program for the first year in the morning and the program for the second year in the evening. Some persons may prefer to repeat the first year, which includes the four Gospels and the Acts, before beginning the second year's program to complete the New Testament.

Read regularly each day. Don't rush too far ahead and then stop.

Read at the same time each day. Irregular reading will not last. Early in the morning is usually the best time.

Read carefully and slowly. Read intelligently. Meditate on the meaning. If you wish, mark any word, line, or verse, neatly with a brief note alongside.

Read prayerfully. Pray before you read and afterwards. Ask God to open your mind to understand His Word. Ask Him to reveal to you Jesus Christ as Saviour and Lord.

Further readings for the whole Bible also are available. For information, write to the Gideons:

THE GIDEONS INTERNATIONAL
IN CANADA

501 IMPERIAL ROAD
GUELPH, ONTARIO N1H 7A2

DAILY READINGS

JANUARY

Matthew

1	1:1—25
2	2:1—15
3	2:16—3:6
4	3:7—17
5	4:1—17
6	4:18—5:16
7	5:17—32
8	5:33—48
9	6:1—23
10	6:24—7:12
11	7:13—29
12	8:1—22
13	8:23—9:8
14	9:9—26
15	9:27—38
16	10:1—15
17	10:16—42
18	11:1—19
19	11:20—30
20	12:1—21
21	12:22—37
22	12:38—50
23	13:1—17
24	13:18—32
25	13:33—46
26	13:47—58
27	14:1—14
28	14:15—36
29	15:1—20
30	15:21—39
31	16:1—12

FEBRUARY

Matthew

1	16:13—28
2	17:1—13
3	17:14—27
4	18:1—14
5	18:15—35
6	19:1—12
7	19:13—30
8	20:1—16
9	20:17—34
10	21:1—16
11	21:17—32
12	21:33—46
13	22:1—10
14	22:11—22
15	22:23—46
16	23:1—22
17	23:23—39
18	24:1—14
19	24:15—28
20	24:29—51
21	25:1—13
22	25:14—30
23	25:31—46
24	26:1—16
25	26:17—35
26	26:36—46
27	26:47—56
28	26:57—75

MARCH

Matthew

1	27:1—18
2	27:19—33
3	27:34—49
4	27:50—66
5	28:1—20

Psalms

6	1 & 2
7	3 & 4
8	5:1—12
9	6:1—10
10	7:1—17
11	8:1—9
12	9:1—20
13	10:1—18

Proverbs

14	1:1—19
15	1:20—33
16	2:1—22

Mark

17	1:1—13
18	1:14—28
19	1:29—45
20	2:1—14
21	2:15—28
22	3:1—13
23	3:14—35
24	4:1—25
25	4:26—41
26	5:1—17
27	5:18—36

DAILY READINGS

DAILY READINGS

2 Corinthians

22	1:1—11
23	1:12—24
24	2:1—17
25	3:1—18
26	4:1—18
27	5:1—11
28	5:12—21
29	6:1—18
30	7:1—16
31	8:1—24

APRIL

2 Corinthians

1	9:1—15
2	10:1—18
3	11:1—17
4	11:18—33
5	12:1—21
6	13:1—14

Psalms

7	68:1—16
8	68:17—35
9	69:1—15
10	69:16—36
11	70:1—5
12	71:1—24

Proverbs

13	13:1—25
14	14:1—15
15	14:16—35

Galatians

16	1:1—12
17	1:13—24
18	2:1—10
19	2:11—21
20	3:1—14
21	3:15—29
22	4:1—14
23	4:15—31
24	5:1—10
25	5:11—26
26	6:1—18

Psalms

27	72:1—20
28	73:1—28
29	74:1—23
30	75:1—10

MAY

Ephesians

1	1:1—14
2	1:15—23
3	2:1—9
4	2:10—22
5	3:1—21
6	4:1—16
7	4:17—32
8	5:1—16
9	5:17—33
10	6:1—12
11	6:13—24

Psalms

12	76:1—12

13	77:1—20
14	78:1—24
15	78:25—49
16	78:50—72
17	79:1—13
18	80:1—19

Proverbs

19	15:1—16
20	15:17—33

Philippians

21	1:1—14
22	1:15—30
23	2:1—13
24	2:14—30
25	3:1—21
26	4:1—13
27	4:14—23

Psalms

28	81:1—16
29	82:1—8
30	83:1—18
31	84:1—12

JUNE

Proverbs

1	16:1—16
2	16:17—33

Colossians

3	1:1—17
4	1:18—29

DAILY READINGS

WHERE TO FIND HELP WHEN:

WHERE TO FIND HELP WHEN:

Teachings of Jesus Christ

CHRISTIAN VIRTUES

SUGGESTED READINGS

Suggested Readings

NATIONAL ANTHEMS

GOD SAVE THE QUEEN

God save our gracious Queen,
Long live our noble Queen,
God save the Queen;
Send her victorious,
Happy and glorious,
Long to reign over us,
God save the Queen.

O CANADA

O Canada! Our home and native land!
True patriot love in all thy sons command.
With glowing hearts we see thee rise,
The True North strong and free!
From far and wide, O Canada,
We stand on guard for thee.

Chorus
God keep our land glorious and free!
O Canada, we stand on guard for thee.
O Canada, we stand on guard for thee.

THE
NEW TESTAMENT
OF OUR LORD AND SAVIOUR
JESUS CHRIST
WITH PSALMS AND PROVERBS

*The New American Standard Bible
translated from the original languages
into contemporary English.*

THE GIDEONS INTERNATIONAL
In Canada

1985 EDITION

Printed & bound
in Canada by
RBW GRAPHICS

3 4 5 6 7 8 9 10 11 12/87 86 85

SCRIPTURAL PROMISE

"The grass withers, the flower fades, but the word of our God stands forever." Isaiah 40:8

FOURFOLD AIM
OF
THE LOCKMAN FOUNDATION

1. These publications shall be true to the original Hebrew, Aramaic, and Greek.

2. They shall be grammatically correct.

3. They shall be understandable to the masses.

4. They shall give the Lord Jesus Christ His proper place, the place which the Word gives Him; therefore, no work will ever be personalized.

FOREWORD

The New American Standard Bible has been produced with the conviction that the words of Scripture as originally penned in the Hebrew, Aramaic, and Greek were inspired by God. Since they are the eternal Word of God, the Holy Scriptures speak with fresh power to each generation, to give wisdom that leads to salvation, that men may serve Christ to the glory of God.

The Editorial Board had a twofold purpose in making this translation: to adhere as closely as possible to the original languages of the Holy Scriptures, and to make the translation in a fluent and readable style according to current English usage.

PREFACE TO THE
NEW AMERICAN STANDARD BIBLE

In the history of English Bible translations, the King James Version is the most prestigious. This time-honored version of 1611, itself a revision of the Bishops' Bible of 1568, became the basis for the English Revised Version appearing in 1881 (New Testament) and 1885 (Old Testament). The American counterpart of this last work was published in 1901 as the American Standard Version. Recognizing the values of the American Standard Version, the Lockman Foundation felt an urgency to update it by incorporating recent discoveries of Hebrew and Greek textual sources and by rendering it into more current English. Therefore, in 1959 a new translation project was launched, based on the ASV. The result is the New American Standard Bible.

The American Standard Version (1901) has been highly regarded for its scholarship and accuracy. A product of both British and American scholarship, it has frequently been used as a standard for other translations. It is still recognized as a valuable tool for study of the Scriptures. The New American Standard Bible has sought to preserve these and other lasting values of the ASV.

Furthermore, in the preparation of this work numerous other translations have been consulted along with the linguistic tools and literature of biblical scholarship. Decisions about English renderings were made by consensus of a team composed of educators and pastors. Subsequently, review and evaluation by other Hebrew and Greek scholars outside the Editorial Board were sought and carefully considered.

The Editorial Board has continued to function since publication of the complete Bible in 1971. Minor revisions and refinements, recommended over the last several years, are presented in this edition.

Explanation of
GENERAL FORMAT

FOOTNOTES are used only where the text especially requires them for clarification. Marginal notes and cross references have been deleted from this edition.

PARAGRAPHS are designated with bold face numbers or letters.

QUOTATION MARKS are used in the text in accordance with modern English usage.

"THOU," "THEE" AND "THY" are not used in this translation except in the language of prayer when addressing Deity.

PERSONAL PRONOUNS are capitalized when pertaining to Deity.

ITALICS are used in the text to indicate words which are not found in the original Hebrew, Aramaic, or Greek but implied by it. Italics are used in the footnotes to signify alternate readings for the text.

SMALL CAPS in the New Testament are used in the text to indicate Old Testament quotations or obvious allusions to Old Testament texts. Variations of Old Testament wording are found in New Testament citations depending on whether the New Testament writer translated from a Hebrew text, used existing Greek or Aramaic translations, or paraphrased the material. It should be noted that modern rules for the indication of direct quotation were not used in biblical times thus allowing freedom for omissions or insertions without specific indication of these.

ASTERISKS are used to mark verbs that are historical presents in the Greek which have been translated with an English past tense in order to conform to modern usage. The translators recognized that in some contexts the present tense seems more unexpected and unjustified to the English reader than a past tense would have been. But Greek authors frequently used the present tense for the sake of heightened vividness, thereby transporting their readers in imagination to the actual scene at the time of occurrence. However, the translators felt that it would be wise to change these historical presents to English past tenses.

Books of the New Testament

THE GOSPEL ACCORDING TO

MATTHEW

THE book of the genealogy of Jesus Christ, the son of David, the son of Abraham.

2 To Abraham was born Isaac; and to Isaac, Jacob; and to Jacob, [1]Judah and his brothers;

3 and to Judah were born Perez and Zerah by Tamar; and to Perez was born Hezron; and to Hezron, Ram;

4 and to Ram was born Amminadab; and to Amminadab, Nahshon; and to Nahshon, Salmon;

5 and to Salmon was born Boaz by Rahab; and to Boaz was born Obed by Ruth; and to Obed, Jesse;

6 and to Jesse was born David the king.

And to David was born Solomon by her *who had been the wife* of Uriah;

7 and to Solomon was born Rehoboam; and to Rehoboam, Abijah; and to Abijah, Asa;

8 and to Asa was born Jehoshaphat; and to Jehoshaphat, Joram; and to Joram, Uzziah;

9 and to Uzziah was born Jotham; and to Jotham, Ahaz; and to Ahaz, Hezekiah;

10 and to Hezekiah was born Manasseh; and to Manasseh, Amon; and to Amon, Josiah;

11 and to Josiah were born Jeconiah and his brothers, at the time of the deportation to Babylon.

12 And after the deportation to Babylon, to Jeconiah was born Shealtiel; and to Shealtiel, Zerubbabel;

13 and to Zerubbabel was born Abiud; and to Abiud, Eliakim; and to Eliakim, Azor;

14 and to Azor was born Zadok; and to Zadok, Achim; and to Achim, Eliud;

15 and to Eliud was born Eleazar; and to Eleazar, Matthan; and to Matthan, Jacob;

16 and to Jacob was born Joseph the husband of Mary, by whom was born Jesus, who is called Christ.

17 Therefore all the generations from Abraham to David are fourteen generations; and from David to the deportation to Babylon fourteen generations; and from the deportation to Babylon to *the time of* Christ fourteen generations.

18 Now the birth of Jesus Christ was as follows. When His mother Mary had been betrothed to Joseph, before they came together she was found to be with child by the Holy Spirit.

19 And Joseph her husband, being a righteous man, and not wanting to disgrace her, desired [2]to put her away secretly.

20 But when he had considered this, behold, an angel of the Lord appeared to him in a dream, saying, "Joseph, son of David, do not be afraid to take Mary as your wife; for that which has been [3]conceived in her is of the Holy Spirit.

21 "And she will bear a Son; and

---

[1] Gr., *Judas*. Names of Old Testament characters will be given in their Old Testament form.   [2] Or, *to divorce her*
[3] Lit., *begotten*

you shall call His name Jesus, for it is He who will save His people from their sins."

22 Now all this took place that what was spoken by the Lord through the prophet might be fulfilled, saying,

23 "BEHOLD, THE VIRGIN SHALL BE WITH CHILD, AND SHALL BEAR A SON, AND THEY SHALL CALL HIS NAME IMMANUEL," which translated means, "GOD WITH US."

24 And Joseph arose from his sleep, and did as the angel of the Lord commanded him, and took *her* as his wife,

25 and [4]kept her a virgin until she gave birth to a Son; and he called His name Jesus.

CHAPTER 2

NOW after Jesus was born in Bethlehem of Judea in the days of Herod the king, behold, [5]magi from the east arrived in Jerusalem, saying,

2 "Where is He who has been born King of the Jews? For we saw His star in the east, and have come to worship Him."

3 And when Herod the king heard it, he was troubled, and all Jerusalem with him.

4 And gathering together all the chief priests and scribes of the people, he *began* to inquire of them where the Christ was to be born.

5 And they said to him, "In Bethlehem of Judea, for so it has been written by the prophet,

6 'AND YOU, BETHLEHEM,
    LAND OF JUDAH,
  ARE BY NO MEANS LEAST
    AMONG THE LEADERS OF
    JUDAH;
  FOR OUT OF YOU SHALL
    COME FORTH A RULER,

WHO WILL SHEPHERD MY
    PEOPLE ISRAEL.' "

7 Then Herod secretly called the magi, and ascertained from them the time the star appeared.

8 And he sent them to Bethlehem, and said, "Go and make careful search for the Child; and when you have found *Him*, report to me, that I too may come and worship Him."

9 And having heard the king, they went their way; and lo, the star, which they had seen in the east, went on before them, until it came and stood over where the Child was.

10 And when they saw the star, they rejoiced exceedingly with great joy.

11 And they came into the house and saw the Child with Mary His mother; and they fell down and worshiped Him; and opening their treasures they presented to Him gifts of gold and frankincense and myrrh.

12 And having been warned *by God* in a dream not to return to Herod, they departed for their own country by another way.

13 Now when they had departed, behold, an angel of the Lord *appeared to Joseph in a dream, saying, "Arise and take the Child and His mother, and flee to Egypt, and remain there until I tell you; for Herod is going to search for the Child to destroy Him."

14 And he arose and took the Child and His mother by night, and departed for Egypt;

15 and was there until the death of Herod, that what was

---

4 Lit., *was not knowing her*
5 Pronounced may-ji, a caste of wise men specializing in astrology, medicine and natural science

spoken by the Lord through the prophet might be fulfilled, saying, "Out of Egypt did I call My Son."

16 Then when Herod saw that he had been tricked by the magi, he became very enraged, and sent and slew all the male children who were in Bethlehem and in all its environs, from two years old and under, according to the time which he had ascertained from the magi.

17 Then that which was spoken through Jeremiah the prophet was fulfilled, saying,

18 "A voice was heard in Ra-
      mah,
      Weeping and great
        mourning,
      Rachel weeping for her
        children;
      And she refused to be
        comforted,
      Because they were no
        more."

19 But when Herod was dead, behold, an angel of the Lord *appeared in a dream to Joseph in Egypt, saying,

20"Arise and take the Child and His mother, and go into the land of Israel; for those who sought the Child's life are dead."

21 And he arose and took the Child and His mother, and came into the land of Israel.

22 But when he heard that Archelaus was reigning over Judea in place of his father Herod, he was afraid to go there. And being warned by God in a dream, he departed for the regions of Galilee,

23 and came and resided in a city called Nazareth, that what was spoken through the prophets might be fulfilled, "He shall be called a Nazarene."

CHAPTER 3

NOW in those days John the Baptist *came, preaching in the wilderness of Judea, saying,

2"Repent, for the kingdom of heaven is at hand."

3 For this is the one referred to by Isaiah the prophet, saying,

    "The voice of one crying
      in the wilderness,
      'Make ready the way of
        the Lord,
        Make   His   paths
          straight!' "

4 Now John himself had a garment of camel's hair, and a leather belt about his waist; and his food was locusts and wild honey.

5 Then Jerusalem was going out to him, and all Judea, and all the district around the Jordan;

6 and they were being baptized by him in the Jordan River, as they confessed their sins.

7 But when he saw many of the Pharisees and Sadducees coming for baptism, he said to them, "You brood of vipers, who warned you to flee from the wrath to come?

8"Therefore bring forth fruit in keeping with repentance;

9 and do not suppose that you can say to yourselves, 'We have Abraham for our father'; for I say to you, that God is able from these stones to raise up children to Abraham.

10"And the axe is already laid at the root of the trees; every tree therefore that does not bear good fruit is cut down and thrown into the fire.

11"As for me, I baptize you

⁶with water for repentance, but He who is coming after me is mightier than I, and I am not fit to remove His sandals; He will baptize you with the Holy Spirit and fire.

12"And His winnowing fork is in His hand, and He will thoroughly clear His threshing floor; and He will gather His wheat into the barn, but He will burn up the chaff with unquenchable fire."

13 Then Jesus *arrived from Galilee at the Jordan *coming* to John, to be baptized by him.

14 But John tried to prevent Him, saying, "I have need to be baptized by You, and do You come to me?"

15 But Jesus answering said to him, "Permit *it* at this time; for in this way it is fitting for us to fulfill all righteousness." Then he *permitted Him.

16 And after being baptized, Jesus went up immediately from the water; and behold, the heavens were opened, and he saw the Spirit of God descending as a dove, *and* coming upon Him,

17 and behold, a voice out of the heavens, saying, "This is ⁷My beloved Son, in whom I am well-pleased."

CHAPTER 4

THEN Jesus was led up by the Spirit into the wilderness to be tempted by the devil.

2 And after He had fasted forty days and forty nights, He ⁸then became hungry.

3 And the tempter came and said to Him, "If You are the Son of God, command that these stones become bread."

4 But He answered and said, "It is written, 'MAN SHALL NOT

LIVE ON BREAD ALONE, BUT ON EVERY WORD THAT PROCEEDS OUT OF THE MOUTH OF GOD.'"

5 Then the devil *took Him into the holy city; and he had Him stand on the pinnacle of the temple,

6 and *said to Him, "If You are the Son of God throw Yourself down; for it is written,

'HE WILL GIVE HIS ANGELS
        CHARGE   CONCERNING
        YOU';
and

'ON *their* HANDS THEY WILL
        BEAR YOU UP,
    LEST YOU STRIKE YOUR
        FOOT AGAINST A STONE.'"

7 Jesus said to him, "On the other hand, it is written, 'YOU SHALL NOT ⁹PUT THE LORD YOUR GOD TO THE TEST.'"

8 Again, the devil *took Him to a very high mountain, and *showed Him all the kingdoms of the world, and their glory;

9 and he said to Him, "All these things will I give You, if You fall down and worship me."

10 Then Jesus *said to him, "Begone, Satan! For it is written, 'YOU SHALL WORSHIP THE LORD YOUR GOD, AND SERVE HIM ONLY.'"

11 Then the devil *left Him; and behold, angels came and *began to minister to Him.

12 Now when He heard that John had been taken into custody, He withdrew into Galilee;

13 and leaving Nazareth, He came and settled in Capernaum, which is by the sea, in the region of Zebulun and Naphtali.

14 *This was* to fulfill what was

---

⁶ The Gr. here can be translated *in, with* or *by*   ⁷ Lit., *My Son, the Beloved*
⁸ Lit., *later, afterward*   ⁹ Or, *tempt . . . God*

spoken through Isaiah the prophet, saying,

15 "THE LAND OF ZEBULUN AND
    THE LAND OF NAPHTALI,
    BY THE WAY OF THE SEA,
    BEYOND THE JORDAN,
    GALILEE OF THE [10]GEN-
    TILES—

16 "THE PEOPLE WHO WERE SIT-
    TING IN DARKNESS SAW A
    GREAT LIGHT,
    AND TO THOSE WHO WERE
    SITTING IN THE LAND AND
    SHADOW OF DEATH,
    UPON THEM A LIGHT
    DAWNED."

17 From that time Jesus began to preach and say, "Repent, for the kingdom of heaven is at hand."

18 And walking by the Sea of Galilee, He saw two brothers, Simon who was called Peter, and Andrew his brother, casting a net into the sea; for they were fishermen.

19 And He *said to them, "Follow Me, and I will make you fishers of men."

20 And they immediately left the nets, and followed Him.

21 And going on from there He saw two other brothers, James the son of Zebedee, and John his brother, in the boat with Zebedee their father, mending their nets; and He called them.

22 And they immediately left the boat and their father, and followed Him.

23 And Jesus was going about in all Galilee, teaching in their synagogues, and proclaiming the gospel of the kingdom, and healing every kind of disease and every kind of sickness among the people.

24 And the news about Him went out into all Syria; and they brought to Him all who were ill, taken with various diseases and pains, demoniacs, epileptics, paralytics; and He healed them.

25 And great multitudes followed Him from Galilee and Decapolis and Jerusalem and Judea and from beyond the Jordan.

CHAPTER 5

AND when He saw the multitudes, He went up on the mountain; and after He sat down, His disciples came to Him.

2 And opening His mouth He began to teach them, saying,

3 "Blessed are the poor in spirit, for theirs is the kingdom of heaven.

4 "Blessed are those who mourn, for they shall be comforted.

5 "Blessed are the [11]gentle, for they shall inherit the earth.

6 "Blessed are those who hunger and thirst for righteousness, for they shall be satisfied.

7 "Blessed are the merciful, for they shall receive mercy.

8 "Blessed are the pure in heart, for they shall see God.

9 "Blessed are the peacemakers, for they shall be called sons of God.

10 "Blessed are those who have been persecuted for the sake of righteousness, for theirs is the kingdom of heaven.

11 "Blessed are you when men cast insults at you, and persecute you, and say all kinds of evil against you falsely, on account of Me.

12 "Rejoice, and be glad, for your reward in heaven is great, for so they persecuted the prophets who were before you.

[10] Or, nations　[11] Or, humble, meek

13 "You are the salt of the earth; but if the salt has become tasteless, how will it be made salty *again*? It is good for nothing anymore, except to be thrown out and trampled under foot by men.

14 "You are the light of the world. A city set on a hill cannot be hidden.

15 "Nor do *men* light a lamp, and put it under the peck-measure, but on the lampstand; and it gives light to all who are in the house.

16 "Let your light shine before men in such a way that they may see your good works, and glorify your Father who is in heaven.

17 "Do not think that I came to abolish the Law or the Prophets; I did not come to abolish, but to fulfill.

18 "For truly I say to you, until heaven and earth pass away, not the smallest letter or stroke shall pass away from the Law, until all is accomplished.

19 "Whoever then annuls one of the least of these commandments, and so teaches others, shall be called least in the kingdom of heaven; but whoever keeps and teaches *them*, he shall be called great in the kingdom of heaven.

20 "For I say to you, that unless your righteousness surpasses *that* of the scribes and Pharisees, you shall not enter the kingdom of heaven.

21 "You have heard that the ancients were told, 'YOU SHALL NOT COMMIT MURDER' and 'Whoever commits murder shall be 12liable to the court.'

22 "But I say to you that everyone who is angry with his brother13 shall be guilty before the court; and whoever shall say to his brother, '14Raca,' shall be guilty before 15the supreme court; and whoever shall say, 'You fool,' shall be guilty *enough to go* into the 16fiery hell.

23 "If therefore you are presenting your offering at the altar, and there remember that your brother has something against you,

24 leave your offering there before the altar, and go your way; first be reconciled to your brother, and then come and present your offering.

25 "Make friends quickly with your opponent at law while you are with him on the way, in order that your opponent may not deliver you to the judge, and the judge to the officer, and you be thrown into prison.

26 "Truly I say to you, you shall not come out of there, until you have paid up the last 17cent.

27 "You have heard that it was said, 'YOU SHALL NOT COMMIT ADULTERY';

28 but I say to you, that everyone who looks on a woman to lust for her has committed adultery with her already in his heart.

29 "And if your right eye makes you stumble, tear it out, and throw it from you; for it is better for you that one of the parts of your body perish, than for your whole body to be thrown into hell.

30 "And if your right hand makes you stumble, cut it off, and throw it from you; for it is better for you that one of the

---

12 Or, *guilty before*
13 Some mss. insert here: *without cause*
14 Aramaic for *empty-head* or, *good for nothing*   15 Lit., *the Sanhedrin*
16 Lit., *Gehenna of fire*
17 Lit., *quadrans* (equaling two lepta or mites), i.e., 1/64 of a denarius

parts of your body perish, than for your whole body to go into hell.

31 "And it was said, 'WHOEVER DIVORCES HIS WIFE, LET HIM GIVE HER A CERTIFICATE OF DISMISSAL';

32 but I say to you that everyone who divorces his wife, except for *the* cause of unchastity, makes her commit adultery; and whoever marries a divorced woman commits adultery.

33 "Again, you have heard that the ancients were told, 'YOU SHALL NOT MAKE FALSE VOWS, BUT SHALL FULFILL YOUR VOWS TO THE LORD.'

34 "But I say to you, make no oath at all, either by heaven, for it is the throne of God,

35 or by the earth, for it is the footstool of His feet, or by Jerusalem, for it is THE CITY OF THE GREAT KING.

36 "Nor shall you make an oath by your head, for you cannot make one hair white or black.

37 "But let your statement be, 'Yes, yes' *or* 'No, no'; and anything beyond these is of evil.

38 "You have heard that it was said, 'AN EYE FOR AN EYE, AND A TOOTH FOR A TOOTH.'

39 "But I say to you, do not resist him who is evil; but whoever slaps you on your right cheek, turn to him the other also.

40 "And if anyone wants to sue you, and take your [18]shirt, let him have your [19]coat also.

41 "And whoever shall force you to go one mile, go with him two.

42 "Give to him who asks of you, and do not turn away from him who wants to borrow from you.

43 "You have heard that it was said, 'YOU SHALL LOVE YOUR NEIGHBOR, and hate your enemy.'

44 "But I say to you, love your enemies, and pray for those who persecute you

45 in order that you may be sons of your Father who is in heaven; for He causes His sun to rise on *the* evil and *the* good, and sends rain on *the* righteous and *the* unrighteous.

46 "For if you love those who love you, what reward have you? Do not even the tax-gatherers do the same?

47 "And if you greet your brothers only, what do you do more *than others*? Do not even the Gentiles do the same?

48 "Therefore you are to be perfect, as your heavenly Father is perfect.

CHAPTER 6

"BEWARE of practicing your righteousness before men to be noticed by them; otherwise you have no reward with your Father who is in heaven.

2 "When therefore you give alms, do not sound a trumpet before you, as the hypocrites do in the synagogues and in the streets, that they may be honored by men. Truly I say to you, they have their reward in full.

3 "But when you give alms, do not let your left hand know what your right hand is doing

4 that your alms may be in secret; and your Father who sees in secret will repay you.

5 "And when you pray, you are not to be as the hypocrites; for they love to stand and pray in the synagogues and on the street corners, in order to be seen by

---

18 Or, *tunic*; i.e., garment worn next to the body   19 Or, *cloak*; i.e., outer garment

men. Truly I say to you, they have their reward in full.

6"But you, when you pray, go into your inner room, and when you have shut your door, pray to your Father who is in secret, and your Father who sees in secret will repay you.

7"And when you are praying, do not use meaningless repetition, as the Gentiles do, for they suppose that they will be heard for their many words.

8"Therefore do not be like them; for your Father knows what you need, before you ask Him.

9"Pray, then, in this way:
'Our Father who art in heaven,
Hallowed be Thy name.
10 Thy kingdom come.
Thy will be done,
On earth as it is in heaven.
11 'Give us this day our daily bread.
12 'And forgive us our debts, as we also have forgiven our debtors.
13 'And do not lead us into temptation, but deliver us from evil. [For Thine is the kingdom, and the power, and the glory, forever. Amen.]'

14"For if you forgive men for their transgressions, your heavenly Father will also forgive you.

15"But if you do not forgive men, then your Father will not forgive your transgressions.

16"And whenever you fast, do not put on a gloomy face as the hypocrites do, for they neglect their appearance in order to be seen fasting by men. Truly I say to you, they have their reward in full.

17"But you, when you fast, anoint your head, and wash your face

18 so that you may not be seen fasting by men, but by your Father who is in secret; and your Father who sees in secret will repay you.

19"Do not lay up for yourselves treasures upon earth, where moth and rust destroy, and where thieves break in and steal.

20"But lay up for yourselves treasures in heaven, where neither moth nor rust destroys, and where thieves do not break in or steal;

21 for where your treasure is, there will your heart be also.

22"The lamp of the body is the eye; if therefore your eye is clear, your whole body will be full of light.

23"But if your eye is bad, your whole body will be full of darkness. If therefore the light that is in you is darkness, how great is the darkness!

24"No one can serve two masters; for either he will hate the one and love the other, or he will hold to one and despise the other. You cannot serve God and 20mammon.

25"For this reason I say to you, do not be anxious for your life, *as to* what you shall eat, or what you shall drink; nor for your body, *as to* what you shall put on. Is not life more than food, and the body than clothing?

26"Look at the birds of the air, that they do not sow, neither do they reap, nor gather into barns, and *yet* your heavenly Father feeds them. Are you not worth much more than they?

20 Or, riches

27"And which of you by being anxious can add a *single* cubit to his life's span?

28"And why are you anxious about clothing? Observe how the lilies of the field grow; they do not toil nor do they spin,

29 yet I say to you that even Solomon in all his glory did not clothe himself like one of these.

30"But if God so arrays the grass of the field, which is *alive* today and tomorrow is thrown into the furnace, *will* He not much more *do so for* you, O men of little faith?

31"Do not be anxious then, saying, 'What shall we eat?' or 'What shall we drink?' or 'With what shall we clothe ourselves?'

32"For all these things the Gentiles eagerly seek; for your heavenly Father knows that you need all these things.

33"But seek first His kingdom and His righteousness; and all these things shall be added to you.

34"Therefore do not be anxious for tomorrow; for tomorrow will care for itself. *Each* day has enough trouble of its own.

CHAPTER 7

"DO not judge lest you be judged.

2"For in the way you judge, you will be judged; and by your standard of measure, it will be measured to you.

3"And why do you look at the speck that is in your brother's eye, but do not notice the log that is in your own eye?

4"Or how can you say to your brother, 'Let me take the speck out of your eye,' and behold, the log is in your own eye?

5"You hypocrite, first take the log out of your own eye, and then you will see clearly to take the speck out of your brother's eye.

6"Do not give what is holy to dogs, and do not throw your pearls before swine, lest they trample them under their feet, and turn and tear you to pieces.

7"Ask, and it shall be given to you; seek, and you shall find; knock, and it shall be opened to you.

8"For everyone who asks receives, and he who seeks finds, and to him who knocks it shall be opened.

9"Or what man is there among you, when his son shall ask him for a loaf, will give him a stone?

10"Or if he shall ask for a fish, he will not give him a snake, will he?

11"If you then, being evil, know how to give good gifts to your children, how much more shall your Father who is in heaven give what is good to those who ask Him!

12"Therefore, however you want people to treat you, so treat them, for this is the Law and the Prophets.

13"Enter by the narrow gate; for the gate is wide, and the way is broad that leads to destruction, and many are those who enter by it.

14"For the gate is small, and the way is narrow that leads to life, and few are those who find it.

15"Beware of the false prophets, who come to you in sheep's clothing, but inwardly are ravenous wolves.

16"You will know them by their fruits. Grapes are not gathered from thorn *bushes*, nor figs from thistles, are they?

17"Even so, every good tree bears good fruit; but the bad tree bears bad fruit.

18"A good tree cannot produce bad fruit, nor can a bad tree produce good fruit.

19"Every tree that does not bear good fruit is cut down and thrown into the fire.

20"So then, you will know them by their fruits.

21"Not everyone who says to Me, 'Lord, Lord,' will enter the kingdom of heaven; but he who does the will of My Father who is in heaven.

22"Many will say to Me on that day, 'Lord, Lord, did we not prophesy in Your name, and in Your name cast out demons, and in Your name perform many miracles?'

23"And then I will declare to them, 'I never knew you; DEPART FROM ME, YOU WHO PRACTICE LAWLESSNESS.'

24"Therefore everyone who hears these words of Mine, and acts upon them, may be compared to a wise man, who built his house upon the rock.

25"And the rain descended, and the floods came, and the winds blew, and burst against that house; and *yet* it did not fall, for it had been founded upon the rock.

26"And everyone who hears these words of Mine, and does not act upon them, will be like a foolish man, who built his house upon the sand.

27"And the rain descended, and the floods came, and the winds blew, and burst against that house; and it fell, and great was its fall."

28 The result was that when Jesus had finished these words, the multitudes were amazed at His teaching;

29 for He was teaching them as *one* having authority, and not as their scribes.

CHAPTER 8

AND when He had come down from the mountain, great multitudes followed Him.

2 And behold, a leper came to Him, and bowed down to Him, saying, "Lord, if You are willing, You can make me clean."

3 And He stretched out His hand and touched him, saying, "I am willing; be cleansed." And immediately his leprosy was cleansed.

4 And Jesus *said to him, "See that you tell no one; but go, show yourself to the priest, and present the offering that Moses commanded, for a testimony to them."

5 And when He had entered Capernaum, a centurion came to Him, entreating Him,

6 and saying, "Lord, my servant is lying paralyzed at home, suffering great pain."

7 And He *said to him, "I will come and heal him."

8 But the centurion answered and said, "Lord, I am not worthy for You to come under my roof, but just say the word, and my servant will be healed.

9"For I, too, am a man under authority, with soldiers under me; and I say to this one, 'Go!' and he goes, and to another, 'Come!' and he comes, and to my slave, 'Do this!' and he does *it*."

10 Now when Jesus heard *this*, He marveled, and said to those

MATTHEW 8

who were following, "Truly I say to you, I have not found such great faith with anyone in Israel.

11 "And I say to you, that many shall come from east and west, and 21recline *at the table* with Abraham, and Isaac, and Jacob, in the kingdom of heaven;

12 but the sons of the kingdom shall be cast out into the outer darkness; in that place there shall be weeping and gnashing of teeth."

13 And Jesus said to the centurion, "Go your way; let it be done to you as you have believed." And the servant was healed that *very* hour.

14 And when Jesus had come to Peter's home, He saw his mother-in-law lying sick in bed with a fever.

15 And He touched her hand, and the fever left her; and she arose, and waited on Him.

16 And when evening had come, they brought to Him many who were demon-possessed; and He cast out the spirits with a word, and healed all who were ill

17 in order that what was spoken through Isaiah the prophet might be fulfilled, saying, "HE HIMSELF TOOK OUR INFIRMITIES, AND CARRIED AWAY OUR DISEASES."

18 Now when Jesus saw a crowd around Him, He gave orders to depart to the other side.

19 And a certain scribe came and said to Him, "Teacher, I will follow You wherever You go."

20 And Jesus *said to him, "The foxes have holes, and the birds of the air *have* nests; but the Son of Man has nowhere to lay His head."

21 And another of the disciples said to Him, "Lord, permit me first to go and bury my father."

22 But Jesus *said to him, "Follow Me; and allow the dead to bury their own dead."

23 And when He got into the boat, His disciples followed Him.

24 And behold, there arose a great storm in the sea, so that the boat was covered with the waves; but He Himself was asleep.

25 And they came to *Him,* and awoke Him, saying, "Save *us,* Lord; we are perishing!"

26 And He *said to them, "Why are you timid, you men of little faith?" Then He arose, and rebuked the winds and the sea; and it became perfectly calm.

27 And the men marveled, saying, "What kind of a man is this, that even the winds and the sea obey Him?"

28 And when He had come to the other side into the country of the Gadarenes, two men who were demon-possessed met Him as they were coming out of the tombs; *they were* so exceedingly violent that no one could pass by that road.

29 And behold, they cried out, saying, "What do we have to do with You, Son of God? Have You come here to torment us before the time?"

30 Now there was at a distance from them a herd of many swine feeding.

31 And the demons *began* to entreat Him, saying, "If You are *going to* cast us out, send us into the herd of swine."

32 And He said to them, "Begone!" And they came out, and went into the swine, and behold, the whole herd rushed down the

21 Or, *dine*

steep bank into the sea and perished in the waters.

33 And the herdsmen ran away, and went to the city, and reported everything, including the *incident* of the demoniacs.

34 And behold, the whole city came out to meet Jesus; and when they saw Him, they entreated *Him* to depart from their region.

CHAPTER 9

AND getting into a boat, He crossed over, and came to His own city.

2 And behold, they were bringing to Him a paralytic, lying on a bed; and Jesus seeing their faith said to the paralytic, "Take courage, My son, your sins are forgiven."

3 And behold, some of the scribes said to themselves, "This *fellow* blasphemes."

4 And Jesus knowing their thoughts said, "Why are you thinking evil in your hearts?

5"For which is easier, to say, 'Your sins are forgiven,' or to say, 'Rise, and walk'?

6"But in order that you may know that the Son of Man has authority on earth to forgive sins"—then He *said to the paralytic—"Rise, take up your bed, and go home."

7 And he rose, and went home.

8 But when the multitudes saw *this,* they were filled with awe, and glorified God, who had given such authority to men.

9 And as Jesus passed on from there, He saw a man, called Matthew, sitting in the tax office; and He *said to him, "Follow

Me!" And he rose, and followed Him.

10 And it happened that as He was reclining *at the table* in the house, behold many tax-gatherers and sinners came and were dining with Jesus and His disciples.

11 And when the Pharisees saw *this,* they said to His disciples, "Why is your Teacher eating with the tax-gatherers and sinners?"

12 But when He heard this, He said, *"It is* not those who are healthy who need a physician, but those who are sick.

13"But go and learn what *this* means, 'I DESIRE COMPASSION, [22]AND NOT SACRIFICE,' for I did not come to call the righteous, but sinners."

14 Then the disciples of John *came to Him, saying, "Why do we and the Pharisees fast, but Your disciples do not fast?"

15 And Jesus said to them, "The attendants of the bridegroom cannot mourn as long as the bridegroom is with them, can they? But the days will come when the bridegroom is taken away from them, and then they will fast.

16"But no one puts a patch of unshrunk cloth on an old garment; for the patch pulls away from the garment, and a worse tear results.

17"Nor do *men* put new wine into old wineskins; otherwise the wineskins burst, and the wine pours out, and the wineskins are ruined; but they put new wine into fresh wineskins, and both are preserved."

18 While He was saying these

[22] I.e., more than

things to them, behold, there
came a *synagogue* official, and
bowed down before Him, saying,
"My daughter has just died; but
come and lay Your hand on her,
and she will live."

19 And Jesus rose and *began* to
follow him, and *so did* His disciples.

20 And behold, a woman who
had been suffering from a hemorrhage for twelve years, came up
behind Him and touched the
fringe of His cloak;

21 for she was saying to herself, "If I only touch His garment,
I shall get well."

22 But Jesus turning and seeing her said, "Daughter, take
courage; your faith has made you
well." And at once the woman
was made well.

23 And when Jesus came into
the official's house, and saw the
flute-players, and the crowd in
noisy disorder,

24 He *began* to say, "Depart;
for the girl has not died, but is
asleep." And they *began* laughing at Him.

25 But when the crowd had
been put out, He entered and
took her by the hand; and the girl
arose.

26 And this news went out into
all that land.

27 And as Jesus passed on
from there, two blind men followed Him, crying out, and saying, "Have mercy on us, Son of
David!"

28 And after He had come into
the house, the blind men came up
to Him, and Jesus *said to them,
"Do you believe that I am able to
do this?" They *said to Him,
"Yes, Lord."

29 Then He touched their eyes,

saying, "Be it done to you according to your faith."

30 And their eyes were opened.
And Jesus sternly warned them,
saying, "See *here,* let no one
know *about this!"*

31 But they went out, and
spread the news about Him in all
that land.

32 And as they were going out,
behold, a dumb man, demon-
possessed, was brought to Him.

33 And after the demon was
cast out, the dumb man spoke;
and the multitudes marveled,
saying, "Nothing like this was
ever seen in Israel."

34 But the Pharisees were saying, "He casts out the demons by
the ruler of the demons."

35 And Jesus was going about
all the cities and the villages,
teaching in their synagogues, and
proclaiming the gospel of the
kingdom, and healing every kind
of disease and every kind of sickness.

36 And seeing the multitudes,
He felt compassion for them, because they were distressed and
downcast like sheep without a
shepherd.

37 Then He *said to His disciples, "The harvest is plentiful,
but the workers are few.

38 "Therefore beseech the Lord
of the harvest to send out workers into His harvest."

CHAPTER 10

AND having summoned His
twelve disciples, He gave
them authority over unclean spirits, to cast them out, and to heal
every kind of disease and every
kind of sickness.

2 Now the names of the
twelve apostles are these: The

first, Simon, who is called Peter, and Andrew his brother; and James the *son* of Zebedee, and John his brother;

3 Philip and Bartholomew; Thomas and Matthew the tax-gatherer; James the *son* of Alphaeus, and Thaddaeus;

4 Simon the Zealot, and Judas Iscariot, the one who betrayed Him.

5 These twelve Jesus sent out after instructing them, saying, "Do not go in *the* way of *the* Gentiles, and do not enter *any* city of the Samaritans;

6 but rather go to the lost sheep of the house of Israel.

7"And as you go, preach, saying, 'The kingdom of heaven is at hand.'

8"Heal *the* sick, raise *the* dead, cleanse *the* lepers, cast out demons; freely you received, freely give.

9"Do not acquire gold, or silver, or copper for your money belts,

10 or a bag for *your* journey, or even two tunics, or sandals, or a staff; for the worker is worthy of his support.

11"And into whatever city or village you enter, inquire who is worthy in it; and abide there until you go away.

12"And as you enter the house, give it your greeting.

13"And if the house is worthy, let your *greeting of* peace come upon it; but if it is not worthy, let your *greeting of* peace return to you.

14"And whoever does not receive you, nor heed your words, as you go out of that house or that city, shake off the dust of your feet.

15"Truly I say to you, it will be more tolerable for *the* land of Sodom and Gomorrah in the day of judgment, than for that city.

16"Behold, I send you out as sheep in the midst of wolves; therefore be shrewd as serpents, and innocent as doves.

17"But beware of men; for they will deliver you up to *the* courts, and scourge you in their synagogues;

18 and you shall even be brought before governors and kings for My sake, as a testimony to them and to the Gentiles.

19"But when they deliver you up, do not become anxious about how or what you will speak; for it shall be given you in that hour what you are to speak.

20"For it is not you who speak, but *it is* the Spirit of your Father who speaks in you.

21"And brother will deliver up brother to death, and a father *his* child; and children will rise up against parents, and cause them to be put to death.

22"And you will be hated by all on account of My name, but it is the one who has endured to the end who will be saved.

23"But whenever they persecute you in this city, flee to the next; for truly I say to you, you shall not finish *going through* the cities of Israel, until the Son of Man comes.

24"A disciple is not above his teacher, nor a slave above his master.

25"It is enough for the disciple that he become as his teacher, and the slave as his master. If they have called the head of the house Beelzebul, how much more the members of his household!

26"Therefore do not fear them,

for there is nothing covered that will not be revealed, and hidden that will not be known.

27"What I tell you in the darkness, speak in the light; and what you hear *whispered* in *your* ear, proclaim upon the housetops.

28"And do not fear those who kill the body, but are unable to kill the soul; but rather fear Him who is able to destroy both soul and body in hell.

29"Are not two sparrows sold for a [23]cent? And *yet* not one of them will fall to the ground apart from your Father.

30"But the very hairs of your head are all numbered.

31"Therefore do not fear; you are of more value than many sparrows.

32"Everyone therefore who shall confess Me before men, I will also confess him before My Father who is in heaven.

33"But whoever shall deny Me before men, I will also deny him before My Father who is in heaven.

34"Do not think that I came to bring peace on the earth; I did not come to bring peace, but a sword.

35"For I came to SET A MAN AGAINST HIS FATHER, AND A DAUGHTER AGAINST HER MOTHER, AND A DAUGHTER-IN-LAW AGAINST HER MOTHER-IN-LAW;

36 and A MAN'S ENEMIES WILL BE THE MEMBERS OF HIS HOUSEHOLD.

37"He who loves father or mother more than Me is not worthy of Me; and he who loves son or daughter more than Me is not worthy of Me.

38"And he who does not take

his cross and follow after Me is not worthy of Me.

39"He who has found his life shall lose it, and he who has lost his life for My sake shall find it.

40"He who receives you receives Me, and he who receives Me receives Him who sent Me.

41"He who receives a prophet in *the* name of a prophet shall receive a prophet's reward; and he who receives a righteous man in the name of a righteous man shall receive a righteous man's reward.

42"And whoever in the name of a disciple gives to one of these little ones even a cup of cold water to drink, truly I say to you he shall not lose his reward."

CHAPTER 11

AND it came about that when Jesus had finished giving instructions to His twelve disciples, He departed from there to teach and preach in their cities.

2 Now when John in prison heard of the works of Christ, he sent *word* by his disciples,

3 and said to Him, "Are You the Expected One, or shall we look for someone else?"

4 And Jesus answered and said to them, "Go and report to John what you hear and see:

5 *the* BLIND RECEIVE SIGHT and *the* lame walk, *the* lepers are cleansed and *the* deaf hear, and *the* dead are raised up, and *the* POOR HAVE THE GOSPEL PREACHED TO THEM.

6"And blessed is he who keeps from stumbling over Me."

7 And as these were going *away*, Jesus began to speak to the multitudes about John, "What did you go out into the

---

[23] Gr., *assarion*, the smallest copper coin

wilderness to look at? A reed shaken by the wind?

8"But what did you go out to see? A man dressed in soft *clothing*? Behold, those who wear soft *clothing* are in kings' palaces.

9"But why did you go out? To see a prophet? Yes, I say to you, and one who is more than a prophet.

10"This is the one about whom it is written,

'BEHOLD, I SEND MY MESSENGER BEFORE YOUR FACE,

WHO WILL PREPARE YOUR WAY BEFORE YOU.'

11"Truly, I say to you, among those born of women there has not arisen *anyone* greater than John the Baptist; yet he who is least in the kingdom of heaven is greater than he.

12"And from the days of John the Baptist until now the kingdom of heaven suffers violence, and violent men take it by force.

13"For all the prophets and the Law prophesied until John.

14"And if you care to accept *it,* he himself is Elijah, who was to come.

15"He who has ears to hear, let him hear.

16"But to what shall I compare this generation? It is like children sitting in the market places, who call out to the other *children,*

17 and say, 'We played the flute for you, and you did not dance; we sang a dirge, and you did not mourn.'

18"For John came neither eating nor drinking, and they say, 'He has a demon!'

19"The Son of Man came eating and drinking, and they say, 'Behold, a gluttonous man and a drunkard, a friend of tax-gathers and sinners!' Yet wisdom is vindicated by her deeds."

20 Then He began to reproach the cities in which most of His miracles were done, because they did not repent.

21"Woe to you, Chorazin! Woe to you, Bethsaida! For if the miracles had occurred in Tyre and Sidon which occurred in you, they would have repented long ago in sackcloth and ashes.

22"Nevertheless I say to you, it shall be more tolerable for Tyre and Sidon in *the* day of judgment, than for you.

23"And you, Capernaum, will not be exalted to heaven, will you? You shall descend to Hades; for if the miracles had occurred in Sodom which occurred in you, it would have remained to this day.

24"Nevertheless I say to you that it shall be more tolerable for the land of Sodom in *the* day of judgment, than for you."

25 At that time Jesus answered and said, "I praise Thee, O Father, Lord of heaven and earth, that Thou didst hide these things from *the* wise and intelligent and didst reveal them to babes.

26"Yes, Father, for thus it was well-pleasing in Thy sight.

27"All things have been handed over to Me by My Father; and no one knows the Son, except the Father; nor does anyone know the Father, except the Son, and anyone to whom the Son wills to reveal *Him.*

28"Come to Me, all who are weary and heavy-laden, and I will give you rest.

29"Take My yoke upon you, and learn from Me, for I am gentle and humble in heart; and YOU SHALL FIND REST FOR YOUR SOULS.

30 "For My yoke is easy, and My load is light."

CHAPTER 12

AT that time Jesus went on the Sabbath through the grainfields, and His disciples became hungry and began to pick the heads of grain and eat.

2 But when the Pharisees saw it, they said to Him, "Behold, Your disciples do what is not lawful to do on a Sabbath."

3 But He said to them, "Have you not read what David did, when he became hungry, he and his companions;

4 how he entered the house of God, and they ate the consecrated bread, which was not lawful for him to eat, nor for those with him, but for the priests alone?

5 "Or have you not read in the Law, that on the Sabbath the priests in the temple break the Sabbath, and are innocent?

6 "But I say to you, that something greater than the temple is here.

7 "But if you had known what this means, 'I DESIRE COMPASSION, AND NOT A SACRIFICE,' you would not have condemned the innocent.

8 "For the Son of Man is Lord of the Sabbath."

9 And departing from there, He went into their synagogue.

10 And behold, there was a man with a withered hand. And they questioned Him, saying, "Is it lawful to heal on the Sabbath?"—in order that they might accuse Him.

11 And He said to them, "What man shall there be among you, who shall have one sheep, and if it falls into a pit on the Sabbath, will he not take hold of it, and lift it out?

12 "Of how much more value then is a man than a sheep! So then, it is lawful to do good on the Sabbath."

13 Then He *said to the man, "Stretch out your hand!" And he stretched it out, and it was restored to normal, like the other.

14 But the Pharisees went out, and counseled together against Him, as to how they might destroy Him.

15 But Jesus, aware of this, withdrew from there. And many followed Him, and He healed them all,

16 and warned them not to make Him known,

17 in order that what was spoken through Isaiah the prophet, might be fulfilled, saying,

18 "BEHOLD, MY SERVANT WHOM I HAVE CHOSEN;
   MY BELOVED IN WHOM MY SOUL IS WELL-PLEASED;
   I WILL PUT MY SPIRIT UPON HIM,
   AND HE SHALL PROCLAIM JUSTICE TO THE GENTILES.
19 "HE WILL NOT QUARREL, NOR CRY OUT;
   NOR WILL ANYONE HEAR HIS VOICE IN THE STREETS.
20 "A BATTERED REED HE WILL NOT BREAK OFF,
   AND A SMOLDERING WICK HE WILL NOT PUT OUT,
   UNTIL HE LEADS JUSTICE TO VICTORY.
21 "AND IN HIS NAME THE GENTILES WILL HOPE."

22 Then there was brought to Him a demon-possessed man who was blind and dumb, and He healed him, so that the dumb man spoke and saw.

23 And all the multitudes were amazed, and *began* to say, "This *man* cannot be the Son of David, can he?"

24 But when the Pharisees heard it, they said, "This man casts out demons only by Beelzebul the ruler of the demons."

25 And knowing their thoughts He said to them, "Any kingdom divided against itself is laid waste; and any city or house divided against itself shall not stand.

26 "And if Satan casts out Satan, he is divided against himself; how then shall his kingdom stand?

27 "And if I by Beelzebul cast out demons, by whom do your sons cast them out? Consequently they shall be your judges.

28 "But if I cast out demons by the Spirit of God, then the kingdom of God has come upon you.

29 "Or how can anyone enter the strong man's house and carry off his property, unless he first binds the strong *man*? And then he will plunder his house.

30 "He who is not with Me is against Me; and he who does not gather with Me scatters.

31 "Therefore I say to you, any sin and blasphemy shall be forgiven men, but blasphemy against the Spirit shall not be forgiven.

32 "And whoever shall speak a word against the Son of Man, it shall be forgiven him; but whoever shall speak against the Holy Spirit, it shall not be forgiven him, either in this age, or in the *age* to come.

33 "Either make the tree good, and its fruit good; or make the tree bad, and its fruit bad; for the tree is known by its fruit.

34 "You brood of vipers, how can you, being evil, speak what is good? For the mouth speaks out of that which fills the heart.

35 "The good man out of *his* good treasure brings forth what is good; and the evil man out of *his* evil treasure brings forth what is evil.

36 "And I say to you, that every careless word that men shall speak, they shall render account for it in the day of judgment.

37 "For by your words you shall be justified, and by your words you shall be condemned."

38 Then some of the scribes and Pharisees answered Him, saying, "Teacher, we want to see a sign from You."

39 But He answered and said to them, "An evil and adulterous generation craves for a sign; and *yet* no sign shall be given to it but the sign of Jonah the prophet;

40 for just as JONAH WAS THREE DAYS AND THREE NIGHTS IN THE BELLY OF THE SEA MONSTER, so shall the Son of Man be three days and three nights in the heart of the earth.

41 "The men of Nineveh shall stand up with this generation at the judgment, and shall condemn it because they repented at the preaching of Jonah; and behold, something greater than Jonah is here.

42 "The Queen of *the* South shall rise up with this generation at the judgment and shall condemn it, because she came from the ends of the earth to hear the wisdom of Solomon; and behold, something greater than Solomon is here.

43 "Now when the unclean

spirit goes out of a man, it passes through waterless places, seeking rest, and does not find *it*.

44"Then it says, 'I will return to my house from which I came'; and when it comes, it finds it unoccupied, swept, and put in order.

45"Then it goes, and takes along with it seven other spirits more wicked than itself, and they go in and live there; and the last state of that man becomes worse than the first. That is the way it will also be with this evil generation."

46 While He was still speaking to the multitudes, behold, His mother and brothers were standing outside, seeking to speak to Him.

47 And someone said to Him, "Behold, Your mother and Your brothers are standing outside seeking to speak to You."

48 But He answered the one who was telling Him and said, "Who is My mother and who are My brothers?"

49 And stretching out His hand toward His disciples, He said, "Behold, My mother and My brothers!

50"For whoever does the will of My Father who is in heaven, he is My brother and sister and mother."

CHAPTER 13

ON that day Jesus went out of the house, and was sitting by the sea.

2 And great multitudes gathered to Him, so that He got into a boat and sat down, and the whole multitude was standing on the beach.

3 And He spoke many things to them in parables, saying, "Behold, the sower went out to sow;

4 and as he sowed, some *seeds* fell beside the road, and the birds came and ate them up.

5"And others fell upon the rocky places, where they did not have much soil; and immediately they sprang up, because they had no depth of soil.

6"But when the sun had risen, they were scorched; and because they had no root, they withered away.

7"And others fell among the thorns, and the thorns came up and choked them out.

8"And others fell on the good soil, and *yielded a crop, some a hundredfold, some sixty, and some thirty.

9"He who has ears, let him hear."

10 And the disciples came and said to Him, "Why do You speak to them in parables?"

11 And He answered and said to them, "To you it has been granted to know the mysteries of the kingdom of heaven, but to them it has not been granted.

12"For whoever has, to him shall *more* be given, and he shall have an abundance; but whoever does not have, even what he has shall be taken away from him.

13"Therefore I speak to them in parables; because while seeing they do not see, and while hearing they do not hear, nor do they understand.

14"And in their case the prophecy of Isaiah is being fulfilled, which says,

   'YOU WILL KEEP ON HEARING, BUT WILL NOT UNDERSTAND;

   AND YOU WILL KEEP ON SEEING, BUT WILL NOT PERCEIVE;

15 FOR THE HEART OF THIS
    PEOPLE HAS BECOME DULL,
    AND WITH THEIR EARS
    THEY SCARCELY HEAR,
    AND THEY HAVE CLOSED
    THEIR EYES
    LEST THEY SHOULD SEE
    WITH THEIR EYES,
    AND HEAR WITH THEIR
    EARS,
    AND UNDERSTAND WITH
    THEIR HEART AND RE-
    TURN,
    AND I SHOULD HEAL THEM.'

16 "But blessed are your eyes,
because they see; and your ears,
because they hear.

17 "For truly I say to you, that
many prophets and righteous
men desired to see what you see,
and did not see *it*; and to hear
what you hear, and did not hear
it.

18 "Hear then the parable of the
sower.

19 "When anyone hears the
word of the kingdom, and does
not understand it, the evil *one*
comes and snatches away what
has been sown in his heart. This
is the one on whom seed was
sown beside the road.

20 "And the one on whom seed
was sown on the rocky places,
this is the man who hears the
word, and immediately receives
it with joy;

21 yet he has no *firm* root in
himself, but is *only* temporary,
and when affliction or persecution arises because of the word,
immediately he falls away.

22 "And the one on whom seed
was sown among the thorns, this
is the man who hears the word,
and the worry of the world, and
the deceitfulness of riches choke
the word, and it becomes unfruitful.

23 "And the one on whom seed

was sown on the good soil, this is
the man who hears the word and
understands it; who indeed bears
fruit, and brings forth, some a
hundredfold, some sixty, and
some thirty."

24 He presented another parable to them, saying, "The kingdom of heaven may be compared
to a man who sowed good seed in
his field.

25 "But while men were sleeping, his enemy came and sowed
²⁴tares also among the wheat,
and went away.

26 "But when the wheat sprang
up and bore grain, then the tares
became evident also.

27 "And the slaves of the landowner came and said to him, 'Sir,
did you not sow good seed in
your field? How then does it have
tares?'

28 "And he said to them, 'An
enemy has done this!' And the
slaves *said to him, 'Do you want
us, then, to go and gather them
up?'

29 "But he *said, 'No; lest while
you are gathering up the tares,
you may root up the wheat with
them.

30 'Allow both to grow together
until the harvest; and in the time
of the harvest I will say to the
reapers, "First gather up the
tares and bind them in bundles to
burn them up; but gather the
wheat into my barn." ' "

31 He presented another parable to them, saying, "The kingdom of heaven is like a mustard
seed, which a man took and
sowed in his field;

32 and this is smaller than all
other seeds; but when it is full
grown, it is larger than the gar-

²⁴ Or, *darnel*, a weed resembling wheat

den plants, and becomes a tree, so that THE BIRDS OF THE AIR come and NEST IN ITS BRANCHES."

33 He spoke another parable to them, "The kingdom of heaven is like leaven, which a woman took, and hid in three pecks of meal, until it was all leavened."

34 All these things Jesus spoke to the multitudes in parables, and He did not speak to them without a parable,

35 so that what was spoken through the prophet might be fulfilled, saying,

"I WILL OPEN MY MOUTH IN PARABLES;

I WILL UTTER THINGS HIDDEN SINCE THE FOUNDATION OF THE WORLD."

36 Then He left the multitudes, and went into the house. And His disciples came to Him, saying, "Explain to us the parable of the tares of the field."

37 And He answered and said, "The one who sows the good seed is the Son of Man,

38 and the field is the world; and *as for* the good seed, these are the sons of the kingdom; and the tares are the sons of the evil *one;*

39 and the enemy who sowed them is the devil, and the harvest is the end of the age; and the reapers are angels.

40"Therefore just as the tares are gathered up and burned with fire, so shall it be at the end of the age.

41"The Son of Man will send forth His angels, and they will gather out of His kingdom all stumbling blocks, and those who commit lawlessness,

42 and will cast them into the furnace of fire; in that place there shall be weeping and gnashing of teeth.

43"Then THE RIGHTEOUS WILL SHINE FORTH AS THE SUN in the kingdom of their Father. He who has ears, let him hear.

44"The kingdom of heaven is like a treasure hidden in the field, which a man found and hid; and from joy over it he goes and sells all that he has, and buys that field.

45"Again, the kingdom of heaven is like a merchant seeking fine pearls,

46 and upon finding one pearl of great value, he went and sold all that he had, and bought it.

47"Again, the kingdom of heaven is like a dragnet cast into the sea, and gathering *fish* of every kind;

48 and when it was filled, they drew it up on the beach; and they sat down, and gathered the good *fish* into containers, but the bad they threw away.

49"So it will be at the end of the age; the angels shall come forth, and take out the wicked from among the righteous,

50 and will cast them into the furnace of fire; there shall be weeping and gnashing of teeth.

51"Have you understood all these things?" They *said to Him, "Yes."

52 And He said to them, "Therefore every scribe who has become a disciple of the kingdom of heaven is like a head of a household, who brings forth out of his treasure things new and old."

53 And it came about that when Jesus had finished these parables, He departed from there.

54 And coming to His home town He *began* teaching them in their synagogue, so that they

became astonished, and said, "Where *did* this man *get* this wisdom, and *these* miraculous powers?

55"Is not this the carpenter's son? Is not His mother called Mary, and His brothers, James and Joseph and Simon and Judas?

56"And His sisters, are they not all with us? Where then *did* this man *get* all these things?"

57 And they took offense at Him. But Jesus said to them, "A prophet is not without honor except in his home town, and in his *own* household."

58 And He did not do many miracles there because of their unbelief.

CHAPTER 14

AT that time Herod the tetrarch heard the news about Jesus,

2 and said to his servants, "This is John the Baptist; he has risen from the dead; and that is why miraculous powers are at work in him."

3 For when Herod had John arrested, he bound him, and put him in prison on account of Herodias, the wife of his brother Philip.

4 For John had been saying to him, "It is not lawful for you to have her."

5 And although he wanted to put him to death, he feared the multitude, because they regarded him as a prophet.

6 But when Herod's birthday came, the daughter of Herodias danced before *them* and pleased Herod.

7 Thereupon he promised with an oath to give her whatever she asked.

8 And having been prompted by her mother, she *said, "Give me here on a platter the head of John the Baptist."

9 And although he was grieved, the king commanded *it* to be given because of his oaths, and because of his dinner guests.

10 And he sent and had John beheaded in the prison.

11 And his head was brought on a platter and given to the girl; and she brought *it* to her mother.

12 And his disciples came and took away the body and buried it; and they went and reported to Jesus.

13 Now when Jesus heard *it*, He withdrew from there in a boat, to a lonely place by Himself; and when the multitudes heard *of this*, they followed Him on foot from the cities.

14 And when He went ashore, He saw a great multitude, and felt compassion for them, and healed their sick.

15 And when it was evening, the disciples came to Him, saying, "The place is desolate, and the time is already past; so send the multitudes away, that they may go into the villages and buy food for themselves."

16 But Jesus said to them, "They do not need to go away; you give them *something* to eat!"

17 And they *said to Him, "We have here only five loaves and two fish."

18 And He said, "Bring them here to Me."

19 And ordering the multitudes to recline on the grass, He took the five loaves and the two fish, and looking up toward heaven, He blessed *the food*, and break-

ing the loaves He gave them to the disciples, and the disciples *gave* to the multitudes,

20 and they all ate, and were satisfied. And they picked up what was left over of the broken pieces, twelve full baskets.

21 And there were about five thousand men who ate, aside from women and children.

22 And immediately He made the disciples get into the boat, and go ahead of Him to the other side, while He sent the multitudes away.

23 And after He had sent the multitudes away, He went up to the mountain by Himself to pray; and when it was evening, He was there alone.

24 But the boat was already many ²⁵stadia away from the land, battered by the waves; for the wind was contrary.

25 And in the ²⁶fourth watch of the night He came to them, walking on the sea.

26 And when the disciples saw Him walking on the sea, they were frightened, saying, "It is a ghost!" And they cried out for fear.

27 But immediately Jesus spoke to them, saying, "Take courage, it is I; do not be afraid."

28 And Peter answered Him and said, "Lord, if it is You, command me to come to You on the water."

29 And He said, "Come!" And Peter got out of the boat, and walked on the water and came toward Jesus.

30 But seeing the wind, he became afraid, and beginning to sink, he cried out, saying, "Lord, save me!"

31 And immediately Jesus stretched out His hand and took hold of him, and *said to him, "O you of little faith, why did you doubt?"

32 And when they got into the boat, the wind stopped.

33 And those who were in the boat worshiped Him, saying, "You are certainly God's Son!"

34 And when they had crossed over, they came to land at Gennesaret.

35 And when the men of that place recognized Him, they sent into all that surrounding district and brought to Him all who were sick;

36 and they *began* to entreat Him that they might just touch the fringe of His cloak; and as many as touched *it* were cured.

CHAPTER 15

THEN some Pharisees and scribes *came to Jesus from Jerusalem, saying,

2"Why do Your disciples transgress the tradition of the elders? For they do not wash their hands when they eat bread."

3 And He answered and said to them, "And why do you yourselves transgress the commandment of God for the sake of your tradition?

4"For God said, 'HONOR YOUR FATHER AND MOTHER,' and, 'HE WHO SPEAKS EVIL OF FATHER OR MOTHER, LET HIM BE PUT TO DEATH.'

5"But you say, 'Whoever shall say to *his* father or mother, "Anything of mine you might have been helped by has been given *to God*,"

6 he is not to honor his father

---

²⁵ A stadion was about 600 feet
²⁶ I.e., 3–6 a.m.

27or his mother28.' And *thus* you invalidated the word of God for the sake of your tradition.

7"You hypocrites, rightly did Isaiah prophesy of you, saying,

8 'THIS PEOPLE HONORS ME
    WITH THEIR LIPS,
    BUT THEIR HEART IS FAR
    AWAY FROM ME.

9 'BUT IN VAIN DO THEY WOR-
    SHIP ME,
    TEACHING AS DOCTRINES
    THE PRECEPTS OF MEN.' "

10 And after He called the multitude to Him, He said to them, "Hear, and understand.

11"Not what enters into the mouth defiles the man, but what proceeds out of the mouth, this defiles the man."

12 Then the disciples *came and *said to Him, "Do You know that the Pharisees were offended when they heard this statement?"

13 But He answered and said, "Every plant which My heavenly Father did not plant shall be rooted up.

14"Let them alone; they are blind guides29of the blind. And if a blind man guides a blind man, both will fall into a pit."

15 And Peter answered and said to Him, "Explain the parable to us."

16 And He said, "Are you still lacking in understanding also?

17"Do you not understand that everything that goes into the mouth passes into the stomach, and is eliminated?

18"But the things that proceed out of the mouth come from the heart, and those defile the man.

19"For out of the heart come evil thoughts, murders, adulteries, fornications, thefts, false witness, slanders.

20"These are the things which defile the man; but to eat with unwashed hands does not defile the man."

21 And Jesus went away from there, and withdrew into the district of Tyre and Sidon.

22 And behold, a Canaanite woman came out from that region, and *began to cry out, saying, "Have mercy on me, O Lord, Son of David; my daughter is cruelly demon-possessed."

23 But He did not answer her a word. And His disciples came to *Him and kept asking Him, saying, "Send her away, for she is shouting out after us."

24 But He answered and said, "I was sent only to the lost sheep of the house of Israel."

25 But she came and *began to bow down before Him, saying, "Lord, help me!"

26 And He answered and said, "It is not good to take the children's bread and throw it to the dogs."

27 But she said, "Yes, Lord; but even the dogs feed on the crumbs which fall from their masters' table."

28 Then Jesus answered and said to her, "O woman, your faith is great; be it done for you as you wish." And her daughter was healed at once.

29 And departing from there, Jesus went along by the Sea of Galilee, and having gone up to the mountain, He was sitting there.

30 And great multitudes came to Him, bringing with them *those who were* lame, crippled, blind, dumb, and many others, and they

27 Many mss. do not contain *or his mother*
28 I.e., by supporting them with it
29 Some mss. do not contain *of the blind*

laid them down at His feet; and He healed them,

so that the multitude marveled as they saw the dumb speaking, the crippled restored, and the lame walking, and the blind seeing; and they glorified the God of Israel.

32 And Jesus called His disciples to Him, and said, "I feel compassion for the multitude, because they have remained with Me now three days and have nothing to eat; and I do not wish to send them away hungry, lest they faint on the way."

33 And the disciples *said to Him, "Where would we get so many loaves in a desolate place to satisfy such a great multitude?"

34 And Jesus *said to them, "How many loaves do you have?" And they said, "Seven, and a few small fish."

35 And He directed the multitude to sit down on the ground;

36 and He took the seven loaves and the fish; and giving thanks, He broke them and started giving them to the disciples, and the disciples *in turn*, to the multitudes.

37 And they all ate, and were satisfied, and they picked up what was left over of the broken pieces, seven large baskets full.

38 And those who ate were four thousand men, besides women and children.

39 And sending away the multitudes, He got into the boat, and came to the region of Magadan.

CHAPTER 16

AND the Pharisees and Sadducees came up, and testing Him asked Him to show them a sign from heaven.

2 But He answered and said to them, "When it is evening, you say, *'It will be* fair weather, for the sky is red.'

3"And in the morning, *'There will be* a storm today, for the sky is red and threatening.' Do you know how to discern the appearance of the sky, but cannot *discern* the signs of the times?

4"An evil and adulterous generation seeks after a sign; and a sign will not be given it, except the sign of Jonah." And He left them, and went away.

5 And the disciples came to the other side and had forgotten to take bread.

6 And Jesus said to them, "Watch out and beware of the leaven of the Pharisees and Sadducees."

7 And they began to discuss among themselves, saying, "It is because we took no bread."

8 But Jesus, aware of this, said, "You men of little faith, why do you discuss among yourselves that you have no bread?

9"Do you not yet understand or remember the five loaves of the five thousand, and how many baskets you took up?

10"Or the seven loaves of the four thousand, and how many large baskets you took up?

11"How is it that you do not understand that I did not speak to you concerning bread? But beware of the leaven of the Pharisees and Sadducees."

12 Then they understood that He did not say to beware of the leaven of bread, but of the teaching of the Pharisees and Sadducees.

13 Now when Jesus came into the district of Caesarea Philippi, He *began* asking His disciples, saying, "Who do people say that the Son of Man is?"

14 And they said, "Some *say* John the Baptist; and others, Elijah; but still others, Jeremiah, or one of the prophets."

15 He *said to them, "But who do you say that I am?"

16 And Simon Peter answered and said, "Thou art the Christ, the Son of the living God."

17 And Jesus answered and said to him, "Blessed are you, Simon Barjona, because flesh and blood did not reveal *this* to you, but My Father who is in heaven.

18 "And I also say to you that you are Peter, and upon this rock I will build My church; and the gates of Hades shall not overpower it.

19 "I will give you the keys of the kingdom of heaven; and whatever you shall bind on earth shall be bound in heaven, and whatever you shall loose on earth shall be loosed in heaven."

20 Then He warned the disciples that they should tell no one that He was the Christ.

21 From that time Jesus Christ began to show His disciples that He must go to Jerusalem, and suffer many things from the elders and chief priests and scribes, and be killed, and be raised up on the third day.

22 And Peter took Him aside and began to rebuke Him, saying, "God forbid *it*, Lord! This shall never happen to You."

23 But He turned and said to Peter, "Get behind Me, Satan! You are a stumbling block to Me; for you are not setting your mind on God's interests, but man's."

24 Then Jesus said to His disciples, "If anyone wishes to come after Me, let him deny himself, and take up his cross, and follow Me.

25 "For whoever wishes to save his life shall lose it; but whoever loses his life for My sake shall find it.

26 "For what will a man be profited, if he gains the whole world, and forfeits his soul? Or what will a man give in exchange for his soul?

27 "For the Son of Man is going to come in the glory of His Father with His angels; and WILL THEN RECOMPENSE EVERY MAN ACCORDING TO HIS DEEDS.

28 "Truly I say to you, there are some of those who are standing here who shall not taste death until they see the Son of Man coming in His kingdom."

CHAPTER 17

AND six days later Jesus *took with Him Peter and James and John his brother, and *brought them up to a high mountain by themselves.

2 And He was transfigured before them; and His face shone like the sun, and His garments became as white as light.

3 And behold, Moses and Elijah appeared to them, talking with Him.

4 And Peter answered and said to Jesus, "Lord, it is good for us to be here; if You wish, I will make three tabernacles here, one for You, and one for Moses, and one for Elijah."

5 While he was still speaking, behold, a bright cloud overshadowed them; and behold, a voice out of the cloud, saying, "This is My beloved Son, with whom I am well-pleased; listen to Him!"

6 And when the disciples heard *this*, they fell on their faces and were much afraid.

7 And Jesus came to *them* and touched them and said, "Arise, and do not be afraid."

8 And lifting up their eyes, they saw no one, except Jesus Himself alone.

9 And as they were coming down from the mountain, Jesus commanded them, saying, "Tell the vision to no one until the Son of Man has risen from the dead."

10 And His disciples asked Him, saying, "Why then do the scribes say that Elijah must come first?"

11 And He answered and said, "Elijah is coming and will restore all things;

12 but I say to you, that Elijah already came, and they did not recognize him, but did to him whatever they wished. So also the Son of Man is going to suffer at their hands."

13 Then the disciples understood that He had spoken to them about John the Baptist.

14 And when they came to the multitude, a man came up to Him, falling on his knees before Him, and saying,

15"Lord, have mercy on my son, for he is a lunatic, and is very ill; for he often falls into the fire, and often into the water.

16"And I brought him to Your disciples, and they could not cure him."

17 And Jesus answered and said, "O unbelieving and perverted generation, how long shall I be with you? How long shall I put up with you? Bring him here to Me."

18 And Jesus rebuked him, and the demon came out of him, and the boy was cured at once.

19 Then the disciples came to Jesus privately and said, "Why could we not cast it out?"

20 And He *said to them, "Because of the littleness of your faith; for truly I say to you, if you have faith as a mustard seed, you shall say to this mountain, 'Move from here to there,' and it shall move; and nothing shall be impossible to you.

21 ["³⁰But this kind does not go out except by prayer and fasting."]

22 And while they were gathering together in Galilee, Jesus said to them, "The Son of Man is going to be delivered into the hands of men;

23 and they will kill Him, and He will be raised on the third day." And they were deeply grieved.

24 And when they had come to Capernaum, those who collected the ³¹two-drachma *tax* came to Peter, and said, "Does your teacher not pay the ³¹two-drachma *tax?*"

25 He *said, "Yes." And when he came into the house, Jesus spoke to him first, saying, "What do you think, Simon? From whom do the kings of the earth collect customs or poll-tax, from their sons or from strangers?"

26 And upon his saying, "From strangers," Jesus said to him, "Consequently the sons are exempt.

27"But, lest we give them offense, go to the sea, and throw in a hook, and take the first fish that comes up; and when you open its

³⁰ Many mss. do not contain this verse
³¹ Equivalent to two denarii or two days' wages paid as a temple tax

mouth, you will find a [32]stater. Take that and give it to them for you and Me."

CHAPTER 18

AT that time the disciples came to Jesus, saying, "Who then is greatest in the kingdom of heaven?"

2 And He called a child to Himself and set him before them,

3 and said, "Truly I say to you, unless you are converted and become like children, you shall not enter the kingdom of heaven.

4 "Whoever then humbles himself as this child, he is the greatest in the kingdom of heaven.

5 "And whoever receives one such child in My name receives Me;

6 but whoever causes one of these little ones who believe in Me to stumble, it is better for him that a heavy millstone be hung around his neck, and that he be drowned in the depth of the sea.

7 "Woe to the world because of *its* stumbling blocks! For it is inevitable that stumbling blocks come; but woe to that man through whom the stumbling block comes!

8 "And if your hand or your foot causes you to stumble, cut it off and throw it from you; it is better for you to enter life crippled or lame, than having two hands or two feet, to be cast into the eternal fire.

9 "And if your eye causes you to stumble, pluck it out, and throw it from you. It is better for you to enter life with one eye, than having two eyes, to be cast into the fiery hell.

10 "See that you do not despise one of these little ones, for I say to you, that their angels in heaven continually behold the face of My Father who is in heaven.

11 ["[33]For the Son of Man has come to save that which was lost.]

12 "What do you think? If any man has a hundred sheep, and one of them has gone astray, does he not leave the ninety-nine on the mountains and go and search for the one that is straying?

13 "And if it turns out that he finds it, truly I say to you, he rejoices over it more than over the ninety-nine which have not gone astray.

14 "Thus it is not *the* will of your Father who is in heaven that one of these little ones perish.

15 "And if your brother sins[34], go and reprove him in private; if he listens to you, you have won your brother.

16 "But if he does not listen *to you*, take one or two more with you, so that BY THE MOUTH OF TWO OR THREE WITNESSES EVERY FACT MAY BE CONFIRMED.

17 "And if he refuses to listen to them, tell it to the church; and if he refuses to listen even to the church, let him be to you as a Gentile and a tax-gatherer.

18 "Truly I say to you, whatever you shall bind on earth shall be bound in heaven; and whatever you loose on earth shall be loosed in heaven.

19 "Again I say to you, that if two of you agree on earth about anything that they may ask, it

[32] Or, *shekel*, worth four drachmas
[33] Most ancient mss. do not contain this verse   [34] Many mss. add here: *against you*

shall be done for them by My Father who is in heaven.

20 "For where two or three have gathered together in My name, there I am in their midst."

21 Then Peter came and said to Him, "Lord, how often shall my brother sin against me and I forgive him? Up to seven times?"

22 Jesus *said to him, "I do not say to you, up to seven times, but up to seventy times seven.

23 "For this reason the kingdom of heaven may be compared to a certain king who wished to settle accounts with his slaves.

24 "And when he had begun to settle *them*, there was brought to him one who owed him 35ten thousand talents.

25 "But since he did not have *the means* to repay, his lord commanded him to be sold, along with his wife and children and all that he had, and repayment to be made.

26 "The slave therefore falling down, prostrated himself before him, saying, 'Have patience with me, and I will repay you everything.'

27 "And the lord of that slave felt compassion and released him and forgave him the debt.

28 "But that slave went out and found one of his fellow slaves who owed him a hundred 36denarii; and he seized him and *began* to choke *him*, saying, 'Pay back what you owe.'

29 "So his fellow slave fell down and *began* to entreat him, saying, 'Have patience with me and I will repay you.'

30 "He was unwilling however,

but went and threw him in prison until he should pay back what was owed.

31 "So when his fellow slaves saw what had happened, they were deeply grieved and came and reported to their lord all that had happened.

32 "Then summoning him, his lord *said to him, 'You wicked slave, I forgave you all that debt because you entreated me.

33 'Should you not also have had mercy on your fellow slave, even as I had mercy on you?'

34 "And his lord, moved with anger, handed him over to the torturers until he should repay all that was owed him.

35 "So shall My heavenly Father also do to you, if each of you does not forgive his brother from your heart."

CHAPTER 19

AND it came about that when Jesus had finished these words, He departed from Galilee, and came into the region of Judea beyond the Jordan;

2 And great multitudes followed Him, and He healed them there.

3 And *some* Pharisees came to Him, testing Him, and saying, "Is it lawful *for a man* to divorce his wife for any cause at all?"

4 And He answered and said, "Have you not read, that He who created *them* from the beginning MADE THEM MALE AND FEMALE,

5 and said, 'FOR THIS CAUSE A MAN SHALL LEAVE HIS FATHER AND MOTHER, AND SHALL CLEAVE TO HIS WIFE; AND THE TWO SHALL BECOME ONE FLESH'?

6 "Consequently they are no longer two, but one flesh. What

---

35 About $10,000,000 in silver content but worth much more in buying power
36 The denarius was equivalent to one day's wage

therefore God has joined together, let no man separate."

7 They *said to Him, "Why then did Moses command to GIVE HER A CERTIFICATE AND DIVORCE HER?"

8 He *said to them, "Because of your hardness of heart, Moses permitted you to divorce your wives; but from the beginning it has not been this way.

9 "And I say to you, whoever divorces his wife, except for immorality, and marries another woman commits adultery."

10 The disciples *said to Him, "If the relationship of the man with his wife is like this, it is better not to marry."

11 But He said to them, "Not all men can accept this statement, but only those to whom it has been given.

12 "For there are eunuchs who were born that way from their mother's womb; and there are eunuchs who were made eunuchs by men; and there are also eunuchs who made themselves eunuchs for the sake of the kingdom of heaven. He who is able to accept this, let him accept it."

13 Then some children were brought to Him so that He might lay His hands on them and pray; and the disciples rebuked them.

14 But Jesus said, "Let the children alone, and do not hinder them from coming to Me; for the kingdom of heaven belongs to such as these."

15 And after laying His hands on them, He departed from there.

16 And behold, one came to Him and said, "Teacher, what good thing shall I do that I may obtain eternal life?"

17 And He said to him, "Why are you asking Me about what is good? There is only One who is good; but if you wish to enter into life, keep the commandments."

18 He *said to Him, "Which ones?" And Jesus said, "You SHALL NOT COMMIT MURDER; YOU SHALL NOT COMMIT ADULTERY; YOU SHALL NOT STEAL; YOU SHALL NOT BEAR FALSE WITNESS;

19 HONOR YOUR FATHER AND MOTHER; and YOU SHALL LOVE YOUR NEIGHBOR AS YOURSELF."

20 The young man *said to Him, "All these things I have kept; what am I still lacking?"

21 Jesus said to him, "If you wish to be complete, go and sell your possessions and give to the poor, and you shall have treasure in heaven; and come, follow Me."

22 But when the young man heard this statement, he went away grieved; for he was one who owned much property.

23 And Jesus said to His disciples, "Truly I say to you, it is hard for a rich man to enter the kingdom of heaven.

24 "And again I say to you, it is easier for a camel to go through the eye of a needle, than for a rich man to enter the kingdom of God."

25 And when the disciples heard this, they were very astonished and said, "Then who can be saved?"

26 And looking upon them Jesus said to them, "With men this is impossible, but with God all things are possible."

27 Then Peter answered and said to Him, "Behold, we have left everything and followed You; what then will there be for us?"

28 And Jesus said to them, "Truly I say to you, that you who have followed Me, in the regen-

eration when the Son of Man will sit on His glorious throne, you also shall sit upon twelve thrones, judging the twelve tribes of Israel.

29 "And everyone who has left houses or brothers or sisters or father or mother[37] or children or farms for My name's sake, shall receive many times as much, and shall inherit eternal life.

30 "But many who are first will be last; and the last, first.

CHAPTER 20

"FOR the kingdom of heaven is like a landowner who went out early in the morning to hire laborers for his vineyard.

2 "And when he had agreed with the laborers for a [38]denarius for the day, he sent them into his vineyard.

3 "And he went out about the [39]third hour and saw others standing idle in the market place;

4 and to those he said, 'You too go into the vineyard, and whatever is right I will give you.' And so they went.

5 "Again he went out about the [40]sixth and the ninth hour, and did the same thing.

6 "And about the [41]eleventh hour he went out, and found others standing; and he *said to them, 'Why have you been standing here idle all day long?'

7 "They *said to him, 'Because no one hired us.' He *said to them, 'You too go into the vineyard.'

8 "And when evening had come, the owner of the vineyard

*said to his foreman, 'Call the laborers and pay them their wages, beginning with the last group to the first.'

9 "And when those hired about the eleventh hour came, each one received a [38]denarius.

10 "And when those hired first came, they thought that they would receive more; and they also received each one a [38]denarius.

11 "And when they received it, they grumbled at the landowner,

12 saying, 'These last men have worked only one hour, and you have made them equal to us who have borne the burden and the scorching heat of the day.'

13 "But he answered and said to one of them, 'Friend, I am doing you no wrong; did you not agree with me for a [38]denarius?

14 'Take what is yours and go your way, but I wish to give to this last man the same as to you.

15 'Is it not lawful for me to do what I wish with what is my own? Or is your eye envious because I am generous?'

16 "Thus the last shall be first, and the first last."

17 And as Jesus was about to go up to Jerusalem, He took the twelve disciples aside by themselves, and on the way He said to them,

18 "Behold, we are going up to Jerusalem; and the Son of Man will be delivered to the chief priests and scribes, and they will condemn Him to death,

19 and will deliver Him to the Gentiles to mock and scourge and crucify Him, and on the third day He will be raised up."

20 Then the mother of the sons of Zebedee came to Him with her

37 Many mss. add here, or wife
38 The denarius was equivalent to one day's wage   39 I.e., 9 a.m.
40 I.e., Noon and 3 p.m.   41 I.e., 5 p.m.

sons, bowing down, and making a request of Him.

21 And He said to her, "What do you wish?" She *said to Him, "Command that in Your kingdom these two sons of mine may sit, one on Your right and one on Your left."

22 But Jesus answered and said, "You do not know what you are asking for. Are you able to drink the cup that I am about to drink?" They *said to Him, "We are able."

23 He *said to them, "My cup you shall drink; but to sit on My right and on My left, this is not Mine to give, but it is for those for whom it has been prepared by My Father."

24 And hearing this, the ten became indignant with the two brothers.

25 But Jesus called them to Himself, and said, "You know that the rulers of the Gentiles lord it over them, and their great men exercise authority over them.

26 "It is not so among you, but whoever wishes to become great among you shall be your servant,

27 and whoever wishes to be first among you shall be your slave;

28 just as the Son of Man did not come to be served, but to serve, and to give His life a ransom for many."

29 And as they were going out from Jericho, a great multitude followed Him.

30 And behold, two blind men sitting by the road, hearing that Jesus was passing by, cried out, saying, "Lord, have mercy on us, Son of David!"

31 And the multitude sternly told them to be quiet; but they cried out all the more, saying, "Lord, have mercy on us, Son of David!"

32 And Jesus stopped and called them, and said, "What do you want Me to do for you?"

33 They *said to Him, "Lord, we want our eyes to be opened."

34 And moved with compassion, Jesus touched their eyes; and immediately they regained their sight and followed Him.

CHAPTER 21

AND when they had approached Jerusalem and had come to Bethphage, to the Mount of Olives, then Jesus sent two disciples,

2 saying to them, "Go into the village opposite you, and immediately you will find a donkey tied there and a colt with her; untie them, and bring them to Me.

3 "And if anyone says something to you, you shall say, 'The Lord has need of them,' and immediately he will send them."

4 Now this took place that what was spoken through the prophet might be fulfilled, saying,

5 "SAY TO THE DAUGHTER OF ZION,
'BEHOLD YOUR KING IS COMING TO YOU,
GENTLE, AND MOUNTED ON A DONKEY,
EVEN ON A COLT, THE FOAL OF A BEAST OF BURDEN.'"

6 And the disciples went and did just as Jesus had directed them,

7 and brought the donkey and the colt, and laid on them their garments, on which He sat.

8 And most of the multitude

spread their garments in the road, and others were cutting branches from the trees, and spreading them in the road.

9 And the multitudes going before Him, and those who followed after were crying out, saying,

"Hosanna to the Son of David;
BLESSED IS HE WHO COMES IN THE NAME OF THE LORD;
Hosanna in the highest!"

10 And when He had entered Jerusalem, all the city was stirred, saying, "Who is this?"

11 And the multitudes were saying, "This is the prophet Jesus, from Nazareth in Galilee."

12 And Jesus entered the temple and cast out all those who were buying and selling in the temple, and overturned the tables of the moneychangers and the seats of those who were selling doves.

13 And He *said to them, "It is written, 'MY HOUSE SHALL BE CALLED A HOUSE OF PRAYER'; but you are making it a ROBBERS' DEN."

14 And the blind and the lame came to Him in the temple, and He healed them.

15 But when the chief priests and the scribes saw the wonderful things that He had done, and the children who were crying out in the temple and saying, "Hosanna to the Son of David," they became indignant,

16 and said to Him, "Do You hear what these are saying?" And Jesus *said to them, "Yes; have you never read, 'OUT OF THE MOUTH OF INFANTS AND NURSING BABES THOU HAST PREPARED PRAISE FOR THYSELF'?"

17 And He left them and went out of the city to Bethany, and lodged there.

18 Now in the morning, when He returned to the city, He became hungry.

19 And seeing a lone fig tree by the road, He came to it, and found nothing on it except leaves only; and He *said to it, "No longer shall there ever be any fruit from you." And at once the fig tree withered.

20 And seeing this, the disciples marveled, saying, "How did the fig tree wither at once?"

21 And Jesus answered and said to them, "Truly I say to you, if you have faith, and do not doubt, you shall not only do what was done to the fig tree, but even if you say to this mountain, 'Be taken up and cast into the sea,' it shall happen.

22 "And all things you ask in prayer, believing, you shall receive."

23 And when He had come into the temple, the chief priests and the elders of the people came to Him as He was teaching, and said, "By what authority are You doing these things, and who gave You this authority?"

24 And Jesus answered and said to them, "I will ask you one thing too, which if you tell Me, I will also tell you by what authority I do these things.

25 "The baptism of John was from what source, from heaven or from men?" And they began reasoning among themselves, saying, "If we say, 'From heaven,' He will say to us, 'Then why did you not believe him?'

26 "But if we say, 'From men,' we fear the multitude; for they all hold John to be a prophet."

27 And answering Jesus, they said, "We do not know." He also said to them, "Neither will I tell you by what authority I do these things.

28 "But what do you think? A man had two sons, and he came to the first and said, 'Son, go work today in the vineyard.'

29 "And he answered and said, 'I will, sir'; and he did not go.

30 "And he came to the second and said the same thing. But he answered and said, 'I will not'; yet he afterward regretted it and went.

31 "Which of the two did the will of his father?" They *said, "The latter." Jesus *said to them, "Truly I say to you that the tax-gatherers and harlots will get into the kingdom of God before you.

32 "For John came to you in the way of righteousness and you did not believe him; but the tax-gatherers and harlots did believe him; and you, seeing this, did not even feel remorse afterward so as to believe him.

33 "Listen to another parable. There was a landowner who PLANTED A VINEYARD AND PUT A WALL AROUND IT AND DUG A WINE PRESS IN IT, AND BUILT A TOWER, and rented it out to vine-growers, and went on a journey.

34 "And when the harvest time approached, he sent his slaves to the vine-growers to receive his produce.

35 "And the vine-growers took his slaves and beat one, and killed another, and stoned a third.

36 "Again he sent another group of slaves larger than the first; and they did the same thing to them.

37 "But afterward he sent his son to them, saying, 'They will respect my son.'

38 "But when the vine-growers saw the son, they said among themselves, 'This is the heir; come, let us kill him, and seize his inheritance.'

39 "And they took him, and threw him out of the vineyard, and killed him.

40 "Therefore when the owner of the vineyard comes, what will he do to those vine-growers?"

41 They *said to Him, "He will bring those wretches to a wretched end, and will rent out the vineyard to other vine-growers, who will pay him the proceeds at the proper seasons."

42 Jesus *said to them, "Did you never read in the Scriptures,
'THE STONE WHICH THE
    BUILDERS REJECTED,
    THIS BECAME THE CHIEF
    CORNER stone;
    THIS CAME ABOUT FROM
    THE LORD,
    AND IT IS MARVELOUS IN
    OUR EYES'?

43 "Therefore I say to you, the kingdom of God will be taken away from you, and be given to a nation producing the fruit of it.

44 "And he who falls on this stone will be broken to pieces; but on whomever it falls, it will scatter him like dust."

45 And when the chief priests and the Pharisees heard His parables, they understood that He was speaking about them.

46 And when they sought to seize Him, they feared the multitudes, because they held Him to be a prophet.

CHAPTER 22

AND Jesus answered and spoke to them again in parables, saying,

2 "The kingdom of heaven may be compared to a king, who gave a wedding feast for his son.

3 "And he sent out his slaves to call those who had been invited to the wedding feast, and they were unwilling to come.

4 "Again he sent out other slaves saying, 'Tell those who have been invited, "Behold, I have prepared my dinner; my oxen and my fattened livestock are *all* butchered and everything is ready; come to the wedding feast."'

5 "But they paid no attention and went their way, one to his own farm, another to his business,

6 and the rest seized his slaves and mistreated them and killed them.

7 "But the king was enraged and sent his armies, and destroyed those murderers, and set their city on fire.

8 "Then he *said to his slaves, 'The wedding is ready, but those who were invited were not worthy.

9 'Go therefore to the main highways, and as many as you find *there*, invite to the wedding feast.'

10 "And those slaves went out into the streets, and gathered together all they found, both evil and good; and the wedding hall was filled with dinner guests.

11 "But when the king came in to look over the dinner guests, he saw there a man not dressed in wedding clothes,

12 and he *said to him, 'Friend, how did you come in here without wedding clothes?' And he was speechless.

13 "Then the king said to the servants, 'Bind him hand and foot, and cast him into the outer darkness; in that place there shall be weeping and gnashing of teeth.'

14 "For many are called, but few *are* chosen."

15 Then the Pharisees went and counseled together how they might trap Him in what He said.

16 And they *sent their disciples to Him, along with the Herodians, saying, "Teacher, we know that You are truthful and teach the way of God in truth, and defer to no one; for You are not partial to any.

17 "Tell us therefore, what do You think? Is it lawful to give a poll-tax to Caesar, or not?"

18 But Jesus perceived their malice, and said, "Why are you testing Me, you hypocrites?

19 "Show Me the coin *used* for the poll-tax." And they brought Him a denarius.

20 And He *said to them, "Whose likeness and inscription is this?"

21 They *said to Him, "Caesar's." Then He *said to them, "Then render to Caesar the things that are Caesar's; and to God the things that are God's."

22 And hearing *this*, they marveled, and leaving Him, they went away.

23 On that day *some* Sadducees (who say there is no resurrection) came to Him and questioned Him,

24 saying, "Teacher, Moses said, 'IF A MAN DIES, HAVING NO CHILDREN, HIS BROTHER AS NEXT OF KIN SHALL MARRY HIS WIFE,

AND RAISE UP AN OFFSPRING TO HIS BROTHER.'

25"Now there were seven brothers with us; and the first married and died, and having no offspring left his wife to his brother;

26 so also the second, and the third, down to the seventh.

27"And last of all, the woman died.

28"In the resurrection therefore whose wife of the seven shall she be? For they all had her."

29 But Jesus answered and said to them, "You are mistaken, not understanding the Scriptures, or the power of God.

30"For in the resurrection they neither marry, nor are given in marriage, but are like angels in heaven.

31"But regarding the resurrection of the dead, have you not read that which was spoken to you by God, saying,

32 'I AM THE GOD OF ABRAHAM, AND THE GOD OF ISAAC, AND THE GOD OF JACOB'? He is not the God of the dead but of the living."

33 And when the multitudes heard *this*, they were astonished at His teaching.

34 But when the Pharisees heard that He had put the Sadducees to silence, they gathered themselves together.

35 And one of them, [42]a lawyer, asked Him *a question*, testing Him,

36"Teacher, which is the great commandment in the Law?"

37 And He said to him, " 'YOU SHALL LOVE THE LORD YOUR GOD WITH ALL YOUR HEART, AND WITH ALL YOUR SOUL, AND WITH ALL YOUR MIND.'

38"This is the great and foremost commandment.

39"The second is like it, 'YOU SHALL LOVE YOUR NEIGHBOR AS YOURSELF.'

40"On these two commandments depend the whole Law and the Prophets."

41 Now while the Pharisees were gathered together, Jesus asked them a question,

42 saying, "What do you think about the Christ, whose son is He?" They *said to Him, "The son of David."

43 He *said to them, "Then how does David in the Spirit call Him 'Lord,' saying,

44 'THE LORD SAID TO MY LORD,
     "SIT AT MY RIGHT HAND,
      UNTIL I PUT THINE ENEMIES
       BENEATH THY FEET" '?

45"If David then calls Him 'Lord,' how is He his son?"

46 And no one was able to answer Him a word, nor did anyone dare from that day on to ask Him another question.

CHAPTER 23

THEN Jesus spoke to the multitudes and to His disciples,

2 saying, "The scribes and the Pharisees have seated themselves in the chair of Moses;

3 therefore all that they tell you, do and observe, but do not do according to their deeds; for they say *things*, and do not do *them*.

4"And they tie up heavy loads, and lay them on men's shoulders; but they themselves are unwilling to move them with *so much as* a finger.

5"But they do all their deeds to be noticed by men; for they broaden their [43]phylacteries, and

---

[42] I.e., an expert in the Mosaic law
[43] I.e., small boxes containing Scripture texts worn for religious purposes

lengthen the tassels *of their garments.*

6 "And they love the place of honor at banquets, and the chief seats in the synagogues,

7 and respectful greetings in the market places, and being called by men, Rabbi.

8 "But do not be called Rabbi; for One is your Teacher, and you are all brothers.

9 "And do not call *anyone* on earth your father; for One is your Father, He who is in heaven.

10 "And do not be called leaders; for One is your Leader, *that is,* Christ.

11 "But the greatest among you shall be your servant.

12 "And whoever exalts himself shall be humbled; and whoever humbles himself shall be exalted.

13 "But woe to you, scribes and Pharisees, hypocrites, because you shut off the kingdom of heaven from men; for you do not enter in yourselves, nor do you allow those who are entering to go in.

14 ["⁴⁴Woe to you, scribes and Pharisees, hypocrites, because you devour widows' houses, even while for a pretense you make long prayers; therefore you shall receive greater condemnation.]

15 "Woe to you, scribes and Pharisees, hypocrites, because you travel about on sea and land to make one proselyte; and when he becomes one, you make him twice as much a son of hell as yourselves.

16 "Woe to you, blind guides, who say, 'Whoever swears by the temple, that is nothing; but whoever swears by the gold of the temple, he is obligated.'

⁴⁴ This verse not found in the earliest mss.

17 "You fools and blind men; which is more important, the gold, or the temple that sanctified the gold?

18 "And, 'Whoever swears by the altar, *that* is nothing, but whoever swears by the offering upon it, he is obligated.'

19 "You blind men, which is more important, the offering or the altar that sanctifies the offering?

20 "Therefore he who swears, swears *both* by the altar and by everything on it.

21 "And he who swears by the temple, swears *both* by the temple and by Him who dwells within it.

22 "And he who swears by heaven, swears *both* by the throne of God and by Him who sits upon it.

23 "Woe to you, scribes and Pharisees, hypocrites! For you tithe the mint and dill and cummin, and have neglected the weightier provisions of the law: justice and mercy and faithfulness; but these are the things you should have done without neglecting the others.

24 "You blind guides, who strain out a gnat and swallow a camel!

25 "Woe to you, scribes and Pharisees, hypocrites! For you clean the outside of the cup and of the dish, but inside they are full of robbery and self-indulgence.

26 "You blind Pharisee, first clean the inside of the cup and of the dish, so that the outside of it may become clean also.

27 "Woe to you, scribes and Pharisees, hypocrites! For you are like whitewashed tombs which on the outside appear

beautiful, but inside they are full of dead men's bones and all uncleanness.

28"Even so you too outwardly appear righteous to men, but inwardly you are full of hypocrisy and lawlessness.

29"Woe to you, scribes and Pharisees, hypocrites! For you build the tombs of the prophets and adorn the monuments of the righteous,

30 and say, 'If we had been *living* in the days of our fathers, we would not have been partners with them in *shedding* the blood of the prophets.'

31"Consequently you bear witness against yourselves, that you are sons of those who murdered the prophets.

32"Fill up then the measure *of the guilt* of your fathers.

33"You serpents, you brood of vipers, how shall you escape the sentence of hell?

34"Therefore, behold, I am sending you prophets and wise men and scribes; some of them you will kill and crucify, and some of them you will scourge in your synagogues, and persecute from city to city,

35 that upon you may fall *the guilt* of all the righteous blood shed on earth, from the blood of righteous Abel to the blood of Zechariah, the son of Berechiah, whom you murdered between the temple and the altar.

36"Truly I say to you, all these things shall come upon this generation.

37"O Jerusalem, Jerusalem, who kills the prophets and stones those who are sent to her! How often I wanted to gather your children together, the way a hen gathers her chicks under her wings, and you were unwilling.

38"Behold, your house is being left to you desolate!

39"For I say to you, from now on you shall not see Me until you say, 'BLESSED IS HE WHO COMES IN THE NAME OF THE LORD!' "

CHAPTER 24

AND Jesus came out from the temple and was going away when His disciples came up to point out the temple buildings to Him.

2 And He answered and said to them, "Do you not see all these things? Truly I say to you, not one stone here shall be left upon another, which will not be torn down."

3 And as He was sitting on the Mount of Olives, the disciples came to Him privately, saying, "Tell us, when will these things be, and what *will be* the sign of Your coming, and of the end of the age?"

4 And Jesus answered and said to them, "See to it that no one misleads you.

5"For many will come in My name, saying, 'I am the Christ,' and will mislead many.

6"And you will be hearing of wars and rumors of wars; see that you are not frightened, for *those things* must take place, but *that* is not yet the end.

7"For nation will rise against nation, and kingdom against kingdom, and in various places there will be famines and earthquakes.

8"But all these things are *merely* the beginning of birth pangs.

9"Then they will deliver you to

tribulation, and will kill you, and you will be hated by all nations on account of My name.

10 "And at that time many will fall away and will deliver up one another and hate one another.

11 "And many false prophets will arise, and will mislead many.

12 "And because lawlessness is increased, most people's love will grow cold.

13 "But the one who endures to the end, he shall be saved.

14 "And this gospel of the kingdom shall be preached in the whole world for a witness to all the nations, and then the end shall come.

15 "Therefore when you see the ABOMINATION OF DESOLATION which was spoken of through Daniel the prophet, standing in the holy place (let the reader understand),

16 then let those who are in Judea flee to the mountains;

17 let him who is on the housetop not go down to get the things out that are in his house;

18 and let him who is in the field not turn back to get his cloak.

19 "But woe to those who are with child and to those who nurse babes in those days!

20 "But pray that your flight may not be in the winter, or on a Sabbath;

21 for then there will be a great tribulation, such as has not occurred since the beginning of the world until now, nor ever shall.

22 "And unless those days had been cut short, no life would have been saved; but for the sake of the elect those days shall be cut short.

23 "Then if anyone says to you, 'Behold, here is the Christ,' or 'There He is,' do not believe him.

24 "For false Christs and false prophets will arise and will show great signs and wonders, so as to mislead, if possible, even the elect.

25 "Behold, I have told you in advance.

26 "If therefore they say to you, 'Behold, He is in the wilderness,' do not go forth, or, 'Behold, He is in the inner rooms,' do not believe them.

27 "For just as the lightning comes from the east, and flashes even to the west, so shall the coming of the Son of Man be.

28 "Wherever the corpse is, there the vultures will gather.

29 "But immediately after the tribulation of those days THE SUN WILL BE DARKENED, AND THE MOON WILL NOT GIVE ITS LIGHT, AND THE STARS WILL FALL from the sky, and the powers of the heavens will be shaken,

30 and then the sign of the Son of Man will appear in the sky, and then all the tribes of the earth will mourn, and they will see the SON OF MAN COMING ON THE CLOUDS OF THE SKY with power and great glory.

31 "And He will send forth His angels with A GREAT TRUMPET and THEY WILL GATHER TOGETHER His elect from the four winds, from one end of the sky to the other.

32 "Now learn the parable from the fig tree: when its branch has already become tender, and puts forth its leaves, you know that summer is near;

33 even so you too, when you see all these things, recognize that He is near, right at the door.

34 "Truly I say to you, this generation will not pass away until

all these things take place.

35"Heaven and earth will pass away, but My words shall not pass away.

36"But of that day and hour no one knows, not even the angels of heaven, nor the Son, but the Father alone.

37"For the coming of the Son of Man will be just like the days of Noah.

38"For as in those days which were before the flood they were eating and drinking, they were marrying and giving in marriage, until the day that Noah entered the ark,

39 and they did not understand until the flood came and took them all away; so shall the coming of the Son of Man be.

40"Then there shall be two men in the field; one will be taken, and one will be left.

41"Two women *will be* grinding at the mill; one will be taken, and one will be left.

42"Therefore be on the alert, for you do not know which day your Lord is coming.

43"But be sure of this, that if the head of the house had known at what time of the night the thief was coming, he would have been on the alert and would not have allowed his house to be broken into.

44"For this reason you be ready too; for the Son of Man is coming at an hour when you do not think *He will.*

45"Who then is the faithful and sensible slave whom his master put in charge of his household to give them their food at the proper time?

46"Blessed is that slave whom his master finds so doing when he comes.

47"Truly I say to you, that he will put him in charge of all his possessions.

48"But if that evil slave says in his heart, 'My master is not coming for a long time,'

49 and shall begin to beat his fellow slaves and eat and drink with drunkards;

50 the master of that slave will come on a day when he does not expect *him* and at an hour which he does not know,

51 and shall cut him in pieces and assign him a place with the hypocrites; weeping shall be there and the gnashing of teeth.

CHAPTER 25

"THEN the kingdom of heaven will be comparable to ten virgins, who took their lamps, and went out to meet the bridegroom.

2"And five of them were foolish, and five were prudent.

3"For when the foolish took their lamps, they took no oil with them,

4 but the prudent took oil in flasks along with their lamps.

5"Now while the bridegroom was delaying, they all got drowsy and *began* to sleep.

6"But at midnight there was a shout, 'Behold, the bridegroom! Come out to meet *him.*'

7"Then all those virgins rose, and trimmed their lamps.

8"And the foolish said to the prudent, 'Give us some of your oil, for our lamps are going out.'

9"But the prudent answered, saying, 'No, there will not be enough for us and you *too*; go instead to the dealers and buy *some* for yourselves.'

10"And while they were going

away to make the purchase, the bridegroom came, and those who were ready went in with him to the wedding feast; and the door was shut.

11 "And later the other virgins also came, saying, 'Lord, lord, open up for us.'

12 "But he answered and said, 'Truly I say to you, I do not know you.'

13 "Be on the alert then, for you do not know the day nor the hour.

14 "For *it is* just like a man *about* to go on a journey, who called his own slaves, and entrusted his possessions to them.

15 "And to one he gave five talents, to another, two, and to another, one, each according to his own ability; and he went on his journey.

16 "Immediately the one who had received the five talents went and traded with them, and gained five more talents.

17 "In the same manner the one who had *received* the two *talents* gained two more.

18 "But he who received the one *talent* went away and dug in the ground, and hid his master's money.

19 "Now after a long time the master of those slaves *came and *settled accounts with them.

20 "And the one who had received the five talents came up and brought five more talents, saying, 'Master, you entrusted five talents to me; see, I have gained five more talents.'

21 "His master said to him, 'Well done, good and faithful slave; you were faithful with a few things, I will put you in charge of many things, enter into the joy of your master.'

22 "The one also who had *received* the two talents came up and said, 'Master, you entrusted to me two talents; see, I have gained two more talents.'

23 "His master said to him, 'Well done, good and faithful slave; you were faithful with a few things, I will put you in charge of many things; enter into the joy of your master.'

24 "And the one also who had received the one talent came up and said, 'Master, I knew you to be a hard man, reaping where you did not sow, and gathering where you scattered no *seed*.

25 'And I was afraid, and went away and hid your talent in the ground; see, you have what is yours.'

26 "But his master answered and said to him, 'You wicked, lazy slave, you knew that I reap where I did not sow, and gather where I scattered no *seed*.

27 'Then you ought to have put my money in the bank, and on my arrival I would have received my *money* back with interest.

28 'Therefore take away the talent from him, and give it to the one who has the ten talents.'

29 "For to everyone who has shall *more* be given, and he shall have an abundance; but from the one who does not have, even what he does have shall be taken away.

30 "And cast out the worthless slave into the outer darkness; in that place there shall be weeping and gnashing of teeth.

31 "But when the Son of Man comes in His glory, and all the angels with Him, then He will sit on His glorious throne.

32 "And all the nations will be gathered before Him; and He will

separate them from one another, as the shepherd separates the sheep from the goats;

33 and He will put the sheep on His right, and the goats on the left.

34 "Then the King will say to those on His right, 'Come, you who are blessed of My Father, inherit the kingdom prepared for you from the foundation of the world.

35 'For I was hungry, and you gave Me *something* to eat; I was thirsty, and you gave Me drink; I was a stranger, and you invited Me in;

36 naked, and you clothed Me; I was sick, and you visited Me; I was in prison, and you came to Me.'

37 "Then the righteous will answer Him, saying, 'Lord, when did we see You hungry, and feed You, or thirsty, and give You drink?

38 'And when did we see You a stranger, and invite You in, or naked, and clothe You?

39 'And when did we see You sick, or in prison, and come to You?'

40 "And the King will answer and say to them, 'Truly I say to you, to the extent that you did it to one of these brothers of Mine, *even* the least *of them,* you did it to Me.'

41 "Then He will also say to those on His left, 'Depart from Me, accursed ones, into the eternal fire which has been prepared for the devil and his angels;

42 for I was hungry, and you gave Me *nothing* to eat; I was thirsty, and you gave Me nothing to drink;

43 I was a stranger, and you did not invite Me in; naked, and

you did not clothe Me; sick, and in prison, and you did not visit Me.'

44 "Then they themselves also will answer, saying, 'Lord, when did we see You hungry, or thirsty, or a stranger, or naked, or sick, or in prison, and did not take care of You?'

45 "Then He will answer them, saying, 'Truly I say to you, to the extent that you did not do it to one of the least of these, you did not do it to Me.'

46 "And these will go away into eternal punishment, but the righteous into eternal life."

CHAPTER 26

AND it came about that when Jesus had finished all these words, He said to His disciples,

2 "You know that after two days the Passover is coming, and the Son of Man is *to be* delivered up for crucifixion."

3 Then the chief priests and the elders of the people were gathered together in the court of the high priest, named Caiaphas;

4 and they plotted together to seize Jesus by stealth, and kill *Him.*

5 But they were saying, "Not during the festival, lest a riot occur among the people."

6 Now when Jesus was in Bethany, at the home of Simon the leper,

7 a woman came to Him with an alabaster vial of very costly perfume, and she poured it upon His head as He reclined *at the table.*

8 But the disciples were indignant when they saw *this,* and said, "Why this waste?

9 "For this *perfume* might have

been sold for a high price and *the money* given to the poor."

10 But Jesus, aware of this, said to them, "Why do you bother the woman? For she has done a good deed to Me.

11 "For the poor you have with you always; but you do not always have Me.

12 "For when she poured this perfume upon My body, she did it to prepare Me for burial.

13 "Truly I say to you, wherever this gospel is preached in the whole world, what this woman has done shall also be spoken of in memory of her."

14 Then one of the twelve, named Judas Iscariot, went to the chief priests,

15 and said, "What are you willing to give me to deliver Him up to you?" And they weighed out to him thirty pieces of silver.

16 And from then on he *began* looking for a good opportunity to betray Him.

17 Now on the first *day* of Unleavened Bread the disciples came to Jesus, saying, "Where do You want us to prepare for You to eat the Passover?"

18 And He said, "Go into the city to a certain man, and say to him, 'The Teacher says, "My time is at hand; I *am* to keep the Passover at your house with My disciples." ' "

19 And the disciples did as Jesus had directed them; and they prepared the Passover.

20 Now when evening had come, He was reclining *at the table* with the twelve disciples.

21 And as they were eating, He said, "Truly I say to you that one of you will betray Me."

22 And being deeply grieved, they each one began to say to Him, "Surely not I, Lord?"

23 And He answered and said, "He who dipped his hand with Me in the bowl is the one who will betray Me.

24 "The Son of Man *is to* go, just as it is written of Him; but woe to that man by whom the Son of Man is betrayed! It would have been good for that man if he had not been born."

25 And Judas, who was betraying Him, answered and said, "Surely it is not I, Rabbi?" He *said to him, "You have said it* yourself."

26 And while they were eating, Jesus took *some* bread, and after a blessing, He broke *it* and gave *it* to the disciples, and said, "Take, eat; this is My body."

27 And when He had taken a cup and given thanks, He gave *it* to them, saying, "Drink from it, all of you;

28 for this is My blood of the covenant, which is poured out for many for forgiveness of sins.

29 "But I say to you, I will not drink of this fruit of the vine from now on until that day when I drink it new with you in My Father's kingdom."

30 And after singing a hymn, they went out to the Mount of Olives.

31 Then Jesus *said to them, "You will all fall away because of Me this night, for it is written, 'I WILL STRIKE DOWN THE SHEPHERD, AND THE SHEEP OF THE FLOCK SHALL BE SCATTERED.'

32 "But after I have been raised, I will go before you to Galilee."

33 But Peter answered and said to Him, "*Even* though all may fall away because of You, I will never fall away."

34 Jesus said to him, "Truly I say to you that this *very* night, before a cock crows, you shall deny Me three times."

35 Peter *said to Him, "Even if I have to die with You, I will not deny You." All the disciples said the same thing too.

36 Then Jesus *came with them to a place called Gethsemane, and *said to His disciples, "Sit here while I go over there and pray."

37 And He took with Him Peter and the two sons of Zebedee, and began to be grieved and distressed.

38 Then He *said to them, "My soul is deeply grieved, to the point of death; remain here and keep watch with Me."

39 And He went a little beyond *them*, and fell on His face and prayed, saying, "My Father, if it is possible, let this cup pass from Me; yet not as I will, but as Thou wilt."

40 And He *came to the disciples and *found them sleeping, and *said to Peter, "So, you *men* could not keep watch with Me for one hour?

41 "Keep watching and praying, that you may not enter into temptation; the spirit is willing, but the flesh is weak."

42 He went away again a second time and prayed, saying, "My Father, if this cannot pass away unless I drink it, Thy will be done."

43 And again He came and found them sleeping, for their eyes were heavy.

44 And He left them again, and went away and prayed a third time, saying the same thing once more.

45 Then He *came to the disciples, and *said to them, "Are you still sleeping and taking your rest? Behold, the hour is at hand and the Son of Man is being betrayed into the hands of sinners.

46 "Arise, let us be going; behold, the one who betrays Me is at hand!"

47 And while He was still speaking, behold, Judas, one of the twelve, came up, accompanied by a great multitude with swords and clubs, from the chief priests and elders of the people.

48 Now he who was betraying Him gave them a sign, saying, "Whomever I shall kiss, He is the one; seize Him."

49 And immediately he went to Jesus and said, "Hail, Rabbi!" and kissed Him.

50 And Jesus said to him, "Friend, *do* what you have come for." Then they came and laid hands on Jesus and seized Him.

51 And behold, one of those who were with Jesus reached and drew out his sword, and struck the slave of the high priest, and cut off his ear.

52 Then Jesus *said to him, "Put your sword back into its place; for all those who take up the sword shall perish by the sword.

53 "Or do you think that I cannot appeal to My Father, and He will at once put at My disposal more than twelve [45]legions of angels?

54 "How then shall the Scriptures be fulfilled, that it must happen this way?"

55 At that time Jesus said to the multitudes, "Have you come out with swords and clubs to arrest Me as against a robber? Ev-

[45] A legion equaled 6,000 troops

ery day I used to sit in the temple teaching and you did not seize Me.

56 "But all this has taken place that the Scriptures of the prophets may be fulfilled." Then all the disciples left Him and fled.

57 And those who had seized Jesus led Him away to Caiaphas, the high priest, where the scribes and the elders were gathered together.

58 But Peter also was following Him at a distance as far as the courtyard of the high priest, and entered in, and sat down with the officers to see the outcome.

59 Now the chief priests and the whole Council kept trying to obtain false testimony against Jesus, in order that they might put Him to death;

60 and they did not find any, even though many false witnesses came forward. But later on two came forward,

61 and said, "This man stated, 'I am able to destroy the temple of God and to rebuild it in three days.'"

62 And the high priest stood up and said to Him, "Do you make no answer? What is it that these men are testifying against You?"

63 But Jesus kept silent. And the high priest said to Him, "I adjure You by the living God, that You tell us whether You are the Christ, the Son of God."

64 Jesus *said to him, "You have said it yourself; nevertheless I tell you, hereafter you shall see THE SON OF MAN SITTING AT THE RIGHT HAND OF POWER, and COMING ON THE CLOUDS OF HEAVEN."

65 Then the high priest tore his robes, saying, "He has blasphemed! What further need do we have of witnesses? Behold, you have now heard the blasphemy;

66 what do you think?" They answered and said, "He is deserving of death!"

67 Then they spat in His face and beat Him with their fists; and others slapped Him,

68 and said, "Prophesy to us, You Christ; who is the one who hit You?"

69 Now Peter was sitting outside in the courtyard, and a certain servant-girl came to him and said, "You too were with Jesus the Galilean."

70 But he denied it before them all, saying, "I do not know what you are talking about."

71 And when he had gone out to the gateway, another servant-girl saw him and *said to those who were there, "This man was with Jesus of Nazareth."

72 And again he denied it with an oath, "I do not know the man."

73 And a little later the bystanders came up and said to Peter, "Surely you too are one of them; for the way you talk gives you away."

74 Then he began to curse and swear, "I do not know the man!" And immediately a cock crowed.

75 And Peter remembered the word which Jesus had said, "Before a cock crows, you will deny Me three times." And he went out and wept bitterly.

CHAPTER 27

NOW when morning had come, all the chief priests and the elders of the people took counsel against Jesus to put Him to death;

2 and they bound Him, and led Him away, and delivered Him up to Pilate the governor.

3 Then when Judas, who had betrayed Him, saw that He had been condemned, he felt remorse and returned the thirty pieces of silver to the chief priests and elders,

4 saying, "I have sinned by betraying innocent blood." But they said, "What is that to us? See *to that* yourself!"

5 And he threw the pieces of silver into the sanctuary and departed; and he went away and hanged himself.

6 And the chief priests took the pieces of silver and said, "It is not lawful to put them into the temple treasury, since it is the price of blood."

7 And they counseled together and with the money bought the Potter's Field as a burial place for strangers.

8 For this reason that field has been called the Field of Blood to this day.

9 Then that which was spoken through Jeremiah the prophet was fulfilled, saying, "AND THEY TOOK THE THIRTY PIECES OF SILVER, THE PRICE OF THE ONE WHOSE PRICE HAD BEEN SET by the sons of Israel;

10 AND THEY GAVE THEM FOR THE POTTER'S FIELD, AS THE LORD DIRECTED ME."

11 Now Jesus stood before the governor, and the governor questioned Him, saying, "Are You the King of the Jews?" And Jesus said to him, "*It is as* you say."

12 And while He was being accused by the chief priests and elders, He made no answer.

13 Then Pilate *said to Him, "Do You not hear how many things they testify against You?"

14 And He did not answer him with regard to even a *single* charge, so that the governor was quite amazed.

15 Now at *the* feast the governor was accustomed to release for the multitude *any* one prisoner whom they wanted.

16 And they were holding at that time a notorious prisoner, called Barabbas.

17 When therefore they were gathered together, Pilate said to them, "Whom do you want me to release for you? Barabbas, or Jesus who is called Christ?"

18 For he knew that because of envy they had delivered Him up.

19 And while he was sitting on the judgment seat, his wife sent to him, saying, "Have nothing to do with that righteous Man; for last night I suffered greatly in a dream because of Him."

20 But the chief priests and the elders persuaded the multitudes to ask for Barabbas, and to put Jesus to death.

21 But the governor answered and said to them, "Which of the two do you want me to release for you?" And they said, "Barabbas."

22 Pilate *said to them, "Then what shall I do with Jesus who is called Christ?" They all *said, "Let Him be crucified!"

23 And he said, "Why, what evil has He done?" But they kept shouting all the more, saying, "Let Him be crucified!"

24 And when Pilate saw that he was accomplishing nothing, but rather that a riot was starting, he took water and washed his hands in front of the multitude, saying, "I am innocent of this Man's blood; see to that yourselves."

25 And all the people answered and said, "His blood be on us and on our children!"

26 Then he released Barabbas for them; but after having Jesus scourged, he delivered Him to be crucified.

27 Then the soldiers of the governor took Jesus into the Praetorium and gathered the whole Roman cohort around Him.

28 And they stripped Him, and put a scarlet robe on Him.

29 And after weaving a crown of thorns, they put it on His head, and a reed in His right hand; and they kneeled down before Him and mocked Him, saying, "Hail, King of the Jews!"

30 And they spat on Him, and took the reed and began to beat Him on the head.

31 And after they had mocked Him, they took His robe off and put His garments on Him, and led Him away to crucify Him.

32 And as they were coming out, they found a man of Cyrene named Simon, whom they pressed into service to bear His cross.

33 And when they had come to a place called Golgotha, which means Place of a Skull,

34 they gave Him wine to drink mingled with gall; and after tasting it, He was unwilling to drink.

35 And when they had crucified Him, they divided up His garments among themselves, casting lots;

36 and sitting down, they began to keep watch over Him there.

37 And they put up above His head the charge against Him which read, "THIS IS JESUS THE KING OF THE JEWS."

38 At that time two robbers *were crucified with Him, one on the right and one on the left.

39 And those passing by were hurling abuse at Him, wagging their heads,

40 and saying, "You who are going to destroy the temple and rebuild it in three days, save Yourself! If You are the Son of God, come down from the cross."

41 In the same way the chief priests also, along with the scribes and elders, were mocking Him, and saying,

42 "He saved others; He cannot save Himself. He is the King of Israel; let Him now come down from the cross, and we shall believe in Him.

43 "HE TRUSTS IN GOD; LET HIM DELIVER Him now, IF HE TAKES PLEASURE IN HIM; for He said, 'I am the Son of God.' "

44 And the robbers also who had been crucified with Him were casting the same insult at Him.

45 Now from the [46]sixth hour darkness fell upon all the land until the [47]ninth hour.

46 And about the ninth hour Jesus cried out with a loud voice, saying, "ELI, ELI, LAMA SABACHTHANI?" that is, "MY GOD, MY GOD, WHY HAST THOU FORSAKEN ME?"

47 And some of those who were standing there, when they heard it, began saying, "This man is calling for Elijah."

48 And immediately one of them ran, and taking a sponge, he filled it with sour wine, and

[46] I.e., noon   [47] I.e., 3 p.m.

put it on a reed, and gave Him a drink.

49 But the rest of them said, "Let us see whether Elijah will come to save Him."[48]

50 And Jesus cried out again with a loud voice, and yielded up His spirit.

51 And behold, the veil of the temple was torn in two from top to bottom, and the earth shook; and the rocks were split;

52 and the tombs were opened; and many bodies of the saints who had fallen asleep were raised;

53 and coming out of the tombs after His resurrection they entered the holy city and appeared to many.

54 Now the centurion, and those who were with him keeping guard over Jesus, when they saw the earthquake and the things that were happening, became very frightened and said, "Truly this was the Son of God!"

55 And many women were there looking on from a distance, who had followed Jesus from Galilee, ministering to Him,

56 among whom was Mary Magdalene, along with Mary the mother of James and Joseph, and the mother of the sons of Zebedee.

57 And when it was evening, there came a rich man from Arimathea, named Joseph, who himself had also become a disciple of Jesus.

58 This man went to Pilate and asked for the body of Jesus. Then Pilate ordered it to be given over to him.

59 And Joseph took the body and wrapped it in a clean linen cloth,

60 and laid it in his own new tomb, which he had hewn out in the rock; and he rolled a large stone against the entrance of the tomb and went away.

61 And Mary Magdalene was there, and the other Mary, sitting opposite the grave.

62 Now on the next day, which is the one after the preparation, the chief priests and the Pharisees gathered together with Pilate,

63 and said, "Sir, we remember that when He was still alive that deceiver said, 'After three days I am to rise again.'

64 "Therefore, give orders for the grave to be made secure until the third day, lest the disciples come and steal Him away and say to the people, 'He has risen from the dead,' and the last deception will be worse than the first."

65 Pilate said to them, "You have a guard; go, make it as secure as you know how."

66 And they went and made the grave secure, and along with the guard they set a seal on the stone.

CHAPTER 28

NOW after the Sabbath, as it began to dawn toward the first day of the week, Mary Magdalene and the other Mary came to look at the grave.

2 And behold, a severe earthquake had occurred, for an angel of the Lord descended from heaven and came and rolled away the stone and sat upon it.

3 And his appearance was like lightning, and his garment as white as snow;

---

[48] Some early mss. add: And another took a spear and pierced His side, and there came out water and blood. (cf. John 19:34)

4 and the guards shook for fear of him, and became like dead men.

5 And the angel answered and said to the women, "Do not be afraid; for I know that you are looking for Jesus who has been crucified.

6 "He is not here, for He has risen, just as He said. Come, see the place where He was lying.

7 "And go quickly and tell His disciples that He has risen from the dead; and behold, He is going before you into Galilee, there you will see Him; behold, I have told you."

8 And they departed quickly from the tomb with fear and great joy and ran to report it to His disciples.

9 And behold, Jesus met them and greeted them. And they came up and took hold of His feet and worshiped Him.

10 Then Jesus *said to them, "Do not be afraid; go and take word to My brethren to leave for Galilee, and there they shall see Me."

11 Now while they were on their way, behold, some of the guard came into the city and reported to the chief priests all that had happened.

12 And when they had assembled with the elders and counseled together, they gave a large sum of money to the soldiers,

13 and said, "You are to say, 'His disciples came by night and stole Him away while we were asleep.'

14 "And if this should come to the governor's ears, we will win him over and keep you out of trouble."

15 And they took the money and did as they had been instructed; and this story was widely spread among the Jews, *and is* to this day.

16 But the eleven disciples proceeded to Galilee, to the mountain which Jesus had designated.

17 And when they saw Him, they worshiped *Him*; but some were doubtful.

18 And Jesus came up and spoke to them, saying, "All authority has been given to Me in heaven and on earth.

19 "Go therefore and make disciples of all the nations, baptizing them in the name of the Father and the Son and the Holy Spirit,

20 teaching them to observe all that I commanded you; and lo, I am with you always, even to the end of the age."

THE GOSPEL ACCORDING TO

MARK

THE beginning of the gospel of Jesus Christ, [1]the Son of God.

2 As it is written in Isaiah the prophet,

> "BEHOLD, I SEND MY MESSENGER BEFORE YOUR FACE,
> WHO WILL PREPARE YOUR WAY;

3 "THE VOICE OF ONE CRYING IN THE WILDERNESS,
> 'MAKE READY THE WAY OF THE LORD,
> MAKE HIS PATHS STRAIGHT.'"

4 John the Baptist appeared in the wilderness [2]preaching a baptism of repentance for the forgiveness of sins.

5 And all the country of Judea was going out to him, and all the people of Jerusalem; and they were being baptized by him in the Jordan River, confessing their sins.

6 And John was clothed with camel's hair and wore a leather belt around his waist, and his diet was locusts and wild honey.

7 And he was preaching, and saying, "After me One is coming who is mightier than I, and I am not fit to stoop down and untie the thong of His sandals.

8 "I baptized you [3]with water; but He will baptize you [3]with the Holy Spirit."

9 And it came about in those days that Jesus came from Nazareth in Galilee, and was baptized by John in the Jordan.

10 And immediately coming up out of the water, He saw the heavens opening, and the Spirit like a dove descending upon Him;

11 and a voice came out of the heavens: "Thou art My beloved Son, in Thee I am well-pleased."

12 And immediately the Spirit *impelled Him to go out into the wilderness.

13 And He was in the wilderness forty days being tempted by Satan; and He was with the wild beasts, and the angels were ministering to Him.

14 And after John had been taken into custody, Jesus came into Galilee, preaching the gospel of God,

15 and saying, "The time is fulfilled, and the kingdom of God is at hand; repent and believe in the gospel."

16 And as He was going along by the Sea of Galilee, He saw Simon and Andrew, the brother of Simon, casting a net in the sea; for they were fishermen.

17 And Jesus said to them, "Follow Me, and I will make you become fishers of men."

18 And they immediately left the nets and followed Him.

19 And going on a little farther, He saw James the son of Zebedee, and John his brother, who were also in the boat mending the nets.

20 And immediately He called them; and they left their father Zebedee in the boat with the

---

[1] Many mss. do not contain the Son of God
[2] Or, proclaiming
[3] The Gr. here can be translated in, with or by

hired servants, and went away to follow Him.

21 And they *went into Capernaum; and immediately on the Sabbath He entered the synagogue and *began* to teach.

22 And they were amazed at His teaching; for He was teaching them as *one* having authority, and not as the scribes.

23 And just then there was in their synagogue a man with an unclean spirit; and he cried out,

24 saying, "What do we have to do with You, Jesus 4of Nazareth? Have You come to destroy us? I know who You are—the Holy One of God!"

25 And Jesus rebuked him, saying, "Be quiet, and come out of him!"

26 And throwing him into convulsions, the unclean spirit cried out with a loud voice, and came out of him.

27 And they were all amazed, so that they debated among themselves, saying, "What is this? A new teaching with authority! He commands even the unclean spirits, and they obey Him."

28 And immediately the news about Him went out everywhere into all the surrounding district of Galilee.

29 And immediately after they had come out of the synagogue, they came into the house of Simon and Andrew, with James and John.

30 Now Simon's mother-in-law was lying sick with a fever; and immediately they *spoke to Him about her.

31 And He came to her and raised her up, taking her by the hand, and the fever left her, and she 5waited on them.

32 And when evening had come, after the sun had set, they *began* bringing to Him all who were ill and those who were demon-possessed.

33 And the whole city had gathered at the door.

34 And He healed many who were ill with various diseases, and cast out many demons; and He was not permitting the demons to speak, because they 6knew who He was.

35 And in the early morning, while it was still dark, He arose and went out and departed to a lonely place, and was praying there.

36 And Simon and his companions hunted for Him;

37 and they found Him, and *said to Him, "Everyone is looking for You."

38 And He *said to them, "Let us go somewhere else to the towns nearby, in order that I may preach there also; for that is what I came out for."

39 And He went into their synagogues throughout all Galilee, preaching and casting out the demons.

40 And a leper *came to Him, beseeching Him and falling on his knees before Him, and saying to Him, "If You are willing, You can make me clean."

41 And moved with compassion, He stretched out His hand, and touched him, and *said to him, "I am willing; be cleansed."

42 And immediately the leprosy left him and he was cleansed.

43 And He sternly warned him and immediately sent him away,

4 Lit., *the Nazarene* 5 Or, *served*
6 Some mss. read: *knew Him to be Christ*

44 and He *said to him, "See that you say nothing to anyone; but go, show yourself to the priest and offer for your cleansing what Moses commanded, for a testimony to them."

45 But he went out and began to proclaim it freely and to spread the news about, to such an extent that Jesus could no longer publicly enter a city, but [7]stayed out in unpopulated areas; and they were coming to Him from everywhere.

CHAPTER 2

AND when He had come back to Capernaum several days afterward, it was heard that He was at home.

2 And many were gathered together, so that there was no longer room, even near the door; and He was speaking the word to them.

3 And they *came, bringing to Him a paralytic, carried by four men.

4 And being unable to get to Him because of the crowd, they removed the roof above Him; and when they had dug an opening, they let down the pallet on which the paralytic was lying.

5 And Jesus seeing their faith *said to the paralytic, "My [8]son, your sins are forgiven."

6 But there were some of the scribes sitting there and reasoning in their hearts,

7 "Why does this man speak that way? He is blaspheming; who can forgive sins but God alone?"

8 And immediately Jesus, aware in His spirit that they were reasoning that way within themselves, *said to them, "Why are you reasoning about these things in your hearts?

9 "Which is easier, to say to the paralytic, 'Your sins are forgiven'; or to say, 'Arise, and take up your pallet and walk'?

10 "But in order that you may know that the Son of Man has authority on earth to forgive sins"—He *said to the paralytic—

11 "I say to you, rise, take up your pallet and go home."

12 And he rose and immediately took up the pallet and went out in the sight of all; so that they were all amazed and were glorifying God, saying, "We have never seen anything like this."

13 And He went out again by the seashore; and all the multitude were coming to Him, and He was teaching them.

14 And as He passed by, He saw Levi the son of Alphaeus sitting in the tax office, and He *said to him, "Follow Me!" And he rose and followed Him.

15 And it came about that He was reclining at the table in his house, and many tax-gatherers and sinners were dining with Jesus and His disciples; for there were many of them, and they were following Him.

16 And when the scribes of the Pharisees saw that He was eating with the sinners and tax-gatherers, they began saying to His disciples, "Why is He eating and drinking with tax-gatherers and sinners?"

17 And hearing this, Jesus *said to them, "It is not those who are healthy who need a physician, but those who are sick; I

7 Lit., was   8 Lit., child

did not come to call the righteous, but sinners."

18 And John's disciples and the Pharisees were fasting; and they *came and *said to Him, "Why do John's disciples and the disciples of the Pharisees fast, but Your disciples do not fast?"

19 And Jesus said to them, "While the bridegroom is with them, the attendants of the bridegroom do not fast, do they? So long as they have the bridegroom with them, they cannot fast.

20 "But the days will come when the bridegroom is taken away from them, and then they will fast in that day.

21 "No one sews a patch of unshrunk cloth on an old garment; otherwise the patch pulls away from it, the new from the old, and a worse tear results.

22 "And no one puts new wine into old wineskins; otherwise the wine will burst the skins, and the wine is lost, and the skins *as well*; but *one puts* new wine into fresh wineskins."

23 And it came about that He was passing through the grainfields on the Sabbath, and His disciples began to make their way along while picking the heads of grain.

24 And the Pharisees were saying to Him, "See here, why are they doing what is not lawful on the Sabbath?"

25 And He *said to them, "Have you never read what David did when he was in need and became hungry, he and his companions:

26 how he entered the house of God in the time of Abiathar *the* high priest, and ate the consecrated bread, which is not lawful for *anyone* to eat except the

priests, and he gave *it* also to those who were with him?"

27 And He was saying to them, "The Sabbath was made for man, and not man for the Sabbath.

28 "Consequently, the Son of Man is Lord even of the Sabbath."

CHAPTER 3

AND He entered again into a synagogue; and a man was there with a withered hand.

2 And they were watching Him *to see* if He would heal him on the Sabbath, in order that they might accuse Him.

3 And He *said to the man with the withered hand, "Rise and *come* forward!"

4 And He *said to them, "Is it lawful on the Sabbath to do good or to do harm, to save a life or to kill?" But they kept silent.

5 And after looking around at them with anger, grieved at their hardness of heart, He *said to the man, "Stretch out your hand." And he stretched it out, and his hand was restored.

6 And the Pharisees went out and immediately *began* taking counsel with the Herodians against Him, *as to* how they might destroy Him.

7 And Jesus withdrew to the sea with His disciples; and a great multitude from Galilee followed; and *also* from Judea,

8 and from Jerusalem, and from Idumea, and beyond the Jordan, and the vicinity of Tyre and Sidon, a great multitude heard of all that He was doing and came to Him.

9 And He told His disciples that a boat should stand ready for Him because of the multitude, in order that they might not crowd Him;

10 for He had healed many, with the result that all those who had afflictions pressed about Him in order to touch Him.

11 And whenever the unclean spirits beheld Him, they would fall down before Him and cry out, saying, "You are the Son of God!"

12 And He earnestly warned them not to make Him known.

13 And He *went up to the mountain and *summoned those whom He Himself wanted, and they came to Him.

14 And He appointed twelve[9], that they might be with Him, and that He might send them out to preach,

15 and to have authority to cast out the demons.

16 And He appointed the twelve: Simon (to whom He gave the name Peter),

17 and James, the son of Zebedee, and John the brother of James (to them He gave the name Boanerges, which means, "Sons of Thunder");

18 and Andrew, and Philip, and Bartholomew, and Matthew, and Thomas, and James the son of Alphaeus, and Thaddaeus, and Simon the Zealot;

19 and Judas Iscariot, who also betrayed Him.

20 And He *came [10]home, and the multitude *gathered again, to such an extent that they could not even eat a meal.

21 And when His own [11]people heard of this, they went out to take custody of Him; for they were saying, "He has lost His senses."

22 And the scribes who came down from Jerusalem were saying, "He is possessed by Beelzebul," and "He casts out the demons by the ruler of the demons."

23 And He called them to Himself and began speaking to them in parables, "How can Satan cast out Satan?

24 "And if a kingdom is divided against itself, that kingdom cannot stand.

25 "And if a house is divided against itself, that house will not be able to stand.

26 "And if Satan has risen up against himself and is divided, he cannot stand, but he is finished!

27 "But no one can enter the strong man's house and plunder his property unless he first binds the strong man, and then he will plunder his house.

28 "Truly I say to you, all sins shall be forgiven the sons of men, and whatever blasphemies they utter;

29 but whoever blasphemes against the Holy Spirit never has forgiveness, but is guilty of an eternal sin"—

30 because they were saying, "He has an unclean spirit."

31 And His mother and His brothers *arrived, and standing outside they sent word to Him, and called Him.

32 And a multitude was sitting around Him, and they *said to Him, "Behold, Your mother and Your brothers[12] are outside looking for You."

33 And answering them, He *said, "Who are My mother and My brothers?"

34 And looking about on those

---

9 Some early mss. add: whom He named apostles   10 Lit. into a house

11 Or, kinsmen

12 Later mss. add: and Your sisters

who were sitting around Him, He *said, "Behold, My mother and My brothers!

35 "For whoever does the will of God, he is My brother and sister and mother."

CHAPTER 4

AND He began to teach again by the sea. And such a very great multitude gathered to Him that He got into a boat in the sea and sat down; and the whole multitude was by the sea on the land.

2 And He was teaching them many things in parables, and was saying to them in His teaching,

3 "Listen to this! Behold, the sower went out to sow;

4 and it came about that as he was sowing, some seed fell beside the road, and the birds came and ate it up.

5 "And other seed fell on the rocky ground where it did not have much soil; and immediately it sprang up because it had no depth of soil.

6 "And after the sun had risen, it was scorched; and because it had no root, it withered away.

7 "And other seed fell among the thorns, and the thorns came up and choked it, and it yielded no crop.

8 "And other seeds fell into the good soil and as they grew up and increased, they yielded a crop and produced thirty, sixty, and a hundredfold."

9 And He was saying, "He who has ears to hear, let him hear."

10 And as soon as He was alone, His followers, along with

13 Or, age

the twelve, began asking Him about the parables.

11 And He was saying to them, "To you has been given the mystery of the kingdom of God; but those who are outside get everything in parables,

12 in order that WHILE SEEING, THEY MAY SEE AND NOT PERCEIVE; AND WHILE HEARING, THEY MAY HEAR AND NOT UNDERSTAND LEST THEY RETURN AND BE FORGIVEN."

13 And He *said to them, "Do you not understand this parable? And how will you understand all the parables?

14 "The sower sows the word.

15 "And these are the ones who are beside the road where the word is sown; and when they hear, immediately Satan comes and takes away the word which has been sown in them.

16 "And in a similar way these are the ones on whom seed was sown on the rocky places, who, when they hear the word, immediately receive it with joy;

17 and they have no firm root in themselves, but are only temporary; then, when affliction or persecution arises because of the word, immediately they fall away.

18 "And others are the ones on whom seed was sown among the thorns; these are the ones who have heard the word,

19 and the worries of the 13world, and the deceitfulness of riches, and the desires for other things enter in and choke the word, and it becomes unfruitful.

20 "And those are the ones on whom seed was sown on the good soil; and they hear the word and accept it, and bear fruit, thirty, sixty, and a hundredfold.

21 And He was saying to them,

"A lamp is not brought to be put under a peck-measure, is it, or under a bed? Is it not *brought* to be put on the lampstand?

22 "For nothing is hidden, except to be revealed; nor has *anything* been secret, but that it should come to light.

23 "If any man has ears to hear, let him hear."

24 And He was saying to them, "Take care what you listen to. By your standard of measure it shall be measured to you; and more shall be given you besides.

25 "For whoever has, to him shall *more* be given; and whoever does not have, even what he has shall be taken away from him."

26 And He was saying, "The kingdom of God is like a man who casts seed upon the soil;

27 and goes to bed at night and gets up by day, and the seed sprouts up and grows—how, he himself does not know.

28 "The soil produces crops by itself; first the blade, then the head, then the mature grain in the head.

29 "But when the crop permits, he immediately puts in the sickle, because the harvest has come."

30 And He said, "How shall we [14]picture the kingdom of God, or by what parable shall we present it?

31 "*It is* like a mustard seed, which, when sown upon the soil, though it is smaller than all the seeds that are upon the soil,

32 yet when it is sown, grows up and becomes larger than all the garden plants and forms large branches; so that THE BIRDS OF THE [15]AIR CAN NEST UNDER ITS SHADE."

33 And with many such parables He was speaking the word to them as they were able to hear it;

34 and He did not speak to them without a parable; but He was explaining everything privately to His own disciples.

35 And on that day, when evening had come, He *said to them, "Let us go over to the other side."

36 And leaving the multitude, they *took Him along with them, just as He was, in the boat; and other boats were with Him.

37 And there *arose a fierce gale of wind, and the waves were breaking over the boat so much that the boat was already filling up.

38 And He Himself was in the stern, asleep on the cushion; and they *awoke Him and *said to Him, "Teacher, do You not care that we are perishing?"

39 And being aroused, He rebuked the wind and said to the sea, "Hush, be still." And the wind died down and it became perfectly calm.

40 And He said to them, "Why are you so timid? How is it that you have no faith?"

41 And they became very much afraid and said to one another, "Who then is this, that even the wind and the sea obey Him?"

CHAPTER 5

AND they came to the other side of the sea, into the country of the Gerasenes.

2 And when He had come out of the boat, immediately a man from the tombs with an unclean spirit met Him,

[14] Lit., *compare*   [15] Or, *sky*

3 and he had his dwelling among the tombs. And no one was able to bind him anymore, even with a chain;

4 because he had often been bound with shackles and chains, and the chains had been torn apart by him, and the shackles broken in pieces, and no one was strong enough to subdue him.

5 And constantly night and day, among the tombs and in the mountains, he was crying out and gashing himself with stones.

6 And seeing Jesus from a distance, he ran up and bowed down before Him;

7 and crying out with a loud voice, he *said, "What do I have to do with You, Jesus, Son of the Most High God? I implore You by God, do not torment me!"

8 For He had been saying to him, "Come out of the man, you unclean spirit!"

9 And He was asking him, "What is your name?" And he *said to Him, "My name is Legion; for we are many."

10 And he *began* to entreat Him earnestly not to send them out of the country.

11 Now there was a big herd of swine feeding there on the mountain.

12 And the demons entreated Him, saying, "Send us into the swine so that we may enter them."

13 And He gave them permission. And coming out, the unclean spirits entered the swine; and the herd rushed down the steep bank into the sea, about two thousand of them; and they were drowned in the sea.

14 And their herdsmen ran

¹⁶ Or, everything that

away and reported it in the city and out in the country. And the people came to see what it was that had happened.

15 And they *came to Jesus and *observed the man who had been demon-possessed sitting down, clothed and in his right mind, the very man who had had the "legion"; and they became frightened.

16 And those who had seen it described to them how it had happened to the demon-possessed man, and all about the swine.

17 And they began to entreat Him to depart from their region.

18 And as He was getting into the boat, the man who had been demon-possessed was entreating Him that he might accompany Him.

19 And He did not let him, but He *said to him, "Go home to your people and report to them ¹⁶what great things the Lord has done for you, and how He had mercy on you."

20 And he went away and began to proclaim in Decapolis what great things Jesus had done for him; and everyone marveled.

21 And when Jesus had crossed over again in the boat to the other side, a great multitude gathered about Him; and He stayed by the seashore.

22 And one of the synagogue officials named Jairus *came up, and upon seeing Him, *fell at His feet,

23 and *entreated Him earnestly, saying, "My little daughter is at the point of death; please come and lay Your hands on her, that she may get well and live."

24 And He went off with him; and a great multitude was

following Him and pressing in on Him.

25 And a woman who had had a hemorrhage for twelve years,

26 and had endured much at the hands of many physicians, and had spent all that she had and was not helped at all, but rather had grown worse,

27 after hearing about Jesus, came up in the crowd behind *Him*, and touched His cloak.

28 For she thought, "If I just touch His garments, I shall get well."

29 And immediately the flow of her blood was dried up; and she felt in her body that she was healed of her affliction.

30 And immediately Jesus, perceiving in Himself that the power *proceeding* from Him had gone forth, turned around in the crowd and said, "Who touched My garments?"

31 And His disciples said to Him, "You see the multitude pressing in on You, and You say, 'Who touched Me?'"

32 And He looked around to see the woman who had done this.

33 But the woman fearing and trembling, aware of what had happened to her, came and fell down before Him, and told Him the whole truth.

34 And He said to her, "Daughter, your faith has made you well; go in peace, and be healed of your affliction."

35 While He was still speaking, they *came from the house of the synagogue official, saying, "Your daughter has died; why trouble the Teacher anymore?"

36 But Jesus, overhearing what was being spoken, *said to the synagogue official, "Do not be afraid *any longer*, only believe."

37 And He allowed no one to follow with Him, except Peter and James and John the brother of James.

38 And they *came to the house of the synagogue official; and He *beheld a commotion, and *people* loudly weeping and wailing.

39 And entering in, He *said to them, "Why make a commotion and weep? The child has not died, but is asleep."

40 And they *began* laughing at Him. But putting them all out, He *took along the child's father and mother and His own companions, and *entered *the room* where the child was.

41 And taking the child by the hand, He *said to her, "Talitha kum!" (which translated means, "Little girl, I say to you, arise!")

42 And immediately the girl rose and *began* to walk; for she was twelve years old. And immediately they were completely astounded.

43 And He gave them strict orders that no one should know about this; and He said that *something* should be given her to eat.

CHAPTER 6

AND He went out from there, and He *came into His home town; and His disciples *followed Him.

2 And when the Sabbath had come, He began to teach in the synagogue; and the many listeners were astonished, saying, "Where did this man *get* these things, and what is *this* wisdom given to Him, and such miracles as these performed by His hands?

3 "Is not this the carpenter, the son of Mary, and brother of James, and Joses, and Judas, and Simon? Are not His sisters here with us?" And they took offense at Him.

4 And Jesus said to them, "A prophet is not without honor except in his home town and among his *own* relatives and in his *own* household."

5 And He could do no miracle there except that He laid His hands upon a few sick people and healed them.

6 And He wondered at their unbelief.

And He was going around the villages teaching.

7 And He *summoned the twelve and began to send them out in pairs; and He was giving them authority over the unclean spirits;

8 and He instructed them that they should take nothing for *their* journey, except a mere staff; no bread, no bag, no money in their belt;

9 but *to* wear sandals; and *He* added, "Do not put on two [17]tunics."

10 And He said to them, "Wherever you enter a house, stay there until you leave town.

11 "And any place that does not receive you or listen to you, as you go out from there, shake off the dust from the soles of your feet for a testimony against them."

12 And they went out and preached that *men* should repent.

13 And they were casting out many demons and were anointing with oil many sick people and healing them.

14 And King Herod heard *of it,* for His name had become well known; and *people* were saying, "John the Baptist has risen from the dead, and that is why these miraculous powers are at work in Him."

15 But others were saying, "*He is* Elijah." And others were saying, "*He is* a prophet, like one of the prophets *of old.*"

16 But when Herod heard *of it,* he kept saying, "John, whom I beheaded, has risen!"

17 For Herod himself had sent and had John arrested and bound in prison on account of Herodias, the wife of his brother Philip, because he had married her.

18 For John had been saying to Herod, "It is not lawful for you to have your brother's wife."

19 And Herodias had a grudge against him and wanted to put him to death and could not *do so;*

20 for Herod was afraid of John, knowing that he was a righteous and holy man, and kept him safe. And when he heard him, he was very perplexed; but he used to enjoy listening to him.

21 And a strategic day came when Herod on his birthday gave a banquet for his lords and military commanders and the leading men of Galilee;

22 and when the daughter of Herodias herself came in and danced, she pleased Herod and his dinner guests; and the king said to the girl, "Ask me for whatever you want and I will give it to you."

23 And he swore to her, "Whatever you ask of me, I will

[17] Or, *inner garments*

give it to you; up to half of my kingdom."

24 And she went out and said to her mother, "What shall I ask for?" And she said, "The head of John the Baptist."

25 And immediately she came in haste before the king and asked, saying, "I want you to give me right away the head of John the Baptist on a platter."

26 And although the king was very sorry, *yet* because of his oaths and because of his dinner guests, he was unwilling to refuse her.

27 And immediately the king sent an executioner and commanded *him* to bring *back* his head. And he went and had him beheaded in the prison,

28 and brought his head on a platter, and gave it to the girl; and the girl gave it to her mother.

29 And when his disciples heard *about this,* they came and took away his body and laid it in a tomb.

30 And the apostles *gathered together with Jesus; and they reported to Him all that they had done and taught.

31 And He *said to them, "Come away by yourselves to a lonely place and rest a while." (For there were many *people* coming and going, and they did not even have time to eat.)

32 And they went away in the boat to a lonely place by themselves.

33 And *the people* saw them going, and many recognized *them,* and they ran there together on foot from all the cities, and got there ahead of them.

34 And when He went ashore, He saw a great multitude, and He felt compassion for them because they were like sheep without a shepherd; and He began to teach them many things.

35 And when it was already quite late, His disciples came up to Him and *began saying, "The place is desolate and it is already quite late;

36 send them away so that they may go into the surrounding countryside and villages and buy themselves something to eat."

37 But He answered and said to them, "You give them *something* to eat!" And they *said to Him, "Shall we go and spend two hundred [18]denarii on bread and give them *something* to eat?"

38 And He *said to them, "How many loaves do you have? Go look!" And when they found out, they *said, "Five and two fish."

39 And He commanded them all to recline by groups on the green grass.

40 And they reclined in companies of hundreds and of fifties.

41 And He took the five loaves and the two fish, and looking up toward heaven, He blessed the *food* and broke the loaves and He kept giving *them* to the disciples to set before them; and He divided up the two fish among them all.

42 And they all ate and were satisfied.

43 And they picked up twelve full baskets of the broken pieces, and also of the fish.

44 And there were five thousand men who ate the loaves.

45 And immediately He made His disciples get into the boat and go ahead of *Him* to the other

[18] The denarius was equivalent to one day's wage

side to Bethsaida, while He Himself was sending the multitude away.

46 And after bidding them farewell, He departed to the mountain to pray.

47 And when it was evening, the boat was in the midst of the sea, and He *was* alone on the land.

48 And seeing them straining at the oars, for the wind was against them, at about the fourth watch of the night, He *came to them, walking on the sea; and He intended to pass by them.

49 But when they saw Him walking on the sea, they supposed that it was a ghost, and cried out;

50 for they all saw Him and were frightened. But immediately He spoke with them and *said to them, "Take courage; it is I, do not be afraid."

51 And He got into the boat with them, and the wind stopped; and they were greatly astonished,

52 for they had not gained any insight from the *incident of* the loaves, but their heart was hardened.

53 And when they had crossed over they came to land at Gennesaret, and moored to the shore.

54 And when they had come out of the boat, immediately *the people* recognized Him,

55 and ran about that whole country and began to carry about on their pallets those who were sick, to the place they heard He was.

56 And wherever He entered villages, or cities, or countryside, they were laying the sick in the market places, and entreating Him that they might just touch the fringe of His cloak; and as many as touched it were being cured.

CHAPTER 7

AND the Pharisees and some of the scribes gathered together around Him when they had come from Jerusalem,

2 and had seen that some of His disciples were eating their bread with impure hands, that is, unwashed.

3 (For the Pharisees and all the Jews do not eat unless they carefully wash their hands, *thus* observing the traditions of the elders;

4 and *when they come* from the market place, they do not eat unless they cleanse themselves; and there are many other things which they have received in order to observe, such as the washing of cups and pitchers and copper pots.)

5 And the Pharisees and the scribes *asked Him, "Why do Your disciples not walk according to the tradition of the elders, but eat their bread with impure hands?"

6 And He said to them, "Rightly did Isaiah prophesy of you hypocrites, as it is written,

'THIS PEOPLE HONORS ME
    WITH THEIR LIPS,
    BUT THEIR HEART IS FAR
      AWAY FROM ME.

7 'BUT IN VAIN DO THEY WORSHIP ME,
    TEACHING AS DOCTRINES
      THE PRECEPTS OF MEN.'

8 "Neglecting the commandment of God, you hold to the tradition of men."

9 He was also saying to them,

"You nicely set aside the commandment of God in order to keep your tradition.

10 "For Moses said, 'HONOR YOUR FATHER AND YOUR MOTHER'; and, 'HE WHO SPEAKS EVIL OF FATHER OR MOTHER, LET HIM BE PUT TO DEATH';

11 but you say, 'If a man says to his father or his mother, anything of mine you have might have been helped by is Corban (that is to say, 19given to God),'

12 you no longer permit him to do anything for his father or his mother;

13 thus invalidating the word of God by your tradition which you have handed down; and you do many things such as that."

14 And after He called the multitude to Him again, He began saying to them, "Listen to Me, all of you, and understand:

15 there is nothing outside the man which going into him can defile him; but the things which proceed out of the man are what defile the man.

16 ["20If any man has ears to hear, let him hear."]

17 And when leaving the multitude, He had entered the house, His disciples questioned Him about the parable.

18 And He *said to them, "Are you so lacking in understanding also? Do you not understand that whatever goes into the man from outside cannot defile him;

19 because it does not go into his heart, but into his stomach, and is eliminated?" (Thus He declared all foods clean.)

20 And He was saying, "That which proceeds out of the man, that is what defiles the man.

21 "For from within, out of the heart of men, proceed the evil thoughts, fornications, thefts, murders, adulteries,

22 deeds of coveting and wickedness, as well as deceit, sensuality, envy, slander, pride and foolishness.

23 "All these evil things proceed from within and defile the man."

24 And from there He arose and went away to the region of Tyre21. And when He had entered a house, He wanted no one to know of it; yet He could not escape notice.

25 But after hearing of Him, a woman whose little daughter had an unclean spirit, immediately came and fell at His feet.

26 Now the woman was a 22Gentile, of the Syrophoenician race. And she kept asking Him to cast the demon out of her daughter.

27 And He was saying to her, "Let the children be satisfied first, for it is not good to take the children's bread and throw it to the dogs."

28 But she answered and *said to Him, "Yes, Lord, but even the dogs under the table feed on the children's crumbs."

29 And He said to her, "Because of this answer go your way; the demon has gone out of your daughter."

30 And going back to her home, she found the child lying on the bed, the demon having departed.

31 And again He went out from the region of Tyre, and came through Sidon to the Sea of Galilee, within the region of Decapolis.

19 Or, a gift, an offering
20 Many mss. do not contain this verse
21 Some early mss. add: and Sidon
22 Lit., Greek

32 And they *brought to Him one who was deaf and spoke with difficulty, and they *entreated Him to lay His hand upon him.

33 And He took him aside from the multitude by himself, and put His fingers into his ears, and after spitting, He touched his tongue *with the saliva;*

34 and looking up to heaven with a deep sigh, He *said to him, "Ephphatha!" that is, "Be opened!"

35 And his ears were opened, and the impediment of his tongue was removed, and he *began* speaking plainly.

36 And He gave them orders not to tell anyone; but the more He ordered them, the more widely they continued to proclaim it.

37 And they were utterly astonished, saying, "He has done all things well; He makes even the deaf to hear, and the dumb to speak."

CHAPTER 8

IN those days again, when there was a great multitude and they had nothing to eat, He called His disciples and *said to them,

2 "I feel compassion for the multitude because they have remained with Me now three days, and have nothing to eat;

3 and if I send them away hungry to their home, they will faint on the way; and some of them have come from a distance."

4 And His disciples answered Him, "Where will anyone be able to *find enough to* satisfy these men with bread here in a desolate place?"

5 And He was asking them, "How many loaves do you have?" And they said, "Seven."

6 And He *directed the multitude to sit down on the ground; and taking the seven loaves, He gave thanks and broke them, and started giving them to His disciples to serve to them, and they served them to the multitude.

7 They also had a few small fish; and after He had blessed them, He ordered these to be served as well.

8 And they ate and were satisfied; and they picked up seven large baskets full of what was left over of the broken pieces.

9 And about four thousand were *there;* and He sent them away.

10 And immediately He entered the boat with His disciples, and came to the district of Dalmanutha.

11 And the Pharisees came out and began to argue with Him, seeking from Him a sign from heaven, to test Him.

12 And sighing deeply in His spirit, He *said, "Why does this generation seek for a sign? Truly I say to you, no sign shall be given to this generation."

13 And leaving them, He again embarked and went away to the other side.

14 And they had forgotten to take bread; and did not have more than one loaf in the boat with them.

15 And He was giving orders to them, saying, "Watch out! Beware of the leaven of the Pharisees and the leaven of Herod."

16 And they *began* to discuss with one another *the fact* that they had no bread.

17 And Jesus, aware of this, *said to them, "Why do you

discuss the fact that you have no bread? Do you not yet see or understand? Do you have a hardened heart?

18 HAVING EYES, DO YOU NOT SEE? AND HAVING EARS, DO YOU NOT HEAR? And do you not remember,

19 when I broke the five loaves for the five thousand, how many baskets full of broken pieces you picked up?" They *said to Him, "Twelve."

20 "And when I broke the seven for the four thousand, how many large baskets full of broken pieces did you pick up?" And they *said to Him, "Seven."

21 And He was saying to them, "Do you not yet understand?"

22 And they *came to Bethsaida. And they *brought a blind man to Him, and *entreated Him to touch him.

23 And taking the blind man by the hand, He brought him out of the village; and after spitting on his eyes, and laying His hands upon him, He asked him, "Do you see anything?"

24 And he looked up and said, "I see men, for I am seeing them like trees, walking about."

25 Then again He laid His hands upon his eyes; and he looked intently and was restored, and began to see everything clearly.

26 And He sent him to his home, saying, "Do not even enter the village."

27 And Jesus went out, along with His disciples, to the villages of Caesarea Philippi; and on the way He questioned His disciples, saying to them, "Who do people say that I am?"

28 And they told Him, saying, "John the Baptist; and others say

Elijah; but others, one of the prophets."

29 And He continued by questioning them, "But who do you say that I am?" Peter *answered and *said to Him, "Thou art the Christ."

30 And He warned them to tell no one about Him.

31 And He began to teach them that the Son of Man must suffer many things and be rejected by the elders and the chief priests and the scribes, and be killed, and after three days rise again.

32 And He was stating the matter plainly. And Peter took Him aside and began to rebuke Him.

33 But turning around and seeing His disciples, He rebuked Peter, and *said, "Get behind Me, Satan; for you are not setting your mind on 23God's interests, but man's."

34 And He summoned the multitude with His disciples, and said to them, "If anyone wishes to come after Me, let him deny himself, and take up his cross, and follow Me.

35 "For whoever wishes to save his life shall lose it; but whoever loses his life for My sake and the gospel's shall save it.

36 "For what does it profit a man to gain the whole world, and forfeit his soul?

37 "For what shall a man give in exchange for his soul?

38 "For whoever is ashamed of Me and My words in this adulterous and sinful generation, the Son of Man will also be ashamed of him when He comes in the glo-

23 Lit., the things of God

ry of His Father with the holy angels."

CHAPTER 9

AND He was saying to them, "Truly I say to you, there are some of those who are standing here who shall not taste death until they see the kingdom of God after it has come with power."

2 And six days later, Jesus *took with Him Peter and James and John, and *brought them up to a high mountain by themselves. And He was transfigured before them;

3 and His garments became radiant and exceedingly white, as no launderer on earth can whiten them.

4 And Elijah appeared to them along with Moses; and they were talking with Jesus.

5 And Peter answered and *said to Jesus, "Rabbi, it is good for us to be here; and let us make three tabernacles, one for You, and one for Moses, and one for Elijah."

6 For he did not know what to answer; for they became terrified.

7 Then a cloud formed, overshadowing them, and a voice came out of the cloud, "This is My beloved Son, listen to Him!"

8 And all at once they looked around and saw no one with them anymore, except Jesus alone.

9 And as they were coming down from the mountain, He gave them orders not to relate to anyone what they had seen, until the Son of Man should rise from the dead.

10 And they seized upon that statement, discussing with one another what rising from the dead might mean.

11 And they asked Him, saying, "Why is it that the scribes say that Elijah must come first?"

12 And He said to them, "Elijah does first come and restore all things. And yet how is it written of the Son of Man that He should suffer many things and be treated with contempt?

13 But I say to you, that Elijah has indeed come, and they did to him whatever they wished, just as it is written of him."

14 And when they came back to the disciples, they saw a large crowd around them, and some scribes arguing with them.

15 And immediately, when the entire crowd saw Him, they were amazed, and began running up to greet Him.

16 And He asked them, "What are you discussing with them?"

17 And one of the crowd answered Him, "Teacher, I brought You my son, possessed with a spirit which makes him mute;

18 and whenever it seizes him, it dashes him to the ground, and he foams at the mouth, and grinds his teeth, and stiffens out. And I told Your disciples to cast it out, and they could not do it."

19 And He *answered them and *said, "O unbelieving generation, how long shall I be with you? How long shall I put up with you? Bring him to Me!"

20 And they brought the boy to Him. And when he saw Him, immediately the spirit threw him into a convulsion, and falling on the ground, he began rolling about and foaming at the mouth.

21 And He asked his father, "How long has this been

happening to him?" And he said, "From childhood.

22 "And it has often thrown him both into the fire and into the water to destroy him. But if You can do anything, take pity on us and help us!"

23 And Jesus said to him, " 'If You can!' All things are possible to him who believes."

24 Immediately the boy's father cried out and *began* saying, "I do believe; help my unbelief."

25 And when Jesus saw that a crowd was rapidly gathering, He rebuked the unclean spirit, saying to it, "You deaf and dumb spirit, I command you, come out of him and do not enter him again."

26 And after crying out and throwing him into terrible convulsions, it came out; and *the boy* became so much like a corpse that most *of them* said, "He is dead!"

27 But Jesus took him by the hand and raised him; and he got up.

28 And when He had come into *the* house, His disciples *began* questioning Him privately, "Why could we not cast it out?"

29 And He said to them, "This kind cannot come out by anything but prayer24."

30 And from there they went out and *began* to go through Galilee, and He was unwilling for anyone to know *about it.*

31 For He was teaching His disciples and telling them, "The Son of Man is to be 25delivered into the hands of men, and they will kill Him; and when He has been killed, He will rise three days later."

32 But they did not understand

this statement, and they were afraid to ask Him.

33 And they came to Capernaum; and when He was in the house, He *began* to question them, "What were you discussing on the way?"

34 But they kept silent, for on the way they had discussed with one another which *of them was* the greatest.

35 And sitting down, He called the twelve and *said to them, "If anyone wants to be first, he shall be last of all, and servant of all."

36 And taking a child, He set him before them, and taking him in His arms, He said to them,

37"Whoever receives one child like this in My name receives Me; and whoever receives Me does not receive Me, but Him who sent Me."

38 John said to Him, "Teacher, we saw someone casting out demons in Your name, and we tried to hinder him because he was not following us."

39 But Jesus said, "Do not hinder him, for there is no one who shall perform a miracle in My name, and be able soon afterward to speak evil of Me.

40"For he who is not against us is 26for us.

41"For whoever gives you a cup of water to drink because of your name as *followers* of Christ, truly I say to you, he shall not lose his reward.

42"And whoever causes one of these little ones who believe to stumble, it would be better for him if, with a heavy millstone hung around his neck, he had been cast into the sea.

24 Many mss. add: *and fasting*
25 Or, *betrayed*   26 Or, *on our side*

43"And if your hand causes you to stumble, cut it off; it is better for you to enter life crippled, than having your two hands, to go into hell, into the unquenchable fire,

44 [27where THEIR WORM DOES NOT DIE, AND THE FIRE IS NOT QUENCHED.]

45"And if your foot causes you to stumble, cut it off; it is better for you to enter life lame, than having your two feet, to be cast into hell,

46 [27where THEIR WORM DOES NOT DIE, AND THE FIRE IS NOT QUENCHED.]

47"And if your eye causes you to stumble, cast it out; it is better for you to enter the kingdom of God with one eye, than having two eyes, to be cast into hell,

48 where THEIR WORM DOES NOT DIE, AND THE FIRE IS NOT QUENCHED.

49"For everyone will be salted with fire.

50"Salt is good; but if the salt becomes unsalty, with what will you make it salty *again*? Have salt in yourselves, and be at peace with one another."

CHAPTER 10

AND rising up, He *went from there to the region of Judea, and beyond the Jordan; and crowds *gathered around Him again, and, according to His custom, He once more *began to teach them.

2 And *some* Pharisees came up to Him, testing Him, and *began* to question Him whether it

was lawful for a man to divorce a wife.

3 And He answered and said to them, "What did Moses command you?"

4 And they said, "Moses permitted *a man* TO WRITE A CERTIFICATE OF DIVORCE AND SEND *her* AWAY."

5 But Jesus said to them, "Because of your hardness of heart he wrote you this commandment.

6"But from the beginning of creation, *God* MADE THEM MALE AND FEMALE.

7"FOR THIS CAUSE A MAN SHALL LEAVE HIS FATHER AND MOTHER,28

8 AND THE TWO SHALL BECOME ONE FLESH; consequently they are no longer two, but one flesh.

9"What therefore God has joined together, let no man separate."

10 And in the house the disciples *began* questioning Him about this again.

11 And He *said to them, "Whoever divorces his wife and marries another woman commits adultery against her;

12 and if she herself divorces her husband and marries another man, she is committing adultery."

13 And they were bringing children to Him so that He might touch them; and the disciples rebuked them.

14 But when Jesus saw this, He was indignant and said to them, "Permit the children to come to Me; do not hinder them; for the kingdom of God belongs to such as these.

15"Truly I say to you, whoever does not receive the kingdom of

---

27 Vv. 44 and 46, which are identical with v. 48, are not found in the best ancient mss.
28 Some mss. add: *and shall cleave to his wife*

God like a child shall not enter it *at all.*"

16 And He took them in His arms and *began* blessing them, laying His hands upon them.

17 And as He was setting out on a journey, a man ran up to Him and knelt before Him, and *began* asking Him, "Good Teacher, what shall I do to inherit eternal life?"

18 And Jesus said to him, "Why do you call Me good? No one is good except God alone.

19 "You know the commandments, 'DO NOT MURDER, DO NOT COMMIT ADULTERY, DO NOT STEAL, DO NOT BEAR FALSE WITNESS, Do not defraud, HONOR YOUR FATHER AND MOTHER.' "

20 And he said to Him, "Teacher, I have kept all these things from my youth up."

21 And looking at him, Jesus felt a love for him, and said to him, "One thing you lack: go and sell all you possess, and give to the poor, and you shall have treasure in heaven; and come, follow Me."

22 But at these words his face fell, and he went away grieved, for he was one who owned much property.

23 And Jesus, looking around, *said to His disciples, "How hard it will be for those who are wealthy to enter the kingdom of God!"

24 And the disciples were amazed at His words. But Jesus *answered again and *said to them, "Children, how hard it is 29 to enter the kingdom of God!

25 "It is easier for a camel to go through the eye of a needle than for a rich man to enter the kingdom of God."

26 And they were even more astonished and said to Him, "Then who can be saved?"

27 Looking upon them, Jesus *said, "With men it is impossible, but not with God; for all things are possible with God."

28 Peter began to say to Him, "Behold, we have left everything and followed You."

29 Jesus said, "Truly I say to you, there is no one who has left house or brothers or sisters or mother or father or children or farms, for My sake and for the gospel's sake,

30 but that he shall receive a hundred times as much now in the present age, houses and brothers and sisters and mothers and children and farms, along with persecutions; and in the age to come, eternal life.

31 "But many *who are* first, will be last; and the last, first."

32 And they were on the road, going up to Jerusalem, and Jesus was walking on ahead of them; and they were amazed, and those who followed were fearful. And again He took the twelve aside and began to tell them what was going to happen to Him,

33 *saying,* "Behold, we are going up to Jerusalem, and the Son of Man will be 30 delivered to the chief priests and the scribes; and they will condemn Him to death, and will deliver Him to the Gentiles.

34 "And they will mock Him and spit upon Him, and scourge Him, and kill *Him,* and three days later He will rise again."

35 And James and John, the two sons of Zebedee, *came up to Him, saying to Him, "Teacher,

---

29 Later mss. insert: *for those who trust in wealth*   30 Or, *betrayed*

we want You to do for us whatever we ask of You."

36 And He said to them, "What do you want Me to do for you?"

37 And they said to Him, "Grant that we may sit in Your glory, one on Your right, and one on Your left."

38 But Jesus said to them, "You do not know what you are asking for. Are you able to drink the cup that I drink, or to be baptized with the baptism with which I am baptized?"

39 And they said to Him, "We are able." And Jesus said to them, "The cup that I drink you shall drink; and you shall be baptized with the baptism with which I am baptized.

40 "But to sit on My right or on My left, this is not Mine to give; but it is for those for whom it has been prepared."

41 And hearing this, the ten began to feel indignant with James and John.

42 And calling them to Himself, Jesus *said to them, "You know that those who are recognized as rulers of the Gentiles lord it over them; and their great men exercise authority over them.

43 "But it is not so among you, but whoever wishes to become great among you shall be your servant;

44 and whoever wishes to be first among you shall be slave of all.

45 "For even the Son of Man did not come to be served, but to serve, and to give His life a ransom for many."

46 And they *came to Jericho. And as He was *going out from Jericho with His disciples and a great multitude, a blind beggar named Bartimaeus, the son of Timaeus, was sitting by the road.

47 And when he heard that it was Jesus the Nazarene, he began to cry out and say, "Jesus, Son of David, have mercy on me!"

48 And many were sternly telling him to be quiet, but he kept crying out all the more, "Son of David, have mercy on me!"

49 And Jesus stopped and said, "Call him here." And they *called the blind man, saying to him, "Take courage, arise! He is calling for you."

50 And casting aside his cloak, he jumped up, and came to Jesus.

51 And answering him, Jesus said, "What do you want Me to do for you?" And the blind man said to Him, "[31]Rabboni, I want to regain my sight!"

52 And Jesus said to him, "Go your way; your faith has made you well." And immediately he regained his sight and began following Him on the road.

CHAPTER 11

AND as they *approached Jerusalem, at Bethphage and Bethany, near the Mount of Olives, He *sent two of His disciples,

2 and *said to them, "Go into the village opposite you, and immediately as you enter it, you will find a colt tied there, on which no one yet has ever sat; untie it and bring it here.

3 "And if anyone says to you, 'Why are you doing this?' you say, 'The Lord has need of it'; and

---

[31] I.e., My Master

immediately he will send it back here."

4 And they went away and found a colt tied at the door outside in the street; and they *untied it.

5 And some of the bystanders were saying to them, "What are you doing, untying the colt?"

6 And they spoke to them just as Jesus had told *them*, and they gave them permission.

7 And they *brought the colt to Jesus and put their garments on it; and He sat upon it.

8 And many spread their garments in the road, and others *spread* leafy branches which they had cut from the fields.

9 And those who went before, and those who followed after, were crying out,
"Hosanna!
BLESSED IS HE WHO COMES IN THE NAME OF THE LORD;

10 Blessed *is* the coming kingdom of our father David;
Hosanna in the highest!"

11 And He entered Jerusalem *and came* into the temple; and after looking all around, He departed for Bethany with the twelve, since it was already late.

12 And on the next day, when they had departed from Bethany, He became hungry.

13 And seeing at a distance a fig tree in leaf, He went *to see* if perhaps He would find anything on it; and when He came to it, He found nothing but leaves, for it was not the season for figs.

14 And He answered and said to it, "May no one ever eat fruit from you again!" And His disciples were listening.

15 And they *came to Jerusalem. And He entered the temple and began to cast out those who were buying and selling in the temple, and overturned the tables of the moneychangers and the seats of those who were selling doves;

16 and He would not permit anyone to carry goods through the temple.

17 And He *began* to teach and say to them, "Is it not written, 'MY HOUSE SHALL BE CALLED A HOUSE OF PRAYER FOR ALL THE NATIONS'? But you have made it a ROBBERS' DEN."

18 And the chief priests and the scribes heard *this*, and *began* seeking how to destroy Him; for they were afraid of Him, for all the multitude was astonished at His teaching.

19 And whenever evening came, they would go out of the city.

20 And as they were passing by in the morning, they saw the fig tree withered from the roots *up*.

21 And being reminded, Peter *said to Him, "Rabbi, behold, the fig tree which You cursed has withered."

22 And Jesus *answered saying to them, "Have faith in God.

23 "Truly I say to you, whoever says to this mountain, 'Be taken up and cast into the sea,' and does not doubt in his heart but believes that what he says is going to happen, it shall be *granted* him.

24 "Therefore I say to you, all things for which you pray and ask, believe that you have received them, and they shall be *granted* you.

25 "And whenever you stand

praying, forgive, if you have anything against anyone; so that your Father also who is in heaven may forgive you your transgressions.

26 [³²But if you do not forgive, neither will your Father who is in heaven forgive your transgressions.]

27 And they *came again to Jerusalem. And as He was walking in the temple, the chief priests, and scribes, and elders *came to Him,

28 and *began* saying to Him, "By what authority are You doing these things, or who gave You this authority to do these things?"

29 And Jesus said to them, "I will ask you one question, and you answer Me, and *then* I will tell you by what authority I do these things.

30 "Was the baptism of John from heaven, or from men? Answer Me."

31 And they *began* reasoning among themselves, saying, "If we say, 'From heaven,' He will say, 'Then why did you not believe him?'

32 "But shall we say, 'From men'?"—they were afraid of the multitude, for all considered John to have been a prophet indeed.

33 And answering Jesus, they *said, "We do not know." And Jesus *said to them, "Neither will I tell you by what authority I do these things."

CHAPTER 12

AND He began to speak to them in parables: "A man PLANTED A VINEYARD, AND PUT A WALL AROUND IT, AND DUG A VAT UNDER THE WINE PRESS, AND BUILT A TOWER, and rented it out to ³³vine-growers and went on a journey.

2 "And at the *harvest* time he sent a slave to the vine-growers, in order to receive *some* of the produce of the vineyard from the vine-growers.

3 "And they took him, and beat him, and sent him away empty-handed.

4 "And again he sent them another slave, and they wounded him in the head, and treated him shamefully.

5 "And he sent another, and that one they killed; and *so with* many others, beating some, and killing others.

6 "He had one more *to send*, a beloved son; he sent him last *of all* to them, saying, 'They will respect my son.'

7 "But those vine-growers said to one another, 'This is the heir; come, let us kill him, and the inheritance will be ours!'

8 "And they took him, and killed him, and threw him out of the vineyard.

9 "What will the owner of the vineyard do? He will come and destroy the vine-growers, and will give the vineyard to others.

10 "Have you not even read this Scripture:

'THE STONE WHICH THE
    BUILDERS REJECTED,
THIS BECAME THE CHIEF
    CORNER *stone*;
11 THIS CAME ABOUT FROM
    THE LORD,
    AND IT IS MARVELOUS IN
    OUR EYES'?"

12 And they were seeking to seize Him; and *yet* they feared

---

³² Many mss. do not contain this verse
³³ Or, *tenant farmers*, also vv. 2, 7, 9

the multitude; for they understood that He spoke the parable against them. And *so* they left Him, and went away.

13 And they *sent some of the Pharisees and Herodians to Him, in order to trap Him in a statement.

14 And they *came and *said to Him, "Teacher, we know that You are truthful, and defer to no one; for You are not partial to any, but teach the way of God in truth. Is it lawful to pay a poll-tax to Caesar, or not?

15 "Shall we pay, or shall we not pay?" But He, knowing their hypocrisy, said to them, "Why are you testing Me? Bring Me a [34]denarius to look at."

16 And they brought *one*. And He *said to them, "Whose likeness and inscription is this?" And they said to Him, "Caesar's."

17 And Jesus said to them, "Render to Caesar the things that are Caesar's, and to God the things that are God's." And they were amazed at Him.

18 And *some* Sadducees (who say that there is no resurrection) *came to Him, and *began* questioning Him, saying,

19 "Teacher, Moses wrote for us that IF A MAN'S BROTHER DIES, and leaves behind a wife, AND LEAVES NO CHILD, HIS BROTHER SHOULD TAKE THE WIFE, AND RAISE UP OFFSPRING TO HIS BROTHER.

20 "There were seven brothers; and the first took a wife, and died, leaving no offspring.

21 "And the second one took her, and died, leaving behind no offspring; and the third likewise;

22 and *so* all seven left no offspring. Last of all the woman died also.

23 "In the resurrection, [35]when they rise again, which one's wife will she be? For all seven had her as wife."

24 Jesus said to them, "Is this not the reason you are mistaken, that you do not understand the Scriptures, or the power of God?

25 "For when they rise from the dead, they neither marry, nor are given in marriage, but are like angels in heaven.

26 "But regarding the fact that the dead rise again, have you not read in the book of Moses, in the *passage about the burning* bush, how God spoke to him, saying, 'I AM THE GOD OF ABRAHAM, AND THE GOD OF ISAAC, AND THE GOD OF JACOB'?

27 "He is not the God of the dead, but of the living; you are greatly mistaken."

28 And one of the scribes came and heard them arguing, and recognizing that He had answered them well, asked Him, "What commandment is the foremost of all?"

29 Jesus answered, "The foremost is, 'HEAR, O ISRAEL! THE LORD OUR GOD IS ONE LORD;

30 AND YOU SHALL LOVE THE LORD YOUR GOD WITH ALL YOUR HEART, AND WITH ALL YOUR SOUL, AND WITH ALL YOUR MIND, AND WITH ALL YOUR STRENGTH.'

31 "The second is this, 'YOU SHALL LOVE YOUR NEIGHBOR AS YOURSELF.' There is no other commandment greater than these."

32 And the scribe said to Him, "Right, Teacher, You have truly

---

[34] The denarius was equivalent to one day's wage

[35] Most ancient mss. do not contain *when they rise again*

stated that HE IS ONE; AND THERE
IS NO ONE ELSE BESIDES HIM;

33 AND TO LOVE HIM WITH ALL
THE HEART AND WITH ALL THE UN-
DERSTANDING AND WITH ALL THE
STRENGTH, AND TO LOVE ONE'S
NEIGHBOR AS HIMSELF, is much
more than all burnt offerings and
sacrifices."

34 And when Jesus saw that he
had answered intelligently, He
said to him, "You are not far
from the kingdom of God." And
after that, no one would venture
to ask Him any more questions.

35 And Jesus answering *began*
to say, as He taught in the temple, "How *is it that* the scribes
say that the Christ is the son of
David?

36"David himself said in the
Holy Spirit,
  'THE LORD SAID TO MY
    LORD,
  "SIT AT MY RIGHT HAND,
    UNTIL I PUT THINE ENEMIES
    BENEATH THY FEET." '

37"David himself calls Him
'Lord'; and *so* in what sense is He
his son?" And the great crowd
enjoyed listening to Him.

38 And in His teaching He was
saying: "Beware of the scribes
who like to walk around in long
robes, and *like* respectful greetings in the market places,

39 and chief seats in the synagogues, and places of honor at
banquets,

40 who devour widows'
houses, and for appearance'
sake offer long prayers; these
will receive greater condemnation."

41 And He sat down opposite
the treasury, and *began* observing how the multitude were put-

ting money into the treasury; and
many rich people were putting in
large sums.

42 And a poor widow came
and put in two small copper
coins, which amount to a cent.

43 And calling His disciples to
Him, He said to them, "Truly I
say to you, this poor widow put
in more than all the contributors
to the treasury;

44 for they all put in out of
their surplus, but she, out of her
poverty, put in all she owned, all
she had to live on."

CHAPTER 13

AND as He was going out of the
temple, one of His disciples
*said to Him, "Teacher, behold
36what wonderful stones and
what wonderful buildings!"

2 And Jesus said to him, "Do
you see these great buildings?
Not one stone shall be left upon
another which will not be torn
down."

3 And as He was sitting on
the Mount of Olives opposite the
temple, Peter and James and
John and Andrew were questioning Him privately,

4"Tell us, when will these
things be, and what *will be* the
sign when all these things are
going to be fulfilled?"

5 And Jesus began to say to
them, "See to it that no one misleads you.

6"Many will come in My
name, saying, 'I am *He!*' and will
mislead many.

7"And when you hear of wars
and rumors of wars, do not be
frightened; *those things* must
take place; but *that is* not yet the
end.

---

36 Lit., *how great*

8"For nation will arise against nation, and kingdom against kingdom; there will be earthquakes in various places; there will *also* be famines. These things are *merely* the beginning of birth pangs.

9"But be on your guard; for they will deliver you to *the* courts, and you will be flogged in *the* synagogues, and you will stand before governors and kings for My sake, as a testimony to them.

10"And the gospel must first be preached to all the nations.

11"And when they arrest you and deliver you up, do not be anxious beforehand about what you are to say, but say whatever is given you in that hour; for it is not you who speak, but *it is* the Holy Spirit.

12"And brother will deliver brother to death, and a father *his* child; and children will rise up against parents and have them put to death.

13"And you will be hated by all on account of My name, but the one who endures to the end, he shall be saved.

14"But when you see the ABOMINATION OF DESOLATION standing where it should not be (let the reader understand), then let those who are in Judea flee to the mountains.

15"And let him who is on the housetop not go down, or enter in, to get anything out of his house;

16 and let him who is in the field not turn back to get his cloak.

17"But woe to those who are with child and to those who nurse babes in those days!

18"But pray that it may not happen in the winter.

19"For those days will be a *time of* tribulation such as has not occurred since the beginning of the creation which God created, until now, and never shall.

20"And unless the Lord had shortened *those* days, no life would have been saved; but for the sake of the elect whom He chose, He shortened the days.

21"And then if anyone says to you, 'Behold, here is the Christ'; or, 'Behold, *He is* there'; do not believe *him*;

22 for false Christs and false prophets will arise, and will show signs and wonders, in order, if possible, to lead the elect astray.

23"But take heed; behold, I have told you everything in advance.

24"But in those days, after that tribulation, THE SUN WILL BE DARKENED, AND THE MOON WILL NOT GIVE ITS LIGHT,

25 AND THE STARS WILL BE FALLING from heaven, and the powers that are in the heavens will be shaken.

26"And then they will see THE SON OF MAN COMING IN CLOUDS with great power and glory.

27"And then He will send forth the angels, and will gather together His elect from the four winds, from the farthest end of the earth, to the farthest end of heaven.

28"Now learn the parable from the fig tree: when its branch has already become tender, and puts forth its leaves, you know that summer is near.

29"Even so, you too, when you see these things happening, recognize that He is near, *right* at the door.

30"Truly I say to you, this [37]generation will not pass away until all these things take place.

31"Heaven and earth will pass away, but My words will not pass away.

32"But of that day or hour no one knows, not even the angels in heaven, nor the Son, but the Father *alone*.

33"Take heed, keep on the alert; for you do not know when the *appointed* time is.

34"*It is* like a man, away on a journey, *who* upon leaving his house and putting his slaves in charge, *assigning* to each one his task, also commanded the door-keeper to stay on the alert.

35"Therefore, be on the alert—for you do not know when the master of the house is coming, whether in the evening, at midnight, at cockcrowing, or in the morning—

36 lest he come suddenly and find you asleep.

37"And what I say to you I say to all, 'Be on the alert!' "

CHAPTER 14

NOW the Passover and Un-leavened Bread was two days off; and the chief priests and the scribes were seeking how to seize Him by stealth, and kill Him;

2 for they were saying, "Not during the festival, lest there be a riot of the people."

3 And while He was in Bethany at the home of Simon the leper, and reclining *at the table*, there came a woman with an alabaster vial of very costly per-

fume of pure nard; *and* she broke the vial and poured it over His head.

4 But some were indignantly *remarking* to one another, "Why has this perfume been wasted?

5"For this perfume might have been sold for over three hundred [38]denarii, and *the money* given to the poor." And they were scolding her.

6 But Jesus said, "Let her alone; why do you bother her? She has done a good deed to Me.

7"For the poor you always have with you, and whenever you wish, you can do them good; but you do not always have Me.

8"She has done what she could; she has anointed My body beforehand for the burial.

9"And truly I say to you, wherever the gospel is preached in the whole world, that also which this woman has done shall be spoken of in memory of her."

10 And Judas Iscariot, who was one of the twelve, went off to the chief priests, in order to betray Him to them.

11 And they were glad when they heard *this*, and promised to give him money. And he *began* seeking how to betray Him at an opportune time.

12 And on the first day of Un-leavened Bread, when the Passover *lamb* was being sacrificed, His disciples *said to Him, "Where do You want us to go and prepare for You to eat the Passover?"

13 And He *sent two of His disciples, and *said to them, "Go into the city, and a man will meet you carrying a pitcher of water; follow him;

14 and wherever he enters, say to the owner of the house, 'The

[37] Or, *race*
[38] The denarius was equivalent to one day's wage

Teacher says, "Where is My guest room in which I may eat the Passover with My disciples?" '

15 "And he himself will show you a large upper room furnished *and* ready; and prepare for us there."

16 And the disciples went out, and came to the city, and found *it* just as He had told them; and they prepared the Passover.

17 And when it was evening He *came with the twelve.

18 And as they were reclining *at the table* and eating, Jesus said, "Truly I say to you that one of you will betray Me—one who is eating with Me."

19 They began to be grieved and to say to Him one by one, "Surely not I?"

20 And He said to them, *"It is* one of the twelve, one who dips with Me in the bowl.

21 "For the Son of Man *is* to go, just as it is written of Him; but woe to that man by whom the Son of Man is betrayed! *It would have been* good for that man if he had not been born."

22 And while they were eating, He took *some* bread, and after a blessing He broke *it;* and gave *it* to them, and said, "Take *it;* this is My body."

23 And when He had taken a cup, *and* given thanks, He gave *it* to them; and they all drank from it.

24 And He said to them, "This is My blood of the covenant, which is poured out for many.

25 "Truly I say to you, I shall never again drink of the fruit of the vine until that day when I drink it new in the kingdom of God."

26 And after singing a hymn, they went out to the Mount of Olives.

27 And Jesus *said to them, "You will all fall away, because it is written, 'I WILL STRIKE DOWN THE SHEPHERD, AND THE SHEEP SHALL BE SCATTERED.'

28 "But after I have been raised, I will go before you to Galilee."

29 But Peter said to Him, *"Even* though all may fall away, yet I will not."

30 And Jesus *said to him, "Truly I say to you, that you yourself this very night, before a cock crows twice, shall three times deny Me."

31 But *Peter* kept saying insistently, *"Even* if I have to die with You, I will not deny You!" And they all were saying the same thing, too.

32 And they *came to a place named Gethsemane; and He *said to His disciples, "Sit here until I have prayed."

33 And He *took with Him Peter and James and John, and began to be very distressed and troubled.

34 And He *said to them, "My soul is deeply grieved to the point of death; remain here and keep watch."

35 And He went a little beyond *them,* and fell to the ground, and *began* to pray that if it were possible, the hour might pass Him by.

36 And He was saying, "Abba! Father! All things are possible for Thee; remove this cup from Me; yet not what I will, but what Thou wilt."

37 And He *came and *found them sleeping, and *said to Peter, "Simon, are you asleep? Could you not keep watch for one hour?

38 "Keep watching and praying, that you may not come into temptation; the spirit is willing, but the flesh is weak."

39 And again He went away and prayed, saying the same words.

40 And again He came and found them sleeping, for their eyes were very heavy; and they did not know what to answer Him.

41 And He *came the third time, and *said to them, "Are you still sleeping and taking your rest? It is enough; the hour has come; behold, the Son of Man is being betrayed into the hands of sinners.

42 "Arise, let us be going; behold, the one who betrays Me is at hand!"

43 And immediately while He was still speaking, Judas, one of the twelve, *came up, accompanied by a multitude with swords and clubs, from the chief priests and the scribes and the elders.

44 Now he who was betraying Him had given them a signal, saying, "Whomever I shall kiss, He is the one; seize Him, and lead Him away under guard."

45 And after coming, he immediately went to Him, saying, "Rabbi!" and kissed Him.

46 And they laid hands on Him, and seized Him.

47 But a certain one of those who stood by drew his sword, and struck the slave of the high priest, and cut off his ear.

48 And Jesus answered and said to them, "Have you come out with swords and clubs to arrest Me, as against a robber?

49 "Every day I was with you in the temple teaching, and you did not seize Me; but this has happened that the Scriptures might be fulfilled."

50 And they all left Him and fled.

51 And a certain young man was following Him, wearing nothing but a linen sheet over his naked body; and they *seized him.

52 But he left the linen sheet behind, and escaped naked.

53 And they led Jesus away to the high priest; and all the chief priests and the elders and the scribes *gathered together.

54 And Peter had followed Him at a distance, right into the courtyard of the high priest; and he was sitting with the officers, and warming himself at the fire.

55 Now the chief priests and the whole 39Council kept trying to obtain testimony against Jesus to put Him to death; and they were not finding any.

56 For many were giving false testimony against Him, and yet their testimony was not consistent.

57 And some stood up and began to give false testimony against Him, saying,

58 "We heard Him say, 'I will destroy this temple made with hands, and in three days I will build another made without hands.'"

59 And not even in this respect was their testimony consistent.

60 And the high priest stood up and came forward and questioned Jesus, saying, "Do You make no answer? What is it that these men are testifying against You?"

61 But He kept silent, and made no answer. Again the high

---

39 Or, Sanhedrin

priest was questioning Him, and saying to Him, "Are You the Christ, the Son of the Blessed One?"

62 And Jesus said, "I am; and you shall see THE SON OF MAN SITTING AT THE RIGHT HAND OF POWER, and COMING WITH THE CLOUDS OF HEAVEN."

63 And tearing his clothes, the high priest *said, "What further need do we have of witnesses?

64 "You have heard the blasphemy; how does it seem to you?" And they all condemned Him to be deserving of death.

65 And some began to spit at Him, and to blindfold Him, and to beat Him with their fists, and to say to Him, "Prophesy!" And the officers received Him with slaps *in the face.*

66 And as Peter was below in the courtyard, one of the servant-girls of the high priest *came,

67 and seeing Peter warming himself, she looked at him, and *said, "You, too, were with Jesus the Nazarene."

68 But he denied *it,* saying, "I neither know nor understand what you are talking about." And he went out onto the porch.[40]

69 And the maid saw him, and began once more to say to the bystanders, "This is *one* of them!"

70 But again he was denying it. And after a little while the bystanders were again saying to Peter, "Surely you are *one* of them, for you are a Galilean too."

71 But he began to curse and swear, "I do not know this man you are talking about!"

72 And immediately a cock crowed a second time. And Peter remembered how Jesus had made the remark to him, "Before a cock crows twice, you will deny Me three times." And he began to weep.

CHAPTER 15

AND early in the morning the chief priests with the elders and scribes, and the whole [41]Council, immediately held a consultation; and binding Jesus, they led Him away, and delivered Him up to Pilate.

2 And Pilate questioned Him, "Are You the King of the Jews?" And answering He *said to him, "It *is as* you say."

3 And the chief priests *began* to accuse Him harshly.

4 And Pilate was questioning Him again, saying, "Do You make no answer? See how many charges they bring against You!"

5 But Jesus made no further answer; so that Pilate was amazed.

6 Now at *the* feast he used to release for them *any* one prisoner whom they requested.

7 And the man named Barabbas had been imprisoned with the insurrectionists who had committed murder in the insurrection.

8 And the multitude went up and began asking him *to do* as he had been accustomed to do for them.

9 And Pilate answered them, saying, "Do you want me to release for you the King of the Jews?"

10 For he was aware that the chief priests had delivered Him up because of envy.

11 But the chief priests stirred

---

[40] Later mss. add: *and a cock crowed*
[41] Or, *Sanhedrin*

up the multitude *to ask* him to release Barabbas for them instead.

12 And answering again, Pilate was saying to them, "Then what shall I do with Him whom you call the King of the Jews?"

13 And they shouted back, "Crucify Him!"

14 But Pilate was saying to them, "Why, what evil has He done?" But they shouted all the more, "Crucify Him!"

15 And wishing to satisfy the multitude, Pilate released Barabbas for them, and after having Jesus scourged, he delivered *Him* to be crucified.

16 And the soldiers took Him away into the palace (that is, the Praetorium), and they *called together the whole *Roman* [42]cohort.

17 And they *dressed Him up in purple, and after weaving a crown of thorns, they put it on Him;

18 and they began to acclaim Him, "Hail, King of the Jews!"

19 And they kept beating His head with a [43]reed, and spitting at Him, and kneeling and bowing before Him.

20 And after they had mocked Him, they took the purple off Him, and put His garments on Him. And they *led Him out to crucify Him.

21 And they *pressed into service a passer-by coming from the country, Simon of Cyrene (the father of Alexander and Rufus), to bear His cross.

22 And they *brought Him to the place Golgotha, which is translated, Place of a Skull.

23 And they tried to give Him wine mixed with myrrh; but He did not take it.

24 And they *crucified Him, and *divided up His garments among themselves, casting lots for them, *to decide* what each should take.

25 And it was the [44]third hour when they crucified Him.

26 And the inscription of the charge against Him read, "THE KING OF THE JEWS."

27 And they *crucified two robbers with Him, one on His right and one on His left.

28 [[45]And the Scripture was fulfilled which says, "And He was numbered with transgressors."]

29 And those passing by were hurling abuse at Him, wagging their heads, and saying, "Ha! You who *are going to* destroy the temple and rebuild it in three days,

30 save Yourself, and come down from the cross!"

31 In the same way the chief priests also, along with the scribes, were mocking *Him* among themselves and saying, "He saved others; He cannot save Himself.

32 "Let *this* Christ, the King of Israel, now come down from the cross, so that we may see and believe!" And those who were crucified with Him were casting the same insult at Him.

33 And when the [46]sixth hour had come, darkness fell over the whole land until the [47]ninth hour.

34 And at the ninth hour Jesus cried out with a loud voice, "ELOI, ELOI, LAMA SABACHTHANI?" which is translated, "MY GOD, MY GOD, WHY HAST THOU FORSAKEN ME?"

---

[42] Or, *battalion*
[43] Or, *staff* (made of a reed)   [44] I.e., 9 a.m.
[45] Many mss. do not contain this verse
[46] I.e., noon   [47] I.e., 3 p.m.

35 And when some of the by-standers heard it, they *began* saying, "Behold, He is calling for Elijah."

36 And someone ran and filled a sponge with sour wine, put it on a reed, and gave Him a drink, saying, "Let us see whether Elijah will come to take Him down."

37 And Jesus uttered a loud cry, and breathed His last.

38 And the veil of the temple was torn in two from top to bottom.

39 And when the centurion, who was standing right in front of Him, saw the way He breathed His last, he said, "Truly this man was the Son of God!"

40 And there were also *some* women looking on from a distance, among whom *were* Mary Magdalene, and Mary the mother of James the Less and Joses, and Salome.

41 And when He was in Galilee, they used to follow Him and minister to Him; and *there were* many other women who had come up with Him to Jerusalem.

42 And when evening had already come, because it was the preparation day, that is, the day before the Sabbath,

43 Joseph of Arimathea came, a prominent member of the Council, who himself was waiting for the kingdom of God; and he gathered up courage and went in before Pilate, and asked for the body of Jesus.

44 And Pilate wondered if He was dead by this time, and summoning the centurion, he questioned him as to whether He was already dead.

45 And ascertaining this from the centurion, he granted the body to Joseph.

46 And *Joseph* bought a linen cloth, took Him down, wrapped Him in the linen cloth, and laid Him in a tomb which had been hewn out in the rock; and he rolled a stone against the entrance of the tomb.

47 And Mary Magdalene and Mary the *mother* of Joses were looking on *to see* where He was laid.

CHAPTER 16

AND when the Sabbath was over, Mary Magdalene, and Mary the *mother* of James, and Salome, bought spices, that they might come and anoint Him.

2 And very early on the first day of the week, they *came to the tomb when the sun had risen.

3 And they were saying to one another, "Who will roll away the stone for us from the entrance of the tomb?"

4 And looking up, they *saw that the stone had been rolled away, although it was extremely large.

5 And entering the tomb, they saw a young man sitting at the right, wearing a white robe; and they were amazed.

6 And he *said to them, "Do not be amazed; you are looking for Jesus the Nazarene, who has been crucified. He is not here; behold, *here is* the place where they laid Him.

7 "But go, tell His disciples and Peter, 'He is going before you into Galilee; there you will see Him, just as He said to you.'"

8 And they went out and fled from the tomb, for trembling and astonishment had gripped them;

and they said nothing to anyone, for they were afraid.

9 [48Now after He had risen early on the first day of the week, He first appeared to Mary Magdalene, from whom He had cast out seven demons.

10 She went and reported to those who had been with Him, while they were mourning and weeping.

11 And when they heard that He was alive, and had been seen by her, they refused to believe it.

12 And after that, He appeared in a different form to two of them, while they were walking along on their way to the country.

13 And they went away and reported it to the others, but they did not believe them either.

14 And afterward He appeared to the eleven themselves as they were reclining *at the table*; and He reproached them for their unbelief and hardness of heart, because they had not believed those who had seen Him after He had risen.

15 And He said to them, "Go into all the world and preach the gospel to all creation.

16 "He who has believed and has been baptized shall be saved; but he who has disbelieved shall be condemned.

17 "And these signs will accompany those who have believed: in My name they will cast out demons, they will speak with new tongues;

18 they will pick up serpents, and if they drink any deadly *poison*, it shall not hurt them; they will lay hands on the sick, and they will recover."

19 So then, when the Lord Jesus had spoken to them, He was received up into heaven, and sat down at the right hand of God.

20 And they went out and preached everywhere, while the Lord worked with them, and confirmed the word by the signs that followed.]

[49And they promptly reported all these instructions to Peter and his companions. And after that, Jesus Himself sent out through them from east to west the sacred and imperishable proclamation of eternal salvation.]

48 Some of the oldest mss. do not contain vv. 9-20

49 A few later mss. and versions contain this paragraph, usually after verse 8; a few have it at the end of chapter.

LUKE

INASMUCH as many have undertaken to compile an account of the things accomplished among us,

2 just as those who from the beginning were eyewitnesses and servants of the [1]word have handed them down to us,

3 it seemed fitting for me as well, having investigated everything carefully from the beginning, to write *it* out for you in consecutive order, most excellent Theophilus;

4 so that you might know the exact truth about the things you have been taught.

5 In the days of Herod, king of Judea, there was a certain priest named Zacharias, of the division of [2]Abijah; and he had a wife [3]from the daughters of Aaron, and her name was Elizabeth.

6 And they were both righteous in the sight of God, walking blamelessly in all the commandments and requirements of the Lord.

7 And they had no child, because Elizabeth was barren, and they were both advanced in years.

8 Now it came about, while he was performing his priestly service before God in the *appointed* order of his division,

9 according to the custom of the priestly office, he was chosen by lot to enter the temple of the Lord and burn incense.

10 And the whole multitude of the people were in prayer outside at the hour of the incense offering.

11 And an angel of the Lord appeared to him, standing to the right of the altar of incense.

12 And Zacharias was troubled when he saw *him*, and fear gripped him.

13 But the angel said to him, "Do not be afraid, Zacharias, for your petition has been heard, and your wife Elizabeth will bear you a son, and you will give him the name John.

14 "And you will have joy and gladness, and many will rejoice at his birth.

15 "For he will be great in the sight of the Lord, and he will drink no wine or liquor; and he will be filled with the Holy Spirit, while yet in his mother's womb.

16 "And he will turn back many of the sons of Israel to the Lord their God.

17 "And it is he who will go *as a forerunner* before Him in the spirit and power of Elijah, TO TURN THE HEARTS OF THE FATHERS BACK TO THE CHILDREN, and the disobedient to the attitude of the righteous; so as to make ready a people prepared for the Lord."

18 And Zacharias said to the angel, "How shall I know this *for certain?* For I am an old man, and my wife is advanced in years."

19 And the angel answered and said to him, "I am Gabriel, who

[1] I.e., gospel [2] Gr., *Abia*
[3] I.e., of priestly descent

stands in the presence of God; and I have been sent to speak to you, and to bring you this good news.

20 "And behold, you shall be silent and unable to speak until the day when these things take place, because you did not believe my words, which shall be fulfilled in their proper time."

21 And the people were waiting for Zacharias, and were wondering at his delay in the temple.

22 But when he came out, he was unable to speak to them; and they realized that he had seen a vision in the temple; and he kept making signs to them, and remained mute.

23 And it came about, when the days of his priestly service were ended, that he went back home.

24 And after these days Elizabeth his wife became pregnant; and she kept herself in seclusion for five months, saying,

25 "This is the way the Lord has dealt with me in the days when He looked *with favor* upon *me*, to take away my disgrace among men."

26 Now in the sixth month the angel Gabriel was sent from God to a city in Galilee, called Nazareth,

27 to a virgin engaged to a man whose name was Joseph, of the descendants of David; and the virgin's name was Mary.

28 And coming in, he said to her, "Hail, favored one! The Lord *is* with you."[4]

29 But she was greatly troubled at *this* statement, and kept pondering what kind of salutation this might be.

30 And the angel said to her, "Do not be afraid, Mary; for you have found favor with God.

31 "And behold, you will conceive in your womb, and bear a son, and you shall name Him Jesus.

32 "He will be great, and will be called the Son of the Most High; and the Lord God will give Him the throne of His father David;

33 and He will reign over the house of Jacob forever; and His kingdom will have no end."

34 And Mary said to the angel, "How can this be, since I am a virgin?"

35 And the angel answered and said to her, "The Holy Spirit will come upon you, and the power of the Most High will overshadow you; and for that reason the holy offspring shall be called the Son of God.

36 "And behold, even your relative Elizabeth has also conceived a son in her old age; and she who was called barren is now in her sixth month.

37 "For nothing will be impossible with God."

38 And Mary said, "Behold, the [5]bondslave of the Lord; be it done to me according to your word." And the angel departed from her.

39 Now at this time Mary arose and went with haste to the hill country, to a city of Judah,

40 and entered the house of Zacharias and greeted Elizabeth.

41 And it came about that when Elizabeth heard Mary's greeting, the baby leaped in her womb; and Elizabeth was filled with the Holy Spirit.

42 And she cried out with a loud voice, and said, "Blessed among women *are* you, and blessed *is* the fruit of your womb!

---

4 Later mss. add: *you are blessed among women* 5 I.e., female slave

43 "And how has it *happened* to me, that the mother of my Lord should come to me?

44 "For behold, when the sound of your greeting reached my ears, the baby leaped in my womb for joy.

45 "And blessed *is* she who believed that there would be a fulfillment of what had been spoken to her by the Lord."

46 And Mary said:

"My soul exalts the Lord,

47 "And my spirit has rejoiced in God my Savior.

48 "For He has had regard for the humble state of His bondslave;
For behold, from this time on all generations will count me blessed.

49 "For the Mighty One has done great things for me;
And holy is His name.

50 "AND HIS MERCY IS UPON GENERATION AFTER GENERATION
TOWARD THOSE WHO FEAR HIM.

51 "He has done mighty deeds with His arm;
He has scattered *those who were* proud in the thoughts of their heart.

52 "He has brought down rulers from *their* thrones,
And has exalted those who were humble.

53 "HE HAS FILLED THE HUNGRY WITH GOOD THINGS;
And sent away the rich empty-handed.

54 "He has given help to Israel His servant,
In remembrance of His mercy,

55 As He spoke to our fathers,
To Abraham and his offspring forever."

56 And Mary stayed with her about three months, and *then* returned to her home.

57 Now the time had come for Elizabeth to give birth, and she brought forth a son.

58 And her neighbors and her relatives heard that the Lord had displayed His great mercy toward her; and they were rejoicing with her.

59 And it came about that on the eighth day they came to circumcise the child, and they were going to call him Zacharias, after his father.

60 And his mother answered and said, "No indeed; but he shall be called John."

61 And they said to her, "There is no one among your relatives who is called by that name."

62 And they made signs to his father, as to what he wanted him called.

63 And he asked for a tablet, and wrote as follows, "His name is John." And they were all astonished.

64 And at once his mouth was opened and his tongue *loosed,* and he *began* to speak in praise of God.

65 And fear came on all those living around them; and all these matters were being talked about in all the hill country of Judea.

66 And all who heard them kept them in mind, saying, "What then will this child *turn out to* be?" For the hand of the Lord was certainly with him.

67 And his father Zacharias was filled with the Holy Spirit, and prophesied, saying:

68 "Blessed *be* the Lord God of Israel,

For He has visited us and accomplished redemption for His people,

69 And has raised up a horn of salvation for us
In the house of David His servant—

70 As He spoke by the mouth of His holy prophets from of old—

71 Salvation FROM OUR ENEMIES,
And FROM THE HAND OF ALL WHO HATE US;

72 To show mercy toward our fathers,
And to remember His holy covenant,

73 The oath which He swore to Abraham our father,

74 To grant us that we, being delivered from the hand of our enemies,
Might serve Him without fear,

75 In holiness and righteousness before Him all our days.

76 "And you, child, will be called the prophet of the Most High;
For you will go on BEFORE THE LORD TO PREPARE HIS WAYS;

77 To give to His people *the* knowledge of salvation
By the forgiveness of their sins,

78 Because of the tender mercy of our God,
With which the Sunrise from on high shall visit us,

79 TO SHINE UPON THOSE WHO SIT IN DARKNESS AND THE SHADOW OF DEATH,

To guide our feet into the way of peace."

80 And the child continued to grow, and to become strong in spirit, and he lived in the deserts until the day of his public appearance to Israel.

CHAPTER 2

NOW it came about in those days that a decree went out from Caesar Augustus, that a census be taken of all [6]the inhabited earth.

2 This was the first census taken while [7]Quirinius was governor of Syria.

3 And all were proceeding to register for the census, everyone to his own city.

4 And Joseph also went up from Galilee, from the city of Nazareth, to Judea, to the city of David, which is called Bethlehem, because he was of the house and family of David,

5 in order to register, along with Mary, who was engaged to him, and was with child.

6 And it came about that while they were there, the days were completed for her to give birth.

7 And she gave birth to her first-born son; and she wrapped Him in cloths, and laid Him in a manger, because there was no room for them in the inn.

8 And in the same region there were *some* shepherds staying out in the fields, and keeping watch over their flock by night.

9 And an angel of the Lord suddenly stood before them, and the glory of the Lord shone around them; and they were terribly frightened.

---

[6] I.e., the Roman empire   [7] Gr., *Kyrenios*

10 And the angel said to them, "Do not be afraid; for behold, I bring you good news of a great joy which shall be for all the people;

11 for today in the city of David there has been born for you a Savior, who is [8]Christ the Lord.

12 "And this *will be* a sign for you: you will find a baby wrapped in cloths, and lying in a manger."

13 And suddenly there appeared with the angel a multitude of the heavenly host praising God, and saying,

14 "Glory to God in the highest,
And on earth peace among men [9]with whom He is pleased."

15 And it came about when the angels had gone away from them into heaven, that the shepherds *began* saying to one another, "Let us go straight to Bethlehem then, and see this thing that has happened which the Lord has made known to us."

16 And they came in haste and found their way to Mary and Joseph, and the baby as He lay in the manger.

17 And when they had seen this, they made known the statement which had been told them about this Child.

18 And all who heard it wondered at the things which were told them by the shepherds.

19 But Mary treasured up all these things, pondering them in her heart.

20 And the shepherds went back, glorifying and praising God for all that they had heard and seen, just as had been told them.

21 And when eight days were completed before His circumcision, His name was *then* called Jesus, the name given by the angel before He was conceived in the womb.

22 And when the days for their purification according to the law of Moses were completed, they brought Him up to Jerusalem to present Him to the Lord

23 (as it is written in the Law of the Lord, "EVERY *first-born* MALE THAT OPENS THE WOMB SHALL BE CALLED HOLY TO THE LORD"),

24 and to offer a sacrifice according to what was said in the Law of the Lord, "A PAIR OF TURTLEDOVES, OR TWO YOUNG PIGEONS."

25 And behold, there was a man in Jerusalem whose name was Simeon; and this man was righteous and devout, looking for the consolation of Israel; and the Holy Spirit was upon him.

26 And it had been revealed to him by the Holy Spirit that he would not see death before he had seen the Lord's Christ.

27 And he came in the Spirit into the temple; and when the parents brought in the child Jesus, to carry out for Him the custom of the Law,

28 then he took Him into his arms, and blessed God, and said,

29 "Now Lord, Thou dost let Thy bond-servant depart In peace, according to Thy word;

30 For my eyes have seen Thy salvation,

31 Which Thou hast prepared in the presence of all peoples,

---

[8] I.e., Messiah
[9] Lit., *of good pleasure;* or possibly, *of good will*

32 A LIGHT OF REVELATION TO
      THE GENTILES,
      And the glory of Thy peo-
      ple Israel."

33 And His father and mother
were amazed at the things which
were being said about Him.

34 And Simeon blessed them,
and said to Mary His mother,
"Behold, this *Child* is appointed
for the fall and rise of many in
Israel, and for a sign to be opposed—

35 and a sword will pierce even
your own soul—to the end that
thoughts from many hearts may
be revealed."

36 And there was a prophetess,
Anna the daughter of Phanuel, of
the tribe of Asher. She was advanced in years, having lived
with a husband seven years after
her marriage,

37 and then as a widow to the
age of eighty-four. And she never
left the temple, serving night and
day with fastings and prayers.

38 And at that very moment
she came up and *began* giving
thanks to God, and continued to
speak of Him to all those who
were looking for the redemption
of Jerusalem.

39 And when they had performed everything according to
the Law of the Lord, they returned to Galilee, to their own
city of Nazareth.

40 And the Child continued to
grow and become strong, increasing in wisdom; and the
grace of God was upon Him.

41 And His parents used to go
to Jerusalem every year at the
Feast of the Passover.

42 And when He became
twelve, they went up *there* according to the custom of the
Feast;

43 and as they were returning,
after spending the full number of
days, the boy Jesus stayed behind in Jerusalem. And His parents were unaware of it,

44 but supposed Him to be in
the caravan, and went a day's
journey; and they *began* looking
for Him among their relatives
and acquaintances.

45 And when they did not find
Him, they returned to Jerusalem,
looking for Him.

46 And it came about that after
three days they found Him in the
temple, sitting in the midst of the
teachers, both listening to them,
and asking them questions.

47 And all who heard Him
were amazed at His understanding and His answers.

48 And when they saw Him,
they were astonished; and His
mother said to Him, "Son, why
have You treated us this way?
Behold, Your father and I have
been anxiously looking for You."

49 And He said to them, "Why
is it that you were looking for
Me? Did you not know that I had
to be in My Father's *house?*"

50 And they did not understand the statement which He
had made to them.

51 And He went down with
them, and came to Nazareth; and
He continued in subjection to
them; and His mother treasured
all *these* things in her heart.

52 And Jesus kept increasing
in wisdom and stature, and in favor with God and men.

CHAPTER 3

N OW in the fifteenth year of
the reign of Tiberius Caesar,
when Pontius Pilate was governor of Judea, and Herod was

tetrarch of Galilee, and his brother Philip was tetrarch of the region of Ituraea and Trachonitis, and Lysanias was tetrarch of Abilene,

2 in the high priesthood of Annas and Caiaphas, the word of God came to John, the son of Zacharias, in the wilderness.

3 And he came into all the district around the Jordan, preaching a baptism of repentance for the forgiveness of sins;

4 as it is written in the book of the words of Isaiah the prophet,

"THE VOICE OF ONE CRYING IN
    THE WILDERNESS,
'MAKE READY THE WAY OF
    THE LORD,
MAKE   HIS   PATHS
    STRAIGHT.

5 'EVERY RAVINE SHALL BE
    FILLED UP,
AND EVERY MOUNTAIN AND
    HILL SHALL BE BROUGHT
    LOW;
AND THE CROOKED SHALL
    BECOME STRAIGHT,
AND THE ROUGH ROADS
    SMOOTH;

6 AND ALL FLESH SHALL SEE
    THE SALVATION OF GOD.'"

7 He therefore began saying to the multitudes who were going out to be baptized by him, "You brood of vipers, who warned you to flee from the wrath to come?

8 "Therefore bring forth fruits in keeping with repentance, and do not begin to say to yourselves, 'We have Abraham for our father,' for I say to you that God is able from these stones to raise up children to Abraham.

9 "And also the axe is already laid at the root of the trees; every tree therefore that does not bear good fruit is cut down and thrown into the fire."

10 And the multitudes were questioning him, saying, "Then what shall we do?"

11 And he would answer and say to them, "Let the man who has two tunics share with him who has none; and let him who has food do likewise."

12 And some [10]tax-gatherers also came to be baptized, and they said to him, "Teacher, what shall we do?"

13 And he said to them, "Collect no more than what you have been ordered to."

14 And some [11]soldiers were questioning him, saying, "And what about us, what shall we do?" And he said to them, "Do not take money from anyone by force, or accuse anyone falsely, and be content with your wages."

15 Now while the people were in a state of expectation and all were wondering in their hearts about John, as to whether he might be the Christ,

16 John answered and said to them all, "As for me, I baptize you with water; but One is coming who is mightier than I, and I am not fit to untie the thong of His sandals; He will baptize you with the Holy Spirit and fire.

17 "And His winnowing fork is in His hand to thoroughly clear His threshing floor, and to gather the wheat into His barn; but He will burn up the chaff with unquenchable fire."

18 So with many other exhortations also he preached the gospel to the people.

19 But when Herod the tetrarch was reproved by him on account of Herodias, his broth-

---

[10] I.e., Collectors of Roman taxes for profit
[11] I.e., men in active military service

er's wife, and on account of all the wicked things which Herod had done,

20 he added this also to them all, that he locked John up in prison.

21 Now it came about when all the people were baptized, that Jesus also was baptized, and while He was praying, heaven was opened,

22 and the Holy Spirit descended upon Him in bodily form like a dove, and a voice came out of heaven, "Thou art My beloved Son, in Thee I am well-pleased."

23 And when He began His ministry, Jesus Himself was about thirty years of age, being supposedly the son of Joseph, the son of Eli,

24 the son of Matthat, the son of Levi, the son of Melchi, the son of Jannai, the son of Joseph,

25 the son of Mattathias, the son of Amos, the son of Nahum, the son of Hesli, the son of Naggai,

26 the son of Maath, the son of Mattathias, the son of Semein, the son of Josech, the son of Joda,

27 the son of Joanan, the son of Rhesa, the son of Zerubbabel, the son of Shealtiel, the son of Neri,

28 the son of Melchi, the son of Addi, the son of Cosam, the son of Elmadam, the son of Er,

29 the son of Joshua, the son of Eliezer, the son of Jorim, the son of Matthat, the son of Levi,

30 the son of Simeon, the son of Judah, the son of Joseph, the son of Jonam, the son of Eliakim,

31 the son of Melea, the son of Menna, the son of Mattatha, the son of Nathan, the son of David,

32 the son of Jesse, the son of

Obed, the son of Boaz, the son of Salmon, the son of Nahshon,

33 the son of Amminadab, the son of Admin, the son of Ram, the son of Hezron, the son of Perez, the son of Judah,

34 the son of Jacob, the son of Isaac, the son of Abraham, the son of Terah, the son of Nahor,

35 the son of Serug, the son of Reu, the son of Peleg, the son of Heber, the son of Shelah,

36 the son of Cainan, the son of Arphaxad, the son of Shem, the son of Noah, the son of Lamech,

37 the son of Methuselah, the son of Enoch, the son of Jared, the son of Mahalaleel, the son of Cainan,

38 the son of Enosh, the son of Seth, the son of Adam, the son of God.

CHAPTER 4

AND Jesus, full of the Holy Spirit, returned from the Jordan and was led about by the Spirit in the wilderness

2 for forty days, being tempted by the devil. And He ate nothing during those days; and when they had ended, He became hungry.

3 And the devil said to Him, "If You are the Son of God, tell this stone to become bread."

4 And Jesus answered him, "It is written, 'MAN SHALL NOT LIVE ON BREAD ALONE.'"

5 And he led Him up and showed Him all the kingdoms of the world in a moment of time.

6 And the devil said to Him, "I will give You all this domain and its glory; for it has been handed over to me, and I give it to whomever I wish.

7"Therefore if You worship before me, it shall all be Yours."

8 And Jesus answered and said to him, "It is written, 'YOU SHALL WORSHIP THE LORD your GOD AND SERVE HIM ONLY.' "

9 And he led Him to Jerusalem and had Him stand on the pinnacle of the temple, and said to Him, "If You are the Son of God, throw Yourself down from here;

10 for it is written,

'HE WILL GIVE HIS ANGELS
   CHARGE CONCERNING YOU
   TO GUARD YOU,'

11 and,

'ON *their* HANDS THEY WILL
   BEAR YOU UP,
 LEST YOU STRIKE YOUR
   FOOT AGAINST A STONE.' "

12 And Jesus answered and said to him, "It is said, 'YOU SHALL NOT [12]PUT THE LORD your GOD TO THE TEST.' "

13 And when the devil had finished every temptation, he departed from Him until an opportune time.

14 And Jesus returned to Galilee in the power of the Spirit; and news about Him spread through all the surrounding district.

15 And He *began* teaching in their synagogues and was praised by all.

16 And He came to Nazareth, where He had been brought up; and as was His custom, He entered the synagogue on the Sabbath, and stood up to read.

17 And the book of the prophet Isaiah was handed to Him. And He opened the book, and found the place where it was written,

18 "THE SPIRIT OF THE LORD IS UPON ME,
 BECAUSE HE ANOINTED ME
   TO PREACH THE GOSPEL TO
   THE POOR.
HE HAS SENT ME TO PRO-
   CLAIM RELEASE TO THE
   CAPTIVES,
AND RECOVERY OF SIGHT TO
   THE BLIND,
TO SET FREE THOSE WHO
   ARE DOWNTRODDEN,

19 TO PROCLAIM THE FAVOR-
   ABLE YEAR OF THE LORD."

20 And He closed the book, and gave it back to the attendant, and sat down; and the eyes of all in the synagogue were fixed upon Him.

21 And He began to say to them, "Today this Scripture has been fulfilled in your hearing."

22 And all were speaking well of Him, and wondering at the gracious words which were falling from His lips; and they were saying, "Is this not Joseph's son?"

23 And He said to them, "No doubt you will quote this proverb to Me, 'Physician, heal yourself! Whatever we heard was done at Capernaum, do here in your home town as well.' "

24 And He said, "Truly I say to you, no prophet is welcome in his home town.

25"But I say to you in truth, there were many widows in Israel in the days of Elijah, when the sky was shut up for three years and six months, when a great famine came over all the land;

26 and yet Elijah was sent to none of them, but only to Zarephath, in the land of Sidon, to a woman who was a widow.

27"And there were many lepers in Israel in the time of Elisha the

12 Or, *tempt . . . God*

prophet; and none of them was cleansed, but only Naaman the Syrian."

28 And all in the synagogue were filled with rage as they heard these things;

29 and they rose up and cast Him out of the city, and led Him to the brow of the hill on which their city had been built, in order to throw Him down the cliff.

30 But passing through their midst, He went His way.

31 And He came down to Capernaum, a city of Galilee. And He was teaching them on the Sabbath;

32 and they were amazed at His teaching, for His message was with authority.

33 And there was a man in the synagogue possessed by the spirit of an unclean demon, and he cried out with a loud voice,

34 "Ha! What do we have to do with You, Jesus of Nazareth? Have You come to destroy us? I know who You are—the Holy One of God!"

35 And Jesus rebuked him, saying, "Be quiet and come out of him!" And when the demon had thrown him down in *their* midst, he came out of him without doing him any harm.

36 And amazement came upon them all, and they *began* discussing with one another saying, "What is this message? For with authority and power He commands the unclean spirits, and they come out."

37 And the report about Him was getting out into every locality in the surrounding district.

38 And He arose and *left* the synagogue, and entered Simon's home. Now Simon's mother-in-law was suffering from a high fever; and they made request of Him on her behalf.

39 And standing over her, He rebuked the fever, and it left her; and she immediately arose and waited on them.

40 And while the sun was setting, all who had any sick with various diseases brought them to Him; and laying His hands on every one of them, He was healing them.

41 And demons also were coming out of many, crying out and saying, "You are the Son of God!" And rebuking them, He would not allow them to speak, because they knew Him to be the Christ.

42 And when day came, He departed and went to a lonely place; and the multitudes were searching for Him, and came to Him, and tried to keep Him from going away from them.

43 But He said to them, "I must preach the kingdom of God to the other cities also, for I was sent for this purpose."

44 And He kept on preaching in the synagogues of [13]Judea.

CHAPTER 5

NOW it came about that while the multitude were pressing around Him and listening to the word of God, He was standing by the lake of Gennesaret;

2 and He saw two boats lying at the edge of the lake; but the fishermen had gotten out of them, and were washing their nets.

3 And He got into one of the boats, which was Simon's, and

---

[13] I.e., the country of the Jews (including Galilee); some mss. read *Galilee*

asked him to put out a little way from the land. And He sat down and *began* teaching the multitudes from the boat.

4 And when He had finished speaking, He said to Simon, "Put out into the deep water and let down your nets for a catch."

5 And Simon answered and said, "Master, we worked hard all night and caught nothing, but at Your bidding I will let down the nets."

6 And when they had done this, they enclosed a great quantity of fish; and their nets *began* to break;

7 and they signaled to their partners in the other boat, for them to come and help them. And they came, and filled both of the boats, so that they began to sink.

8 But when Simon Peter saw *that*, he fell down at Jesus' feet, saying, "Depart from me, for I am a sinful man, O Lord!"

9 For amazement had seized him and all his companions because of the catch of fish which they had taken;

10 and so also James and John, sons of Zebedee, who were partners with Simon. And Jesus said to Simon, "Do not fear, from now on you will be catching men."

11 And when they had brought their boats to land, they left everything and followed Him.

12 And it came about that while He was in one of the cities, behold, *there was* a man full of leprosy; and when he saw Jesus, he fell on his face and implored Him, saying, "Lord, if You are willing, You can make me clean."

13 And He stretched out His hand, and touched him, saying,

"I am willing; be cleansed." And immediately the leprosy left him.

14 And He ordered him to tell no one, "But go and show yourself to the priest, and make an offering for your cleansing, just as Moses commanded, for a testimony to them."

15 But the news about Him was spreading even farther, and great multitudes were gathering to hear *Him* and to be healed of their sicknesses.

16 But He Himself would *often* slip away to the wilderness and pray.

17 And it came about one day that He was teaching; and there were *some* Pharisees and teachers of the law sitting *there*, who had come from every village of Galilee and Judea and *from* Jerusalem; and the power of the Lord was *present* for Him to perform healing.

18 And behold, *some* men *were* carrying on a bed a man who was paralyzed; and they were trying to bring him in, and to set him down in front of Him.

19 And not finding any *way* to bring him in because of the crowd, they went up on the roof and let him down through the tiles with his stretcher, right in the center, in front of Jesus.

20 And seeing their faith, He said, "Friend, your sins are forgiven you."

21 And the scribes and the Pharisees began to reason, saying, "Who is this *man* who speaks blasphemies? Who can forgive sins, but God alone?"

22 But Jesus, aware of their reasonings, answered and said to them, "Why are you reasoning in your hearts?

23"Which is easier, to say, 'Your sins have been forgiven you,' or to say, 'Rise and walk?'

24"But in order that you may know that the Son of Man has authority on earth to forgive sins,"—He said to the paralytic—"I say to you, rise, and take up your stretcher and go home."

25 And at once he rose up before them, and took up what he had been lying on, and went home, glorifying God.

26 And they were all seized with astonishment and began glorifying God; and they were filled with fear, saying, "We have seen remarkable things today."

27 And after that He went out, and noticed a [14]tax-gatherer named Levi, sitting in the tax office, and He said to him, "Follow Me."

28 And he left everything behind, and rose and began to follow Him.

29 And Levi gave a big reception for Him in his house; and there was a great crowd of tax-gatherers and other *people* who were reclining *at the table* with them.

30 And the Pharisees and their scribes *began* grumbling at His disciples, saying, "Why do you eat and drink with the tax-gatherers and sinners?"

31 And Jesus answered and said to them, "*It is* not those who are well who need a physician, but those who are sick.

32"I have not come to call the righteous but sinners to repentance."

33 And they said to Him, "The disciples of John often fast and offer prayers; the *disciples* of the Pharisees also do the same; but Yours eat and drink."

34 And Jesus said to them, "You cannot make the attendants of the bridegroom fast while the bridegroom is with them, can you?

35"But *the* days will come; and when the bridegroom is taken away from them, then they will fast in those days."

36 And He was also telling them a parable: "No one tears a piece from a new garment and puts it on an old garment; otherwise he will both tear the new, and the piece from the new will not match the old.

37"And no one puts new wine into old wineskins; otherwise the new wine will burst the skins, and it will be spilled out, and the skins will be ruined.

38"But new wine must be put into fresh wineskins.

39"And no one, after drinking old *wine* wishes for new; for he says, 'The old is good *enough.'*"

CHAPTER 6

NOW it came about that on a *certain* Sabbath He was passing through *some* grainfields; and His disciples were picking and eating the heads *of grain*, rubbing them in their hands.

2 But some of the Pharisees said, "Why do you do what is not lawful on the Sabbath?"

3 And Jesus answering them said, "Have you not even read what David did when he was hungry, he and those who were with him,

4 how he entered the house of God, and took and ate the

---

[14] I.e., Collector of Roman taxes for profit

15consecrated bread which is not lawful for any to eat except the priests alone, and gave it to his companions?"

5 And He was saying to them, "The Son of Man is Lord of the Sabbath."

6 And it came about on another Sabbath, that He entered the synagogue and was teaching; and there was a man there whose right hand was withered.

7 And the scribes and the Pharisees were watching Him closely, *to see* if He healed on the Sabbath, in order that they might find *reason* to accuse Him.

8 But He knew what they were thinking, and He said to the man with the withered hand, "Rise and come forward!" And he rose and came forward.

9 And Jesus said to them, "I ask you, is it lawful on the Sabbath to do good, or to do harm, to save a life, or to destroy it?"

10 And after looking around at them all, He said to him, "Stretch out your hand!" And he did *so;* and his hand was restored.

11 But they themselves were filled with rage, and discussed together what they might do to Jesus.

12 And it was at this time that He went off to the mountain to pray, and He spent the whole night in prayer to God.

13 And when day came, He called His disciples to Him; and chose twelve of them, whom He also named as apostles:

14 Simon, whom He also named Peter, and Andrew his brother; and James and John; and Philip and Bartholomew;

15 and Matthew and Thomas; James *the son* of Alphaeus, and Simon who was called the Zealot;

16 Judas *the son* of James, and Judas Iscariot, who became a traitor.

17 And He descended with them, and stood on a level place; and *there was* a great multitude of His disciples, and a great throng of people from all Judea and Jerusalem and the coastal region of Tyre and Sidon,

18 who had come to hear Him, and to be healed of their diseases; and those who were troubled with unclean spirits were being cured.

19 And all the multitude were trying to touch Him, for power was coming from Him and healing *them* all.

20 And turning His gaze on His disciples, He *began* to say, "Blessed *are* you *who are* poor, for yours is the kingdom of God.

21"Blessed *are* you who hunger now, for you shall be satisfied. Blessed *are* you who weep now, for you shall laugh.

22"Blessed *are* you when men hate you, and ostracize you, and cast insults at you, and spurn your name as evil, for the sake of the Son of Man.

23"Be glad in that day, and leap *for joy,* for behold, your reward is great in heaven; for in the same way their fathers used to treat the prophets.

24"But woe to you who are rich, for you are receiving your comfort in full.

25"Woe to you who are well-fed now, for you shall be hungry. Woe *to you* who laugh now, for you shall mourn and weep.

26"Woe *to you* when all men speak well of you, for in the same

15 Or, *showbread,* lit., *loaves of presentation*

way their fathers used to treat the false prophets.

27"But I say to you who hear, love your enemies, do good to those who hate you,

28 bless those who curse you, pray for those who mistreat you.

29"Whoever hits you on the cheek, offer him the other also; and whoever takes away your coat, do not withhold your shirt from him either.

30"Give to everyone who asks of you, and whoever takes away what is yours, do not demand it back.

31"And just as you want people to treat you, treat them in the same way.

32"And if you love those who love you, what credit is *that* to you? For even sinners love those who love them.

33"And if you do good to those who do good to you, what credit is *that* to you? For even sinners do the same.

34"And if you lend to those from whom you expect to receive, what credit is *that* to you? Even sinners lend to sinners, in order to receive back the same *amount.*

35"But love your enemies, and do good, and lend, expecting nothing in return; and your reward will be great, and you will be sons of the Most High; for He Himself is kind to ungrateful and evil *men.*

36"Be merciful, just as your Father is merciful.

37"And do not judge and you will not be judged; and do not condemn, and you will not be condemned; pardon, and you will be pardoned.

38"Give, and it will be given to you; good measure, pressed down, shaken together, running over, they will pour into your lap. For by your standard of measure it will be measured to you in return."

39 And He also spoke a parable to them: "A blind man cannot guide a blind man, can he? Will they not both fall into a pit?

40"A pupil is not above his teacher; but everyone, after he has been fully trained, will be like his teacher.

41"And why do you look at the speck that is in your brother's eye, but do not notice the log that is in your own eye?

42"Or how can you say to your brother, 'Brother, let me take out the speck that is in your eye,' when you yourself do not see the log that is in your own eye? You hypocrite, first take the log out of your own eye, and then you will see clearly to take out the speck that is in your brother's eye.

43"For there is no good tree which produces bad fruit; nor, on the other hand, a bad tree which produces good fruit.

44"For each tree is known by its own fruit. For men do not gather figs from thorns, nor do they pick grapes from a briar bush.

45"The good man out of the good treasure of his heart brings forth what is good; and the evil *man* out of the evil *treasure* brings forth what is evil; for his mouth speaks from that which fills his heart.

46"And why do you call Me, 'Lord, Lord,' and do not do what I say?

47"Everyone who comes to Me, and hears My words, and acts upon them, I will show you whom he is like:

48 he is like a man building a house, who dug deep and laid a foundation upon the rock; and when a flood rose, the torrent burst against that house and could not shake it, because it had been well built.

49 "But the one who has heard, and has not acted *accordingly*, is like a man who built a house upon the ground without any foundation; and the torrent burst against it and immediately it collapsed, and the ruin of that house was great."

CHAPTER 7

WHEN He had completed all His discourse in the hearing of the people, He went to Capernaum.

2 And a certain centurion's slave, who was highly regarded by him, was sick and about to die.

3 And when he heard about Jesus, he sent some Jewish elders asking Him to come and save the life of his slave.

4 And when they had come to Jesus, they earnestly entreated Him, saying, "He is worthy for You to grant this to him;

5 for he loves our nation, and it was he who built us our synagogue."

6 Now Jesus *started* on His way with them; and when He was already not far from the house, the centurion sent friends, saying to Him, "Lord, do not trouble Yourself further, for I am not worthy for You to come under my roof;

7 for this reason I did not even consider myself worthy to come to You, but just say the word, and my servant will be healed.

8 "For I, too, am a man under authority, with soldiers under me; and I say to this one, 'Go!' and he goes; and to another, 'Come!' and he comes; and to my slave, 'Do this!' and he does it."

9 Now when Jesus heard this, He marveled at him, and turned and said to the multitude that was following Him, "I say to you, not even in Israel have I found such great faith."

10 And when those who had been sent returned to the house, they found the slave in good health.

11 And it came about soon afterwards, that He went to a city called Nain; and His disciples were going along with Him, accompanied by a large multitude.

12 Now as He approached the gate of the city, behold, a dead man was being carried out, the only son of his mother, and she was a widow; and a sizeable crowd from the city was with her.

13 And when the Lord saw her, He felt compassion for her, and said to her, "Do not weep."

14 And He came up and touched the coffin; and the bearers came to a halt. And He said, "Young man, I say to you, arise!"

15 And the dead man sat up, and began to speak. And *Jesus* gave him back to his mother.

16 And fear gripped them all, and they *began* glorifying God, saying, "A great prophet has arisen among us!" and, "God has visited His people!"

17 And this report concerning Him went out all over Judea, and in all the surrounding district.

18 And the disciples of John

reported to him about all these things.

19 And summoning two of his disciples, John sent them to the Lord, saying, "Are You the Expected One, or do we look for someone else?"

20 And when the men had come to Him, they said, "John the Baptist has sent us to You, saying, 'Are You the Expected One, or do we look for someone else?' "

21 At that very time He cured many *people* of diseases and afflictions and evil spirits; and He granted sight to many *who were* blind.

22 And He answered and said to them, "Go and report to John what you have seen and heard: *the* BLIND RECEIVE SIGHT, *the* lame walk, *the* lepers are cleansed, and *the* deaf hear, *the* dead are raised up, the POOR HAVE THE GOSPEL PREACHED TO THEM.

23 "And blessed is he who keeps from stumbling over Me."

24 And when the messengers of John had left, He began to speak to the multitudes about John, "What did you go out into the wilderness to look at? A reed shaken by the wind?

25 "But what did you go out to see? A man dressed in soft clothing? Behold, those who are splendidly clothed and live in luxury are *found* in royal palaces.

26 "But what did you go out to see? A prophet? Yes, I say to you, and one who is more than a prophet.

27 "This is the one about whom it is written,

'BEHOLD, I SEND MY MESSENGER BEFORE YOUR FACE,
WHO WILL PREPARE YOUR WAY BEFORE YOU.'

28 "I say to you, among those born of women, there is no one greater than John; yet he who is least in the kingdom of God is greater than he."

29 And when all the people and the [16]tax-gatherers heard *this*, they acknowledged God's justice, having been baptized with the baptism of John.

30 But the Pharisees and the [17]lawyers rejected God's purpose for themselves, not having been baptized by John.

31 "To what then shall I compare the men of this generation, and what are they like?

32 "They are like children who sit in the market place and call to one another; and they say, 'We played the flute for you, and you did not dance; we sang a dirge, and you did not weep.'

33 "For John the Baptist has come eating no bread and drinking no wine; and you say, 'He has a demon!'

34 "The Son of Man has come eating and drinking; and you say, 'Behold, a gluttonous man, and a drunkard, a friend of tax-gatherers and sinners!'

35 "Yet wisdom is vindicated by all her children."

36 Now one of the Pharisees was requesting Him to dine with him. And He entered the Pharisee's house, and reclined *at the table.*

37 And behold, there was a woman in the city who was a sinner; and when she learned that He was reclining *at the table* in

[16] I.e., Collectors of Roman taxes for profit
[17] I.e., experts in the Mosaic law

the Pharisee's house, she brought an alabaster vial of perfume,

38 and standing behind *Him* at His feet, weeping, she began to wet His feet with her tears, and kept wiping them with the hair of her head, and kissing His feet, and anointing them with the perfume.

39 Now when the Pharisee who had invited Him saw this, he said to himself, "If this man were a prophet He would know who and what sort of person this woman is who is touching Him, that she is a sinner."

40 And Jesus answered and said to him, "Simon, I have something to say to you." And he replied, "Say it, Teacher."

41 "A certain moneylender had two debtors: one owed five hundred [18]denarii, and the other fifty.

42 "When they were unable to repay, he graciously forgave them both. Which of them therefore will love him more?"

43 Simon answered and said, "I suppose the one whom he forgave more." And He said to him, "You have judged correctly."

44 And turning toward the woman, He said to Simon, "Do you see this woman? I entered your house; you gave Me no water for My feet, but she has wet My feet with her tears, and wiped them with her hair.

45 "You gave Me no kiss; but she, since the time I came in, has not ceased to kiss My feet.

46 "You did not anoint My head with oil, but she anointed My feet with perfume.

47 "For this reason I say to you, her sins, which are many, have been forgiven, for she loved much; but he who is forgiven little, loves little."

48 And He said to her, "Your sins have been forgiven."

49 And those who were reclining *at the table* with Him began to say to themselves, "Who is this *man* who even forgives sins?"

50 And He said to the woman, "Your faith has saved you; go in peace."

CHAPTER 8

AND it came about soon afterwards, that He *began* going about from one city and village to another, proclaiming and preaching the kingdom of God; and the twelve were with Him,

2 and *also* some women who had been healed of evil spirits and sicknesses: Mary who was called Magdalene, from whom seven demons had gone out,

3 and Joanna the wife of Chuza, Herod's steward, and Susanna, and many others who were contributing to their support out of their private means.

4 And when a great multitude were coming together, and those from the various cities were journeying to Him, He spoke by way of a parable:

5 "The sower went out to sow his seed; and as he sowed, some fell beside the road; and it was trampled under foot, and the birds of the air ate it up.

6 "And other *seed* fell on rocky *soil*, and as soon as it grew up, it withered away, because it had no moisture.

7 "And other *seed* fell among the thorns; and the thorns grew up with it, and choked it out.

[18] The denarius was equivalent to one day's wage

8"And other *seed* fell into the good soil, and grew up, and produced a crop a hundred times as great." As He said these things, He would call out, "He who has ears to hear, let him hear."

9 And His disciples *began* questioning Him as to what this parable might be.

10 And He said, "To you it has been granted to know the mysteries of the kingdom of God, but to the rest *it is* in parables, in order that SEEING THEY MAY NOT SEE, AND HEARING THEY MAY NOT UNDERSTAND.

11"Now the parable is this: the seed is the word of God.

12"And those beside the road are those who have heard; then the devil comes and takes away the word from their heart, so that they may not believe and be saved.

13"And those on the rocky *soil are* those who, when they hear, receive the word with joy; and these have no *firm* root; they believe for a while, and in time of temptation fall away.

14"And the *seed* which fell among the thorns, these are the ones who have heard, and as they go on their way they are choked with worries and riches and pleasures of *this* life, and bring no fruit to maturity.

15"And the *seed* in the good soil, these are the ones who have heard the word in an honest and good heart, and hold it fast, and bear fruit with perseverance.

16"Now no one after lighting a lamp covers it over with a container, or puts it under a bed; but he puts it on a lampstand, in order that those who come in may see the light.

17"For nothing is hidden that

shall not become evident, nor *anything* secret that shall not be known and come to light.

18"Therefore take care how you listen; for whoever has, to him shall *more* be given; and whoever does not have, even what he thinks he has shall be taken away from him."

19 And His mother and brothers came to Him, and they were unable to get to Him because of the crowd.

20 And it was reported to Him, "Your mother and Your brothers are standing outside, wishing to see You."

21 But He answered and said to them, "My mother and My brothers are these who hear the word of God and do it."

22 Now it came about on one of *those* days, that He and His disciples got into a boat, and He said to them, "Let us go over to the other side of the lake." And they launched out.

23 But as they were sailing along He fell asleep; and a fierce gale of wind descended upon the lake, and they *began* to be swamped and to be in danger.

24 And they came to Him and woke Him up, saying, "Master, Master, we are perishing!" And being aroused, He rebuked the wind and the surging waves, and they stopped, and it became calm.

25 And He said to them, "Where is your faith?" And they were fearful and amazed, saying to one another, "Who then is this, that He commands even the winds and the water, and they obey Him?"

26 And they sailed to the country of the Gerasenes, which is opposite Galilee.

27 And when He had come out onto the land, He was met by a certain man from the city who was possessed with demons; and who had not put on any clothing for a long time, and was not living in a house, but in the tombs.

28 And seeing Jesus, he cried out and fell before Him, and said in a loud voice, "What do I have to do with You, Jesus, Son of the Most High God? I beg You, do not torment me."

29 For He had been commanding the unclean spirit to come out of the man. For it had seized him many times; and he was bound with chains and shackles and kept under guard; and *yet* he would burst his fetters and be driven by the demon into the desert.

30 And Jesus asked him, "What is your name?" And he said, "Legion"; for many demons had entered him.

31 And they were entreating Him not to command them to depart into the abyss.

32 Now there was a herd of many swine feeding there on the mountain; and *the demons* entreated Him to permit them to enter the swine. And He gave them permission.

33 And the demons came out from the man and entered the swine; and the herd rushed down the steep bank into the lake, and were drowned.

34 And when the herdsmen saw what had happened, they ran away and reported it in the city and *out* in the country.

35 And *the people* went out to see what had happened; and they came to Jesus, and found the man from whom the demons had gone out, sitting down at the feet of Jesus, clothed and in his right mind; and they became frightened.

36 And those who had seen it reported to them how the man who was demon-possessed had been made well.

37 And all the people of the country of the Gerasenes and the surrounding district asked Him to depart from them; for they were gripped with great fear; and He got into a boat, and returned.

38 But the man from whom the demons had gone out was begging Him that he might accompany Him; but He sent him away, saying,

39 "Return to your house and describe what great things God has done for you." And he went away, proclaiming throughout the whole city what great things Jesus had done for him.

40 And as Jesus returned, the multitude welcomed Him, for they had all been waiting for Him.

41 And behold, there came a man named Jairus, and he was an official of the synagogue; and he fell at Jesus' feet, and *began* to entreat Him to come to his house;

42 for he had an only daughter, about twelve years old, and she was dying. But as He went, the multitudes were pressing against Him.

43 And a woman who had a hemorrhage for twelve years, [19]and could not be healed by anyone,

44 came up behind Him, and touched the fringe of His cloak; and immediately her hemorrhage stopped.

[19] Some mss. add *who had spent all her living upon physicians*

45 And Jesus said, "Who is the one who touched Me?" And while they were all denying it, Peter said, "Master, the multitudes are crowding and pressing upon You."

46 But Jesus said, "Someone did touch Me, for I was aware that power had gone out of Me."

47 And when the woman saw that she had not escaped notice, she came trembling and fell down before Him, and declared in the presence of all the people the reason why she had touched Him, and how she had been immediately healed.

48 And He said to her, "Daughter, your faith has made you well; go in peace."

49 While He was still speaking, someone *came from the house of the synagogue official, saying, "Your daughter has died; do not trouble the Teacher anymore."

50 But when Jesus heard this, He answered him, "Do not be afraid any longer; only believe, and she shall be made well."

51 And when He had come to the house, He did not allow anyone to enter with Him, except Peter and John and James, and the girl's father and mother.

52 Now they were all weeping and lamenting for her; but He said, "Stop weeping, for she has not died, but is asleep."

53 And they began laughing at Him, knowing that she had died.

54 He, however, took her by the hand and called, saying, "Child, arise!"

55 And her spirit returned, and she rose immediately; and He gave orders for something to be given her to eat.

56 And her parents were amazed; but He instructed them to tell no one what had happened.

CHAPTER 9

AND He called the twelve together, and gave them power and authority over all the demons, and to heal diseases.

2 And He sent them out to proclaim the kingdom of God, and to perform healing.

3 And He said to them, "Take nothing for your journey, neither a staff, nor a bag, nor bread, nor money; and do not even have two tunics apiece.

4 "And whatever house you enter, stay there, and take your leave from there.

5 "And as for those who do not receive you, as you go out from that city, shake off the dust from your feet as a testimony against them."

6 And departing, they began going about among the villages, preaching the gospel, and healing everywhere.

7 Now Herod the tetrarch heard of all that was happening; and he was greatly perplexed, because it was said by some that John had risen from the dead,

8 and by some that Elijah had appeared, and by others, that one of the prophets of old had risen again.

9 And Herod said, "I myself had John beheaded; but who is this man about whom I hear such things?" And he kept trying to see Him.

10 And when the apostles returned, they gave an account to Him of all that they had done. And taking them with Him, He

withdrew by Himself to a city called Bethsaida.

11 But the multitudes were aware of this and followed Him; and welcoming them, He *began* speaking to them about the kingdom of God and curing those who had need of healing.

12 And the day began to decline, and the twelve came and said to Him, "Send the multitude away, that they may go into the surrounding villages and countryside and find lodging and get something to eat; for here we are in a desolate place."

13 But He said to them, "You give them *something* to eat!" And they said, "We have no more than five loaves and two fish, unless perhaps we go and buy food for all these people."

14 (For there were about five thousand men.) And He said to His disciples, "Have them recline *to eat* in groups of about fifty each."

15 And they did so, and had them all recline.

16 And He took the five loaves and the two fish, and looking up to heaven, He blessed them, and broke *them*, and kept giving *them* to the disciples to set before the multitude.

17 And they all ate and were satisfied; and the broken pieces which they had left over were picked up, twelve baskets *full*.

18 And it came about that while He was praying alone, the disciples were with Him, and He questioned them, saying, "Who do the multitudes say that I am?"

19 And they answered and said, "John the Baptist, and others *say* Elijah; but others, that one of the prophets of old has risen again."

20 And He said to them, "But who do you say that I am?" And Peter answered and said, "The Christ of God."

21 But He warned them, and instructed *them* not to tell this to anyone,

22 saying, "The Son of Man must suffer many things, and be rejected by the elders and chief priests and scribes, and be killed, and be raised up on the third day."

23 And He was saying to *them* all, "If anyone wishes to come after Me, let him deny himself, and take up his cross daily, and follow Me.

24 "For whoever wishes to save his life shall lose it, but whoever loses his life for My sake, he is the one who will save it.

25 "For what is a man profited if he gains the whole world, and loses or forfeits himself?

26 "For whoever is ashamed of Me and My words, of him will the Son of Man be ashamed when He comes in His glory, and *the glory* of the Father and of the holy angels.

27 "But I say to you truthfully, there are some of those standing here who shall not taste death until they see the kingdom of God."

28 And some eight days after these sayings, it came about that He took along Peter and John and James, and went up to the mountain to pray.

29 And while He was praying, the appearance of His face became different, and His clothing *became* white *and* gleaming.

30 And behold, two men were talking with Him; and they were Moses and Elijah,

31 who, appearing in glory,

were speaking of His departure which He was about to accomplish at Jerusalem.

32 Now Peter and his companions had been overcome with sleep; but when they were fully awake, they saw His glory and the two men standing with Him.

33 And it came about, as these were parting from Him, Peter said to Jesus, "Master, it is good for us to be here; and let us make three tabernacles: one for You, and one for Moses, and one for Elijah"—not realizing what he was saying.

34 And while he was saying this, a cloud formed and *began* to overshadow them; and they were afraid as they entered the cloud.

35 And a voice came out of the cloud, saying, "This is My Son, My Chosen One; listen to Him!"

36 And when the voice had spoken, Jesus was found alone. And they kept silent, and reported to no one in those days any of the things which they had seen.

37 And it came about on the next day, that when they had come down from the mountain, a great multitude met Him.

38 And behold, a man from the multitude shouted out, saying, "Teacher, I beg You to look at my son, for he is my only *boy*,

39 and behold, a spirit seizes him, and he suddenly screams, and it throws him into a convulsion with foaming *at the mouth*, and as it mauls him, it scarcely leaves him.

40"And I begged Your disciples to cast it out, and they could not."

41 And Jesus answered and said, "O unbelieving and perverted generation, how long shall I be with you, and put up with you? Bring your son here."

42 And while he was still approaching, the demon dashed him *to the ground*, and threw him into a convulsion. But Jesus rebuked the unclean spirit, and healed the boy, and gave him back to his father.

43 And they were all amazed at the greatness of God.

But while everyone was marveling at all that He was doing, He said to His disciples,

44"Let these words sink into your ears; for the Son of Man is going to be delivered into the hands of men."

45 But they did not understand this statement, and it was concealed from them so that they might not perceive it; and they were afraid to ask Him about this statement.

46 And an argument arose among them as to which of them might be the greatest.

47 But Jesus, knowing what they were thinking in their heart, took a child and stood him by His side,

48 and said to them, "Whoever receives this child in My name receives Me; and whoever receives Me receives Him who sent Me; for he who is least among you, this is the one who is great."

49 And John answered and said, "Master, we saw someone casting out demons in Your name; and we tried to hinder him because he does not follow along with us."

50 But Jesus said to him, "Do not hinder *him;* for he who is not against you is for you."

51 And it came about, when the days were approaching for

His ascension, that He resolutely set His face to go to Jerusalem;

52 and He sent messengers on ahead of Him. And they went, and entered a village of the Samaritans, to make arrangements for Him.

53 And they did not receive Him, because He was journeying with His face toward Jerusalem.

54 And when His disciples James and John saw *this*, they said, "Lord, do You want us to command fire to come down from heaven and consume them?"

55 But He turned and rebuked them, [and said, "You do not know what kind of spirit you are of;

56 for the Son of Man did not come to destroy men's lives, but to save them."] And they went on to another village.

57 And as they were going along the road, someone said to Him, "I will follow You wherever You go."

58 And Jesus said to him, "The foxes have holes, and the birds of the air *have* nests, but the Son of Man has nowhere to lay His head."

59 And He said to another, "Follow Me." But he said, "[20]Permit me first to go and bury my father."

60 But He said to him, "Allow the dead to bury their own dead; but as for you, go and proclaim everywhere the kingdom of God."

61 And another also said, "I will follow You, Lord; but first permit me to say good-bye to those at home."

62 But Jesus said to him, "No one, after putting his hand to the plow and looking back, is fit for the kingdom of God."

CHAPTER 10

NOW after this the Lord appointed seventy others, and sent them two and two ahead of Him to every city and place where He Himself was going to come.

2 And He was saying to them, "The harvest is plentiful, but the laborers are few; therefore beseech the Lord of the harvest to send out laborers into His harvest.

3 "Go your ways; behold, I send you out as lambs in the midst of wolves.

4 "Carry no purse, no bag, no shoes; and greet no one on the way.

5 "And whatever house you enter, first say, 'Peace *be* to this house.'

6 "And if a man of peace is there, your peace will rest upon him; but if not, it will return to you.

7 "And stay in that house, eating and drinking what they give you; for the laborer is worthy of his wages. Do not keep moving from house to house.

8 "And whatever city you enter, and they receive you, eat what is set before you;

9 and heal those in it who are sick, and say to them, 'The kingdom of God has come near to you.'

10 "But whatever city you enter and they do not receive you, go out into its streets and say,

11 'Even the dust of your city which clings to our feet, we wipe

[20] Some mss. add *Lord*

off *in protest* against you; yet be sure of this, that the kingdom of God has come near.'

12 "I say to you, it will be more tolerable in that day for Sodom, than for that city.

13 "Woe to you, Chorazin! Woe to you, Bethsaida! For if the miracles had been performed in Tyre and Sidon which occurred in you, they would have repented long ago, sitting in sackcloth and ashes.

14 "But it will be more tolerable for Tyre and Sidon in the judgment, than for you.

15 "And you, Capernaum, will not be exalted to heaven, will you? You will be brought down to Hades!

16 "The one who listens to you listens to Me, and the one who rejects you rejects Me; and he who rejects Me rejects the One who sent Me."

17 And the seventy returned with joy, saying, "Lord, even the demons are subject to us in Your name."

18 And He said to them, "I was watching Satan fall from heaven like lightning.

19 "Behold, I have given you authority to tread upon serpents and scorpions, and over all the power of the enemy, and nothing shall injure you.

20 "Nevertheless do not rejoice in this, that the spirits are subject to you, but rejoice that your names are recorded in heaven."

21 At that very time He rejoiced greatly in the Holy Spirit, and said, "I praise Thee, O Father, Lord of heaven and earth, that Thou didst hide these things from *the* wise and intelligent and didst reveal them to babes. Yes, Father, for thus it was well-pleasing in Thy sight.

22 "All things have been handed over to Me by My Father, and no one knows who the Son is except the Father, and who the Father is except the Son, and anyone to whom the Son wills to reveal *Him*."

23 And turning to the disciples, He said privately, "Blessed *are* the eyes which see the things you see,

24 for I say to you, that many prophets and kings wished to see the things which you see, and did not see *them*, and to hear the things which you hear, and did not hear *them*."

25 And behold, a certain lawyer stood up and put Him to the test, saying, "Teacher, what shall I do to inherit eternal life?"

26 And He said to him, "What is written in the Law? How does it read to you?"

27 And he answered and said, "YOU SHALL LOVE THE LORD YOUR GOD WITH ALL YOUR HEART, AND WITH ALL YOUR SOUL, AND WITH ALL YOUR STRENGTH, AND WITH ALL YOUR MIND; AND YOUR NEIGHBOR AS YOURSELF."

28 And He said to him, "You have answered correctly; DO THIS, AND YOU WILL LIVE."

29 But wishing to justify himself, he said to Jesus, "And who is my neighbor?"

30 Jesus replied and said, "A certain man was going down from Jerusalem to Jericho; and he fell among robbers, and they stripped him and beat him, and went off leaving him half dead.

31 "And by chance a certain priest was going down on that road, and when he saw him, he passed by on the other side.

32"And likewise a Levite also, when he came to the place and saw him, passed by on the other side.

33"But a certain Samaritan, who was on a journey, came upon him; and when he saw him, he felt compassion,

34 and came to him, and bandaged up his wounds, pouring oil and wine on *them;* and he put him on his own beast, and brought him to an inn, and took care of him.

35"And on the next day he took out two [21]denarii and gave them to the innkeeper and said, 'Take care of him; and whatever more you spend, when I return, I will repay you.'

36"Which of these three do you think proved to be a neighbor to the man who fell into the robbers' *hands?*"

37 And he said, "The one who showed mercy toward him." And Jesus said to him, "Go and do the same."

38 Now as they were traveling along, He entered a certain village; and a woman named Martha welcomed Him into her home.

39 And she had a sister called Mary, who moreover was listening to the Lord's word, seated at His feet.

40 But Martha was distracted with all her preparations; and she came up *to Him,* and said, "Lord, do You not care that my sister has left me to do all the serving alone? Then tell her to help me."

41 But the Lord answered and said to her, "Martha, Martha, you are worried and bothered about so many things;

42 but *only* a few things are necessary, really *only* one, for Mary has chosen the good part, which shall not be taken away from her."

CHAPTER 11

AND it came about that while He was praying in a certain place, after He had finished, one of His disciples said to Him, "Lord, teach us to pray just as John also taught his disciples."

2 And He said to them, "When you pray, say:
'[22]Father, hallowed be Thy name.
Thy kingdom come.
3 'Give us each day our daily bread.
4 'And forgive us our sins, For we ourselves also forgive everyone who is indebted to us.
And lead us not into temptation.' "

5 And He said to them, "Suppose one of you shall have a friend, and shall go to him at midnight, and say to him, 'Friend, lend me three loaves;

6 for a friend of mine has come to me from a journey, and I have nothing to set before him';

7 and from inside he shall answer and say, 'Do not bother me; the door has already been shut and my children and I are in bed; I cannot get up and give you *anything.*'

8"I tell you, even though he will not get up and give him *anything* because he is his friend, yet because of his persistence he will get up and give him as much as he needs.

---

21 The denarius was equivalent to one day's wage
22 Some mss. insert phrases from Matt. 6:9-13 to make the two passages closely similar

9"And I say to you, ask, and it shall be given to you; seek, and you shall find; knock, and it shall be opened to you.

10"For everyone who asks, receives; and he who seeks, finds; and to him who knocks, it shall be opened.

11"Now suppose one of you fathers is asked by his son for a fish; he will not give him a snake instead of a fish, will he?

12"Or *if* he is asked for an egg, he will not give him a scorpion, will he?

13"If you then, being evil, know how to give good gifts to your children, how much more shall *your* heavenly Father give the Holy Spirit to those who ask Him?"

14 And He was casting out a demon, *and it was* dumb; and it came about that when the demon had gone out, the dumb man spoke; and the multitudes marveled.

15 But some of them said, "He casts out demons by Beelzebul, the ruler of the demons."

16 And others, to test *Him,* were demanding of Him a sign from heaven.

17 But He knew their thoughts, and said to them, "Any kingdom divided against itself is laid waste; and a house *divided* against itself falls.

18"And if Satan also is divided against himself, how shall his kingdom stand? For you say that I cast out demons by Beelzebul.

19"And if I by Beelzebul cast out demons, by whom do your sons cast them out? Consequently they shall be your judges.

20"But if I cast out demons by the finger of God, then the kingdom of God has come upon you.

21"When a strong *man,* fully armed, guards his own homestead, his possessions are undisturbed;

22 but when someone stronger than he attacks him and overpowers him, he takes away from him all his armor on which he had relied, and distributes his plunder.

23"He who is not with Me is against Me; and he who does not gather with Me, scatters.

24"When the unclean spirit goes out of a man, it passes through waterless places seeking rest, and not finding any, it says, 'I will return to my house from which I came.'

25"And when it comes, it finds it swept and put in order.

26"Then it goes and takes *along* seven other spirits more evil than itself, and they go in and live there; and the last state of that man becomes worse than the first."

27 And it came about while He said these things, one of the women in the crowd raised her voice, and said to Him, "Blessed is the womb that bore You, and the breasts at which You nursed."

28 But He said, "On the contrary, blessed are those who hear the word of God, and observe it."

29 And as the crowds were increasing, He began to say, "This generation is a wicked generation; it seeks for a sign, and *yet* no sign shall be given to it but the sign of Jonah.

30"For just as Jonah became a sign to the Ninevites, so shall the Son of Man be to this generation.

31"The Queen of the South

shall rise up with the men of this generation at the judgment and condemn them, because she came from the ends of the earth to hear the wisdom of Solomon; and behold, something greater than Solomon is here.

32 "The men of Nineveh shall stand up with this generation at the judgment and condemn it, because they repented at the preaching of Jonah; and behold, something greater than Jonah is here.

33 "No one, after lighting a lamp, puts it away in a cellar, nor under a peck-measure, but on the lampstand, in order that those who enter may see the light.

34 "The lamp of your body is your eye; when your eye is clear, your whole body also is full of light; but when it is bad, your body also is full of darkness.

35 "Then watch out that the light in you may not be darkness.

36 "If therefore your whole body is full of light, with no dark part in it, it shall be wholly illumined, as when the lamp illumines you with its rays."

37 Now when He had spoken, a Pharisee *asked Him to have lunch with him; and He went in, and reclined at the table.

38 And when the Pharisee saw it, he was surprised that He had not first ceremonially washed before the meal.

39 But the Lord said to him, "Now you Pharisees clean the outside of the cup and of the platter; but inside of you, you are full of robbery and wickedness.

40 "You foolish ones, did not He who made the outside make the inside also?

41 "But give that which is within as charity, and then all things are clean for you.

42 "But woe to you Pharisees! For you pay tithe of mint and rue and every kind of garden herb, and yet disregard justice and the love of God; but these are the things you should have done without neglecting the others.

43 "Woe to you Pharisees! For you love the front seats in the synagogues, and the respectful greetings in the market places.

44 "Woe to you! For you are like concealed tombs, and the people who walk over them are unaware of it."

45 And one of the 23lawyers *said to Him in reply, "Teacher, when You say this, You insult us too."

46 But He said, "Woe to you lawyers as well! For you weigh men down with burdens hard to bear, while you yourselves will not even touch the burdens with one of your fingers.

47 "Woe to you! For you build the tombs of the prophets, and it was your fathers who killed them.

48 "Consequently, you are witnesses and approve the deeds of your fathers; because it was they who killed them, and you build their tombs.

49 "For this reason also the wisdom of God said, 'I will send to them prophets and apostles, and some of them they will kill and some they will persecute,

50 in order that the blood of all the prophets, shed since the foundation of the world, may be charged against this generation,

51 from the blood of Abel to the blood of Zechariah, who per-

23 I.e., experts in the Mosaic law

ished between the altar and the house of God; yes, I tell you, it shall be charged against this generation.'

52 "Woe to you lawyers! For you have taken away the key of knowledge; you did not enter in yourselves, and those who were entering in you hindered."

53 And when He left there, the scribes and the Pharisees began to be very hostile and to question Him closely on many subjects,

54 plotting against Him, to catch Him in something He might say.

CHAPTER 12

UNDER these circumstances, after so many thousands of the multitude had gathered together that they were stepping on one another, He began saying to His disciples first of all, "Beware of the leaven of the Pharisees, which is hypocrisy.

2 "But there is nothing covered up that will not be revealed, and hidden that will not be known.

3 "Accordingly, whatever you have said in the dark shall be heard in the light, and what you have whispered in the inner rooms shall be proclaimed upon the housetops.

4 "And I say to you, My friends, do not be afraid of those who kill the body, and after that have no more that they can do.

5 "But I will warn you whom to fear: fear the One who after He has killed has authority to cast into hell; yes, I tell you, fear Him!

6 "Are not five sparrows sold for two cents? And yet not one of them is forgotten before God.

7 "Indeed, the very hairs of your head are all numbered. Do not fear; you are of more value than many sparrows.

8 "And I say to you, everyone who confesses Me before men, the Son of Man shall confess him also before the angels of God;

9 but he who denies Me before men shall be denied before the angels of God.

10 "And everyone who will speak a word against the Son of Man, it shall be forgiven him; but he who blasphemes against the Holy Spirit, it shall not be forgiven him.

11 "And when they bring you before the synagogues and the rulers and the authorities, do not become anxious about how or what you should speak in your defense, or what you should say;

12 for the Holy Spirit will teach you in that very hour what you ought to say."

13 And someone in the crowd said to Him, "Teacher, tell my brother to divide the family inheritance with me."

14 But He said to him, "Man, who appointed Me a judge or arbiter over you?"

15 And He said to them, "Beware, and be on your guard against every form of greed; for not even when one has an abundance does his life consist of his possessions."

16 And He told them a parable, saying, "The land of a certain rich man was very productive.

17 "And he began reasoning to himself, saying, 'What shall I do, since I have no place to store my crops?'

18 "And he said, 'This is what I will do: I will tear down my barns and build larger ones, and there I will store all my grain and my goods.

19 'And I will say to my soul, "Soul, you have many goods laid up for many years *to come*; take your ease, eat, drink *and* be merry." '

20 "But God said to him, 'You fool! This *very* night your soul is required of you; and *now* who will own what you have prepared?'

21 "So is the man who lays up treasure for himself, and is not rich toward God."

22 And He said to His disciples, "For this reason I say to you, do not be anxious for your life, *as to* what you shall eat; nor for your body, *as to* what you shall put on.

23 "For life is more than food, and the body than clothing.

24 "Consider the ravens, for they neither sow nor reap; and they have no storeroom nor barn; and *yet* God feeds them; how much more valuable you are than the birds!

25 "And which of you by being anxious can add a *single* [24]cubit to his [25]life's span?

26 "If then you cannot do even a very little thing, why are you anxious about other matters?

27 "Consider the lilies, how they grow; they neither toil nor spin; but I tell you, even Solomon in all his glory did not clothe himself like one of these.

28 "But if God so arrays the grass in the field, which is *alive* today and tomorrow is thrown into the furnace, how much more *will He clothe* you, O men of little faith!

29 "And do not seek what you shall eat, and what you shall drink, and do not keep worrying.

30 "For all these things the nations of the world eagerly seek;

but your Father knows that you need these things.

31 "But seek for His kingdom, and these things shall be added to you.

32 "Do not be afraid, little flock, for your Father has chosen gladly to give you the kingdom.

33 "Sell your possessions and give to charity; make yourselves purses which do not wear out, an unfailing treasure in heaven, where no thief comes near, nor moth destroys.

34 "For where your treasure is, there will your heart be also.

35 "Be dressed in readiness, and *keep* your lamps alight.

36 "And be like men who are waiting for their master when he returns from the wedding feast, so that they may immediately open *the door* to him when he comes and knocks.

37 "Blessed are those slaves whom the master shall find on the alert when he comes; truly I say to you, that he will gird himself *to serve*, and have them recline *at the table*, and will come up and wait on them.

38 "Whether he comes in the [26]second watch, or even in the [27]third, and finds *them* so, blessed are those *slaves*.

39 "And be sure of this, that if the head of the house had known at what hour the thief was coming, he would not have allowed his house to be broken into.

40 "You too, be ready; for the Son of Man is coming at an hour that you do not expect."

41 And Peter said, "Lord, are

[24] I.e., One cubit equals approx. 18 in.
[25] Or, *height*
[26] I.e., 9 p.m. to midnight
[27] I.e., midnight to 3 a.m.

You addressing this parable to us, or to everyone *else* as well?"

42 And the Lord said, "Who then is the faithful and sensible steward, whom his master will put in charge of his servants, to give them their rations at the proper time?

43 "Blessed is that slave whom his master finds so doing when he comes.

44 "Truly I say to you, that he will put him in charge of all his possessions.

45 "But if that slave says in his heart, 'My master will be a long time in coming,' and begins to beat the slaves, *both* men and women, and to eat and drink and get drunk;

46 the master of that slave will come on a day when he does not expect *him,* and at an hour he does not know, and will cut him in pieces, and assign him a place with the unbelievers.

47 "And that slave who knew his master's will and did not get ready or act in accord with his will, shall receive many lashes.

48 but the one who did not know *it,* and committed deeds worthy of a flogging, will receive but few. And from everyone who has been given much shall much be required; and to whom they entrusted much, of him they will ask all the more.

49 "I have come to cast fire upon the earth; and how I wish it were already kindled!

50 "But I have a baptism to undergo, and how distressed I am until it is accomplished!

51 "Do you suppose that I came to grant peace on earth? I tell you, no, but rather division;

52 for from now on five *members* in one household will be di-

vided, three against two, and two against three.

53 "They will be divided, father against son, and son against father; mother against daughter, and daughter against mother; mother-in-law against daughter-in-law, and daughter-in-law against mother-in-law."

54 And He was also saying to the multitudes, "When you see a cloud rising in the west, immediately you say, 'A shower is coming,' and so it turns out.

55 "And when *you see* a south wind blowing, you say, 'It will be a hot day,' and it turns out *that way.*

56 "You hypocrites! You know how to analyze the appearance of the earth and the sky, but why do you not analyze this present time?

57 "And why do you not even on your own initiative judge what is right?

58 "For while you are going with your opponent to appear before the magistrate, on *your* way *there* make an effort to settle with him, in order that he may not drag you before the judge, and the judge turn you over to the constable, and the constable throw you into prison.

59 "I say to you, you shall not get out of there until you have paid the very last cent."

CHAPTER 13

NOW on the same occasion there were some present who reported to Him about the Galileans, whose blood Pilate had mingled with their sacrifices.

2 And He answered and said to them, "Do you suppose that these Galileans were *greater*

sinners than all *other* Galileans, because they suffered this *fate*?

3 "I tell you, no, but, unless you repent, you will all likewise perish.

4 "Or do you suppose that those eighteen on whom the tower in Siloam fell and killed them, were *worse* culprits than all the men who live in Jerusalem?

5 "I tell you, no, but unless you repent, you will all likewise perish."

6 And He *began* telling this parable: "A certain man had a fig tree which had been planted in his vineyard; and he came looking for fruit on it, and did not find any.

7 "And he said to the vineyard-keeper, 'Behold, for three years I have come looking for fruit on this fig tree without finding any. Cut it down! Why does it even use up the ground?'

8 "And he answered and said to him, 'Let it alone, sir, for this year too, until I dig around it and put in fertilizer;

9 and if it bears fruit next year, *fine*; but if not, cut it down.' "

10 And He was teaching in one of the synagogues on the Sabbath.

11 And behold, there was a woman who for eighteen years had had a sickness caused by a spirit; and she was bent double, and could not straighten up at all.

12 And when Jesus saw her, He called her over and said to her, "Woman, you are freed from your sickness."

13 And He laid His hands upon her; and immediately she was made erect again, and *began* glorifying God.

14 And the synagogue official, indignant because Jesus had healed on the Sabbath, *began* saying to the multitude in response, "There are six days in which work should be done; therefore come during them and get healed, and not on the Sabbath day."

15 But the Lord answered him and said, "You hypocrites, does not each of you on the Sabbath untie his ox or his donkey from the stall, and lead him away to water *him*?

16 "And this woman, a daughter of Abraham as she is, whom Satan has bound for eighteen long years, should she not have been released from this bond on the Sabbath day?"

17 And as He said this, all His opponents were being humiliated; and the entire multitude was rejoicing over all the glorious things being done by Him.

18 Therefore He was saying, "What is the kingdom of God like, and to what shall I compare it?

19 "It is like a mustard seed, which a man took and threw into his own garden; and it grew and became a tree; and THE BIRDS OF THE AIR NESTED IN ITS BRANCHES."

20 And again He said, "To what shall I compare the kingdom of God?

21 "It is like leaven, which a woman took and hid in three pecks of meal, until it was all leavened."

22 And He was passing through from one city and village to another, teaching, and proceeding on His way to Jerusalem.

23 And someone said to Him, "Lord, are there *just* a few who

are being saved?" And He said to them,

24"Strive to enter by the narrow door; for many, I tell you, will seek to enter and will not be able.

25"Once the head of the house gets up and shuts the door, and you begin to stand outside and knock on the door, saying, 'Lord, open up to us!' then He will answer and say to you, 'I do not know where you are from.'

26"Then you will begin to say, 'We ate and drank in Your presence, and You taught in our streets';

27 and He will say, 'I tell you, I do not know where you are from; DEPART FROM ME, ALL YOU EVIL-DOERS.'

28"There will be weeping and gnashing of teeth there when you see Abraham and Isaac and Jacob and all the prophets in the kingdom of God, but yourselves being cast out.

29"And they will come from east and west, and from north and south, and will recline *at the table* in the kingdom of God.

30"And behold, *some* are last who will be first and *some* are first who will be last."

31 Just at that time some Pharisees came up, saying to Him, "Go away and depart from here, for Herod wants to kill You."

32 And He said to them, "Go and tell that fox, 'Behold, I cast out demons and perform cures today and tomorrow, and the third *day* I reach My goal.'

33"Nevertheless I must journey on today and tomorrow and the next *day;* for it cannot be that a prophet should perish outside of Jerusalem.

34"O Jerusalem, Jerusalem, *the city* that kills the prophets and stones those sent to her! How often I wanted to gather your children together, just as a hen *gathers* her brood under her wings, and you would not *have it!*

35"Behold, your house is left to you *desolate;* and I say to you, you shall not see Me until *the time* comes when you say, 'BLESSED IS HE WHO COMES IN THE NAME OF THE LORD!' "

CHAPTER 14

AND it came about when He went into the house of one of the leaders of the Pharisees on *the* Sabbath to eat bread, that they were watching Him closely.

2 And there, in front of Him was a certain man suffering from dropsy.

3 And Jesus answered and spoke to the lawyers and Pharisees, saying, "Is it lawful to heal on the Sabbath, or not?"

4 But they kept silent. And He took hold of him, and healed him, and sent him away.

5 And He said to them, "Which one of you shall have a son or an ox fall into a well, and will not immediately pull him out on a Sabbath day?"

6 And they could make no reply to this.

7 And He *began* speaking a parable to the invited guests when He noticed how they had been picking out the places of honor *at the table;* saying to them,

8"When you are invited by someone to a wedding feast, do not take the place of honor, lest someone more distinguished than you may have been invited by him,

9 and he who invited you both shall come and say to you, 'Give place to this man,' and then in disgrace you proceed to occupy the last place.

10"But when you are invited, go and recline at the last place, so that when the one who has invited you comes, he may say to you, 'Friend, move up higher'; then you will have honor in the sight of all who are at the table with you.

11"For everyone who exalts himself shall be humbled, and he who humbles himself shall be exalted."

12 And He also went on to say to the one who had invited Him, "When you give a luncheon or a dinner, do not invite your friends or your brothers or your relatives or rich neighbors, lest they also invite you in return, and repayment come to you.

13"But when you give a reception, invite *the* poor, *the* crippled, *the* lame, *the* blind,

14 and you will be blessed, since they do not have *the means* to repay you; for you will be repaid at the resurrection of the righteous."

15 And when one of those who were reclining *at the table* with Him heard this, he said to Him, "Blessed is everyone who shall eat bread in the kingdom of God!"

16 But He said to him, "A certain man was giving a big dinner, and he invited many;

17 and at the dinner hour he sent his slave to say to those who had been invited, 'Come; for everything is ready now.'

18"But they all alike began to make excuses. The first one said to him, 'I have bought a piece of land and I need to go out and look at it; please consider me excused.'

19"And another one said, 'I have bought five yoke of oxen, and I am going to try them out; please consider me excused.'

20"And another one said, 'I have married a wife, and for that reason I cannot come.'

21"And the slave came *back* and reported this to his master. Then the head of the household became angry and said to his slave, 'Go out at once into the streets and lanes of the city and bring in here the poor and crippled and blind and lame.'

22"And the slave said, 'Master, what you commanded has been done, and still there is room.'

23"And the master said to the slave, 'Go out into the highways and along the hedges, and compel *them* to come in, that my house may be filled.

24 'For I tell you, none of those men who were invited shall taste of my dinner.' "

25 Now great multitudes were going along with Him; and He turned and said to them,

26"If anyone comes to Me, and does not [28]hate his own father and mother and wife and children and brothers and sisters, yes, and even his own life, he cannot be My disciple.

27"Whoever does not carry his own cross and come after Me cannot be My disciple.

28"For which one of you, when he wants to build a tower, does not first sit down and calculate

[28] I.e., by comparison of his love for Me

the cost, to see if he has enough to complete it?

29 "Otherwise, when he has laid a foundation, and is not able to finish, all who observe it begin to ridicule him,

30 saying, 'This man began to build and was not able to finish.'

31 "Or what king, when he sets out to meet another king in battle, will not first sit down and take counsel whether he is strong enough with ten thousand *men* to encounter the one coming against him with twenty thousand?

32 "Or else, while the other is still far away, he sends a delegation and asks terms of peace.

33 "So therefore, no one of you can be My disciple who does not give up all his own possessions.

34 "Therefore, salt is good; but if even salt has become tasteless, with what will it be seasoned?

35 "It is useless either for the soil or for the manure pile; it is thrown out. He who has ears to hear, let him hear."

CHAPTER 15

NOW all the tax-gatherers and the sinners were coming near Him to listen to Him.

2 And both the Pharisees and the scribes *began* to grumble, saying, "This man receives sinners and eats with them."

3 And He told them this parable, saying,

4 "What man among you, if he has a hundred sheep and has lost one of them, does not leave the ninety-nine in the open pasture, and go after the one which is lost, until he finds it?

5 "And when he has found it,

he lays it on his shoulders, rejoicing.

6 "And when he comes home, he calls together his friends and his neighbors, saying to them, 'Rejoice with me, for I have found my sheep which was lost!'

7 "I tell you that in the same way, there will be *more* joy in heaven over one sinner who repents, than over ninety-nine righteous persons who need no repentance.

8 "Or what woman, if she has ten silver coins and loses one coin, does not light a lamp and sweep the house and search carefully until she finds it?

9 "And when she has found it, she calls together her friends and neighbors, saying, 'Rejoice with me, for I have found the coin which I had lost!'

10 "In the same way, I tell you, there is joy in the presence of the angels of God over one sinner who repents."

11 And He said, "A certain man had two sons;

12 and the younger of them said to his father, 'Father, give me the share of the estate that falls to me.' And he divided them his wealth between them.

13 "And not many days later, the younger son gathered everything together and went on a journey into a distant country, and there he squandered his estate with loose living.

14 "Now when he had spent everything, a severe famine occurred in that country, and he began to be in need.

15 "And he went and attached himself to one of the citizens of that country, and he sent him into his fields to feed swine.

16 "And he was longing to fill

his stomach with the pods that the swine were eating, and no one was giving *anything* to him.

17"But when he came to his senses, he said, 'How many of my father's hired men have more than enough bread, but I am dying here with hunger!

18 'I will get up and go to my father, and will say to him, "Father, I have sinned against heaven, and in your sight;

19"I am no longer worthy to be called your son; make me as one of your hired men." '

20"And he got up and came to his father. But while he was still a long way off, his father saw him, and felt compassion *for him*, and ran and embraced him, and kissed him.

21"And the son said to him, 'Father, I have sinned against heaven and in your sight; I am no longer worthy to be called your son.'

22"But the father said to his slaves, 'Quickly bring out the best robe and put it on him, and put a ring on his hand and sandals on his feet;

23 and bring the fattened calf, kill it, and let us eat and be merry;

24 for this son of mine was dead, and has come to life again; he was lost, and has been found.' And they began to be merry.

25"Now his older son was in the field, and when he came and approached the house, he heard music and dancing.

26"And he summoned one of the servants and *began* inquiring what these things might be.

27"And he said to him, 'Your brother has come, and your father has killed the fattened calf,

because he has received him back safe and sound.'

28"But he became angry, and was not willing to go in; and his father came out and *began* entreating him.

29"But he answered and said to his father, 'Look! For so many years I have been serving you, and I have never neglected a command of yours; and *yet* you have never given me a kid, that I might be merry with my friends;

30 but when this son of yours came, who has devoured your wealth with harlots, you killed the fattened calf for him.'

31"And he said to him, 'My child, you have always been with me, and all that is mine is yours.

32 'But we had to be merry and rejoice, for this brother of yours was dead and *has begun* to live, and *was* lost and has been found.' "

CHAPTER 16

NOW He was also saying to the disciples, "There was a certain rich man who had a steward, and this *steward* was reported to him as squandering his possessions.

2"And he called him and said to him, 'What is this I hear about you? Give an account of your stewardship, for you can no longer be steward.'

3"And the steward said to himself, 'What shall I do, since my master is taking the stewardship away from me? I am not strong enough to dig; I am ashamed to beg.

4 'I know what I shall do, so that when I am removed from the stewardship, they will receive me into their homes.'

5 "And he summoned each one of his master's debtors, and he *began* saying to the first, 'How much do you owe my master?'

6 "And he said, 'A hundred measures of oil.' And he said to him, 'Take your bill, and sit down quickly and write fifty.'

7 "Then he said to another, 'And how much do you owe?' And he said, 'A hundred measures of wheat.' He *said to him, 'Take your bill, and write eighty.'

8 "And his master praised the unrighteous steward because he had acted shrewdly; for the sons of this age are more shrewd in relation to their own kind than the sons of light.

9 "And I say to you, make friends for yourselves by means of the [29]mammon of unrighteousness; that when it fails, they may receive you into the eternal dwellings.

10 "He who is faithful in a very little thing is faithful also in much; and he who is unrighteous in a very little thing is unrighteous also in much.

11 "If therefore you have not been faithful in the *use of* unrighteous mammon, who will entrust the true *riches* to you?

12 "And if you have not been faithful in *the use of* that which is another's, who will give you that which is your own?

13 "No servant can serve two masters; for either he will hate the one, and love the other, or else he will hold to one, and despise the other. You cannot serve God and mammon."

14 Now the Pharisees, who were lovers of money, were lis-

tening to all these things, and they were scoffing at Him.

15 And He said to them, "You are those who justify yourselves in the sight of men, but God knows your hearts; for that which is highly esteemed among men is detestable in the sight of God.

16 "The Law and the Prophets *were* proclaimed until John; since then the gospel of the kingdom of God is preached, and everyone is forcing his way into it.

17 "But it is easier for heaven and earth to pass away than for one stroke of a letter of the Law to fail.

18 "Everyone who divorces his wife and marries another commits adultery; and he who marries one who is divorced from a husband commits adultery.

19 "Now there was a certain rich man, and he habitually dressed in purple and fine linen, gaily living in splendor every day.

20 "And a certain poor man named Lazarus was laid at his gate, covered with sores,

21 and longing to be fed with the *crumbs* which were falling from the rich man's table; besides, even the dogs were coming and licking his sores.

22 "Now it came about that the poor man died and he was carried away by the angels to Abraham's bosom; and the rich man also died and was buried.

23 "And in Hades he lifted up his eyes, being in torment, and *saw Abraham far away, and Lazarus in his bosom.

24 "And he cried out and said, 'Father Abraham, have mercy on me, and send Lazarus, that he may dip the tip of his finger in

[29] Or, *riches*

water and cool off my tongue; for I am in agony in this flame.'

25"But Abraham said, 'Child, remember that during your life you received your good things, and likewise Lazarus bad things; but now he is being comforted here, and you are in agony.

26 'And besides all this, between us and you there is a great chasm fixed, in order that those who wish to come over from here to you may not be able, and *that* none may cross over from there to us.'

27"And he said, 'Then I beg you, Father, that you send him to my father's house—

28 for I have five brothers— that he may warn them, lest they also come to this place of torment.'

29"But Abraham *said, 'They have Moses and the Prophets; let them hear them.'

30"But he said, 'No, Father Abraham, but if someone goes to them from the dead, they will repent!'

31"But he said to him, 'If they do not listen to Moses and the Prophets, neither will they be persuaded if someone rises from the dead.' "

CHAPTER 17

AND He said to His disciples, "It is inevitable that stumbling blocks should come, but woe to him through whom they come!

2"It would be better for him if a millstone were hung around his neck and he were thrown into the sea, than that he should cause one of these little ones to stumble.

3"Be on your guard! If your brother sins, rebuke him; and if he repents, forgive him.

4"And if he sins against you seven times a day, and returns to you seven times, saying, 'I repent,' forgive him."

5 And the apostles said to the Lord, "Increase our faith!"

6 And the Lord said, "If you had faith like a mustard seed, you would say to this mulberry tree, 'Be uprooted and be planted in the sea'; and it would obey you.

7"But which of you, having a slave plowing or tending sheep, will say to him when he has come in from the field, 'Come immediately and sit down to eat'?

8"But will he not say to him, 'Prepare something for me to eat, and *properly* clothe yourself and serve me until I have eaten and drunk; and afterward you will eat and drink'?

9"He does not thank the slave because he did the things which were commanded, does he?

10"So you too, when you do all the things which are commanded you, say, 'We are unworthy slaves; we have done *only* that which we ought to have done.' "

11 And it came about while He was on the way to Jerusalem, that He was passing between Samaria and Galilee.

12 And as He entered a certain village, ten leprous men who stood at a distance met Him;

13 and they raised their voices, saying, "Jesus, Master, have mercy on us!"

14 And when He saw them, He said to them, "Go and show yourselves to the priests." And it came about that as they were going, they were cleansed.

15 Now one of them, when he

saw that he had been healed, turned back, glorifying God with a loud voice,

16 and he fell on his face at His feet, giving thanks to Him. And he was a Samaritan.

17 And Jesus answered and said, "Were there not ten cleansed? But the nine—where are they?

18 "Was no one found who turned back to give glory to God, except this foreigner?"

19 And He said to him, "Rise, and go your way; your faith [30]has made you well."

20 Now having been questioned by the Pharisees as to when the kingdom of God was coming, He answered them and said, "The kingdom of God is not coming with signs to be observed;

21 nor will they say, 'Look, here *it is!*' or, 'There *it is!*' For behold, the kingdom of God is in your midst."

22 And He said to the disciples, "The days shall come when you will long to see one of the days of the Son of Man, and you will not see it.

23 "And they will say to you, 'Look there! Look here!' Do not go away, and do not run after *them.*

24 "For just as the lightning, when it flashes out of one part of the sky, shines to the other part of the sky, so will the Son of Man be in His day.

25 "But first He must suffer many things and be rejected by this generation.

26 "And just as it happened in the days of Noah, so it shall be also in the days of the Son of Man:

27 they were eating, they were drinking, they were marrying, they were being given in marriage, until the day that Noah entered the ark, and the flood came and destroyed them all.

28 "It was the same as happened in the days of Lot: they were eating, they were drinking, they were buying, they were selling, they were planting, they were building;

29 but on the day that Lot went out from Sodom it rained fire and brimstone from heaven and destroyed them all.

30 "It will be just the same on the day that the Son of Man is revealed.

31 "On that day, let not the one who is on the housetop and whose goods are in the house go down to take them away; and likewise let not the one who is in the field turn back.

32 "Remember Lot's wife.

33 "Whoever seeks to keep his life shall lose it, and whoever loses *his life* shall preserve it.

34 "I tell you, on that night there will be two men in one bed; one will be taken, and the other will be left.

35 "There will be two women grinding at the same place; one will be taken, and the other will be left.

36 ["[31]Two men will be in the field; one will be taken and the other will be left."]

37 And answering they *said to Him, "Where, Lord?" And He said to them, "Where the body *is,* there also will the vultures be gathered."

---

[30] Or, *has saved you*
[31] Many mss. do not contain this verse

CHAPTER 18

N OW He was telling them a parable to show that at all times they ought to pray and not to lose heart,

2 saying, "There was in a certain city a judge who did not fear God, and did not respect man.

3 "And there was a widow in that city, and she kept coming to him, saying, 'Give me legal protection from my opponent.'

4 "And for a while he was unwilling; but afterward he said to himself, 'Even though I do not fear God nor respect man,

5 yet because this widow bothers me, I will give her legal protection, lest by continually coming she wear me out.' "

6 And the Lord said, "Hear what the unrighteous judge *said;

7 now shall not God bring about justice for His elect, who cry to Him day and night, and will He delay long over them?

8 "I tell you that He will bring about justice for them speedily. However, when the Son of Man comes, will He find faith on the earth?"

9 And He also told this parable to certain ones who trusted in themselves that they were righteous, and viewed others with contempt:

10 "Two men went up into the temple to pray, one a Pharisee, and the other a tax-gatherer.

11 "The Pharisee stood and was praying thus to himself, 'God, I thank Thee that I am not like other people: swindlers, unjust, adulterers, or even like this tax-gatherer.

12 'I fast twice a week; I pay tithes of all that I get.'

13 "But the tax-gatherer, standing some distance away, was even unwilling to lift up his eyes to heaven, but was beating his breast, saying, 'God, be merciful to me, the sinner!'

14 "I tell you, this man went down to his house justified rather than the other; for everyone who exalts himself shall be humbled, but he who humbles himself shall be exalted."

15 And they were bringing even their babies to Him so that He might touch them, but when the disciples saw it, they began rebuking them.

16 But Jesus called for them, saying, "Permit the children to come to Me, and do not hinder them, for the kingdom of God belongs to such as these.

17 "Truly I say to you, whoever does not receive the kingdom of God like a child shall not enter it at all."

18 And a certain ruler questioned Him, saying, "Good Teacher, what shall I do to inherit eternal life?"

19 And Jesus said to him, "Why do you call Me good? No one is good except God alone.

20 "You know the commandments, 'DO NOT COMMIT ADULTERY, DO NOT MURDER, DO NOT STEAL, DO NOT BEAR FALSE WITNESS, HONOR YOUR FATHER AND MOTHER.' "

21 And he said, "All these things I have kept from my youth."

22 And when Jesus heard this, He said to him, "One thing you still lack; sell all that you possess, and distribute it to the poor, and you shall have treasure in heaven; and come, follow Me."

23 But when he had heard

these things, he became very sad; for he was extremely rich.

24 And Jesus looked at him and said, "How hard it is for those who are wealthy to enter the kingdom of God!

25 "For it is easier for a camel to go through the eye of a needle, than for a rich man to enter the kingdom of God."

26 And they who heard it said, "Then who can be saved?"

27 But He said, "The things impossible with men are possible with God."

28 And Peter said, "Behold, we have left our own *homes*, and followed You."

29 And He said to them, "Truly I say to you, there is no one who has left house or wife or brothers or parents or children, for the sake of the kingdom of God,

30 who shall not receive many times as much at this time and in the age to come, eternal life."

31 And He took the twelve aside and said to them, "Behold, we are going up to Jerusalem, and all things which are written through the prophets about the Son of Man will be accomplished.

32 "For He will be delivered to the Gentiles, and will be mocked and mistreated and spit upon,

33 and after they have scourged Him, they will kill Him; and the third day He will rise again."

34 And they understood none of these things, and this saying was hidden from them, and they did not comprehend the things that were said.

35 And it came about that as He was approaching Jericho, a certain blind man was sitting by the road, begging.

36 Now hearing a multitude going by, he *began* to inquire what this might be.

37 And they told him that Jesus of Nazareth was passing by.

38 And he called out, saying, "Jesus, Son of David, have mercy on me!"

39 And those who led the way were sternly telling him to be quiet; but he kept crying out all the more, "Son of David, have mercy on me!"

40 And Jesus stopped and commanded that he be brought to Him; and when he had come near, He questioned him,

41 "What do you want Me to do for you?" And he said, "Lord, I want to regain my sight!"

42 And Jesus said to him, "Receive your sight; your faith has made you well."

43 And immediately he regained his sight, and *began* following Him, glorifying God; and when all the people saw it, they gave praise to God.

CHAPTER 19

AND He entered and was passing through Jericho.

2 And behold, there was a man called by the name of Zaccheus; and he was a chief tax-gatherer, and he was rich.

3 And he was trying to see who Jesus was, and he was unable because of the crowd, for he was small in stature.

4 And he ran on ahead and climbed up into a sycamore tree in order to see Him, for He was about to pass through that way.

5 And when Jesus came to the place, He looked up and said to him, "Zaccheus, hurry and come

down, for today I must stay at your house."

6 And he hurried and came down, and received Him gladly.

7 And when they saw it, they all *began* to grumble, saying, "He has gone to be the guest of a man who is a sinner."

8 And Zaccheus stopped and said to the Lord, "Behold, Lord, half of my possessions I will give to the poor, and if I have defrauded anyone of anything, I will give back four times as much."

9 And Jesus said to him, "Today salvation has come to this house, because he, too, is a son of Abraham.

10 "For the Son of Man has come to seek and to save that which was lost."

11 And while they were listening to these things, He went on to tell a parable, because He was near Jerusalem, and they supposed that the kingdom of God was going to appear immediately.

12 He said therefore, "A certain nobleman went to a distant country to receive a kingdom for himself, and *then* return.

13 "And he called ten of his slaves, and gave them ten [32]minas, and said to them, 'Do business *with this* until I come *back.*'

14 "But his citizens hated him, and sent a delegation after him, saying, 'We do not want this man to reign over us.'

15 "And it came about that when he returned, after receiving the kingdom, he ordered that these slaves, to whom he had given the money, be called to him in order that he might know what business they had done.

16 "And the first appeared, saying, 'Master, your mina has made ten minas more.'

17 "And he said to him, 'Well done, good slave, because you have been faithful in a very little thing, be in authority over ten cities.'

18 "And the second came, saying, 'Your mina, master, has made five minas.'

19 "And he said to him also, 'And you are to be over five cities.'

20 "And another came, saying, 'Master, behold your mina, which I kept put away in a handkerchief;

21 for I was afraid of you, because you are an exacting man; you take up what you did not lay down, and reap what you did not sow.'

22 "He *said to him, 'By your own words I will judge you, you worthless slave. Did you know that I am an exacting man, taking up what I did not lay down, and reaping what I did not sow?

23 'Then why did you not put the money in the bank, and having come, I would have collected it with interest?'

24 "And he said to the bystanders, 'Take the mina away from him, and give it to the one who has the ten minas.'

25 "And they said to him, 'Master, he has ten minas *already.*'

26 "I tell you, that to everyone who has shall *more* be given, but from the one who does not have, even what he does have shall be taken away.

27 "But these enemies of mine, who did not want me to reign

---

[32] A mina is equal to about 100 days' wages or nearly $20

over them, bring them here and slay them in my presence."

28 And after He had said these things, He was going on ahead, ascending to Jerusalem.

29 And it came about that when He approached Bethphage and Bethany, near the mount that is called Olivet, He sent two of the disciples,

30 saying, "Go into the village opposite *you*, in which as you enter you will find a colt tied, on which no one yet has ever sat; untie it, and bring it *here*.

31 "And if anyone asks you, 'Why are you untying it?' thus shall you speak, 'The Lord has need of it.' "

32 And those who were sent went away and found it just as He had told them.

33 And as they were untying the colt, its owners said to them, "Why are you untying the colt?"

34 And they said, "The Lord has need of it."

35 And they brought it to Jesus, and they threw their garments on the colt, and put Jesus *on it.*

36 And as He was going, they were spreading their garments in the road.

37 And as He was now approaching, near the descent of the Mount of Olives, the whole multitude of the disciples began to praise God joyfully with a loud voice for all the miracles which they had seen,

38 saying,

"BLESSED IS THE King WHO
    COMES IN THE NAME OF
    THE LORD;
  Peace in heaven and glory
    in the highest!"

39 And some of the Pharisees in the multitude said to Him,

"Teacher, rebuke Your disciples."

40 And He answered and said, "I tell you, if these become silent, the stones will cry out!"

41 And when He approached, He saw the city and wept over it,

42 saying, "If you had known in this day, even you, the things which make for peace! But now they have been hidden from your eyes.

43 "For the days shall come upon you when your enemies will throw up a bank before you, and surround you, and hem you in on every side,

44 and will level you to the ground and your children within you, and they will not leave in you one stone upon another, because you did not recognize the time of your visitation."

45 And He entered the temple and began to cast out those who were selling,

46 saying to them, "It is written, 'AND MY HOUSE SHALL BE A HOUSE OF PRAYER,' but you have made it a ROBBERS' DEN."

47 And He was teaching daily in the temple; but the chief priests and the scribes and the leading men among the people were trying to destroy Him,

48 and they could not find anything that they might do, for all the people were hanging upon His words.

CHAPTER 20

AND it came about on one of the days while He was teaching the people in the temple and preaching the gospel, that the chief priests and the scribes with the elders confronted *Him,*

2 and they spoke, saying to

Him, "Tell us by what authority You are doing these things, or who is the one who gave You this authority?"

3 And He answered and said to them, "I shall also ask you a question, and you tell Me:

4 "Was the baptism of John from heaven or from men?"

5 And they reasoned among themselves, saying, "If we say, 'From heaven,' He will say, 'Why did you not believe him?'

6 "But if we say, 'From men,' all the people will stone us to death, for they are convinced that John was a prophet."

7 And they answered that they did not know where *it* came from.

8 And Jesus said to them, "Neither will I tell you by what authority I do these things."

9 And He began to tell the people this parable: "A man planted a vineyard and rented it out to vine-growers, and went on a journey for a long time.

10 "And at the *harvest* time he sent a slave to the vine-growers, in order that they might give him *some* of the produce of the vineyard; but the vine-growers beat him and sent him away empty-handed.

11 "And he proceeded to send another slave; and they beat him also and treated him shamefully, and sent him away empty-handed.

12 "And he proceeded to send a third; and this one also they wounded and cast out.

13 "And the owner of the vineyard said, 'What shall I do? I will send my beloved son; perhaps they will respect him.'

14 "But when the vine-growers saw him, they reasoned with one another, saying, 'This is the heir; let us kill him that the inheritance may be ours.'

15 "And they threw him out of the vineyard and killed him. What, therefore, will the owner of the vineyard do to them?

16 "He will come and destroy these vine-growers and will give the vineyard to others." And when they heard it, they said, "May it never be!"

17 But He looked at them and said, "What then is this that is written,

'THE STONE WHICH THE BUILDERS REJECTED,
THIS BECAME THE CHIEF CORNER *stone*'?

18 "Everyone who falls on that stone will be broken to pieces; but on whomever it falls, it will scatter him like dust."

19 And the scribes and the chief priests tried to lay hands on Him that very hour, and they feared the people; for they understood that He spoke this parable against them.

20 And they watched Him, and sent spies who pretended to be righteous, in order that they might catch Him in some statement, so as to deliver Him up to the rule and the authority of the governor.

21 And they questioned Him, saying, "Teacher, we know that You speak and teach correctly, and You are not partial to any, but teach the way of God in truth.

22 "Is it lawful for us to pay taxes to Caesar, or not?"

23 But He detected their trickery and said to them,

24 "Show Me a ³³denarius.

³³ The denarius was equivalent to one day's wage

Whose likeness and inscription does it have?" And they said, "Caesar's."

25 And He said to them, "Then render to Caesar the things that are Caesar's, and to God the things that are God's."

26 And they were unable to catch Him in a saying in the presence of the people; and marveling at His answer, they became silent.

27 Now there came to Him some of the Sadducees (who say that there is no resurrection),

28 and they questioned Him, saying, "Teacher, Moses wrote for us that IF A MAN'S BROTHER DIES, having a wife, AND HE IS CHILDLESS, HIS BROTHER SHOULD TAKE THE WIFE AND RAISE UP OFFSPRING TO HIS BROTHER.

29"Now there were seven brothers; and the first took a wife, and died childless;

30 and the second

31 and the third took her; and in the same way all seven died, leaving no children.

32"Finally the woman died also.

33"In the resurrection therefore, which one's wife will she be? For all seven had her as wife."

34 And Jesus said to them, "The sons of this age marry and are given in marriage,

35 but those who are considered worthy to attain to that age and the resurrection from the dead, neither marry, nor are given in marriage;

36 for neither can they die anymore, for they are like angels, and are sons of God, being sons of the resurrection.

37"But that the dead are raised, even Moses showed, in the *passage about the burning bush*, where he calls the Lord THE GOD OF ABRAHAM, AND THE GOD OF ISAAC, AND THE GOD OF JACOB.

38"Now He is not the God of the dead, but of the living; for all live to Him."

39 And some of the scribes answered and said, "Teacher, You have spoken well."

40 For they did not have courage to question Him any longer about anything.

41 And He said to them, "How *is it that* they say ³⁴the Christ is David's son?

42"For David himself says in the book of Psalms,

THE LORD SAID TO MY LORD,

"SIT AT MY RIGHT HAND,

43 UNTIL I MAKE THINE ENEMIES A FOOTSTOOL FOR THY FEET." '

44"David therefore calls Him 'Lord,' and how is He his son?"

45 And while all the people were listening, He said to the disciples,

46"Beware of the scribes, who like to walk around in long robes, and love respectful greetings in the market places, and chief seats in the synagogues, and places of honor at banquets,

47 who devour widows' houses, and for appearance' sake offer long prayers; these will receive greater condemnation."

CHAPTER 21

AND He looked up and saw the rich putting their gifts into the treasury.

2 And He saw a certain poor

---

³⁴ I.e., the Messiah

widow putting in two small copper coins.

3 And He said, "Truly I say to you, this poor widow put in more than all of them;

4 for they all out of their surplus put into the offering; but she out of her poverty put in all that she had to live on."

5 And while some were talking about the temple, that it was adorned with beautiful stones and votive gifts, He said,

6"As for these things which you are looking at, the days will come in which there will not be left one stone upon another which will not be torn down."

7 And they questioned Him, saying, "Teacher, when therefore will these things be? And what will be the sign when these things are about to take place?"

8 And He said, "See to it that you be not misled; for many will come in My name, saying, 'I am He,' and, 'The time is at hand'; do not go after them.

9"And when you hear of wars and disturbances, do not be terrified; for these things must take place first, but the end does not follow immediately."

10 Then He continued by saying to them, "Nation will rise against nation, and kingdom against kingdom,

11 and there will be great earthquakes, and in various places plagues and famines; and there will be terrors and great signs from heaven.

12"But before all these things, they will lay their hands on you and will persecute you, delivering you to the synagogues and prisons, bringing you before kings and governors for My name's sake.

13"It will lead to an opportunity for your testimony.

14"So make up your minds not to prepare beforehand to defend yourselves;

15 for I will give you utterance and wisdom which none of your opponents will be able to resist or refute.

16"But you will be delivered up even by parents and brothers and relatives and friends, and they will put some of you to death,

17 and you will be hated by all on account of My name.

18"Yet not a hair of your head will perish.

19"By your endurance you will gain your lives.

20"But when you see Jerusalem surrounded by armies, then recognize that her desolation is at hand.

21"Then let those who are in Judea flee to the mountains, and let those who are in the midst of the city depart, and let not those who are in the country enter the city;

22 because these are days of vengeance, in order that all things which are written may be fulfilled.

23"Woe to those who are with child and to those who nurse babes in those days; for there will be great distress upon the land, and wrath to this people,

24 and they will fall by the edge of the sword, and will be led captive into all the nations; and Jerusalem will be trampled under foot by the Gentiles until the times of the Gentiles be fulfilled.

25"And there will be signs in sun and moon and stars, and upon the earth dismay among nations, in perplexity at the roaring of the sea and the waves,

26 men fainting from fear and the expectation of the things which are coming upon the world; for the powers of the heavens will be shaken.

27"And then they will see THE SON OF MAN COMING IN A CLOUD with power and great glory.

28"But when these things begin to take place, straighten up and lift up your heads, because your redemption is drawing near."

29 And He told them a parable: "Behold the fig tree and all the trees;

30 as soon as they put forth *leaves*, you see it and know for yourselves that summer is now near.

31"Even so you, too, when you see these things happening, recognize that the kingdom of God is near.

32"Truly I say to you, this generation will not pass away until all things take place.

33"Heaven and earth will pass away, but My words will not pass away.

34"Be on guard, that your hearts may not be weighted down with dissipation and drunkenness and the worries of life, and that day come on you suddenly like a trap;

35 for it will come upon all those who dwell on the face of all the earth.

36"But keep on the alert at all times, praying in order that you may have strength to escape all these things that are about to take place, and to stand before the Son of Man."

37 Now during the day He was teaching in the temple, but at evening He would go out and spend the night on the mount that is called Olivet.

38 And all the people would get up early in the morning *to come* to Him in the temple to listen to Him.

CHAPTER 22

NOW the Feast of Unleavened Bread, which is called the Passover, was approaching.

2 And the chief priests and the scribes were seeking how they might put Him to death; for they were afraid of the people.

3 And Satan entered into Judas who was called Iscariot, belonging to the number of the twelve.

4 And he went away and discussed with the chief priests and officers how he might betray Him to them.

5 And they were glad, and agreed to give him money.

6 And he consented, and *began* seeking a good opportunity to betray Him to them apart from the multitude.

7 Then came the *first* day of Unleavened Bread on which the Passover *lamb* had to be sacrificed.

8 And He sent Peter and John, saying, "Go and prepare the Passover for us, that we may eat it."

9 And they said to Him, "Where do You want us to prepare it?"

10 And He said to them, "Behold, when you have entered the city, a man will meet you carrying a pitcher of water; follow him into the house that he enters.

11"And you shall say to the owner of the house, 'The Teacher says to you, "Where is the guest room in which I may eat the Passover with My disciples?"'

12"And he will show you a large, furnished, upper room; prepare it there."

13 And they departed and found *everything* just as He had told them; and they prepared the Passover.

14 And when the hour had come He reclined *at the table*, and the apostles with Him.

15 And He said to them, "I have earnestly desired to eat this Passover with you before I suffer;

16 for I say to you, I shall never again eat it until it is fulfilled in the kingdom of God."

17 And when He had taken a cup *and* given thanks, He said, "Take this and share it among yourselves;

18 for I say to you, I will not drink of the fruit of the vine from now on until the kingdom of God comes."

19 And when He had taken *some* bread *and* given thanks, He broke *it*, and gave *it* to them, saying, "This is My body 35which is given for you; do this in remembrance of Me."

20 And in the same way He *took* the cup after they had eaten, saying, "This cup which is poured out for you is the new covenant in My blood.

21"But behold, the hand of the one betraying Me is with Me on the table.

22"For indeed, the Son of Man is going as it has been determined; but woe to that man by whom He is betrayed!"

23 And they began to discuss among themselves which one of them it might be who was going to do this thing.

24 And there arose also a dispute among them *as to* which one of them was regarded to be greatest.

25 And He said to them, "The kings of the Gentiles lord it over them; and those who have authority over them are called 'Benefactors.'

26"But not so with you, but let him who is the greatest among you become as the youngest, and the leader as the servant.

27"For who is greater, the one who reclines *at the table*, or the one who serves? Is it not the one who reclines *at the table*? But I am among you as the one who serves.

28"And you are those who have stood by Me in My trials;

29 and just as My Father has granted Me a kingdom, I grant you

30 that you may eat and drink at My table in My kingdom, and you will sit on thrones judging the twelve tribes of Israel.

31"Simon, Simon, behold, Satan has demanded *permission* to sift you like wheat;

32 but I have prayed for you, that your faith may not fail; and you, when once you have turned again, strengthen your brothers."

33 And he said to Him, "Lord, with You I am ready to go both to prison and to death!"

34 And He said, "I say to you, Peter, the cock will not crow today until you have denied three times that you know Me."

35 And He said to them, "When I sent you out without purse and bag and sandals, you did not lack anything, did you?" And they said, "No, nothing."

36 And He said to them, "But

35 Some ancient mss. do not contain the remainder of v. 19 nor any of v. 20

now, let him who has a purse take it along, likewise also a bag, and let him who has no sword sell his robe and buy one.

37 "For I tell you, that this which is written must be fulfilled in Me, 'AND HE WAS NUMBERED WITH TRANSGRESSORS'; for that which refers to Me has *its* fulfillment."

38 And they said, "Lord, look, here are two swords." And He said to them, "It is enough."

39 And He came out and proceeded as was His custom to the Mount of Olives; and the disciples also followed Him.

40 And when He arrived at the place, He said to them, "Pray that you may not enter into temptation."

41 And He withdrew from them about a stone's throw, and He knelt down and *began* to pray,

42 saying, "Father, if Thou art willing, remove this cup from Me; yet not My will, but Thine be done."

43 Now an angel from heaven appeared to Him, strengthening Him.

44 And being in agony He was praying very fervently; and His sweat became like drops of blood, falling down upon the ground.

45 And when He rose from prayer, He came to the disciples and found them sleeping from sorrow,

46 and said to them, "Why are you sleeping? Rise and pray that you may not enter into temptation."

47 While He was still speaking, behold, a multitude *came*, and the one called Judas, one of the twelve, was preceding them; and he approached Jesus to kiss Him.

48 But Jesus said to him, "Judas, are you betraying the Son of Man with a kiss?"

49 And when those who were around Him saw what was going to happen, they said, "Lord, shall we strike with the sword?"

50 And a certain one of them struck the slave of the high priest and cut off his right ear.

51 But Jesus answered and said, "Stop! No more of this." And He touched his ear and healed him.

52 And Jesus said to the chief priests and officers of the temple and elders who had come against Him, "Have you come out with swords and clubs as against a robber?

53 "While I was with you daily in the temple, you did not lay hands on Me; but this hour and the power of darkness are yours."

54 And having arrested Him, they led Him *away*, and brought Him to the house of the high priest; but Peter was following at a distance.

55 And after they had kindled a fire in the middle of the courtyard and had sat down together, Peter was sitting among them.

56 And a certain servant-girl, seeing him as he sat in the firelight, and looking intently at him, said, "This man was with Him too."

57 But he denied *it*, saying, "Woman, I do not know Him."

58 And a little later, another saw him and said, "You are *one* of them too!" But Peter said, "Man, I am not!"

59 And after about an hour had

CHAPTER 23

passed, another man *began* to insist, saying, "Certainly this man also was with Him, for he is a Galilean too."

60 But Peter said, "Man, I do not know what you are talking about." And immediately, while he was still speaking, a cock crowed.

61 And the Lord turned and looked at Peter. And Peter remembered the word of the Lord, how He had told him, "Before a cock crows today, you will deny Me three times."

62 And he went out and wept bitterly.

63 And the men who were holding Jesus in custody were mocking Him, and beating Him,

64 and they blindfolded Him and were asking Him, saying, "Prophesy, who is the one who hit You?"

65 And they were saying many other things against Him, blaspheming.

66 And when it was day, the ³⁶Council of elders of the people assembled, both chief priests and scribes, and they led Him away to their council *chamber*, saying,

67"If you are the Christ, tell us." But He said to them, "If I tell you, you will not believe;

68 and if I ask a question, you will not answer.

69"But from now on THE SON OF MAN WILL BE SEATED AT THE RIGHT HAND of the power OF GOD."

70 And they all said, "Are You the Son of God, then?" And He said to them, "Yes, I am."

71 And they said, "What further need do we have of testimony? For we have heard it ourselves from His own mouth."

THEN the whole body of them arose and brought Him before Pilate.

2 And they began to accuse Him, saying, "We found this man misleading our nation and forbidding to pay taxes to Caesar, and saying that He Himself is Christ, a King."

3 And Pilate asked Him, saying, "Are You the King of the Jews?" And He answered him and said, "*It is as* you say."

4 And Pilate said to the chief priests and the multitudes, "I find no guilt in this man."

5 But they kept on insisting, saying, "He stirs up the people, teaching all over Judea, starting from Galilee, even as far as this place."

6 But when Pilate heard it, he asked whether the man was a Galilean.

7 And when he learned that He belonged to Herod's jurisdiction, he sent Him to Herod, who himself also was in Jerusalem at that time.

8 Now Herod was very glad when he saw Jesus; for he had wanted to see Him for a long time, because he had been hearing about Him and was hoping to see some sign performed by Him.

9 And he questioned Him at some length; but He answered him nothing.

10 And the chief priests and the scribes were standing there, accusing Him vehemently.

11 And Herod with his soldiers, after treating Him with contempt and mocking Him, dressed Him

³⁶ Or, *Sanhedrin*

in a gorgeous robe and sent Him back to Pilate.

12 Now Herod and Pilate became friends with one another that very day; for before they had been at enmity with each other.

13 And Pilate summoned the chief priests and the rulers and the people,

14 and said to them, "You brought this man to me as one who incites the people to rebellion, and behold, having examined Him before you, I have found no guilt in this man regarding the charges which you make against Him.

15"No, nor has Herod, for he sent Him back to us; and behold, nothing deserving death has been done by Him.

16"I will therefore punish Him and release Him."

17 [37Now he was obliged to release to them at the feast one prisoner.]

18 But they cried out all together, saying, "Away with this man, and release for us Barabbas!"

19 (He was one who had been thrown into prison for a certain insurrection made in the city, and for murder.)

20 And Pilate, wanting to release Jesus, addressed them again,

21 but they kept on calling out, saying, "Crucify, crucify Him!"

22 And he said to them the third time, "Why, what evil has this man done? I have found in Him no guilt *demanding* death; I will therefore punish Him and release Him."

23 But they were insistent, with loud voices asking that He

_____
37 Many mss. do not contain this verse

be crucified. And their voices *began* to prevail.

24 And Pilate pronounced sentence that their demand should be granted.

25 And he released the man they were asking for who had been thrown into prison for insurrection and murder, but he delivered Jesus to their will.

26 And when they laid Him away, they laid hold of one Simon of Cyrene, coming in from the country, and placed on him the cross to carry behind Jesus.

27 And there were following Him a great multitude of the people, and of women who were mourning and lamenting Him.

28 But Jesus turning to them said, "Daughters of Jerusalem, stop weeping for Me, but weep for yourselves and for your children.

29"For behold, the days are coming when they will say, 'Blessed are the barren, and the wombs that never bore, and the breasts that never nursed.'

30"Then they will begin to SAY TO THE MOUNTAINS, 'FALL ON US,' AND TO THE HILLS, 'COVER US.'

31"For if they do these things in the green tree, what will happen in the dry?"

32 And two others also, who were criminals, were being led away to be put to death with Him.

33 And when they came to the place called The Skull, there they crucified Him and the criminals, one on the right and the other on the left.

34 But Jesus was saying, "Father, forgive them; for they do not know what they are doing." And they cast lots, dividing up His garments among themselves.

35 And the people stood by, looking on. And even the rulers were sneering at Him, saying, "He saved others; let Him save Himself if this is the Christ of God, His Chosen One."

36 And the soldiers also mocked Him, coming up to Him, offering Him sour wine,

37 and saying, "If You are the King of the Jews, save Yourself!"

38 Now there was also an inscription above Him, "THIS IS THE KING OF THE JEWS."

39 And one of the criminals who were hanged *there* was hurling abuse at Him, saying, "Are You not the Christ? Save Yourself and us!"

40 But the other answered, and rebuking him said, "Do you not even fear God, since you are under the same sentence of condemnation?

41 "And we indeed justly, for we are receiving what we deserve for our deeds; but this man has done nothing wrong."

42 And he was saying, "Jesus, remember me when You come in Your kingdom!"

43 And He said to him, "Truly I say to you, today you shall be with Me in Paradise."

44 And it was now about [38]the sixth hour, and darkness fell over the whole land until [39]the ninth hour,

45 the sun being obscured; and the veil of the temple was torn in two.

46 And Jesus, crying out with a loud voice, said, "Father, INTO THY HANDS I COMMIT MY SPIRIT." And having said this, He breathed His last.

47 Now when the centurion saw what had happened, he *be-gan* praising God, saying, "Certainly this man was innocent."

48 And all the multitudes who came together for this spectacle, when they observed what had happened, *began* to return, beating their breasts.

49 And all His acquaintances and the women who accompanied Him from Galilee, were standing at a distance, seeing these things.

50 And behold, a man named Joseph, who was a member of the Council, a good and righteous man

51 (he had not consented to their plan and action), *a man* from Arimathea, a city of the Jews, who was waiting for the kingdom of God;

52 this man went to Pilate and asked for the body of Jesus.

53 And he took it down and wrapped it in a linen cloth, and laid Him in a tomb cut into the rock, where no one had ever lain.

54 And it was the preparation day, and the Sabbath was about to begin.

55 Now the women who had come with Him out of Galilee followed after, and saw the tomb and how His body was laid.

56 And they returned and prepared spices and perfumes.

And on the Sabbath they rested according to the commandment.

CHAPTER 24

BUT on the first day of the week, at early dawn, they came to the tomb, bringing the spices which they had prepared.

2 And they found the stone rolled away from the tomb,

[38] I.e., 12 noon   [39] I.e., 3 p.m.

3 but when they entered, they did not find the body of the Lord Jesus.

4 And it happened that while they were perplexed about this, behold, two men suddenly stood near them in dazzling apparel;

5 and as *the women* were terrified and bowed their faces to the ground, *the men* said to them, "Why do you seek the living One among the dead?

6 "He is not here, but He has risen. Remember how He spoke to you while He was still in Galilee,

7 saying that the Son of Man must be delivered into the hands of sinful men, and be crucified, and the third day rise again."

8 And they remembered His words,

9 and returned from the tomb and reported all these things to the eleven and to all the rest.

10 Now they were Mary Magdalene and Joanna and Mary the *mother* of James; also the other women with them were telling these things to the apostles.

11 And these words appeared to them as nonsense, and they would not believe them.

12 [⁴⁰But Peter arose and ran to the tomb; stooping and looking in, he *saw the linen wrappings only; and he went away to his home, marveling at that which had happened.]

13 And behold, two of them were going that very day to a village named Emmaus, which was ⁴¹about seven miles from Jerusalem.

14 And they were conversing with each other about all these things which had taken place.

15 And it came about that while they were conversing and discussing, Jesus Himself approached, and *began* traveling with them.

16 But their eyes were prevented from recognizing Him.

17 And He said to them, "What are these words that you are exchanging with one another as you are walking?" And they stood still, looking sad.

18 And one of them, named Cleopas, answered and said to Him, "Are You the only one visiting Jerusalem and unaware of the things which have happened here in these days?"

19 And He said to them, "What things?" And they said to Him, "The things about Jesus the Nazarene, who was a prophet mighty in deed and word in the sight of God and all the people,

20 and how the chief priests and our rulers delivered Him up to the sentence of death, and crucified Him.

21 "But we were hoping that it was He who was going to redeem Israel. Indeed, besides all this, it is the third day since these things happened.

22 "But also some women among us amazed us. When they were at the tomb early in the morning,

23 and did not find His body, they came, saying that they had also seen a vision of angels, who said that He was alive.

24 "And some of those who were with us went to the tomb and found it just exactly as the women also had said; but Him they did not see."

25 And He said to them, "O foolish men and slow of heart to

⁴⁰ Some ancient mss. do not contain v. 12
⁴¹ I.e., 60 stadia, one stadion was about 600 feet

believe in all that the prophets have spoken!

26 "Was it not necessary for the Christ to suffer these things and to enter into His glory?"

27 And beginning with Moses and with all the prophets, He explained to them the things concerning Himself in all the Scriptures.

28 And they approached the village where they were going, and He acted as though He would go farther.

29 And they urged Him, saying, "Stay with us, for it is getting toward evening, and the day is now nearly over." And He went in to stay with them.

30 And it came about that when He had reclined at the table with them, He took the bread and blessed it, and breaking it, He began giving it to them.

31 And their eyes were opened and they recognized Him; and He vanished from their sight.

32 And they said to one another, "Were not our hearts burning within us while He was speaking to us on the road, while He was explaining the Scriptures to us?"

33 And they arose that very hour and returned to Jerusalem, and found gathered together the eleven and those who were with them,

34 saying, "The Lord has really risen, and has appeared to Simon."

35 And they began to relate their experiences on the road and how He was recognized by them in the breaking of the bread.

36 And while they were telling these things, He Himself stood in their midst.[42]

37 But they were startled and frightened and thought that they were seeing a spirit.

38 And He said to them, "Why are you troubled, and why do doubts arise in your hearts?

39 "See My hands and My feet, that it is I Myself; touch Me and see, for a spirit does not have flesh and bones as you see that I have."

40 [43And when He had said this, He showed them His hands and His feet.]

41 And while they still could not believe it for joy and were marveling, He said to them, "Have you anything here to eat?"

42 And they gave Him a piece of a broiled fish;

43 and He took it and ate it before them.

44 Now He said to them, "These are My words which I spoke to you while I was still with you, that all things which are written about Me in the Law of Moses and the Prophets and the Psalms must be fulfilled."

45 Then He opened their minds to understand the Scriptures,

46 and He said to them, "Thus it is written, that the Christ should suffer and rise again from the dead the third day;

47 and that repentance for forgiveness of sins should be proclaimed in His name to all the nations, beginning from Jerusalem.

48 "You are witnesses of these things.

49 "And behold, I am sending forth the promise of My Father upon you; but you are to stay in the city until you are clothed with power from on high."

50 And He led them out as far

---

42 Some ancient mss. insert And He says to them, "Peace be to you."

43 Many mss. do not contain this verse

as Bethany, and He lifted up His hands and blessed them.

51 And it came about that while He was blessing them, He parted from them.[44]

52 And they[45] returned to Jerusalem with great joy,

53 and were continually in the temple, praising God.

[44] Some mss. add *and was carried up into heaven*
[45] Some mss. insert *worshiped Him, and*

THE GOSPEL ACCORDING TO

JOHN

IN the beginning was the Word, and the Word was with God, and the Word was God.

2 He was in the beginning with God.

3 All things came into being by Him, and apart from Him nothing came into being that has come into being.

4 In Him was life, and the life was the light of men.

5 And the light shines in the darkness, and the darkness did not [1]comprehend it.

6 There [2]came a man, sent from God, whose name was John.

7 He came for a witness, that he might bear witness of the light, that all might believe through him.

8 He was not the light, but *came* that he might bear witness of the light.

9 There was the true light [3]which, coming into the world, enlightens every man.

10 He was in the world, and the world was made through Him, and the world did not know Him.

11 He came to His [4]own, and those who were His own did not receive Him.

12 But as many as received Him, to them He gave the right to become children of God, *even* to those who believe in His name,

13 who were born not of blood, nor of the will of the flesh, nor of the will of man, but of God.

14 And the Word became flesh, and dwelt among us, and we beheld His glory, glory as of the only begotten from the Father, full of grace and truth.

15 John *bore witness of Him, and cried out, saying, "This was He of whom I said, 'He who comes after me has a higher rank than I, for He existed before me.'"

16 For of His fulness we have all received, and grace upon grace.

17 For the Law was given through Moses; grace and truth were realized through Jesus Christ.

18 No man has seen God at any time; the only begotten [5]God, who is in the bosom of the Father, He has explained *Him*.

19 And this is the witness of John, when the Jews sent to him

[1] Or, *overpower* [2] Or, *came into being*
[3] Or, *which enlightens every man coming into the world*
[4] Or, *own things, possessions, domain*
[5] Some later mss. read *Son*

priests and Levites from Jerusalem to ask him, "Who are you?"

20 And he confessed, and did not deny, and he confessed, "I am not the Christ."

21 And they asked him, "What then? Are you Elijah?" And he *said, "I am not." "Are you the Prophet?" And he answered, "No."

22 They said then to him, "Who are you, so that we may give an answer to those who sent us? What do you say about yourself?"

23 He said, "I am a VOICE OF ONE CRYING IN THE WILDERNESS, 'MAKE STRAIGHT THE WAY OF THE LORD,' as Isaiah the prophet said."

24 Now they had been sent from the Pharisees.

25 And they asked him, and said to him, "Why then are you baptizing, if you are not the Christ, nor Elijah, nor the Prophet?"

26 John answered them saying, "I baptize 6in water, but among you stands One whom you do not know.

27"It is He who comes after me, the thong of whose sandal I am not worthy to untie."

28 These things took place in Bethany beyond the Jordan, where John was baptizing.

29 The next day he *saw Jesus coming to him, and *said, "Behold, the Lamb of God who takes away the sin of the world!

30"This is He on behalf of whom I said, 'After me comes a Man who has a higher rank than I, for He existed before me.'

31"And I did not recognize Him, but in order that He might be manifested to Israel, I came baptizing 6in water."

32 And John bore witness saying, "I have beheld the Spirit descending as a dove out of heaven, and He remained upon Him.

33"And I did not recognize Him, but He who sent me to baptize 6in water said to me, 'He upon whom you see the Spirit descending and remaining upon Him, this is the one who baptizes in the Holy Spirit.'

34"And I have seen, and have borne witness that this is the Son of God."

35 Again the next day John was standing with two of his disciples,

36 and he looked upon Jesus as He walked, and *said, "Behold, the Lamb of God!"

37 And the two disciples heard him speak, and they followed Jesus.

38 And Jesus turned, and beheld them following, and *said to them, "What do you seek?" And they said to Him, "Rabbi (which translated means Teacher), where are You staying?"

39 He *said to them, "Come, and you will see." They came therefore and saw where He was staying; and they stayed with Him that day, for it was about the 7tenth hour.

40 One of the two who heard John speak, and followed Him, was Andrew, Simon Peter's brother.

41 He *found first his own brother Simon, and *said to him, "We have found the Messiah" (which translated means Christ).

42 He brought him to Jesus. Jesus looked at him, and said, "You are Simon the son of John;

6 The Gr. here can be translated in, with or by   7 Perhaps 10 a.m. (Roman time)

you shall be called Cephas" (which translated means Peter).

43 The next day He purposed to go forth into Galilee, and He *found Philip. And Jesus *said to him, "Follow Me."

44 Now Philip was from Bethsaida, of the city of Andrew and Peter.

45 Philip *found Nathanael and *said to him, "We have found Him of whom Moses in the Law and *also* the Prophets wrote, Jesus of Nazareth, the son of Joseph."

46 And Nathanael *said to him, "Can any good thing come out of Nazareth?" Philip *said to him, "Come and see."

47 Jesus saw Nathanael coming to Him, and *said of him, "Behold, an Israelite indeed, in whom is no guile!"

48 Nathanael *said to Him, "How do You know me?" Jesus answered and said to him, "Before Philip called you, when you were under the fig tree, I saw you."

49 Nathanael answered Him, "Rabbi, You are the Son of God; You are the King of Israel."

50 Jesus answered and said to him, "Because I said to you that I saw you under the fig tree, do you believe? You shall see greater things than these."

51 And He *said to him, "Truly, truly, I say to you, you shall see the heavens opened, and the angels of God ascending and descending on the Son of Man."

CHAPTER 2

AND on the third day there was a wedding in Cana of Gali-

⁸ Or, *steward*

lee, and the mother of Jesus was there;

2 and Jesus also was invited, and His disciples, to the wedding.

3 And when the wine gave out, the mother of Jesus *said to Him, "They have no wine."

4 And Jesus *said to her, "Woman, what do I have to do with you? My hour has not yet come."

5 His mother *said to the servants, "Whatever He says to you, do it."

6 Now there were six stone waterpots set there for the Jewish custom of purification, containing twenty or thirty gallons each.

7 Jesus *said to them, "Fill the waterpots with water." And they filled them up to the brim.

8 And He *said to them, "Draw *some* out now, and take it to the ⁸headwaiter." And they took it *to him.*

9 And when the headwaiter tasted the water which had become wine, and did not know where it came from (but the servants who had drawn the water knew), the headwaiter *called the bridegroom,

10 and *said to him, "Every man serves the good wine first, and when *men* have drunk freely, *then* that which is poorer; you have kept the good wine until now."

11 This beginning of *His* signs Jesus did in Cana of Galilee, and manifested His glory, and His disciples believed in Him.

12 After this He went down to Capernaum, He and His mother, and *His* brothers, and His disciples; and there they stayed a few days.

13 And the Passover of the

Jews was at hand, and Jesus went up to Jerusalem.

14 And He found in the temple those who were selling oxen and sheep and doves, and the money-changers seated.

15 And He made a scourge of cords, and drove *them* all out of the temple, with the sheep and the oxen; and He poured out the coins of the moneychangers, and overturned their tables;

16 and to those who were selling the doves He said, "Take these things away; stop making My Father's house a house of merchandise."

17 His disciples remembered that it was written, "ZEAL FOR THY HOUSE WILL CONSUME ME."

18 The Jews therefore answered and said to Him, "What sign do You show to us, seeing that You do these things?"

19 Jesus answered and said to them, "Destroy this temple, and in three days I will raise it up."

20 The Jews therefore said, "It took forty-six years to build this temple, and will You raise it up in three days?"

21 But He was speaking of the temple of His body.

22 When therefore He was raised from the dead, His disciples remembered that He said this; and they believed the Scripture, and the word which Jesus had spoken.

23 Now when He was in Jerusalem at the Passover, during the feast, many believed in His name, beholding His signs which He was doing.

24 But Jesus, on His part, was not entrusting Himself to them, for He knew all men,

25 and because He did not need anyone to bear witness concerning man for He Himself knew what was in man.

CHAPTER 3

NOW there was a man of the Pharisees, named Nicodemus, a ruler of the Jews;

2 this man came to Him by night, and said to Him, "Rabbi, we know that You have come from God *as* a teacher; for no one can do these signs that You do unless God is with him."

3 Jesus answered and said to him, "Truly, truly, I say to you, unless one is born again, he cannot see the kingdom of God."

4 Nicodemus *said to Him, "How can a man be born when he is old? He cannot enter a second time into his mother's womb and be born, can he?"

5 Jesus answered, "Truly, truly, I say to you, unless one is born of water and the Spirit, he cannot enter into the kingdom of God.

6 "That which is born of the flesh is flesh, and that which is born of the Spirit is spirit.

7 "Do not marvel that I said to you, 'You must be born again.'

8 "The wind blows where it wishes and you hear the sound of it, but do not know where it comes from and where it is going; so is everyone who is born of the Spirit."

9 Nicodemus answered and said to Him, "How can these things be?"

10 Jesus answered and said to him, "Are you the teacher of Israel, and do not understand these things?

11 "Truly, truly, I say to you, we speak that which we know, and bear witness of that which we

have seen; and you do not receive our witness.

12 "If I told you earthly things and you do not believe, how shall you believe if I tell you heavenly things?

13 "And no one has ascended into heaven, but He who descended from heaven, *even* the Son of Man.

14 "And as Moses lifted up the serpent in the wilderness, even so must the Son of Man be lifted up;

15 that whoever [9]believes may in Him have eternal life.

16 "For God so loved the world, that He gave His only begotten Son, that whoever believes in Him should not perish, but have eternal life.

17 "For God did not send the Son into the world to judge the world, but that the world should be saved through Him.

18 "He who believes in Him is not judged; he who does not believe has been judged already, because he has not believed in the name of the only begotten Son of God.

19 "And this is the judgment, that the light is come into the world, and men loved the darkness rather than the light; for their deeds were evil.

20 "For everyone who does evil hates the light, and does not come to the light, lest his deeds should be exposed.

21 "But he who practices the truth comes to the light, that his deeds may be manifested as having been wrought in God."

22 After these things Jesus and His disciples came into the land of Judea, and there He was spending time with them and baptizing.

23 And John also was baptizing in Aenon near Salim, because there was much water there; and they were coming and were being baptized.

24 For John had not yet been thrown into prison.

25 There arose therefore a discussion on the part of John's disciples with a Jew about purification.

26 And they came to John and said to him, "Rabbi, He who was with you beyond the Jordan, to whom you have borne witness, behold, He is baptizing, and all are coming to Him."

27 John answered and said, "A man can receive nothing, unless it has been given him from heaven.

28 "You yourselves bear me witness, that I said, 'I am not the Christ,' but, 'I have been sent before Him.'

29 "He who has the bride is the bridegroom; but the friend of the bridegroom, who stands and hears him, rejoices greatly because of the bridegroom's voice. And so this joy of mine has been made full.

30 "He must increase, but I must decrease.

31 "He who comes from above is above all, he who is of the earth is from the earth and speaks of the earth. He who comes from heaven is above all.

32 "What He has seen and heard, of that He bears witness; and no man receives His witness.

33 "He who has received His witness has set his seal to *this*, that God is true.

[9] Some mss. read *believes in Him may have eternal life*

34"For He whom God has sent speaks the words of God; for He gives the Spirit without measure.

35"The Father loves the Son, and has given all things into His hand.

36"He who believes in the Son has eternal life; but he who does not obey the Son shall not see life, but the wrath of God abides on him."

CHAPTER 4

WHEN therefore the Lord knew that the Pharisees had heard that Jesus was making and baptizing more disciples than John

2 (although Jesus Himself was not baptizing, but His disciples were),

3 He left Judea, and departed again into Galilee.

4 And He had to pass through Samaria.

5 So He *came to a city of Samaria, called Sychar, near the parcel of ground that Jacob gave to his son Joseph;

6 and Jacob's well was there. Jesus therefore, being wearied from His journey, was sitting thus by the well. It was about [10]the sixth hour.

7 There *came a woman of Samaria to draw water. Jesus *said to her, "Give Me a drink."

8 For His disciples had gone away into the city to buy food.

9 The Samaritan woman therefore *said to Him, "How is it that You, being a Jew, ask me for a drink since I am a Samaritan woman?" (For Jews have no dealings with Samaritans.)

10 Jesus answered and said to her, "If you knew the gift of God, and who it is who says to you,

'Give Me a drink,' you would have asked Him, and He would have given you living water."

11 She *said to Him, "Sir, You have nothing to draw with and the well is deep; where then do You get that living water?

12"You are not greater than our father Jacob, are You, who gave us the well, and drank of it himself, and his sons, and his cattle?"

13 Jesus answered and said to her, "Everyone who drinks of this water shall thirst again;

14 but whoever drinks of the water that I shall give him shall never thirst; but the water that I shall give him shall become in him a well of water springing up to eternal life."

15 The woman *said to Him, "Sir, give me this water, so I will not be thirsty, nor come all the way here to draw."

16 He *said to her, "Go, call your husband, and come here."

17 The woman answered and said, "I have no husband." Jesus *said to her, "You have well said, 'I have no husband';

18 for you have had five husbands, and the one whom you now have is not your husband; this you have said truly."

19 The woman *said to Him, "Sir, I perceive that You are a prophet.

20"Our fathers worshiped in this mountain, and you *people* say that in Jerusalem is the place where men ought to worship."

21 Jesus *said to her, "Woman, believe Me, an hour is coming when neither in this mountain, nor in Jerusalem, shall you worship the Father.

22"You worship that which you

[10] Perhaps 6 p.m. (Roman time)

do not know; we worship that which we know, for salvation is from the Jews.

23"But an hour is coming, and now is, when the true worshipers shall worship the Father in spirit and truth; for such people the Father seeks to be His worshipers.

24"God is spirit, and those who worship Him must worship in spirit and truth."

25 The woman *said to Him, "I know that Messiah is coming (He who is called Christ); when that One comes, He will declare all things to us."

26 Jesus *said to her, "I who speak to you am *He."

27 And at this point His disciples came, and they marveled that He had been speaking with a woman; yet no one said, "What do You seek?" or, "Why do You speak with her?"

28 So the woman left her waterpot, and went into the city, and *said to the men,

29"Come, see a man who told me all the things that I *have done; this is not the Christ, is it?"

30 They went out of the city, and were coming to Him.

31 In the meanwhile the disciples were requesting Him, saying, "Rabbi, eat."

32 But He said to them, "I have food to eat that you do not know about."

33 The disciples therefore were saying to one another, "No one brought Him *anything* to eat, did he?"

34 Jesus *said to them, "My food is to do the will of Him who sent Me, and to accomplish His work.

35"Do you not say, 'There are yet four months, and *then* comes the harvest'? Behold, I say to you, lift up your eyes, and look on the fields, that they are white for harvest.

36"Already he who reaps is receiving wages, and is gathering fruit for life eternal; that he who sows and he who reaps may rejoice together.

37"For in this *case* the saying is true, 'One sows, and another reaps.'

38"I sent you to reap that for which you have not labored; others have labored, and you have entered into their labor."

39 And from that city many of the Samaritans believed in Him because of the word of the woman who testified, "He told me all the things that I *have* done."

40 So when the Samaritans came to Him, they were asking Him to stay with them; and He stayed there two days.

41 And many more believed because of His word;

42 and they were saying to the woman, "It is no longer because of what you said that we believe, for we have heard for ourselves and know that this One is indeed the Savior of the world."

43 And after the two days He went forth from there into Galilee.

44 For Jesus Himself testified that a prophet has no honor in his own country.

45 So when He came to Galilee, the Galileans received Him, having seen all the things that He did in Jerusalem at the feast; for they themselves also went to the feast.

46 He came therefore again to Cana of Galilee where He had made the water wine. And there was a certain royal official,

whose son was sick at Capernaum.

47 When he heard that Jesus had come out of Judea into Galilee, he went to Him, and was requesting *Him* to come down and heal his son; for he was at the point of death.

48 Jesus therefore said to him, "Unless you *people* see signs and wonders, you *simply* will not believe."

49 The royal official *said to Him, "Sir, come down before my child dies."

50 Jesus *said to him, "Go your way; your son lives." The man believed the word that Jesus spoke to him, and he started off.

51 And as he was now going down, *his* slaves met him, saying that his son was living.

52 So he inquired of them the hour when he began to get better. They said therefore to him, "Yesterday at the [11]seventh hour the fever left him."

53 So the father knew that *it was* at that hour in which Jesus said to him, "Your son lives"; and he himself believed, and his whole household.

54 This is again a second sign that Jesus performed, when He had come out of Judea into Galilee.

CHAPTER 5

AFTER these things there was [12]a feast of the Jews, and Jesus went up to Jerusalem.

2 Now there is in Jerusalem by the sheep *gate* a pool, which is called in Hebrew Bethesda, having five porticoes.

3 In these lay a multitude of those who were sick, blind, lame, and withered, [[13]waiting for the moving of the waters;

4 for an angel of the Lord went down at certain seasons into the pool, and stirred up the water; whoever then first, after the stirring up of the water, stepped in was made well from whatever disease with which he was afflicted.]

5 And a certain man was there, who had been thirty-eight years in his sickness.

6 When Jesus saw him lying there, and knew that he had already been a long time in *that condition,* He *said to him, "Do you wish to get well?"

7 The sick man answered Him, "Sir, I have no man to put me into the pool when the water is stirred up, but while I am coming, another steps down before me."

8 Jesus *said to him, "Arise, take up your pallet, and walk."

9 And immediately the man became well, and took up his pallet and *began to walk.

Now it was the Sabbath on that day.

10 Therefore the Jews were saying to him who was cured, "It is the Sabbath, and it is not permissible for you to carry your pallet."

11 But he answered them, "He who made me well was the one who said to me, 'Take up your pallet and walk.' "

12 They asked him, "Who is the man who said to you, 'Take up *your* pallet, and walk'?"

13 But he who was healed did not know who it was; for Jesus

[11] Perhaps 7 p.m. (Roman time)
[12] Many mss. read *the feast,* i.e., the Passover
[13] Many mss. do not contain the remainder of v. 3 nor v. 4

had slipped away while there was a crowd in *that* place.

14 Afterward Jesus *found him in the temple, and said to him, "Behold, you have become well; do not sin anymore, so that nothing worse may befall you."

15 The man went away, and told the Jews that it was Jesus who had made him well.

16 And for this reason the Jews were persecuting Jesus, because He was doing these things on the Sabbath.

17 But He answered them, "My Father is working until now, and I Myself am working."

18 For this cause therefore the Jews were seeking all the more to kill Him, because He not only was breaking the Sabbath, but also was calling God His own Father, making Himself equal with God.

19 Jesus therefore answered and was saying to them, "Truly, truly, I say to you, the Son can do nothing of Himself, unless *it is* something He sees the Father doing; for whatever *the Father* does, these things the Son also does in like manner.

20 "For the Father loves the Son, and shows Him all things that He Himself is doing; and greater works than these will He show Him, that you may marvel.

21 "For just as the Father raises the dead and gives them life, even so the Son also gives life to whom He wishes.

22 "For not even the Father judges anyone, but He has given all judgment to the Son,

23 in order that all may honor the Son, even as they honor the Father. He who does not honor the Son does not honor the Father who sent Him.

24 "Truly, truly, I say to you, he who hears My word, and believes Him who sent Me, has eternal life, and does not come into judgment, but has passed out of death into life.

25 "Truly, truly, I say to you, an hour is coming and now is, when the dead shall hear the voice of the Son of God; and those who hear shall live.

26 "For just as the Father has life in Himself, even so He gave to the Son also to have life in Himself;

27 and He gave Him authority to execute judgment, because He is *the* Son of Man.

28 "Do not marvel at this; for an hour is coming, in which all who are in the tombs shall hear His voice,

29 and shall come forth; those who did the good *deeds* to a resurrection of life, those who committed the evil *deeds* to a resurrection of judgment.

30 "I can do nothing on My own initiative. As I hear, I judge; and My judgment is just, because I do not seek My own will, but the will of Him who sent Me.

31 "If I *alone* bear witness of Myself, My testimony is not true.

32 "There is another who bears witness of Me, and I know that the testimony which He bears of Me is true.

33 "You have sent to John, and he has borne witness to the truth.

34 "But the witness which I receive is not from man, but I say these things that you may be saved.

35 "He was the lamp that was burning and was shining and you were willing to rejoice for a while in his light.

36 "But the witness which I

have is greater than *that of* John; for the works which the Father has given Me to accomplish, the very works that I do, bear witness of Me, that the Father has sent Me.

37"And the Father who sent Me, He has borne witness of Me. You have neither heard His voice at any time, nor seen His form.

38"And you do not have His word abiding in you, for you do not believe Him whom He sent.

39"[14]You search the Scriptures, because you think that in them you have eternal life; and it is these that bear witness of Me;

40 and you are unwilling to come to Me, that you may have life.

41"I do not receive glory from men;

42 but I know you, that you do not have the love of God in yourselves.

43"I have come in My Father's name, and you do not receive Me; if another shall come in his own name, you will receive him.

44"How can you believe, when you receive glory from one another, and you do not seek the glory that is from the *one and only* God?

45"Do not think that I will accuse you before the Father; the one who accuses you is Moses, in whom you have set your hope.

46"For if you believed Moses, you would believe Me; for he wrote of Me.

47"But if you do not believe his writings, how will you believe My words?"

CHAPTER 6

AFTER these things Jesus went away to the other side of the Sea of Galilee (or Tiberias).

2 And a great multitude was following Him, because they were seeing the signs which He was performing on those who were sick.

3 And Jesus went up on the mountain, and there He sat with His disciples.

4 Now the Passover, the feast of the Jews, was at hand.

5 Jesus therefore lifting up His eyes, and seeing that a great multitude was coming to Him, *said to Philip, "Where are we to buy bread, that these may eat?"

6 And this He was saying to test him; for He Himself knew what He was intending to do.

7 Philip answered Him, "Two hundred [15]denarii worth of bread is not sufficient for them, for everyone to receive a little."

8 One of His disciples, Andrew, Simon Peter's brother, *said to Him,

9"There is a lad here who has five barley loaves and two fish, but what are these for so many people?"

10 Jesus said, "Have the people sit down." Now there was much grass in the place. So the men sat down, in number about five thousand.

11 Jesus therefore took the loaves; and having given thanks, He distributed to those who were seated; likewise also of the fish as much as they wanted.

12 And when they were filled, He *said to His disciples, "Gather up the leftover fragments that nothing may be lost."

13 And so they gathered them up, and filled twelve baskets with fragments from the five barley

[14] Or, (a command) *Search the Scriptures!*
[15] The *denarius* was equivalent to one day's wage

loaves, which were left over by those who had eaten.

14 When therefore the people saw the sign which He had performed, they said, "This is of a truth the Prophet who is to come into the world."

15 Jesus therefore perceiving that they were intending to come and take Him by force, to make Him king, withdrew again to the mountain by Himself alone.

16 Now when evening came, His disciples went down to the sea,

17 and after getting into a boat, they *started to* cross the sea to Capernaum. And it had already become dark, and Jesus had not yet come to them.

18 And the sea *began* to be stirred up because a strong wind was blowing.

19 When therefore they had rowed about three or four miles, they *beheld Jesus walking on the sea and drawing near to the boat; and they were frightened.

20 But He *said to them, "It is I; do not be afraid."

21 They were willing therefore to receive Him into the boat; and immediately the boat was at the land to which they were going.

22 The next day the multitude that stood on the other side of the sea saw that there was no other small boat there, except one, and that Jesus had not entered with His disciples into the boat, but *that* His disciples had gone away alone.

23 There came other small boats from Tiberias near to the place where they ate the bread after the Lord had given thanks.

24 When the multitude therefore saw that Jesus was not there, nor His disciples, they themselves got into the small boats, and came to Capernaum, seeking Jesus.

25 And when they found Him on the other side of the sea, they said to Him, "Rabbi, when did You get here?"

26 Jesus answered them and said, "Truly, truly, I say to you, you seek Me, not because you saw signs, but because you ate of the loaves, and were filled.

27 "Do not work for the food which perishes, but for the food which endures to eternal life, which the Son of Man shall give to you, for on Him the Father, *even* God, has set His seal."

28 They said therefore to Him, "What shall we do, that we may work the works of God?"

29 Jesus answered and said to them, "This is the work of God, that you believe in Him whom He has sent."

30 They said therefore to Him, "What then do You do for a sign, that we may see, and believe You? What work do You perform?

31 "Our fathers ate the manna in the wilderness; as it is written, 'HE GAVE THEM BREAD OUT OF HEAVEN TO EAT.'"

32 Jesus therefore said to them, "Truly, truly, I say to you, it is not Moses who has given you the bread out of heaven, but it is My Father who gives you the true bread out of heaven.

33 "For the bread of God is [16]that which comes down out of heaven, and gives life to the world."

34 They said therefore to Him,

[16] Or, He who comes

"Lord, evermore give us this bread."

35 Jesus said to them, "I am the bread of life; he who comes to Me shall not hunger, and he who believes in Me shall never thirst.

36"But I said to you, that you have seen Me, and yet do not believe.

37"All that the Father gives Me shall come to Me, and the one who comes to Me I will certainly not cast out.

38"For I have come down from heaven, not to do My own will, but the will of Him who sent Me.

39"And this is the will of Him who sent Me, that of all that He has given Me I lose nothing, but raise it up on the last day.

40"For this is the will of My Father, that everyone who beholds the Son and believes in Him, may have eternal life; and I Myself will raise him up on the last day."

41 The Jews therefore were grumbling about Him, because He said, "I am the bread that came down out of heaven."

42 And they were saying, "Is not this Jesus, the son of Joseph, whose father and mother we know? How does He now say, 'I have come down out of heaven'?"

43 Jesus answered and said to them, "Do not grumble among yourselves.

44"No one can come to Me, unless the Father who sent Me draws him; and I will raise him up on the last day.

45"It is written in the prophets, 'AND THEY SHALL ALL BE TAUGHT OF GOD.' Everyone who has heard and learned from the Father, comes to Me.

46"Not that any man has seen the Father, except the One who is from God; He has seen the Father.

47"Truly, truly, I say to you, he who believes has eternal life.

48"I am the bread of life.

49"Your fathers ate the manna in the wilderness, and they died.

50"This is the bread which comes down out of heaven, so that one may eat of it and not die.

51"I am the living bread that came down out of heaven; if anyone eats of this bread, he shall live forever; and the bread also which I shall give for the life of the world is My flesh."

52 The Jews therefore *began* to argue with one another, saying, "How can this man give us *His* flesh to eat?"

53 Jesus therefore said to them, "Truly, truly, I say to you, unless you eat the flesh of the Son of Man and drink His blood, you have no life in yourselves.

54"He who eats My flesh and drinks My blood has eternal life, and I will raise him up on the last day.

55"For My flesh is true food, and My blood is true drink.

56"He who eats My flesh and drinks My blood abides in Me, and I in him.

57"As the living Father sent Me, and I live because of the Father, so he who eats Me, he also shall live because of Me.

58"This is the bread which came down out of heaven; not as the fathers ate, and died; he who eats this bread shall live forever."

59 These things He said in the synagogue, as He taught in Capernaum.

60 Many therefore of His disciples, when they heard *this* said,

"This is a difficult statement; who can listen to it?"

61 But Jesus, conscious that His disciples grumbled at this, said to them, "Does this cause you to stumble?

62 *What* then if you should behold the Son of Man ascending where He was before?

63 "It is the Spirit who gives life; the flesh profits nothing; the words that I have spoken to you are spirit and are life.

64 "But there are some of you who do not believe." For Jesus knew from the beginning who they were who did not believe, and who it was that would betray Him.

65 And He was saying, "For this reason I have said to you, that no one can come to Me, unless it has been granted him from the Father."

66 As a result of this many of His disciples withdrew, and were not walking with Him anymore.

67 Jesus said therefore to the twelve, "You do not want to go away also, do you?"

68 Simon Peter answered Him, "Lord, to whom shall we go? You have words of eternal life.

69 "And we have believed and have come to know that You are the Holy One of God."

70 Jesus answered them, "Did I Myself not choose you, the twelve, and *yet* one of you is a devil?"

71 Now He meant Judas *the son* of Simon Iscariot, for he, one of the twelve, was going to betray Him.

CHAPTER 7

AND after these things Jesus was walking in Galilee; for He was unwilling to walk in Ju-

dea, because the Jews were seeking to kill Him.

2 Now the feast of the Jews, the Feast of Booths, was at hand.

3 His brothers therefore said to Him, "Depart from here, and go into Judea, that Your disciples also may behold Your works which You are doing.

4 "For no one does anything in secret, when he himself seeks to be *known* publicly. If You do these things, show Yourself to the world."

5 For not even His brothers were believing in Him.

6 Jesus therefore *said to them, "My time is not yet at hand, but your time is always opportune.

7 "The world cannot hate you; but it hates Me because I testify of it, that its deeds are evil.

8 "Go up to the feast yourselves; I do not go up to this feast because My time has not yet fully come."

9 And having said these things to them, He stayed in Galilee.

10 But when His brothers had gone up to the feast, then He Himself also went up, not publicly, but as it were, in secret.

11 The Jews therefore were seeking Him at the feast, and were saying, "Where is He?"

12 And there was much grumbling among the multitudes concerning Him; some were saying, "He is a good man"; others were saying, "No, on the contrary, He leads the multitude astray."

13 Yet no one was speaking openly of Him for fear of the Jews.

14 But when it was now the midst of the feast Jesus went up

into the temple, and *began to* teach.

15 The Jews therefore were marveling, saying, "How has this man become learned, having never been educated?"

16 Jesus therefore answered them, and said, "My teaching is not Mine, but His who sent Me.

17"If any man is willing to do His will, he shall know of the teaching, whether it is of God, or *whether* I speak from Myself.

18"He who speaks from himself seeks his own glory; but He who is seeking the glory of the one who sent Him, He is true, and there is no unrighteousness in Him.

19"Did not Moses give you the law, and *yet* none of you carries out the law? Why do you seek to kill Me?"

20 The multitude answered, "You have a demon! Who seeks to kill You?"

21 Jesus answered and said to them, "I did one deed, and you all marvel.

22"On this account Moses has given you circumcision (not because it is from Moses, but from the fathers), and on *the* Sabbath you circumcise a man.

23"If a man receives circumcision on *the* Sabbath that the Law of Moses may not be broken, are you angry with Me because I made an entire man well on *the* Sabbath?

24"Do not judge according to appearance, but judge with righteous judgment."

25 Therefore some of the people of Jerusalem were saying, "Is this not the man whom they are seeking to kill?

26"And look, He is speaking publicly, and they are saying nothing to Him. The rulers do not really know that this is the Christ, do they?

27"However, we know where this man is from; but whenever the Christ may come, no one knows where He is from."

28 Jesus therefore cried out in the temple, teaching and saying, "You both know Me and know where I am from; and I have not come of Myself, but He who sent Me is true, whom you do not know.

29"I know Him; because I am from Him, and He sent Me."

30 They were seeking therefore to seize Him; and no man laid his hand on Him, because His hour had not yet come.

31 But many of the multitude believed in Him; and they were saying, "When the Christ shall come, He will not perform more signs than those which this man has, will He?"

32 The Pharisees heard the multitude muttering these things about Him; and the chief priests and the Pharisees sent officers to seize Him.

33 Jesus therefore said, "For a little while longer I am with you, then I go to Him who sent Me.

34"You shall seek Me, and shall not find Me; and where I am, you cannot come."

35 The Jews therefore said to one another, "Where does this man intend to go that we shall not find Him? He is not intending to go to the Dispersion among the Greeks, and teach the Greeks, is He?

36"What is this statement that He said, 'You will seek Me, and will not find Me; and where I am, you cannot come'?"

37 Now on the last day, the great *day* of the feast, Jesus stood and cried out, saying, "If any man is thirsty, let him come to Me and drink.

38"He who believes in Me, as the Scripture said, 'From his innermost being shall flow rivers of living water.' "

39 But this He spoke of the Spirit, whom those who believed in Him were to receive; for the Spirit was not yet *given*, because Jesus was not yet glorified.

40 *Some* of the multitude therefore, when they heard these words, were saying, "This certainly is the Prophet."

41 Others were saying, "This is the Christ." Still others were saying, "Surely the Christ is not going to come from Galilee, is He?

42"Has not the Scripture said that the Christ comes from the offspring of David, and from Bethlehem, the village where David was?"

43 So there arose a division in the multitude because of Him.

44 And some of them wanted to seize Him, but no one laid hands on Him.

45 The officers therefore came to the chief priests and Pharisees, and they said to them, "Why did you not bring Him?"

46 The officers answered, "Never did a man speak the way this man speaks."

47 The Pharisees therefore answered them, "You have not also been led astray, have you?

48"No one of the rulers or Pharisees has believed in Him, has he?

49"But this multitude which does not know the Law is accursed."

50 Nicodemus *said to them (he who came to Him before, being one of them),

51"Our Law does not judge a man, unless it first hears from him and knows what he is doing, does it?"

52 They answered and said to him, "You are not also from Galilee, are you? Search, and see that no prophet arises out of Galilee."

53 [17And everyone went to his home.

CHAPTER 8

BUT Jesus went to the Mount of Olives.

2 And early in the morning He came again into the temple, and all the people were coming to Him; and He sat down and *began* to teach them.

3 And the scribes and the Pharisees *brought a woman caught in adultery, and having set her in the midst,

4 they *said to Him, "Teacher, this woman has been caught in adultery, in the very act.

5"Now in the Law Moses commanded us to stone such women; what then do You say?"

6 And they were saying this, testing Him, in order that they might have grounds for accusing Him. But Jesus stooped down, and with His finger wrote on the ground.

7 But when they persisted in asking Him, He straightened up, and said to them, "He who is without sin among you, let him *be the* first to throw a stone at her."

17 John 7:53–8:11 is not found in most of the old mss.

8 And again He stooped down, and wrote on the ground.

9 And when they heard it, they *began* to go out one by one, beginning with the older ones, and He was left alone, and the woman, *where she had been,* in the midst.

10 And straightening up, Jesus said to her, "Woman, where are they? Did no one condemn you?"

11 And she said, "No one, Lord." And Jesus said, ["Neither do I condemn you; go your way. From now on sin no more."]

12 Again therefore Jesus spoke to them, saying, "I am the light of the world; he who follows Me shall not walk in the darkness, but shall have the light of life."

13 The Pharisees therefore said to Him, "You are bearing witness of Yourself; Your witness is not true."

14 Jesus answered and said to them, "Even if I bear witness of Myself, My witness is true; for I know where I came from, and where I am going; but you do not know where I come from, or where I am going.

15 "You people judge according to the flesh; I am not judging anyone.

16 "But even if I do judge, My judgment is true; for I am not alone *in it,* but I and [18]He who sent Me.

17 "Even in your law it has been written, that the testimony of two men is true.

18 "I am He who bears witness of Myself, and the Father who sent Me bears witness of Me."

19 And so they were saying to Him, "Where is Your Father?" Jesus answered, "You know neither Me, nor My Father; if you knew Me, you would know My Father also."

20 These words He spoke in the treasury, as He taught in the temple; and no one seized Him, because His hour had not yet come.

21 He said therefore again to them, "I go away, and you shall seek Me, and shall die in your sin; where I am going, you cannot come."

22 Therefore the Jews were saying, "Surely He will not kill Himself, will He, since He says, 'Where I am going, you cannot come'?"

23 And He was saying to them, "You are from below, I am from above; you are of this world, I am not of this world.

24 "I said therefore to you, that you shall die in your sins; for unless you believe that I am *He,* you shall die in your sins."

25 And so they were saying to Him, "Who are You?" Jesus said to them, "What have I been saying to you *from* the beginning?

26 "I have many things to speak and to judge concerning you, but He who sent Me is true; and the things which I heard from Him, these I speak to the world."

27 They did not realize that He had been speaking to them about the Father.

28 Jesus therefore said, "When you lift up the Son of Man, then you will know that I am *He,* and I do nothing on My own initiative, but I speak these things as the Father taught Me.

29 "And He who sent Me is with Me; He has not left Me alone, for I always do the things that are pleasing to Him."

[18] Many ancient mss. read *the Father who sent Me*

30 As He spoke these things, many came to believe in Him.

31 Jesus therefore was saying to those Jews who had believed Him, "If you abide in My word, *then* you are truly disciples of Mine;

32 and you shall know the truth, and the truth shall make you free."

33 They answered Him, "We are Abraham's offspring, and have never yet been enslaved to anyone; how is it that You say, 'You shall become free'?"

34 Jesus answered them, "Truly, truly, I say to you, everyone who commits sin is the slave of sin.

35 "And the slave does not remain in the house forever; the son does remain forever.

36 "If therefore the Son shall make you free, you shall be free indeed.

37 "I know that you are Abraham's offspring; yet you seek to kill Me, because My word has no place in you.

38 "I speak the things which I have seen with My Father; therefore you also do the things which you heard from *your* father."

39 They answered and said to Him, "Abraham is our father." Jesus *said to them, "If you are Abraham's children, do the deeds of Abraham.

40 "But as it is, you are seeking to kill Me, a man who has told you the truth, which I heard from God; this Abraham did not do.

41 "You are doing the deeds of your father." They said to Him, "We were not born of fornication; we have one Father, *even* God."

42 Jesus said to them, "If God were your Father, you would love Me; for I proceeded forth and have come from God, for I have not even come on My own initiative, but He sent Me.

43 "Why do you not understand what I am saying? *It is* because you cannot hear My word.

44 "You are of *your* father the devil, and you want to do the desires of your father. He was a murderer from the beginning, and does not stand in the truth, because there is no truth in him. Whenever he speaks a lie, he speaks from his own *nature*; for he is a liar, and the father of lies.

45 "But because I speak the truth, you do not believe Me.

46 "Which one of you convicts Me of sin? If I speak truth, why do you not believe Me?

47 "He who is of God hears the words of God; for this reason you do not hear *them*, because you are not of God."

48 The Jews answered and said to Him, "Do we not say rightly that You are a Samaritan and have a demon?"

49 Jesus answered, "I do not have a demon; but I honor My Father, and you dishonor Me.

50 "But I do not seek My glory; there is One who seeks and judges.

51 "Truly, truly, I say to you, if anyone keeps My word he shall never see death."

52 The Jews said to Him, "Now we know that You have a demon. Abraham died, and the prophets *also*; and You say, 'If anyone keeps My word, he shall never taste of death.'

53 "Surely You are not greater than our father Abraham, who died? The prophets died too; whom do You make Yourself out to *be*?"

54 Jesus answered, "If I glorify Myself, My glory is nothing; it is My Father who glorifies Me, of whom you say, 'He is our God';

55 and you have not come to know Him, but I know Him; and if I say that I do not know Him, I shall be a liar like you, but I do know Him, and keep His word.

56 "Your father Abraham rejoiced to see My day, and he saw *it* and was glad."

57 The Jews therefore said to Him, "You are not yet fifty years old, and have You seen Abraham?"

58 Jesus said to them, "Truly, truly, I say to you, before Abraham was born, I am."

59 Therefore they picked up stones to throw at Him; but Jesus hid Himself, and went out of the temple.

CHAPTER 9

AND as He passed by, He saw a man blind from birth.

2 And His disciples asked Him, saying, "Rabbi, who sinned, this man or his parents, that he should be born blind?"

3 Jesus answered, "*It was* neither *that* this man sinned, nor his parents; but *it was* in order that the works of God might be displayed in him.

4 "We must work the works of Him who sent Me, as long as it is day; night is coming, when no man can work.

5 "While I am in the world, I am the light of the world."

6 When He had said this, He spat on the ground, and made clay of the spittle, and applied the clay to his eyes,

7 and said to him, "Go, wash in the pool of Siloam" (which is translated, Sent). And so he went away and washed, and came *back* seeing.

8 The neighbors therefore, and those who previously saw him as a beggar, were saying, "Is not this the one who used to sit and beg?"

9 Others were saying, "This is he," *still* others were saying, "No, but he is like him." He kept saying, "I am the one."

10 Therefore they were saying to him, "How then were your eyes opened?"

11 He answered, "The man who is called Jesus made clay, and anointed my eyes, and said to me, 'Go to Siloam, and wash'; so I went away and washed, and I received sight."

12 And they said to him, "Where is He?" He *said, "I do not know."

13 They *brought to the Pharisees him who was formerly blind.

14 Now it was a Sabbath on the day when Jesus made the clay, and opened his eyes.

15 Again, therefore, the Pharisees also were asking him how he received his sight. And he said to them, "He applied clay to my eyes, and I washed, and I see."

16 Therefore some of the Pharisees were saying, "This man is not from God, because He does not keep the Sabbath." But others were saying, "How can a man who is a sinner perform such signs?" And there was a division among them.

17 They *said therefore to the blind man again, "What do you say about Him, since He opened your eyes?" And he said, "He is a prophet."

18 The Jews therefore did not

believe it of him, that he had been blind, and had received sight, until they called the parents of the very one who had received his sight,

19 and questioned them, saying, "Is this your son, who you say was born blind? Then how does he now see?"

20 His parents answered them and said, "We know that this is our son, and that he was born blind;

21 but how he now sees, we do not know; or who opened his eyes, we do not know. Ask him; he is of age, he shall speak for himself."

22 His parents said this because they were afraid of the Jews; for the Jews had already agreed, that if anyone should confess Him to be Christ, he should be put out of the synagogue.

23 For this reason his parents said, "He is of age; ask him."

24 So a second time they called the man who had been blind, and said to him, "Give glory to God; we know that this man is a sinner."

25 He therefore answered, "Whether He is a sinner, I do not know; one thing I do know, that, whereas I was blind, now I see."

26 They said therefore to him, "What did He do to you? How did He open your eyes?"

27 He answered them, "I told you already, and you did not listen; why do you want to hear it again? You do not want to become His disciples too, do you?"

28 And they reviled him, and said, "You are His disciple, but we are disciples of Moses.

29 "We know that God has spoken to Moses; but as for this man, we do not know where He is from."

30 The man answered and said to them, "Well, here is an amazing thing, that you do not know where He is from, and yet He opened my eyes.

31 "We know that God does not hear sinners; but if anyone is God-fearing, and does His will, He hears him.

32 "Since the beginning of time it has never been heard that anyone opened the eyes of a person born blind.

33 "If this man were not from God, He could do nothing."

34 They answered and said to him, "You were born entirely in sins, and are you teaching us?" And they put him out.

35 Jesus heard that they had put him out; and finding him, He said, "Do you believe in the Son of Man?"

36 He answered and said, "And who is He, Lord, that I may believe in Him?"

37 Jesus said to him, "You have both seen Him, and He is the one who is talking with you."

38 And he said, "Lord, I believe." And he worshiped Him.

39 And Jesus said, "For judgment I came into this world, that those who do not see may see; and that those who see may become blind."

40 Those of the Pharisees who were with Him heard these things, and said to Him, "We are not blind too, are we?"

41 Jesus said to them, "If you were blind, you would have no sin; but since you say, 'We see,' your sin remains.

CHAPTER 10

"TRULY, truly, I say to you, he who does not enter by the door into the fold of the sheep, but climbs up some other way, he is a thief and a robber.

2 "But he who enters by the door is a shepherd of the sheep.

3 "To him the doorkeeper opens, and the sheep hear his voice, and he calls his own sheep by name, and leads them out.

4 "When he puts forth all his own, he goes before them, and the sheep follow him because they know his voice.

5 "And a stranger they simply will not follow, but will flee from him, because they do not know the voice of strangers."

6 This figure of speech Jesus spoke to them, but they did not understand what those things were which He had been saying to them.

7 Jesus therefore said to them again, "Truly, truly, I say to you, I am the door of the sheep.

8 "All who came before Me are thieves and robbers, but the sheep did not hear them.

9 "I am the door; if anyone enters through Me, he shall be saved, and shall go in and out, and find pasture.

10 "The thief comes only to steal, and kill, and destroy; I came that they might have life, and might have *it* abundantly.

11 "I am the good shepherd; the good shepherd lays down His life for the sheep.

12 "He who is a hireling, and not a shepherd, who is not the owner of the sheep, beholds the wolf coming, and leaves the sheep, and flees, and the wolf snatches them, and scatters *them*.

13 "*He flees* because he is a hireling, and is not concerned about the sheep.

14 "I am the good shepherd; and I know My own, and My own know Me,

15 even as the Father knows Me and I know the Father; and I lay down My life for the sheep.

16 "And I have other sheep, which are not of this fold; I must bring them also, and they shall hear My voice; and they shall become one flock *with* one shepherd.

17 "For this reason the Father loves Me, because I lay down My life that I may take it again.

18 "No one [19]has taken it away from Me, but I lay it down on My own initiative. I have authority to lay it down, and I have authority to take it up again. This commandment I received from My Father."

19 There arose a division again among the Jews because of these words.

20 And many of them were saying, "He has a demon and is insane. Why do you listen to Him?"

21 Others were saying, "These are not the sayings of one demon-possessed. A demon cannot open the eyes of the blind, can he?"

22 At that time the Feast of the Dedication took place at Jerusalem;

23 it was winter, and Jesus was walking in the temple in the portico of Solomon.

24 The Jews therefore gathered around Him, and were saying to Him, "How long will You keep us

[19] Many Gr. mss. read *takes*

in suspense? If You are the Christ, tell us plainly."

25 Jesus answered them, "I told you, and you do not believe; the works that I do in My Father's name, these bear witness of Me.

26 "But you do not believe, because you are not of My sheep.

27 "My sheep hear My voice, and I know them, and they follow Me;

28 and I give eternal life to them, and they shall never perish; and no one shall snatch them out of My hand.

29 "[20]My Father, who has given *them* to Me, is greater than all; and no one is able to snatch them out of the Father's hand.

30 "I and the Father are one."

31 The Jews took up stones again to stone Him.

32 Jesus answered them, "I showed you many good works from the Father; for which of them are you stoning Me?"

33 The Jews answered Him, "For a good work we do not stone You, but for blasphemy; and because You, being a man, make Yourself out *to be* God."

34 Jesus answered them, "Has it not been written in your Law, 'I SAID, YOU ARE GODS'?

35 "If he called them gods, to whom the word of God came (and the Scripture cannot be broken),

36 do you say of Him, whom the Father sanctified and sent into the world, 'You are blaspheming,' because I said, 'I am the Son of God'?

37 "If I do not do the works of My Father, do not believe Me;

38 but if I do them, though you

do not believe Me, believe the works, that you may know and understand that the Father is in Me, and I in the Father."

39 Therefore they were seeking again to seize Him, and He eluded their grasp.

40 And He went away again beyond the Jordan to the place where John was first baptizing, and He was staying there.

41 And many came to Him and were saying, "While John performed no sign, yet everything John said about this man was true."

42 And many believed in Him there.

CHAPTER 11

NOW a certain man was sick, Lazarus of Bethany, the village of Mary and her sister Martha.

2 And it was the Mary who anointed the Lord with ointment, and wiped His feet with her hair, whose brother Lazarus was sick.

3 The sisters therefore sent to Him, saying, "Lord, behold, he whom You love is sick."

4 But when Jesus heard it, He said, "This sickness is not unto death, but for the glory of God, that the Son of God may be glorified by it."

5 Now Jesus loved Martha, and her sister, and Lazarus.

6 When therefore He heard that he was sick, He stayed then two days *longer* in the place where He was.

7 Then after this He *said to the disciples, "Let us go to Judea again."

8 The disciples *said to Him, "Rabbi, the Jews were just now

[20] Some early mss. read *What My Father has given Me is greater than all*

seeking to stone You, and are You going there again?"

9 Jesus answered, "Are there not twelve hours in the day? If anyone walks in the day, he does not stumble, because he sees the light of this world.

10 "But if anyone walks in the night, he stumbles, because the light is not in him."

11 This He said, and after that He *said to them, "Our friend Lazarus has fallen asleep; but I go, that I may awaken him out of sleep."

12 The disciples therefore said to Him, "Lord, if he has fallen asleep, he will recover."

13 Now Jesus had spoken of his death, but they thought that He was speaking of literal sleep.

14 Then Jesus therefore said to them plainly, "Lazarus is dead,

15 and I am glad for your sakes that I was not there, so that you may believe; but let us go to him."

16 Thomas therefore, who is called Didymus, said to his fellow disciples, "Let us also go, that we may die with Him."

17 So when Jesus came, He found that he had already been in the tomb four days.

18 Now Bethany was near Jerusalem, about two miles off;

19 and many of the Jews had come to Martha and Mary, to console them concerning their brother.

20 Martha therefore, when she heard that Jesus was coming, went to meet Him; but Mary still sat in the house.

21 Martha therefore said to Jesus, "Lord, if You had been here, my brother would not have died.

22 "Even now I know that whatever You ask of God, God will give You."

23 Jesus *said to her, "Your brother shall rise again."

24 Martha *said to Him, "I know that he will rise again in the resurrection on the last day."

25 Jesus said to her, "I am the resurrection and the life; he who believes in Me shall live even if he dies,

26 and everyone who lives and believes in Me shall never die. Do you believe this?"

27 She *said to Him, "Yes, Lord; I have believed that You are the Christ, the Son of God, even He who comes into the world."

28 And when she had said this, she went away, and called Mary her sister, saying secretly, "The Teacher is here, and is calling for you."

29 And when she heard it, she *arose quickly, and was coming to Him.

30 Now Jesus had not yet come into the village, but was still in the place where Martha met Him.

31 The Jews then who were with her in the house, and consoling her, when they saw that Mary rose up quickly and went out, followed her, supposing that she was going to the tomb to weep there.

32 Therefore, when Mary came where Jesus was, she saw Him, and fell at His feet, saying to Him, "Lord, if You had been here, my brother would not have died."

33 When Jesus therefore saw her weeping, and the Jews who came with her, also weeping, He was deeply moved in spirit, and was troubled,

34 and said, "Where have you laid him?" They *said to Him, "Lord, come and see."

35 Jesus wept.

36 And so the Jews were saying, "Behold how He loved him!"

37 But some of them said, "Could not this man, who opened the eyes of him who was blind, have kept this man also from dying?"

38 Jesus therefore again being deeply moved within, *came to the tomb. Now it was a cave, and a stone was lying against it.

39 Jesus *said, "Remove the stone." Martha, the sister of the deceased, *said to Him, "Lord, by this time there will be a stench, for he has been *dead* four days."

40 Jesus *said to her, "Did I not say to you, if you believe, you will see the glory of God?"

41 And so they removed the stone. And Jesus raised His eyes, and said, "Father, I thank Thee that Thou heardest Me.

42 "And I knew that Thou hearest Me always; but because of the people standing around I said it, that they may believe that Thou didst send Me."

43 And when He had said these things, He cried out with a loud voice, "Lazarus, come forth."

44 He who had died came forth, bound hand and foot with wrappings; and his face was wrapped around with a cloth. Jesus *said to them, "Unbind him, and let him go."

45 Many therefore of the Jews, who had come to Mary and beheld what He had done, believed in Him.

46 But some of them went away to the Pharisees, and told them the things which Jesus had done.

47 Therefore the chief priests and the Pharisees convened a council, and were saying, "What are we doing? For this man is performing many signs.

48 "If we let Him go on like this, all men will believe in Him, and the Romans will come and take away both our place and our nation."

49 But a certain one of them, Caiaphas, who was high priest that year, said to them, "You know nothing at all,

50 nor do you take into account that it is expedient for you that one man should die for the people, and that the whole nation should not perish."

51 Now this he did not say on his own initiative; but being high priest that year, he prophesied that Jesus was going to die for the nation,

52 and not for the nation only, but that He might also gather together into one the children of God who are scattered abroad.

53 So from that day on they planned together to kill Him.

54 Jesus therefore no longer continued to walk publicly among the Jews, but went away from there to the country near the wilderness, into a city called Ephraim; and there He stayed with the disciples.

55 Now the Passover of the Jews was at hand, and many went up to Jerusalem out of the country before the Passover, to purify themselves.

56 Therefore they were seeking for Jesus, and were saying to one another, as they stood in the temple, "What do you think; that He will not come to the feast at all?"

57 Now the chief priests and the Pharisees had given orders that if anyone knew where He was, he should report it, that they might seize Him.

CHAPTER 12

JESUS, therefore, six days before the Passover, came to Bethany where Lazarus was, whom Jesus had raised from the dead.

2 So they made Him a supper there, and Martha was serving; but Lazarus was one of those reclining *at the table* with Him.

3 Mary therefore took a pound of very costly perfume of pure nard, and anointed the feet of Jesus, and wiped His feet with her hair; and the house was filled with the fragrance of the perfume.

4 But Judas Iscariot, one of His disciples, who was intending to betray Him, *said,

5 "Why was this perfume not sold for 21three hundred denarii, and given to poor *people?*"

6 Now he said this, not because he was concerned about the poor, but because he was a thief, and as he had the money box, he used to pilfer what was put into it.

7 Jesus therefore said, "Let her alone, in order that she may keep 22it for the day of My burial.

8 "For the poor you always have with you, but you do not always have Me."

9 The great multitude therefore of the Jews learned that He was there; and they came, not for Jesus' sake only, but that they might also see Lazarus, whom He raised from the dead.

10 But the chief priests took counsel that they might put Lazarus to death also;

11 because on account of him many of the Jews were going away, and were believing in Jesus.

12 On the next day the great multitude who had come to the feast, when they heard that Jesus was coming to Jerusalem,

13 took the branches of the palm trees, and went out to meet Him, and *began* to cry out, "Hosanna! BLESSED IS HE WHO COMES IN THE NAME OF THE LORD, even the King of Israel."

14 And Jesus, finding a young donkey, sat on it; as it is written,

15 "FEAR NOT, DAUGHTER OF ZION; BEHOLD, YOUR KING IS COMING, SEATED ON A DONKEY'S COLT."

16 These things His disciples did not understand at the first; but when Jesus was glorified, then they remembered that these things were written of Him, and that they had done these things to Him.

17 And so the multitude who were with Him when He called Lazarus out of the tomb, and raised him from the dead, were bearing Him witness.

18 For this cause also the multitude went and met Him, because they heard that He had performed this sign.

19 The Pharisees therefore said to one another, "You see that you are not doing any good; look, the world has gone after Him."

20 Now there were certain Greeks among those who were going up to worship at the feast;

21 these therefore came to

21 Equivalent to 11 months' wages
22 I.e., The custom of anointing for burial

Philip, who was from Bethsaida of Galilee, and *began to* ask him, saying, "Sir, we wish to see Jesus."

22 Philip *came and *told Andrew; Andrew and Philip *came, and they *told Jesus.

23 And Jesus *answered them, saying, "The hour has come for the Son of Man to be glorified.

24 "Truly, truly, I say to you, unless a grain of wheat falls into the earth and dies, it remains by itself alone; but if it dies, it bears much fruit.

25 "He who loves his life loses it; and he who hates his life in this world shall keep it to life eternal.

26 "If anyone serves Me, let him follow Me; and where I am, there shall My servant also be; if anyone serves Me, the Father will honor him.

27 "Now My soul has become troubled; and what shall I say, 'Father, save Me from this hour'? But for this purpose I came to this hour.

28 "Father, glorify Thy name." There came therefore a voice out of heaven: "I have both glorified it, and will glorify it again."

29 The multitude therefore, who stood by and heard it, were saying that it had thundered; others were saying, "An angel has spoken to Him."

30 Jesus answered and said, "This voice has not come for My sake, but for your sakes.

31 "Now judgment is upon this world; now the ruler of this world shall be cast out.

32 "And I, if I be lifted up from the earth, will draw all men to Myself."

33 But He was saying this to indicate the kind of death by which He was to die.

34 The multitude therefore answered Him, "We have heard out of the Law that the Christ is to remain forever; and how can You say, 'The Son of Man must be lifted up'? Who is this Son of Man?"

35 Jesus therefore said to them, "For a little while longer the light is among you. Walk while you have the light, that darkness may not overtake you; he who walks in the darkness does not know where he goes.

36 "While you have the light, believe in the light, in order that you may become sons of light." These things Jesus spoke, and He departed and hid Himself from them.

37 But though He had performed so many signs before them, *yet* they were not believing in Him;

38 that the word of Isaiah the prophet might be fulfilled, which he spoke, "LORD, WHO HAS BELIEVED OUR REPORT? AND TO WHOM HAS THE ARM OF THE LORD BEEN REVEALED?"

39 For this cause they could not believe, for Isaiah said again,

40 "HE HAS BLINDED THEIR EYES, AND HE HARDENED THEIR HEART; LEST THEY SEE WITH THEIR EYES, AND PERCEIVE WITH THEIR HEART, AND BE CONVERTED, AND I HEAL THEM."

41 These things Isaiah said, because he saw His glory, and he spoke of Him.

42 Nevertheless many even of the rulers believed in Him, but because of the Pharisees they were not confessing *Him*, lest they should be put out of the synagogue;

43 for they loved the approval of men rather than the approval of God.

44 And Jesus cried out and said, "He who believes in Me does not believe in Me, but in Him who sent Me.

45 "And he who beholds Me beholds the One who sent Me.

46 "I have come *as* light into the world, that everyone who believes in Me may not remain in darkness.

47 "And if anyone hears My sayings, and does not keep them, I do not judge him; for I did not come to judge the world, but to save the world.

48 "He who rejects Me, and does not receive My sayings, has one who judges him; the word I spoke is what will judge him at the last day.

49 "For I did not speak on My own initiative, but the Father Himself who sent Me has given Me commandment, what to say, and what to speak.

50 "And I know that His commandment is eternal life; therefore the things I speak, I speak just as the Father has told Me."

CHAPTER 13

NOW before the Feast of the Passover, Jesus knowing that His hour had come that He should depart out of this world to the Father, having loved His own who were in the world, He loved them to the end.

2 And during supper, the devil having already put into the heart of Judas Iscariot, *the son* of Simon, to betray Him,

3 *Jesus*, knowing that the Father had given all things into His hands, and that He had come forth from God, and was going back to God,

4 *rose from supper, and *laid aside His garments; and taking a towel, He girded Himself about.

5 Then He *poured water into the basin, and began to wash the disciples' feet, and to wipe them with the towel with which He was girded.

6 And so He *came to Simon Peter. He *said to Him, "Lord, do You wash my feet?"

7 Jesus answered and said to him, "What I do you do not realize now, but you shall understand hereafter."

8 Peter *said to Him, "Never shall You wash my feet!" Jesus answered him, "If I do not wash you, you have no part with Me."

9 Simon Peter *said to Him, "Lord, not my feet only, but also my hands and my head."

10 Jesus *said to him, "He who has bathed needs only to wash his feet, but is completely clean; and you are clean, but not all *of you."*

11 For He knew the one who was betraying Him; for this reason He said, "Not all of you are clean."

12 And so when He had washed their feet, and taken His garments, and reclined *at the table* again, He said to them, "Do you know what I have done to you?

13 "You call Me Teacher and Lord; and you are right, for so I am.

14 "If I then, the Lord and the Teacher, washed your feet, you also ought to wash one another's feet.

15 "For I gave you an example that you also should do as I did to you.

16"Truly, truly, I say to you, a slave is not greater than his master; neither is one who is sent greater than the one who sent him.

17"If you know these things, you are blessed if you do them.

18"I do not speak of all of you. I know the ones I have chosen; but it is that the Scripture may be fulfilled, 'HE WHO EATS MY BREAD HAS LIFTED UP HIS HEEL AGAINST ME.'

19"From now on I am telling you before it comes to pass, so that when it does occur, you may believe that I am He.

20"Truly, truly, I say to you, he who receives whomever I send receives Me; and he who receives Me receives Him who sent Me."

21 When Jesus had said this, He became troubled in spirit, and testified, and said, "Truly, truly, I say to you, that one of you will betray Me."

22 The disciples began looking at one another, at a loss to know of which one He was speaking.

23 There was reclining on Jesus' breast one of His disciples, whom Jesus loved.

24 Simon Peter therefore *gestured to him, and *said to him, "Tell us who it is of whom He is speaking."

25 He, leaning back thus on Jesus' breast, *said to Him, "Lord, who is it?"

26 Jesus therefore *answered, "That is the one for whom I shall dip the morsel and give it to him." So when He had dipped the morsel, He *took and *gave it to Judas, the son of Simon Iscariot.

27 And after the morsel, Satan then entered into him. Jesus therefore *said to him, "What you do, do quickly."

28 Now no one of those reclining at the table knew for what purpose He had said this to him.

29 For some were supposing, because Judas had the money box, that Jesus was saying to him, "Buy the things we have need of for the feast"; or else, that he should give something to the poor.

30 And so after receiving the morsel he went out immediately; and it was night.

31 When therefore he had gone out, Jesus *said, "Now is the Son of Man glorified, and God is glorified in Him;

32 if God is glorified in Him, God will also glorify Him in Himself, and will glorify Him immediately.

33"Little children, I am with you a little while longer. You shall seek Me; and as I said to the Jews, I now say to you also, 'Where I am going, you cannot come.'

34"A new commandment I give to you, that you love one another, even as I have loved you, that you also love one another.

35"By this all men will know that you are My disciples, if you have love for one another."

36 Simon Peter *said to Him, "Lord, where are You going?" Jesus answered, "Where I go, you cannot follow Me now; but you shall follow later."

37 Peter *said to Him, "Lord, why can I not follow You right now? I will lay down my life for You."

38 Jesus *answered, "Will you lay down your life for Me? Truly, truly, I say to you, a cock shall

not crow, until you deny Me three times.

CHAPTER 14

"LET not your heart be troubled; [23]believe in God, believe also in Me.

2"In My Father's house are many dwelling places; if it were not so, I would have told you; for I go to prepare a place for you.

3"And if I go and prepare a place for you, I will come again, and receive you to Myself; that where I am, *there* you may be also.

4"[24]And you know the way where I am going."

5 Thomas *said to Him, "Lord, we do not know where You are going, how do we know the way?"

6 Jesus *said to him, "I am the way, and the truth, and the life; no one comes to the Father, but through Me.

7"If you had known Me, you would have known My Father also; from now on you know Him, and have seen Him."

8 Philip *said to Him, "Lord, show us the Father, and it is enough for us."

9 Jesus *said to him, "Have I been so long with you, and *yet* you have not come to know Me, Philip? He who has seen Me has seen the Father; how do you say, 'Show us the Father'?

10"Do you not believe that I am in the Father, and the Father is in Me? The words that I say to you I do not speak on My own initiative, but the Father abiding in Me does His works.

11"Believe Me that I am in the Father, and the Father in Me; otherwise believe on account of the works themselves.

12"Truly, truly, I say to you, he who believes in Me, the works that I do shall he do also; and greater *works* than these shall he do; because I go to the Father.

13"And whatever you ask in My name, that will I do, that the Father may be glorified in the Son.

14"If you ask Me anything in My name, I will do *it.*

15"If you love Me, you will keep My commandments.

16"And I will ask the Father, and He will give you another Helper, that He may be with you forever;

17 *that is* the Spirit of truth, whom the world cannot receive, because it does not behold Him or know Him, *but* you know Him because He abides with you, and will be in you.

18"I will not leave you as orphans; I will come to you.

19"After a little while the world will behold Me no more; but you *will* behold Me; because I live, you shall live also.

20"In that day you shall know that I am in My Father, and you in Me, and I in you.

21"He who has My commandments and keeps them, he it is who loves Me; and he who loves Me shall be loved by My Father, and I will love him, and will disclose Myself to him."

22 Judas (not Iscariot) *said to Him, "Lord, what then has happened that You are going to disclose Yourself to us, and not to the world?"

23 Jesus answered and said to him, "If anyone loves Me, he will

[23] Or, *you believe in God*
[24] Many ancient authorities read *And where I go you know, and the way you know*

keep My word; and My Father will love him, and We will come to him, and make Our abode with him.

24"He who does not love Me does not keep My words; and the word which you hear is not Mine, but the Father's who sent Me.

25"These things I have spoken to you, while abiding with you.

26"But the Helper, the Holy Spirit, whom the Father will send in My name, He will teach you all things, and bring to your remembrance all that I said to you.

27"Peace I leave with you; My peace I give to you; not as the world gives, do I give to you. Let not your heart be troubled, nor let it be fearful.

28"You heard that I said to you, 'I go away, and I will come to you.' If you loved Me, you would have rejoiced, because I go to the Father; for the Father is greater than I.

29"And now I have told you before it comes to pass, that when it comes to pass, you may believe.

30"I will not speak much more with you, for the ruler of the world is coming, and he has nothing in Me;

31 but that the world may know that I love the Father, and as the Father gave Me commandment, even so I do. Arise, let us go from here.

CHAPTER 15

"I AM the true vine, and My Father is the vinedresser.

2"Every branch in Me that does not bear fruit, He takes away; and every branch that bears fruit, He 25prunes it, that it

may bear more fruit.

3"You are already clean because of the word which I have spoken to you.

4"Abide in Me, and I in you. As the branch cannot bear fruit of itself, unless it abides in the vine, so neither can you, unless you abide in Me.

5"I am the vine, you are the branches; he who abides in Me, and I in him, he bears much fruit; for apart from Me you can do nothing.

6"If anyone does not abide in Me, he is thrown away as a branch, and dries up; and they gather them, and cast them into the fire, and they are burned.

7"If you abide in Me, and My words abide in you, ask whatever you wish, and it shall be done for you.

8"By this is My Father glorified, that you bear much fruit, and so prove to be My disciples.

9"Just as the Father has loved Me, I have also loved you; abide in My love.

10"If you keep My commandments, you will abide in My love; just as I have kept My Father's commandments, and abide in His love.

11"These things I have spoken to you, that My joy may be in you, and that your joy may be made full.

12"This is My commandment, that you love one another, just as I have loved you.

13"Greater love has no one than this, that one lay down his life for his friends.

14"You are My friends, if you do what I command you.

15"No longer do I call you slaves, for the slave does not

25 Lit., cleanses

know what his master is doing; but I have called you friends, for all things that I have heard from My Father I have made known to you.

16"You did not choose Me, but I chose you, and appointed you, that you should go and bear fruit, and *that* your fruit should remain, that whatever you ask of the Father in My name, He may give to you.

17"This I command you, that you love one another.

18"If the world hates you, you know that it has hated Me before *it hated* you.

19"If you were of the world, the world would love its own; but because you are not of the world, but I chose you out of the world, therefore the world hates you.

20"Remember the word that I said to you, 'A slave is not greater than his master.' If they persecuted Me, they will also persecute you; if they kept My word, they will keep yours also.

21"But all these things they will do to you for My name's sake, because they do not know the One who sent Me.

22"If I had not come and spoken to them, they would not have sin, but now they have no excuse for their sin.

23"He who hates Me hates My Father also.

24"If I had not done among them the works which no one else did, they would not have sin; but now they have both seen and hated Me and My Father as well.

25"But *they have done this* in order that the word may be fulfilled that is written in their Law, 'THEY HATED ME WITHOUT A CAUSE.'

26"When the Helper comes, whom I will send to you from the Father, *that is* the Spirit of truth, who proceeds from the Father, He will bear witness of Me,

27 and you *will* bear witness also, because you have been with Me from the beginning.

CHAPTER 16

"THESE things I have spoken to you, that you may be kept from stumbling.

2"They will make you outcasts from the synagogue, but an hour is coming for everyone who kills you to think that he is offering service to God.

3"And these things they will do, because they have not known the Father, or Me.

4"But these things I have spoken to you, that when their hour comes, you may remember that I told you of them. And these things I did not say to you at the beginning, because I was with you.

5"But now I am going to Him who sent Me; and none of you asks Me, 'Where are You going?'

6"But because I have said these things to you, sorrow has filled your heart.

7"But I tell you the truth, it is to your advantage that I go away; for if I do not go away, the Helper shall not come to you; but if I go, I will send Him to you.

8"And He, when He comes, will convict the world concerning sin, and righteousness, and judgment;

9 concerning sin, because they do not believe in Me;

10 and concerning righteousness, because I go to the Father, and you no longer behold Me;

11 and concerning judgment, because the ruler of this world has been judged.

12 "I have many more things to say to you, but you cannot bear *them* now.

13 "But when He, the Spirit of truth, comes, He will guide you into all the truth; for He will not speak on His own initiative, but whatever He hears, He will speak; and He will disclose to you what is to come.

14 "He shall glorify Me; for He shall take of Mine, and shall disclose *it* to you.

15 "All things that the Father has are Mine; therefore I said, that He takes of Mine, and will disclose *it* to you.

16 "A little while, and you will no longer behold Me; and again a little while, and you will see Me."

17 *Some* of His disciples therefore said to one another, "What is this thing He is telling us, 'A little while, and you will not behold Me; and again a little while, and you will see Me'; and, because I go to the Father'?"

18 And so they were saying, "What is this that He says, 'A little while'? We do not know what He is talking about."

19 Jesus knew that they wished to question Him, and He said to them, "Are you deliberating together about this, that I said, 'A little while, and you will not behold Me, and again a little while, and you will see Me'?

20 "Truly, truly, I say to you, that you will weep and lament, but the world will rejoice; you will be sorrowful, but your sorrow will be turned to joy.

21 "Whenever a woman is in travail she has sorrow, because her hour has come; but when she gives birth to the child, she remembers the anguish no more, for joy that a child has been born into the world.

22 "Therefore you too now have sorrow; but I will see you again, and your heart will rejoice, and no one takes your joy away from you.

23 "And in that day you will ask Me no question. Truly, truly, I say to you, if you shall ask the Father for anything, He will give it to you in My name.

24 "Until now you have asked for nothing in My name; ask, and you will receive, that your joy may be made full.

25 "These things I have spoken to you in figurative language; an hour is coming when I will speak no more to you in figurative language, but will tell you plainly of the Father.

26 "In that day you will ask in My name, and I do not say to you that I will request the Father on your behalf;

27 for the Father Himself loves you, because you have loved Me, and have believed that I came forth from the Father.

28 "I came forth from the Father, and have come into the world; I am leaving the world again, and going to the Father."

29 His disciples *said, "Lo, now You are speaking plainly, and are not using a figure of speech.

30 "Now we know that You know all things, and have no need for anyone to question You; by this we believe that You came from God."

31 Jesus answered them, "Do you now believe?

32 "Behold, an hour is coming, and has *already* come, for you to

be scattered, each to his own *home,* and to leave Me alone; and *yet* I am not alone, because the Father is with Me.

33"These things I have spoken to you, that in Me you may have peace. In the world you have tribulation, but take courage; I have overcome the world."

CHAPTER 17

THESE things Jesus spoke; and lifting up His eyes to heaven, He said, "Father, the hour has come; glorify Thy Son, that the Son may glorify Thee,

2 even as Thou gavest Him authority over all mankind, that to all whom Thou hast given Him, He may give eternal life.

3"And this is eternal life, that they may know Thee, the only true God, and Jesus Christ whom Thou hast sent.

4"I glorified Thee on the earth, having accomplished the work which Thou hast given Me to do.

5"And now, glorify Thou Me together with Thyself, Father, with the glory which I had with Thee before the world was.

6"I manifested Thy name to the men whom Thou gavest Me out of the world; Thine they were, and Thou gavest them to Me, and they have kept Thy word.

7"Now they have come to know that everything Thou hast given Me is from Thee;

8 for the words which Thou gavest Me I have given to them; and they received *them,* and truly understood that I came forth from Thee, and they believed that Thou didst send Me.

9"I ask on their behalf; I do not ask on behalf of the world, but of those whom Thou hast given Me; for they are Thine;

10 and all things that are Mine are Thine, and Thine are Mine; and I have been glorified in them.

11"And I am no more in the world; and *yet* they themselves are in the world, and I come to Thee. Holy Father, keep them in Thy name, *the name* which Thou hast given Me, that they may be one, even as We *are.*

12"While I was with them, I was keeping them in Thy name which Thou hast given Me; and I guarded them, and not one of them perished but the son of perdition, that the Scripture might be fulfilled.

13"But now I come to Thee; and these things I speak in the world, that they may have My joy made full in themselves.

14"I have given them Thy word; and the world has hated them, because they are not of the world, even as I am not of the world.

15"I do not ask Thee to take them out of the world, but to keep them from the evil *one.*

16"They are not of the world, even as I am not of the world.

17"Sanctify them in the truth; Thy word is truth.

18"As Thou didst send Me into the world, I also have sent them into the world.

19"And for their sakes I sanctify Myself, that they themselves also may be sanctified in truth.

20"I do not ask in behalf of these alone, but for those also who believe in Me through their word;

21 that they may all be one; even as Thou, Father, *art* in Me, and I in Thee, that they also may be in Us; that the world may believe that Thou didst send Me.

22"And the glory which Thou hast given Me I have given to them; that they may be one, just as We are one;

23 I in them, and Thou in Me, that they may be perfected in unity, that the world may know that Thou didst send Me, and didst love them, even as Thou didst love Me.

24"Father, I desire that they also, whom Thou hast given Me, be with Me where I am, in order that they may behold My glory, which Thou hast given Me; for Thou didst love Me before the foundation of the world.

25"O righteous Father, although the world has not known Thee, yet I have known Thee; and these have known that Thou didst send Me;

26 and I have made Thy name known to them, and will make it known; that the love wherewith Thou didst love Me may be in them, and I in them."

CHAPTER 18

WHEN Jesus had spoken these words, He went forth with His disciples over the ravine of the Kidron, where there was a garden, into which He Himself entered, and His disciples.

2 Now Judas also, who was betraying Him, knew the place; for Jesus had often met there with His disciples.

3 Judas then, having received the *Roman* cohort, and officers from the chief priests and the Pharisees, *came there with lanterns and torches and weapons.

4 Jesus therefore, knowing all the things that were coming upon Him, went forth, and *said to them, "Whom do you seek?"

5 They answered Him, "Jesus the Nazarene." He *said to them, "I am *He*." And Judas also who was betraying Him, was standing with them.

6 When therefore He said to them, "I am *He*," they drew back, and fell to the ground.

7 Again therefore He asked them, "Whom do you seek?" And they said, "Jesus the Nazarene."

8 Jesus answered, "I told you that I am *He*; if therefore you seek Me, let these go their way;"

9 that the word might be fulfilled which He spoke, "Of those whom Thou hast given Me I lost not one."

10 Simon Peter therefore having a sword, drew it, and struck the high priest's slave, and cut off his right ear; and the slave's name was Malchus.

11 Jesus therefore said to Peter, "Put the sword into the sheath; the cup which the Father has given Me, shall I not drink it?"

12 So the *Roman* cohort and the commander, and the officers of the Jews, arrested Jesus and bound Him,

13 and led Him to Annas first; for he was father-in-law of Caiaphas, who was high priest that year.

14 Now Caiaphas was the one who had advised the Jews that it was expedient for one man to die on behalf of the people.

15 And Simon Peter was following Jesus, and *so was* another disciple. Now that disciple was known to the high priest, and entered with Jesus into the court of the high priest,

16 but Peter was standing at the door outside. So the other disciple, who was known to the

high priest, went out and spoke to the doorkeeper, and brought in Peter.

17 The slave-girl therefore who kept the door *said to Peter, "You are not also one of this man's disciples, are you?" He *said, "I am not."

18 Now the slaves and the officers were standing there, having made a charcoal fire, for it was cold and they were warming themselves; and Peter also was with them, standing and warming himself.

19 The high priest therefore questioned Jesus about His disciples, and about His teaching.

20 Jesus answered him, "I have spoken openly to the world; I always taught in synagogues, and in the temple, where all the Jews come together; and I spoke nothing in secret.

21 "Why do you question Me? Question those who have heard what I spoke to them; behold, these know what I said."

22 And when He had said this, one of the officers standing by gave Jesus a blow, saying, "Is that the way You answer the high priest?"

23 Jesus answered him, "If I have spoken wrongly, bear witness of the wrong; but if rightly, why do you strike Me?"

24 Annas therefore sent Him bound to Caiaphas the high priest.

25 Now Simon Peter was standing and warming himself. They said therefore to him, "You are not also one of His disciples, are you?" He denied it, and said, "I am not."

26 One of the slaves of the high priest, being a relative of the one whose ear Peter cut off, *said,

"Did I not see you in the garden with Him?"

27 Peter therefore denied it again; and immediately a cock crowed.

28 They *led Jesus therefore from Caiaphas into the 26Praetorium, and it was early; and they themselves did not enter into the Praetorium in order that they might not be defiled, but might eat the Passover.

29 Pilate therefore went out to them, and *said, "What accusation do you bring against this Man?"

30 They answered and said to him, "If this Man were not an evildoer, we would not have delivered Him up to you."

31 Pilate therefore said to them, "Take Him yourselves, and judge Him according to your law." The Jews said to him, "We are not permitted to put anyone to death,"

32 that the word of Jesus might be fulfilled, which He spoke, signifying by what kind of death He was about to die.

33 Pilate therefore entered again into the 26Praetorium, and summoned Jesus, and said to Him, "Are You the King of the Jews?"

34 Jesus answered, "Are you saying this on your own initiative, or did others tell you about Me?"

35 Pilate answered, "I am not a Jew, am I? Your own nation and the chief priests delivered You up to me; what have You done?"

36 Jesus answered, "My kingdom is not of this world. If My kingdom were of this world, then My servants would be fighting,

26 I.e., governor's official residence

that I might not be delivered up to the Jews; but as it is, My kingdom is not [27]of this realm."

37 Pilate therefore said to Him, "So You are a king?" Jesus answered, "You say *correctly* that I am a king. For this I have been born, and for this I have come into the world, to bear witness to the truth. Everyone who is of the truth hears My voice."

38 Pilate *said to Him, "What is truth?"

And when he had said this, he went out again to the Jews, and *said to them, "I find no guilt in Him.

39"But you have a custom, that I should release someone for you at the Passover; do you wish then that I release for you the King of the Jews?"

40 Therefore they cried out again, saying, "Not this Man, but Barabbas." Now Barabbas was a robber.

CHAPTER 19

THEN Pilate therefore took Jesus, and scourged Him.

2 And the soldiers wove a crown of thorns and put it on His head, and arrayed Him in a purple robe;

3 and they *began* to come up to Him, and say, "Hail, King of the Jews!" and to give Him blows in the face.

4 And Pilate came out again, and *said to them, "Behold, I am bringing Him out to you, that you may know that I find no guilt in Him."

5 Jesus therefore came out, wearing the crown of thorns and the purple robe. And *Pilate* *said to them, "Behold, the Man!"

6 When therefore the chief priests and the officers saw Him, they cried out, saying, "Crucify, crucify!" Pilate *said to them, "Take Him yourselves, and crucify Him, for I find no guilt in Him."

7 The Jews answered him, "We have a law, and by that law He ought to die because He made Himself out *to be* the Son of God."

8 When Pilate therefore heard this statement, he was the more afraid;

9 and he entered into the [28]Praetorium again, and *said to Jesus, "Where are You from?" But Jesus gave him no answer.

10 Pilate therefore *said to Him, "You do not speak to me? Do You not know that I have authority to release You, and I have authority to crucify You?"

11 Jesus answered, "You would have no authority over Me, unless it had been given you from above; for this reason he who delivered Me up to you has *the* greater sin."

12 As a result of this Pilate made efforts to release Him, but the Jews cried out, saying, "If you release this Man, you are no friend of Caesar; everyone who makes himself out *to be* a king opposes Caesar."

13 When Pilate therefore heard these words, he brought Jesus out, and sat down on the judgment seat at a place called The Pavement, but in Hebrew, Gabbatha.

14 Now it was the day of preparation for the Passover; it was about the [29]sixth hour. And he

---

[27] Lit., *from here*
[28] I.e., governor's official residence
[29] Perhaps 6 a.m. (Roman time)

*said to the Jews, "Behold, your King!"

15 They therefore cried out, "Away with *Him*, away with *Him*, crucify Him!" Pilate *said to them, "Shall I crucify your King?" The chief priests answered, "We have no king but Caesar."

16 So he then delivered Him to them to be crucified.

17 They took Jesus therefore, and He went out, bearing His own cross, to the place called the Place of a Skull, which is called in Hebrew, Golgotha.

18 There they crucified Him, and with Him two other men, one on either side, and Jesus in between.

19 And Pilate wrote an inscription also, and put it on the cross. And it was written, "JESUS THE NAZARENE, THE KING OF THE JEWS."

20 Therefore this inscription many of the Jews read, for the place where Jesus was crucified was near the city; and it was written in Hebrew, Latin, *and* in Greek.

21 And so the chief priests of the Jews were saying to Pilate, "Do not write, 'The King of the Jews'; but that He said, 'I am King of the Jews.'"

22 Pilate answered, "What I have written I have written."

23 The soldiers therefore, when they had crucified Jesus, took His outer garments and made four parts, a part to every soldier and *also* the [30]tunic; now the tunic was seamless, woven in one piece.

24 They said therefore to one another, "Let us not tear it, but cast lots for it, *to decide* whose it shall be"; that the Scripture

might be fulfilled, "THEY DIVIDED MY OUTER GARMENTS AMONG THEM, AND FOR MY CLOTHING THEY CAST LOTS."

25 Therefore the soldiers did these things. But there were standing by the cross of Jesus His mother, and His mother's sister, Mary the *wife* of Clopas, and Mary Magdalene.

26 When Jesus therefore saw His mother, and the disciple whom He loved standing nearby, He *said to His mother, "Woman, behold, your son!"

27 Then He *said to the disciple, "Behold, your mother!" And from that hour the disciple took her into his own *household.*

28 After this, Jesus, knowing that all things had already been accomplished, in order that the Scripture might be fulfilled, *said, "I am thirsty."

29 A jar full of sour wine was standing there; so they put a sponge full of the sour wine upon *a branch of* hyssop, and brought it up to His mouth.

30 When Jesus therefore had received the sour wine, He said, "It is finished!" And He bowed His head, and gave up His spirit.

31 The Jews therefore, because it was the day of preparation, so that the bodies should not remain on the cross on the Sabbath (for that Sabbath was a high *day*), asked Pilate that their legs might be broken, and *that* they might be taken away.

32 The soldiers therefore came, and broke the legs of the first man, and of the other man who was crucified with Him;

33 but coming to Jesus, when

[30] Gr., *khiton*, the garment worn next to the skin

they saw that He was already dead, they did not break His legs;

34 but one of the soldiers pierced His side with a spear, and immediately there came out blood and water.

35 And he who has seen has borne witness, and his witness is true; and he knows that he is telling the truth, so that you also may believe.

36 For these things came to pass, that the Scripture might be fulfilled, "NOT A BONE OF HIM SHALL BE BROKEN."

37 And again another Scripture says, "THEY SHALL LOOK ON HIM WHOM THEY PIERCED."

38 And after these things Joseph of Arimathea, being a disciple of Jesus, but a secret one, for fear of the Jews, asked Pilate that he might take away the body of Jesus; and Pilate granted permission. He came therefore, and took away His body.

39 And Nicodemus came also, who had first come to Him by night; bringing a mixture of myrrh and aloes, about a hundred pounds weight.

40 And so they took the body of Jesus, and bound it in linen wrappings with the spices, as is the burial custom of the Jews.

41 Now in the place where He was crucified there was a garden; and in the garden a new tomb, in which no one had yet been laid.

42 Therefore on account of the Jewish day of preparation, because the tomb was nearby, they laid Jesus there.

CHAPTER 20

NOW on the first day of the week Mary Magdalene *came early to the tomb, while it *was still dark, and *saw the stone already taken away from the tomb.

2 And so she *ran and *came to Simon Peter, and to the other disciple whom Jesus loved, and *said to them, "They have taken away the Lord out of the tomb, and we do not know where they have laid Him."

3 Peter therefore went forth, and the other disciple, and they were going to the tomb.

4 And the two were running together; and the other disciple ran ahead faster than Peter, and came to the tomb first;

5 and stooping and looking in, he *saw the linen wrappings lying there; but he did not go in.

6 Simon Peter therefore also *came, following him, and entered the tomb; and he *beheld the linen wrappings lying there,

7 and the face-cloth, which had been on His head, not lying with the linen wrappings, but rolled up in a place by itself.

8 So the other disciple who had first come to the tomb entered then also, and he saw and believed.

9 For as yet they did not understand the Scripture, that He must rise again from the dead.

10 So the disciples went away again to their own homes.

11 But Mary was standing outside the tomb weeping; and so, as she wept, she stooped and looked into the tomb;

12 and she *beheld two angels in white sitting, one at the head, and one at the feet, where the body of Jesus had been lying.

13 And they *said to her, "Woman, why are you weeping?" She *said to them, "Because they have taken away my

Lord, and I do not know where they have laid Him."

14 When she had said this, she turned around, and *beheld Jesus standing *there, and did not know that it was Jesus.

15 Jesus *said to her, "Woman, why are you weeping? Whom are you seeking?" Supposing Him to be the gardener, she *said to Him, "Sir, if you have carried Him away, tell me where you have laid Him, and I will take Him away."

16 Jesus *said to her, "Mary!" She *turned and *said to Him in Hebrew, "Rabboni!" (which means, Teacher).

17 Jesus *said to her, "Stop clinging to Me, for I have not yet ascended to the Father; but go to My brethren, and say to them, 'I ascend to My Father and your Father, and My God and your God.'"

18 Mary Magdalene *came, announcing to the disciples, "I have seen the Lord," and *that He had said these things to her.

19 When therefore it was evening, on that day, the first *day of the week, and when the doors were shut where the disciples were, for fear of the Jews, Jesus came and stood in their midst, and *said to them, "Peace *be with you."

20 And when He had said this, He showed them both His hands and His side. The disciples therefore rejoiced when they saw the Lord.

21 Jesus therefore said to them again, "Peace *be with you; as the Father has sent Me, I also send you."

22 And when He had said this, He breathed on them, and *said to them, "Receive the Holy Spirit.

23 "If you forgive the sins of any, *their sins have been forgiven them; if you retain the *sins of any, they have been retained."

24 But Thomas, one of the twelve, called Didymus, was not with them when Jesus came.

25 The other disciples therefore were saying to him, "We have seen the Lord!" But he said to them, "Unless I shall see in His hands the imprint of the nails, and put my finger into the place of the nails, and put my hand into His side, I will not believe."

26 And after eight days again His disciples were inside, and Thomas with them. Jesus *came, the doors having been shut, and stood in their midst, and said, "Peace *be with you."

27 Then He *said to Thomas, "Reach here your finger, and see My hands; and reach here your hand, and put it into My side; and be not unbelieving, but believing."

28 Thomas answered and said to Him, "My Lord and my God!"

29 Jesus *said to him, "Because you have seen Me, have you believed? Blessed *are they who did not see, and *yet believed."

30 Many other signs therefore Jesus also performed in the presence of the disciples, which are not written in this book;

31 but these have been written that you may believe that Jesus is the Christ, the Son of God; and that believing you may have life in His name.

CHAPTER 21

AFTER these things Jesus manifested Himself again to the disciples at the Sea of Tiberias, and He manifested *Himself* in this way.

2 There were together Simon Peter, and Thomas called Didymus, and Nathanael of Cana in Galilee, and the *sons* of Zebedee, and two others of His disciples.

3 Simon Peter *said to them, "I am going fishing." They *said to him, "We will also come with you." They went out, and got into the boat; and that night they caught nothing.

4 But when the day was now breaking, Jesus stood on the beach; yet the disciples did not know that it was Jesus.

5 Jesus therefore *said to them, "Children, you do not have any fish, do you?" They answered Him, "No."

6 And He said to them, "Cast the net on the right-hand side of the boat, and you will find *a catch.*" They cast therefore, and then they were not able to haul it in because of the great number of fish.

7 That disciple therefore whom Jesus loved *said to Peter, "It is the Lord." And so when Simon Peter heard that it was the Lord, he put his outer garment on (for he was stripped *for work*), and threw himself into the sea.

8 But the other disciples came in the little boat, for they were not far from the land, but about one hundred yards away, dragging the net *full* of fish.

9 And so when they got out upon the land, they *saw a charcoal fire *already* laid, and fish placed on it, and bread.

10 Jesus *said to them, "Bring some of the fish which you have now caught."

11 Simon Peter went up, and drew the net to land, full of large fish, a hundred and fifty-three; and although there were so many, the net was not torn.

12 Jesus *said to them, "Come *and* have breakfast." None of the disciples ventured to question Him, "Who are You?" knowing that it was the Lord.

13 Jesus *came and *took the bread, and *gave them, and the fish likewise.

14 This is now the third time that Jesus was manifested to the disciples, after He was raised from the dead.

15 So when they had finished breakfast, Jesus *said to Simon Peter, "Simon, *son* of John, do you love Me more than these?" He *said to Him, "Yes, Lord; You know that I love You." He *said to him, "Tend My lambs."

16 He *said to him again a second time, "Simon, *son* of John, do you love Me?" He *said to Him, "Yes, Lord; You know that I love You." He *said to him, "Shepherd My sheep."

17 He *said to him the third time, "Simon, *son* of John, do you love Me?" Peter was grieved because He said to him the third time, "Do you love Me?" And he said to Him, "Lord, You know all things; You know that I love You." Jesus *said to him, "Tend My sheep.

18 "Truly, truly, I say to you, when you were younger, you used to gird yourself, and walk wherever you wished; but when you grow old, you will stretch out your hands, and someone else will gird you, and bring you where you do not wish to go."

19 Now this He said, signifying by what kind of death he would glorify God. And when He had

spoken this, He *said to him, "Follow Me!"

20 Peter, turning around, *saw the disciple whom Jesus loved following *them;* the one who also had leaned back on His breast at the supper, and said, "Lord, who is the one who betrays You?"

21 Peter therefore seeing him *said to Jesus, "Lord, and what about this man?"

22 Jesus *said to him, "If I want him to remain until I come, what *is that* to you? You follow Me!"

23 This saying therefore went out among the brethren that that disciple would not die; yet Jesus did not say to him that he would not die, but *only,* "If I want him to remain until I come, what *is that* to you?"

24 This is the disciple who bears witness of these things, and wrote these things; and we know that his witness is true.

25 And there are also many other things which Jesus did, which if they *were written in detail, I suppose that even the world itself *would not contain the books which *were written.

THE
ACTS OF THE APOSTLES

THE first account I composed, Theophilus, about all that Jesus began to do and teach,

2 until the day when He was taken up, after He had by the Holy Spirit given orders to the apostles whom He had chosen.

3 To these He also presented Himself alive, after His suffering, by many convincing proofs, appearing to them over *a period of* forty days, and speaking of the things concerning the kingdom of God.

4 And gathering them together, He commanded them not to leave Jerusalem, but to wait for what the Father had promised, "Which," *He said,* "you heard of from Me;

5 for John baptized with water, but you shall be baptized with the Holy Spirit not many days from now."

6 And so when they had come together, they were asking Him, saying, "Lord, is it at this time You are restoring the kingdom to Israel?"

7 He said to them, "It is not for you to know times or epochs which the Father has fixed by His own authority;

8 but you shall receive power when the Holy Spirit has come upon you; and you shall be My witnesses both in Jerusalem, and in all Judea and Samaria, and even to the remotest part of the earth."

9 And after He had said these things, He was lifted up while they were looking on, and a cloud received Him out of their sight.

10 And as they were gazing intently into the sky while He was departing, behold, two men in

white clothing stood beside them;

11 and they also said, "Men of Galilee, why do you stand looking into the sky? This Jesus, who has been taken up from you into heaven, will come in just the same way as you have watched Him go into heaven."

12 Then they returned to Jerusalem from the mount called Olivet, which is near Jerusalem, a Sabbath day's journey away.

13 And when they had entered, they went up to the upper room, where they were staying; that is, Peter and John and James and Andrew, Philip and Thomas, Bartholomew and Matthew, James *the son* of Alphaeus, and Simon the Zealot, and Judas *the son* of James.

14 These all with one mind were continually devoting themselves to prayer, along with *the* women, and Mary the mother of Jesus, and with His brothers.

15 And at this time Peter stood up in the midst of the brethren (a gathering of about one hundred and twenty persons was there together), and said,

16 "Brethren, the Scripture had to be fulfilled, which the Holy Spirit foretold by the mouth of David concerning Judas, who became a guide to those who arrested Jesus.

17 "For he was counted among us, and received his portion in this ministry."

18 (Now this man acquired a field with the price of his wickedness; and falling headlong, he burst open in the middle and all his bowels gushed out.

19 And it became known to all who were living in Jerusalem; so that in their own language that field was called Hakeldama, that is, Field of Blood.)

20 "For it is written in the book of Psalms,

'LET HIS HOMESTEAD BE
    MADE DESOLATE,
AND LET NO MAN DWELL IN
    IT';
and,
'HIS OFFICE LET ANOTHER
    MAN TAKE.'

21 "It is therefore necessary that of the men who have accompanied us all the time that the Lord Jesus went in and out among us—

22 beginning with the baptism of John, until the day that He was taken up from us—one of these should become a witness with us of His resurrection."

23 And they put forward two men, Joseph called Barsabbas (who was also called Justus), and Matthias.

24 And they prayed, and said, "Thou, Lord, who knowest the hearts of all men, show which one of these two Thou hast chosen

25 to occupy this ministry and apostleship from which Judas turned aside to go to his own place."

26 And they drew lots for them, and the lot fell to Matthias; and he was numbered with the eleven apostles.

CHAPTER 2

AND when the day of Pentecost had come, they were all together in one place.

2 And suddenly there came from heaven a noise like a violent, rushing wind, and it filled the whole house where they were sitting.

3 And there appeared to them tongues as of fire distributing themselves, and they rested on each one of them.

4 And they were all filled with the Holy Spirit and began to speak with other tongues, as the Spirit was giving them utterance.

5 Now there were Jews living in Jerusalem, devout men, from every nation under heaven.

6 And when this sound occurred, the multitude came together, and were bewildered, because they were each one hearing them speak in his own language.

7 And they were amazed and marveled, saying, "Why, are not all these who are speaking Galileans?

8 "And how is it that we each hear *them* in our own language to which we were born?

9 "Parthians and Medes and Elamites, and residents of Mesopotamia, Judea and Cappadocia, Pontus and Asia,

10 Phrygia and Pamphylia, Egypt and the districts of Libya around Cyrene, and visitors from Rome, both Jews and [1]proselytes,

11 Cretans and Arabs—we hear them in our *own* tongues speaking of the mighty deeds of God."

12 And they continued in amazement and great perplexity, saying to one another, "What does this mean?"

13 But others were mocking and saying, "They are full of sweet wine."

14 But Peter, taking his stand with the eleven, raised his voice and declared to them: "Men of Judea, and all you who live in Jerusalem, let this be known to you, and give heed to my words.

15 "For these men are not drunk, as you suppose, for it is only the [2]third hour of the day;

16 but this is what was spoken of through the prophet Joel:

17 'AND IT SHALL BE IN THE LAST DAYS,' God says,
    'THAT I WILL POUR FORTH OF MY SPIRIT UPON ALL MANKIND;
    AND YOUR SONS AND YOUR DAUGHTERS SHALL PROPHESY,
    AND YOUR YOUNG MEN SHALL SEE VISIONS,
    AND YOUR OLD MEN SHALL DREAM DREAMS;

18 EVEN UPON MY BONDSLAVES, BOTH MEN AND WOMEN,
    I WILL IN THOSE DAYS POUR FORTH OF MY SPIRIT
    And they shall prophesy.

19 'AND I WILL GRANT WONDERS IN THE SKY ABOVE,
    AND SIGNS ON THE EARTH BENEATH,
    BLOOD, AND FIRE, AND VAPOR OF SMOKE.

20 'THE SUN SHALL BE TURNED INTO DARKNESS,
    AND THE MOON INTO BLOOD,
    BEFORE THE GREAT AND GLORIOUS DAY OF THE LORD SHALL COME.

21 'AND IT SHALL BE, THAT EVERYONE WHO CALLS ON THE NAME OF THE LORD SHALL BE SAVED.'

22 "Men of Israel, listen to these words: Jesus the Nazarene, a man attested to you by God with miracles and wonders and signs which God performed through Him in your midst, just as you yourselves know—

---

[1] I.e., Gentile converts to Judaism
[2] I.e., 9 a.m.

23 this *Man*, delivered up by the predetermined plan and fore-knowledge of God, you nailed to a cross by the hands of godless men and put *Him* to death.

24 "And God raised Him up again, putting an end to the agony of death, since it was impossible for Him to be held in its power.

25 "For David says of Him,

'I WAS ALWAYS BEHOLDING THE LORD IN MY PRESENCE;
FOR HE IS AT MY RIGHT HAND, THAT I MAY NOT BE SHAKEN.

26 'THEREFORE MY HEART WAS GLAD AND MY TONGUE EXULTED;
MOREOVER MY FLESH ALSO WILL ABIDE IN HOPE;

27 BECAUSE THOU WILT NOT ABANDON MY SOUL TO HADES,
NOR ALLOW THY HOLY ONE TO UNDERGO DECAY.

28 'THOU HAST MADE KNOWN TO ME THE WAYS OF LIFE;
THOU WILT MAKE ME FULL OF GLADNESS WITH THY PRESENCE.'

29 "Brethren, I may confidently say to you regarding the patriarch David that he both died and was buried, and his tomb is with us to this day.

30 "And so, because he was a prophet, and knew that GOD HAD SWORN TO HIM WITH AN OATH TO SEAT *one* OF HIS DESCENDANTS UPON HIS THRONE,

31 he looked ahead and spoke of the resurrection of [3]the Christ, that HE WAS NEITHER ABANDONED TO HADES, NOR DID His flesh SUFFER DECAY.

[3] I.e., the Messiah   [4] I.e., persons

32 "This Jesus God raised up again, to which we are all witnesses.

33 "Therefore having been exalted to the right hand of God, and having received from the Father the promise of the Holy Spirit, He has poured forth this which you both see and hear.

34 "For it was not David who ascended into heaven, but he himself says:

'THE LORD SAID TO MY LORD,
"SIT AT MY RIGHT HAND,

35 UNTIL I MAKE THINE ENEMIES A FOOTSTOOL FOR THY FEET." '

36 "Therefore let all the house of Israel know for certain that God has made Him both Lord and Christ—this Jesus whom you crucified."

37 Now when they heard *this*, they were pierced to the heart, and said to Peter and the rest of the apostles, "Brethren, what shall we do?"

38 And Peter *said* to them, "Repent, and let each of you be baptized in the name of Jesus Christ for the forgiveness of your sins; and you shall receive the gift of the Holy Spirit.

39 "For the promise is for you and your children, and for all who are far off, as many as the Lord our God shall call to Himself."

40 And with many other words he solemnly testified and kept on exhorting them, saying, "Be saved from this perverse generation!"

41 So then, those who had received his word were baptized; and there were added that day about three thousand [4]souls.

42 And they were continually

devoting themselves to the apostles' teaching and to fellowship, to the breaking of bread and to prayer.

43 And everyone kept feeling a sense of awe; and many wonders and signs were taking place through the apostles[5].

44 And all those who had believed [6]were together, and had all things in common;

45 and they *began* selling their property and possessions, and were sharing them with all, as anyone might have need.

46 And day by day continuing with one mind in the temple, and breaking bread from house to house, they were taking their meals together with gladness and sincerity of heart,

47 praising God, and having favor with all the people. And the Lord was adding to their number day by day those who were being saved.

CHAPTER 3

NOW Peter and John were going up to the temple at the [7]ninth *hour*, the hour of prayer.

2 And a certain man who had been lame from his mother's womb was being carried along, whom they used to set down every day at the gate of the temple which is called Beautiful, in order to beg [8]alms of those who were entering the temple.

3 And when he saw Peter and John about to go into the temple, he *began* asking to receive alms.

4 And Peter, along with John, fixed his gaze upon him and said, "Look at us!"

5 And he *began* to give them his attention, expecting to receive something from them.

6 But Peter said, "I do not possess silver and gold, but what I do have I give to you: In the name of Jesus Christ the Nazarene—walk!"

7 And seizing him by the right hand, he raised him up; and immediately his feet and his ankles were strengthened.

8 And with a leap, he stood upright and *began* to walk; and he entered the temple with them, walking and leaping and praising God.

9 And all the people saw him walking and praising God;

10 and they were taking note of him as being the one who used to sit at the Beautiful Gate of the temple to *beg* alms, and they were filled with wonder and amazement at what had happened to him.

11 And while he was clinging to Peter and John, all the people ran together to them at the so-called portico of Solomon, full of amazement.

12 But when Peter saw *this*, he replied to the people, "Men of Israel, why do you marvel at this, or why do you gaze at us, as if by our own power or piety we had made him walk?

13"The God of Abraham, Isaac, and Jacob, the God of our fathers, has glorified His servant Jesus, *the one* whom you delivered up, and disowned in the presence of Pilate, when he had decided to release Him.

14"But you disowned the Holy and Righteous One, and asked for a murderer to be granted to you,

---

[5] Some ancient mss. add *in Jerusalem; and great fear was upon all*
[6] Some ancient mss. do not contain *were*
[7] I.e., 3 p.m.   [8] Or, *a gift of charity*

15 but put to death the Prince of life, *the one* whom God raised from the dead, *a fact* to which we are witnesses.

16 "And on the basis of faith in His name, *it is* the name of Jesus which has strengthened this man whom you see and know; and the faith which *comes* through Him has given him this perfect health in the presence of you all.

17 "And now, brethren, I know that you acted in ignorance, just as your rulers did also.

18 "But the things which God announced beforehand by the mouth of all the prophets, that His Christ should suffer, He has thus fulfilled.

19 "Repent therefore and return, that your sins may be wiped away, in order that times of refreshing may come from the presence of the Lord;

20 and that He may send Jesus, the Christ appointed for you,

21 whom heaven must receive until *the* period of restoration of all things about which God spoke by the mouth of His holy prophets from ancient time.

22 "Moses said, 'THE LORD GOD SHALL RAISE UP FOR YOU A PROPHET LIKE ME FROM YOUR BRETHREN; TO HIM YOU SHALL GIVE HEED in everything He says to you.

23 'And it shall be that every soul that does not heed that prophet shall be utterly destroyed from among the people.'

24 "And likewise, all the prophets who have spoken, from Samuel and *his* successors onward, also announced these days.

25 "It is you who are the sons of the prophets, and of the covenant which God made with your fathers, saying to Abraham, 'AND IN YOUR SEED ALL THE FAMILIES OF THE EARTH SHALL BE BLESSED.'

26 "For you first, God raised up His Servant, and sent Him to bless you by turning every one *of you* from your wicked ways."

CHAPTER 4

AND as they were speaking to the people, the priests and the captain of the temple *guard,* and the Sadducees, came upon them,

2 being greatly disturbed because they were teaching the people and proclaiming in Jesus the resurrection from the dead.

3 And they laid hands on them, and put them in jail until the next day, for it was already evening.

4 But many of those who had heard the message believed; and the number of the men came to be about five thousand.

5 And it came about on the next day, that their rulers and elders and scribes were gathered together in Jerusalem;

6 and Annas the high priest *was there,* and Caiaphas and John and Alexander, and all who were of high-priestly descent.

7 And when they had placed them in the center, they *began to* inquire, "By what power, or in what name, have you done this?"

8 Then Peter, filled with the Holy Spirit, said to them, "Rulers and elders of the people,

9 if we are on trial today for a benefit done to a sick man, as to how this man has been made well,

10 let it be known to all of you, and to all the people of Israel, that by the name of Jesus Christ the Nazarene, whom you

crucified, whom God raised from the dead—by this *name* this man stands here before you in good health.

11"He is the STONE WHICH WAS REJECTED by you, THE BUILDERS, *but* WHICH BECAME THE VERY CORNER *stone*.

12"And there is salvation in no one else; for there is no other name under heaven that has been given among men, by which we must be saved."

13 Now as they observed the confidence of Peter and John, and understood that they were uneducated and untrained men, they were marveling, and *began* to recognize them as having been with Jesus.

14 And seeing the man who had been healed standing with them, they had nothing to say in reply.

15 But when they had ordered them to go aside out of the Council, they *began* to confer with one another,

16 saying, "What shall we do with these men? For the fact that a noteworthy miracle has taken place through them is apparent to all who live in Jerusalem, and we cannot deny it.

17"But in order that it may not spread any further among the people, let us warn them to speak no more to any man in this name."

18 And when they had summoned them, they commanded them not to speak or teach at all in the name of Jesus.

19 But Peter and John answered and said to them, "Whether it is right in the sight of God to give heed to you rather than to God, you be the judge;

20 for we cannot stop speaking what we have seen and heard."

21 And when they had threatened them further, they let them go (finding no basis on which they might punish them) on account of the people, because they were all glorifying God for what had happened;

22 for the man was more than forty years old on whom this miracle of healing had been performed.

23 And when they had been released, they went to their own *companions*, and reported all that the chief priests and the elders had said to them.

24 And when they heard *this*, they lifted their voices to God with one accord and said, "O Lord, it is Thou who DIDST MAKE THE HEAVEN AND THE EARTH AND THE SEA, AND ALL THAT IS IN THEM,

25 who by the Holy Spirit, *through* the mouth of our father David Thy servant, didst say,

'WHY DID THE [9]GENTILES
 RAGE,
AND THE PEOPLES DEVISE
 FUTILE THINGS?

26 'THE KINGS OF THE EARTH
 TOOK THEIR STAND,
AND THE RULERS WERE
 GATHERED TOGETHER
AGAINST THE LORD, AND
 AGAINST HIS CHRIST.'

27"For truly in this city there were gathered together against Thy holy servant Jesus, whom Thou didst anoint, both Herod and Pontius Pilate, along with the Gentiles and the peoples of Israel,

28 to do whatever Thy hand and Thy purpose predestined to occur.

[9] Or, *nations*

29 "And now, Lord, take note of their threats, and grant that Thy bond-servants may speak Thy word with all confidence,

30 while Thou dost extend Thy hand to heal, and signs and wonders take place through the name of Thy holy servant Jesus."

31 And when they had prayed, the place where they had gathered together was shaken, and they were all filled with the Holy Spirit, and *began* to speak the word of God with boldness.

32 And the congregation of those who believed were of one heart and soul; and not one *of them* claimed that anything belonging to him was his own; but all things were common property to them.

33 And with great power the apostles were giving witness to the resurrection of the Lord Jesus, and abundant grace was upon them all.

34 For there was not a needy person among them, for all who were owners of land or houses would sell them and bring the proceeds of the sales,

35 and lay them at the apostles' feet; and they would be distributed to each, as any had need.

36 And Joseph, a Levite of Cyprian birth, who was also called Barnabas by the apostles (which translated means, Son of Encouragement),

37 and who owned a tract of land, sold it and brought the money and laid it at the apostles' feet.

CHAPTER 5

BUT a certain man named Ananias, with his wife Sapphira, sold a piece of property,

2 and kept back *some* of the price for himself, with his wife's full knowledge, and bringing a portion of it, he laid it at the apostles' feet.

3 But Peter said, "Ananias, why has Satan filled your heart to lie to the Holy Spirit, and to keep back *some* of the price of the land?

4 "While it remained *unsold*, did it not remain your own? And after it was sold, was it not under your control? Why is it that you have conceived this deed in your heart? You have not lied to men, but to God."

5 And as he heard these words, Ananias fell down and breathed his last; and great fear came upon all who heard of it.

6 And the young men arose and covered him up, and after carrying him out, they buried him.

7 Now there elapsed an interval of about three hours, and his wife came in, not knowing what had happened.

8 And Peter responded to her, "Tell me whether you sold the land for such and such a price?" And she said, "Yes, that was the price."

9 Then Peter *said* to her, "Why is it that you have agreed together to put the Spirit of the Lord to the test? Behold, the feet of those who have buried your husband are at the door, and they shall carry you out *as well*."

10 And she fell immediately at his feet, and breathed her last; and the young men came in and found her dead, and they carried her out and buried her beside her husband.

11 And great fear came upon

the whole church, and upon all who heard of these things.

12 And at the hands of the apostles many signs and wonders were taking place among the people; and they were all with one accord in Solomon's portico.

13 But none of the rest dared to associate with them; however, the people held them in high esteem.

14 And all the more believers in the Lord, multitudes of men and women, were constantly added to *their* number;

15 to such an extent that they even carried the sick out into the streets, and laid them on cots and pallets, so that when Peter came by, at least his shadow might fall on any one of them.

16 And also the people from the cities in the vicinity of Jerusalem were coming together, bringing people who were sick [10]or afflicted with unclean spirits; and they were all being healed.

17 But the high priest rose up, along with all his associates (that is the sect of the Sadducees), and they were filled with jealousy;

18 and they laid hands on the apostles, and put them in a public jail.

19 But an angel of the Lord during the night opened the gates of the prison, and taking them out he said,

20"Go your way, stand and speak to the people in the temple the whole message of this Life."

21 And upon hearing *this*, they entered into the temple about daybreak, and *began* to teach. Now when the high priest and his associates had come, they called the Council together, even all the Senate of the sons of Israel, and

sent *orders* to the prison house for them to be brought.

22 But the officers who came did not find them in the prison; and they returned, and reported back,

23 saying, "We found the prison house locked quite securely and the guards standing at the doors; but when we had opened up, we found no one inside."

24 Now when the captain of the temple *guard* and the chief priests heard these words, they were greatly perplexed about them as to what would come of this.

25 But someone came and reported to them, "Behold, the men whom you put in prison are standing in the temple and teaching the people!"

26 Then the captain went along with the officers and *proceeded* to bring them *back* without violence (for they were afraid of the people, lest they should be stoned).

27 And when they had brought them, they stood them before the Council. And the high priest questioned them,

28 saying, "We gave you strict orders not to continue teaching in this name, and behold, you have filled Jerusalem with your teaching, and intend to bring this man's blood upon us."

29 But Peter and the apostles answered and said, "We must obey God rather than men.

30"The God of our fathers raised up Jesus, whom you had put to death by hanging Him on a cross.

31"He is the one whom God ex-

[10] Lit., *and*

alted to His right hand as a Prince and a Savior, to grant repentance to Israel, and forgiveness of sins.

32"And we are witnesses[11] of these things; and so is the Holy Spirit, whom God has given to those who obey Him."

33 But when they heard this, they were cut to the quick and were intending to slay them.

34 But a certain Pharisee named Gamaliel, a teacher of the Law, respected by all the people, stood up in the Council and gave orders to put the men outside for a short time.

35 And he said to them, "Men of Israel, take care what you propose to do with these men.

36"For some time ago Theudas rose up, claiming to be somebody; and a group of about four hundred men joined up with him. And he was slain; and all who followed him were dispersed and came to nothing.

37"After this man Judas of Galilee rose up in the days of the census, and drew away some people after him, he too perished, and all those who followed him were scattered.

38"And so in the present case, I say to you, stay away from these men and let them alone, for if this plan or action should be of men, it will be overthrown;

39 but if it is of God, you will not be able to overthrow them; or else you may even be found fighting against God."

40 And they took his advice; and after calling the apostles in, they flogged them and ordered them to speak no more in the name of Jesus, and then released them.

41 So they went on their way from the presence of the Council, rejoicing that they had been considered worthy to suffer shame for His name.

42 And every day, in the temple and from house to house, they kept right on teaching and preaching Jesus as the Christ.

CHAPTER 6

NOW at this time while the disciples were increasing in number, a complaint arose on the part of the [12]Hellenistic Jews against the native Hebrews, because their widows were being overlooked in the daily serving of food.

2 And the twelve summoned the congregation of the disciples and said, "It is not desirable for us to neglect the word of God in order to serve tables.

3"But select from among you, brethren, seven men of good reputation, full of the Spirit and of wisdom, whom we may put in charge of this task.

4"But we will devote ourselves to prayer, and to the ministry of the word."

5 And the statement found approval with the whole congregation; and they chose Stephen, a man full of faith and of the Holy Spirit, and Philip, Prochorus, Nicanor, Timon, Parmenas and Nicolas, a [13]proselyte from Antioch.

6 And these they brought before the apostles; and after praying, they laid their hands on them.

7 And the word of God kept on spreading; and the number of

---

[11] Some mss. add in Him, or, of Him
[12] I.e., non-Palestinian Jews who normally spoke Greek
[13] I.e., a Gentile convert to Judaism

the disciples continued to increase greatly in Jerusalem, and a great many of the priests were becoming obedient to the faith.

8 And Stephen, full of grace and power, was performing great wonders and signs among the people.

9 But some men from what was called the Synagogue of the Freedmen, *including* both Cyrenians and Alexandrians, and some from Cilicia and Asia, rose up and argued with Stephen.

10 And *yet* they were unable to cope with the wisdom and the Spirit with which he was speaking.

11 Then they secretly induced men to say, "We have heard him speak blasphemous words against Moses and *against* God."

12 And they stirred up the people, the elders and the scribes, and they came upon him and dragged him away, and brought him before the Council.

13 And they put forward false witnesses who said, "This man incessantly speaks against this holy place, and the Law;

14 for we have heard him say that this Nazarene, Jesus, will destroy this place and alter the customs which Moses handed down to us."

15 And fixing their gaze on him, all who were sitting in the Council saw his face like the face of an angel.

CHAPTER 7

AND the high priest said, "Are these things so?"

2 And he said, "Hear me, brethren and fathers! The God of glory appeared to our father Abraham when he was in Mesopotamia, before he lived in Haran,

3 and said to him, 'DEPART FROM YOUR COUNTRY AND YOUR RELATIVES, AND COME INTO THE LAND THAT I WILL SHOW YOU.'

4 "Then he departed from the land of the Chaldeans, and settled in Haran. And from there, after his father died, *God* removed him into this country in which you are now living.

5 "And He gave him no inheritance in it, not even a foot of ground; and *yet*, even when he had no child, He promised that HE WOULD GIVE IT TO HIM AS A POSSESSION, AND TO HIS OFF-SPRING AFTER HIM.

6 "But God spoke to this effect, that his OFFSPRING WOULD BE ALIENS IN A FOREIGN LAND, AND THAT THEY WOULD BE ENSLAVED AND MISTREATED FOR FOUR HUN-DRED YEARS.

7 "'AND WHATEVER NATION TO WHICH THEY SHALL BE IN BOND-AGE I MYSELF WILL JUDGE,' said God, 'AND AFTER THAT THEY WILL COME OUT AND [14]SERVE ME IN THIS PLACE.'

8 "And He gave him the covenant of circumcision; and so *Abraham* became the father of Isaac, and circumcised him on the eighth day; and Isaac *became the father of* Jacob, and Jacob *of* the twelve patriarchs.

9 "And the patriarchs became jealous of Joseph and sold him into Egypt. And *yet* God was with him,

10 and rescued him from all his afflictions, and granted him favor and wisdom in the sight of Pharaoh, king of Egypt; and he made

[14] Or, *worship*

11 "Now a famine came over all Egypt and Canaan, and great affliction *with it;* and our fathers could find no food.

12 "But when Jacob heard that there was grain in Egypt, he sent our fathers *there* the first time.

13 "And on the second *visit* Joseph made himself known to his brothers, and Joseph's family was disclosed to Pharaoh.

14 "And Joseph sent *word* and invited Jacob his father and all his relatives to come to him, seventy-five persons *in all.*

15 "And Jacob went down to Egypt and *there* passed away, he and our fathers.

16 "And *from there* they were removed to Shechem, and laid in the tomb which Abraham had purchased for a sum of money from the sons of Hamor in Shechem.

17 "But as the time of the promise was approaching which God had assured to Abraham, the people increased and multiplied in Egypt,

18 until THERE AROSE ANOTHER KING OVER EGYPT WHO KNEW NOTHING ABOUT JOSEPH.

19 "It was he who took shrewd advantage of our race, and mistreated our fathers so that they would expose their infants and they would not survive.

20 "And it was at this time that Moses was born; and he was lovely in the sight of God; and he was nurtured three months in his father's home.

21 "And after he had been exposed, Pharaoh's daughter took him away, and nurtured him as her own son.

22 "And Moses was educated in all the learning of the Egyptians, and he was a man of power in words and deeds.

23 "But when he was approaching the age of forty, it entered his mind to visit his brethren, the sons of Israel.

24 "And when he saw one *of them* being treated unjustly, he defended him and took vengeance for the oppressed by striking down the Egyptian.

25 "And he supposed that his brethren understood that God was granting them deliverance through him; but they did not understand.

26 "And on the following day he appeared to them as they were fighting together, and he tried to reconcile them in peace, saying, 'Men, you are brethren, why do you injure one another?'

27 "But the one who was injuring his neighbor pushed him away, saying, 'WHO MADE YOU A RULER AND JUDGE OVER US?

28 'YOU DO NOT MEAN TO KILL ME AS YOU KILLED THE EGYPTIAN YESTERDAY, DO YOU?'

29 "And at this remark MOSES FLED, AND BECAME AN ALIEN IN THE LAND OF MIDIAN, where he became the father of two sons.

30 "And after forty years had passed, AN ANGEL APPEARED TO HIM IN THE WILDERNESS OF MOUNT Sinai, IN THE FLAME OF A BURNING THORN BUSH.

31 "And when Moses saw it, he *began* to marvel at the sight; and as he approached to look *more* closely, there came the voice of the Lord:

32 'I AM THE GOD OF YOUR FATHERS, THE GOD OF ABRAHAM AND ISAAC AND JACOB.' And

Moses shook with fear and would not venture to look.

33"BUT THE LORD SAID TO HIM, 'TAKE OFF THE SANDALS FROM YOUR FEET, FOR THE PLACE ON WHICH YOU ARE STANDING IS HOLY GROUND.

34 'I HAVE CERTAINLY SEEN THE OPPRESSION OF MY PEOPLE IN EGYPT, AND HAVE HEARD THEIR GROANS, AND I HAVE COME DOWN TO DELIVER THEM; COME NOW, AND I WILL SEND YOU TO EGYPT.'

35"This Moses whom they disowned, saying, 'WHO MADE YOU A RULER AND A JUDGE?' is the one whom God sent *to be* both a ruler and a deliverer with the help of the angel who appeared to him in the thorn bush.

36"This man led them out, performing wonders and signs in the land of Egypt and in the Red Sea and in the wilderness for forty years.

37"This is the Moses who said to the sons of Israel, 'GOD SHALL RAISE UP FOR YOU A PROPHET LIKE ME FROM YOUR BRETHREN.'

38"This is the one who was in the congregation in the wilderness together with the angel who was speaking to him on Mount Sinai, and *who was* with our fathers; and he received living oracles to pass on to you.

39"And our fathers were unwilling to be obedient to him, but repudiated him and in their hearts turned back to Egypt,

40 SAYING TO AARON, 'MAKE FOR US GODS WHO WILL GO BEFORE US; FOR THIS MOSES WHO LED US OUT OF THE LAND OF EGYPT—WE DO NOT KNOW WHAT HAPPENED TO HIM.'

41"And at that time they made a calf and brought a sacrifice to the idol, and were rejoicing in the works of their hands.

42"But God turned away and delivered them up to serve the host of heaven; as it is written in the book of the prophets, 'IT WAS NOT TO ME THAT YOU OFFERED VICTIMS AND SACRIFICES FORTY YEARS IN THE WILDERNESS, WAS IT, O HOUSE OF ISRAEL?

43 'YOU ALSO TOOK ALONG THE TABERNACLE OF MOLOCH AND THE STAR OF THE GOD ROMPHA, THE IMAGES WHICH YOU MADE TO WORSHIP THEM. I ALSO WILL REMOVE YOU BEYOND BABYLON.'

44"Our fathers had the tabernacle of testimony in the wilderness, just as He who spoke to Moses directed *him* to make it according to the pattern which he had seen.

45"And having received it in their turn, our fathers brought it in with Joshua upon dispossessing the nations whom God drove out before our fathers, until the time of David.

46"And *David* found favor in God's sight, and asked that he might find a dwelling place for the [15]God of Jacob.

47"But it was Solomon who built a house for Him.

48"However, the Most High does not dwell in *houses* made by *human* hands; as the prophet says:

49 'HEAVEN IS MY THRONE,
        AND EARTH IS THE FOOT-
            STOOL OF MY FEET;
        WHAT KIND OF HOUSE WILL
            YOU BUILD FOR ME?' says
            the Lord;
        'OR WHAT PLACE IS THERE
            FOR MY REPOSE?

---

[15] The earliest mss. read *house* instead of *God*; the Septuagint reads *God*

50 'Was it not My hand which made all these things?'

51 "You men who are stiff-necked and uncircumcised in heart and ears are always resisting the Holy Spirit; you are doing just as your fathers did.

52 "Which one of the prophets did your fathers not persecute? And they killed those who had previously announced the coming of the Righteous One, whose betrayers and murderers you have now become;

53 you who received the law as ordained by angels, and *yet* did not keep it."

54 Now when they heard this, they were cut to the quick, and they *began* gnashing their teeth at him.

55 But being full of the Holy Spirit, he gazed intently into heaven and saw the glory of God, and Jesus standing at the right hand of God;

56 and he said, "Behold, I see the heavens opened up and the Son of Man standing at the right hand of God."

57 But they cried out with a loud voice, and covered their ears, and they rushed upon him with one impulse.

58 And when they had driven him out of the city, they *began* stoning *him*, and the witnesses laid aside their robes at the feet of a young man named Saul.

59 And they went on stoning Stephen as he called upon *the Lord* and said, "Lord Jesus, receive my spirit!"

60 And falling on his knees, he cried out with a loud voice, "Lord, do not hold this sin against them!" And having said this, he fell asleep.

CHAPTER 8

AND Saul was in hearty agreement with putting him to death.

And on that day a great persecution arose against the church in Jerusalem; and they were all scattered throughout the regions of Judea and Samaria, except the apostles.

2 And *some* devout men buried Stephen, and made loud lamentation over him.

3 But Saul *began* ravaging the church, entering house after house; and dragging off men and women, he would put them in prison.

4 Therefore, those who had been scattered went about preaching the word.

5 And Philip went down to the city of Samaria and *began* proclaiming Christ to them.

6 And the multitudes with one accord were giving attention to what was said by Philip, as they heard and saw the signs which he was performing.

7 For *in the case of* many who had unclean spirits, they were coming out *of them* shouting with a loud voice; and many who had been paralyzed and lame were healed.

8 And there was much rejoicing in that city.

9 Now there was a certain man named Simon, who formerly was practicing magic in the city, and astonishing the people of Samaria, claiming to be someone great;

10 and they all, from smallest to greatest, were giving attention to him, saying, "This man is what is called the Great Power of God."

11 And they were giving him attention because he had for a long time astonished them with his magic arts.

12 But when they believed Philip preaching the good news about the kingdom of God and the name of Jesus Christ, they were being baptized, men and women alike.

13 And even Simon himself believed; and after being baptized, he continued on with Philip; and as he observed signs and great miracles taking place, he was constantly amazed.

14 Now when the apostles in Jerusalem heard that Samaria had received the word of God, they sent them Peter and John,

15 who came down and prayed for them, that they might receive the Holy Spirit.

16 For He had not yet fallen upon any of them; they had simply been baptized in the name of the Lord Jesus.

17 Then they *began* laying their hands on them, and they were receiving the Holy Spirit.

18 Now when Simon saw that the Spirit was bestowed through the laying on of the apostles' hands, he offered them money,

19 saying, "Give this authority to me as well, so that everyone on whom I lay my hands may receive the Holy Spirit."

20 But Peter said to him, "May your silver perish with you, because you thought you could obtain the gift of God with money!

21 "You have no part or portion in this matter, for your heart is not right before God.

22 "Therefore repent of this wickedness of yours, and pray the Lord that if possible, the intention of your heart may be forgiven you.

23 "For I see that you are in the gall of bitterness and in the bondage of iniquity."

24 But Simon answered and said, "Pray to the Lord for me yourselves, so that nothing of what you have said may come upon me."

25 And so, when they had solemnly testified and spoken the word of the Lord, they started back to Jerusalem, and were preaching the gospel to many villages of the Samaritans.

26 But an angel of the Lord spoke to Philip saying, "Arise and go south to the road that descends from Jerusalem to Gaza." (This is a desert *road.*)

27 And he arose and went; and behold, there was an Ethiopian eunuch, a court official of Candace, queen of the Ethiopians, who was in charge of all her treasure; and he had come to Jerusalem to worship.

28 And he was returning and sitting in his chariot, and was reading the prophet Isaiah.

29 And the Spirit said to Philip, "Go up and join this chariot."

30 And when Philip had run up, he heard him reading Isaiah the prophet, and said, "Do you understand what you are reading?"

31 And he said, "Well, how could I, unless someone guides me?" And he invited Philip to come up and sit with him.

32 Now the passage of Scripture which he was reading was this:

"HE WAS LED AS A SHEEP TO SLAUGHTER;
AND AS A LAMB BEFORE ITS SHEARER IS SILENT,

So He does not open His
mouth.

33 "In humiliation His judgment was taken away;
Who shall relate His
generation?
For His life is removed
from the earth.''

34 And the eunuch answered
Philip and said, "Please tell me,
of whom does the prophet say
this? Of himself, or of someone
else?"

35 And Philip opened his
mouth, and beginning from this
Scripture he preached Jesus to
him.

36 And as they went along the
road they came to some water;
and the eunuch *said, "Look!
Water! What prevents me from
being baptized?"

37 [16And Philip said, "If you
believe with all your heart, you
may." And he answered and said,
"I believe that Jesus Christ is the
Son of God."]

38 And he ordered the chariot
to stop; and they both went down
into the water, Philip as well as
the eunuch; and he baptized him.

39 And when they came up out
of the water, the Spirit of the
Lord snatched Philip away; and
the eunuch saw him no more, but
went on his way rejoicing.

40 But Philip found himself at
Azotus; and as he passed through
he kept preaching the gospel to
all the cities, until he came to
Caesarea.

CHAPTER 9

NOW Saul, still breathing
threats and murder against

the disciples of the Lord, went to
the high priest,

2 and asked for letters from
him to the synagogues at Damascus, so that if he found any belonging to the Way, both men
and women, he might bring them
bound to Jerusalem.

3 And it came about that as
he journeyed, he was approaching Damascus, and suddenly a
light from heaven flashed around
him;

4 and he fell to the ground,
and heard a voice saying to him,
"Saul, Saul, why are you persecuting Me?"

5 And he said, "Who art
Thou, Lord?" And He said, "I am
Jesus whom you are persecuting,

6 but rise, and enter the city,
and it shall be told you what you
must do."

7 And the men who traveled
with him stood speechless, hearing the voice, but seeing no one.

8 And Saul got up from the
ground, and though his eyes
were open, he could see nothing;
and leading him by the hand,
they brought him into Damascus.

9 And he was three days without sight, and neither ate nor
drank.

10 Now there was a certain
disciple at Damascus, named
Ananias; and the Lord said to
him in a vision, "Ananias." And
he said, "Behold, here am I,
Lord."

11 And the Lord said to him,
"Arise and go to the street called
Straight, and inquire at the house
of Judas for a man from Tarsus
named Saul, for behold, he is
praying,

12 and he has seen 17in a vision
a man named Ananias come in

16 Many mss. do not contain this verse
17 Some mss. do not contain in a vision

and lay his hands on him, so that he might regain his sight."

13 But Ananias answered, "Lord, I have heard from many about this man, how much harm he did to Thy saints at Jerusalem;

14 and here he has authority from the chief priests to bind all who call upon Thy name."

15 But the Lord said to him, "Go, for he is a chosen [18]instrument of Mine, to bear My name before the Gentiles and kings and the sons of Israel;

16 for I will show him how much he must suffer for My name's sake."

17 And Ananias departed and entered the house, and after laying his hands on him said, "Brother Saul, the Lord Jesus, who appeared to you on the road by which you were coming, has sent me so that you may regain your sight, and be filled with the Holy Spirit."

18 And immediately there fell from his eyes something like scales, and he regained his sight, and he arose and was baptized;

19 and he took food and was strengthened.

Now for several days he was with the disciples who were at Damascus,

20 and immediately he *began* to proclaim Jesus in the synagogues, saying, "He is the Son of God."

21 And all those hearing him continued to be amazed, and were saying, "Is this not he who in Jerusalem destroyed those who called on this name, and *who* had come here for the purpose of bringing them bound before the chief priests?"

22 But Saul kept increasing in strength and confounding the Jews who lived at Damascus by proving that this *Jesus* is the Christ.

23 And when many days had elapsed, the Jews plotted together to do away with him,

24 but their plot became known to Saul. And they were also watching the gates day and night so that they might put him to death;

25 but his disciples took him by night, and let him down through *an opening in* the wall, lowering him in a large basket.

26 And when he had come to Jerusalem, he was trying to associate with the disciples; and they were all afraid of him, not believing that he was a disciple.

27 But Barnabas took hold of him and brought him to the apostles and described to them how he had seen the Lord on the road, and that He had talked to him, and how at Damascus he had spoken out boldly in the name of Jesus.

28 And he was with them moving about freely in Jerusalem, speaking out boldly in the name of the Lord.

29 And he was talking and arguing with the Hellenistic *Jews*; but they were attempting to put him to death.

30 But when the brethren learned *of it*, they brought him down to Caesarea and sent him away to Tarsus.

31 So the church throughout all Judea and Galilee and Samaria enjoyed peace, being built up; and, going on in the fear of the Lord and in the comfort of the Holy Spirit, it continued to increase.

18 Or, *vessel*

32 Now it came about that as Peter was traveling through all *those parts,* he came down also to the saints who lived at Lydda.

33 And there he found a certain man named Aeneas, who had been bedridden eight years, for he was paralyzed.

34 And Peter said to him, "Aeneas, Jesus Christ heals you; arise, and make your bed." And immediately he arose.

35 And all who lived at Lydda and Sharon saw him, and they turned to the Lord.

36 Now in Joppa there was a certain disciple named Tabitha (which translated in *Greek* is called Dorcas); this woman was abounding with deeds of kindness and charity, which she continually did.

37 And it came about at that time that she fell sick and died; and when they had washed her body, they laid it in an upper room.

38 And since Lydda was near Joppa, the disciples, having heard that Peter was there, sent two men to him, entreating him, "Do not delay to come to us."

39 And Peter arose and went with them. And when he had come, they brought him into the upper room; and all the widows stood beside him weeping, and showing all the [19]tunics and garments that Dorcas used to make while she was with them.

40 But Peter sent them all out and knelt down and prayed, and turning to the body, he said, "Tabitha, arise." And she opened her eyes, and when she saw Peter, she sat up.

41 And he gave her his hand and raised her up; and calling the saints and widows, he presented her alive.

42 And it became known all over Joppa, and many believed in the Lord.

43 And it came about that he stayed many days in Joppa with a certain tanner, Simon.

CHAPTER 10

NOW *there was* a certain man at Caesarea named Cornelius, a centurion of what was called the Italian [20]cohort,

2 a devout man, and one who feared God with all his household, and gave many [21]alms to the *Jewish* people, and prayed to God continually.

3 About the [22]ninth hour of the day he clearly saw in a vision an angel of God who had *just* come in to him, and said to him, "Cornelius!"

4 And fixing his gaze upon him and being much alarmed, he said, "What is it, Lord?" And he said to him, "Your prayers and [23]alms have ascended as a memorial before God.

5 "And now dispatch *some* men to Joppa, and send for a man *named* Simon, who is also called Peter;

6 he is staying with a certain tanner *named* Simon, whose house is by the sea."

7 And when the angel who was speaking to him had departed, he summoned two of his servants and a devout soldier of those who were in constant attendance upon him,

8 and after he had explained everything to them, he sent them to Joppa.

---

[19] Or, *inner garments*   [20] Or, *battalion*
[21] Or, *gifts of charity*   [22] I.e., 3 p.m.
[23] Or, *deeds of charity*

9 And on the next day, as they were on their way, and approaching the city, Peter went up on the housetop about the [24]sixth hour to pray.

10 And he became hungry, and was desiring to eat; but while they were making preparations, he fell into a trance;

11 and he *beheld the sky opened up, and a certain [25]object like a great sheet coming down, lowered by four corners to the ground,

12 and there were in it all *kinds of* four-footed animals and [26]crawling creatures of the earth and birds of the air.

13 And a voice came to him, "Arise, Peter, kill and eat!"

14 But Peter said, "By no means, Lord, for I have never eaten anything unholy and unclean."

15 And again a voice *came* to him a second time, "What God has cleansed, no *longer* consider unholy."

16 And this happened three times; and immediately the object was taken up into the sky.

17 Now while Peter was greatly perplexed in mind as to what the vision which he had seen might be, behold, the men who had been sent by Cornelius, having asked directions for Simon's house, appeared at the gate;

18 and calling out, they were asking whether Simon, who was also called Peter, was staying there.

19 And while Peter was reflecting on the vision, the Spirit said to him, "Behold, three men are looking for you.

20 "But arise, go downstairs, and accompany them without misgivings; for I have sent them Myself."

21 And Peter went down to the men and said, "Behold, I am the one you are looking for; what is the reason for which you have come?"

22 And they said, "Cornelius, a centurion, a righteous and God-fearing man well spoken of by the entire nation of the Jews, was *divinely* directed by a holy angel to send for you *to come* to his house and hear a message from you."

23 And so he invited them in and gave them lodging.

And on the next day he arose and went away with them, and some of the brethren from Joppa accompanied him.

24 And on the following day he entered Caesarea. Now Cornelius was waiting for them, and had called together his relatives and close friends.

25 And when it came about that Peter entered, Cornelius met him, and fell at his feet and worshiped *him*.

26 But Peter raised him up, saying, "Stand up; I too am *just* a man."

27 And as he talked with him, he entered, and found many people assembled.

28 And he said to them, "You yourselves know how unlawful it is for a man who is a Jew to associate with a foreigner or to visit him; and *yet* God has shown me that I should not call any man unholy or unclean.

29 "That is why I came without even raising any objection when I was sent for. And so I ask for

[24] I.e., noon   [25] Or, *vessel*
[26] Or possibly, *reptiles*

what reason you have sent for me."

30 And Cornelius said, "Four days ago to this hour, I was praying in my house during the [27]ninth hour; and behold, a man stood before me in shining garments,

31 and he *said, 'Cornelius, your prayer has been heard and your alms have been remembered before God.

32 'Send therefore to Joppa and invite Simon, who is also called Peter, to come to you; he is staying at the house of Simon the tanner by the sea.'

33 "And so I sent to you immediately, and you have been kind enough to come. Now then, we are all here present before God to hear all that you have been commanded by the Lord."

34 And opening his mouth, Peter said:

"I most certainly understand now that God is not one to show partiality,

35 but in every nation the man who fears Him and does what is right, is welcome to Him.

36 "The word which He sent to the sons of Israel, preaching peace through Jesus Christ (He is Lord of all)—

37 you yourselves know the thing which took place throughout all Judea, starting from Galilee, after the baptism which John proclaimed.

38 "You know of Jesus of Nazareth, how God anointed Him with the Holy Spirit and with power, and how He went about doing good, and healing all who were oppressed by the devil; for God was with Him.

39 "And we are witnesses of all the things He did both in the land of the Jews and in Jerusalem. And they also put Him to death by hanging Him on a cross,

40 "God raised Him up on the third day, and granted that He should become visible,

41 not to all the people, but to witnesses who were chosen beforehand by God, that is, to us, who ate and drank with Him after He arose from the dead.

42 "And He ordered us to preach to the people, and solemnly to testify that this is the One who has been appointed by God as Judge of the living and the dead.

43 "Of Him all the prophets bear witness that through His name everyone who believes in Him receives forgiveness of sins."

44 While Peter was still speaking these words, the Holy Spirit fell upon all those who were listening to the message.

45 And all the circumcised believers who had come with Peter were amazed, because the gift of the Holy Spirit had been poured out upon the Gentiles also.

46 For they were hearing them speaking with tongues and exalting God. Then Peter answered,

47 "Surely no one can refuse the water for these to be baptized who have received the Holy Spirit just as we did, can he?"

48 And he ordered them to be baptized in the name of Jesus Christ. Then they asked him to stay on for a few days.

CHAPTER 11

NOW the apostles and the brethren who were throughout Judea heard that the Gentiles

[27] I.e., 3 to 4 p.m.

also had received the word of God.

2 And when Peter came up to Jerusalem, those who were circumcised took issue with him,

3 saying, "You went to uncircumcised men and ate with them."

4 But Peter began *speaking* and *proceeded* to explain to them in orderly sequence, saying,

5 "I was in the city of Joppa praying; and in a trance I saw a vision, a certain object coming down like a great sheet lowered by four corners from the sky; and it came right down to me,

6 and when I had fixed my gaze upon it and was observing it I saw the four-footed animals of the earth and the wild beasts and the [28]crawling creatures and the birds of the air.

7 "And I also heard a voice saying to me, 'Arise, Peter; kill and eat.'

8 "But I said, 'By no means, Lord, for nothing unholy or unclean has ever entered my mouth.'

9 "But a voice from heaven answered a second time, 'What God has cleansed, no longer consider unholy.'

10 "And this happened three times, and everything was drawn back up into the sky.

11 "And behold, at that moment three men appeared before the house in which we were *staying*, having been sent to me from Caesarea.

12 "And the Spirit told me to go with them without misgivings. And these six brethren also went with me, and we entered the man's house.

13 "And he reported to us how he had seen the angel standing in his house, and saying, 'Send to Joppa, and have Simon, who is also called Peter, brought here;

14 and he shall speak words to you by which you will be saved, you and all your household.'

15 "And as I began to speak, the Holy Spirit fell upon them, just as *He* did upon us at the beginning.

16 "And I remembered the word of the Lord, how He used to say, 'John baptized with water, but you shall be baptized with the Holy Spirit.'

17 "If God therefore gave to them the same gift as *He* gave to us also after believing in the Lord Jesus Christ, who was I that I could stand in God's way?"

18 And when they heard this, they quieted down, and glorified God, saying, "Well then, God has granted to the Gentiles also the repentance *that leads* to life."

19 So then those who were scattered because of the persecution that arose in connection with Stephen made their way to Phoenicia and Cyprus and Antioch, speaking the word to no one except to Jews alone.

20 But there were some of them, men of Cyprus and Cyrene, who came to Antioch and *began* speaking to the [29]Greeks also, preaching the Lord Jesus.

21 And the hand of the Lord was with them, and a large number who believed turned to the Lord.

22 And the news about them reached the ears of the church at Jerusalem, and they sent Barnabas off to Antioch.

23 Then when he had come and

[28] Or possibly, *reptiles*
[29] Some mss. read *Greek-speaking Jews*

witnessed the grace of God, he rejoiced and *began* to encourage them all with resolute heart to remain *true* to the Lord;

24 for he was a good man, and full of the Holy Spirit and of faith. And considerable numbers were brought to the Lord.

25 And he left for Tarsus to look for Saul;

26 and when he had found him, he brought him to Antioch. And it came about that for an entire year they met with the church, and taught considerable numbers; and the disciples were first called Christians in Antioch.

27 Now at this time some prophets came down from Jerusalem to Antioch.

28 And one of them named Agabus stood up and *began* to indicate by the Spirit that there would certainly be a great famine all over the world. And this took place in the *reign* of Claudius.

29 And in the proportion that any of the disciples had means, each of them determined to send *a contribution* for the relief of the brethren living in Judea.

30 And this they did, sending it in charge of Barnabas and Saul to the elders.

CHAPTER 12

NOW about that time Herod the king laid hands on some who belonged to the church, in order to mistreat them.

2 And he had James the brother of John put to death with a sword.

3 And when he saw that it pleased the Jews, he proceeded to arrest Peter also. Now it was during the days of Unleavened Bread.

4 And when he had seized him, he put him in prison, delivering him to four squads of soldiers to guard him, intending after the Passover to bring him out before the people.

5 So Peter was kept in the prison, but prayer for him was being made fervently by the church to God.

6 And on the very night when Herod was about to bring him forward, Peter was sleeping between two soldiers, bound with two chains; and guards in front of the door were watching over the prison.

7 And behold, an angel of the Lord suddenly appeared, and a light shone in the cell; and he struck Peter's side and roused him, saying, "Get up quickly." And his chains fell off his hands.

8 And the angel said to him, "Gird yourself and put on your sandals." And he did so. And he *said to him, "Wrap your cloak around you and follow me."

9 And he went out and continued to follow, and he did not know that what was being done by the angel was real, but thought he was seeing a vision.

10 And when they had passed the first and second guard, they came to the iron gate that leads into the city, which opened for them by itself; and they went out and went along one street; and immediately the angel departed from him.

11 And when Peter came to himself, he said, "Now I know for sure that the Lord has sent forth His angel and rescued me from the hand of Herod and from all that the Jewish people were expecting."

12 And when he realized *this*, he went to the house of Mary, the mother of John who was also called Mark, where many were gathered together and were praying.

13 And when he knocked at the door of the gate, a servant-girl named Rhoda came to answer.

14 And when she recognize Peter's voice, because of her joy she did not open the gate, but ran in and announced that Peter was standing in front of the gate.

15 And they said to her, "You are out of your mind!" But she kept insisting that it was so. And they kept saying, "It is his angel."

16 But Peter continued knocking; and when they had opened *the door*, they saw him and were amazed.

17 But motioning to them with his hand to be silent, he described to them how the Lord had led him out of the prison. And he said, "Report these things to James and the brethren." And he departed and went to another place.

18 Now when day came, there was no small disturbance among the soldiers *as to* what could have become of Peter.

19 And when Herod had searched for him and had not found him, he examined the guards and ordered that they be led away *to execution*. And he went down from Judea to Caesarea and was spending time there.

20 Now he was very angry with the people of Tyre and Sidon; and with one accord they came to him, and having won over Blastus the king's chamberlain, they were asking for peace, because their country was fed by the king's country.

21 And on an appointed day Herod, having put on his royal apparel, took his seat on the rostrum and *began* delivering an address to them.

22 And the people kept crying out, "The voice of a god and not of a man!"

23 And immediately an angel of the Lord struck him because he did not give God the glory, and he was eaten by worms and died.

24 But the word of the Lord continued to grow and to be multiplied.

25 And Barnabas and Saul returned from Jerusalem when they had fulfilled their mission, taking along with *them* John, who was also called Mark.

CHAPTER 13

NOW there were at Antioch, in the church that was *there*, prophets and teachers: Barnabas, and Simeon who was called Niger, and Lucius of Cyrene, and Manaen who had been brought up with Herod the tetrarch, and Saul.

2 And while they were ministering to the Lord and fasting, the Holy Spirit said, "Set apart for Me Barnabas and Saul for the work to which I have called them."

3 Then, when they had fasted and prayed and laid their hands on them, they sent them away.

4 So, being sent out by the Holy Spirit, they went down to Seleucia and from there they sailed to Cyprus.

5 And when they reached Salamis, they *began* to proclaim the

word of God in the synagogues of the Jews; and they also had John as their helper.

6 And when they had gone through the whole island as far as Paphos, they found a certain magician, a Jewish false prophet whose name was Bar-Jesus,

7 who was with the proconsul, Sergius Paulus, a man of intelligence. This man summoned Barnabas and Saul and sought to hear the word of God.

8 But Elymas the magician (for thus his name is translated) was opposing them, seeking to turn the proconsul away from the faith.

9 But Saul, who was also known as Paul, filled with the Holy Spirit, fixed his gaze upon him,

10 and said, "You who are full of all deceit and fraud, you son of the devil, you enemy of all righteousness, will you not cease to make crooked the straight ways of the Lord?

11 "And now, behold, the hand of the Lord is upon you, and you will be blind and not see the sun for a time." And immediately a mist and a darkness fell upon him, and he went about seeking those who would lead him by the hand.

12 Then the proconsul believed when he saw what had happened, being amazed at the teaching of the Lord.

13 Now Paul and his companions put out to sea from Paphos and came to Perga in Pamphylia; and John left them and returned to Jerusalem.

14 But going on from Perga, they arrived at Pisidian Antioch, and on the Sabbath day they went into the synagogue and sat down.

15 And after the reading of the Law and the Prophets the synagogue officials sent to them, saying, "Brethren, if you have any word of exhortation for the people, say it."

16 And Paul stood up, and motioning with his hand, he said,

"Men of Israel, and you who fear God, listen:

17 "The God of this people Israel chose our fathers, and made the people great during their stay in the land of Egypt, and with an uplifted arm He led them out from it.

18 "And for a period of about forty years He put up with them in the wilderness.

19 "And when He had destroyed seven nations in the land of Canaan, He distributed their land as an inheritance—all of which took about four hundred and fifty years.

20 "And after these things He gave them judges until Samuel the prophet.

21 "And then they asked for a king, and God gave them Saul the son of Kish, a man of the tribe of Benjamin, for forty years.

22 "And after He had removed him, He raised up David to be their king, concerning whom He also testified and said, 'I HAVE FOUND DAVID the son of Jesse, A MAN AFTER MY HEART, who will do all My will.'

23 "From the offspring of this man, according to promise, God has brought to Israel a Savior, Jesus,

24 after John had proclaimed before His coming a baptism of

repentance to all the people of Israel.

25"And while John was completing his course, he kept saying, 'What do you suppose that I am? I am not *He*. But behold, one is coming after me the sandals of whose feet I am not worthy to untie.'

26"Brethren, sons of Abraham's family, and those among you who fear God, to us the word of this salvation is sent out.

27"For those who live in Jerusalem, and their rulers, recognizing neither Him nor the utterances of the prophets which are read every Sabbath, fulfilled *these* by condemning *Him*.

28"And though they found no ground for *putting Him to* death, they asked Pilate that He be executed.

29"And when they had carried out all that was written concerning Him, they took Him down from the cross and laid Him in a tomb.

30"But God raised Him from the dead;

31 and for many days He appeared to those who came up with Him from Galilee to Jerusalem, the very ones who are now His witnesses to the people.

32"And we preach to you the good news of the promise made to the fathers,

33 that God has fulfilled this *promise* to our children in that He raised up Jesus, as it is also written in the second Psalm, 'THOU ART MY SON; TODAY I HAVE BEGOTTEN THEE.'

34"*And as for the fact* that He raised Him up from the dead, no more to return to decay, He has spoken in this way: 'I WILL GIVE YOU THE HOLY *and* SURE *blessings* OF DAVID.'

35"Therefore He also says in another *Psalm*, 'THOU WILT NOT ALLOW THY HOLY ONE TO UNDERGO DECAY.'

36"For David, after he had served the purpose of God in his own generation, fell asleep, and was laid among his fathers, and underwent decay;

37 but He whom God raised did not undergo decay.

38"Therefore let it be known to you, brethren, that through Him forgiveness of sins is proclaimed to you,

39 and through Him everyone who believes is freed from all things, from which you could not be freed through the Law of Moses.

40"Take heed therefore, so that the thing spoken of in the Prophets may not come upon *you*:

41 'BEHOLD, YOU SCOFFERS,
     AND MARVEL, AND PERISH;
   FOR I AM ACCOMPLISHING A
     WORK IN YOUR DAYS,
     A WORK WHICH YOU WILL
       NEVER BELIEVE, THOUGH
       SOMEONE SHOULD DE-
       SCRIBE IT TO YOU.' "

42 And as Paul and Barnabas were going out, the people kept begging that these things might be spoken to them the next Sabbath.

43 Now when *the meeting of* the synagogue had broken up, many of the Jews and of the God-fearing proselytes followed Paul and Barnabas, who, speaking to them, were urging them to continue in the grace of God.

44 And the next Sabbath nearly the whole city assembled to hear the word of God.

45 But when the Jews saw the crowds, they were filled with jealousy, and *began* contradicting the things spoken by Paul, and were blaspheming.

46 And Paul and Barnabas spoke out boldly and said, "It was necessary that the word of God should be spoken to you first; since you repudiate it, and judge yourselves unworthy of eternal life, behold, we are turning to the Gentiles.

47 "For thus the Lord has commanded us,

'I HAVE PLACED YOU AS A LIGHT FOR THE GENTILES, THAT YOU SHOULD BRING SALVATION TO THE END OF THE EARTH.'"

48 And when the Gentiles heard this, they *began* rejoicing and glorifying the word of the Lord; and as many as had been appointed to eternal life believed.

49 And the word of the Lord was being spread through the whole region.

50 But the Jews aroused the devout women of prominence and the leading men of the city, and instigated a persecution against Paul and Barnabas, and drove them out of their district.

51 But they shook off the dust of their feet *in protest* against them and went to Iconium.

52 And the disciples were continually filled with joy and with the Holy Spirit.

CHAPTER 14

AND it came about that in Iconium they entered the synagogue of the Jews together, and spoke in such a manner that a great multitude believed, both of Jews and of Greeks.

2 But the Jews who disbelieved stirred up the minds of the Gentiles, and embittered them against the brethren.

3 Therefore they spent a long time *there* speaking boldly *with reliance* upon the Lord, who was bearing witness to the word of His grace, granting that signs and wonders be done by their hands.

4 But the multitude of the city was divided; and some sided with the Jews, and some with the apostles.

5 And when an attempt was made by both the Gentiles and the Jews with their rulers, to mistreat and to stone them,

6 they became aware of it and fled to the cities of Lycaonia, Lystra and Derbe, and the surrounding region;

7 and there they continued to preach the gospel.

8 And at Lystra there was sitting a certain man, without strength in his feet, lame from his mother's womb, who had never walked.

9 This man was listening to Paul as he spoke, who, when he had fixed his gaze upon him, and had seen that he had faith to be made well,

10 said with a loud voice, "Stand upright on your feet." And he leaped up and *began* to walk.

11 And when the multitudes saw what Paul had done, they raised their voice, saying in the Lycaonian language, "The gods have become like men and have come down to us."

12 And they *began* calling Barnabas, Zeus, and Paul, Hermes, because he was the chief speaker.

13 And the priest of Zeus, whose *temple* was just outside the city, brought oxen and garlands to the gates, and wanted to offer sacrifice with the crowds.

14 But when the apostles, Barnabas and Paul, heard of it, they tore their robes and rushed out into the crowd, crying out

15 and saying, "Men, why are you doing these things? We are also men of the same nature as you, and preach the gospel to you in order that you should turn from these ³⁰vain things to a living God, WHO MADE THE HEAVEN AND THE EARTH AND THE SEA, AND ALL THAT IS IN THEM.

16 "And in the generations gone by He permitted all the nations to go their own ways;

17 and yet He did not leave Himself without witness, in that He did good and gave you rains from heaven and fruitful seasons, satisfying your hearts with food and gladness."

18 And *even* saying these things, they with difficulty restrained the crowds from offering sacrifice to them.

19 But Jews came from Antioch and Iconium, and having won over the multitudes, they stoned Paul and dragged him out of the city, supposing him to be dead.

20 But while the disciples stood around him, he arose and entered the city. And the next day he went away with Barnabas to Derbe.

21 And after they had preached the gospel to that city and had made many disciples, they returned to Lystra and to Iconium and to Antioch,

22 strengthening the souls of the disciples, encouraging them to continue in the faith, and *saying*, "Through many tribulations we must enter the kingdom of God."

23 And when they had appointed elders for them in every church, having prayed with fasting, they commended them to the Lord in whom they had believed.

24 And they passed through Pisidia and came into Pamphylia.

25 And when they had spoken the word in Perga, they went down to Attalia;

26 and from there they sailed to Antioch, from which they had been commended to the grace of God for the work that they had accomplished.

27 And when they had arrived and gathered the church together, they *began* to report all things that God had done with them and how He had opened a door of faith to the Gentiles.

28 And they spent a long time with the disciples.

CHAPTER 15

AND some men came down from Judea and *began* teaching the brethren, "Unless you are circumcised according to the custom of Moses, you cannot be saved."

2 And when Paul and Barnabas had great dissension and debate with them, *the brethren* determined that Paul and Barnabas and certain others of them should go up to Jerusalem to the apostles and elders concerning this issue.

3 Therefore, being sent on their way by the church, they were passing through both Phoe-

---

³⁰ I.e., idols

nicia and Samaria, describing in detail the conversion of the Gentiles, and were bringing great joy to all the brethren.

4 And when they arrived at Jerusalem, they were received by the church and the apostles and the elders, and they reported all that God had done with them.

5 But certain ones of the sect of the Pharisees who had believed, stood up, saying, "It is necessary to circumcise them, and to direct them to observe the Law of Moses."

6 And the apostles and the elders came together to look into this matter.

7 And after there had been much debate, Peter stood up and said to them, "Brethren, you know that in the early days God made a choice among you, that by my mouth the Gentiles should hear the word of the gospel and believe.

8 "And God, who knows the heart, bore witness to them, giving them the Holy Spirit, just as He also did to us;

9 and He made no distinction between us and them, cleansing their hearts by faith.

10 "Now therefore why do you put God to the test by placing upon the neck of the disciples a yoke which neither our fathers nor we have been able to bear?

11 "But we believe that we are saved through the grace of the Lord Jesus, in the same way as they also are."

12 And all the multitude kept silent, and they were listening to Barnabas and Paul as they were relating what signs and wonders God had done through them among the Gentiles.

13 And after they had stopped speaking, James answered, saying, "Brethren, listen to me.

14 "Simeon has related how God first concerned Himself about taking from among the Gentiles a people for His name.

15 "And with this the words of the Prophets agree, just as it is written,

16   'After these things I will
      return,
      And I will rebuild the
        tabernacle of David
        which has fallen,
      And I will rebuild its
        ruins,
      And I will restore it,

17   In order that the rest of
      mankind may seek the
      Lord,
      And all the Gentiles
      who are called by My
      name,'

18   Says the Lord, who
      makes these things
      known from of old.

19 "Therefore it is my judgment that we do not trouble those who are turning to God from among the Gentiles,

20 but that we write to them that they abstain from things contaminated by idols and from fornication and from what is strangled and from blood.

21 "For Moses from ancient generations has in every city those who preach him, since he is read in the synagogues every Sabbath."

22 Then it seemed good to the apostles and the elders, with the whole church, to choose men from among them to send to Antioch with Paul and Barnabas—Judas called Barsabbas, and Silas, leading men among the brethren,

23 and they sent this letter by them,

> "The apostles and the brethren who are elders, to the brethren in Antioch and Syria and Cilicia who are from the Gentiles, greetings.

24 "Since we have heard that some of our number to whom we gave no instruction have disturbed you with *their* words, unsettling your souls,

25 it seemed good to us, having become of one mind, to select men to send to you with our beloved Barnabas and Paul,

26 men who have risked their lives for the name of our Lord Jesus Christ.

27 "Therefore we have sent Judas and Silas, who themselves will also report the same things by word *of mouth.*

28 "For it seemed good to the Holy Spirit and to us to lay upon you no greater burden than these essentials:

29 that you abstain from things sacrificed to idols and from blood and from things strangled and from fornication; if you keep yourselves free from such things, you will do well. Farewell."

30 So, when they were sent away, they went down to Antioch; and having gathered the congregation together, they delivered the letter.

31 And when they had read it, they rejoiced because of its encouragement.

32 And Judas and Silas, also being prophets themselves, encouraged and strengthened the brethren with a lengthy message.

33 And after they had spent time *there,* they were sent away from the brethren in peace to those who had sent them out.

34 [[31]But it seemed good to Silas to remain there.]

35 But Paul and Barnabas stayed in Antioch, teaching and preaching, with many others also, the word of the Lord.

36 And after some days Paul said to Barnabas, "Let us return and visit the brethren in every city in which we proclaimed the word of the Lord, *and see* how they are."

37 And Barnabas was desirous of taking John, called Mark, along with them also.

38 But Paul kept insisting that they should not take him along who had deserted them in Pamphylia and had not gone with them to the work.

39 And there arose such a sharp disagreement that they separated from one another, and Barnabas took Mark with him and sailed away to Cyprus.

40 But Paul chose Silas and departed, being committed by the brethren to the grace of the Lord.

41 And he was traveling through Syria and Cilicia, strengthening the churches.

---

[31] Many mss. do not contain this verse

CHAPTER 16

AND he came also to Derbe and to Lystra. And behold, a certain disciple was there, named Timothy, the son of a Jewish woman who was a believer, but his father was a Greek,

2 and he was well spoken of by the brethren who were in Lystra and Iconium.

3 Paul wanted this man to go with him; and he took him and circumcised him because of the Jews who were in those parts, for they all knew that his father was a Greek.

4 Now while they were passing through the cities, they were delivering the decrees, which had been decided upon by the apostles and elders who were in Jerusalem, for them to observe.

5 So the churches were being strengthened in the faith, and were increasing in number daily.

6 And they passed through the Phrygian and Galatian region, having been forbidden by the Holy Spirit to speak the word in Asia;

7 and when they had come to Mysia, they were trying to go into Bithynia, and the Spirit of Jesus did not permit them;

8 and passing by Mysia, they came down to Troas.

9 And a vision appeared to Paul in the night: a certain man of Macedonia was standing and appealing to him, and saying, "Come over to Macedonia and help us."

10 And when he had seen the vision, immediately we sought to go into Macedonia, concluding that God had called us to preach the gospel to them.

11 Therefore putting out to sea from Troas, we ran a straight course to Samothrace, and on the day following to Neapolis;

12 and from there to Philippi, which is a leading city of the district of Macedonia, a *Roman* colony; and we were staying in this city for some days.

13 And on the Sabbath day we went outside the gate to a riverside, where we were supposing that there would be a place of prayer; and we sat down and began speaking to the women who had assembled.

14 And a certain woman named Lydia, from the city of Thyatira, a seller of purple fabrics, a worshiper of God, was listening; and the Lord opened her heart to respond to the things spoken by Paul.

15 And when she and her household had been baptized, she urged us, saying, "If you have judged me to be faithful to the Lord, come into my house and stay." And she prevailed upon us.

16 And it happened that as we were going to the place of prayer, a certain slave-girl having a spirit of divination met us, who was bringing her masters much profit by fortunetelling.

17 Following after Paul and us, she kept crying out, saying, "These men are bond-servants of the Most High God, who are proclaiming to you the way of salvation."

18 And she continued doing this for many days. But Paul was greatly annoyed, and turned and said to the spirit, "I command you in the name of Jesus Christ to come out of her!" And it came out at that very moment.

19 But when her masters saw that their hope of profit was gone, they seized Paul and Silas and dragged them into the market place before the authorities,

20 and when they had brought them to the chief magistrates, they said, "These men are throwing our city into confusion, being Jews,

21 and are proclaiming customs which it is not lawful for us to accept or to observe, being Romans."

22 And the crowd rose up together against them, and the chief magistrates tore their robes off them, and proceeded to order *them* to be beaten with rods.

23 And when they had inflicted many blows upon them, they threw them into prison, commanding the jailer to guard them securely;

24 and he, having received such a command, threw them into the inner prison, and fastened their feet in the stocks.

25 But about midnight Paul and Silas were praying and singing hymns of praise to God, and the prisoners were listening to them;

26 and suddenly there came a great earthquake, so that the foundations of the prison house were shaken; and immediately all the doors were opened, and everyone's chains were unfastened.

27 And when the jailer had been roused out of sleep and had seen the prison doors opened, he drew his sword and was about to kill himself, supposing that the prisoners had escaped.

28 But Paul cried out with a loud voice, saying, "Do yourself no harm, for we are all here!"

29 And he called for lights and rushed in and, trembling with fear, he fell down before Paul and Silas,

30 and after he brought them out, he said, "Sirs, what must I do to be saved?"

31 And they said, "Believe in the Lord Jesus, and you shall be saved, you and your household."

32 And they spoke the word of the Lord to him together with all who were in his house.

33 And he took them that *very* hour of the night and washed their wounds, and immediately he was baptized, he and all his *household.*

34 And he brought them into his house and set food before them, and rejoiced greatly, having believed in God with his whole household.

35 Now when day came, the chief magistrates sent their policemen, saying, "Release those men."

36 And the jailer reported these words to Paul, *saying,* "The chief magistrates have sent to release you. Now therefore, come out and go in peace."

37 And Paul said to them, "They have beaten us in public without trial, men who are Romans, and have thrown us into prison; and now are they sending us away secretly? No indeed! But let them come themselves and bring us out."

38 And the policemen reported these words to the chief magistrates. And they were afraid when they heard that they were Romans,

39 and they came and appealed to them, and when they had brought them out, they kept begging them to leave the city.

40 And they went out of the prison and entered *the house of* Lydia, and when they saw the brethren, they encouraged them and departed.

CHAPTER 17

NOW when they had traveled through Amphipolis and Apollonia, they came to Thessalonica, where there was a synagogue of the Jews.

2 And according to Paul's custom, he went to them, and for three Sabbaths reasoned with them from the Scriptures,

3 explaining and giving evidence that the Christ had to suffer and rise again from the dead, and *saying,* "This Jesus whom I am proclaiming to you is the Christ."

4 And some of them were persuaded and joined Paul and Silas, along with a great multitude of the God-fearing Greeks and a number of the leading women.

5 But the Jews, becoming jealous and taking along some wicked men from the market place, formed a mob and set the city in an uproar; and coming upon the house of Jason, they were seeking to bring them out to the people.

6 And when they did not find them, they *began* dragging Jason and some brethren before the city authorities, shouting, "These men who have upset [32]the world have come here also;

7 and Jason has welcomed them, and they all act contrary to the decrees of Caesar, saying that there is another king, Jesus."

[32] Lit., *the inhabited earth*

8 And they stirred up the crowd and the city authorities who heard these things.

9 And when they had received a pledge from Jason and the others, they released them.

10 Now the brethren immediately sent Paul and Silas away by night to Berea; and when they arrived, they went into the synagogue of the Jews.

11 Now these were more noble-minded than those in Thessalonica, for they received the word with great eagerness, examining the Scriptures daily, *to see* whether these things were so.

12 Many of them therefore believed, along with a number of prominent Greek women and men.

13 But when the Jews of Thessalonica found out that the word of God had been proclaimed by Paul in Berea also, they came there likewise, agitating and stirring up the crowds.

14 And then immediately the brethren sent Paul out to go as far as the sea; and Silas and Timothy remained there.

15 Now those who conducted Paul brought him as far as Athens; and receiving a command for Silas and Timothy to come to him as soon as possible, they departed.

16 Now while Paul was waiting for them at Athens, his spirit was being provoked within him as he was beholding the city full of idols.

17 So he was reasoning in the synagogue with the Jews and the God-fearing *Gentiles,* and in the market place every day with those who happened to be present.

18 And also some of the Epicurean and Stoic philosophers were conversing with him. And some were saying, "What would this idle babbler wish to say?" Others, "He seems to be a proclaimer of strange deities,"—because he was preaching Jesus and the resurrection.

19 And they took him and brought him to the Areopagus, saying, "May we know what this new teaching is which you are proclaiming?

20 "For you are bringing some strange things to our ears; we want to know therefore what these things mean."

21 (Now all the Athenians and the strangers visiting there used to spend their time in nothing other than telling or hearing something new.)

22 And Paul stood in the midst of the Areopagus and said, "Men of Athens, I observe that you are very religious in all respects.

23 "For while I was passing through and examining the objects of your worship, I also found an altar with this inscription, 'TO AN UNKNOWN GOD.' What therefore you worship in ignorance, this I proclaim to you.

24 "The God who made the world and all things in it, since He is Lord of heaven and earth, does not dwell in temples made with hands;

25 neither is He served by human hands, as though He needed anything, since He Himself gives to all life and breath and all things;

26 and He made from [33]one, every nation of mankind to live on all the face of the earth, having determined *their* appointed times, and the boundaries of their habitation,

27 that they should seek God, if perhaps they might grope for Him and find Him, though He is not far from each one of us;

28 for in Him we live and move and exist, as even some of your own poets have said, 'For we also are His offspring.'

29 "Being then the offspring of God, we ought not to think that the Divine Nature is like gold or silver or stone, an image formed by the art and thought of man.

30 "Therefore having overlooked the times of ignorance, God is now declaring to men that all everywhere should repent,

31 because He has fixed a day in which He will judge the world in righteousness through a Man whom He has appointed, having furnished proof to all men by raising Him from the dead."

32 Now when they heard of the resurrection of the dead, some *began* to sneer, but others said, "We shall hear you again concerning this."

33 So Paul went out of their midst.

34 But some men joined him and believed, among whom also was Dionysius the Areopagite and a woman named Damaris and others with them.

CHAPTER 18

AFTER these things he left Athens and went to Corinth.

2 And he found a certain Jew named Aquila, a native of Pontus, having recently come from Italy with his wife Priscilla, because Claudius had commanded

[33] Some later mss. read one blood

all the Jews to leave Rome. He came to them,

3 and because he was of the same trade, he stayed with them and they were working; for by trade they were tent-makers.

4 And he was reasoning in the synagogue every Sabbath and trying to persuade Jews and Greeks.

5 But when Silas and Timothy came down from Macedonia, Paul *began* devoting himself completely to the word, solemnly testifying to the Jews that Jesus was the Christ.

6 And when they resisted and blasphemed, he shook out his garments and said to them, "Your blood *be* upon your own heads! I am clean. From now on I shall go to the Gentiles."

7 And he departed from there and went to the house of a certain man named Titius Justus, a worshiper of God, whose house was next to the synagogue.

8 And Crispus, the leader of the synagogue, believed in the Lord with all his household, and many of the Corinthians when they heard were believing and being baptized.

9 And the Lord said to Paul in the night by a vision, "Do not be afraid *any longer*, but go on speaking and do not be silent;

10 for I am with you, and no man will attack you in order to harm you, for I have many people in this city."

11 And he settled *there* a year and six months, teaching the word of God among them.

12 But while Gallio was proconsul of Achaia, the Jews with one accord rose up against Paul and brought him before the judgment seat,

13 saying, "This man persuades men to worship God contrary to the law."

14 But when Paul was about to open his mouth, Gallio said to the Jews, "If it were a matter of wrong or of vicious crime, O Jews, it would be reasonable for me to put up with you;

15 but if there are questions about words and names and your own law, look after it yourselves; I am unwilling to be a judge of these matters."

16 And he drove them away from the judgment seat.

17 And they all took hold of Sosthenes, the leader of the synagogue, and *began* beating him in front of the judgment seat. And Gallio was not concerned about any of these things.

18 And Paul, having remained many days longer, took leave of the brethren and put out to sea for Syria, and with him were Priscilla and Aquila. In Cenchrea he had his hair cut, for he was keeping a vow.

19 And they came to Ephesus, and he left them there. Now he himself entered the synagogue and reasoned with the Jews.

20 And when they asked him to stay for a longer time, he did not consent,

21 but taking leave of them and saying, "I will return to you again if God wills," he set sail from Ephesus.

22 And when he had landed at Caesarea, he went up and greeted the church, and went down to Antioch.

23 And having spent some time *there*, he departed and passed successively through the Galatian region and Phrygia, strengthening all the disciples.

24 Now a certain Jew named Apollos, an Alexandrian by birth, an eloquent man, came to Ephesus; and he was mighty in the Scriptures.

25 This man had been instructed in the way of the Lord; and being fervent in spirit, he was speaking and teaching accurately the things concerning Jesus, being acquainted only with the baptism of John;

26 and he began to speak out boldly in the synagogue. But when Priscilla and Aquila heard him, they took him aside and explained to him the way of God more accurately.

27 And when he wanted to go across to Achaia, the brethren encouraged him and wrote to the disciples to welcome him; and when he had arrived, he helped greatly those who had believed through grace;

28 for he powerfully refuted the Jews in public, demonstrating by the Scriptures that Jesus was the Christ.

CHAPTER 19

AND it came about that while Apollos was at Corinth, Paul having passed through the upper country came to Ephesus, and found some disciples,

2 and he said to them, "Did you receive the Holy Spirit when you believed?" And they said to him, "No, we have not even heard whether there is a Holy Spirit."

3 And he said, "Into what then were you baptized?" And they said, "Into John's baptism."

4 And Paul said, "John baptized with the baptism of repentance, telling the people to believe in Him who was coming after him, that is, in Jesus."

5 And when they heard this, they were baptized in the name of the Lord Jesus.

6 And when Paul had laid his hands upon them, the Holy Spirit came on them, and they *began* speaking with tongues and prophesying.

7 And there were in all about twelve men.

8 And he entered the synagogue and continued speaking out boldly for three months, reasoning and persuading *them* about the kingdom of God.

9 But when some were becoming hardened and disobedient, speaking evil of the Way before the multitude, he withdrew from them and took away the disciples, reasoning daily in the school of Tyrannus.

10 And this took place for two years, so that all who lived in Asia heard the word of the Lord, both Jews and Greeks.

11 And God was performing extraordinary miracles by the hands of Paul,

12 so that handkerchiefs or aprons were even carried from his body to the sick, and the diseases left them and the evil spirits went out.

13 But also some of the Jewish exorcists, who went from place to place, attempted to name over those who had the evil spirits the name of the Lord Jesus, saying, "I adjure you by Jesus whom Paul preaches."

14 And seven sons of one Sceva, a Jewish chief priest, were doing this.

15 And the evil spirit answered and said to them, "I recognize

Jesus, and I know about Paul, but who are you?"

16 And the man, in whom was the evil spirit, leaped on them and subdued all of them and overpowered them, so that they fled out of that house naked and wounded.

17 And this became known to all, both Jews and Greeks, who lived in Ephesus; and fear fell upon them all and the name of the Lord Jesus was being magnified.

18 Many also of those who had believed kept coming, confessing and disclosing their practices.

19 And many of those who practiced magic brought their books together and *began* burning them in the sight of all; and they counted up the price of them and found it fifty thousand pieces of silver.

20 So the word of the Lord was growing mightily and prevailing.

21 Now after these things were finished, Paul purposed in the spirit to go to Jerusalem after he had passed through Macedonia and Achaia, saying, "After I have been there, I must also see Rome."

22 And having sent into Macedonia two of those who ministered to him, Timothy and Erastus, he himself stayed in Asia for a while.

23 And about that time there arose no small disturbance concerning the Way.

24 For a certain man named Demetrius, a silversmith, who made silver shrines of Artemis, was bringing no little business to the craftsmen;

25 these he gathered together with the workmen of similar *trades,* and said, "Men, you know that our prosperity depends upon this business.

26 "And you see and hear that not only in Ephesus, but in almost all of Asia, this Paul has persuaded and turned away a considerable number of people, saying that gods made with hands are no gods *at all.*

27 "And not only is there danger that this trade of ours fall into disrepute, but also that the temple of the great goddess Artemis be regarded as worthless and that she whom all of Asia and the world worship should even be dethroned from her magnificence."

28 And when they heard *this* and were filled with rage, they *began* crying out, saying, "Great is Artemis of the Ephesians!"

29 And the city was filled with the confusion, and they rushed with one accord into the theater, dragging along Gaius and Aristarchus, Paul's traveling companions from Macedonia.

30 And when Paul wanted to go into the assembly, the disciples would not let him.

31 And also some of the ³⁴Asiarchs who to him and were friends of his son and repeatedly urged him not to venture into the theater.

32 So then, some were shouting one thing and some another, for the assembly was in confusion, and the majority did not know for what cause they had come together.

33 And some of the crowd concluded *it was* Alexander, since the Jews had put him forward;

³⁴ I.e., political or religious officials of the province of Asia

and having motioned with his hand, Alexander was intending to make a defense to the assembly.

34 But when they recognized that he was a Jew, a *single* outcry arose from them all as they shouted for about two hours, "Great is Artemis of the Ephesians!"

35 And after quieting the multitude, the town clerk *said, "Men of Ephesus, what man is there after all who does not know that the city of the Ephesians is guardian of the temple of the great Artemis, and of the *image* which fell down from heaven?

36 "Since then these are undeniable facts, you ought to keep calm and to do nothing rash.

37 "For you have brought these men *here* who are neither robbers of temples nor blasphemers of our goddess.

38 "So then, if Demetrius and the craftsmen who are with him have a complaint against any man, the courts are in session and proconsuls are *available*; let them bring charges against one another.

39 "But if you want anything beyond this, it shall be settled in the lawful assembly.

40 "For indeed we are in danger of being accused of a riot in connection with today's affair, since there is no *real* cause *for it*; and in this connection we shall be unable to account for this disorderly gathering."

41 And after saying this he dismissed the assembly.

CHAPTER 20

AND after the uproar had ceased, Paul sent for the disciples and when he had exhorted them and taken his leave of them, he departed to go to Macedonia.

2 And when he had gone through those districts and had given them much exhortation, he came to Greece.

3 And *there* he spent three months, and when a plot was formed against him by the Jews as he was about to set sail for Syria, he determined to return through Macedonia.

4 And he was accompanied by Sopater of Berea, *the son* of Pyrrhus; and by Aristarchus and Secundus of the Thessalonians; and Gaius of Derbe, and Timothy; and Tychicus and Trophimus of Asia.

5 But these had gone on ahead and were waiting for us at Troas.

6 And we sailed from Philippi after the days of Unleavened Bread, and came to them at Troas within five days; and there we stayed seven days.

7 And on the first day of the week, when we were gathered together to break bread, Paul *began* talking to them, intending to depart the next day, and he prolonged his message until midnight.

8 And there were many lamps in the upper room where we were gathered together.

9 And there was a certain young man named Eutychus sitting on the window sill, sinking into a deep sleep; and as Paul kept on talking, he was overcome by sleep and fell down from the third floor, and was picked up dead.

10 But Paul went down and fell upon him and after embracing

him, he said, "Do not be troubled, for his life is in him."

11 And when he had gone *back* up, and had broken the bread and eaten, he talked with them a long while, until daybreak, and so departed.

12 And they took away the boy alive, and were greatly comforted.

13 But we, going ahead to the ship, set sail for Assos, intending from there to take Paul on board; for thus he had arranged it, intending himself to go by land.

14 And when he met us at Assos, we took him on board and came to Mitylene.

15 And sailing from there, we arrived the following day opposite Chios; and the next day we crossed over to Samos; and the day following we came to Miletus.

16 For Paul had decided to sail past Ephesus in order that he might not have to spend time in Asia; for he was hurrying to be in Jerusalem, if possible, on the day of Pentecost.

17 And from Miletus he sent to Ephesus and called to him the elders of the church.

18 And when they had come to him, he said to them,

"You yourselves know, from the first day that I set foot in Asia, how I was with you the whole time,

19 serving the Lord with all humility and with tears and with trials which came upon me through the plots of the Jews;

20 how I did not shrink from declaring to you anything that was profitable, and teaching you publicly and from house to house,

21 solemnly testifying to both Jews and Greeks of repentance toward God and faith in our Lord Jesus Christ.

22 "And now, behold, bound in spirit, I am on my way to Jerusalem, not knowing what will happen to me there,

23 except that the Holy Spirit solemnly testifies to me in every city, saying that bonds and afflictions await me.

24 "But I do not consider my life of any account as dear to myself, in order that I may finish my course, and the ministry which I received from the Lord Jesus, to testify solemnly of the gospel of the grace of God.

25 "And now, behold, I know that all of you, among whom I went about preaching the kingdom, will see my face no more.

26 "Therefore I testify to you this day, that I am innocent of the blood of all men.

27 "For I did not shrink from declaring to you the whole purpose of God.

28 "Be on guard for yourselves and for all the flock, among which the Holy Spirit has made you overseers, to shepherd the church of God which He purchased with His own blood.

29 "I know that after my departure savage wolves will come in among you, not sparing the flock;

30 and from among your own selves men will arise, speaking perverse things, to draw away the disciples after them.

31 "Therefore be on the alert, remembering that night and day for a period of three years I did not cease to admonish each one with tears.

32 "And now I commend you to God and to the word of His

grace, which is able to build *you* up and to give *you* the inheritance among all those who are sanctified.

33 "I have coveted no one's silver or gold or clothes.

34 "You yourselves know that these hands ministered to my *own* needs and to the men who were with me.

35 "In everything I showed you that by working hard in this manner you must help the weak and remember the words of the Lord Jesus, that He Himself said, 'It is more blessed to give than to receive.'"

36 And when he had said these things, he knelt down and prayed with them all.

37 And they *began* to weep aloud and embraced Paul, and repeatedly kissed him,

38 grieving especially over the word which he had spoken, that they should see his face no more. And they were accompanying him to the ship.

CHAPTER 21

AND when it came about that we had parted from them and had set sail, we ran a straight course to Cos and the next day to Rhodes and from there to Patara;

2 and having found a ship crossing over to Phoenicia, we went aboard and set sail.

3 And when we had come in sight of Cyprus, leaving it on the left, we kept sailing to Syria and landed at Tyre; for there the ship was to unload its cargo.

4 And after looking up the disciples, we stayed there seven days; and they kept telling Paul through the Spirit not to set foot in Jerusalem.

5 And when it came about that our days there were ended, we departed and started on our journey, while they all, with wives and children, escorted us until *we were* out of the city. And after kneeling down on the beach and praying, we said farewell to one another.

6 Then we went on board the ship, and they returned home again.

7 And when we had finished the voyage from Tyre, we arrived at Ptolemais; and after greeting the brethren, we stayed with them for a day.

8 And on the next day we departed and came to Caesarea; and entering the house of Philip the evangelist, who was one of the seven, we stayed with him.

9 Now this man had four virgin daughters who were prophetesses.

10 And as we were staying there for some days, a certain prophet named Agabus came down from Judea.

11 And coming to us, he took Paul's belt and bound his own feet and hands, and said, "This is what the Holy Spirit says: 'In this way the Jews at Jerusalem will bind the man who owns this belt and deliver him into the hands of the Gentiles.'"

12 And when we had heard this, we as well as the local residents *began* begging him not to go up to Jerusalem.

13 Then Paul answered, "What are you doing, weeping and breaking my heart? For I am ready not only to be bound, but even to die at Jerusalem for the name of the Lord Jesus."

14 And since he would not be persuaded, we fell silent, remark-

ing, "The will of the Lord be done!"

15 And after these days we got ready and started on our way up to Jerusalem.

16 And *some* of the disciples from Caesarea also came with us, taking us to Mnason of Cyprus, a disciple of long standing with whom we were to lodge.

17 And when we had come to Jerusalem, the brethren received us gladly.

18 And now the following day Paul went in with us to James, and all the elders were present.

19 And after he had greeted them, he *began* to relate one by one the things which God had done among the Gentiles through his ministry.

20 And when they heard it they *began* glorifying God; and they said to him, "You see, brother, how many thousands there are among the Jews of those who have believed, and they are all zealous for the Law;

21 and they have been told about you, that you are teaching all the Jews who are among the Gentiles to forsake Moses, telling them not to circumcise their children nor to walk according to the customs.

22 "What, then, is *to be done?* They will certainly hear that you have come.

23 "Therefore do this that we tell you. We have four men who are under a vow;

24 take them and purify yourself along with them, and pay their expenses in order that they may shave their heads; and all will know that there is nothing to the things which they have been

told about you, but that you yourself also walk orderly, keeping the Law.

25 "But concerning the Gentiles who have believed, we wrote, having decided that they should abstain from meat sacrificed to idols and from blood and from what is strangled and from fornication."

26 Then Paul took the men, and the next day, purifying himself along with them, went into the temple, giving notice of the completion of the days of purification, until the sacrifice was offered for each one of them.

27 And when the seven days were almost over, the Jews from Asia, upon seeing him in the temple, *began* to stir up all the multitude and laid hands on him,

28 crying out, "Men of Israel, come to our aid! This is the man who preaches to all men everywhere against our people, and the Law, and this place; and besides he has even brought Greeks into the temple and has defiled this holy place."

29 For they had previously seen Trophimus the Ephesian in the city with him, and they supposed that Paul had brought him into the temple.

30 And all the city was aroused, and the people rushed together; and taking hold of Paul, they dragged him out of the temple; and immediately the doors were shut.

31 And while they were seeking to kill him, a report came up to the [35]commander of the *Roman* cohort that all Jerusalem was in confusion.

32 And at once he took along *some* soldiers and centurions, and ran down to them; and when

[35] I.e., chiliarch, in command of one thousand troops

they saw the commander and the soldiers, they stopped beating Paul.

33 Then the commander came up and took hold of him, and ordered him to be bound with two chains; and he *began* asking who he was and what he had done.

34 But among the crowd some were shouting one thing *and* some another, and when he could not find out the facts on account of the uproar, he ordered him to be brought into the barracks.

35 And when he got to the stairs, it so happened that he was carried by the soldiers because of the violence of the mob;

36 for the multitude of the people kept following behind, crying out, "Away with him!"

37 And as Paul was about to be brought into the barracks, he said to the commander, "May I say something to you?" And he *said, "Do you know Greek?

38 "Then you are not the Egyptian who some time ago stirred up a revolt and led the four thousand men of the Assassins out into the wilderness?"

39 But Paul said, "I am a Jew of Tarsus in Cilicia, a citizen of no insignificant city; and I beg you, allow me to speak to the people."

40 And when he had given him permission, Paul, standing on the stairs, motioned to the people with his hand; and when there was a great hush, he spoke to them in the Hebrew dialect, saying,

CHAPTER 22

"BRETHREN and fathers, hear my defense which I now *offer* to you."

2 And when they heard that he was addressing them in the Hebrew dialect, they became even more quiet; and he *said,

3 "I am a Jew, born in Tarsus of Cilicia, but brought up in this city, educated under Gamaliel, strictly according to the law of our fathers, being zealous for God, just as you all are today.

4 "And I persecuted this Way to the death, binding and putting both men and women into prisons,

5 as also the high priest and all the Council of the elders can testify. From them I also received letters to the brethren, and started off for Damascus in order to bring even those who were there to Jerusalem as prisoners to be punished.

6 "And it came about that as I was on my way, approaching Damascus about noontime, a very bright light suddenly flashed from heaven all around me,

7 and I fell to the ground and heard a voice saying to me, 'Saul, Saul, why are you persecuting Me?'

8 "And I answered, 'Who art Thou, Lord?' And He said to me, 'I am Jesus the Nazarene, whom you are persecuting.'

9 "And those who were with me beheld the light, to be sure, but did not understand the voice of the One who was speaking to me.

10 "And I said, 'What shall I do, Lord?' And the Lord said to me, 'Arise and go on into Damascus; and there you will be told of all that has been appointed for you to do.'

11 "But since I could not see because of the brightness of that

light, I was led by the hand by those who were with me, and came into Damascus.

12 "And a certain Ananias, a man who was devout by the standard of the Law, *and* well spoken of by all the Jews who lived there,

13 came to me, and standing near said to me, 'Brother Saul, receive your sight!' And at that very time I looked up at him.

14 "And he said, 'The God of our fathers has appointed you to know His will, and to see the Righteous One, and to hear an utterance from His mouth.

15 'For you will be a witness for Him to all men of what you have seen and heard.

16 'And now why do you delay? Arise, and be baptized, and wash away your sins, calling on His name.'

17 "And it came about when I returned to Jerusalem and was praying in the temple, that I fell into a trance,

18 and I saw Him saying to me, 'Make haste, and get out of Jerusalem quickly, because they will not accept your testimony about Me.'

19 "And I said, 'Lord, they themselves understand that in one synagogue after another I used to imprison and beat those who believed in Thee.

20 'And when the blood of Thy witness Stephen was being shed, I also was standing by approving, and watching out for the cloaks of those who were slaying him.'

21 "And He said to me, 'Go! For I will send you far away to the Gentiles.'"

36 I.e., chiliarch, in command of one thousand troops

22 And they listened to him up to this statement, and *then* they raised their voices and said, "Away with such a fellow from the earth, for he should not be allowed to live!"

23 And as they were crying out and throwing off their cloaks and tossing dust into the air,

24 the 36commander ordered him to be brought into the barracks, stating that he should be examined by scourging so that he might find out the reason why they were shouting against him that way.

25 And when they stretched him out with thongs, Paul said to the centurion who was standing by, "Is it lawful for you to scourge a man who is a Roman and uncondemned?"

26 And when the centurion heard *this,* he went to the commander and told him, saying, "What are you about to do? For this man is a Roman."

27 And the commander came and said to him, "Tell me, are you a Roman?" And he said, "Yes."

28 And the commander answered, "I acquired this citizenship with a large sum of money." And Paul said, "But I was actually born *a citizen.*"

29 Therefore those who were about to examine him immediately let go of him; and the commander also was afraid when he found out that he was a Roman, and because he had put him in chains.

30 But on the next day, wishing to know for certain why he had been accused by the Jews, he released him and ordered the chief priests and all the Council

to assemble, and brought Paul down and set him before them.

CHAPTER 23

AND Paul, looking intently at the Council, said, "Brethren, I have lived my life with a perfectly good conscience before God up to this day."

2 And the high priest Ananias commanded those standing beside him to strike him on the mouth.

3 Then Paul said to him, "God is going to strike you, you whitewashed wall! And do you sit to try me according to the Law, and in violation of the Law order me to be struck?"

4 But the bystanders said, "Do you revile God's high priest?"

5 And Paul said, "I was not aware, brethren, that he was high priest; for it is written, 'YOU SHALL NOT SPEAK EVIL OF A RULER OF YOUR PEOPLE.'"

6 But perceiving that one part were Sadducees and the other Pharisees, Paul *began* crying out in the Council, "Brethren, I am a Pharisee, a son of Pharisees; I am on trial for the hope and resurrection of the dead!"

7 And as he said this, there arose a dissension between the Pharisees and Sadducees; and the assembly was divided.

8 For the Sadducees say that there is no resurrection, nor an angel, nor a spirit; but the Pharisees acknowledge them all.

9 And there arose a great uproar; and some of the scribes of the Pharisaic party stood up and *began* to argue heatedly, saying, "We find nothing wrong with this man; suppose a spirit or an angel has spoken to him?"

10 And as a great dissension was developing, the [37]commander was afraid Paul would be torn to pieces by them and ordered the troops to go down and take him away from them by force, and bring him into the barracks.

11 But on the night *immediately* following, the Lord stood at his side and said, "Take courage; for as you have solemnly witnessed to My cause at Jerusalem, so you must witness at Rome also."

12 And when it was day, the Jews formed a conspiracy and bound themselves under an oath, saying that they would neither eat nor drink until they had killed Paul.

13 And there were more than forty who formed this plot.

14 And they came to the chief priests and the elders, and said, "We have bound ourselves under a solemn oath to taste nothing until we have killed Paul.

15 "Now, therefore, you and the Council notify the commander to bring him down to you, as though you were going to determine his case by a more thorough investigation; and we for our part are ready to slay him before he comes near *the place*."

16 But the son of Paul's sister heard of their ambush, and he came and entered the barracks and told Paul.

17 And Paul called one of the centurions to him and said, "Lead this young man to the commander, for he has something to report to him."

[37] I.e., chiliarch, in command of one thousand troops

18 So he took him and led him to the commander and *said, "Paul the prisoner called me to him and asked me to lead this young man to you since he has something to tell you."

19 And the commander took him by the hand and stepping aside, *began* to inquire of him privately, "What is it that you have to report to me?"

20 And he said, "The Jews have agreed to ask you to bring Paul down tomorrow to the Council, as though they were going to inquire somewhat more thoroughly about him.

21 "So do not listen to them, for more than forty of them are lying in wait for him who have bound themselves under a curse not to eat or drink until they slay him; and now they are ready and waiting for the promise from you."

22 Therefore the commander let the young man go, instructing him, "Tell no one that you have notified me of these things."

23 And he called to him two of the centurions, and said, "Get two hundred soldiers ready by [38]the third hour of the night to proceed to Caesarea, with seventy horsemen and two hundred spearmen.

24 *They were* also to provide mounts to put Paul on and bring him safely to Felix the governor.

25 And he wrote a letter having this form:

26 "Claudius Lysias, to the most excellent governor Felix, greetings.

27 "When this man was arrested by the Jews and was about to be slain by them, I came upon them with the troops and rescued him, having learned that he was a Roman.

28 "And wanting to ascertain the charge for which they were accusing him, I brought him down to their Council;

29 and I found him to be accused over questions about their Law, but under no accusation deserving death or imprisonment.

30 "And when I was informed that there would be a plot against the man, I sent him to you at once, also instructing his accusers to bring charges against him before you."

31 So the soldiers, in accordance with their orders, took Paul and brought him by night to Antipatris.

32 But the next day, leaving the horsemen to go on with him, they returned to the barracks.

33 And when these had come to Caesarea and delivered the letter to the governor, they also presented Paul to him.

34 And when he had read it, he asked from what province he was; and when he learned that he was from Cilicia,

35 he said, "I will give you a hearing after your accusers arrive also," giving orders for him to be kept in Herod's [39]Praetorium.

[38] I.e., 9 p.m.
[39] I.e., governor's official residence

CHAPTER 24

AND after five days the high priest Ananias came down with some elders, with a certain attorney *named* Tertullus; and they brought charges to the governor against Paul.

2 And after *Paul* had been summoned, Tertullus began to accuse him, saying *to the governor,*

"Since we have through you attained much peace, and since by your providence reforms are being carried out for this nation,

3 we acknowledge *this* in every way and everywhere, most excellent Felix, with all thankfulness.

4 "But, that I may not weary you any further, I beg you to grant us, by your kindness, a brief hearing.

5 "For we have found this man a real pest and a fellow who stirs up dissension among all the Jews throughout [40]the world, and a ringleader of the sect of the Nazarenes.

6 "And he even tried to desecrate the temple; and then we arrested him. [[41]And we wanted to judge him according to our own Law.

7 "But Lysias the commander came along, and with much violence took him out of our hands,

8 ordering his accusers to come before you.] And by examining him yourself concerning all these matters, you will be able to ascertain the things of which we accuse him."

9 And the Jews also joined in the attack, asserting that these things were so.

10 And when the governor had nodded for him to speak, Paul responded:

"Knowing that for many years you have been a judge to this nation, I cheerfully make my defense,

11 since you can take note of the fact that no more than twelve days ago I went up to Jerusalem to worship.

12 "And neither in the temple, nor in the synagogues, nor in the city *itself* did they find me carrying on a discussion with anyone or causing a riot.

13 "Nor can they prove to you the charges of which they now accuse me.

14 "But this I admit to you, that according to the Way which they call a sect I do serve the God of our fathers, believing everything that is in accordance with the Law, and that is written in the Prophets;

15 having a hope in God, which these men cherish themselves, that there shall certainly be a resurrection of both the righteous and the wicked.

16 "In view of this, I also do my best to maintain always a blameless conscience *both* before God and before men.

17 "Now after several years I came to bring [42]alms to my nation and to present offerings;

18 in which they found me occupied in the temple, having been purified, without *any* crowd or uproar. But *there were* certain Jews from Asia—

19 who ought to have been

---

[40] Lit., *the inhabited earth*
[41] Many mss. do not contain the remainder of v. 6, v. 7, nor the first part of v. 8
[42] Or, *gifts to charity*

present before you, and to make accusation, if they should have anything against me.

20 "Or else let these men themselves tell what misdeed they found when I stood before the Council,

21 other than for this one statement which I shouted out while standing among them, 'For the resurrection of the dead I am on trial before you today.'"

22 But Felix, having a more exact knowledge about the Way, put them off, saying, "When Lysias the 43commander comes down, I will decide your case."

23 And he gave orders to the centurion for him to be kept in custody and yet have some freedom, and not to prevent any of his friends from ministering to him.

24 But some days later, Felix arrived with Drusilla, his wife who was a Jewess, and sent for Paul, and heard him speak about faith in Christ Jesus.

25 And as he was discussing righteousness, self-control and the judgment to come, Felix became frightened and said, "Go away for the present, and when I find time, I will summon you."

26 At the same time too, he was hoping that money would be given him by Paul; therefore he also used to send for him quite often and converse with him.

27 But after two years had passed, Felix was succeeded by Porcius Festus; and wishing to do the Jews a favor, Felix left Paul imprisoned.

43 I.e., chiliarch, in command of one thousand troops

CHAPTER 25

FESTUS therefore, having arrived in the province, three days later went up to Jerusalem from Caesarea.

2 And the chief priests and the leading men of the Jews brought charges against Paul; and they were urging him,

3 requesting a concession against Paul, that he might have him brought to Jerusalem (at the same time, setting an ambush to kill him on the way).

4 Festus then answered that Paul was being kept in custody at Caesarea and that he himself was about to leave shortly.

5 "Therefore," he *said, "let the influential men among you go there with me, and if there is anything wrong about the man, let them prosecute him."

6 And after he had spent not more than eight or ten days among them, he went down to Caesarea; and on the next day he took his seat on the tribunal and ordered Paul to be brought.

7 And after he had arrived, the Jews who had come down from Jerusalem stood around him, bringing many and serious charges against him which they could not prove;

8 while Paul said in his own defense, "I have committed no offense either against the Law of the Jews or against the temple or against Caesar."

9 But Festus, wishing to do the Jews a favor, answered Paul and said, "Are you willing to go up to Jerusalem and stand trial before me on these charges?"

10 But Paul said, "I am standing before Caesar's tribunal, where I ought to be tried. I have

done no wrong to the Jews, as you also very well know.

11 "If then I am a wrongdoer, and have committed anything worthy of death, I do not refuse to die; but if none of those things is true of which these men accuse me, no one can hand me over to them. I appeal to Caesar."

12 Then when Festus had conferred with his council, he answered, "You have appealed to Caesar, to Caesar you shall go."

13 Now when several days had elapsed, King Agrippa and Bernice arrived at Caesarea, and paid their respects to Festus.

14 And while they were spending many days there, Festus laid Paul's case before the king, saying, "There is a certain man left a prisoner by Felix;

15 and when I was at Jerusalem, the chief priests and the elders of the Jews brought charges against him, asking for a sentence of condemnation upon him.

16 "And I answered them that it is not the custom of the Romans to hand over any man before the accused meets his accusers face to face, and has an opportunity to make his defense against the charges.

17 "And so after they had assembled here, I made no delay, but on the next day took my seat on the tribunal, and ordered the man to be brought.

18 "And when the accusers stood up, they began bringing charges against him not of such crimes as I was expecting;

19 but they simply had some points of disagreement with him about their own religion and about a certain dead man, Jesus, whom Paul asserted to be alive.

20 "And being at a loss how to investigate such matters, I asked whether he was willing to go to Jerusalem and there stand trial on these matters.

21 "But when Paul appealed to be held in custody for [44]the Emperor's decision, I ordered him to be kept in custody until I send him to Caesar."

22 And Agrippa said to Festus, "I also would like to hear the man myself." "Tomorrow," he *said, "you shall hear him."

23 And so, on the next day when Agrippa had come together with Bernice, amid great pomp, and had entered the auditorium [45]accompanied by the commanders and the prominent men of the city, at the command of Festus, Paul was brought in.

24 And Festus *said, "King Agrippa, and all you gentlemen here present with us, you behold this man about whom all the people of the Jews appealed to me, both at Jerusalem and here, loudly declaring that he ought not to live any longer.

25 "But I found that he had committed nothing worthy of death; and since he himself appealed to the Emperor, I decided to send him.

26 "Yet I have nothing definite about him to write to my lord. Therefore I have brought him before you all and especially before you, King Agrippa, so that after the investigation has taken place, I may have something to write.

27 "For it seems absurd to me in sending a prisoner, not to indicate also the charges against him."

[44] Lit., the Augustus' (in this case Nero)
[45] Lit., and with

CHAPTER 26

AND Agrippa said to Paul, "You are permitted to speak for yourself." Then Paul stretched out his hand and *proceeded* to make his defense:

2 "In regard to all the things of which I am accused by the Jews, I consider myself fortunate, King Agrippa, that I am about to make my defense before you today;

3 especially because you are an expert in all customs and questions among *the* Jews; therefore I beg you to listen to me patiently.

4 "So then, all Jews know my manner of life from my youth up, which from the beginning was spent among my *own* nation and at Jerusalem;

5 since they have known about me for a long time previously, if they are willing to testify, that I lived *as* a Pharisee according to the strictest sect of our religion.

6 "And now I am standing trial for the hope of the promise made by God to our fathers;

7 *the* promise to which our twelve tribes hope to attain, as they earnestly serve *God* night and day. And for this hope, O King, I am being accused by Jews.

8 "Why is it considered incredible among you *people* if God does raise the dead?

9 "So then, I thought to myself that I had to do many things hostile to the name of Jesus of Nazareth.

10 "And this is just what I did in Jerusalem; not only did I lock up many of the saints in prisons, having received authority from the chief priests, but also when they were being put to death I cast my vote against them.

11 "And as I punished them often in all the synagogues, I tried to force them to blaspheme; and being furiously enraged at them, I kept pursuing them even to foreign cities.

12 "While thus engaged as I was journeying to Damascus with the authority and commission of the chief priests,

13 at midday, O King, I saw on the way a light from heaven, brighter than the sun, shining all around me and those who were journeying with me.

14 "And when we had all fallen to the ground, I heard a voice saying to me in the Hebrew dialect, 'Saul, Saul, why are you persecuting Me? It is hard for you to kick against the goads.'

15 "And I said, 'Who art Thou, Lord?' And the Lord said, 'I am Jesus whom you are persecuting.

16 'But arise, and stand on your feet; for this purpose I have appeared to you, to appoint you a minister and a witness not only to the things which you have seen, but also to the things in which I will appear to you;

17 delivering you from the *Jewish* people and from the Gentiles, to whom I am sending you,

18 to open their eyes so that they may turn from darkness to light and from the dominion of Satan to God, in order that they may receive forgiveness of sins and an inheritance among those who have been sanctified by faith in Me.'

19 "Consequently, King Agrippa, I did not prove disobedient to the heavenly vision,

20 but *kept* declaring both to those of Damascus first, and *also*

at Jerusalem and *then* throughout all the region of Judea, and *even* to the Gentiles, that they should repent and turn to God, performing deeds appropriate to repentance.

21 "For this reason *some* Jews seized me in the temple and tried to put me to death.

22 "And so, having obtained help from God, I stand to this day testifying both to small and great, stating nothing but what the Prophets and Moses said was going to take place;

23 that the Christ was to suffer, *and* that by reason of *His* resurrection from the dead He should be the first to proclaim light both to the *Jewish* people and to the Gentiles."

24 And while *Paul* was saying this in his defense, Festus *said in a loud voice, "Paul, you are out of your mind! *Your* great learning is driving you mad."

25 But Paul *said, "I am not out of my mind, most excellent Festus, but I utter words of sober truth.

26 "For the king knows about these matters, and I speak to him also with confidence, since I am persuaded that none of these things escape his notice; for this has not been done in a corner.

27 "King Agrippa, do you believe the Prophets? I know that you do."

28 And Agrippa *replied* to Paul, "In a short time you will persuade me to become a Christian."

29 And Paul *said,* "I would to God, that whether in a short or long time, not only you, but also all who hear me this day, might become such as I am, except for these chains."

30 And the king arose and the governor and Bernice, and those who were sitting with them,

31 and when they had drawn aside, they *began* talking to one another, saying, "This man is not doing anything worthy of death or imprisonment."

32 And Agrippa said to Festus, "This man might have been set free if he had not appealed to Caesar."

CHAPTER 27

AND when it was decided that we should sail for Italy, they proceeded to deliver Paul and some other prisoners to a centurion of the Augustan [46]cohort named Julius.

2 And embarking in an Adramyttian ship, which was about to sail to the regions along the coast of Asia, we put out to sea, accompanied by Aristarchus, a Macedonian of Thessalonica.

3 And the next day we put in at Sidon; and Julius treated Paul with consideration and allowed him to go to his friends and receive care.

4 And from there we put out to sea and sailed under the shelter of Cyprus because the winds were contrary.

5 And when we had sailed through the sea along the coast of Cilicia and Pamphylia, we landed at Myra in Lycia.

6 And there the centurion found an Alexandrian ship sailing for Italy, and he put us aboard it.

7 And when we had sailed slowly for a good many days, and with difficulty had arrived · off

[46] Or, *battalion*

Cnidus, since the wind did not permit us to go farther, we sailed under the shelter of Crete, off Salmone;

8 and with difficulty sailing past it we came to a certain place called Fair Havens, near which was the city of Lasea.

9 And when considerable time had passed and the voyage was now dangerous, since even the ⁴⁷fast was already over, Paul began to admonish them,

10 and said to them, "Men, I perceive that the voyage will certainly be attended with damage and great loss, not only of the cargo and the ship, but also of our lives."

11 But the centurion was more persuaded by the pilot and the captain of the ship, than by what was being said by Paul.

12 And because the harbor was not suitable for wintering, the majority reached a decision to put out to sea from there, if somehow they could reach Phoenix, a harbor of Crete, facing southwest and northwest, and spend the winter there.

13 And when a moderate south wind came up, supposing that they had gained their purpose, they weighed anchor and began sailing along Crete, close inshore.

14 But before very long there rushed down from the land a violent wind, called ⁴⁸Euraquilo;

15 and when the ship was caught in it, and could not face the wind, we gave way to it, and let ourselves be driven along.

16 And running under the shelter of a small island called

Clauda, we were scarcely able to get the ship's boat under control.

17 And after they had hoisted it up, they used supporting cables in undergirding the ship; and fearing that they might run aground on the shallows of Syrtis, they let down the sea anchor, and so let themselves be driven along.

18 The next day as we were being violently storm-tossed, they began to jettison the cargo;

19 and on the third day they threw the ship's tackle overboard with their own hands.

20 And since neither sun nor stars appeared for many days, and no small storm was assailing us, from then on all hope of our being saved was gradually abandoned.

21 And when they had gone a long time without food, then Paul stood up in their midst and said, "Men, you ought to have followed my advice and not to have set sail from Crete, and incurred this damage and loss.

22 "And yet now I urge you to keep up your courage, for there shall be no loss of life among you, but only of the ship.

23 "For this very night an angel of the God to whom I belong and whom I serve stood before me,

24 saying, 'Do not be afraid, Paul; you must stand before Caesar; and behold, God has granted you all those who are sailing with you.'

25 "Therefore, keep up your courage, men, for I believe God, that it will turn out exactly as I have been told.

26 "But we must run aground on a certain island."

27 But when the fourteenth night had come, as we were

⁴⁷ I.e., Day of Atonement in September or October ⁴⁸ I.e., a northeaster

being driven about in the Adriatic Sea, about midnight the sailors *began* to surmise that they were approaching some land.

28 And they took soundings, and found *it to be* twenty fathoms; and a little farther on they took another sounding and found *it to be* fifteen fathoms.

29 And fearing that we might run aground somewhere on the rocks, they cast four anchors from the stern and wished for daybreak.

30 And as the sailors were trying to escape from the ship, and had let down the *ship's* boat into the sea, on the pretense of intending to lay out anchors from the bow,

31 Paul said to the centurion and to the soldiers, "Unless these men remain in the ship, you yourselves cannot be saved."

32 Then the soldiers cut away the ropes of the *ship's* boat, and let it fall away.

33 And until the day was about to dawn, Paul was encouraging them all to take some food, saying, "Today is the fourteenth day that you have been constantly watching and going without eating, having taken nothing.

34 "Therefore I encourage you to take some food, for this is for your preservation; for not a hair from the head of any of you shall perish."

35 And having said this, he took bread and gave thanks to God in the presence of all; and he broke it and began to eat.

36 And all of them were encouraged, and they themselves also took food.

37 And all of us in the ship were two hundred and seventy-six persons.

38 And when they had eaten enough, they *began* to lighten the ship by throwing out the wheat into the sea.

39 And when day came, they could not recognize the land; but they did observe a certain bay with a beach, and they resolved to [49]drive the ship onto it if they could.

40 And casting off the anchors, they left them in the sea while at the same time they were loosening the ropes of the rudders, and hoisting the foresail to the wind, they were heading for the beach.

41 But striking a reef where two seas met, they ran the vessel aground; and the prow stuck fast and remained immovable, but the stern *began* to be broken up by the force of *the waves.*

42 And the soldiers' plan was to kill the prisoners, that none of *them* should swim away and escape;

43 but the centurion, wanting to bring Paul safely through, kept them from their intention, and commanded that those who could swim should jump overboard first and get to land,

44 and the rest *should follow*, some on planks, and others on various things from the ship. And thus it happened that they all were brought safely to land.

CHAPTER 28

AND when they had been brought safely through, then we found out that the island was called Malta.

2 And the natives showed us extraordinary kindness; for be-

---

[49] Some ancient mss. read *bring the ship safely ashore*

cause of the rain that had set in and because of the cold, they kindled a fire and received us all.

3 But when Paul had gathered a bundle of sticks and laid them on the fire, a viper came out because of the heat, and fastened on his hand.

4 And when the natives saw the creature hanging from his hand, they *began* saying to one another, "Undoubtedly this man is a murderer, and though he has been saved from the sea, justice has not allowed him to live."

5 However he shook the creature off into the fire and suffered no harm.

6 But they were expecting that he was about to swell up or suddenly fall down dead. But after they had waited a long time and had seen nothing unusual happen to him, they changed their minds and *began* to say that he was a god.

7 Now in the neighborhood of that place were lands belonging to the leading man of the island, named Publius, who welcomed us and entertained us courteously three days.

8 And it came about that the father of Publius was lying in *bed* afflicted with *recurrent* fever and dysentery; and Paul went in *to see* him and after he had prayed, he laid his hands on him and healed him.

9 And after this had happened, the rest of the people on the island who had diseases were coming to him and getting cured.

10 And they also honored us with many marks of respect; and when we were setting sail, they supplied *us* with all we needed.

11 And at the end of three months we set sail on an Alexan-

drian ship which had wintered at the island, and which had the Twin Brothers for its figurehead.

12 And after we put in at Syracuse, we stayed there for three days.

13 And from there we sailed around and arrived at Rhegium, and a day later a south wind sprang up, and on the second day we came to Puteoli.

14 There we found *some* brethren, and were invited to stay with them for seven days; and thus we came to Rome.

15 And the brethren, when they heard about us, came from there as far as the Market of Appius and Three Inns to meet us; and when Paul saw them, he thanked God and took courage.

16 And when we entered Rome, Paul was allowed to stay by himself, with the soldier who was guarding him.

17 And it happened that after three days he called together those who were the leading men of the Jews, and when they had come together, he *began* saying to them, "Brethren, though I had done nothing against our people, or the customs of our fathers, yet I was delivered prisoner from Jerusalem into the hands of the Romans.

18 "And when they had examined me, they were willing to release me because there was no ground for putting me to death.

19 "But when the Jews objected, I was forced to appeal to Caesar; not that I had any accusation against my nation.

20 "For this reason therefore, I requested to see you and to speak with you, for I am wearing this chain for the sake of the hope of Israel."

21 And they said to him, "We have neither received letters from Judea concerning you, nor have any of the brethren come here and reported or spoken anything bad about you.

22 "But we desire to hear from you what your views are; for concerning this sect, it is known to us that it is spoken against everywhere."

23 And when they had set a day for him, they came to him at his lodging in large numbers; and he was explaining to them by solemnly testifying about the kingdom of God, and trying to persuade them concerning Jesus, from both the Law of Moses and from the Prophets, from morning until evening.

24 And some were being persuaded by the things spoken, but others would not believe.

25 And when they did not agree with one another, they *began* leaving after Paul had spoken one parting word, "The Holy Spirit rightly spoke through Isaiah the prophet to your fathers,

26 saying,

'GO TO THIS PEOPLE AND SAY,
"YOU WILL KEEP ON HEARING, BUT WILL NOT UNDERSTAND;

AND YOU WILL KEEP ON SEEING, BUT WILL NOT PERCEIVE;

27 FOR THE HEART OF THIS PEOPLE HAS BECOME DULL,
AND WITH THEIR EARS THEY SCARCELY HEAR,
AND THEY HAVE CLOSED THEIR EYES;
LEST THEY SHOULD SEE WITH THEIR EYES,
AND HEAR WITH THEIR EARS,
AND UNDERSTAND WITH THEIR HEART AND RETURN,
AND I SHOULD HEAL THEM." '

28 "Let it be known to you therefore, that this salvation of God has been sent to the Gentiles; they will also listen."

29 [50 And when he had spoken these words, the Jews departed, having a great dispute among themselves.]

30 And he stayed two full years in his own rented quarters, and was welcoming all who came to him,

31 preaching the kingdom of God, and teaching concerning the Lord Jesus Christ with all openness, unhindered.

50 Many mss. do not contain this verse

ROMANS

PAUL, a bond-servant of Christ Jesus, called *as* an apostle, set apart for the gospel of God,

2 which He promised beforehand through His prophets in the holy Scriptures,

3 concerning His Son, who was born of a descendant of David according to the flesh,

4 who was declared the Son of God with power [1]by the resurrection from the dead, according to the spirit of holiness, Jesus Christ our Lord,

5 through whom we have received grace and apostleship to bring about *the* obedience of faith among all the Gentiles, for His name's sake,

6 among whom you also are the called of Jesus Christ;

7 to all who are beloved of God in Rome, called *as* saints: Grace to you and peace from God our Father and the Lord Jesus Christ.

8 First, I thank my God through Jesus Christ for you all, because your faith is being proclaimed throughout the whole world.

9 For God, whom I serve in my spirit in the *preaching of the* gospel of His Son, is my witness *as to* how unceasingly I make mention of you,

10 always in my prayers making request, if perhaps now at last by the will of God I may succeed in coming to you.

11 For I long to see you in order that I may impart some spiritual gift to you, that you may be established;

12 that is, that I may be encouraged together with you *while* among you, each of us by the other's faith, both yours and mine.

13 And I do not want you to be unaware, brethren, that often I have planned to come to you (and have been prevented thus far) in order that I might obtain some fruit among you also, even as among the rest of the Gentiles.

14 I am [2]under obligation both to Greeks and to barbarians, both to the wise and to the foolish.

15 Thus, for my part, I am eager to preach the gospel to you also who are in Rome.

16 For I am not ashamed of the gospel, for it is the power of God for salvation to everyone who believes, to the Jew first and also to the Greek.

17 For in it *the* righteousness of God is revealed from faith to faith; as it is written, "BUT THE RIGHTEOUS *man* SHALL LIVE BY FAITH."

18 For the wrath of God is revealed from heaven against all ungodliness and unrighteousness of men, who suppress the truth in unrighteousness,

19 because that which is known about God is evident within them; for God made it evident to them.

20 For since the creation of the world His invisible attributes, His eternal power and divine nature, have been clearly seen,

[1] Or, *as a result of* [2] Lit., *debtor*

being understood through what has been made, so that they are without excuse.

21 For even though they knew God, they did not [3]honor Him as God, or give thanks; but they became futile in their speculations, and their foolish heart was darkened.

22 Professing to be wise, they became fools,

23 and exchanged the glory of the incorruptible God for an image in the form of corruptible man and of birds and four-footed animals and [4]crawling creatures.

24 Therefore God gave them over in the lusts of their hearts to impurity, that their bodies might be dishonored among them.

25 For they exchanged the truth of God for a lie, and worshiped and served the creature rather than the Creator, who is blessed forever. Amen.

26 For this reason God gave them over to degrading passions; for their women exchanged the natural function for that which is unnatural,

27 and in the same way also the men abandoned the natural function of the woman and burned in their desire toward one another, men with men committing indecent acts and receiving in their own persons the due penalty of their error.

28 And just as they did not see fit to acknowledge God any longer, God gave them over to a depraved mind, to do those things which are not proper,

29 being filled with all unrighteousness, wickedness, greed, evil; full of envy, murder, strife, deceit, malice; *they are* gossips,

30 slanderers, haters of God, insolent, arrogant, boastful, inventors of evil, disobedient to parents,

31 without understanding, untrustworthy, unloving, unmerciful;

32 and, although they know the ordinance of God, that those who practice such things are worthy of death, they not only do the same, but also give hearty approval to those who practice them.

CHAPTER 2

THEREFORE you are without excuse, every man *of you* who passes judgment, for in that you judge another, you condemn yourself; for you who judge practice the same things.

2 And we know that the judgment of God rightly falls upon those who practice such things.

3 And do you suppose this, O man, when you pass judgment upon those who practice such things and do the same *yourself,* that you will escape the judgment of God?

4 Or do you think lightly of the riches of His kindness and forbearance and patience, not knowing that the kindness of God leads you to repentance?

5 But because of your stubbornness and unrepentant heart you are storing up wrath for yourself in the day of wrath and revelation of the righteous judgment of God,

6 who WILL RENDER TO EVERY MAN ACCORDING TO HIS DEEDS:

7 to those who by perseverance in doing good seek for glory and honor and immortality, eternal life;

[3] Lit., *glorify* [4] Or possibly, *reptiles*

8 but to those who are selfishly ambitious and do not obey the truth, but obey unrighteousness, wrath and indignation.

9 *There will be* tribulation and distress for every soul of man who does evil, of the Jew first and also of the Greek,

10 but glory and honor and peace to every man who does good, to the Jew first and also to the Greek.

11 For there is no partiality with God.

12 For all who have sinned without the Law will also perish without the Law; and all who have sinned under the Law will be judged by the Law;

13 for not the hearers of the Law are just before God, but the doers of the Law will be justified.

14 For when Gentiles who do not have the Law do instinctively the things of the Law, these, not having the Law, are a law to themselves,

15 in that they show the work of the Law written in their hearts, their conscience bearing witness, and their thoughts alternately accusing or else defending them,

16 on the day when, according to my gospel, God will judge the secrets of men through Christ Jesus.

17 But if you bear the name "Jew," and rely upon the Law, and boast in God,

18 and know *His* will, and approve the things that are essential, being instructed out of the Law,

19 and are confident that you yourself are a guide to the blind, a light to those who are in darkness,

20 a corrector of the foolish, a teacher of the immature, having in the Law the embodiment of knowledge and of the truth,

21 you, therefore, who teach another, do you not teach yourself? You who preach that one should not steal, do you steal?

22 You who say that one should not commit adultery, do you commit adultery? You who abhor idols, do you rob temples?

23 You who boast in the Law, through your breaking the Law, do you dishonor God?

24 For "THE NAME OF GOD IS BLASPHEMED AMONG THE GENTILES BECAUSE OF YOU," just as it is written.

25 For indeed circumcision is of value, if you practice the Law; but if you are a transgressor of the Law, your circumcision has become uncircumcision.

26 If therefore the uncircumcised man keeps the requirements of the Law, will not his uncircumcision be regarded as circumcision?

27 And will not he who is physically uncircumcised, if he keeps the Law, will he not judge you who though having the letter *of the Law* and circumcision are a transgressor of the Law?

28 For he is not a Jew who is one outwardly; neither is circumcision that which is outward in the flesh.

29 But he is a Jew who is one inwardly; and circumcision is that which is of the heart, by the Spirit, not by the letter; and his praise is not from men, but from God.

CHAPTER 3

THEN what advantage has the Jew? Or what is the benefit of circumcision?

2 Great in every respect. First of all, that they were entrusted with the oracles of God.

3 What then? If some did not believe, their unbelief will not nullify the faithfulness of God, will it?

4 May it never be! Rather, let God be found true, though every man *be found* a liar, as it is written,

> "THAT THOU MIGHTEST BE JUSTIFIED IN THY WORDS, AND MIGHTEST PREVAIL WHEN THOU ART JUDGED."

5 But if our unrighteousness demonstrates the righteousness of God, what shall we say? The God who inflicts wrath is not unrighteous, is He? (I am speaking in human terms.)

6 May it never be! For otherwise how will God judge the world?

7 But if through my lie the truth of God abounded to His glory, why am I also still being judged as a sinner?

8 And why not *say* (as we are slanderously reported and as some affirm that we say), "Let us do evil that good may come"? Their condemnation is just.

9 What then? Are we better than they? Not at all; for we have already charged that both Jews and Greeks are all under sin;

10 as it is written,

> "THERE IS NONE RIGHTEOUS, NOT EVEN ONE;

11 THERE IS NONE WHO UNDERSTANDS,
    THERE IS NONE WHO SEEKS FOR GOD;

12 ALL HAVE TURNED ASIDE, TOGETHER THEY HAVE BECOME USELESS;

    THERE IS NONE WHO DOES GOOD,
    THERE IS NOT EVEN ONE."

13 "THEIR THROAT IS AN OPEN GRAVE,
    WITH THEIR TONGUES THEY KEEP DECEIVING,"
    "THE POISON OF ASPS IS UNDER THEIR LIPS";

14 "WHOSE MOUTH IS FULL OF CURSING AND BITTERNESS";

15 "THEIR FEET ARE SWIFT TO SHED BLOOD,

16 DESTRUCTION AND MISERY ARE IN THEIR PATHS,

17 AND THE PATH OF PEACE HAVE THEY NOT KNOWN."

18 "THERE IS NO FEAR OF GOD BEFORE THEIR EYES."

19 Now we know that whatever the Law says, it speaks to those who are under the Law, that every mouth may be closed, and all the world may become accountable to God;

20 because by the works of the Law no flesh will be justified in His sight; for through the Law *comes* the knowledge of sin.

21 But now apart from the Law *the* righteousness of God has been manifested, being witnessed by the Law and the Prophets,

22 even *the* righteousness of God through faith in Jesus Christ for all those who believe; for there is no distinction;

23 for all have sinned and fall short of the glory of God,

24 being justified as a gift by His grace through the redemption which is in Christ Jesus;

25 whom God displayed publicly as a propitiation in His blood through faith. *This was* to demonstrate His righteousness, because in the forbearance of

God He passed over the sins previously committed;

26 for the demonstration, *I say*, of His righteousness at the present time, that He might be just and the justifier of the one who has faith in Jesus.

27 Where then is boasting? It is excluded. By what kind of law? Of works? No, but by a law of faith.

28 For we maintain that a man is justified by faith apart from works of the Law.

29 Or is God *the God* of Jews only? Is He not *the God* of Gentiles also? Yes, of Gentiles also,

30 since indeed God who will justify the circumcised by faith and the uncircumcised through faith is one.

31 Do we then nullify the Law through faith? May it never be! On the contrary, we establish the Law.

CHAPTER 4

WHAT then shall we say that Abraham, our forefather according to the flesh, has found?

2 For if Abraham was justified by works, he has something to boast about; but not before God.

3 For what does the Scripture say? "AND ABRAHAM BELIEVED GOD, AND IT WAS RECKONED TO HIM AS RIGHTEOUSNESS."

4 Now to the one who works, his wage is not reckoned as a favor, but as what is due.

5 But to the one who does not work, but believes in Him who justifies the ungodly, his faith is reckoned as righteousness,

6 just as David also speaks of the blessing upon the man to whom God reckons righteousness apart from works:

7 "BLESSED ARE THOSE WHOSE
   LAWLESS DEEDS HAVE
   BEEN FORGIVEN,
   AND WHOSE SINS HAVE
   BEEN COVERED.

8 "BLESSED IS THE MAN
   WHOSE SIN THE LORD
   WILL NOT TAKE INTO AC-
   COUNT."

9 Is this blessing then upon the circumcised, or upon the uncircumcised also? For we say, "FAITH WAS RECKONED TO ABRAHAM AS RIGHTEOUSNESS."

10 How then was it reckoned? While he was circumcised, or uncircumcised? Not while circumcised, but while uncircumcised;

11 and he received the sign of circumcision, a seal of the righteousness of the faith which he had while uncircumcised, that he might be the father of all who believe without being circumcised, that righteousness might be reckoned to them,

12 and the father of circumcision to those who not only are of the circumcision, but who also follow in the steps of the faith of our father Abraham which he had while uncircumcised.

13 For the promise to Abraham or to his descendants that he would be heir of the world was not through the Law, but through the righteousness of faith.

14 For if those who are of the Law are heirs, faith is made void and the promise is nullified;

15 for the Law brings about wrath, but where there is no law, neither is there violation.

16 For this reason *it is* by faith, that *it might be* in accordance with grace, in order that the promise may be certain to all the

descendants, not only to those who are of the Law, but also to those who are of the faith of Abraham, who is the father of us all,

17 (as it is written, "A FATHER OF MANY NATIONS HAVE I MADE YOU") in the sight of Him whom he believed, *even* God, who gives life to the dead and calls into being that which does not exist.

18 In hope against hope he believed, in order that he might become a father of many nations, according to that which had been spoken, "SO SHALL YOUR DESCENDANTS BE."

19 And without becoming weak in faith he contemplated his own body, now as good as dead since he was about a hundred years old, and the deadness of Sarah's womb;

20 yet, with respect to the promise of God, he did not waver in unbelief, but grew strong in faith, giving glory to God,

21 and being fully assured that what He had promised, He was able also to perform.

22 Therefore also IT WAS RECKONED TO HIM AS RIGHTEOUSNESS.

23 Now not for his sake only was it written, that it was reckoned to him,

24 but for our sake also, to whom it will be reckoned, as those who believe in Him who raised Jesus our Lord from the dead,

25 *He* who was delivered up because of our transgressions, and was raised because of our justification.

CHAPTER 5

THEREFORE having been justified by faith, we have peace with God through our Lord Jesus Christ,

2 through whom also we have obtained our introduction by faith into this grace in which we stand; and we exult in hope of the glory of God.

3 And not only this, but we also exult in our tribulations, knowing that tribulation brings about perseverance;

4 and perseverance, proven character; and proven character, hope;

5 and hope does not disappoint, because the love of God has been poured out within our hearts through the Holy Spirit who was given to us.

6 For while we were still helpless, at the right time Christ died for the ungodly.

7 For one will hardly die for a righteous man; though perhaps for the good man someone would dare even to die.

8 But God demonstrates His own love toward us, in that while we were yet sinners, Christ died for us.

9 Much more then, having now been justified by His blood, we shall be saved from the wrath *of God* through Him.

10 For if while we were enemies, we were reconciled to God through the death of His Son, much more, having been reconciled, we shall be saved by His life.

11 And not only this, but we also exult in God through our Lord Jesus Christ, through whom we have now received the reconciliation.

12 Therefore, just as through one man sin entered into the world, and death through sin,

and so death spread to all men, because all sinned—

13 for until the Law sin was in the world; but sin is not imputed when there is no law.

14 Nevertheless death reigned from Adam until Moses, even over those who had not sinned in the likeness of the offense of Adam, who is a [5]type of Him who was to come.

15 But the free gift is not like the transgression. For if by the transgression of the one the many died, much more did the grace of God and the gift by the grace of the one Man, Jesus Christ, abound to the many.

16 And the gift is not like *that which came* through the one who sinned; for on the one hand the judgment *arose* from one *transgression* resulting in condemnation, but on the other hand the free gift *arose* from many transgressions resulting in justification.

17 For if by the transgression of the one, death reigned through the one, much more those who receive the abundance of grace and of the gift of righteousness will reign in life through the One, Jesus Christ.

18 So then as through one transgression there resulted condemnation to all men, even so through one act of righteousness there resulted justification of life to all men.

19 For as through the one man's disobedience the many were made sinners, even so through the obedience of the One the many will be made righteous.

20 And the Law came in that the transgression might increase;

[5] Or, *foreshadowing*

but where sin increased, grace abounded all the more,

21 that, as sin reigned in death, even so grace might reign through righteousness to eternal life through Jesus Christ our Lord.

CHAPTER 6

WHAT shall we say then? Are we to continue in sin that grace might increase?

2 May it never be! How shall we who died to sin still live in it?

3 Or do you not know that all of us who have been baptized into Christ Jesus have been baptized into His death?

4 Therefore we have been buried with Him through baptism into death, in order that as Christ was raised from the dead through the glory of the Father, so we too might walk in newness of life.

5 For if we have become united with *Him* in the likeness of His death, certainly we shall be also *in the likeness* of His resurrection,

6 knowing this, that our old self was crucified with *Him*, that our body of sin might be done away with, that we should no longer be slaves to sin;

7 for he who has died is freed from sin.

8 Now if we have died with Christ, we believe that we shall also live with Him,

9 knowing that Christ, having been raised from the dead, is never to die again; death no longer is master over Him.

10 For the death that He died, He died to sin, once for all; but the life that He lives, He lives to God.

11 Even so consider yourselves to be dead to sin, but alive to God in Christ Jesus.

12 Therefore do not let sin reign in your mortal body that you should obey its lusts,

13 and do not go on presenting the members of your body to sin *as* instruments of unrighteousness; but present yourselves to God as those alive from the dead, and your members *as* instruments of righteousness to God.

14 For sin shall not be master over you, for you are not under law, but under grace.

15 What then? Shall we sin because we are not under law but under grace? May it never be!

16 Do you not know that when you present yourselves to someone *as* slaves for obedience, you are slaves of the one whom you obey, either of sin resulting in death, or of obedience resulting in righteousness?

17 But thanks be to God that though you were slaves of sin, you became obedient from the heart to that form of teaching to which you were committed,

18 and having been freed from sin, you became slaves of righteousness.

19 I am speaking in human terms because of the weakness of your flesh. For just as you presented your members *as* slaves to impurity and to lawlessness, resulting in *further* lawlessness, so now present your members *as* slaves to righteousness, resulting in sanctification.

20 For when you were slaves of sin, you were free in regard to righteousness.

21 Therefore what benefit were you then deriving from the things of which you are now ashamed? For the outcome of those things is death.

22 But now having been freed from sin and enslaved to God, you derive your benefit, resulting in sanctification, and the outcome, eternal life.

23 For the wages of sin is death, but the free gift of God is eternal life in Christ Jesus our Lord.

CHAPTER 7

OR do you not know, brethren (for I am speaking to those who know the law), that the law has jurisdiction over a person as long as he lives?

2 For the married woman is bound by law to her husband while he is living; but if her husband dies, she is released from the law concerning the husband.

3 So then if, while her husband is living, she is joined to another man, she shall be called an adulteress; but if her husband dies, she is free from the law, so that she is not an adulteress, though she is joined to another man.

4 Therefore, my brethren, you also were made to die to the Law through the body of Christ, that you might be joined to another, to Him who was raised from the dead, that we might bear fruit for God.

5 For while we were in the flesh, the sinful passions, which were *aroused* by the Law, were at work in the members of our body to bear fruit for death.

6 But now we have been released from the Law, having died to that by which we were bound, so that we serve in newness of

the [6]Spirit and not in oldness of the letter.

7 What shall we say then? Is the Law sin? May it never be! On the contrary, I would not have come to know sin except through the Law; for I would not have known about coveting if the Law had not said, "YOU SHALL NOT COVET."

8 But sin, taking opportunity through the commandment, produced in me coveting of every kind; for apart from the Law sin *is* dead.

9 And I was once alive apart from the Law; but when the commandment came, sin became alive, and I died;

10 and this commandment, which was to result in life, proved to result in death for me;

11 for sin, taking opportunity through the commandment, deceived me, and through it killed me.

12 So then, the Law is holy, and the commandment is holy and righteous and good.

13 Therefore did that which is good become *a cause of* death for me? May it never be! Rather it was sin, in order that it might be shown to be sin by effecting my death through that which is good, that through the commandment sin might become utterly sinful.

14 For we know that the Law is spiritual; but I am of flesh, sold into bondage to sin.

15 For that which I am doing, I do not understand; for I am not practicing what I *would* like to *do*, but I am doing the very thing I hate.

16 But if I do the very thing I

do not wish *to do,* I agree with the Law, *confessing* that it is good.

17 So now, no longer am I the one doing it, but sin which indwells me.

18 For I know that nothing good dwells in me, that is, in my flesh; for the wishing is present in me, but the doing of the good *is* not.

19 For the good that I wish, I do not do; but I practice the very evil that I do not wish.

20 But if I am doing the very thing I do not wish, I am no longer the one doing it, but sin which dwells in me.

21 I find then the principle that evil is present in me, the one who wishes to do good.

22 For I joyfully concur with the law of God in the inner man,

23 but I see a different law in the members of my body, waging war against the law of my mind, and making me a prisoner of the law of sin which is in my members.

24 Wretched man that I am! Who will set me free from the body of this death?

25 Thanks be to God through Jesus Christ our Lord! So then, on the one hand I myself with my mind am serving the law of God, but on the other, with my flesh the law of sin.

CHAPTER 8

THERE is therefore now no condemnation for those who are in Christ Jesus.

2 For the law of the Spirit of life in Christ Jesus has set [7]you free from the law of sin and of death.

3 For what the Law could not

[6] Or, *spirit*   [7] Some ancient mss. read *me*

do, weak as it was through the flesh, God *did*: sending His own Son in the likeness of sinful flesh and *as an offering* for sin, He condemned sin in the flesh,

4 in order that the requirement of the Law might be fulfilled in us, who do not walk according to the flesh, but according to the Spirit.

5 For those who are according to the flesh set their minds on the things of the flesh, but those who are according to the Spirit, the things of the Spirit.

6 For the mind set on the flesh is death, but the mind set on the Spirit is life and peace,

7 because the mind set on the flesh is hostile toward God; for it does not subject itself to the law of God, for it is not even able *to do so*;

8 and those who are in the flesh cannot please God.

9 However, you are not in the flesh but in the Spirit, if indeed the Spirit of God dwells in you. But if anyone does not have the Spirit of Christ, he does not belong to Him.

10 And if Christ is in you, though the body is dead because of sin, yet the spirit is alive because of righteousness.

11 But if the Spirit of Him who raised Jesus from the dead dwells in you, He who raised Christ Jesus from the dead will also give life to your mortal bodies 8through His Spirit who indwells you.

12 So then, brethren, we are under obligation, not to the flesh, to live according to the flesh—

13 for if you are living according to the flesh, you must die; but if by the Spirit you are putting to death the deeds of the body, you will live.

14 For all who are being led by the Spirit of God, these are sons of God.

15 For you have not received a spirit of slavery leading to fear again, but you have received a spirit of adoption as sons by which we cry out, "Abba! Father!"

16 The Spirit Himself bears witness with our spirit that we are children of God,

17 and if children, heirs also, heirs of God and fellow heirs with Christ, if indeed we suffer with *Him* in order that we may also be glorified with *Him.*

18 For I consider that the sufferings of this present time are not worthy to be compared with the glory that is to be revealed to us.

19 For the anxious longing of the creation waits eagerly for the revealing of the sons of God.

20 For the creation was subjected to futility, not of its own will, but because of Him who subjected it, 9in hope

21 that the creation itself also will be set free from its slavery to corruption into the freedom of the glory of the children of God.

22 For we know that the whole creation groans and suffers the pains of childbirth together until now.

23 And not only this, but also we ourselves, having the first fruits of the Spirit, even we ourselves groan within ourselves, waiting eagerly for *our* adoption as sons, the redemption of our body.

---

8 Some ancient mss. read *because of*
9 Some ancient mss. read *in hope; because the creation*

24 For in hope we have been saved, but hope that is seen is not hope; for [10]why does one also hope for what he sees?

25 But if we hope for what we do not see, with perseverance we wait eagerly for it.

26 And in the same way the Spirit also helps our weakness; for we do not know how to pray as we should, but the Spirit Himself intercedes for *us* with groanings too deep for words;

27 and He who searches the hearts knows what the mind of the Spirit is, because He intercedes for the saints according to *the will of* God.

28 And we know that [11]God causes all things to work together for good to those who love God, to those who are called according to *His* purpose.

29 For whom He foreknew, He also predestined *to become* conformed to the image of His Son, that He might be the first-born among many brethren;

30 and whom He predestined, these He also called; and whom He called, these He also justified; and whom He justified, these He also glorified.

31 What then shall we say to these things? If God *is* for us, who is against us?

32 He who did not spare His own Son, but delivered Him up for us all, how will He not also with Him freely give us all things?

33 Who will bring a charge against God's elect? God is the one who justifies;

34 who is the one who condemns? Christ Jesus is He who died, yes, rather who was [12]raised, who is at the right hand of God, who also intercedes for us.

35 Who shall separate us from the love of [13]Christ? Shall tribulation, or distress, or persecution, or famine, or nakedness, or peril, or sword?

36 Just as it is written,

"FOR THY SAKE WE ARE
BEING PUT TO DEATH ALL
DAY LONG;
WE WERE CONSIDERED AS
SHEEP TO BE SLAUGH-
TERED."

37 But in all these things we overwhelmingly conquer through Him who loved us.

38 For I am convinced that neither death, nor life, nor angels, nor principalities, nor things present, nor things to come, nor powers,

39 nor height, nor depth, nor any other created thing, shall be able to separate us from the love of God, which is in Christ Jesus our Lord.

CHAPTER 9

I AM telling the truth in Christ, I am not lying, my conscience bearing me witness in the Holy Spirit,

2 that I have great sorrow and unceasing grief in my heart.

3 For I could wish that I myself were accursed, *separated* from Christ for the sake of my brethren, my kinsmen according to the flesh,

4 who are Israelites, to whom belongs the adoption as sons and the glory and the covenants and

[10] Some ancient mss. read *who hopes for what he sees?*
[11] Some ancient mss. read *all things work together for good*
[12] Some ancient mss. read *raised from the dead*   [13] Some ancient mss. read *God*

the giving of the Law and the *temple* service and the promises,

5 whose are the fathers, and from whom is the Christ according to the flesh, who is over all, God blessed forever. Amen.

6 But *it is* not as though the word of God has failed. For they are not all Israel who are *descended* from Israel;

7 neither are they all children because they are Abraham's descendants, but: "THROUGH ISAAC YOUR DESCENDANTS WILL BE NAMED."

8 That is, it is not the children of the flesh who are children of God, but the children of the promise are regarded as descendants.

9 For this is a word of promise: "AT THIS TIME I WILL COME, AND SARAH SHALL HAVE A SON."

10 And not only this, but there was Rebekah also, when she had conceived *twins* by one man, our father Isaac;

11 for though *the twins* were not yet born, and had not done anything good or bad, in order that God's purpose according to *His* choice might stand, not because of works, but because of Him who calls,

12 it was said to her, "THE OLDER WILL SERVE THE YOUNGER."

13 Just as it is written, "JACOB I LOVED, BUT ESAU I HATED."

14 What shall we say then? There is no injustice with God, is there? May it never be!

15 For He says to Moses, "I WILL HAVE MERCY ON WHOM I HAVE MERCY, AND I WILL HAVE COMPASSION ON WHOM I HAVE COMPASSION."

16 So then it *does* not *depend* on the man who wills or the man

who runs, but on God who has mercy.

17 For the Scripture says to Pharaoh, "FOR THIS VERY PURPOSE I RAISED YOU UP, TO DEMONSTRATE MY POWER IN YOU, AND THAT MY NAME MIGHT BE PROCLAIMED THROUGHOUT THE WHOLE EARTH."

18 So then He has mercy on whom He desires, and He hardens whom He desires.

19 You will say to me then, "Why does He still find fault? For who resists His will?"

20 On the contrary, who are you, O man, who answers back to God? The thing molded will not say to the molder, "Why did you make me like this," will it?

21 Or does not the potter have a right over the clay, to make from the same lump one vessel for honorable use, and another for common use?

22 What if God, although willing to demonstrate His wrath and to make His power known, endured with much patience vessels of wrath prepared for destruction?

23 And *He did so* in order that He might make known the riches of His glory upon vessels of mercy, which He prepared beforehand for glory,

24 *even* us, whom He also called, not from among Jews only, but also from among Gentiles.

25 As He says also in Hosea,

"I WILL CALL THOSE WHO WERE NOT MY PEOPLE, 'MY PEOPLE,' AND HER WHO WAS NOT BELOVED, 'BELOVED.' "

26 "AND IT SHALL BE THAT IN THE PLACE WHERE IT WAS

SAID TO THEM, 'YOU ARE
NOT MY PEOPLE,'
THERE THEY SHALL BE
CALLED SONS OF THE LIV-
ING GOD."

27 And Isaiah cries out con-
cerning Israel, "THOUGH THE
NUMBER OF THE SONS OF ISRAEL
BE AS THE SAND OF THE SEA, IT IS
THE REMNANT THAT WILL BE
SAVED;

28 FOR THE LORD WILL EXECUTE
HIS WORD UPON THE EARTH,
THOROUGHLY AND QUICKLY."

29 And just as Isaiah foretold,
"EXCEPT THE LORD OF SABA-
OTH HAD LEFT TO US A
POSTERITY,
WE WOULD HAVE BECOME
AS SODOM, AND WOULD
HAVE RESEMBLED GOMOR-
RAH."

30 What shall we say then?
That Gentiles, who did not pursue righteousness, attained righteousness, even the righteousness
which is by faith;

31 but Israel, pursuing a law of
righteousness, did not arrive at
that law.

32 Why? Because *they did* not
pursue it by faith, but as though
it were by works. They stumbled
over the stumbling stone,

33 just as it is written,
"BEHOLD, I LAY IN ZION A
STONE OF STUMBLING AND
A ROCK OF OFFENSE,
AND HE WHO BELIEVES IN
HIM WILL NOT BE DISAP-
POINTED."

CHAPTER 10

BRETHREN, my heart's desire
and my prayer to God for
them is for *their* salvation.

2 For I bear them witness that

they have a zeal for God, but not
in accordance with knowledge.

3 For not knowing about
God's righteousness, and seeking
to establish their own, they did
not subject themselves to the
righteousness of God.

4 For Christ is the end of the
law for righteousness to everyone who believes.

5 For Moses writes that the
man who practices the righteousness which is based on law shall
live by that righteousness.

6 But the righteousness based
on faith speaks thus, "DO NOT
SAY IN YOUR HEART, 'WHO WILL
ASCEND INTO HEAVEN?' (that is, to
bring Christ down),

7 or 'WHO WILL DESCEND INTO
THE ABYSS?' (that is, to bring
Christ up from the dead)."

8 But what does it say? "THE
WORD IS NEAR YOU, IN YOUR
MOUTH AND IN YOUR HEART"—
that is, the word of faith which
we are preaching,

9 that if you confess with
your mouth Jesus *as* Lord, and
believe in your heart that God
raised Him from the dead, you
shall be saved;

10 for with the heart man believes, resulting in righteousness,
and with the mouth he confesses,
resulting in salvation.

11 For the Scripture says,
"WHOEVER BELIEVES IN HIM WILL
NOT BE DISAPPOINTED."

12 For there is no distinction
between Jew and Greek; for the
same *Lord* is Lord of all, abounding in riches for all who call upon
Him;

13 for "WHOEVER WILL CALL
UPON THE NAME OF THE LORD
WILL BE SAVED."

14 How then shall they call
upon Him in whom they have not

believed? And how shall they believe in Him whom they have not heard? And how shall they hear without a preacher?

15 And how shall they preach unless they are sent? Just as it is written, "HOW BEAUTIFUL ARE THE FEET OF THOSE WHO BRING GLAD TIDINGS OF GOOD THINGS!"

16 However, they did not all heed the glad tidings; for Isaiah says, "LORD, WHO HAS BELIEVED OUR REPORT?"

17 So faith *comes* from hearing, and hearing by the word of Christ.

18 But I say, surely they have never heard, have they? Indeed they have;

"THEIR VOICE HAS GONE OUT
INTO ALL THE EARTH,
AND THEIR WORDS TO THE
ENDS OF THE WORLD."

19 But I say, surely Israel did not know, did they? At the first Moses says,

"I WILL MAKE YOU JEALOUS
BY THAT WHICH IS NOT A
NATION,
BY A NATION WITHOUT UN-
DERSTANDING WILL I AN-
GER YOU."

20 And Isaiah is very bold and says,

"I WAS FOUND BY THOSE
WHO SOUGHT ME NOT,
I BECAME MANIFEST TO
THOSE WHO DID NOT ASK
FOR ME."

21 But as for Israel He says, "ALL THE DAY LONG I HAVE STRETCHED OUT MY HANDS TO A DISOBEDIENT AND OBSTINATE PEOPLE."

CHAPTER 11

I SAY then, God has not rejected His people, has He? May it never be! For I too am an Israelite, a descendant of Abraham, of the tribe of Benjamin.

2 God has not rejected His people whom He foreknew. Or do you not know what the Scripture says in *the passage about* Elijah, how he pleads with God against Israel?

3 "Lord, THEY HAVE KILLED THY PROPHETS, THEY HAVE TORN DOWN THINE ALTARS, AND I ALONE AM LEFT, AND THEY ARE SEEKING MY LIFE."

4 But what is the divine response to him? "I HAVE KEPT for Myself SEVEN THOUSAND MEN WHO HAVE NOT BOWED THE KNEE TO BAAL."

5 In the same way then, there has also come to be at the present time a remnant according to *God's* gracious choice.

6 But if it is by grace, it is no longer on the basis of works, otherwise grace is no longer grace.

7 What then? That which Israel is seeking for, it has not obtained, but those who were chosen obtained it, and the rest were hardened;

8 just as it is written,

"GOD GAVE THEM A SPIRIT
OF STUPOR,
EYES TO SEE NOT AND EARS
TO HEAR NOT,
DOWN TO THIS VERY DAY."

9 And David says,

"LET THEIR TABLE BECOME A
SNARE AND A TRAP,
AND A STUMBLING BLOCK
AND A RETRIBUTION TO
THEM.

10 "LET THEIR EYES BE DARK-
ENED TO SEE NOT,
AND BEND THEIR BACKS
FOREVER."

11 I say then, they did not stumble so as to fall, did they?

May it never be! But by their transgression salvation *has come* to the Gentiles, to make them jealous.

12 Now if their transgression be riches for the world and their failure be riches for the Gentiles, how much more will their fulfillment be!

13 But I am speaking to you who are Gentiles. Inasmuch then as I am an apostle of Gentiles, I magnify my ministry,

14 if somehow I might move to jealousy my fellow countrymen and save some of them.

15 For if their rejection be the reconciliation of the world, what will *their* acceptance be but life from the dead?

16 And if the first piece *of dough* be holy, the lump is also; and if the root be holy, the branches are too.

17 But if some of the branches were broken off, and you, being a wild olive, were grafted in among them and became partaker with them of the rich root of the olive tree,

18 do not be arrogant toward the branches; but if you are arrogant, *remember that* it is not you who supports the root, but the root *supports* you.

19 You will say then, "Branches were broken off so that I might be grafted in."

20 Quite right, they were broken off for their unbelief, but you stand by your faith. Do not be conceited, but fear;

21 for if God did not spare the natural branches, neither will He spare you.

22 Behold then the kindness and severity of God; to those who fell, severity, but to you, God's kindness, if you continue in His kindness; otherwise you also will be cut off.

23 And they also, if they do not continue in their unbelief, will be grafted in; for God is able to graft them in again.

24 For if you were cut off from what is by nature a wild olive tree, and were grafted contrary to nature into a cultivated olive tree, how much more shall these who are the natural *branches* be grafted into their own olive tree?

25 For I do not want you, brethren, to be uninformed of this mystery, lest you be wise in your own estimation, that a partial hardening has happened to Israel until the fulness of the Gentiles has come in;

26 and thus all Israel will be saved; just as it is written,

> "THE DELIVERER WILL COME
> FROM ZION,
> HE WILL REMOVE UNGODLI-
> NESS FROM JACOB."

27 "AND THIS IS MY COVENANT
> WITH THEM,
> WHEN I TAKE AWAY THEIR
> SINS."

28 From the standpoint of the gospel they are enemies for your sake, but from the standpoint of God's choice they are beloved for the sake of the fathers;

29 for the gifts and the calling of God are irrevocable.

30 For just as you once were disobedient to God, but now have been shown mercy because of their disobedience,

31 so these also now have been disobedient, in order that because of the mercy shown to you they also may now be shown mercy.

32 For God has shut up all in

disobedience that He might show mercy to all.

33 Oh, the depth of the riches both of the wisdom and knowledge of God! How unsearchable are His judgments and unfathomable His ways!

34 For WHO HAS KNOWN THE MIND OF THE LORD, OR WHO BECAME HIS COUNSELOR?

35 Or WHO HAS FIRST GIVEN TO HIM THAT IT MIGHT BE PAID BACK TO HIM AGAIN?

36 For from Him and through Him and to Him are all things. To Him *be* the glory forever. Amen.

CHAPTER 12

I URGE you therefore, brethren, by the mercies of God, to present your bodies a living and holy sacrifice, acceptable to God, *which is* your spiritual service of worship.

2 And do not be conformed to this world, but be transformed by the renewing of your mind, that you may prove what the will of God is, that which is good and acceptable and perfect.

3 For through the grace given to me I say to every man among you not to think more highly of himself than he ought to think; but to think so as to have sound judgment, as God has allotted to each a measure of faith.

4 For just as we have many members in one body and all the members do not have the same function,

5 so we, who are many, are one body in Christ, and individually members one of another.

6 And since we have gifts that differ according to the grace given to us, *let each exercise them accordingly:* if prophecy, according to the proportion of his faith;

7 if service, in his serving; or he who teaches, in his teaching;

8 or he who exhorts, in his exhortation; he who gives, with 14liberality; he who leads, with diligence; he who shows mercy, with cheerfulness.

9 Let love be without hypocrisy. Abhor what is evil; cling to what is good.

10 Be devoted to one another in brotherly love; give preference to one another in honor;

11 not lagging behind in diligence, fervent in spirit, serving the Lord;

12 rejoicing in hope, persevering in tribulation, devoted to prayer,

13 contributing to the needs of the saints, practicing hospitality.

14 Bless those who persecute 15you; bless and curse not.

15 Rejoice with those who rejoice, and weep with those who weep.

16 Be of the same mind toward one another; do not be haughty in mind, but associate with the lowly. Do not be wise in your own estimation.

17 Never pay back evil for evil to anyone. Respect what is right in the sight of all men.

18 If possible, so far as it depends on you, be at peace with all men.

19 Never take your own revenge, beloved, but leave room for the wrath *of God*, for it is written, "VENGEANCE IS MINE, I WILL REPAY," says the Lord.

20"BUT IF YOUR ENEMY IS HUNGRY, FEED HIM, AND IF HE IS THIRSTY, GIVE HIM A DRINK; FOR

14 Or, *simplicity*
15 Some ancient mss. do not contain *you*

IN SO DOING YOU WILL HEAP BURN-
ING COALS UPON HIS HEAD."

21 Do not be overcome by evil,
but overcome evil with good.

CHAPTER 13

LET every person be in subjection to the governing au-
thorities. For there is no authority except from God, and those
which exist are established by
God.

2 Therefore he who resists authority has opposed the ordinance of God; and they who have
opposed will receive condemnation upon themselves.

3 For rulers are not a cause of
fear for good behavior, but for
evil. Do you want to have no fear
of authority? Do what is good,
and you will have praise from the
same;

4 for it is a minister of God to
you for good. But if you do what
is evil, be afraid; for it does not
bear the sword for nothing; for it
is a minister of God, an avenger
who brings wrath upon the one
who practices evil.

5 Wherefore it is necessary to
be in subjection, not only because of wrath, but also for conscience' sake.

6 For because of this you also
pay taxes, for *rulers* are servants
of God, devoting themselves to
this very thing.

7 Render to all what is due
them: tax to whom tax *is due;*
custom to whom custom; fear to
whom fear; honor to whom hon-
or.

8 Owe nothing to anyone except to love one another; for he
who loves his neighbor has fulfilled *the* law.

9 For this, "YOU SHALL NOT
COMMIT ADULTERY, YOU SHALL
NOT MURDER, YOU SHALL NOT
STEAL, YOU SHALL NOT COVET,"
and if there is any other com-
mandment, it is summed up in
this saying, "YOU SHALL LOVE
YOUR NEIGHBOR AS YOURSELF."

10 Love does no wrong to a
neighbor; love therefore is the
fulfillment of *the* law.

11 And this *do,* knowing the
time, that it is already the hour
for you to awaken from sleep; for
now [16]salvation is nearer to us
than when we believed.

12 The night is almost gone,
and the day is at hand. Let us
therefore lay aside the deeds of
darkness and put on the armor of
light.

13 Let us behave properly as in
the day, not in carousing and
drunkenness, not in sexual pro-
miscuity and sensuality, not in
strife and jealousy.

14 But put on the Lord Jesus
Christ, and make no provision
for the flesh in regard to *its* lusts.

CHAPTER 14

NOW accept the one who is
weak in faith, *but* not for *the
purpose of* passing judgment on
his opinions.

2 One man has faith that he
may eat all things, but he who is
weak eats vegetables *only.*

3 Let not him who eats regard
with contempt him who does not
eat, and let not him who does not
eat judge him who eats, for God
has accepted him.

4 Who are you to judge the
servant of another? To his own
master he stands or falls; and
stand he will, for the Lord is able
to make him stand.

[16] Or, *our salvation is nearer than when*

5 One man regards one day above another, another regards every day *alike.* Let each man be fully convinced in his own mind.

6 He who observes the day, observes it for the Lord, and he who eats, does so for the Lord, for he gives thanks to God; and he who eats not, for the Lord he does not eat, and gives thanks to God.

7 For not one of us lives for himself, and not one dies for himself;

8 for if we live, we live for the Lord, or if we die, we die for the Lord; therefore whether we live or die, we are the Lord's.

9 For to this end Christ died and lived *again,* that He might be Lord both of the dead and of the living.

10 But you, why do you judge your brother? Or you again, why do you regard your brother with contempt? For we shall all stand before the judgment seat of God.

11 For it is written,
"As I live, says the Lord, every knee shall bow to Me,
And every tongue shall give praise to God."

12 So then each one of us shall give account of himself to God.

13 Therefore let us not judge one another anymore, but rather determine this—not to put an obstacle or a stumbling block in a brother's way.

14 I know and am convinced in the Lord Jesus that nothing is unclean in itself; but to him who thinks anything to be unclean, to him it is unclean.

15 For if because of food your brother is hurt, you are no longer walking according to love. Do not destroy with your food him for whom Christ died.

16 Therefore do not let what is for you a good thing be spoken of as evil;

17 for the kingdom of God is not eating and drinking, but righteousness and peace and joy in the Holy Spirit.

18 For he who in this *way* serves Christ is acceptable to God and approved by men.

19 So then [17]let us pursue the things which make for peace and the building up of one another.

20 Do not tear down the work of God for the sake of food. All things indeed are clean, but they are evil for the man who eats and gives offense.

21 It is good not to eat meat or to drink wine, or *to do anything* by which your brother stumbles.

22 The faith which you have, have as your own conviction before God. Happy is he who does not condemn himself in what he approves.

23 But he who doubts is condemned if he eats, because *his eating is* not from faith; and whatever is not from faith is sin.

CHAPTER 15

NOW we who are strong ought to bear the weaknesses of those without strength and not *just* please ourselves.

2 Let each of us please his neighbor for his good, to his edification.

3 For even Christ did not please Himself; but as it is written, "The reproaches of those who reproached Thee fell upon Me."

[17] Many ancient mss. read *we pursue*

4 For whatever was written in earlier times was written for our instruction, that through perseverance and the encouragement of the Scriptures we might have hope.

5 Now may the God who gives perseverance and encouragement grant you to be of the same mind with one another according to Christ Jesus;

6 that with one accord you may with one voice glorify the God and Father of our Lord Jesus Christ.

7 Wherefore, accept one another, just as Christ also accepted us to the glory of God.

8 For I say that Christ has become a servant to the circumcision on behalf of the truth of God to confirm the promises *given* to the fathers,

9 and for the Gentiles to glorify God for His mercy; as it is written,

"THEREFORE I WILL GIVE
    PRAISE TO THEE AMONG
    THE GENTILES,
AND I WILL SING TO THY
    NAME."

10 And again he says,

"REJOICE, O GENTILES, WITH
    HIS PEOPLE."

11 And again,

"PRAISE THE LORD ALL YOU
    GENTILES,
AND LET ALL THE PEOPLES
    PRAISE HIM."

12 And again Isaiah says,

"THERE SHALL COME THE
    ROOT OF JESSE,
AND HE WHO ARISES TO
    RULE OVER THE GENTILES,
IN HIM SHALL THE GEN-
    TILES HOPE."

13 Now may the God of hope fill you with all joy and peace in believing, that you may abound in hope by the power of the Holy Spirit.

14 And concerning you, my brethren, I myself also am convinced that you yourselves are full of goodness, filled with all knowledge, and able also to admonish one another.

15 But I have written very boldly to you on some points, so as to remind you again, because of the grace that was given me from God,

16 to be a minister of Christ Jesus to the Gentiles, ministering as a priest the gospel of God, that *my* offering of the Gentiles might become acceptable, sanctified by the Holy Spirit.

17 Therefore in Christ Jesus I have found reason for boasting in things pertaining to God.

18 For I will not presume to speak of anything except what Christ has accomplished through me, resulting in the obedience of the Gentiles by word and deed,

19 in the power of signs and wonders, in the power of the Spirit; so that from Jerusalem and round about as far as Illyricum I have fully preached the gospel of Christ.

20 And thus I aspired to preach the gospel, not where Christ was *already* named, that I might not build upon another man's foundation;

21 but as it is written,

"THEY WHO HAD NO NEWS OF
    HIM SHALL SEE,
AND THEY WHO HAVE NOT
    HEARD SHALL UNDER-
    STAND."

22 For this reason I have often been hindered from coming to you;

23 but now, with no further place for me in these regions, and

since I have had for many years a longing to come to you

24 whenever I go to Spain—for I hope to see you in passing, and to be helped on my way there by you, when I have first enjoyed your company for a while—

25 but now, I am going to Jerusalem serving the saints.

26 For Macedonia and Achaia have been pleased to make a contribution for the poor among the saints in Jerusalem.

27 Yes, they were pleased *to do so,* and they are indebted to them. For if the Gentiles have shared in their spiritual things, they are indebted to minister to them also in material things.

28 Therefore, when I have finished this, and have put my seal on this fruit of theirs, I will go on by way of you to Spain.

29 And I know that when I come to you, I will come in the fulness of the blessing of Christ.

30 Now I urge you, brethren, by our Lord Jesus Christ and by the love of the Spirit, to strive together with me in your prayers to God for me,

31 that I may be delivered from those who are disobedient in Judea, and *that* my service for Jerusalem may prove acceptable to the saints;

32 so that I may come to you in joy by the will of God and find *refreshing* rest in your company.

33 Now the God of peace be with you all. Amen.

CHAPTER 16

I COMMEND to you our sister Phoebe, who is a servant of the church which is at Cenchrea;

2 that you receive her in the Lord in a manner worthy of the saints, and that you help her in whatever matter she may have need of you; for she herself has also been a helper of many, and of myself as well.

3 Greet Prisca and Aquila, my fellow workers in Christ Jesus,

4 who for my life risked their own necks, to whom not only do I give thanks, but also all the churches of the Gentiles;

5 also *greet* the church that is in their house. Greet Epaenetus, my beloved, who is the first convert to Christ from Asia.

6 Greet Mary, who has worked hard for you.

7 Greet Andronicus and Junias, my kinsmen, and my fellow prisoners, who are outstanding among the apostles, who also were in Christ before me.

8 Greet Ampliatus, my beloved in the Lord.

9 Greet Urbanus, our fellow worker in Christ, and Stachys my beloved.

10 Greet Apelles, the approved in Christ. Greet those who are of the *household* of Aristobulus.

11 Greet Herodion, my kinsman. Greet those of the *household* of Narcissus, who are in the Lord.

12 Greet Tryphaena and Tryphosa, workers in the Lord. Greet Persis the beloved, who has worked hard in the Lord.

13 Greet Rufus, a choice man in the Lord, also his mother and mine.

14 Greet Asyncritus, Phlegon, Hermes, Patrobas, Hermas and the brethren with them.

15 Greet Philologus and Julia, Nereus and his sister, and Olympas, and all the saints who are with them.

16 Greet one another with a holy kiss. All the churches of Christ greet you.

17 Now I urge you, brethren, keep your eye on those who cause dissensions and hindrances contrary to the teaching which you learned, and turn away from them.

18 For such men are slaves, not of our Lord Christ but of their own appetites; and by their smooth and flattering speech they deceive the hearts of the unsuspecting.

19 For the report of your obedience has reached to all; therefore I am rejoicing over you, but I want you to be wise in what is good, and innocent in what is evil.

20 And the God of peace will soon crush Satan under your feet.

The grace of our Lord Jesus be with you.

21 Timothy my fellow worker

greets you, and so do Lucius and Jason and Sosipater, my kinsmen.

22 I, Tertius, who write this letter, greet you in the Lord.

23 Gaius, host to me and to the whole church, greets you. Erastus, the city treasurer greets you, and Quartus, the brother.

24 [18The grace of our Lord Jesus Christ be with you all. Amen.]

25 Now to Him who is able to establish you according to my gospel and the preaching of Jesus Christ, according to the revelation of the mystery which has been kept secret for long ages past,

26 but now is manifested, and by the Scriptures of the prophets, according to the commandment of the eternal God, has been made known to all the nations, *leading* to obedience of faith;

27 to the only wise God, through Jesus Christ, be the glory forever. Amen.

---

18 Many mss. do not contain this verse

THE FIRST EPISTLE OF PAUL TO THE

CORINTHIANS

PAUL, called *as* an apostle of Jesus Christ by the will of God, and Sosthenes our brother,

2 to the church of God which is at Corinth, to those who have been sanctified in Christ Jesus, saints by calling, with all who in every place call upon the name of our Lord Jesus Christ, their *Lord* and ours:

3 Grace to you and peace

from God our Father and the Lord Jesus Christ.

4 I thank 1my God always concerning you, for the grace of God which was given you in Christ Jesus,

5 that in everything you were enriched in Him, in all speech and all knowledge,

6 even as the testimony concerning Christ was confirmed in you,

---

1 Some ancient mss. do not contain *my*

7 so that you are not lacking in any gift, awaiting eagerly the revelation of our Lord Jesus Christ,

8 who shall also confirm you to the end, blameless in the day of our Lord Jesus Christ.

9 God is faithful, through whom you were called into fellowship with His Son, Jesus Christ our Lord.

10 Now I exhort you, brethren, by the name of our Lord Jesus Christ, that you all agree, and there be no divisions among you, but you be made complete in the same mind and in the same judgment.

11 For I have been informed concerning you, my brethren, by Chloe's *people*, that there are quarrels among you.

12 Now I mean this, that each one of you is saying, "I am of Paul," and "I of Apollos," and "I of Cephas," and "I of Christ."

13 Has Christ been divided? Paul was not crucified for you, was he? Or were you baptized in the name of Paul?

14 [2]I thank God that I baptized none of you except Crispus and Gaius,

15 that no man should say you were baptized in my name.

16 Now I did baptize also the household of Stephanas; beyond that, I do not know whether I baptized any other.

17 For Christ did not send me to baptize, but to preach the gospel, not in cleverness of speech, that the cross of Christ should not be made void.

18 For the word of the cross is to those who are perishing foolishness, but to us who are being saved it is the power of God.

19 For it is written,

"I WILL DESTROY THE WIS-
DOM OF THE WISE,
AND THE CLEVERNESS OF
THE CLEVER I WILL SET
ASIDE."

20 Where is the wise man? Where is the scribe? Where is the debater of this age? Has not God made foolish the wisdom of the world?

21 For since in the wisdom of God the world through its wisdom did not *come to* know God, God was well-pleased through the foolishness of the message preached to save those who believe.

22 For indeed Jews ask for signs, and Greeks search for wisdom;

23 but we preach [3]Christ crucified, to Jews a stumbling block, and to Gentiles foolishness;

24 but to those who are the called, both Jews and Greeks, Christ the power of God and the wisdom of God.

25 Because the foolishness of God is wiser than men, and the weakness of God is stronger than men.

26 For consider your calling, brethren, that there were not many wise according to the flesh, not many mighty, not many noble;

27 but God has chosen the foolish things of the world to shame the wise, and God has chosen the weak things of the world to shame the things which are strong,

28 and the base things of the world and the despised, God has chosen, the things that are not,

2 Some ancient mss. read *I give thanks that*
3 I.e., Messiah

that He might nullify the things that are,

29 that no man should boast before God.

30 But by His doing you are in Christ Jesus, who became to us wisdom from God, and righteousness and sanctification, and redemption,

31 that, just as it is written, "LET HIM WHO BOASTS, BOAST IN THE LORD."

CHAPTER 2

AND when I came to you, brethren, I did not come with superiority of speech or of wisdom, proclaiming to you the [4]testimony of God.

2 For I determined to know nothing among you except Jesus Christ, and Him crucified.

3 And I was with you in weakness and in fear and in much trembling.

4 And my message and my preaching were not in persuasive words of wisdom, but in demonstration of the Spirit and of power,

5 that your faith should not rest on the wisdom of men, but on the power of God.

6 Yet we do speak wisdom among those who are mature; a wisdom, however, not of this age, nor of the rulers of this age, who are passing away;

7 but we speak God's wisdom in a mystery, the hidden *wisdom*, which God predestined before the ages to our glory;

8 *the wisdom* which none of the rulers of this age has understood; for if they had understood

it, they would not have crucified the Lord of glory;

9 but just as it is written,
"THINGS WHICH EYE HAS NOT SEEN AND EAR HAS NOT HEARD,
AND *which* HAVE NOT ENTERED THE HEART OF MAN,
ALL THAT GOD HAS PREPARED FOR THOSE WHO LOVE HIM."

10 [5]For to us God revealed *them* through the Spirit; for the Spirit searches all things, even the depths of God.

11 For who among men knows the *thoughts* of a man except the spirit of the man, which is in him? Even so the *thoughts* of God no one knows except the Spirit of God.

12 Now we have received, not the spirit of the world, but the Spirit who is from God, that we might know the things freely given to us by God,

13 which things we also speak, not in words taught by human wisdom, but in those taught by the Spirit, combining spiritual *thoughts* with spiritual *words*.

14 But a natural man does not accept the things of the Spirit of God; for they are foolishness to him, and he cannot understand them, because they are spiritually appraised.

15 But he who is spiritual appraises all things, yet he himself is appraised by no man.

16 For WHO HAS KNOWN THE MIND OF THE LORD, THAT HE SHOULD INSTRUCT HIM? But we have the mind of Christ.

CHAPTER 3

AND I, brethren, could not speak to you as to spiritual

---

[4] Some ancient mss. read *mystery*
[5] Some ancient mss. use *But*

men, but as to men of flesh, as to babes in Christ.

2 I gave you milk to drink, not solid food; for you were not yet able *to receive it*. Indeed, even now you are not yet able,

3 for you are still fleshly. For since there is jealousy and strife among you, are you not fleshly, and are you not walking like mere men?

4 For when one says, "I am of Paul," and another, "I am of Apollos," are you not *mere* men?

5 What then is Apollos? And what is Paul? Servants through whom you believed, even as the Lord gave *opportunity* to each one.

6 I planted, Apollos watered, but God was causing the growth.

7 So then neither the one who plants nor the one who waters is anything, but God who causes the growth.

8 Now he who plants and he who waters are one; but each will receive his own reward according to his own labor.

9 For we are God's fellow workers; you are God's field, God's building.

10 According to the grace of God which was given to me, as a wise master builder I laid a foundation, and another is building upon it. But let each man be careful how he builds upon it.

11 For no man can lay a foundation other than the one which is laid, which is Jesus Christ.

12 Now if any man builds upon the foundation with gold, silver, precious stones, wood, hay, straw,

13 each man's work will become evident; for the day will show it, because it is *to be* revealed with fire; and the fire itself will test the quality of each man's work.

14 If any man's work which he has built upon it remains, he shall receive a reward.

15 If any man's work is burned up, he shall suffer loss; but he himself shall be saved, yet so as through fire.

16 Do you not know that you are a temple of God, and *that* the Spirit of God dwells in you?

17 If any man destroys the temple of God, God will destroy him, for the temple of God is holy, and that is what you are.

18 Let no man deceive himself. If any man among you thinks that he is wise in this age, let him become foolish that he may become wise.

19 For the wisdom of this world is foolishness before God. For it is written, "He is THE ONE WHO CATCHES THE WISE IN THEIR CRAFTINESS";

20 and again, "THE LORD KNOWS THE REASONINGS of the wise, THAT THEY ARE USELESS."

21 So then let no one boast in men. For all things belong to you,

22 whether Paul or Apollos or Cephas or the world or life or death or things present or things to come; all things belong to you,

23 and you belong to Christ; and Christ belongs to God.

CHAPTER 4

LET a man regard us in this manner, as servants of Christ, and stewards of the mysteries of God.

2 In this case, moreover, it is required of stewards that one be found trustworthy.

3 But to me it is a very small thing that I should be examined

by you, or by *any* human court; in fact, I do not even examine myself.

4 I am conscious of nothing against myself, yet I am not by this acquitted; but the one who examines me is the Lord.

5 Therefore do not go on passing judgment before [6]the time, *but wait* until the Lord comes who will both bring to light the things hidden in the darkness and disclose the motives of *men's* hearts; and then each man's praise will come to him from God.

6 Now these things, brethren, I have figuratively applied to myself and Apollos for your sakes, that in us you might learn not to exceed what is written, in order that no one of you might become arrogant in behalf of one against the other.

7 For who regards you as superior? And what do you have that you did not receive? But if you did receive it, why do you boast as if you had not received it?

8 You are already filled, you have already become rich, you have become kings without us; and *I* would indeed that you had become kings so that we also might reign with you.

9 For, I think, God has exhibited us apostles last of all, as men condemned to death; because we have become a spectacle to the world, both to angels and to men.

10 We are fools for Christ's sake, but you are prudent in Christ; we are weak, but you are strong; you are distinguished, but we are without honor.

11 To this present hour we are both hungry and thirsty, and are poorly clothed, and are roughly treated, and are homeless;

12 and we toil, working with our own hands; when we are reviled, we bless; when we are persecuted, we endure;

13 when we are slandered, we try to conciliate; we have become as the scum of the world, the dregs of all things, *even* until now.

14 I do not write these things to shame you, but to admonish you as my beloved children.

15 For if you were to have countless tutors in Christ, yet *you* would not *have* many fathers; for in Christ Jesus I became your father through the gospel.

16 I exhort you therefore, be imitators of me.

17 For this reason I have sent to you Timothy, who is my beloved and faithful child in the Lord, and he will remind you of my ways which are in Christ, just as I teach everywhere in every church.

18 Now some have become arrogant, as though I were not coming to you.

19 But I will come to you soon, if the Lord wills, and I shall find out, not the words of those who are arrogant, but their power.

20 For the kingdom of God does not consist in words, but in power.

21 What do you desire? Shall I come to you with a rod or with love and a spirit of gentleness?

CHAPTER 5

IT is actually reported that there is immorality among you, and immorality of such a

---

[6] I.e., the appointed time of judgment

kind as does not exist even among the Gentiles, that someone has his father's wife.

2 And you have become arrogant, and have not mourned instead, in order that the one who had done this deed might be removed from your midst.

3 For I, on my part, though absent in body but present in spirit, have already judged him who has so committed this, as though I were present.

4 In the name of our Lord Jesus, when you are assembled, and I with you in spirit, with the power of our Lord Jesus,

5 I have decided to deliver such a one to Satan for the destruction of his flesh, that his spirit may be saved in the day of the Lord [7]Jesus.

6 Your boasting is not good. Do you not know that a little leaven leavens the whole lump of dough?

7 Clean out the old leaven, that you may be a new lump, just as you are in fact unleavened. For Christ our Passover also has been sacrificed.

8 Let us therefore celebrate the feast, not with old leaven, nor with the leaven of malice and wickedness, but with the unleavened bread of sincerity and truth.

9 I wrote to you in my letter not to associate with immoral people;

10 I did not at all mean with the immoral people of this world, or with the covetous and swindlers, or with idolaters; for then you would have to go out of the world.

11 But actually, I wrote to you not to associate with any so-called brother if he should be an immoral person, or covetous, or an idolater, or a reviler, or a drunkard, or a swindler—not even to eat with such a one.

12 For what have I to do with judging outsiders? Do you not judge those who are within the church?

13 But those who are outside, God judges. REMOVE THE WICKED MAN FROM AMONG YOURSELVES.

CHAPTER 6

DOES any one of you, when he has a case against his neighbor, dare to go to law before the unrighteous, and not before the saints?

2 Or do you not know that the saints will judge the world? And if the world is judged by you, are you not competent to constitute the smallest law courts?

3 Do you not know that we shall judge angels? How much more, matters of this life?

4 If then you have law courts dealing with matters of this life, do you appoint them as judges who are of no account in the church?

5 I say this to your shame. Is it so, that there is not among you one wise man who will be able to decide between his brethren,

6 but brother goes to law with brother, and that before unbelievers?

7 Actually, then, it is already a defeat for you, that you have lawsuits with one another. Why not rather be wronged? Why not rather be defrauded?

8 On the contrary, you yourselves wrong and defraud, and that your brethren.

9 Or do you not know that the

---

[7] Some ancient mss. do not contain Jesus

unrighteous shall not inherit the kingdom of God? Do not be deceived; neither fornicators, nor idolaters, nor adulterers, nor 8effeminate, nor homosexuals,

10 nor thieves, nor *the* covetous, nor drunkards, nor revilers, nor swindlers, shall inherit the kingdom of God.

11 And such were some of you; but you were washed, but you were sanctified, but you were justified in the name of the Lord Jesus Christ, and in the Spirit of our God.

12 All things are lawful for me, but not all things are profitable. All things are lawful for me, but I will not be mastered by anything.

13 Food is for the stomach, and the stomach is for food; but God will do away with both of them. Yet the body is not for immorality, but for the Lord; and the Lord is for the body.

14 Now God has not only raised the Lord, but will also raise us up through His power.

15 Do you not know that your bodies are members of Christ? Shall I then take away the members of Christ and make them members of a harlot? May it never be!

16 Or do you not know that the one who joins himself to a harlot is one body *with her*? For He says, "THE TWO WILL BECOME ONE FLESH."

17 But the one who joins himself to the Lord is one spirit *with Him.*

18 Flee immorality. Every *other* sin that a man commits is outside the body, but the immoral man sins against his own body.

19 Or do you not know that your body is a temple of the Holy Spirit who is in you, whom you have from God, and that you are not your own?

20 For you have been bought with a price: therefore glorify God in your body.

CHAPTER 7

NOW concerning the things about which you wrote, it is good for a man not to touch a woman.

2 But because of immoralities, let each man have his own wife, and let each woman have her own husband.

3 Let the husband fulfill his duty to his wife, and likewise also the wife to her husband.

4 The wife does not have authority over her own body, but the husband *does*; and likewise also the husband does not have authority over his own body, but the wife *does.*

5 Stop depriving one another, except by agreement for a time that you may devote yourselves to prayer, and come together again lest Satan tempt you because of your lack of self-control.

6 But this I say by way of concession, not of command.

7 9Yet I wish that all men were even as I myself am. However, each man has his own gift from God, one in this manner, and another in that.

8 But I say to the unmarried and to widows that it is good for them if they remain even as I.

9 But if they do not have self-control, let them marry; for it is better to marry than to burn.

10 But to the married I give instructions, not I, but the Lord,

---

8 I.e., effeminate by perversion

9 Some ancient mss. read *For*

that the wife should not leave her husband

11 (but if she does leave, let her remain unmarried, or else be reconciled to her husband), and that the husband should not send his wife away.

12 But to the rest I say, not the Lord, that if any brother has a wife who is an unbeliever, and she consents to live with him, let him not send her away.

13 And a woman who has an unbelieving husband, and he consents to live with her, let her not send her husband away.

14 For the unbelieving husband is sanctified through his wife, and the unbelieving wife is sanctified through her believing husband; for otherwise your children are unclean, but now they are holy.

15 Yet if the unbelieving one leaves, let him leave; the brother or the sister is not under bondage in such *cases*, but God has called [10]us to peace.

16 For how do you know, O wife, whether you will save your husband? Or how do you know, O husband, whether you will save your wife?

17 Only, as the Lord has assigned to each one, as God has called each, in this manner let him walk. And thus I direct in all the churches.

18 Was any man called *already* circumcised? Let him not become uncircumcised. Has anyone been called in uncircumcision? Let him not be circumcised.

19 Circumcision is nothing, and uncircumcision is nothing, but *what matters is* the keeping of the commandments of God.

20 Let each man remain in that condition in which he was called.

21 Were you called while a slave? Do not worry about it; but if you are able also to become free, rather do that.

22 For he who was called in the Lord while a slave, is the Lord's freedman; likewise he who was called while free, is Christ's slave.

23 You were bought with a price; do not become slaves of men.

24 Brethren, let each man remain with God in that *condition* in which he was called.

25 Now concerning virgins I have no command of the Lord, but I give an opinion as one who by the mercy of the Lord is trustworthy.

26 I think then that this is good in view of the present distress, that it is good for a man to remain as he is.

27 Are you bound to a wife? Do not seek to be released. Are you released from a wife? Do not seek a wife.

28 But if you should marry, you have not sinned; and if a virgin should marry, she has not sinned. Yet such will have trouble in this life, and I am trying to spare you.

29 But this I say, brethren, the time has been shortened, so that from now on those who have wives should be as though they had none;

30 and those who weep, as though they did not weep; and those who rejoice, as though they did not rejoice; and those who buy, as though they did not possess;

31 and those who use the world, as though they did not

---

[10] Some ancient mss. read you

make full use of it; for the form of this world is passing away.

32 But I want you to be free from concern. One who is unmarried is concerned about the things of the Lord, how he may please the Lord;

33 but one who is married is concerned about the things of the world, how he may please his [11]wife,

34 and *his interests* are divided. And the woman who is unmarried, and the virgin, is concerned about the things of the Lord, that she may be holy both in body and spirit; but one who is married is concerned about the things of the world, how she may please her husband.

35 And this I say for your own benefit; not to put a restraint upon you, but to promote what is seemly, and *to secure* undistracted devotion to the Lord.

36 But if any man thinks that he is acting unbecomingly toward his virgin *daughter*, if she should be of full age, and if it must be so, let him do what he wishes, he does not sin; let her marry.

37 But he who stands firm in his heart, being under no constraint, but has authority over his own will, and has decided this in his own heart, to keep his own virgin *daughter*, he will do well.

38 So then both he who gives his own virgin *daughter* in marriage does well, and he who does not give her in marriage will do better.

39 A wife is bound as long as her husband lives; but if her husband is dead, she is free to be married to whom she wishes, only in the Lord.

40 But in my opinion she is happier if she remains as she is; and I think that I also have the Spirit of God.

CHAPTER 8

NOW concerning things sacrificed to idols, we know that we all have knowledge. Knowledge makes arrogant, but love edifies.

2 If anyone supposes that he knows anything, he has not yet known as he ought to know;

3 but if anyone loves God, he is known by Him.

4 Therefore concerning the eating of things sacrificed to idols, we know that [12]there is no such thing as an idol in the world, and that there is no God but one.

5 For even if there are so-called gods whether in heaven or on earth, as indeed there are many gods and many lords,

6 yet for us there is *but* one God, the Father, from whom are all things, and we *exist* for Him; and one Lord, Jesus Christ, by whom are all things, and we *exist* through Him.

7 However not all men have this knowledge; but some, being accustomed to the idol until now, eat food as if it were sacrificed to an idol; and their conscience being weak is defiled.

8 But food will not commend us to God; we are neither the worse if we do not eat, nor the better if we do eat.

9 But take care lest this liberty of yours somehow become a stumbling block to the weak.

---

[11] Some mss. read *wife. And there is a difference also between the wife and the virgin. One who is unmarried is concerned . . .*
[12] I.e., has no real existence

10 For if someone sees you, who have knowledge, dining in an idol's temple, will not his conscience, if he is weak, be strengthened to eat things sacrificed to idols?

11 For through your knowledge he who is weak is ruined, the brother for whose sake Christ died.

12 And thus, by sinning against the brethren and wounding their conscience when it is weak, you sin against Christ.

13 Therefore, if food causes my brother to stumble, I will never eat meat again, that I might not cause my brother to stumble.

CHAPTER 9

AM I not free? Am I not an apostle? Have I not seen Jesus our Lord? Are you not my work in the Lord?

2 If to others I am not an apostle, at least I am to you; for you are the seal of my apostleship in the Lord.

3 My defense to those who examine me is this:

4 Do we not have a right to eat and drink?

5 Do we not have a right to take along a believing wife, even as the rest of the apostles, and the brothers of the Lord, and Cephas?

6 Or do only Barnabas and I not have a right to refrain from working?

7 Who at any time serves as a soldier at his own expense? Who plants a vineyard, and does not eat the fruit of it? Or who tends a flock and does not use the milk of the flock?

8 I am not speaking these things according to human judgment, am I? Or does not the Law also say these things?

9 For it is written in the Law of Moses, "YOU SHALL NOT MUZZLE THE OX WHILE HE IS THRESHING." God is not concerned about oxen, is He?

10 Or is He speaking altogether for our sake? Yes, for our sake it was written, because the plowman ought to plow in hope, and the thresher to thresh in hope of sharing the crops.

11 If we sowed spiritual things in you, is it too much if we should reap material things from you?

12 If others share the right over you, do we not more? Nevertheless, we did not use this right, but we endure all things, that we may cause no hindrance to the gospel of Christ.

13 Do you not know that those who perform sacred services eat the food of the temple, and those who attend regularly to the altar have their share with the altar?

14 So also the Lord directed those who proclaim the gospel to get their living from the gospel.

15 But I have used none of these things. And I am not writing these things that it may be done so in my case; for it would be better for me to die than have any man make my boast an empty one.

16 For if I preach the gospel, I have nothing to boast of, for I am under compulsion; for woe is me if I do not preach the gospel.

17 For if I do this voluntarily, I have a reward; but if against my will, I have a stewardship entrusted to me.

18 What then is my reward? That, when I preach the gospel, I may offer the gospel without

charge, so as not to make full use of my right in the gospel.

19 For though I am free from all *men*, I have made myself a slave to all, that I might win the more.

20 And to the Jews I became as a Jew, that I might win Jews; to those who are under the Law, as under the Law, though not being myself under the Law, that I might win those who are under the Law;

21 to those who are without law, as without law, though not being without the law of God but under the law of Christ, that I might win those who are without law.

22 To the weak I became weak, that I might win the weak; I have become all things to all men, that I may by all means save some.

23 And I do all things for the sake of the gospel, that I may become a fellow partaker of it.

24 Do you not know that those who run in a race all run, but *only* one receives the prize? Run in such a way that you may win.

25 And everyone who competes in the games exercises self-control in all things. They then *do it* to receive a perishable wreath, but we an imperishable.

26 Therefore I run in such a way, as not without aim; I box in such a way, as not beating the air;

27 but I buffet my body and make it my slave, lest possibly, after I have preached to others, I myself should be disqualified.

CHAPTER 10

FOR I do not want you to be unaware, brethren, that our fathers were all under the cloud, and all passed through the sea;

2 and all [13]were baptized into Moses in the cloud and in the sea;

3 and all ate the same spiritual food;

4 and all drank the same spiritual drink, for they were drinking from a spiritual rock which followed them; and the rock was Christ.

5 Nevertheless, with most of them God was not well-pleased; for they were laid low in the wilderness.

6 Now these things happened as examples for us, that we should not crave evil things, as they also craved.

7 And do not be idolaters, as some of them were; as it is written, "THE PEOPLE SAT DOWN TO EAT AND DRINK, AND STOOD UP TO PLAY."

8 Nor let us act immorally, as some of them did, and twenty-three thousand fell in one day.

9 Nor let us try the Lord, as some of them did, and were destroyed by the serpents.

10 Nor grumble, as some of them did, and were destroyed by the destroyer.

11 Now these things happened to them as an example, and they were written for our instruction, upon whom the ends of the ages have come.

12 Therefore let him who thinks he stands take heed lest he fall.

13 No temptation has overtaken you but such as is common to man; and God is faithful, who will not allow you to be tempted beyond what you are able, but with the temptation will provide the way of escape also, that you may be able to endure it.

[13] Some ancient mss. read *received baptism*

14 Therefore, my beloved, flee from idolatry.

15 I speak as to wise men; you judge what I say.

16 Is not the cup of blessing which we bless a sharing in the blood of Christ? Is not the bread which we break a sharing in the body of Christ?

17 Since there is one bread, we who are many are one body; for we all partake of the one bread.

18 Look at the nation Israel; are not those who eat the sacrifices sharers in the altar?

19 What do I mean then? That a thing sacrificed to idols is anything, or that an idol is anything?

20 No, but I *say* that the things which the Gentiles sacrifice, they sacrifice to demons, and not to God; and I do not want you to become sharers in demons.

21 You cannot drink the cup of the Lord and the cup of demons; you cannot partake of the table of the Lord and the table of demons.

22 Or do we provoke the Lord to jealousy? We are not stronger than He, are we?

23 All things are lawful, but not all things are profitable. All things are lawful, but not all things edify.

24 Let no one seek his own *good*, but that of his neighbor.

25 Eat anything that is sold in the meat market, without asking questions for conscience' sake;

26 FOR THE EARTH IS THE LORD'S, AND ALL IT CONTAINS.

27 If one of the unbelievers invites you, and you wish to go, eat anything that is set before you, without asking questions for conscience' sake.

28 But if anyone should say to you, "This is meat sacrificed to idols," do not eat *it*, for the sake of the one who informed *you*, and for conscience' sake;

29 I mean not your own conscience, but the other *man's*; for why is my freedom judged by another's conscience?

30 If I partake with thankfulness, why am I slandered concerning that for which I give thanks?

31 Whether, then, you eat or drink or whatever you do, do all to the glory of God.

32 Give no offense either to Jews or to Greeks or to the church of God;

33 just as I also please all men in all things, not seeking my own profit, but the *profit* of the many, that they may be saved.

CHAPTER 11

BE imitators of me, just as I also am of Christ.

2 Now I praise you because you remember me in everything, and hold firmly to the traditions, just as I delivered them to you.

3 But I want you to understand that Christ is the head of every man, and the man is the head of a woman, and God is the head of Christ.

4 Every man who has *something* on his head while praying or prophesying, disgraces his head.

5 But every woman who has her head uncovered while praying or prophesying, disgraces her head; for she is one and the same with her whose head is shaved.

6 For if a woman does not cover her head, let her also have her hair cut off; but if it is disgraceful for a woman to have her

hair cut off or her head shaved, let her cover her head.

7 For a man ought not to have his head covered, since he is the image and glory of God; but the woman is the glory of man.

8 For man does not originate from woman, but woman from man;

9 for indeed man was not created for the woman's sake, but woman for the man's sake.

10 Therefore the woman ought to have *a symbol of* authority on her head, because of the angels.

11 However, in the Lord, neither is woman independent of man, nor is man independent of woman.

12 For as the woman originates from the man, so also the man has his birth through the woman; and all things originate from God.

13 Judge for yourselves: is it proper for a woman to pray to God *with head* uncovered?

14 Does not even nature itself teach you that if a man has long hair, it is a dishonor to him,

15 but if a woman has long hair, it is a glory to her? For her hair is given to her for a covering.

16 But if one is inclined to be contentious, we have no other practice, nor have the churches of God.

17 But in giving this instruction, I do not praise you, because you come together not for the better but for the worse.

18 For, in the first place, when you come together as a church, I hear that divisions exist among you; and in part, I believe it.

19 For there must also be fac-

tions among you, in order that those who are approved may have become evident among you.

20 Therefore when you meet together, it is not to eat the Lord's Supper.

21 For in your eating each one takes his own supper first; and one is hungry and another is drunk.

22 What! Do you not have houses in which to eat and drink? Or do you despise the church of God, and shame those who have nothing? What shall I say to you? Shall I praise you? In this I will not praise you.

23 For I received from the Lord that which I also delivered to you, that the Lord Jesus in the night in which He was betrayed took bread;

24 and when He had given thanks, He broke it, and said, "This is My body, which [14]is for you; do this in remembrance of Me."

25 In the same way *He took* the cup also, after supper, saying, "This cup is the new covenant in My blood; do this, as often as you drink *it*, in remembrance of Me."

26 For as often as you eat this bread and drink the cup, you proclaim the Lord's death until He comes.

27 Therefore whoever eats the bread or drinks the cup of the Lord in an unworthy manner, shall be guilty of the body and the blood of the Lord.

28 But let a man examine himself, and so let him eat of the bread and drink of the cup.

29 For he who eats and drinks, eats and drinks judgment to himself, if he does not judge the body rightly.

30 For this reason many

[14] Some ancient mss. read *is broken*

among you are weak and sick, and a number sleep.

31 But if we judged ourselves rightly, we should not be judged.

32 But when we are judged, we are disciplined by the Lord in order that we may not be condemned along with the world.

33 So then, my brethren, when you come together to eat, wait for one another.

34 If anyone is hungry, let him eat at home, so that you may not come together for judgment. And the remaining matters I shall arrange when I come.

CHAPTER 12

NOW concerning spiritual *gifts*, brethren, I do not want you to be unaware.

2 You know that when you were pagans, *you were* led astray to the dumb idols, however you were led.

3 Therefore I make known to you, that no one speaking by the Spirit of God says, "Jesus is accursed"; and no one can say, "Jesus is Lord," except by the Holy Spirit.

4 Now there are varieties of gifts, but the same Spirit.

5 And there are varieties of ministries, and the same Lord.

6 And there are varieties of effects, but the same God who works all things in all *persons*.

7 But to each one is given the manifestation of the Spirit for the common good.

8 For to one is given the word of wisdom through the Spirit, and to another the word of knowledge according to the same Spirit;

9 to another faith by the same Spirit, and to another gifts of healing by the one Spirit,

10 and to another the effecting of miracles, and to another prophecy, and to another the distinguishing of spirits, to another *various* kinds of tongues, and to another the interpretation of tongues.

11 But one and the same Spirit works all these things, distributing to each one individually just as He wills.

12 For even as the body is one and *yet* has many members, and all the members of the body, though they are many, are one body, so also is Christ.

13 For by one Spirit we were all baptized into one body, whether Jews or Greeks, whether slaves or free, and we were all made to drink of one Spirit.

14 For the body is not one member, but many.

15 If the foot should say, "Because I am not a hand, I am not *a part* of the body," it is not for this reason any the less *a part* of the body.

16 And if the ear should say, "Because I am not an eye, I am not *a part* of the body," it is not for this reason any the less *a part* of the body.

17 If the whole body were an eye, where would the hearing be? If the whole were hearing, where would the sense of smell be?

18 But now God has placed the members, each one of them, in the body, just as He desired.

19 And if they were all one member, where would the body be?

20 But now there are many members, but one body.

21 And the eye cannot say to

the hand, "I have no need of you"; or again the head to the feet, "I have no need of you."

22 On the contrary, it is much truer that the members of the body which seem to be weaker are necessary;

23 and those *members* of the body, which we deem less honorable, on these we bestow more abundant honor, and our unseemly *members come to* have more abundant seemliness.

24 whereas our seemly *members* have no need *of it.* But God has *so* composed the body, giving more abundant honor to that *member* which lacked,

25 that there should be no division in the body, but *that* the members should have the same care for one another.

26 And if one member suffers, all the members suffer with it; if *one* member is honored, all the members rejoice with it.

27 Now you are Christ's body, and individually members of it.

28 And God has appointed in the church, first apostles, second prophets, third teachers, then miracles, then gifts of healings, helps, administrations, *various* kinds of tongues.

29 All are not apostles, are they? All are not prophets, are they? All are not teachers, are they? All are not *workers of* miracles, are they?

30 All do not have gifts of healings, do they? All do not speak with tongues, do they? All do not interpret, do they?

31 But earnestly desire the greater gifts.

And I show you a still more excellent way.

CHAPTER 13

IF I speak with the tongues of men and of angels, but do not have love, I have become a noisy gong or a clanging cymbal.

2 And if I have *the gift of* prophecy, and know all mysteries and all knowledge; and if I have all faith, so as to remove mountains, but do not have love, I am nothing.

3 And if I give all my possessions to feed *the poor,* and if I deliver my body [15]to be burned, but do not have love, it profits me nothing.

4 Love is patient, love is kind, *and* is not jealous; love does not brag *and* is not arrogant,

5 does not act unbecomingly; it does not seek its own, is not provoked, does not take into account a wrong *suffered,*

6 does not rejoice in unrighteousness, but rejoices with the truth;

7 bears all things, believes all things, hopes all things, endures all things.

8 Love never fails; but if *there are gifts of* prophecy, they will be done away; if *there are* tongues, they will cease; if *there is* knowledge, it will be done away.

9 For we know in part, and we prophesy in part;

10 but when the perfect comes, the partial will be done away.

11 When I was a child, I used to speak as a child, think as a child, reason as a child; when I became a man, I did away with childish things.

12 For now we see in a mirror dimly, but then face to face; now I know in part, but then I shall know fully just as I also have been fully known.

[15] Some ancient mss. read *that I may boast*

13 But now abide faith, hope, love, these three; but the greatest of these is love.

CHAPTER 14

PURSUE love, yet desire earnestly spiritual *gifts*, but especially that you may prophesy.

2 For one who speaks in a tongue does not speak to men, but to God; for no one understands, but in *his* spirit he speaks mysteries.

3 But one who prophesies speaks to men for edification and exhortation and consolation.

4 One who speaks in a tongue edifies himself; but one who prophesies edifies the church.

5 Now I wish that you all spoke in tongues, but *even* more that you would prophesy; and greater is one who prophesies than one who speaks in tongues, unless he interprets, so that the church may receive edifying.

6 But now, brethren, if I come to you speaking in tongues, what shall I profit you, unless I speak to you either by way of revelation or of knowledge or of prophecy or of teaching?

7 Yet *even* lifeless things, either flute or harp, in producing a sound, if they do not produce a distinction in the tones, how will it be known what is played on the flute or on the harp?

8 For if the bugle produces an indistinct sound, who will prepare himself for battle?

9 So also you, unless you utter by the tongue speech that is clear, how will it be known what is spoken? For you will be speaking into the air.

10 There are, perhaps, a great many kinds of languages in the world, and no *kind* is without meaning.

11 If then I do not know the meaning of the language, I shall be to the one who speaks a barbarian, and the one who speaks will be a barbarian to me.

12 So also you, since you are zealous of spiritual *gifts,* seek to abound for the edification of the church.

13 Therefore let one who speaks in a tongue pray that he may interpret.

14 For if I pray in a tongue, my spirit prays, but my mind is unfruitful.

15 What is *the outcome* then? I shall pray with the spirit and I shall pray with the mind also; I shall sing with the spirit and I shall sing with the mind also.

16 Otherwise if you bless in the spirit *only,* how will the one who fills the place of the ungifted say the "Amen" at your giving of thanks, since he does not know what you are saying?

17 For you are giving thanks well enough, but the other man is not edified.

18 I thank God, I speak in tongues more than you all;

19 however, in the church I desire to speak five words with my mind, that I may instruct others also, rather than ten thousand words in a tongue.

20 Brethren, do not be children in your thinking; yet in evil be babes, but in your thinking be mature.

21 In the Law it is written, "BY MEN OF STRANGE TONGUES AND BY THE LIPS OF STRANGERS I WILL SPEAK TO THIS PEOPLE, AND EVEN SO THEY WILL NOT LISTEN TO ME," says the Lord.

22 So then tongues are for a

sign, not to those who believe, but to unbelievers; but prophecy *is for a sign*, not to unbelievers, but to those who believe.

23 If therefore the whole church should assemble together and all speak in tongues, and ungifted men or unbelievers enter, will they not say that you are mad?

24 But if all prophesy, and an unbeliever or an ungifted man enters, he is convicted by all, he is called to account by all;

25 the secrets of his heart are disclosed; and so he will fall on his face and worship God, declaring that God is certainly among you.

26 What is *the outcome* then, brethren? When you assemble, each one has a psalm, has a teaching, has a revelation, has a tongue, has an interpretation. Let all things be done for edification.

27 If anyone speaks in a tongue, *it should be* by two or at the most three, and *each* in turn, and let one interpret;

28 but if there is no interpreter, let him keep silent in the church; and let him speak to himself and to God.

29 And let two or three prophets speak, and let the others pass judgment.

30 But if a revelation is made to another who is seated, let the first keep silent.

31 For you can all prophesy one by one, so that all may learn and all may be exhorted;

32 and the spirits of prophets are subject to prophets;

33 for God is not *a God* of confusion but of peace, as in all the churches of the saints.

34 Let the women keep silent in the churches; for they are not permitted to speak, but let them subject themselves, just as the Law also says.

35 And if they desire to learn anything, let them ask their own husbands at home; for it is improper for a woman to speak in church.

36 Was it from you that the word of God *first* went forth? Or has it come to you only?

37 If anyone thinks he is a prophet or spiritual, let him recognize that the things which I write to you are the Lord's commandment.

38 But if anyone [16]does not recognize *this*, he is not recognized.

39 Therefore, my brethren, desire earnestly to prophesy, and do not forbid to speak in tongues.

40 But let all things be done properly and in an orderly manner.

CHAPTER 15

NOW I make known to you, brethren, the gospel which I preached to you, which also you received, in which also you stand,

2 by which also you are saved, if you hold fast the word which I preached to you, unless you believed in vain.

3 For I delivered to you as of first importance what I also received, that Christ died for our sins according to the Scriptures,

4 and that He was buried, and that He was raised on the third day according to the Scriptures,

5 and that He appeared to Cephas, then to the twelve.

6 After that He appeared to more than five hundred brethren at one time, most of whom

[16] Some ancient mss. read *is ignorant, let him be ignorant*

remain until now, but some have fallen asleep;

7 then He appeared to James, then to all the apostles;

8 and last of all, as it were to one untimely born, He appeared to me also.

9 For I am the least of the apostles, who am not fit to be called an apostle, because I persecuted the church of God.

10 But by the grace of God I am what I am, and His grace toward me did not prove vain; but I labored even more than all of them, yet not I, but the grace of God with me.

11 Whether then *it was* I or they, so we preach and so you believed.

12 Now if Christ is preached, that He has been raised from the dead, how do some among you say that there is no resurrection of the dead?

13 But if there is no resurrection of the dead, not even Christ has been raised;

14 and if Christ has not been raised, then our preaching is vain, your faith also is vain.

15 Moreover we are even found *to be* false witnesses of God, because we witnessed against God that He raised [17]Christ, whom He did not raise, if in fact the dead are not raised.

16 For if the dead are not raised, not even Christ has been raised;

17 and if Christ has not been raised, your faith is worthless; you are still in your sins.

18 Then those also who have fallen asleep in Christ have perished.

19 If we have hoped in Christ in this life only, we are of all men most to be pitied.

20 But now Christ has been raised from the dead, the first fruits of those who are asleep.

21 For since by a man *came* death, by a man also *came* the resurrection of the dead.

22 For as in Adam all die, so also in Christ all shall be made alive.

23 But each in his own order: Christ the first fruits, after that those who are Christ's at His coming,

24 then *comes* the end, when He delivers up the kingdom to the God and Father, when He has abolished all rule and all authority and power.

25 For He must reign until He has put all His enemies under His feet.

26 The last enemy that will be abolished is death.

27 For HE HAS PUT ALL THINGS IN SUBJECTION UNDER HIS FEET. But when He says, "All things are put in subjection," it is evident that He is excepted who put all things in subjection to Him.

28 And when all things are subjected to Him, then the Son Himself also will be subjected to the One who subjected all things to Him, that God may be all in all.

29 Otherwise, what will those do who are baptized for the dead? If the dead are not raised at all, why then are they baptized for them?

30 Why are we also in danger every hour?

31 I protest, brethren, by the boasting in you, which I have in Christ Jesus our Lord, I die daily.

32 If from human motives I fought with wild beasts at Eph-

---

[17] I.e., the Messiah

esus, what does it profit me? If the dead are not raised, LET US EAT AND DRINK, FOR TOMORROW WE DIE.

33 Do not be deceived: "Bad company corrupts good morals."

34 Become sober-minded as you ought, and stop sinning; for some have no knowledge of God. I speak *this* to your shame.

35 But someone will say, "How are the dead raised? And with what kind of body do they come?"

36 You fool! That which you sow does not come to life unless it dies;

37 and that which you sow, you do not sow the body which is to be, but a bare grain, perhaps of wheat or of something else.

38 But God gives it a body just as He wished, and to each of the seeds a body of its own.

39 All flesh is not the same flesh, but there is *one flesh* of men, and another flesh of beasts, and another flesh of birds, and another of fish.

40 There are also heavenly bodies and earthly bodies, but the glory of the heavenly is one, and the *glory* of the earthly is another.

41 There is one glory of the sun, and another glory of the moon, and another glory of the stars; for star differs from star in glory.

42 So also is the resurrection of the dead. It is sown a perishable *body*, it is raised an imperishable *body*;

43 it is sown in dishonor, it is raised in glory; it is sown in weakness, it is raised in power;

44 it is sown a natural body, it is raised a spiritual body. If there is a natural body, there is also a spiritual *body*.

45 So also it is written, "The first MAN, Adam, BECAME A LIVING SOUL." The last Adam *became* a life-giving spirit.

46 However, the spiritual is not first, but the natural; then the spiritual.

47 The first man is from the earth, earthy; the second man is from heaven.

48 As is the earthy, so also are those who are earthy; and as is the heavenly, so also are those who are heavenly.

49 And just as we have borne the image of the earthy, [18]we shall also bear the image of the heavenly.

50 Now I say this, brethren, that flesh and blood cannot inherit the kingdom of God; nor does the perishable inherit the imperishable.

51 Behold, I tell you a mystery; we shall not all sleep, but we shall all be changed,

52 in a moment, in the twinkling of an eye, at the last trumpet; for the trumpet will sound, and the dead will be raised imperishable, and we shall be changed.

53 For this perishable must put on the imperishable, and this mortal must put on immortality.

54 But when this perishable will have put on the imperishable, and this mortal will have put on immortality, then will come about the saying that is written, "DEATH IS SWALLOWED UP in victory.

55 "O DEATH, WHERE IS YOUR VICTORY? O DEATH, WHERE IS YOUR STING?"

[18] Some ancient mss. read *let us also*

56 The sting of death is sin, and the power of sin is the law;

57 but thanks be to God, who gives us the victory through our Lord Jesus Christ.

58 Therefore, my beloved brethren, be steadfast, immovable, always abounding in the work of the Lord, knowing that your toil is not *in* vain in the Lord.

CHAPTER 16

NOW concerning the collection for the saints, as I directed the churches of Galatia, so do you also.

2 On the first day of every week let each one of you put aside and save, as he may prosper, that no collections be made when I come.

3 And when I arrive, whomever you may approve, I shall send them with letters to carry your gift to Jerusalem;

4 and if it is fitting for me to go also, they will go with me.

5 But I shall come to you after I go through Macedonia, for I am going through Macedonia;

6 and perhaps I shall stay with you, or even spend the winter, that you may send me on my way wherever I may go.

7 For I do not wish to see you now *just* in passing; for I hope to remain with you for some time, if the Lord permits.

8 But I shall remain in Ephesus until Pentecost;

9 for a wide door for effective *service* has opened to me, and there are many adversaries.

10 Now if Timothy comes, see that he is with you without cause to be afraid; for he is doing the Lord's work, as I also am.

11 Let no one therefore despise him. But send him on his way in peace, so that he may come to me; for I expect him with the brethren.

12 But concerning Apollos our brother, I encouraged him greatly to come to you with the brethren; and it was not at all *his* desire to come now, but he will come when he has opportunity.

13 Be on the alert, stand firm in the faith, act like men, be strong.

14 Let all that you do be done in love.

15 Now I urge you, brethren (you know the household of Stephanas, that they were the first fruits of Achaia, and that they have devoted themselves for ministry to the saints),

16 that you also be in subjection to such men and to everyone who helps in the work and labors.

17 And I rejoice over the coming of Stephanas and Fortunatus and Achaicus; because they have supplied what was lacking on your part.

18 For they have refreshed my spirit and yours. Therefore acknowledge such men.

19 The churches of Asia greet you. Aquila and Prisca greet you heartily in the Lord, with the church that is in their house.

20 All the brethren greet you. Greet one another with a holy kiss.

21 The greeting is in my own hand—Paul.

22 If anyone does not love the Lord, let him be accursed. Maranatha.

23 The grace of the Lord Jesus be with you.

24 My love be with you all in Christ Jesus. Amen.

CORINTHIANS

PAUL, an apostle of Christ Jesus by the will of God, and Timothy *our* brother, to the church of God which is at Corinth with all the saints who are throughout Achaia:

2 Grace to you and peace from God our Father and the Lord Jesus Christ.

3 Blessed be the God and Father of our Lord Jesus Christ, the Father of mercies and God of all comfort;

4 who comforts us in all our affliction so that we may be able to comfort those who are in any affliction with the comfort with which we ourselves are comforted by God.

5 For just as the sufferings of Christ are ours in abundance, so also our comfort is abundant through Christ.

6 But if we are afflicted, it is for your comfort and salvation; or if we are comforted, it is for your comfort, which is effective in the patient enduring of the same sufferings which we also suffer;

7 and our hope for you is firmly grounded, knowing that as you are sharers of our sufferings, so also you are *sharers* of our comfort.

8 For we do not want you to be unaware, brethren, of our affliction which came *to us* in Asia, that we were burdened excessively, beyond our strength, so that we despaired even of life;

9 indeed, we had the sentence of death within ourselves in order that we should not trust in ourselves, but in God who raises the dead;

10 who delivered us from so great a *peril of* death, and will deliver *us*, He on whom we have set our hope. And He will yet deliver us,

11 you also joining in helping us through your prayers, that thanks may be given by many persons on our behalf for the favor bestowed upon us through *the prayers of* many.

12 For our proud confidence is this, the testimony of our conscience, that in holiness and godly sincerity, not in fleshly wisdom but in the grace of God, we have conducted ourselves in the world, and especially toward you.

13 For we write nothing else to you than what you read and understand, and I hope you will understand until the end;

14 just as you also partially did understand us, that we are your reason to be proud as you also are ours, in the day of our Lord Jesus.

15 And in this confidence I intended at first to come to you, that you might twice receive a blessing;

16 that is, to pass your way into Macedonia, and again from Macedonia to come to you, and by you to be helped on my journey to Judea.

17 Therefore, I was not vacillating when I intended to do this, was I? Or that which I purpose,

do I purpose according to the flesh, that with me there should be yes, yes and no, no *at the same time?*

18 But as God is faithful, our word to you is not yes and no.

19 For the Son of God, Christ Jesus, who was preached among you by us—by me and Silvanus and Timothy—was not yes and no, but is yes in Him.

20 For as many as may be the promises of God, in Him they are yes; wherefore also by Him is our Amen to the glory of God through us.

21 Now He who establishes us with you in Christ and anointed us is God,

22 who also sealed us and gave *us* the Spirit in our hearts as a pledge.

23 But I call God as witness to my soul, that to spare you I came no more to Corinth.

24 Not that we lord it over your faith, but are workers with you for your joy; for in your faith you are standing firm.

CHAPTER 2

BUT I determined this for my own sake, that I would not come to you in sorrow again.

2 For if I cause you sorrow, who then makes me glad but the one whom I made sorrowful?

3 And this is the very thing I wrote you, lest, when I came, I should have sorrow from those who ought to make me rejoice; having confidence in you all, that my joy would be *the joy* of you all.

4 For out of much affliction and anguish of heart I wrote to you with many tears; not that you should be made sorrowful,

but that you might know the love which I have especially for you.

5 But if any has caused sorrow, he has caused sorrow not to me, but in some degree—in order not to say too much—to all of you.

6 Sufficient for such a one is this punishment which was *inflicted by* the majority,

7 so that on the contrary you should rather forgive and comfort *him*, lest somehow such a one be overwhelmed by excessive sorrow.

8 Wherefore I urge you to reaffirm *your* love for him.

9 For to this end also I wrote that I might put you to the test, whether you are obedient in all things.

10 But whom you forgive anything, I *forgive* also; for indeed what I have forgiven, if I have forgiven anything, I *did it* for your sakes in the presence of Christ,

11 in order that no advantage be taken of us by Satan; for we are not ignorant of his schemes.

12 Now when I came to Troas for the gospel of Christ and when a door was opened for me in the Lord,

13 I had no rest for my spirit, not finding Titus my brother; but taking my leave of them, I went on to Macedonia.

14 But thanks be to God, who always leads us in His triumph in Christ, and manifests through us the sweet aroma of the knowledge of Him in every place.

15 For we are a fragrance of Christ to God among those who are being saved and among those who are perishing;

16 to the one an aroma from death to death, to the other an

aroma from life to life. And who is adequate for these things?

17 For we are not like many, [1]peddling the word of God, but as from sincerity, but as from God, we speak in Christ in the sight of God.

CHAPTER 3

ARE we beginning to commend ourselves again? Or do we need, as some, letters of commendation to you or from you?

2 You are our letter, written in our hearts, known and read by all men;

3 being manifested that you are a letter of Christ, cared for by us, written not with ink, but with the Spirit of the living God, not on tablets of stone, but on tablets of human hearts.

4 And such confidence we have through Christ toward God.

5 Not that we are adequate in ourselves to consider anything as *coming* from ourselves, but our adequacy is from God,

6 who also made us adequate *as* servants of a new covenant, not of the letter, but of the Spirit; for the letter kills, but the Spirit gives life.

7 But if the ministry of death, in letters engraved on stones, came with glory, so that the sons of Israel could not look intently at the face of Moses because of the glory of his face, fading *as* it was,

8 how shall the ministry of the Spirit fail to be even more with glory?

9 For if the ministry of condemnation has glory, much more

does the ministry of righteousness abound in glory.

10 For indeed what had glory, in this case has no glory on account of the glory that surpasses *it*.

11 For if that which fades away *was* with glory, much more that which remains *is* in glory.

12 Having therefore such a hope, we use great boldness in *our* speech,

13 and *are* not as Moses, *who* used to put a veil over his face that the sons of Israel might not look intently at the end of what was fading away.

14 But their minds were hardened; for until this very day at the reading of the old covenant the same veil remains unlifted, because it is removed in Christ.

15 But to this day whenever Moses is read, a veil lies over their heart;

16 but whenever a man turns to the Lord, the veil is taken away.

17 Now the Lord is the Spirit; and where the Spirit of the Lord is, *there* is liberty.

18 But we all, with unveiled face beholding as in a mirror the glory of the Lord, are being transformed into the same image from glory to glory, just as from the Lord, the Spirit.

CHAPTER 4

THEREFORE, since we have this ministry, as we received mercy, we do not lose heart,

2 but we have renounced the things hidden because of shame, not walking in craftiness or adulterating the word of God, but by the manifestation of truth commending ourselves to every

---

[1] Or, *corrupting*

man's conscience in the sight of God.

3 And even if our gospel is veiled, it is veiled to those who are perishing,

4 in whose case the god of this world has blinded the minds of the unbelieving, that they might not see the light of the gospel of the glory of Christ, who is the image of God.

5 For we do not preach ourselves but Christ Jesus as Lord, and ourselves as your bond-servants for Jesus' sake.

6 For God, who said, "Light shall shine out of darkness," is the One who has shone in our hearts to give the light of the knowledge of the glory of God in the face of Christ.

7 But we have this treasure in earthen vessels, that the surpassing greatness of the power may be of God and not from ourselves;

8 *we are* afflicted in every way, but not crushed; perplexed, but not despairing;

9 persecuted, but not forsaken; struck down, but not destroyed;

10 always carrying about in the body the dying of Jesus, that the life of Jesus also may be manifested in our body.

11 For we who live are constantly being delivered over to death for Jesus' sake, that the life of Jesus also may be manifested in our mortal flesh.

12 So death works in us, but life in you.

13 But having the same spirit of faith, according to what is written, "I BELIEVED, THEREFORE I SPOKE," we also believe, therefore also we speak;

14 knowing that He who raised the Lord Jesus will raise us also with Jesus and will present us with you.

15 For all things *are* for your sakes, that the grace which is spreading to more and more people may cause the giving of thanks to abound to the glory of God.

16 Therefore we do not lose heart, but though our outer man is decaying, yet our inner man is being renewed day by day.

17 For momentary, light affliction is producing for us an eternal weight of glory far beyond all comparison,

18 while we look not at the things which are seen, but at the things which are not seen; for the things which are seen are temporal, but the things which are not seen are eternal.

CHAPTER 5

FOR we know that if the earthly tent which is our house is torn down, we have a building from God, a house not made with hands, eternal in the heavens.

2 For indeed in this *house* we groan, longing to be clothed with our dwelling from heaven;

3 inasmuch as we, having put it on, shall not be found naked.

4 For indeed while we are in this tent, we groan, being burdened, because we do not want to be unclothed, but to be clothed, in order that what is mortal may be swallowed up by life.

5 Now He who prepared us for this very purpose is God, who gave to us the Spirit as a pledge.

6 Therefore, being always of good courage, and knowing that

while we are at home in the body we are absent from the Lord—

7 for we walk by faith, not by sight—

8 we are of good courage, I say, and prefer rather to be absent from the body and to be at home with the Lord.

9 Therefore also we have as our ambition, whether at home or absent, to be pleasing to Him.

10 For we must all appear before the judgment seat of Christ, that each one may be recompensed for his deeds in the body, according to what he has done, whether good or bad.

11 Therefore knowing the fear of the Lord, we persuade men, but we are made manifest to God; and I hope that we are made manifest also in your consciences.

12 We are not again commending ourselves to you but *are* giving you an occasion to be proud of us, that you may have *an answer* for those who take pride in appearance, and not in heart.

13 For if we are beside ourselves, it is for God; if we are of sound mind, it is for you.

14 For the love of Christ controls us, having concluded this, that one died for all, therefore all died;

15 and He died for all, that they who live should no longer live for themselves, but for Him who died and rose again on their behalf.

16 Therefore from now on we recognize no man according to the flesh; even though we have known Christ according to the flesh, yet now we know *Him* thus no longer.

17 Therefore if any man is in Christ, *he is* a new creature; the old things passed away; behold, new things have come.

18 Now all *these* things are from God, who reconciled us to Himself through Christ, and gave us the ministry of reconciliation,

19 namely, that God was in Christ reconciling the world to Himself, not counting their trespasses against them, and He has committed to us the word of reconciliation.

20 Therefore, we are ambassadors for Christ, as though God were entreating through us; we beg you on behalf of Christ, be reconciled to God.

21 He made Him who knew no sin *to be* sin on our behalf, that we might become the righteousness of God in Him.

CHAPTER 6

AND working together *with Him*, we also urge you not to receive the grace of God in vain—

2 for He says,

"AT THE ACCEPTABLE TIME I
LISTENED TO YOU,
AND ON THE DAY OF SALVA-
TION I HELPED YOU";

behold, now is "THE ACCEPTABLE TIME," behold, now is "THE DAY OF SALVATION"—

3 giving no cause for offense in anything, in order that the ministry be not discredited,

4 but in everything commending ourselves as servants of God, in much endurance, in afflictions, in hardships, in distresses,

5 in beatings, in imprisonments, in tumults, in labors, in sleeplessness, in hunger,

6 in purity, in knowledge, in patience, in kindness, in the Holy Spirit, in genuine love,

7 in the word of truth, in the power of God; by the weapons of righteousness for the right hand and the left,

8 by glory and dishonor, by evil report and good report; *regarded* as deceivers and yet true;

9 as unknown yet well-known, as dying yet behold, we live; as punished yet not put to death,

10 as sorrowful yet always rejoicing, as poor yet making many rich, as having nothing yet possessing all things.

11 Our mouth has spoken freely to you, O Corinthians, our heart is opened wide.

12 You are not restrained by us, but you are restrained in your own affections.

13 Now in a like exchange—I speak as to children—open wide *to us* also.

14 Do not be bound together with unbelievers; for what partnership have righteousness and lawlessness, or what fellowship has light with darkness?

15 Or what harmony has Christ with Belial, or what has a believer in common with an unbeliever?

16 Or what agreement has the temple of God with idols? For we are the temple of the living God; just as God said,

"I WILL DWELL IN THEM AND WALK AMONG THEM;
AND I WILL BE THEIR GOD,
AND THEY SHALL BE MY PEOPLE.

17 "Therefore, COME OUT FROM THEIR MIDST AND BE SEPARATE," says the Lord.

"AND DO NOT TOUCH WHAT IS UNCLEAN;
And I will welcome you.

18 "And I will be a father to you,
And you shall be sons and daughters to Me,"
Says the Lord Almighty.

CHAPTER 7

THEREFORE, having these promises, beloved, let us cleanse ourselves from all defilement of flesh and spirit, perfecting holiness in the fear of God.

2 Make room for us *in your hearts;* we wronged no one, we corrupted no one, we took advantage of no one.

3 I do not speak to condemn you; for I have said before that you are in our hearts to die together and to live together.

4 Great is my confidence in you, great is my boasting on your behalf; I am filled with comfort. I am overflowing with joy in all our affliction.

5 For even when we came into Macedonia our flesh had no rest, but we were afflicted on every side: conflicts without, fears within.

6 But God, who comforts the depressed, comforted us by the coming of Titus;

7 and not only by his coming, but also by the comfort with which he was comforted in you, as he reported to us your longing, your mourning, your zeal for me; so that I rejoiced even more.

8 For though I caused you sorrow by my letter, I do not regret it; though I did regret it—*for* I see that that letter caused you sorrow, though only for a while—

9 I now rejoice, not that you were made sorrowful, but that you were made sorrowful to the point of repentance; for you were made sorrowful according to the will of God, in order that you might not suffer loss in anything through us.

10 For the sorrow that is according to the will of God produces a repentance without regret, leading to salvation; but the sorrow of the world produces death.

11 For behold what earnestness this very thing, this godly sorrow, has produced in you: what vindication of yourselves, what indignation, what fear, what longing, what zeal, what avenging of wrong! In everything you demonstrated yourselves to be innocent in the matter.

12 So although I wrote to you it was not for the sake of the offender, nor for the sake of the one offended, but that your earnestness on our behalf might be made known to you in the sight of God.

13 For this reason we have been comforted.

And besides our comfort, we rejoiced even much more for the joy of Titus, because his spirit has been refreshed by you all.

14 For if in anything I have boasted to him about you, I was not put to shame; but as we spoke all things to you in truth, so also our boasting before Titus proved to be the truth.

15 And his affection abounds all the more toward you, as he remembers the obedience of you all, how you received him with fear and trembling.

² Lit., love from us in you; some ancient mss. read your love for us

16 I rejoice that in everything I have confidence in you.

CHAPTER 8

NOW, brethren, we wish to make known to you the grace of God which has been given in the churches of Macedonia,

2 that in a great ordeal of affliction their abundance of joy and their deep poverty overflowed in the wealth of their liberality.

3 For I testify that according to their ability, and beyond their ability they gave of their own accord,

4 begging us with much entreaty for the favor of participation in the support of the saints,

5 and this, not as we had expected, but they first gave themselves to the Lord and to us by the will of God.

6 Consequently we urged Titus that as he had previously made a beginning, so he would also complete in you this gracious work as well.

7 But just as you abound in everything, in faith and utterance and knowledge and in all earnestness and in the ²love we inspired in you, see that you abound in this gracious work also.

8 I am not speaking this as a command, but as proving through the earnestness of others the sincerity of your love also.

9 For you know the grace of our Lord Jesus Christ, that though He was rich, yet for your sake He became poor, that you through His poverty might become rich.

10 And I give my opinion in this matter, for this is to your

advantage, who were the first to begin a year ago not only to do *this*, but also to desire *to do it*.

11 But now finish doing it also; that just as *there was* the readiness to desire it, so *there may be* also the completion of it by your ability.

12 For if the readiness is present, it is acceptable according to what *a man* has, not according to what he does not have.

13 For *this* is not for the ease of others *and* for your affliction, but by way of equality—

14 at this present time your abundance *being a supply* for their want, that their abundance also may become *a supply* for your want, that there may be equality;

15 as it is written, "HE WHO *gathered* MUCH DID NOT HAVE TOO MUCH, AND HE WHO *gathered* LITTLE HAD NO LACK."

16 But thanks be to God, who puts the same earnestness on your behalf in the heart of Titus.

17 For he not only accepted our appeal, but being himself very earnest, he has gone to you of his own accord.

18 And we have sent along with him the brother whose fame in *the things of* the gospel *has spread* through all the churches;

19 and not only *this*, but he has also been appointed by the churches to travel with us in this gracious work, which is being administered by us for the glory of the Lord Himself, and *to show* our readiness,

20 taking precaution that no one should discredit us in our administration of this generous gift;

21 for we have regard for what is honorable, not only in the sight of the Lord, but also in the sight of men.

22 And we have sent with them our brother, whom we have often tested and found diligent in many things, but now even more diligent, because of *his* great confidence in you.

23 As for Titus, *he is* my partner and fellow worker among you; as for our brethren, *they are* messengers of the churches, a glory to Christ.

24 Therefore openly before the churches show them the proof of your love and of our reason for boasting about you.

CHAPTER 9

FOR it is superfluous for me to write to you about this ministry to the saints;

2 for I know your readiness, of which I boast about you to the Macedonians, *namely,* that Achaia has been prepared since last year, and your zeal has stirred up most of them.

3 But I have sent the brethren, that our boasting about you may not be made empty in this case, that, as I was saying, you may be prepared;

4 lest if any Macedonians come with me and find you unprepared, we (not to speak of you) should be put to shame by this confidence.

5 So I thought it necessary to urge the brethren that they would go on ahead to you and arrange beforehand your previously promised bountiful gift, that the same might be ready as a bountiful gift, and not affected by covetousness.

6 Now this *I say,* he who sows sparingly shall also reap sparingly; and he who sows bountifully shall also reap bountifully.

7 Let each one *do* just as he has purposed in his heart; not grudgingly or under compulsion; for God loves a cheerful giver.

8 And God is able to make all grace abound to you, that always having all sufficiency in everything, you may have an abundance for every good deed;

9 as it is written,

"HE SCATTERED ABROAD, HE
    GAVE TO THE POOR,
HIS RIGHTEOUSNESS ABIDES
    FOREVER."

10 Now He who supplies seed to the sower and bread for food, will supply and multiply your seed for sowing and increase the harvest of your righteousness;

11 you will be enriched in everything for all liberality, which through us is producing thanksgiving to God.

12 For the ministry of this service is not only fully supplying the needs of the saints, but is also overflowing through many thanksgivings to God.

13 Because of the proof given by this ministry they will glorify God for *your* obedience to your confession of the gospel of Christ, and for the liberality of your contribution to them and to all,

14 while they also, by prayer on your behalf, yearn for you because of the surpassing grace of God in you.

15 Thanks be to God for His indescribable gift!

CHAPTER 10

NOW I, Paul, myself urge you by the meekness and gentleness of Christ—I who am meek

when face to face with you, but bold toward you when absent!

2 I ask that when I am present I may not be bold with the confidence with which I propose to be courageous against some, who regard us as if we walked according to the flesh.

3 For though we walk in the flesh, we do not war according to the flesh,

4 for the weapons of our warfare are not of the flesh, but divinely powerful for the destruction of fortresses.

5 *We are* destroying speculations and every lofty thing raised up against the knowledge of God, and *we are* taking every thought captive to the obedience of Christ,

6 and we are ready to punish all disobedience, whenever your obedience is complete.

7 You are looking at things as they are outwardly. If anyone is confident in himself that he is Christ's, let him consider this again within himself, that just as he is Christ's, so also are we.

8 For even if I should boast somewhat further about our authority, which the Lord gave for building you up and not for destroying you, I shall not be put to shame,

9 for I do not wish to seem as if I would terrify you by my letters.

10 For they say, "His letters are weighty and strong, but his personal presence is unimpressive, and his speech contemptible."

11 Let such a person consider this, that what we are in word by letters when absent, such persons *we are* also in deed when present.

12 For we are not bold to class or compare ourselves with some of those who commend themselves; but when they measure themselves by themselves, and compare themselves with themselves, they are without understanding.

13 But we will not boast beyond *our* measure, but within the measure of the sphere which God apportioned to us as a measure, to reach even as far as you.

14 For we are not overextending ourselves, as if we did not reach to you, for we were the first to come even as far as you in the gospel of Christ;

15 not boasting beyond *our* measure, *that is,* in other men's labors, but with the hope that as your faith grows, we shall be, within our sphere, enlarged even more by you,

16 so as to preach the gospel even to the regions beyond you, *and* not to boast in what has been accomplished in the sphere of another.

17 But HE WHO BOASTS, LET HIM BOAST IN THE LORD.

18 For not he who commends himself is approved, but whom the Lord commends.

CHAPTER 11

I WISH that you would bear with me in a little foolishness; but indeed you are bearing with me.

2 For I am jealous for you with a godly jealousy; for I betrothed you to one husband, that to Christ I might present you *as* a pure virgin.

3 But I am afraid, lest as the serpent deceived Eve by his craftiness, your minds should be led astray from the simplicity and purity *of devotion* to Christ.

4 For if one comes and preaches another Jesus whom we have not preached, or you receive a different spirit which you have not received, or a different gospel which you have not accepted, you bear *this* beautifully.

5 For I consider myself not in the least inferior to the most eminent apostles.

6 But even if I am unskilled in speech, yet I am not *so* in knowledge; in fact, in every way we have made *this* evident to you in all things.

7 Or did I commit a sin in humbling myself that you might be exalted, because I preached the gospel of God to you without charge?

8 I robbed other churches, taking wages *from them* to serve you;

9 and when I was present with you and was in need, I was not a burden to anyone; for when the brethren came from Macedonia, they fully supplied my need, and in everything I kept myself from being a burden to you, and will continue to do so.

10 As the truth of Christ is in me, this boasting of mine will not be stopped in the regions of Achaia.

11 Why? Because I do not love you? God knows I do!

12 But what I am doing, I will continue to do, that I may cut off opportunity from those who desire an opportunity to be regarded just as we are in the matter about which they are boasting.

13 For such men are false apostles, deceitful workers, dis-

guising themselves as apostles of Christ.

14 And no wonder, for even Satan disguises himself as an angel of light.

15 Therefore it is not surprising if his servants also disguise themselves as servants of righteousness; whose end shall be according to their deeds.

16 Again I say, let no one think me foolish; but if *you do*, receive me even as foolish, that I also may boast a little.

17 That which I am speaking, I am not speaking as the Lord would, but as in foolishness, in this confidence of boasting.

18 Since many boast according to the flesh, I will boast also.

19 For you, being *so* wise, bear with the foolish gladly.

20 For you bear with anyone if he enslaves you, if he devours you, if he takes advantage of you, if he exalts himself, if he hits you in the face.

21 To *my* shame I *must* say that we have been weak *by comparison*. But in whatever respect anyone *else* is bold (I speak in foolishness), I am just as bold myself.

22 Are they Hebrews? So am I. Are they Israelites? So am I. Are they descendants of Abraham? So am I.

23 Are they servants of Christ? (I speak as if insane) I more so; in far more labors, in far more imprisonments, beaten times without number, often in danger of death.

24 Five times I received from the Jews thirty-nine *lashes.*

25 Three times I was beaten with rods, once I was stoned, three times I was shipwrecked, a night and a day I have spent in the deep.

26 *I have been* on frequent journeys, in dangers from rivers, dangers from robbers, dangers from *my* countrymen, dangers from the Gentiles, dangers in the city, dangers in the wilderness, dangers on the sea, dangers among false brethren;

27 *I have been* in labor and hardship, through many sleepless nights, in hunger and thirst, often without food, in cold and exposure.

28 Apart from *such* external things, there is the daily pressure upon me *of* concern for all the churches.

29 Who is weak without my being weak? Who is led into sin without my intense concern?

30 If I have to boast, I will boast of what pertains to my weakness.

31 The God and Father of the Lord Jesus, He who is blessed forever, knows that I am not lying.

32 In Damascus the ethnarch under Aretas the king was guarding the city of the Damascenes in order to seize me,

33 and I was let down in a basket through a window in the wall, and *so* escaped his hands.

CHAPTER 12

BOASTING is necessary, though it is not profitable; but I will go on to visions and revelations of the Lord.

2 I know a man in Christ who fourteen years ago—whether in the body I do not know, or out of the body I do not know, God knows—such a man was caught up to the third heaven.

3 And I know how such a man—whether in the body or apart from the body I do not know, God knows—

4 was caught up into Paradise, and heard inexpressible words, which a man is not permitted to speak.

5 On behalf of such a man will I boast; but on my own behalf I will not boast, except in regard to *my* weaknesses.

6 For if I do wish to boast I shall not be foolish, for I shall be speaking the truth; but I refrain *from this,* so that no one may credit me with more than he sees *in* me or hears from me.

7 And because of the surpassing greatness of the revelations, for this reason, to keep me from exalting myself, there was given me a thorn in the flesh, a messenger of Satan to buffet me—to keep me from exalting myself!

8 Concerning this I entreated the Lord three times that it might depart from me.

9 And He has said to me, "My grace is sufficient for you, for [3]power is perfected in weakness." Most gladly, therefore, I will rather boast about my weaknesses, that the power of Christ may dwell in me.

10 Therefore I am well content with weaknesses, with insults, with distresses, with persecutions, with difficulties, for Christ's sake; for when I am weak, then I am strong.

11 I have become foolish; you yourselves compelled me. Actually I should have been commended by you, for in no respect was I inferior to the most eminent apostles, even though I am a nobody.

12 The signs of a true apostle were performed among you with all perseverance, by signs and wonders and miracles.

13 For in what respect were you treated as inferior to the rest of the churches, except that I myself did not become a burden to you? Forgive me this wrong!

14 Here for this third time I am ready to come to you, and I will not be a burden to you; for I do not seek what is yours, but you; for children are not responsible to save up for *their* parents, but parents for *their* children.

15 And I will most gladly spend and be expended for your souls. If I love you the more, am I to be loved the less?

16 But be that as it may, I did not burden you myself; nevertheless, crafty fellow that I am, I took you in by deceit.

17 Certainly I have not taken advantage of you through any of those whom I have sent to you, have I?

18 I urged Titus *to go,* and sent the brother with him. Titus did not take any advantage of you, did he? Did we not conduct ourselves in the same spirit *and* walk in the same steps?

19 All this time you have been thinking that we are defending ourselves to you. *Actually,* it is in the sight of God that we have been speaking in Christ; and all for your upbuilding, beloved.

20 For I am afraid that perhaps when I come I may find you to be not what I wish and may be found by you to be not what you wish; that perhaps *there may be* strife, jealousy, angry tempers,

[3] Later mss. read *My power*

disputes, slanders, gossip, arrogance, disturbances;

21 I am afraid that when I come again my God may humiliate me before you, and I may mourn over many of those who have sinned in the past and not repented of the impurity, immorality and sensuality which they have practiced.

CHAPTER 13

THIS is the third time I am coming to you. EVERY FACT IS TO BE CONFIRMED BY THE TESTIMONY OF TWO OR THREE WITNESSES.

2 I have previously said when present the second time, and though now absent I say in advance to those who have sinned in the past and to all the rest as well, that if I come again, I will not spare *anyone,*

3 since you are seeking for proof of the Christ who speaks in me, and who is not weak toward you, but mighty in you.

4 For indeed He was crucified because of weakness, yet He lives because of the power of God. For we also are weak [4]in Him, yet we shall live with Him because of the power of God *directed* toward you.

5 Test yourselves *to see* if you are in the faith; examine yourselves! Or do you not recognize this about yourselves, that Jesus Christ is in you—unless indeed you fail the test?

6 But[I trust that you will realize that we ourselves do not fail the test.

7 Now we pray to God that you do no wrong; not that we ourselves may appear approved, but that you may do what is right, even though we should appear unapproved.

8 For we can do nothing against the truth, but *only* for the truth.

9 For we rejoice when we ourselves are weak but you are strong; this we also pray for, that you be made complete.

10 For this reason I am writing these things while absent, in order that when present I may not use severity, in accordance with the authority which the Lord gave me, for building up and not for tearing down.

11 Finally, brethren, rejoice, be made complete, be comforted, be like-minded, live in peace; and the God of love and peace shall be with you.

12 Greet one another with a holy kiss.

13 All the saints greet you.

14 The grace of the Lord Jesus Christ, and the love of God, and the fellowship of the Holy Spirit, be with you all.

[4] Some early mss. read *with Him*

GALATIANS

PAUL, an apostle (not *sent* from men, nor through the agency of man, but through Jesus Christ, and God the Father, who raised Him from the dead),

2 and all the brethren who are with me, to the churches of Galatia:

3 Grace to you and peace from God our Father, and the Lord Jesus Christ,

4 who gave Himself for our sins, that He might deliver us out of this present evil age, according to the will of our God and Father,

5 to whom *be* the glory forevermore. Amen.

6 I am amazed that you are so quickly deserting Him who called you by the grace of Christ, for a different gospel;

7 which is *really* not another; only there are some who are disturbing you, and want to distort the gospel of Christ.

8 But even though we, or an angel from heaven, should preach to you a gospel contrary to that which we have preached to you, let him be accursed.

9 As we have said before, so I say again now, if any man is preaching to you a gospel contrary to that which you received, let him be accursed.

10 For am I now seeking the favor of men, or of God? Or am I striving to please men? If I were still trying to please men, I would not be a bond-servant of Christ.

11 For I would have you know, brethren, that the gospel which was preached by me is not according to man.

12 For I neither received it from man, nor was I taught it, but *I received it* through a revelation of Jesus Christ.

13 For you have heard of my former manner of life in Judaism, how I used to persecute the church of God beyond measure, and tried to destroy it;

14 and I was advancing in Judaism beyond many of my contemporaries among my countrymen, being more extremely zealous for my ancestral traditions.

15 But when He who had set me apart, *even* from my mother's womb, and called me through His grace, was pleased

16 to reveal His Son in me, that I might preach Him among the Gentiles, I did not immediately consult with flesh and blood,

17 nor did I go up to Jerusalem to those who were apostles before me; but I went away to Arabia, and returned once more to Damascus.

18 Then three years later I went up to Jerusalem to become acquainted with Cephas, and stayed with him fifteen days.

19 But I did not see any other of the apostles except James, the Lord's brother.

20 (Now in what I am writing to you, I assure you before God *that* I am not lying.)

21 Then I went into the regions of Syria and Cilicia.

22 And I was *still* unknown by

sight to the churches of Judea which were in Christ;

23 but only, they kept hearing, "He who once persecuted us is now preaching the faith which he once tried to destroy."

24 And they were glorifying God because of me.

CHAPTER 2

THEN after an interval of fourteen years I went up again to Jerusalem with Barnabas, taking Titus along also.

2 And it was because of a revelation that I went up; and I submitted to them the gospel which I preach among the Gentiles, but I did so in private to those who were of reputation, for fear that I might be running, or had run, in vain.

3 But not even Titus who was with me, though he was a Greek, was compelled to be circumcised.

4 But *it was* because of the false brethren who had sneaked in to spy out our liberty which we have in Christ Jesus, in order to bring us into bondage.

5 But we did not yield in subjection to them for even an hour, so that the truth of the gospel might remain with you.

6 But from those who were of high reputation (what they were makes no difference to me; God shows no partiality)—well, those who were of reputation contributed nothing to me.

7 But on the contrary, seeing that I had been entrusted with the gospel to the uncircumcised, just as Peter *had been* to the circumcised

8 (for He who effectually worked for Peter in *his* apostle-ship to the circumcised effectually worked for me also to the Gentiles),

9 and recognizing the grace that had been given to me, James and Cephas and John, who were reputed to be pillars, gave to me and Barnabas the right hand of fellowship, that we might go to the Gentiles, and they to the circumcised.

10 *They* only *asked* us to remember the poor—the very thing I also was eager to do.

11 But when Cephas came to Antioch, I opposed him to his face, because he stood condemned.

12 For prior to the coming of certain men from James, he used to eat with the Gentiles; but when they came, he *began* to withdraw and hold himself aloof, fearing the party of the circumcision.

13 And the rest of the Jews joined him in hypocrisy, with the result that even Barnabas was carried away by their hypocrisy.

14 But when I saw that they were not straightforward about the truth of the gospel, I said to Cephas in the presence of all, "If you, being a Jew, live like the Gentiles and not like the Jews, how *is it that* you compel the Gentiles to live like Jews?

15 "We *are* Jews by nature, and not sinners from among the Gentiles;

16 nevertheless knowing that a man is not justified by the works of the Law but through faith in Christ Jesus, even we have believed in Christ Jesus, that we may be justified by faith in Christ, and not by the works of the Law; since by the works of

the Law shall no flesh be justified.

17"But if, while seeking to be justified in Christ, we ourselves have also been found sinners, is Christ then a minister of sin? May it never be!

18"For if I rebuild what I have *once* destroyed, I prove myself to be a transgressor.

19"For through the Law I died to the Law, that I might live to God.

20"I have been crucified with Christ; and it is no longer I who live, but Christ lives in me; and the *life* which I now live in the flesh I live by faith in the Son of God, who loved me, and delivered Himself up for me.

21"I do not nullify the grace of God; for if righteousness *comes* through the Law, then Christ died needlessly."

CHAPTER 3

YOU foolish Galatians, who has bewitched you, before whose eyes Jesus Christ was publicly portrayed *as* crucified?

2 This is the only thing I want to find out from you: did you receive the Spirit by the works of the Law, or by hearing with faith?

3 Are you so foolish? Having begun by the Spirit, are you now being perfected by the flesh?

4 Did you suffer so many things in vain—if indeed it was in vain?

5 Does He then, who provides you with the Spirit and works miracles among you, do it by the works of the Law, or by hearing with faith?

6 Even so Abraham BELIEVED GOD, AND IT WAS RECKONED TO HIM AS RIGHTEOUSNESS.

7 Therefore, be sure that it is those who are of faith who are sons of Abraham.

8 And the Scripture, foreseeing that God would justify the Gentiles by faith, preached the gospel beforehand to Abraham, *saying,* "ALL THE NATIONS SHALL BE BLESSED IN YOU."

9 So then those who are of faith are blessed with Abraham, the believer.

10 For as many as are of the works of the Law are under a curse; for it is written, "CURSED IS EVERYONE WHO DOES NOT ABIDE BY ALL THINGS WRITTEN IN THE BOOK OF THE LAW, TO PERFORM THEM."

11 Now that no one is justified by the Law before God is evident; for, "THE RIGHTEOUS MAN SHALL LIVE BY FAITH."

12 However, the Law is not of faith; on the contrary, "HE WHO PRACTICES THEM SHALL LIVE BY THEM."

13 Christ redeemed us from the curse of the Law, having become a curse for us—for it is written, "CURSED IS EVERYONE WHO HANGS ON A TREE"—

14 in order that in Christ Jesus the blessing of Abraham might come to the Gentiles, so that we might receive the promise of the Spirit through faith.

15 Brethren, I speak in terms of human relations: even though it is *only* a man's covenant, yet when it has been ratified, no one sets it aside or adds conditions to it.

16 Now the promises were spoken to Abraham and to his seed. He does not say, "And to seeds," as *referring* to many, but *rather* to one, "And to your seed," that is, Christ.

17 What I am saying is this: the Law, which came four hundred and thirty years later, does not invalidate a covenant previously ratified by God, so as to nullify the promise.

18 For if the inheritance is based on law, it is no longer based on a promise; but God has granted it to Abraham by means of a promise.

19 Why the Law then? It was added because of transgressions, having been ordained through angels by the agency of a mediator, until the seed should come to whom the promise had been made.

20 Now a mediator is not for one *party only*; whereas God is *only one.*

21 Is the Law then contrary to the promises of God? May it never be! For if a law had been given which was able to impart life, then righteousness would indeed have been based on law.

22 But the Scripture has shut up all men under sin, that the promise by faith in Jesus Christ might be given to those who believe.

23 But before faith came, we were kept in custody under the law, being shut up to the faith which was later to be revealed.

24 Therefore the Law has become our tutor *to lead us to* Christ, that we may be justified by faith.

25 But now that faith has come, we are no longer under a tutor.

26 For you are all sons of God through faith in Christ Jesus.

27 For all of you who were baptized into Christ have clothed yourselves with Christ.

28 There is neither Jew nor Greek, there is neither slave nor free man, there is neither male nor female; for you are all one in Christ Jesus.

29 And if you belong to Christ, then you are Abraham's offspring, heirs according to promise.

CHAPTER 4

NOW I say, as long as the heir is a child, he does not differ at all from a slave although he is owner of everything,

2 but he is under guardians and managers until the date set by the father.

3 So also we, while we were children, were held in bondage under the elemental things of the world.

4 But when the fulness of the time came, God sent forth His Son, born of a woman, born under the Law,

5 in order that He might redeem those who were under the Law, that we might receive the adoption as sons.

6 And because you are sons, God has sent forth the Spirit of His Son into our hearts, crying, "Abba! Father!"

7 Therefore you are no longer a slave, but a son; and if a son, then an heir through God.

8 However at that time, when you did not know God, you were slaves to those which by nature are no gods.

9 But now that you have come to know God, or rather to be known by God, how is it that you turn back again to the weak and worthless elemental things, to which you desire to be enslaved all over again?

10 You observe days and months and seasons and years.

11 I fear for you, that perhaps I have labored over you in vain.

12 I beg of you, brethren, become as I *am*, for I also *have become* as you *are*. You have done me no wrong;

13 but you know that it was because of a bodily illness that I preached the gospel to you the first time;

14 and that which was a trial to you in my bodily condition you did not despise or loathe, but you received me as an angel of God, as Christ Jesus *Himself*.

15 Where then is that sense of blessing you had? For I bear you witness, that if possible, you would have plucked out your eyes and given them to me.

16 Have I therefore become your enemy by telling you the truth?

17 They eagerly seek you, not commendably, but they wish to shut you out, in order that you may seek them.

18 But it is good always to be eagerly sought in a commendable manner, and not only when I am present with you.

19 My children, with whom I am again in labor until Christ is formed in you—

20 but I could wish to be present with you now and to change my tone, for I am perplexed about you.

21 Tell me, you who want to be under law, do you not listen to the law?

22 For it is written that Abraham had two sons, one by the bondwoman and one by the free woman.

23 But the son by the bondwoman was born according to the flesh, and the son by the free woman through the promise.

24 This is allegorically speaking: for these *women* are two covenants, one *proceeding* from Mount Sinai bearing children who are to be slaves; she is Hagar.

25 Now this Hagar is Mount Sinai in Arabia, and corresponds to the present Jerusalem, for she is in slavery with her children.

26 But the Jerusalem above is free; she is our mother.

27 For it is written,

"REJOICE, BARREN WOMAN
   WHO DOES NOT BEAR;
BREAK FORTH AND SHOUT,
   YOU WHO ARE NOT IN LABOR;
FOR MORE ARE THE CHILDREN OF THE DESOLATE
THAN OF THE ONE WHO HAS
   A HUSBAND."

28 And you brethren, like Isaac, are children of promise.

29 But as at that time he who was born according to the flesh persecuted him *who was born* according to the Spirit, so it is now also.

30 But what does the Scripture say?

"CAST OUT THE BONDWOMAN
   AND HER SON,
FOR THE SON OF THE BONDWOMAN SHALL NOT BE AN
HEIR WITH THE SON OF
THE FREE WOMAN."

31 So then, brethren, we are not children of a bondwoman, but of the free woman.

CHAPTER 5

IT was for freedom that Christ set us free; therefore keep standing firm and do not be subject again to a yoke of slavery.

2 Behold I, Paul, say to you that if you receive circumcision, Christ will be of no benefit to you.

3 And I testify again to every man who receives circumcision, that he is under obligation to keep the whole Law.

4 You have been severed from Christ, you who are seeking to be justified by law; you have fallen from grace.

5 For we through the Spirit, by faith, are waiting for the hope of righteousness.

6 For in Christ Jesus neither circumcision nor uncircumcision means anything, but faith working through love.

7 You were running well; who hindered you from obeying the truth?

8 This persuasion *did* not *come* from Him who calls you.

9 A little leaven leavens the whole lump *of dough.*

10 I have confidence in you in the Lord, that you will adopt no other view; but the one who is disturbing you shall bear his judgment, whoever he is.

11 But I, brethren, if I still preach circumcision, why am I still persecuted? Then the stumbling block of the cross has been abolished.

12 Would that those who are troubling you would even mutilate themselves.

13 For you were called to freedom, brethren; only *do not turn* your freedom into an opportunity for the flesh, but through love serve one another.

14 For the whole Law is fulfilled in one word, in the *statement,* "YOU SHALL LOVE YOUR NEIGHBOR AS YOURSELF."

15 But if you bite and devour one another, take care lest you be consumed by one another.

16 But I say, walk by the Spirit, and you will not carry out the desire of the flesh.

17 For the flesh sets its desire against the Spirit, and the Spirit against the flesh; for these are in opposition to one another, so that you may not do the things that you please.

18 But if you are led by the Spirit, you are not under the Law.

19 Now the deeds of the flesh are evident, which are: immorality, impurity, sensuality,

20 idolatry, sorcery, enmities, strife, jealousy, outbursts of anger, disputes, dissensions, factions,

21 envying, drunkenness, carousing, and things like these, of which I forewarn you just as I have forewarned you that those who practice such things shall not inherit the kingdom of God.

22 But the fruit of the Spirit is love, joy, peace, patience, kindness, goodness, faithfulness,

23 gentleness, self-control; against such things there is no law.

24 Now those who belong to Christ Jesus have crucified the flesh with its passions and desires.

25 If we live by the Spirit, let us also walk by the Spirit.

26 Let us not become boastful, challenging one another, envying one another.

CHAPTER 6

BRETHREN, even if a man is caught in any trespass, you who are spiritual, restore such a one in a spirit of gentleness; *each one* looking to yourself, lest you too be tempted.

2 Bear one another's burdens, and thus fulfill the law of Christ.

3 For if anyone thinks he is something when he is nothing, he deceives himself.

4 But let each one examine his own work, and then he will have *reason for* boasting in regard to himself alone, and not in regard to another.

5 For each one shall bear his own load.

6 And let the one who is taught the word share all good things with him who teaches.

7 Do not be deceived, God is not mocked; for whatever a man sows, this he will also reap.

8 For the one who sows to his own flesh shall from the flesh reap corruption, but the one who sows to the Spirit shall from the Spirit reap eternal life.

9 And let us not lose heart in doing good, for in due time we shall reap if we do not grow weary.

10 So then, while we have opportunity, let us do good to all men, and especially to those who are of the household of the faith.

11 See with what large letters I am writing to you with my own hand.

12 Those who desire to make a good showing in the flesh try to compel you to be circumcised, simply that they may not be persecuted for the cross of Christ.

13 For those who ¹are circumcised do not even keep the Law themselves, but they desire to have you circumcised, that they may boast in your flesh.

14 But may it never be that I should boast, except in the cross of our Lord Jesus Christ, through which the world has been crucified to me, and I to the world.

15 For neither is circumcision anything, nor uncircumcision, but a new creation.

16 And those who will walk by this rule, peace and mercy *be* upon them, and upon the Israel of God.

17 From now on let no one cause trouble for me, for I bear on my body the brand-marks of Jesus.

18 The grace of our Lord Jesus Christ be with your spirit, brethren. Amen.

¹ Some ancient mss. read *have been*

EPHESIANS

PAUL, an apostle of Christ Jesus by the will of God, to the saints who are [1]at Ephesus, and who are faithful in Christ Jesus:

2 Grace to you and peace from God our Father and the Lord Jesus Christ.

3 Blessed be the God and Father of our Lord Jesus Christ, who has blessed us with every spiritual blessing in the heavenly places in Christ,

4 just as He chose us in Him before the foundation of the world, that we should be holy and blameless before [2]Him. In love

5 He predestined us to adoption as sons through Jesus Christ to Himself, according to the kind intention of His will,

6 to the praise of the glory of His grace, which He freely bestowed on us in the Beloved.

7 In Him we have redemption through His blood, the forgiveness of our trespasses, according to the riches of His grace,

8 which He lavished upon us. In all wisdom and insight

9 He made known to us the mystery of His will, according to His kind intention which He purposed in Him

10 with a view to an administration suitable to the fulness of the times, that is, the summing up of all things in Christ, things in the heavens and things upon the earth. In Him

11 also we have obtained an inheritance, having been predestined according to His purpose who works all things after the counsel of His will,

12 to the end that we who were the first to hope in [3]Christ should be to the praise of His glory.

13 In Him, you also, after listening to the message of truth, the gospel of your salvation— having also believed, you were sealed in Him with the Holy Spirit of promise,

14 who is given as a pledge of our inheritance, with a view to the redemption of God's own possession, to the praise of His glory.

15 For this reason I too, having heard of the faith in the Lord Jesus which exists among you, and [4]your love for all the saints,

16 do not cease giving thanks for you, while making mention of you in my prayers,

17 that the God of our Lord Jesus Christ, the Father of glory, may give to you a spirit of wisdom and of revelation in the knowledge of Him.

18 I pray that the eyes of your heart may be enlightened, so that you may know what is the hope of His calling, what are the riches of the glory of His inheritance in the saints,

19 and what is the surpassing greatness of His power toward us who believe. These are in

---

[1] Some ancient mss. do not contain at Ephesus [2] Or, Him, in love.
[3] I.e., the Messiah
[4] Many ancient mss. do not contain your love

accordance with the working of the strength of His might

20 which He brought about in Christ, when He raised Him from the dead, and seated Him at His right hand in the heavenly *places*,

21 far above all rule and authority and power and dominion, and every name that is named, not only in this age, but also in the one to come.

22 And He put all things in subjection under His feet, and gave Him as head over all things to the church,

23 which is His body, the fulness of Him who fills all in all.

CHAPTER 2

AND you were dead in your trespasses and sins,

2 in which you formerly walked according to the course of this world, according to the prince of the power of the air, of the spirit that is now working in the sons of disobedience.

3 Among them we too all formerly lived in the lusts of our flesh, indulging the desires of the flesh and of the mind, and were by nature children of wrath, even as the rest.

4 But God, being rich in mercy, because of His great love with which He loved us,

5 even when we were dead in our transgressions, made us alive together [5]with Christ (by grace you have been saved),

6 and raised us up with Him, and seated us with Him in the heavenly *places*, in Christ Jesus,

7 in order that in the ages to come He might show the surpassing riches of His grace in kindness toward us in Christ Jesus.

8 For by grace you have been saved through faith; and that not of yourselves, *it is* the gift of God;

9 not as a result of works, that no one should boast.

10 For we are His workmanship, created in Christ Jesus for good works, which God prepared beforehand, that we should walk in them.

11 Therefore remember, that formerly you, the Gentiles in the flesh, who are called "Uncircumcision" by the so-called "Circumcision," *which is* performed in the flesh by human hands—

12 *remember* that you were at that time separate from Christ, excluded from the commonwealth of Israel, and strangers to the covenants of promise, having no hope and without God in the world.

13 But now in Christ Jesus you who formerly were far off have been brought near by the blood of Christ.

14 For He Himself is our peace, who made both *groups into* one, and broke down the barrier of the dividing wall,

15 by abolishing in His flesh the enmity, *which is* the Law of commandments *contained* in ordinances, that in Himself He might make the two into one new man, *thus* establishing peace,

16 and might reconcile them both in one body to God through the cross, by it having put to death the enmity.

17 AND HE CAME AND PREACHED PEACE TO YOU WHO WERE FAR AWAY, AND PEACE TO THOSE WHO WERE NEAR;

18 for through Him we both

---

[5] Some ancient mss. read *in Christ*

have our access in one Spirit to the Father.

19 So then you are no longer strangers and aliens, but you are fellow citizens with the saints, and are of God's household,

20 having been built upon the foundation of the apostles and prophets, Christ Jesus Himself being the corner *stone,*

21 in whom the whole building, being fitted together is growing into a holy temple in the Lord;

22 in whom you also are being built together into a dwelling of God in the Spirit.

CHAPTER 3

FOR this reason I, Paul, the prisoner of Christ Jesus for the sake of you Gentiles—

2 if indeed you have heard of the stewardship of God's grace which was given to me for you;

3 that by revelation there was made known to me the mystery, as I wrote before in brief.

4 And by referring to this, when you read you can understand my insight into the mystery of Christ,

5 which in other generations was not made known to the sons of men, as it has now been revealed to His holy apostles and prophets in the Spirit;

6 *to be specific,* that the Gentiles are fellow heirs and fellow members of the body, and fellow partakers of the promise in Christ Jesus through the gospel,

7 of which I was made a minister, according to the gift of God's grace which was given to me according to the working of His power.

8 To me, the very least of all saints, this grace was given, to preach to the Gentiles the unfathomable riches of Christ,

9 and to bring to light what is the administration of the mystery which for ages has been hidden in God, who created all things;

10 in order that the manifold wisdom of God might now be made known through the church to the rulers and the authorities in the heavenly *places.*

11 *This was* in accordance with the eternal purpose which He carried out in Christ Jesus our Lord,

12 in whom we have boldness and confident access through faith in Him.

13 Therefore I ask you not to lose heart at my tribulations on your behalf, for they are your glory.

14 For this reason, I bow my knees before the Father,

15 from whom every family in heaven and on earth derives its name,

16 that He would grant you, according to the riches of His glory, to be strengthened with power through His Spirit in the inner man;

17 so that Christ may dwell in your hearts through faith; *and* that you, being rooted and grounded in love,

18 may be able to comprehend with all the saints what is the breadth and length and height and depth,

19 and to know the love of Christ which surpasses knowledge, that you may be filled up to all the fulness of God.

20 Now to Him who is able to do exceeding abundantly beyond all that we ask or think,

according to the power that works within us,

21 to Him *be* the glory in the church and in Christ Jesus to all generations forever and ever. Amen.

CHAPTER 4

I, THEREFORE, the prisoner of the Lord, entreat you to walk in a manner worthy of the calling with which you have been called,

2 with all humility and gentleness, with patience, showing forbearance to one another in love,

3 being diligent to preserve the unity of the Spirit in the bond of peace.

4 *There is* one body and one Spirit, just as also you were called in one hope of your calling;

5 one Lord, one faith, one baptism,

6 one God and Father of all who is over all and through all and in all.

7 But to each one of us grace was given according to the measure of Christ's gift.

8 Therefore it says,
"WHEN HE ASCENDED ON
   HIGH,
HE LED CAPTIVE A HOST OF
   CAPTIVES,
AND HE GAVE GIFTS TO
   MEN."

9 (Now this *expression,* "He ascended," what does it mean except that He also had descended into the lower parts of the earth?

10 He who descended is Himself also He who ascended far above all the heavens, that He might fill all things.)

11 And He gave some *as* apostles, and some *as* prophets, and

some *as* evangelists, and some *as* pastors and teachers,

12 for the equipping of the saints for the work of service, to the building up of the body of Christ;

13 until we all attain to the unity of the faith, and of the knowledge of the Son of God, to a mature man, to the measure of the stature which belongs to the fulness of Christ.

14 As a result, we are no longer to be children, tossed here and there by waves, and carried about by every wind of doctrine, by the trickery of men, by craftiness in deceitful scheming;

15 but speaking the truth in love, we are to grow up in all *aspects* into Him, who is the head, *even* Christ,

16 from whom the whole body, being fitted and held together by that which every joint supplies, according to the proper working of each individual part, causes the growth of the body for the building up of itself in love.

17 This I say therefore, and affirm together with the Lord, that you walk no longer just as the Gentiles also walk, in the futility of their mind,

18 being darkened in their understanding, excluded from the life of God, because of the ignorance that is in them, because of the hardness of their heart;

19 and they, having become callous, have given themselves over to sensuality, for the practice of every kind of impurity with greediness.

20 But you did not learn Christ in this way,

21 if indeed you have heard

Him and have been taught in Him, just as truth is in Jesus,

22 that, in reference to your former manner of life, you lay aside the old self, which is being corrupted in accordance with the lusts of deceit,

23 and that you be renewed in the spirit of your mind,

24 and put on the new self, which in *the likeness* of God has been created in righteousness and holiness of the truth.

25 Therefore, laying aside falsehood, SPEAK TRUTH, EACH ONE *of you*, WITH HIS NEIGHBOR, for we are members of one another.

26 BE ANGRY, AND *yet* DO NOT SIN; do not let the sun go down on your anger,

27 and do not give the devil an opportunity.

28 Let him who steals steal no longer; but rather let him labor, performing with his own hands what is good, in order that he may have *something* to share with him who has need.

29 Let no unwholesome word proceed from your mouth, but only such *a word* as is good for edification according to the need *of the moment*, that it may give grace to those who hear.

30 And do not grieve the Holy Spirit of God, by whom you were sealed for the day of redemption.

31 Let all bitterness and wrath and anger and clamor and slander be put away from you, along with all malice.

32 And be kind to one another, tender-hearted, forgiving each other, just as God in Christ also has forgiven [6]you.

6 Some ancient mss. read *us*

CHAPTER 5

THEREFORE be imitators of God, as beloved children;

2 and walk in love, just as Christ also loved [6]you, and gave Himself up for us, an offering and a sacrifice to God as a fragrant aroma.

3 But do not let immorality or any impurity or greed even be named among you, as is proper among saints;

4 and *there must be no* filthiness and silly talk, or coarse jesting, which are not fitting, but rather giving of thanks.

5 For this you know with certainty, that no immoral or impure person or covetous man, who is an idolater, has an inheritance in the kingdom of Christ and God.

6 Let no one deceive you with empty words, for because of these things the wrath of God comes upon the sons of disobedience.

7 Therefore do not be partakers with them;

8 for you were formerly darkness, but now you are light in the Lord; walk as children of light

9 (for the fruit of the light *consists* in all goodness and righteousness and truth),

10 trying to learn what is pleasing to the Lord.

11 And do not participate in the unfruitful deeds of darkness, but instead even expose them;

12 for it is disgraceful even to speak of the things which are done by them in secret.

13 But all things become visible when they are exposed by the light, for everything that becomes visible is light.

14 For this reason it says,

"Awake, sleeper,

And arise from the dead,
And Christ will shine on
you."

15 Therefore be careful how you walk, not as unwise men, but as wise,

16 making the most of your time, because the days are evil.

17 So then do not be foolish, but understand what the will of the Lord is.

18 And do not get drunk with wine, for that is dissipation, but be filled with the Spirit,

19 speaking to one another in psalms and hymns and spiritual songs, singing and making melody with your heart to the Lord;

20 always giving thanks for all things in the name of our Lord Jesus Christ to God, even the Father;

21 and be subject to one another in the fear of Christ.

22 Wives, *be subject* to your own husbands, as to the Lord.

23 For the husband is the head of the wife, as Christ also is the head of the church, He Himself *being* the Savior of the body.

24 But as the church is subject to Christ, so also the wives *ought to be* to their husbands in everything.

25 Husbands, love your wives, just as Christ also loved the church and gave Himself up for her;

26 that He might sanctify her, having cleansed her by the washing of water with the word,

27 that He might present to Himself the church in all her glory, having no spot or wrinkle or any such thing; but that she should be holy and blameless.

28 So husbands ought also to love their own wives as their own bodies. He who loves his own wife loves himself;

29 for no one ever hated his own flesh, but nourishes and cherishes it, just as Christ also *does* the church,

30 because we are members of His body.

31 FOR THIS CAUSE A MAN SHALL LEAVE HIS FATHER AND MOTHER, AND SHALL CLEAVE TO HIS WIFE; AND THE TWO SHALL BECOME ONE FLESH.

32 This mystery is great; but I am speaking with reference to Christ and the church.

33 Nevertheless let each individual among you also love his own wife even as himself; and *let* the wife *see to it* that she respect her husband.

CHAPTER 6

CHILDREN, obey your parents in the Lord, for this is right.

2 HONOR YOUR FATHER AND MOTHER (which is the first commandment with a promise),

3 THAT IT MAY BE WELL WITH YOU, AND THAT YOU MAY LIVE LONG ON THE EARTH.

4 And, fathers, do not provoke your children to anger; but bring them up in the discipline and instruction of the Lord.

5 Slaves, be obedient to those who are your masters according to the flesh, with fear and trembling, in the sincerity of your heart, as to Christ;

6 not by way of eyeservice, as men-pleasers, but as slaves of Christ, doing the will of God from the heart.

7 With good will render service, as to the Lord, and not to men,

8 knowing that whatever good thing each one does, this he will receive back from the Lord, whether slave or free.

9 And, masters, do the same things to them, and give up threatening, knowing that both their Master and yours is in heaven, and there is no partiality with Him.

10 Finally, be strong in the Lord, and in the strength of His might.

11 Put on the full armor of God, that you may be able to stand firm against the schemes of the devil.

12 For our struggle is not against flesh and blood, but against the rulers, against the powers, against the world forces of this darkness, against the spiritual *forces* of wickedness in the heavenly *places.*

13 Therefore, take up the full armor of God, that you may be able to resist in the evil day, and having done everything, to stand firm.

14 Stand firm therefore, HAVING GIRDED YOUR LOINS WITH TRUTH, and HAVING PUT ON THE BREASTPLATE OF RIGHTEOUSNESS,

15 and having shod YOUR FEET WITH THE PREPARATION OF THE GOSPEL OF PEACE;

7 Some ancient mss. read *I may speak it boldly*

16 in addition to all, taking up the shield of faith with which you will be able to extinguish all the flaming missiles of the evil *one.*

17 And take THE HELMET OF SALVATION, and the sword of the Spirit, which is the word of God.

18 With all prayer and petition pray at all times in the Spirit, and with this in view, be on the alert with all perseverance and petition for all the saints,

19 and *pray* on my behalf, that utterance may be given to me in the opening of my mouth, to make known with boldness the mystery of the gospel,

20 for which I am an ambassador in chains; that [7] *proclaiming* it I may speak boldly, as I ought to speak.

21 But that you also may know about my circumstances, how I am doing, Tychicus, the beloved brother and faithful minister in the Lord, will make everything known to you.

22 And I have sent him to you for this very purpose, so that you may know about us, and that he may comfort your hearts.

23 Peace be to the brethren, and love with faith, from God the Father and the Lord Jesus Christ.

24 Grace be with all those who love our Lord Jesus Christ with *a love* incorruptible.

PHILIPPIANS

PAUL and Timothy, bond-servants of Christ Jesus, to all the saints in Christ Jesus who are in Philippi, including the overseers and deacons:

2 Grace to you and peace from God our Father and the Lord Jesus Christ.

3 I thank my God in all my remembrance of you,

4 always offering prayer with joy in my every prayer for you all,

5 in view of your participation in the gospel from the first day until now.

6 *For I am* confident of this very thing, that He who began a good work in you will perfect it until the day of Christ Jesus.

7 For it is only right for me to feel this way about you all, because I have you in my heart, since both in my imprisonment and in the defense and confirmation of the gospel, you all are partakers of grace with me.

8 For God is my witness, how I long for you all with the affection of Christ Jesus.

9 And this I pray, that your love may abound still more and more in real knowledge and all discernment,

10 so that you may approve the things that are excellent, in order to be sincere and blameless until the day of Christ;

11 having been filled with the fruit of righteousness which *comes* through Jesus Christ, to the glory and praise of God.

12 Now I want you to know, brethren, that my circumstances have turned out for the greater progress of the gospel,

13 so that my imprisonment in *the cause of* Christ has become well known throughout the whole [1]praetorian guard and to everyone else,

14 and that most of the brethren, trusting in the Lord because of my imprisonment, have far more courage to speak the word of God without fear.

15 Some, to be sure, are preaching Christ even from envy and strife, but some also from good will;

16 [2]the latter *do it* out of love, knowing that I am appointed for the defense of the gospel;

17 the former proclaim Christ out of selfish ambition, rather than from pure motives, thinking to cause me distress in my imprisonment.

18 What then? Only that in every way, whether in pretense or in truth, Christ is proclaimed; and in this I rejoice, yes, and I will rejoice.

19 For I know that this shall turn out for my deliverance through your prayers and the provision of the Spirit of Jesus Christ,

20 according to my earnest expectation and hope, that I shall not be put to shame in anything, but *that* with all boldness, Christ shall even now, as always, be exalted in my body, whether by life or by death.

[1] Or, *governor's palace*
[2] Some later mss. reverse the order of vv. 16 and 17

21 For to me, to live is Christ, and to die is gain.

22 But if *I am* to live *on* in the flesh, this *will mean* fruitful labor for me; and I do not know which to choose.

23 But I am hard-pressed from both *directions*, having the desire to depart and be with Christ, for *that* is very much better;

24 yet to remain on in the flesh is more necessary for your sake.

25 And convinced of this, I know that I shall remain and continue with you all for your progress and joy in the faith,

26 so that your proud confidence in me may abound in Christ Jesus through my coming to you again.

27 Only conduct yourselves in a manner worthy of the gospel of Christ; so that whether I come and see you or remain absent, I may hear of you that you are standing firm in one spirit, with one mind striving together for the faith of the gospel;

28 in no way alarmed by *your* opponents—which is a sign of destruction for them, but of salvation for you, and that *too*, from God.

29 For to you it has been granted for Christ's sake, not only to believe in Him, but also to suffer for His sake,

30 experiencing the same conflict which you saw in me, and now hear *to be* in me.

CHAPTER 2

IF therefore there is any encouragement in Christ, if there is any consolation of love, if there is any fellowship of the Spirit, if any affection and compassion,

2 make my joy complete by being of the same mind, maintaining the same love, united in spirit, intent on one purpose.

3 Do nothing from selfishness or empty conceit, but with humility of mind let each of you regard one another as more important than himself;

4 do not *merely* look out for your own personal interests, but also for the interests of others.

5 Have this attitude in yourselves which was also in Christ Jesus,

6 who, although He existed in the form of God, did not regard equality with God a thing to be grasped,

7 but ³emptied Himself, taking the form of a bond-servant, *and* being made in the likeness of men.

8 And being found in appearance as a man, He humbled Himself by becoming obedient to the point of death, even death on a cross.

9 Therefore also God highly exalted Him, and bestowed on Him the name which is above every name,

10 that at the name of Jesus EVERY KNEE SHOULD BOW, of those who are in heaven, and on earth, and under the earth,

11 and that every tongue should confess that Jesus Christ is Lord, to the glory of God the Father.

12 So then, my beloved, just as you have always obeyed, not as in my presence only, but now much more in my absence, work out your salvation with fear and trembling;

13 for it is God who is at work

³ I.e., laid aside His privileges

in you, both to will and to work for *His* good pleasure.

14 Do all things without grumbling or disputing;

15 that you may prove yourselves to be blameless and innocent, children of God above reproach in the midst of a crooked and perverse generation, among whom you appear as lights in the world,

16 holding fast the word of life, so that in the day of Christ I may have cause to glory because I did not run in vain nor toil in vain.

17 But even if I am being poured out as a drink offering upon the sacrifice and service of your faith, I rejoice and share my joy with you all.

18 And you too, *I urge you*, rejoice in the same way and share your joy with me.

19 But I hope in the Lord Jesus to send Timothy to you shortly, so that I also may be encouraged when I learn of your condition.

20 For I have no one *else* of kindred spirit who will genuinely be concerned for your welfare.

21 For they all seek after their own interests, not those of Christ Jesus.

22 But you know of his proven worth that he served with me in the furtherance of the gospel like a child *serving* his father.

23 Therefore I hope to send him immediately, as soon as I see how things go with me;

24 and I trust in the Lord that I myself also shall be coming shortly.

25 But I thought it necessary to send to you Epaphroditus, my brother and fellow worker and fellow soldier, who is also your messenger and minister to my need;

26 because he was longing [*]for you all and was distressed because you had heard that he was sick.

27 For indeed he was sick to the point of death, but God had mercy on him, and not on him only but also on me, lest I should have sorrow upon sorrow.

28 Therefore I have sent him all the more eagerly in order that when you see him again you may rejoice and I may be less concerned *about you.*

29 Therefore receive him in the Lord with all joy, and hold men like him in high regard;

30 because he came close to death for the work of Christ, risking his life to complete what was deficient in your service to me.

CHAPTER 3

FINALLY, my brethren, rejoice in the Lord. To write the same things *again* is no trouble to me, and it is a safeguard for you.

2 Beware of the dogs, beware of the evil workers, beware of the false circumcision;

3 for we are the *true* circumcision, who worship in the Spirit of God and glory in Christ Jesus and put no confidence in the flesh,

4 although I myself might have confidence even in the flesh. If anyone else has a mind to put confidence in the flesh, I far more:

5 circumcised the eighth day, of the nation of Israel, of the tribe of Benjamin, a Hebrew of Hebrews; as to the Law, a Pharisee;

---

[*] Some ancient mss. read *to see you all*

6 as to zeal, a persecutor of the church; as to the righteousness which is in the Law, found blameless.

7 But whatever things were gain to me, those things I have counted as loss for the sake of Christ.

8 More than that, I count all things to be loss in view of the surpassing value of knowing Christ Jesus my Lord, for whom I have suffered the loss of all things, and count them but rubbish in order that I may gain Christ,

9 and may be found in Him, not having a righteousness of my own derived from the Law, but that which is through faith in Christ, the righteousness which comes from God on the basis of faith,

10 that I may know Him, and the power of His resurrection and the fellowship of His sufferings, being conformed to His death;

11 in order that I may attain to the resurrection from the dead.

12 Not that I have already obtained it, or have already become perfect, but I press on in order that I may lay hold of that for which also I was laid hold of by Christ Jesus.

13 Brethren, I do not regard myself as having laid hold of it yet; but one thing I do: forgetting what lies behind and reaching forward to what lies ahead,

14 I press on toward the goal for the prize of the upward call of God in Christ Jesus.

15 Let us therefore, as many as are perfect, have this attitude; and if in anything you have a different attitude, God will reveal that also to you;

16 however, let us keep living by that same standard to which we have attained.

17 Brethren, join in following my example, and observe those who walk according to the pattern you have in us.

18 For many walk, of whom I often told you, and now tell you even weeping, that they are enemies of the cross of Christ,

19 whose end is destruction, whose god is their appetite, and whose glory is in their shame, who set their minds on earthly things.

20 For our citizenship is in heaven, from which also we eagerly wait for a Savior, the Lord Jesus Christ;

21 who will transform the body of our humble state into conformity with the body of His glory, by the exertion of the power that He has even to subject all things to Himself.

CHAPTER 4

THEREFORE, my beloved brethren whom I long to see, my joy and crown, so stand firm in the Lord, my beloved.

2 I urge Euodia and I urge Syntyche to live in harmony in the Lord.

3 Indeed, true comrade, I ask you also to help these women who have shared my struggle in the cause of the gospel, together with Clement also, and the rest of my fellow workers, whose names are in the book of life.

4 Rejoice in the Lord always; again I will say, rejoice!

5 Let your forbearing spirit be known to all men. The Lord is near.

6 Be anxious for nothing, but in everything by prayer and supplication with thanksgiving let your requests be made known to God.

7 And the peace of God, which surpasses all comprehension, shall guard your hearts and your minds in Christ Jesus.

8 Finally, brethren, whatever is true, whatever is honorable, whatever is right, whatever is pure, whatever is lovely, whatever is of good repute, if there is any excellence and if anything worthy of praise, let your mind dwell on these things.

9 The things you have learned and received and heard and seen in me, practice these things; and the God of peace shall be with you.

10 But I rejoiced in the Lord greatly, that now at last you have revived your concern for me; indeed, you were concerned *before*, but you lacked opportunity.

11 Not that I speak from want; for I have learned to be content in whatever circumstances I am.

12 I know how to get along with humble means, and I also know how to live in prosperity; in any and every circumstance I have learned the secret of being filled and going hungry, both of having abundance and suffering need.

13 I can do all things through Him who strengthens me.

14 Nevertheless, you have done well to share *with me* in my affliction.

15 And you yourselves also know, Philippians, that at the first preaching of the gospel, after I departed from Macedonia, no church shared with me in the matter of giving and receiving but you alone;

16 for even in Thessalonica you sent *a gift* more than once for my needs.

17 Not that I seek the gift itself, but I seek for the profit which increases to your account.

18 But I have received everything in full, and have an abundance; I am amply supplied, having received from Epaphroditus what you have sent, a fragrant aroma, an acceptable sacrifice, well-pleasing to God.

19 And my God shall supply all your needs according to His riches in glory in Christ Jesus.

20 Now to our God and Father *be* the glory forever and ever. Amen.

21 Greet every saint in Christ Jesus. The brethren who are with me greet you.

22 All the saints greet you, especially those of Caesar's household.

23 The grace of the Lord Jesus Christ be with your spirit.

COLOSSIANS

PAUL, an apostle of Jesus Christ by the will of God, and Timothy our brother,

2 to the saints and faithful brethren in Christ *who are* at Colossae: Grace to you and peace from God our Father.

3 We give thanks to God, the Father of our Lord Jesus Christ, praying always for you,

4 since we heard of your faith in Christ Jesus and the love which you have for all the saints;

5 because of the hope laid up for you in heaven, of which you previously heard in the word of truth, the gospel,

6 which has come to you, just as in all the world also it is constantly bearing fruit and increasing, even as *it has been doing* in you also since the day you heard *of it* and understood the grace of God in truth;

7 just as you learned *it* from Epaphras, our beloved fellow bond-servant, who is a faithful servant of Christ on [1]our behalf,

8 and he also informed us of your love in the Spirit.

9 For this reason also, since the day we heard *of it*, we have not ceased to pray for you and to ask that you may be filled with the knowledge of His will in all spiritual wisdom and understanding,

10 so that you may walk in a manner worthy of the Lord, to please *Him* in all respects, bearing fruit in every good work and increasing in the knowledge of God;

11 strengthened with all power, according to His glorious might, for the attaining of all steadfastness and patience; joyously

12 giving thanks to the Father, who has qualified us to share in the inheritance of the saints in light.

13 For He delivered us from the domain of darkness, and transferred us to the kingdom of His beloved Son,

14 in whom we have redemption, the forgiveness of sins.

15 And He is the image of the invisible God, the first-born of all creation.

16 For by Him all things were created, *both* in the heavens and on earth, visible and invisible, whether thrones or dominions or rulers or authorities—all things have been created by Him and for Him.

17 And He is before all things, and in Him all things hold together.

18 He is also head of the body, the church; and He is the beginning, the first-born from the dead; so that He Himself might come to have first place in everything.

19 For it was the *Father's* good pleasure for all the fulness to dwell in Him,

20 and through Him to reconcile all things to Himself, having made peace through the blood of His cross; through Him, *I say,*

[1] Some later mss. read *your*

whether things on earth or things in heaven.

21 And although you were formerly alienated and hostile in mind, *engaged* in evil deeds,

22 yet He has now reconciled you in His fleshly body through death, in order to present you before Him holy and blameless and beyond reproach—

23 if indeed you continue in the faith firmly established and steadfast, and not moved away from the hope of the gospel that you have heard, which was proclaimed in all creation under heaven, and of which I, Paul, was made a minister.

24 Now I rejoice in my sufferings for your sake, and in my flesh I do my share on behalf of His body (which is the church) in filling up that which is lacking in Christ's afflictions.

25 Of *this church* I was made a minister according to the stewardship from God bestowed on me for your benefit, that I might fully carry out the *preaching of* the word of God,

26 *that is,* the mystery which has been hidden from the *past* ages and generations; but has now been manifested to His saints,

27 to whom God willed to make known what is the riches of the glory of this mystery among the Gentiles, which is Christ in you, the hope of glory.

28 And we proclaim Him, admonishing every man and teaching every man with all wisdom, that we may present every man complete in Christ.

29 And for this purpose also I labor, striving according to His power, which mightily works within me.

CHAPTER 2

FOR I want you to know how great a struggle I have on your behalf, and for those who are at Laodicea, and for all those who have not personally seen my face,

2 that their hearts may be encouraged, having been knit together in love, and *attaining* to all the wealth that comes from the full assurance of understanding, *resulting* in a true knowledge of God's mystery, *that is,* Christ *Himself*,

3 in whom are hidden all the treasures of wisdom and knowledge.

4 I say this in order that no one may delude you with persuasive argument.

5 For even though I am absent in body, nevertheless I am with you in spirit, rejoicing to see your good discipline and the stability of your faith in Christ.

6 As you therefore have received Christ Jesus the Lord, *so* walk in Him,

7 having been firmly rooted *and now* being built up in Him and established [2]in your faith, just as you were instructed, *and* overflowing with gratitude.

8 See to it that no one takes you captive through philosophy and empty deception, according to the tradition of men, according to the elementary principles of the world, rather than according to Christ.

9 For in Him all the fulness of Deity dwells in bodily form,

10 and in Him you have been made complete, and He is the

[2] Or, *by*

head over all rule and authority;

11 and in Him you were also circumcised with a circumcision made without hands, in the removal of the body of the flesh by the circumcision of Christ;

12 having been buried with Him in baptism, in which you were also raised up with Him through faith in the working of God, who raised Him from the dead.

13 And when you were dead in your transgressions, and the uncircumcision of your flesh, He made you alive together with Him, having forgiven us all our transgressions,

14 having canceled out the certificate of debt consisting of decrees against us *and* which was hostile to us; and He has taken it out of the way, having nailed it to the cross.

15 When He had disarmed the rulers and authorities, He made a public display of them, having triumphed over them through Him.

16 Therefore let no one act as your judge in regard to food or drink or in respect to a festival or a new moon or a Sabbath day—

17 things which are a *mere* shadow of what is to come; but the substance belongs to Christ.

18 Let no one keep defrauding you of your prize by delighting in self-abasement and the worship of the angels, taking his stand on *visions* he has seen, inflated without cause by his fleshly mind,

19 and not holding fast to the head, from whom the entire body, being supplied and held together by the joints and liga-

ments, grows with a growth which is from God.

20 If you have died with Christ to the elementary principles of the world, why, as if you were living in the world, do you submit yourself to decrees, such as,

21 "Do not handle, do not taste, do not touch!"

22 (which all *refer to* things destined to perish with the using)—in accordance with the commandments and teachings of men?

23 These are matters which have, to be sure, the appearance of wisdom in self-made religion and self-abasement and severe treatment of the body, *but are* of no value against fleshly indulgence.

CHAPTER 3

IF then you have been raised up with Christ, keep seeking the things above, where Christ is, seated at the right hand of God.

2 Set your mind on the things above, not on the things that are on earth.

3 For you have died and your life is hidden with Christ in God.

4 When Christ, who is our life, is revealed, then you also will be revealed with Him in glory.

5 Therefore consider the members of your earthly body as dead to immorality, impurity, passion, evil desire, and greed, which amounts to idolatry.

6 For it is on account of these things that the wrath of God will come[3],

7 and in them you also once walked, when you were living in them.

8 But now you also, put them

[3] Some early mss. add *upon the sons of disobedience*

all aside: anger, wrath, malice, slander, *and* abusive speech from your mouth.

9 Do not lie to one another, since you laid aside the old self with its *evil* practices,

10 and have put on the new self who is being renewed to a true knowledge according to the image of the One who created him

11 —*a renewal* in which there is no *distinction between* Greek and Jew, circumcised and uncircumcised, barbarian, Scythian, slave and freeman, but Christ is all, and in all.

12 And so, as those who have been chosen of God, holy and beloved, put on a heart of compassion, kindness, humility, gentleness and patience;

13 bearing with one another, and forgiving each other, whoever has a complaint against anyone; just as the Lord forgave you, so also should you.

14 And beyond all these things *put on* love, which is the perfect bond of unity.

15 And let the peace of Christ rule in your hearts, to which indeed you were called in one body; and be thankful.

16 Let the word of [4]Christ richly dwell within you, with all wisdom teaching and admonishing one another with psalms *and* hymns *and* spiritual songs, singing with thankfulness in your hearts to God.

17 And whatever you do in word or deed, *do* all in the name of the Lord Jesus, giving thanks through Him to God the Father.

18 Wives, be subject to your husbands, as is fitting in the Lord.

19 Husbands, love your wives,

and do not be embittered against them.

20 Children, be obedient to your parents in all things, for this is well-pleasing to the Lord.

21 Fathers, do not [5]exasperate your children, that they may not lose heart.

22 Slaves, in all things obey those who are your masters on earth, not with external service, as those who *merely* please men, but with sincerity of heart, fearing the Lord.

23 Whatever you do, do your work heartily, as for the Lord rather than for men;

24 knowing that from the Lord you will receive the reward of the inheritance. It is the Lord Christ whom you serve.

25 For he who does wrong will receive the consequences of the wrong which he has done, and that without partiality.

CHAPTER 4

MASTERS, grant to your slaves justice and fairness, knowing that you too have a Master in heaven.

2 Devote yourselves to prayer, keeping alert in it with *an attitude of* thanksgiving;

3 praying at the same time for us as well, that God may open up to us a door for the word, so that we may speak forth the mystery of Christ, for which I have also been imprisoned;

4 in order that I may make it clear in the way I ought to speak.

5 Conduct yourselves with wisdom toward outsiders, mak-

---

[4] Some mss. read *the Lord;* others read *God*
[5] Some early mss. read *provoke to anger*

ing the most of the opportunity.

6 Let your speech always be with grace, seasoned, *as it were*, with salt, so that you may know how you should respond to each person.

7 As to all my affairs, Tychicus, *our* beloved brother and faithful servant and fellow bondservant in the Lord, will bring you information.

8 For I have sent him to you for this very purpose, that you may know *about* our circumstances and that he may encourage your hearts;

9 and with him Onesimus, *our* faithful and beloved brother, who is one of your *number*. They will inform you about the whole situation here.

10 Aristarchus, my fellow prisoner, sends you his greetings; and *also* Barnabas' cousin Mark (about whom you received instructions: if he comes to you, welcome him);

11 and *also* Jesus who is called Justus; these are the only fellow workers for the kingdom of God who are from the circumcision;

and they have proved to be an encouragement to me.

12 Epaphras, who is one of your number, a bondslave of Jesus Christ, sends you his greetings, always laboring earnestly for you in his prayers, that you may stand perfect and fully assured in all the will of God.

13 For I bear him witness that he has a deep concern for you and for those who are in Laodicea and Hierapolis.

14 Luke, the beloved physician, sends you his greetings, and *also* Demas.

15 Greet the brethren who are in Laodicea and also [6]Nympha and the church that is in her house.

16 And when this letter is read among you, have it also read in the church of the Laodiceans; and you, for your part read my letter *that is coming* from Laodicea.

17 And say to Archippus, "Take heed to the ministry which you have received in the Lord, that you may fulfill it."

18 I, Paul, write this greeting with my own hand. Remember my imprisonment. Grace be with you.

[6] Or, *Nymphas* (masc.)

THESSALONIANS

Paul and Silvanus and Timothy to the church of the Thessalonians in God the Father and the Lord Jesus Christ: Grace to you and peace.

2 We give thanks to God always for all of you, making mention of you in our prayers;

3 constantly bearing in mind your work of faith and labor of love and steadfastness of hope in our Lord Jesus Christ in the presence of our God and Father,

4 knowing, brethren beloved by God, *His* choice of you;

5 for our gospel did not come to you in word only, but also in power and in the Holy Spirit and with full conviction; just as you know what kind of men we proved to be among you for your sake.

6 You also became imitators of us and of the Lord, having received the word in much tribulation with the joy of the Holy Spirit,

7 so that you became an example to all the believers in Macedonia and in Achaia.

8 For the word of the Lord has sounded forth from you, not only in Macedonia and Achaia, but also in every place your faith toward God has gone forth, so that we have no need to say anything.

9 For they themselves report about us what kind of a reception we had with you, and how you turned to God from idols to serve a living and true God,

10 and to wait for His Son from heaven, whom He raised from the dead, *that is* Jesus, who delivers us from the wrath to come.

CHAPTER 2

For you yourselves know, brethren, that our coming to you was not in vain,

2 but after we had already suffered and been mistreated in Philippi, as you know, we had the boldness in our God to speak to you the gospel of God amid much opposition.

3 For our exhortation does not *come* from error or impurity or by way of deceit;

4 but just as we have been approved by God to be entrusted with the gospel, so we speak, not as pleasing men but God, who examines our hearts.

5 For we never came with flattering speech, as you know, nor with a pretext for greed—God is witness—

6 nor did we seek glory from men, either from you or from others, even though as apostles of Christ we might have asserted our authority.

7 But we proved to be [1]gentle among you, as a nursing *mother* tenderly cares for her own children.

8 Having thus a fond affection for you, we were well-pleased to impart to you not only the gospel of God but also our own lives, because you had become very dear to us.

[1] Some ancient mss. read *babes*

9 For you recall, brethren, our labor and hardship, *how* working night and day so as not to be a burden to any of you, we proclaimed to you the gospel of God.

10 You are witnesses, and *so is* God, how devoutly and uprightly and blamelessly we behaved toward you believers;

11 just as you know how we *were* exhorting and encouraging and imploring each one of you as a father *would* his own children,

12 so that you may walk in a manner worthy of the God who calls you into His own kingdom and glory.

13 And for this reason we also constantly thank God that when you received from us the word of God's message, you accepted *it* not *as* the word of men, but *for* what it really is, the word of God, which also performs its work in you who believe.

14 For you, brethren, became imitators of the churches of God in Christ Jesus that are in Judea, for you also endured the same sufferings at the hands of your own countrymen, even as they *did* from the Jews,

15 who both killed the Lord Jesus and the prophets, and drove us out. They are not pleasing to God, but hostile to all men,

16 hindering us from speaking to the Gentiles that they might be saved; with the result that they always fill up the measure of their sins. But wrath has come upon them [2]to the utmost.

17 But we, brethren, having been bereft of you for a short while—in person, not in spirit— were all the more eager with great desire to see your face.

18 For we wanted to come to you—I, Paul, more than once— and *yet* Satan thwarted us.

19 For who is our hope or joy or crown of exultation? Is it not even you, in the presence of our Lord Jesus at His coming?

20 For you are our glory and joy.

CHAPTER 3

THEREFORE when we could endure *it* no longer, we thought it best to be left behind at Athens alone;

2 and we sent Timothy, our brother and God's fellow worker in the gospel of Christ, to strengthen and encourage you as to your faith,

3 so that no man may be disturbed by these afflictions; for you yourselves know that we have been destined for this.

4 For indeed when we were with you, we *kept* telling you in advance that we were going to suffer affliction; and so it came to pass, as you know.

5 For this reason, when I could endure *it* no longer, I also sent to find out about your faith, for fear that the tempter might have tempted you, and our labor should be in vain.

6 But now that Timothy has come to us from you, and has brought us good news of your faith and love, and that you always think kindly of us, longing to see us just as we also long to see you,

7 for this reason, brethren, in all our distress and affliction we were comforted about you through your faith;

8 for now we *really* live, if you stand firm in the Lord.

[2] Or, *forever; or, altogether*

9 For what thanks can we render to God for you in return for all the joy with which we rejoice before our God on your account,

10 as we night and day keep praying most earnestly that we may see your face, and may complete what is lacking in your faith?

11 Now may our God and Father Himself and Jesus our Lord direct our way to you;

12 and may the Lord cause you to increase and abound in love for one another, and for all men, just as we also *do* for you;

13 so that He may establish your hearts unblamable in holiness before our God and Father at the coming of our Lord Jesus with all His saints.

CHAPTER 4

FINALLY then, brethren, we request and exhort you in the Lord Jesus, that, as you received from us *instruction* as to how you ought to walk and please God (just as you actually do [3]walk), that you may excel still more.

2 For you know what commandments we gave you [4]by the *authority* of the Lord Jesus.

3 For this is the will of God, your sanctification; *that is*, that you abstain from sexual immorality;

4 that each of you know how to possess his own [5]vessel in sanctification and honor,

5 not in lustful passion, like the Gentiles who do not know God;

6 *and* that no man transgress and defraud his brother in the matter because the Lord is the

avenger in all these things, just as we also told you before and solemnly warned *you*.

7 For God has not called us for the purpose of impurity, but in sanctification.

8 Consequently, he who rejects *this* is not rejecting man but the God who gives His Holy Spirit to you.

9 Now as to the love of the brethren, you have no need for *anyone* to write to you, for you yourselves are taught by God to love one another;

10 for indeed you do practice it toward all the brethren who are in all Macedonia. But we urge you, brethren, to excel still more,

11 and to make it your ambition to lead a quiet life and attend to your own business and work with your own hands, just as we commanded you;

12 so that you may behave properly toward outsiders and not be in any need.

13 But we do not want you to be uninformed, brethren, about those who are asleep, that you may not grieve, as do the rest who have no hope.

14 For if we believe that Jesus died and rose again, even so God will bring with Him those who have fallen asleep in Jesus.

15 For this we say to you by the word of the Lord, that we who are alive, and remain until the coming of the Lord, shall not precede those who have fallen asleep.

16 For the Lord Himself will descend from heaven with a shout, with the voice of *the* archangel, and with the trumpet of

---

3 Or, *conduct yourselves*
4 Lit., *through the Lord*
5 I.e., *body*; or possibly, *wife*

God; and the dead in Christ shall rise first.

17 Then we who are alive and remain shall be caught up together with them in the clouds to meet the Lord in the air, and thus we shall always be with the Lord.

18 Therefore comfort one another with these words.

CHAPTER 5

NOW as to the times and the epochs, brethren, you have no need of anything to be written to you.

2 For you yourselves know full well that the day of the Lord will come just like a thief in the night.

3 While they are saying, "Peace and safety!" then destruction will come upon them suddenly like birth pangs upon a woman with child; and they shall not escape.

4 But you, brethren, are not in darkness, that the day should overtake you like a thief;

5 for you are all sons of light and sons of day. We are not of night nor of darkness;

6 so then let us not sleep as others do, but let us be alert and ⁶sober.

7 For those who sleep do their sleeping at night, and those who get drunk get drunk at night.

8 But since we are of *the* day, let us be ⁶sober, having put on the breastplate of faith and love, and as a helmet, the hope of salvation.

9 For God has not destined us for wrath, but for obtaining salvation through our Lord Jesus Christ,

10 who died for us, that whether we are awake or asleep, we may live together with Him.

11 Therefore encourage one another, and build up one another, just as you also are doing.

12 But we request of you, brethren, that you appreciate those who diligently labor among you, and have charge over you in the Lord and give you instruction,

13 and that you esteem them very highly in love because of their work. Live in peace with one another.

14 And we urge you, brethren, admonish the unruly, encourage the fainthearted, help the weak, be patient with all men.

15 See that no one repays another with evil for evil, but always seek after that which is good for one another and for all men.

16 Rejoice always;

17 pray without ceasing;

18 in everything give thanks; for this is God's will for you in Christ Jesus.

19 Do not quench the Spirit;

20 do not despise prophetic ⁷utterances.

21 But examine everything *carefully*; hold fast to that which is good;

22 abstain from every ⁸form of evil.

23 Now may the God of peace Himself sanctify you entirely; and may your spirit and soul and body be preserved complete, without blame at the coming of our Lord Jesus Christ.

24 Faithful is He who calls you, and He also will bring it to pass.

25 Brethren, pray for us⁹.

26 Greet all the brethren with a holy kiss.

27 I adjure you by the Lord to

---

⁶ Or, *self-controlled*   ⁷ Or, *gifts*
⁸ Or, *appearance*   ⁹ Some mss. add *also*

have this letter read to all the brethren.

28 The grace of our Lord Jesus Christ be with you.

THE SECOND EPISTLE OF PAUL TO THE

THESSALONIANS

PAUL and Silvanus and Timothy to the church of the Thessalonians in God our Father and the Lord Jesus Christ:

2 Grace to you and peace from God the Father and the Lord Jesus Christ.

3 We ought always to give thanks to God for you, brethren, as is *only* fitting, because your faith is greatly enlarged, and the love of each one of you toward one another grows *ever* greater;

4 therefore, we ourselves speak proudly of you among the churches of God for your perseverance and faith in the midst of all your persecutions and afflictions which you endure.

5 *This is* a plain indication of God's righteous judgment so that you may be considered worthy of the kingdom of God, for which indeed you are suffering.

6 For after all it is *only* just for God to repay with affliction those who afflict you,

7 and *to give* relief to you who are afflicted and to us as well when the Lord Jesus shall be revealed from heaven with His mighty angels in flaming fire,

8 dealing out retribution to those who do not know God and to those who do not obey the gospel of our Lord Jesus.

9 And these will pay the penalty of eternal destruction, away from the presence of the Lord and from the glory of His power,

10 when He comes to be glorified in His saints on that day, and to be marveled at among all who have believed—for our testimony to you was believed.

11 To this end also we pray for you always that our God may count you worthy of your calling, and fulfill every desire for goodness and the work of faith with power;

12 in order that the name of our Lord Jesus may be glorified in you, and you in Him, according to the grace of our God and the Lord Jesus Christ.

CHAPTER 2

NOW we request you, brethren, with regard to the coming of our Lord Jesus Christ, and our gathering together to Him,

2 that you may not be quickly shaken from your composure or be disturbed either by a spirit or a message or a letter as if from us, to the effect that the day of the Lord has come.

3 Let no one in any way deceive you, for *it will not come* unless the [1]apostasy comes first,

---

1 Or, *falling away from the faith*

and the man of lawlessness is revealed, the son of destruction,

4 who opposes and exalts himself above every so-called god or object of worship, so that he takes his seat in the temple of God, displaying himself as being God.

5 Do you not remember that while I was still with you, I was telling you these things?

6 And you know what restrains him now, so that in his time he may be revealed.

7 For the mystery of lawlessness is already at work; only he who now restrains *will do so* until he is taken out of the way.

8 And then that lawless one will be revealed whom the Lord will slay with the breath of His mouth and bring to an end by the appearance of His coming;

9 *that is,* the one whose coming is in accord with the activity of Satan, with all power and signs and false wonders,

10 and with all the deception of wickedness for those who perish, because they did not receive the love of the truth so as to be saved.

11 And for this reason God will send upon them a deluding influence so that they might believe what is false,

12 in order that they all may be judged who did not believe the truth, but took pleasure in wickedness.

13 But we should always give thanks to God for you, brethren beloved by the Lord, because God has chosen you ²from the beginning for salvation through sanctification by the Spirit and faith in the truth.

14 And it was for this He called you through our gospel, that you may gain the glory of our Lord Jesus Christ.

15 So then, brethren, stand firm and hold to the traditions which you were taught, whether by word *of mouth* or by letter from us.

16 Now may our Lord Jesus Christ Himself and God our Father, who has loved us and given us eternal comfort and good hope by grace,

17 comfort and strengthen your hearts in every good work and word.

CHAPTER 3

FINALLY, brethren, pray for us that the word of the Lord may spread rapidly and be glorified, just as *it* did also with you;

2 and that we may be delivered from perverse and evil men; for not all have faith.

3 But the Lord is faithful, and He will strengthen and protect you from the evil *one.*

4 And we have confidence in the Lord concerning you, that you are doing and will continue to do what we command.

5 And may the Lord direct your hearts into the love of God and into the steadfastness of Christ.

6 Now we command you, brethren, in the name of our Lord Jesus Christ, that you keep aloof from every brother who leads an unruly life and not according to the tradition which you received from us.

7 For you yourselves know how you ought to follow our example, because we did not act in an undisciplined manner among you,

---

² Some ancient mss. read *first fruits*

8 nor did we eat anyone's bread without paying for it, but with labor and hardship we *kept* working night and day so that we might not be a burden to any of you;

9 not because we do not have the right *to this*, but in order to offer ourselves as a model for you, that you might follow our example.

10 For even when we were with you, we used to give you this order: if anyone will not work, neither let him eat.

11 For we hear that some among you are leading an undisciplined life, doing no work at all, but acting like busybodies.

12 Now such persons we command and exhort in the Lord Jesus Christ to work in quiet fashion and eat their own bread.

13 But as for you, brethren, do not grow weary of doing good.

14 And if anyone does not obey our instruction in this letter, take special note of that man and do not associate with him, so that he may be put to shame.

15 And *yet* do not regard him as an enemy, but admonish him as a brother.

16 Now may the Lord of peace Himself continually grant you peace in every circumstance. The Lord be with you all!

17 I, Paul, write this greeting with my own hand, and this is a distinguishing mark in every letter; this is the way I write.

18 The grace of our Lord Jesus Christ be with you all.

THE FIRST EPISTLE OF PAUL TO

TIMOTHY

PAUL, an apostle of Christ Jesus according to the commandment of God our Savior, and of Christ Jesus, *who is* our hope;

2 to Timothy, *my* true child in *the* faith: Grace, mercy *and* peace from God the Father and Christ Jesus our Lord.

3 As I urged you upon my departure for Macedonia, remain on at Ephesus, in order that you may instruct certain men not to teach strange doctrines,

4 nor to pay attention to myths and endless genealogies, which give rise to mere speculation rather than *furthering* the administration of God which is by faith.

5 But the goal of our instruction is love from a pure heart and a good conscience and a sincere faith.

6 For some men, straying from these things, have turned aside to fruitless discussion,

7 wanting to be teachers of the Law, even though they do not understand either what they are saying or the matters about which they make confident assertions.

8 But we know that the Law is good, if one uses it lawfully,

9 realizing the fact that law is

not made for a righteous man, but for those who are lawless and rebellious, for the ungodly and sinners, for the unholy and profane, for those who kill their fathers or mothers, for murderers

10 and immoral men and homosexuals and kidnappers and liars and perjurers, and whatever else is contrary to sound teaching,

11 according to the glorious gospel of the blessed God, with which I have been entrusted.

12 I thank Christ Jesus our Lord, who has strengthened me, because He considered me faithful, putting me into service;

13 even though I was formerly a blasphemer and a persecutor and a violent aggressor. And yet I was shown mercy, because I acted ignorantly in unbelief;

14 and the grace of our Lord was more than abundant, with the faith and love which are *found* in Christ Jesus.

15 It is a trustworthy statement, deserving full acceptance, that Christ Jesus came into the world to save sinners, among whom I am foremost *of all*.

16 And yet for this reason I found mercy, in order that in me as the foremost, Jesus Christ might demonstrate His perfect patience, as an example for those who would believe in Him for eternal life.

17 Now to the King eternal, immortal, invisible, the only God, *be* honor and glory forever and ever. Amen.

18 This command I entrust to you, Timothy, my son, in accordance with the prophecies previously made concerning you, that by them you may fight the good fight,

19 keeping faith and a good conscience, which some have rejected and suffered shipwreck in regard to their faith.

20 Among these are Hymenaeus and Alexander, whom I have delivered over to Satan, so that they may be taught not to blaspheme.

CHAPTER 2

FIRST of all, then, I urge that entreaties *and* prayers, petitions *and* thanksgivings, be made on behalf of all men,

2 for kings and all who are in authority, in order that we may lead a tranquil and quiet life in all godliness and dignity.

3 This is good and acceptable in the sight of God our Savior,

4 who desires all men to be saved and to come to the knowledge of the truth.

5 For there is one God, *and* one mediator also between God and men, *the* man Christ Jesus,

6 who gave Himself as a ransom for all, the testimony *borne* at the proper time.

7 And for this I was appointed a preacher and an apostle (I am telling the truth, I am not lying) as a teacher of the Gentiles in faith and truth.

8 Therefore I want the men in every place to pray, lifting up holy hands, without wrath and dissension.

9 Likewise, *I want* women to adorn themselves with proper clothing, modestly and discreetly, not with braided hair and gold or pearls or costly garments;

10 but rather by means of good works, as befits women making a claim to godliness.

11 Let a woman quietly receive

instruction with entire submissiveness.

12 But I do not allow a woman to teach or exercise authority over a man, but to remain quiet.

13 For it was Adam who was first created, *and* then Eve.

14 And *it was* not Adam who was deceived, but the woman being quite deceived, fell into transgression.

15 But *women* shall be preserved through the bearing of children if they continue in faith and love and sanctity with self-restraint.

CHAPTER 3

IT is a trustworthy statement: if any man aspires to the office of overseer, it is a fine work he desires *to do*.

2 An overseer, then, must be above reproach, the husband of one wife, temperate, prudent, respectable, hospitable, able to teach,

3 not addicted to wine or pugnacious, but gentle, uncontentious, free from the love of money.

4 *He must be* one who manages his own household well, keeping his children under control with all dignity

5 (but if a man does not know how to manage his own household, how will he take care of the church of God?);

6 *and* not a new convert, lest he become conceited and fall into the condemnation incurred by the devil.

7 And he must have a good reputation with those outside *the church,* so that he may not fall into reproach and the snare of the devil.

8 Deacons likewise *must be*

men of dignity, not double-tongued, or addicted to much wine or fond of sordid gain,

9 *but* holding to the mystery of the faith with a clear conscience.

10 And let these also first be tested; then let them serve as deacons if they are beyond reproach.

11 Women *must* likewise *be* dignified, not malicious gossips, but temperate, faithful in all things.

12 Let deacons be husbands of only one wife, *and* good managers of *their* children and their own households.

13 For those who have served well as deacons obtain for themselves a high standing and great confidence in the faith that is in Christ Jesus.

14 I am writing these things to you, hoping to come to you before long;

15 but in case I am delayed, *I write* so that you may know how one ought to conduct himself in the household of God, which is the church of the living God, the pillar and support of the truth.

16 And by common confession great is the mystery of godliness:

¹He who was revealed in the flesh,
Was vindicated in the Spirit,
Beheld by angels,
Proclaimed among the nations,
Believed on in the world,
Taken up in glory.

CHAPTER 4

BUT the Spirit explicitly says that in later times some will

¹ Some later mss. read *God*

fall away from the faith, paying attention to deceitful spirits and doctrines of demons,

2 by means of the hypocrisy of liars seared in their own conscience as with a branding iron,

3 *men* who forbid marriage *and advocate* abstaining from foods, which God has created to be gratefully shared in by those who believe and know the truth.

4 For everything created by God is good, and nothing is to be rejected, if it is received with gratitude;

5 for it is sanctified by means of the word of God and prayer.

6 In pointing out these things to the brethren, you will be a good servant of Christ Jesus, *constantly* nourished on the words of the faith and of the sound doctrine which you have been following.

7 But have nothing to do with worldly fables fit only for old women. On the other hand, discipline yourself for the purpose of godliness;

8 for bodily discipline is only of little profit, but godliness is profitable for all things, since it holds promise for the present life and *also* for the *life* to come.

9 It is a trustworthy statement deserving full acceptance.

10 For it is for this we labor and strive, because we have fixed our hope on the living God, who is the Savior of all men, especially of believers.

11 Prescribe and teach these things.

12 Let no one look down on your youthfulness, but *rather* in speech, conduct, love, faith *and* purity, show yourself an example of those who believe.

13 Until I come, give attention to the *public* reading *of Scripture,* to exhortation and teaching.

14 Do not neglect the spiritual gift within you, which was bestowed upon you through prophetic utterance with the laying on of hands by the presbytery.

15 Take pains with these things; be *absorbed* in them, so that your progress may be evident to all.

16 Pay close attention to yourself and to your teaching; persevere in these things; for as you do this you will insure salvation both for yourself and for those who hear you.

CHAPTER 5

DO not sharply rebuke an older man, *but rather* appeal to him as a father, *to* the younger men as brothers,

2 the older women as mothers, *and* the younger women as sisters, in all purity.

3 Honor widows who are widows indeed;

4 but if any widow has children or grandchildren, let them first learn to practice piety in regard to their own family, and to make some return to their parents; for this is acceptable in the sight of God.

5 Now she who is a widow indeed, and who has been left alone has fixed her hope on God, and continues in entreaties and prayers night and day.

6 But she who gives herself to wanton pleasure is dead even while she lives.

7 Prescribe these things as well, so that they may be above reproach.

8 But if anyone does not provide for his own, and especially

for those of his household, he has denied the faith, and is worse than an unbeliever.

9 Let a widow be put on the list only if she is not less than sixty years old, *having been* the wife of one man,

10 having a reputation for good works; *and* if she has brought up children, if she has shown hospitality to strangers, if she has washed the saints' feet, if she has assisted those in distress, *and* if she has devoted herself to every good work.

11 But refuse *to put* younger widows *on the list*, for when they feel sensual desires in disregard of Christ, they want to get married,

12 *thus* incurring condemnation, because they have set aside their previous pledge.

13 And at the same time they also learn *to be* idle, as they go around from house to house; and not merely idle, but also gossips and busybodies, talking about things not proper *to mention.*

14 Therefore, I want younger *widows* to get married, bear children, keep house, *and* give the enemy no occasion for reproach;

15 for some have already turned aside to follow Satan.

16 If any woman who is a believer has *dependent* widows, let her assist them, and let not the church be burdened, so that it may assist those who are widows indeed.

17 Let the elders who rule well be considered worthy of double honor, especially those who work hard at preaching and teaching.

18 For the Scripture says, "YOU SHALL NOT MUZZLE THE OX WHILE HE IS THRESHING," and "The laborer is worthy of his wages."

19 Do not receive an accusation against an elder except on the basis of two or three witnesses.

20 Those who continue in sin, rebuke in the presence of all, so that the rest also may be fearful *of sinning.*

21 I solemnly charge you in the presence of God and of Christ Jesus and of *His* chosen angels, to maintain these *principles* without bias, doing nothing in a *spirit of* partiality.

22 Do not lay hands upon anyone *too* hastily and thus share *responsibility for* the sins of others; keep yourself free from sin.

23 No longer drink water *exclusively*, but use a little wine for the sake of your stomach and your frequent ailments.

24 The sins of some men are quite evident, going before them to judgment; for others, their *sins* follow after.

25 Likewise also, deeds that are good are quite evident, and those which are otherwise cannot be concealed.

CHAPTER 6

LET all who are under the yoke as slaves regard their own masters as worthy of all honor so that the name of God and *our* doctrine may not be spoken against.

2 And let those who have believers as their masters not be disrespectful to them because they are brethren, but let them serve them all the more, because those who partake of the benefit are believers and beloved. Teach and preach these *principles.*

3 If anyone advocates a different doctrine, and does not agree with sound words, those of our Lord Jesus Christ, and with the doctrine conforming to godliness,

4 he is conceited *and* understands nothing; but he has a morbid interest in controversial questions and disputes about words, out of which arise envy, strife, abusive language, evil suspicions,

5 and constant friction between men of depraved mind and deprived of the truth, who suppose that godliness is a means of gain.

6 But godliness *actually* is a means of great gain, when accompanied by contentment.

7 For we have brought nothing into the world, ²so we cannot take anything out of it either.

8 And if we have food and covering, with these we shall be content.

9 But those who want to get rich fall into temptation and a snare and many foolish and harmful desires which plunge men into ruin and destruction.

10 For the love of money is a root of all sorts of evil, and some by longing for it have wandered away from the faith, and pierced themselves with many a pang.

11 But flee from these things, you man of God; and pursue righteousness, godliness, faith, love, perseverance *and* gentleness.

12 Fight the good fight of faith; take hold of the eternal life to which you were called, and you made the good confession in the presence of many witnesses.

13 I charge you in the presence of God, who gives life to all things, and of Christ Jesus, who testified the good confession before Pontius Pilate,

14 that you keep the commandment without stain or reproach until the appearing of our Lord Jesus Christ,

15 which He will bring about at the proper time—He who is the blessed and only Sovereign, the King of kings and Lord of lords;

16 who alone possesses immortality and dwells in unapproachable light; whom no man has seen or can see. To Him *be* honor and eternal dominion! Amen.

17 Instruct those who are rich in this present world not to be conceited or to fix their hope on the uncertainty of riches, but on God, who richly supplies us with all things to enjoy.

18 *Instruct them* to do good, to be rich in good works, to be generous and ready to share,

19 storing up for themselves the treasure of a good foundation for the future, so that they may take hold of that which is life indeed.

20 O Timothy, guard what has been entrusted to you, avoiding worldly *and* empty chatter *and* the opposing arguments of what is falsely called "knowledge"—

21 which some have professed and thus gone astray from the faith.

Grace be with you.

---

² Later mss. read *it is clear that*

TIMOTHY

PAUL, an apostle of Christ Jesus by the will of God, according to the promise of life in Christ Jesus,

2 to Timothy, my beloved son: Grace, mercy *and* peace from God the Father and Christ Jesus our Lord.

3 I thank God, whom I serve with a clear conscience the way my forefathers did, as I constantly remember you in my prayers night and day,

4 longing to see you, even as I recall your tears, so that I may be filled with joy.

5 For I am mindful of the sincere faith within you, which first dwelt in your grandmother Lois, and your mother Eunice, and I am sure that *it is* in you as well.

6 And for this reason I remind you to kindle afresh the gift of God which is in you through the laying on of my hands.

7 For God has not given us a spirit of timidity, but of power and love and discipline.

8 Therefore do not be ashamed of the testimony of our Lord, or of me His prisoner; but join with *me* in suffering for the gospel according to the power of God,

9 who has saved us, and called us with a holy calling, not according to our works, but according to His own purpose and grace which was granted us in Christ Jesus from all eternity,

10 but now has been revealed by the appearing of our Savior Christ Jesus, who abolished death, and brought life and immortality to light through the gospel,

11 for which I was appointed a preacher and an apostle and a teacher.

12 For this reason I also suffer these things, but I am not ashamed; for I know whom I have believed and I am convinced that He is able to guard what I have entrusted to Him until that day.

13 Retain the standard of sound words which you have heard from me, in the faith and love which are in Christ Jesus.

14 Guard, through the Holy Spirit who dwells in us, the treasure which has been entrusted to *you*.

15 You are aware of the fact that all who are in Asia turned away from me, among whom are Phygelus and Hermogenes.

16 The Lord grant mercy to the house of Onesiphorus for he often refreshed me, and was not ashamed of my chains;

17 but when he was in Rome, he eagerly searched for me, and found me—

18 the Lord grant the Lord to him to find mercy from the Lord on that day—and you know very well what services he rendered at Ephesus.

CHAPTER 2

YOU therefore, my son, be strong in the grace that is in Christ Jesus.

2 And the things which you have heard from me in the presence of many witnesses, these entrust to faithful men, who will be able to teach others also.

3 Suffer hardship with *me*, as a good soldier of Christ Jesus.

4 No soldier in active service entangles himself in the affairs of everyday life, so that he may please the one who enlisted him as a soldier.

5 And also if anyone competes as an athlete, he does not win the prize unless he competes according to the rules.

6 The hard-working farmer ought to be the first to receive his share of the crops.

7 Consider what I say, for the Lord will give you understanding in everything.

8 Remember Jesus Christ, risen from the dead, descendant of David, according to my gospel,

9 for which I suffer hardship even to imprisonment as a criminal; but the word of God is not imprisoned.

10 For this reason I endure all things for the sake of those who are chosen, that they also may obtain the salvation which is in Christ Jesus *and* with *it* eternal glory.

11 It is a trustworthy statement:

For if we died with Him, we shall also live with Him;

12 If we endure, we shall also reign with Him;

If we deny Him, He also will deny us;

13 If we are faithless, He remains faithful; for He cannot deny Himself.

14 Remind *them* of these things, and solemnly charge *them* in the presence of God not to wrangle about words, which is useless, *and* leads to the ruin of the hearers.

15 Be diligent to present yourself approved to God as a workman who does not need to be ashamed, handling accurately the word of truth.

16 But avoid worldly *and* empty chatter, for it will lead to further ungodliness,

17 and their talk will spread like ¹gangrene. Among them are Hymenaeus and Philetus,

18 *men* who have gone astray from the truth saying that the resurrection has already taken place, and thus they upset the faith of some.

19 Nevertheless, the firm foundation of God stands, having this seal, "The Lord knows those who are His," and, "Let everyone who names the name of the Lord abstain from wickedness."

20 Now in a large house there are not only gold and silver vessels, but also vessels of wood and of earthenware, and some to honor and some to dishonor.

21 Therefore, if a man cleanses himself from these *things*, he will be a vessel for honor, sanctified, useful to the Master, prepared for every good work.

22 Now flee from youthful lusts, and pursue righteousness, faith, love *and* peace, with those who call on the Lord from a pure heart.

23 But refuse foolish and ignorant speculations, knowing that they produce quarrels.

24 And the Lord's bond-servant must not be quarrelsome,

¹ Or, *cancer*

but be kind to all, able to teach, patient when wronged,

25 with gentleness correcting those who are in opposition, if perhaps God may grant them repentance leading to the knowledge of the truth,

26 and they may come to their senses *and escape* from the snare of the devil, having been held captive by him to do his will.

CHAPTER 3

BUT realize this, that in the last days difficult times will come.

2 For men will be lovers of self, lovers of money, boastful, arrogant, revilers, disobedient to parents, ungrateful, unholy,

3 unloving, irreconcilable, malicious gossips, without self-control, brutal, haters of good,

4 treacherous, reckless, conceited, lovers of pleasure rather than lovers of God;

5 holding to a form of godliness, although they have denied its power; and avoid such men as these.

6 For among them are those who enter into households and captivate weak women weighed down with sins, led on by various impulses,

7 always learning and never able to come to the knowledge of the truth.

8 And just as Jannes and Jambres opposed Moses, so these *men* also oppose the truth, men of depraved mind, rejected as regards the faith.

9 But they will not make further progress; for their folly will be obvious to all, as also that of those *two* came to be.

10 But you followed my teach-

ing, conduct, purpose, faith, patience, love, perseverance,

11 persecutions, *and* sufferings, such as happened to me at Antioch, at Iconium *and* at Lystra; what persecutions I endured, and out of them all the Lord delivered me!

12 And indeed, all who desire to live godly in Christ Jesus will be persecuted.

13 But evil men and impostors will proceed *from bad* to worse, deceiving and being deceived.

14 You, however, continue in the things you have learned and become convinced of, knowing from whom you have learned *them*;

15 and that from childhood you have known the sacred writings which are able to give you the wisdom that leads to salvation through faith which is in Christ Jesus.

16 [2]All Scripture is inspired by God and profitable for teaching, for reproof, for correction, for training in righteousness;

17 that the man of God may be adequate, equipped for every good work.

CHAPTER 4

I SOLEMNLY charge *you* in the presence of God and of Christ Jesus, who is to judge the living and the dead, and by His appearing and His kingdom:

2 preach the word; be ready in season *and* out of season; reprove, rebuke, exhort, with great patience and instruction.

3 For the time will come when they will not endure sound doctrine; but *wanting* to have their

[2] Or possibly, *Every Scripture inspired by God is also profitable*

ears tickled, they will accumulate for themselves teachers in accordance to their own desires;

4 and will turn away their ears from the truth, and will turn aside to myths.

5 But you, be sober in all things, endure hardship, do the work of an evangelist, fulfill your ministry.

6 For I am already being poured out as a drink offering, and the time of my departure has come.

7 I have fought the good fight, I have finished the course, I have kept the faith;

8 in the future there is laid up for me the crown of righteousness, which the Lord, the righteous Judge, will award to me on that day; and not only to me, but also to all who have loved His appearing.

9 Make every effort to come to me soon;

10 for Demas, having loved this present world, has deserted me and gone to Thessalonica; Crescens *has gone* to Galatia, Titus to Dalmatia.

11 Only Luke is with me. Pick up Mark and bring him with you, for he is useful to me for service.

12 But Tychicus I have sent to Ephesus.

13 When you come bring the cloak which I left at Troas with Carpus, and the books, especially the parchments.

14 Alexander the coppersmith did me much harm; the Lord will repay him according to his deeds.

15 Be on guard against him yourself, for he vigorously opposed our teaching.

16 At my first defense no one supported me, but all deserted me; may it not be counted against them.

17 But the Lord stood with me, and strengthened me, in order that through me the proclamation might be fully accomplished, and that all the Gentiles might hear; and I was delivered out of the lion's mouth.

18 The Lord will deliver me from every evil deed, and will bring me safely to His heavenly kingdom; to Him *be* the glory forever and ever. Amen.

19 Greet Prisca and Aquila, and the household of Onesiphorus.

20 Erastus remained at Corinth, but Trophimus I left sick at Miletus.

21 Make every effort to come before winter. Eubulus greets you, also Pudens and Linus and Claudia and all the brethren.

22 The Lord be with your spirit. Grace be with you.

TITUS

PAUL, a bond-servant of God, and an apostle of Jesus Christ, for the faith of those chosen of God and the knowledge of the truth which is according to godliness,

2 in the hope of eternal life, which God, who cannot lie, promised long ages ago,

3 but at the proper time manifested, *even* His word, in the proclamation with which I was entrusted according to the commandment of God our Savior;

4 to Titus, my true child in a common faith: Grace and peace from God the Father and Christ Jesus our Savior.

5 For this reason I left you in Crete, that you might set in order what remains, and appoint elders in every city as I directed you,

6 namely, if any man be above reproach, the husband of one wife, having children who believe, not accused of dissipation or rebellion.

7 For the overseer must be above reproach as God's steward, not self-willed, not quick-tempered, not addicted to wine, not pugnacious, not fond of sordid gain,

8 but hospitable, loving what is good, sensible, just, devout, self-controlled,

9 holding fast the faithful word which is in accordance with the teaching, that he may be able both to exhort in sound doctrine and to refute those who contradict.

10 For there are many rebellious men, empty talkers and deceivers, especially those of the circumcision,

11 who must be silenced because they are upsetting whole families, teaching things they should not *teach*, for the sake of sordid gain.

12 One of themselves, a prophet of their own, said, "Cretans are always liars, evil beasts, lazy gluttons."

13 This testimony is true. For this cause reprove them severely that they may be sound in the faith,

14 not paying attention to Jewish myths and commandments of men who turn away from the truth.

15 To the pure, all things are pure; but to those who are defiled and unbelieving, nothing is pure, but both their mind and their conscience are defiled.

16 They profess to know God, but by *their* deeds they deny Him, being detestable and disobedient, and worthless for any good deed.

CHAPTER 2

BUT as for you, speak the things which are fitting for sound doctrine.

2 Older men are to be temperate, dignified, sensible, sound in faith, in love, in perseverance.

3 Older women likewise are to be reverent in their behavior, not malicious gossips, nor enslaved to much wine, teaching what is good,

4 that they may encourage the young women to love their husbands, to love their children,

5 *to be* sensible, pure, workers at home, kind, being subject to their own husbands, that the word of God may not be dishonored.

6 Likewise urge the young men to be sensible;

7 in all things show yourself to be an example of good deeds, *with* purity in doctrine, dignified,

8 sound *in* speech which is beyond reproach, in order that the opponent may be put to shame, having nothing bad to say about us.

9 Urge bondslaves to be subject to their own masters in everything, to be well-pleasing, not argumentative,

10 not pilfering, but showing all good faith that they may adorn the doctrine of God our Savior in every respect.

11 For the grace of God has appeared, bringing salvation to all men,

12 instructing us to deny ungodliness and worldly desires and to live sensibly, righteously and godly in the present age,

13 looking for the blessed hope and the appearing of the glory of our great God and Savior, Christ Jesus;

14 who gave Himself for us, that He might redeem us from every lawless deed and purify for Himself a people for His own possession, zealous for good deeds.

15 These things speak and exhort and reprove with all authority. Let no one disregard you.

CHAPTER 3

REMIND them to be subject to rulers, to authorities, to be obedient, to be ready for every good deed,

2 to malign no one, to be uncontentious, gentle, showing every consideration for all men.

3 For we also once were foolish ourselves, disobedient, deceived, enslaved to various lusts and pleasures, spending our life in malice and envy, hateful, hating one another.

4 But when the kindness of God our Savior and *His* love for mankind appeared,

5 He saved us, not on the basis of deeds which we have done in righteousness, but according to His mercy, by the washing of regeneration and renewing by the Holy Spirit,

6 whom He poured out upon us richly through Jesus Christ our Savior,

7 that being justified by His grace we might be made heirs according to *the* hope of eternal life.

8 This is a trustworthy statement; and concerning these things I want you to speak confidently, so that those who have believed God may be careful to engage in good deeds. These things are good and profitable for men.

9 But shun foolish controversies and genealogies and strife and disputes about the Law; for they are unprofitable and worthless.

10 Reject a factious man after a first and second warning,

11 knowing that such a man is perverted and is sinning, being self-condemned.

12 When I send Artemas or Tychicus to you, make every effort to come to me at Nicopolis, for I have decided to spend the winter there.

13 Diligently help Zenas the lawyer and Apollos on their way so that nothing is lacking for them.

14 And let our *people* also learn to engage in good deeds to meet pressing needs, that they may not be unfruitful.

15 All who are with me greet you. Greet those who love us in *the* faith.

Grace be with you all.

THE EPISTLE OF PAUL TO

PHILEMON

PAUL, a prisoner of Christ Jesus, and Timothy our brother, to Philemon our beloved *brother* and fellow worker,

2 and to Apphia our sister, and to Archippus our fellow soldier, and to the church in your house:

3 Grace to you and peace from God our Father and the Lord Jesus Christ.

4 I thank my God always, making mention of you in my prayers,

5 because I hear of your love, and of the faith which you have toward the Lord Jesus, and toward all the saints;

6 *and I pray* that the fellowship of your faith may become effective [1]through the knowledge of every good thing which is in [2]you for Christ's sake.

7 For I have come to have much joy and comfort in your love, because the hearts of the saints have been refreshed through you, brother.

8 Therefore, though I have

enough confidence in Christ to order you *to do* that which is proper,

9 yet for love's sake I rather appeal *to you*—since I am such a person as Paul, the aged, and now also a prisoner of Christ Jesus—

10 I appeal to you for my child, whom I have begotten in my imprisonment, [3]Onesimus,

11 who formerly was useless to you, but now is useful both to you and to me.

12 And I have sent him back to you in person, that is, *sending* my very heart,

13 whom I wished to keep with me, that in your behalf he might minister to me in my imprisonment for the gospel;

14 but without your consent I did not want to do anything, that your goodness should not be as it were by compulsion, but of your own free will.

[1] Or, *in*
[2] Some ancient mss. read *us*   [3] I.e., useful

15 For perhaps he was for this reason parted *from you* for a while, that you should have him back forever,

16 no longer as a slave, but more than a slave, a beloved brother, especially to me, but how much more to you, both in the flesh and in the Lord.

17 If then you regard me a partner, accept him as *you would* me.

18 But if he has wronged you in any way, or owes you anything, charge that to my account;

19 I, Paul, am writing this with my own hand, I will repay it (lest I should mention to you that you owe to me even your own self as well).

20 Yes, brother, let me benefit from you in the Lord; refresh my heart in Christ.

21 Having confidence in your obedience, I write to you, since I know that you will do even more than what I say.

22 And at the same time also prepare me a lodging; for I hope that through your prayers I shall be given to you.

23 Epaphras, my fellow prisoner in Christ Jesus, greets you,

24 *as do* Mark, Aristarchus, Demas, Luke, my fellow workers.

25 The grace of the Lord Jesus Christ be with your spirit.[4]

⁴ Some ancient mss. add *Amen*

THE EPISTLE TO THE

HEBREWS

GOD, after He spoke long ago to the fathers in the prophets in many portions and in many ways,

2 in these last days has spoken to us in *His* Son, whom He appointed heir of all things, through whom also He made the world.

3 And He is the radiance of His glory and the exact representation of His nature, and upholds all things by the word of His power. When He had made purification of sins, He sat down at the right hand of the Majesty on high;

4 having become as much better than the angels, as He has inherited a more excellent name than they.

5 For to which of the angels did He ever say,

"THOU ART MY SON,
    TODAY I HAVE BEGOTTEN
        THEE"?
And again,
    "I WILL BE A FATHER TO
        HIM,
    AND HE SHALL BE A SON TO
        ME"?

6 And when He again brings the first-born into the world, He says,

"AND LET ALL THE ANGELS
    OF GOD WORSHIP HIM."

7 And of the angels He says,
"WHO MAKES HIS ANGELS
    WINDS,
    AND HIS MINISTERS A
        FLAME OF FIRE."

8 But of the Son *He says,*
> "THY THRONE, O GOD, IS
>   FOREVER AND EVER,
> AND THE RIGHTEOUS SCEP-
>   TER IS THE SCEPTER OF
>   [1]HIS KINGDOM.

9 "THOU HAST LOVED RIGHT-
>   EOUSNESS   AND   HATED
>   LAWLESSNESS;
> THEREFORE GOD, THY GOD,
>   HATH ANOINTED THEE
> WITH THE OIL OF GLADNESS
>   ABOVE THY COMPANIONS."

10 And,
> "THOU, LORD, IN THE BEGIN-
>   NING   DIDST   LAY   THE
>   FOUNDATION   OF   THE
>   EARTH,
> AND THE HEAVENS ARE THE
>   WORKS OF THY HANDS;

11 THEY WILL PERISH, BUT
>   THOU REMAINEST;
> AND THEY ALL WILL BE-
>   COME OLD AS A GARMENT,

12 AND AS A MANTLE THOU
>   WILT ROLL THEM UP;
> AS A GARMENT THEY WILL
>   ALSO BE CHANGED.
> BUT THOU ART THE SAME,
> AND THY YEARS WILL NOT
>   COME TO AN END."

13 But to which of the angels
has He ever said,
> "SIT AT MY RIGHT HAND,
> UNTIL I MAKE THINE EN-
>   EMIES
> A   FOOTSTOOL   FOR   THY
>   FEET"?

14 Are they not all ministering
spirits, sent out to render service
for the sake of those who will inherit salvation?

CHAPTER 2

FOR this reason we must pay
much closer attention to what
we have heard, lest we drift away
from it.

2 For if the word spoken
through angels proved unalter-
able, and every transgression and
disobedience received a just recompense,

3 how shall we escape if we
neglect so great a salvation? After it was at the first spoken
through the Lord, it was confirmed to us by those who heard,

4 God also bearing witness
with them, both by signs and
wonders and by various miracles
and by gifts of the Holy Spirit according to His own will.

5 For He did not subject to
angels the world to come, concerning which we are speaking.

6 But one has testified somewhere, saying,
> "WHAT IS MAN, THAT THOU
>   REMEMBEREST HIM?
> OR THE SON OF MAN, THAT
>   THOU   ART   CONCERNED
>   ABOUT HIM?

7 "THOU HAST MADE HIM FOR
>   A   LITTLE   WHILE   LOWER
>   THAN THE ANGELS;
> THOU HAST CROWNED HIM
>   WITH GLORY AND HONOR,
> [2]AND HAST APPOINTED HIM
>   OVER THE WORKS OF THY
>   HANDS;

8 THOU HAST PUT ALL THINGS
>   IN SUBJECTION UNDER HIS
>   FEET."

For in subjecting all things to
him, He left nothing that is not
subject to him. But now we do
not yet see all things subjected to
him.

9 But we do see Him who has
been made for a little while lower
than the angels, *namely,* Jesus,
because of the suffering of death

---

[1] Some mss. read *Thy*
[2] Some ancient mss. do not contain
And . . . hands

crowned with glory and honor, that by the grace of God He might taste death for everyone.

10 For it was fitting for Him, for whom are all things, and through whom are all things, in bringing many sons to glory, to perfect the author of their salvation through sufferings.

11 For both He who sanctifies and those who are sanctified are all from one *Father;* for which reason He is not ashamed to call them brethren,

12 saying,

"I WILL PROCLAIM THY NAME
TO MY BRETHREN,
IN THE MIDST OF THE CON-
GREGATION I WILL SING
THY PRAISE."

13 And again,

"I WILL PUT MY TRUST IN
HIM."

And again,

"BEHOLD, I AND THE CHIL-
DREN WHOM GOD HAS GIV-
EN ME."

14 Since then the children share in flesh and blood, He Himself likewise also partook of the same, that through death He might render powerless him who had the power of death, that is, the devil;

15 and might deliver those who through fear of death were subject to slavery all their lives.

16 For assuredly He does not give help to angels, but He gives help to the descendant of Abraham.

17 Therefore, He had to be made like His brethren in all things, that He might become a merciful and faithful high priest in things pertaining to God, to make propitiation for the sins of the people.

18 For since He Himself was tempted in that which He has suffered, He is able to come to the aid of those who are tempted.

CHAPTER 3

THEREFORE, holy brethren, partakers of a heavenly calling, consider Jesus, the Apostle and High Priest of our confession.

2 He was faithful to Him who appointed Him, as Moses also was in all His house.

3 For He has been counted worthy of more glory than Moses, by just so much as the builder of the house has more honor than the house.

4 For every house is built by someone, but the builder of all things is God.

5 Now Moses was faithful in all His house as a servant, for a testimony of those things which were to be spoken later;

6 but Christ *was faithful* as a Son over His house whose house we are, if we hold fast our confidence and the boast of our hope firm until the end.

7 Therefore, just as the Holy Spirit says,

"TODAY IF YOU HEAR HIS
VOICE,

8 DO NOT HARDEN YOUR
HEARTS AS WHEN THEY
PROVOKED ME,
AS IN THE DAY OF TRIAL IN
THE WILDERNESS,

9 WHERE YOUR FATHERS
TRIED *Me* BY TESTING *Me,*
AND SAW MY WORKS FOR
FORTY YEARS.

10 "THEREFORE I WAS ANGRY
WITH THIS GENERATION,
AND SAID, 'THEY ALWAYS
GO ASTRAY IN THEIR
HEART;

AND THEY DID NOT KNOW
MY WAYS';

11 As I SWORE IN MY WRATH,
'THEY SHALL NOT ENTER MY
REST.' "

12 Take care, brethren, lest
there should be in any one of you
an evil, unbelieving heart, in falling away from the living God.

13 But encourage one another
day after day, as long as it is *still*
called "Today," lest any one of
you be hardened by the deceitfulness of sin.

14 For we have become partakers of Christ, if we hold fast the
beginning of our assurance firm
until the end;

15 while it is said,

"TODAY IF YOU HEAR HIS
VOICE,
DO NOT HARDEN YOUR
HEARTS, AS WHEN THEY
PROVOKED ME."

16 For who provoked *Him*
when they had heard? Indeed,
did not all those who came out of
Egypt *led* by Moses?

17 And with whom was He angry for forty years? Was it not
with those who sinned, whose
bodies fell in the wilderness?

18 And to whom did He swear
that they should not enter His
rest, but to those who were disobedient?

19 And *so* we see that they
were not able to enter because of
unbelief.

CHAPTER 4

THEREFORE, let us fear lest,
while a promise remains of
entering His rest, any one of you
should seem to have come short
of it.

2 For indeed we have had
good news preached to us, just as

they also; but the word they
heard did not profit them, because it was not united by faith
in those who heard.

3 [3]For we who have believed
enter that rest, just as He has
said,

"AS I SWORE IN MY WRATH,
THEY SHALL NOT ENTER MY
REST,"

although His works were finished
from the foundation of the world.

4 For He has thus said somewhere concerning the seventh
day, "AND GOD RESTED ON THE
SEVENTH DAY FROM ALL HIS
WORKS";

5 and again in this *passage,*
"THEY SHALL NOT ENTER MY
REST."

6 Since therefore it remains
for some to enter it, and those
who formerly had good news
preached to them failed to enter
because of disobedience,

7 He again fixes a certain day,
"Today," saying through David
after so long a time just as has
been said before,

"TODAY IF YOU HEAR HIS
VOICE,
DO NOT HARDEN YOUR
HEARTS."

8 For if Joshua had given
them rest, He would not have
spoken of another day after that.

9 There remains therefore a
Sabbath rest for the people of
God.

10 For the one who has entered
His rest has himself also rested
from his works, as God did from
His.

11 Let us therefore be diligent
to enter that rest, lest anyone fall
through *following* the same example of disobedience.

[3] Some ancient mss. read *Therefore*

12 For the word of God is living and active and sharper than any two-edged sword, and piercing as far as the division of soul and spirit, of both joints and marrow, and able to judge the thoughts and intentions of the heart.

13 And there is no creature hidden from His sight, but all things are open and laid bare to the eyes of Him with whom we have to do.

14 Since then we have a great high priest who has passed through the heavens, Jesus the Son of God, let us hold fast our confession.

15 For we do not have a high priest who cannot sympathize with our weaknesses, but one who has been tempted in all things as *we are, yet* without sin.

16 Let us therefore draw near with confidence to the throne of grace, that we may receive mercy and may find grace to help in time of need.

CHAPTER 5

FOR every high priest taken from among men is appointed on behalf of men in things pertaining to God, in order to offer both gifts and sacrifices for sins;

2 he can deal gently with the ignorant and misguided, since he himself also is beset with weakness;

3 and because of it he is obligated to offer *sacrifices* for sins, as for the people, so also for himself.

4 And no one takes the honor to himself, but *receives it* when he is called by God, even as Aaron was.

5 So also Christ did not glorify Himself so as to become a high priest, but He who said to Him,

"THOU ART MY SON,
TODAY I HAVE BEGOTTEN THEE";

6 just as He says also in another *passage,*

"THOU ART A PRIEST FOREVER
ACCORDING TO THE ORDER OF MELCHIZEDEK."

7 In the days of His flesh, He offered up both prayers and supplications with loud crying and tears to the One able to save Him from death, and He was heard because of His piety.

8 Although He was a Son, He learned obedience from the things which He suffered.

9 And having been made perfect, He became to all those who obey Him the source of eternal salvation,

10 being designated by God as a high priest according to the order of Melchizedek.

11 Concerning 4him we have much to say, and *it is* hard to explain, since you have become dull of hearing.

12 For though by this time you ought to be teachers, you have need again for someone to teach you the elementary principles of the oracles of God, and you have come to need milk and not solid food.

13 For everyone who partakes *only* of milk is not accustomed to the word of righteousness, for he is a babe.

14 But solid food is for the mature, who because of practice have their senses trained to discern good and evil.

4 Or, *Him; or, this*

CHAPTER 6

THEREFORE leaving the elementary teaching about the Christ, let us press on to maturity, not laying again a foundation of repentance from dead works and of faith toward God,

2 of instruction about washings, and laying on of hands, and the resurrection of the dead, and eternal judgment.

3 And this we shall do, if God permits.

4 For in the case of those who have once been enlightened and have tasted of the heavenly gift and have been made partakers of the Holy Spirit,

5 and have tasted the good word of God and the powers of the age to come,

6 and *then* have fallen away, it is impossible to renew them again to repentance, since they again crucify to themselves the Son of God, and put Him to open shame.

7 For ground that drinks the rain which often falls upon it and brings forth vegetation useful to those for whose sake it is also tilled, receives a blessing from God;

8 but if it yields thorns and thistles, it is worthless and close to being cursed, and it ends up being burned.

9 But, beloved, we are convinced of better things concerning you, and things that accompany salvation, though we are speaking in this way.

10 For God is not unjust so as to forget your work and the love which you have shown toward His name, in having ministered and in still ministering to the saints.

11 And we desire that each one of you show the same diligence so as to realize the full assurance of hope until the end,

12 that you may not be sluggish, but imitators of those who through faith and patience inherit the promises.

13 For when God made the promise to Abraham, since He could swear by no one greater, He swore by Himself,

14 saying, "I WILL SURELY BLESS YOU, AND I WILL SURELY MULTIPLY YOU."

15 And thus, having patiently waited, he obtained the promise.

16 For men swear by one greater *than themselves,* and with them an oath *given* as confirmation is an end of every dispute.

17 In the same way God, desiring even more to show to the heirs of the promise the unchangeableness of His purpose, interposed with an oath,

18 in order that by two unchangeable things, in which it is impossible for God to lie, we may have strong encouragement, we who have fled for refuge in laying hold of the hope set before us.

19 This hope we have as an anchor of the soul, a *hope* both sure and steadfast and one which enters within the veil,

20 where Jesus has entered as a forerunner for us, having become a high priest forever according to the order of Melchizedek.

CHAPTER 7

FOR this Melchizedek, king of Salem, priest of the Most High God, who met Abraham as he was returning from the slaughter of the kings and blessed him,

2 to whom also Abraham apportioned a tenth part of all *the spoils*, was first of all, by the translation *of his name*, king of righteousness, and then also king of Salem, which is king of peace.

3 Without father, without mother, without genealogy, having neither beginning of days nor end of life, but made like the Son of God, he abides a priest perpetually.

4 Now observe how great this man was to whom Abraham, the patriarch, gave a tenth of the choicest spoils.

5 And those indeed of the sons of Levi who receive the priest's office have commandment in the Law to collect a tenth from the people, that is, from their brethren, although these are descended from Abraham.

6 But the one whose genealogy is not traced from them collected a tenth from Abraham, and blessed the one who had the promises.

7 But without any dispute the lesser is blessed by the greater.

8 And in this case mortal men receive tithes, but in that case one *receives them*, of whom it is witnessed that he lives on.

9 And, so to speak, through Abraham even Levi, who received tithes, paid tithes,

10 for he was still in the loins of his father when Melchizedek met him.

11 Now if perfection was through the Levitical priesthood (for on the basis of it the people received the Law), what further need *was there* for another priest to arise according to the order of Melchizedek, and not be desig-

nated according to the order of Aaron?

12 For when the priesthood is changed, of necessity there takes place a change of law also.

13 For the one concerning whom these things are spoken belongs to another tribe, from which no one has officiated at the altar.

14 For it is evident that our Lord was descended from Judah, a tribe with reference to which Moses spoke nothing concerning priests.

15 And this is clearer still, if another priest arises according to the likeness of Melchizedek,

16 who has become *such* on the basis of a law of physical requirement, but according to the power of an indestructible life.

17 For it is witnessed *of Him*,
"Thou art a priest forever
According to the order of Melchizedek."

18 For, on the one hand, there is a setting aside of a former commandment because of its weakness and uselessness

19 (for the Law made nothing perfect), and on the other hand there is a bringing in of a better hope, through which we draw near to God.

20 And inasmuch as *it was* not without an oath

21 (for they indeed became priests without an oath, but He with an oath through the One who said to Him,
"The Lord has sworn
And will not change His mind,
'Thou art a priest forever'");

22 so much the more also Jesus

has become the guarantee of a better covenant.

23 And the *former* priests, on the one hand, existed in greater numbers, because they were prevented by death from continuing,

24 but He, on the other hand, because He abides forever, holds His priesthood permanently.

25 Hence, also, He is able to save forever those who draw near to God through Him, since He always lives to make intercession for them.

26 For it was fitting that we should have such a high priest, holy, innocent, undefiled, separated from sinners and exalted above the heavens;

27 who does not need daily, like those high priests, to offer up sacrifices, first for His own sins, and then for the *sins* of the people, because this He did once for all when He offered up Himself.

28 For the Law appoints men as high priests who are weak, but the word of the oath, which came after the Law, *appoints* a Son, made perfect forever.

CHAPTER 8

NOW the main point in what has been said *is this*: we have such a high priest, who has taken His seat at the right hand of the throne of the Majesty in the heavens,

2 a minister in the sanctuary, and in the true tabernacle, which the Lord pitched, not man.

3 For every high priest is appointed to offer both gifts and sacrifices; hence it is necessary that this *high priest* also have something to offer.

4 Now if He were on earth, He would not be a priest at all, since there are those who offer the gifts according to the Law;

5 who serve a copy and shadow of the heavenly things, just as Moses was warned *by* God when he was about to erect the tabernacle; for, "SEE," He says, "THAT YOU MAKE all things ACCORDING TO THE PATTERN WHICH WAS SHOWN YOU ON THE MOUNTAIN."

6 But now He has obtained a more excellent ministry, by as much as He is also the mediator of a better covenant, which has been enacted on better promises.

7 For if that first *covenant* had been faultless, there would have been no occasion sought for a second.

8 For finding fault with them, He says,

"BEHOLD, DAYS ARE COMING,
    SAYS THE LORD,
    WHEN I WILL EFFECT A
      NEW COVENANT
    WITH THE HOUSE OF ISRAEL
      AND WITH THE HOUSE OF
      JUDAH;
9 NOT LIKE THE COVENANT
    WHICH I MADE WITH THEIR
      FATHERS
    ON THE DAY WHEN I TOOK
      THEM BY THE HAND
    TO LEAD THEM OUT OF THE
      LAND OF EGYPT;
    FOR THEY DID NOT CON-
      TINUE IN MY COVENANT,
    AND I DID NOT CARE FOR
      THEM, SAYS THE LORD.
10 "FOR THIS IS THE COVENANT
    THAT I WILL MAKE WITH
      THE HOUSE OF ISRAEL
    AFTER THOSE DAYS, SAYS
      THE LORD:
    I WILL PUT MY LAWS INTO
      THEIR MINDS,
    AND I WILL WRITE THEM
      UPON THEIR HEARTS.

AND I WILL BE THEIR GOD,
AND THEY SHALL BE MY
PEOPLE.

11 "AND THEY SHALL NOT
TEACH EVERYONE HIS FEL-
LOW CITIZEN,
AND EVERYONE HIS
BROTHER, SAYING, 'KNOW
THE LORD,'
FOR ALL SHALL KNOW ME,
FROM THE LEAST TO THE
GREATEST OF THEM.

12 "FOR I WILL BE MERCIFUL TO
THEIR INIQUITIES,
AND I WILL REMEMBER
THEIR SINS NO MORE."

13 When He said, "A new covenant," He has made the first obsolete. But whatever is becoming
obsolete and growing old is
ready to disappear.

CHAPTER 9

NOW even the first covenant
had regulations of divine
worship and the earthly sanctuary.

2 For there was a tabernacle
prepared, the outer one, in which
were the lampstand and the table
and the sacred bread; this is
called the holy place.

3 And behind the second veil,
there was a tabernacle which is
called the Holy of Holies,

4 having a golden altar of incense and the ark of the covenant
covered on all sides with gold, in
which was a golden jar holding
the manna, and Aaron's rod
which budded, and the tables of
the covenant.

5 And above it were the
cherubim of glory overshadowing the mercy seat; but of these
things we cannot now speak in
detail.

6 Now when these things
have been thus prepared, the
priests are continually entering
the outer tabernacle, performing
the divine worship,

7 but into the second only the
high priest enters, once a year,
not without taking blood, which
he offers for himself and for the
sins of the people committed in
ignorance.

8 The Holy Spirit is signifying
this, that the way into the holy
place has not yet been disclosed,
while the outer tabernacle is still
standing,

9 which is a symbol for the
present time. Accordingly both
gifts and sacrifices are offered
which cannot make the worshiper perfect in conscience,

10 since they relate only to
food and drink and various washings, regulations for the body im-
posed until a time of reformation.

11 But when Christ appeared
as a high priest of the good
things [5]to come, He entered
through the greater and more
perfect tabernacle, not made
with hands, that is to say, not of
this creation;

12 and not through the blood of
goats and calves, but through His
own blood, He entered the holy
place once for all, having obtained eternal redemption.

13 For if the blood of goats and
bulls and the ashes of a heifer
sprinkling those who have been
defiled, sanctify for the cleansing
of the flesh,

14 how much more will the
blood of Christ, who through the
eternal Spirit offered Himself
without blemish to God, cleanse
your conscience from dead
works to serve the living God?

15 And for this reason He is the

[5] Some ancient mss. read that have come

mediator of a new covenant, in order that since a death has taken place for the redemption of the transgressions that were *committed* under the first covenant, those who have been called may receive the promise of the eternal inheritance.

16 For where a covenant is, there must of necessity be the death of the one who made it.

17 For a covenant is valid *only* when men are dead, [6]for it is never in force while the one who made it lives.

18 Therefore even the first *covenant* was not inaugurated without blood.

19 For when every commandment had been spoken by Moses to all the people according to the Law, he took the blood of the calves and the goats, with water and scarlet wool and hyssop, and sprinkled both the book itself and all the people,

20 saying, "THIS IS THE BLOOD OF THE COVENANT WHICH GOD COMMANDED YOU."

21 And in the same way he sprinkled both the tabernacle and all the vessels of the ministry with the blood.

22 And according to the Law, *one may* almost *say*, all things are cleansed with blood, and without shedding of blood there is no forgiveness.

23 Therefore it was necessary for the copies of the things in the heavens to be cleansed with these, but the heavenly things themselves with better sacrifices than these.

24 For Christ did not enter a holy place made with hands, a *mere* copy of the true one, but into heaven itself, now to appear in the presence of God for us;

25 nor was it that He should offer Himself often, as the high priest enters the holy place year by year with blood not his own.

26 Otherwise, He would have needed to suffer often since the foundation of the world; but now once at the consummation of the ages He has been manifested to put away sin by the sacrifice of Himself.

27 And inasmuch as it is appointed for men to die once and after this *comes* judgment,

28 so Christ also, having been offered once to bear the sins of many, shall appear a second time for salvation without *reference to* sin, to those who eagerly await Him.

CHAPTER 10

FOR the Law, since it has *only* a shadow of the good things to come *and* not the very form of things, [7]can never by the same sacrifices year by year, which they offer continually, make perfect those who draw near.

2 Otherwise, would they not have ceased to be offered, because the worshipers, having once been cleansed, would no longer have had consciousness of sins?

3 But in those *sacrifices* there is a reminder of sins year by year.

4 For it is impossible for the blood of bulls and goats to take away sins.

5 Therefore, when He comes into the world, He says,

"SACRIFICE AND OFFERING
THOU HAST NOT DESIRED,

---

[6] Some ancient mss. read *for is it then . . . lives?*

[7] Some ancient mss. read *they can*

BUT A BODY THOU HAST PREPARED FOR ME;

6 IN WHOLE BURNT OFFERINGS AND *sacrifices* FOR SIN THOU HAST TAKEN NO PLEASURE.

7 "THEN I SAID, 'BEHOLD, I HAVE COME (IN THE ROLL OF THE BOOK IT IS WRITTEN OF ME) TO DO THY WILL, O GOD.'"

8 After saying above, "SACRIFICES AND OFFERINGS AND WHOLE BURNT OFFERINGS AND *sacrifices* FOR SIN THOU HAST NOT DESIRED, NOR HAST THOU TAKEN PLEASURE *in them*" (which are offered according to the Law),

9 then He said, "BEHOLD, I HAVE COME TO DO THY WILL." He takes away the first in order to establish the second.

10 By this will we have been sanctified through the offering of the body of Jesus Christ once for all.

11 And every priest stands daily ministering and offering time after time the same sacrifices, which can never take away sins;

12 but He, having offered one sacrifice for sins for all time, SAT DOWN AT THE RIGHT HAND OF GOD,

13 waiting from that time onward UNTIL HIS ENEMIES BE MADE A FOOTSTOOL FOR HIS FEET.

14 For by one offering He has perfected for all time those who are sanctified.

15 And the Holy Spirit also bears witness to us; for after saying,

16 "THIS IS THE COVENANT THAT I WILL MAKE WITH THEM AFTER THOSE DAYS, SAYS THE LORD:

I WILL PUT MY LAWS UPON THEIR HEART, AND UPON THEIR MIND I WILL WRITE THEM,"

He then says,

17 "AND THEIR SINS AND THEIR LAWLESS DEEDS I WILL REMEMBER NO MORE."

18 Now where there is forgiveness of these things, there is no longer *any* offering for sin.

19 Since therefore, brethren, we have confidence to enter the holy place by the blood of Jesus,

20 by a new and living way which He inaugurated for us through the veil, that is, His flesh,

21 and since *we have* a great priest over the house of God,

22 let us draw near with a sincere heart in full assurance of faith, having our hearts sprinkled *clean* from an evil conscience and our bodies washed with pure water.

23 Let us hold fast the confession of our hope without wavering, for He who promised is faithful;

24 and let us consider how to stimulate one another to love and good deeds,

25 not forsaking our own assembling together, as is the habit of some, but encouraging *one another*; and all the more, as you see the day drawing near.

26 For if we go on sinning willfully after receiving the knowledge of the truth, there no longer remains a sacrifice for sins,

27 but a certain terrifying expectation of judgment, and THE FURY OF A FIRE WHICH WILL CONSUME THE ADVERSARIES.

28 Anyone who has set aside the Law of Moses dies without

mercy on *the testimony of* two or three witnesses.

29 How much severer punishment do you think he will deserve who has trampled under foot the Son of God, and has regarded as unclean the blood of the covenant by which he was sanctified, and has insulted the Spirit of grace?

30 For we know Him who said, "VENGEANCE IS MINE, I WILL REPAY." And again, "THE LORD WILL JUDGE HIS PEOPLE."

31 It is a terrifying thing to fall into the hands of the living God.

32 But remember the former days, when, after being enlightened, you endured a great conflict of sufferings,

33 partly, by being made a public spectacle through reproaches and tribulations, and partly by becoming sharers with those who were so treated.

34 For you showed sympathy to the prisoners, and accepted joyfully the seizure of your property, knowing that you have for yourselves a better possession and an abiding one.

35 Therefore, do not throw away your confidence, which has a great reward.

36 For you have need of endurance, so that when you have done the will of God, you may receive what was promised.

37 FOR YET IN A VERY LITTLE
WHILE,
HE WHO IS COMING WILL
COME, AND WILL NOT DELAY.

38 BUT MY RIGHTEOUS ONE
SHALL LIVE BY FAITH;
AND IF HE SHRINKS BACK,
MY SOUL HAS NO PLEASURE IN HIM.

39 But we are not of those who shrink back to destruction, but of those who have faith to the preserving of the soul.

CHAPTER 11

NOW faith is the assurance of *things* hoped for, the conviction of things not seen.

2 For by it the men of old gained approval.

3 By faith we understand that the worlds were prepared by the word of God, so that what is seen was not made out of things which are visible.

4 By faith Abel offered to God a better sacrifice than Cain, through which he obtained the testimony that he was righteous, God testifying about his gifts, and through faith, though he is dead, he still speaks.

5 By faith Enoch was taken up so that he should not see death; AND HE WAS NOT FOUND BECAUSE GOD TOOK HIM UP; for he obtained the witness that before his being taken up he was pleasing to God.

6 And without faith it is impossible to please *Him*, for he who comes to God must believe that He is, and *that* He is a rewarder of those who seek Him.

7 By faith Noah, being warned *by God* about things not yet seen, in reverence prepared an ark for the salvation of his household, by which he condemned the world, and became an heir of the righteousness which is according to faith.

8 By faith Abraham, when he was called, obeyed by going out to a place which he was to receive for an inheritance; and he went out, not knowing where he was going.

9 By faith he lived as an alien in the land of promise, as in a foreign land, dwelling in tents with Isaac and Jacob, fellow heirs of the same promise;

10 for he was looking for the city which has foundations, whose architect and builder is God.

11 By faith even Sarah herself received ability to conceive, even beyond the proper time of life, since she considered Him faithful who had promised;

12 therefore, also, there was born of one man, and him as good as dead at that, *as many descendants* AS THE STARS OF HEAVEN IN NUMBER, AND INNUMERABLE AS THE SAND WHICH IS BY THE SEASHORE.

13 All these died in faith, without receiving the promises, but having seen them and having welcomed them from a distance, and having confessed that they were strangers and exiles on the earth.

14 For those who say such things make it clear that they are seeking a country of their own.

15 And indeed if they had been thinking of that *country* from which they went out, they would have had opportunity to return.

16 But as it is, they desire a better *country*, that is a heavenly one. Therefore God is not ashamed to be called their God; for He has prepared a city for them.

17 By faith Abraham, when he was tested, offered up Isaac; and he who had received the promises was offering up his only begotten *son*;

18 *it was he* to whom it was said, "IN ISAAC YOUR DESCENDANTS SHALL BE CALLED."

19 He considered that God is able to raise *men* even from the dead; from which he also received him back as a type.

20 By faith Isaac blessed Jacob and Esau, even regarding things to come.

21 By faith Jacob, as he was dying, blessed each of the sons of Joseph, and worshiped, *leaning* on the top of his staff.

22 By faith Joseph, when he was dying, made mention of the exodus of the sons of Israel, and gave orders concerning his bones.

23 By faith Moses, when he was born, was hidden for three months by his parents, because they saw he was a beautiful child; and they were not afraid of the king's edict.

24 By faith Moses, when he had grown up, refused to be called the son of Pharaoh's daughter;

25 choosing rather to endure ill-treatment with the people of God, than to enjoy the passing pleasures of sin;

26 considering the reproach of Christ greater riches than the treasures of Egypt; for he was looking to the reward.

27 By faith he left Egypt, not fearing the wrath of the king; for he endured, as seeing Him who is unseen.

28 By faith he kept the Passover and the sprinkling of the blood, so that he who destroyed the first-born might not touch them.

29 By faith they passed through the Red Sea as though *they were passing* through dry land; and the Egyptians, when they attempted it, were drowned.

30 By faith the walls of Jericho fell down, after they had been encircled for seven days.

31 By faith Rahab the harlot did not perish along with those who were disobedient, after she had welcomed the spies in peace.

32 And what more shall I say? For time will fail me if I tell of Gideon, Barak, Samson, Jephthah, of David and Samuel and the prophets,

33 who by faith conquered kingdoms, performed *acts of righteousness*, obtained promises, shut the mouths of lions,

34 quenched the power of fire, escaped the edge of the sword, from weakness were made strong, became mighty in war, put foreign armies to flight.

35 Women received *back* their dead by resurrection; and others were tortured, not accepting their release, in order that they might obtain a better resurrection;

36 and others experienced mockings and scourgings, yes, also chains and imprisonment.

37 They were stoned, they were sawn in two, [8]they were tempted, they were put to death with the sword; they went about in sheepskins, in goatskins, being destitute, afflicted, ill-treated

38 (*men* of whom the world was not worthy), wandering in deserts and mountains and caves and holes in the ground.

39 And all these, having gained approval through their faith, did not receive what was promised,

40 because God had provided something better for us, so that apart from us they should not be made perfect.

CHAPTER 12

THEREFORE, since we have so great a cloud of witnesses surrounding us, let us also lay aside every encumbrance, and the sin which so easily entangles us, and let us run with endurance the race that is set before us,

2 fixing our eyes on Jesus, the author and perfecter of faith, who for the joy set before Him endured the cross, despising the shame, and has sat down at the right hand of the throne of God.

3 For consider Him who has endured such hostility by sinners against Himself, so that you may not grow weary and lose heart.

4 You have not yet resisted to the point of shedding blood in your striving against sin;

5 and you have forgotten the exhortation which is addressed to you as sons,

"MY SON, DO NOT REGARD LIGHTLY THE DISCIPLINE OF THE LORD,
   NOR FAINT WHEN YOU ARE REPROVED BY HIM;
6 FOR THOSE WHOM THE LORD LOVES HE DISCIPLINES,
   AND HE SCOURGES EVERY SON WHOM HE RECEIVES."

7 It is for discipline that you endure; God deals with you as with sons; for what son is there whom *his* father does not discipline?

8 But if you are without discipline, of which all have become partakers, then you are illegitimate children and not sons.

9 Furthermore, we had earthly fathers to discipline us, and we respected them; shall we

[8] Some mss. do not contain *they were tempted*

not much rather be subject to the Father of spirits, and live?

10 For they disciplined us for a short time as seemed best to them, but He disciplines us for *our* good, that we may share His holiness.

11 All discipline for the moment seems not to be joyful, but sorrowful; yet to those who have been trained by it, afterwards it yields the peaceful fruit of righteousness.

12 Therefore, strengthen the hands that are weak and the knees that are feeble,

13 and make straight paths for your feet, so that *the limb* which is lame may not be put out of joint, but rather be healed.

14 Pursue peace with all men, and the sanctification without which no one will see the Lord.

15 See to it that no one comes short of the grace of God; that no root of bitterness springing up causes trouble, and by it many be defiled;

16 that *there be* no immoral or godless person like Esau, who sold his own birthright for a *single* meal.

17 For you know that even afterwards, when he desired to inherit the blessing, he was rejected, for he found no place for repentance, though he sought for it with tears.

18 For you have not come to *a mountain* that may be touched and to a blazing fire, and to darkness and gloom and whirlwind,

19 and to the blast of a trumpet and the sound of words which *sound was such that* those who heard begged that no further word should be spoken to them.

20 For they could not bear the command, "IF EVEN A BEAST

TOUCHES THE MOUNTAIN, IT WILL BE STONED."

21 And so terrible was the sight, *that* Moses said, "I AM FULL OF FEAR and trembling."

22 But you have come to Mount Zion and to the city of the living God, the heavenly Jerusalem, and to myriads of angels,

23 to the general assembly and church of the first-born who are enrolled in heaven, and to God, the Judge of all, and to the spirits of righteous men made perfect,

24 and to Jesus, the mediator of a new covenant, and to the sprinkled blood, which speaks better than *the blood* of Abel.

25 See to it that you do not refuse Him who is speaking. For if those did not escape when they refused him who warned *them* on earth, much less *shall* we *escape* who turn away from Him who *warns* from heaven.

26 And His voice shook the earth then, but now He has promised, saying, "YET ONCE MORE I WILL SHAKE NOT ONLY THE EARTH, BUT ALSO THE HEAVEN."

27 And this *expression*, "Yet once more," denotes the removing of those things which can be shaken, as of created things, in order that those things which cannot be shaken may remain.

28 Therefore, since we receive a kingdom which cannot be shaken, let us show gratitude, by which we may offer to God an acceptable service with reverence and awe;

29 for our God is a consuming fire.

CHAPTER 13

LET love of the brethren continue.

2 Do not neglect to show

hospitality to strangers, for by this some have entertained angels without knowing it.

3 Remember the prisoners, as though in prison with them, and those who are ill-treated, since you yourselves also are in the body.

4 *Let* marriage *be held* in honor among all, and let the *marriage* bed *be* undefiled; for fornicators and adulterers God will judge.

5 Let your character be free from the love of money, being content with what you have; for He Himself has said, "I WILL NEVER DESERT YOU, NOR WILL I EVER FORSAKE YOU,"

6 so that we confidently say,

"THE LORD IS MY HELPER, I WILL NOT BE AFRAID. WHAT SHALL MAN DO TO ME?"

7 Remember those who led you, who spoke the word of God to you; and considering the result of their conduct, imitate their faith.

8 Jesus Christ *is* the same yesterday and today, *yes* and forever.

9 Do not be carried away by varied and strange teachings; for it is good for the heart to be strengthened by grace, not by foods, through which those who were thus occupied were not benefited.

10 We have an altar, from which those who serve the tabernacle have no right to eat.

11 For the bodies of those animals whose blood is brought into the holy place by the high priest *as an offering* for sin, are burned outside the camp.

12 Therefore Jesus also, that He might sanctify the people through His own blood, suffered outside the gate.

13 Hence, let us go out to Him outside the camp, bearing His reproach.

14 For here we do not have a lasting city, but we are seeking *the city* which is to come.

15 Through Him then, let us continually offer up a sacrifice of praise to God, that is, the fruit of lips that give thanks to His name.

16 And do not neglect doing good and sharing; for with such sacrifices God is pleased.

17 Obey your leaders, and submit *to them*; for they keep watch over your souls, as those who will give an account. Let them do this with joy and not with grief, for this would be unprofitable for you.

18 Pray for us, for we are sure that we have a good conscience, desiring to conduct ourselves honorably in all things.

19 And I urge *you* all the more to do this, that I may be restored to you the sooner.

20 Now the God of peace, who brought up from the dead the great Shepherd of the sheep through the blood of the eternal covenant, *even* Jesus our Lord,

21 equip you in every good thing to do His will, working in us that which is pleasing in His sight, through Jesus Christ, to whom *be* the glory forever and ever. Amen.

22 But I urge you, brethren, bear with this word of exhortation, for I have written to you briefly.

23 Take notice that our brother Timothy has been released, with

whom, if he comes soon, I shall see you.

24 Greet all of your leaders and all the saints. Those from Italy greet you.

25 Grace be with you all.

THE EPISTLE OF

JAMES

JAMES, a bond-servant of God and of the Lord Jesus Christ, to the twelve tribes who are dispersed abroad, greetings.

2 Consider it all joy, my brethren, when you encounter various trials,

3 knowing that the testing of your faith produces endurance.

4 And let endurance have *its* perfect result, that you may be perfect and complete, lacking in nothing.

5 But if any of you lacks wisdom, let him ask of God, who gives to all men generously and without reproach, and it will be given to him.

6 But let him ask in faith without any doubting, for the one who doubts is like the surf of the sea driven and tossed by the wind.

7 For let not that man expect that he will receive anything from the Lord,

8 *being* a double-minded man, unstable in all his ways.

9 But let the brother of humble circumstances glory in his high position;

10 and *let* the rich man *glory* in his humiliation, because like flowering grass he will pass away.

11 For the sun rises with a scorching wind, and withers the grass; and its flower falls off, and the beauty of its appearance is destroyed; so too the rich man in the midst of his pursuits will fade away.

12 Blessed is a man who perseveres under trial; for once he has been approved, he will receive the crown of life, which *the Lord* has promised to those who love Him.

13 Let no one say when he is tempted, "I am being tempted by God"; for God cannot be tempted by evil, and He Himself does not tempt anyone.

14 But each one is tempted when he is carried away and enticed by his own lust.

15 Then when lust has conceived, it gives birth to sin; and when sin is accomplished, it brings forth death.

16 Do not be deceived, my beloved brethren.

17 Every good thing bestowed and every perfect gift is from above, coming down from the Father of lights, with whom there is no variation, or shifting shadow.

18 In the exercise of His will He brought us forth by the word of truth, so that we might be, as it were, the first fruits among His creatures.

19 ¹*This* you know, my beloved brethren. But let everyone be quick to hear, slow to speak *and* slow to anger;

20 for the anger of man does not achieve the righteousness of God.

21 Therefore putting aside all filthiness and *all* that remains of wickedness, in humility receive the word implanted, which is able to save your souls.

22 But prove yourselves doers of the word, and not merely hearers who delude themselves.

23 For if anyone is a hearer of the word and not a doer, he is like a man who looks at his natural face in a mirror;

24 for *once* he has looked at himself and gone away, he has immediately forgotten what kind of person he was.

25 But one who looks intently at the perfect law, the *law* of liberty, and abides by it, not having become a forgetful hearer but an effectual doer, this man shall be blessed in what he does.

26 If anyone thinks himself to be religious, and yet does not bridle his tongue but deceives his *own* heart, this man's religion is worthless.

27 This is pure and undefiled religion in the sight of *our* God and Father, to visit orphans and widows in their distress, *and* to keep oneself unstained by the world.

CHAPTER 2

MY brethren, do not hold your faith in our glorious Lord Jesus Christ with *an attitude of* personal favoritism.

2 For if a man comes into your assembly with a gold ring and dressed in fine clothes, and there also comes in a poor man in dirty clothes,

3 and you pay special attention to the one who is wearing the fine clothes, and say, "You sit here in a good place," and you say to the poor man, "You stand over there, or sit down by my footstool,"

4 have you not made distinctions among yourselves, and become judges with evil motives?

5 Listen, my beloved brethren: did not God choose the poor of this world *to be* rich in faith and heirs of the kingdom which He promised to those who love Him?

6 But you have dishonored the poor man. Is it not the rich who oppress you and personally drag you into court?

7 Do they not blaspheme the fair name by which you have been called?

8 If, however, you are fulfilling the royal law, according to the Scripture, "YOU SHALL LOVE YOUR NEIGHBOR AS YOURSELF," you are doing well.

9 But if you show partiality, you are committing sin *and* are convicted by the law as transgressors.

10 For whoever keeps the whole law and yet stumbles in one *point*, he has become guilty of all.

11 For He who said, "DO NOT COMMIT ADULTERY," also said, "DO NOT COMMIT MURDER." Now if you do not commit adultery, but do commit murder, you have become a transgressor of the law.

12 So speak and so act, as

¹ Or, *Know this*

those who are to be judged by *the* law of liberty.

13 For judgment *will be* merciless to one who has shown no mercy; mercy triumphs over judgment.

14 What use is it, my brethren, if a man says he has faith, but he has no works? Can that faith save him?

15 If a brother or sister is without clothing and in need of daily food,

16 and one of you says to them, "Go in peace, be warmed and be filled," and yet you do not give them what is necessary for *their* body, what use is that?

17 Even so faith, if it has no works, is dead, *being* by itself.

18 But someone may *well* say, "You have faith, and I have works; show me your faith without the works, and I will show you my faith by my works."

19 You believe that [2]God is one. You do well; the demons also believe, and shudder.

20 But are you willing to recognize, you foolish fellow, that faith without works is useless?

21 Was not Abraham our father justified by works, when he offered up Isaac his son on the altar?

22 You see that faith was working with his works, and as a result of the works, faith was perfected;

23 and the Scripture was fulfilled which says, "AND ABRAHAM BELIEVED GOD, AND IT WAS RECKONED TO HIM AS RIGHTEOUSNESS," and he was called the friend of God.

24 You see that a man is justified by works, and not by faith alone.

25 And in the same way was not Rahab the harlot also justified by works, when she received the messengers and sent them out by another way?

26 For just as the body without *the* spirit is dead, so also faith without works is dead.

CHAPTER 3

LET not many of *you* become teachers, my brethren, knowing that as such we shall incur a stricter judgment.

2 For we all stumble in many *ways*. If anyone does not stumble in what he says, he is a perfect man, able to bridle the whole body as well.

3 Now if we put the bits into the horses' mouths so that they may obey us, we direct their entire body as well.

4 Behold, the ships also, though they are so great and are driven by strong winds, are still directed by a very small rudder, wherever the inclination of the pilot desires.

5 So also the tongue is a small part of the body, and *yet* it boasts of great things. Behold, how great a forest is set aflame by such a small fire!

6 And the tongue is a fire, the *very* world of iniquity; the tongue is set among our members as that which defiles the entire body, and sets on fire the course of *our* life, and is set on fire by hell.

7 For every species of beasts and birds, of reptiles and creatures of the sea, is tamed, and has been tamed by the human race.

[2] Or, *there is one God*

8 But no one can tame the tongue; *it is* a restless evil *and* full of deadly poison.

9 With it we bless *our* Lord and Father; and with it we curse men, who have been made in the likeness of God;

10 from the same mouth come *both* blessing and cursing. My brethren, these things ought not to be this way.

11 Does a fountain send out from the same opening *both* fresh and bitter *water*?

12 Can a fig tree, my brethren, produce olives, or a vine produce figs? Neither *can* salt water produce fresh.

13 Who among you is wise and understanding? Let him show by his good behavior his deeds in the gentleness of wisdom.

14 But if you have bitter jealousy and selfish ambition in your heart, do not be arrogant and *so* lie against the truth.

15 This wisdom is not that which comes down from above, but is earthly, natural, demonic.

16 For where jealousy and selfish ambition exist, there is disorder and every evil thing.

17 But the wisdom from above is first pure, then peaceable, gentle, reasonable, full of mercy and good fruits, unwavering, without hypocrisy.

18 And the seed whose fruit is righteousness is sown in peace by those who make peace.

CHAPTER 4

WHAT is the source of quarrels and conflicts among you? Is not the source your pleasures that wage war in your members?

2 You lust and do not have; so

you commit murder. And you are envious and cannot obtain; *so* you fight and quarrel. You do not have because you do not ask.

3 You ask and do not receive, because you ask with wrong motives, so that you may spend *it* on your pleasures.

4 You adulteresses, do you not know that friendship with the world is hostility toward God? Therefore whoever wishes to be a friend of the world makes himself an enemy of God.

5 Or do you think that the Scripture speaks to no purpose: "[3]He jealously desires the Spirit which He has made to dwell in us"?

6 But He gives a greater grace. Therefore *it* says, "GOD IS OPPOSED TO THE PROUD, BUT GIVES GRACE TO THE HUMBLE."

7 Submit therefore to God. Resist the devil and he will flee from you.

8 Draw near to God and He will draw near to you. Cleanse your hands, you sinners; and purify your hearts, you double-minded.

9 Be miserable and mourn and weep; let your laughter be turned into mourning, and your joy to gloom.

10 Humble yourselves in the presence of the Lord, and He will exalt you.

11 Do not speak against one another, brethren. He who speaks against a brother, or judges his brother, speaks against the law, and judges the law; but if you judge the law, you are not a doer of the law, but a judge *of it.*

12 There is *only* one Lawgiver

---

[3] Or, *The Spirit which He has made to dwell in us jealously desires us*

and Judge, the One who is able to save and to destroy; but who are you who judge your neighbor?

13 Come now, you who say, "Today or tomorrow, we shall go to such and such a city, and spend a year there and engage in business and make a profit."

14 Yet you do not know what your life will be like tomorrow. You are *just* a vapor that appears for a little while and then vanishes away.

15 Instead, *you* ought to say, "If the Lord wills, we shall live and also do this or that."

16 But as it is, you boast in your arrogance; all such boasting is evil.

17 Therefore, to one who knows the right thing to do, and does not do it, to him it is sin.

CHAPTER 5

COME now, you rich, weep and howl for your miseries which are coming upon you.

2 Your riches have rotted and your garments have become moth-eaten.

3 Your gold and your silver have rusted; and their rust will be a witness against you and will consume your flesh like fire. It is in the last days that you have stored up your treasure!

4 Behold, the pay of the laborers who mowed your fields, *and* which has been withheld by you, cries out *against you*; and the outcry of those who did the harvesting has reached the ears of the Lord of Sabaoth.

5 You have lived luxuriously on the earth and led a life of wanton pleasure; you have fattened your hearts in a day of slaughter.

6 You have condemned and put to death the righteous *man*; he does not resist you.

7 Be patient, therefore, brethren, until the coming of the Lord. Behold, the farmer waits for the precious produce of the soil, being patient about it, until it gets the early and late rains.

8 You too be patient; strengthen your hearts, for the coming of the Lord is at hand.

9 Do not complain, brethren, against one another, that you yourselves may not be judged; behold, the Judge is standing right at the door.

10 As an example, brethren, of suffering and patience, take the prophets who spoke in the name of the Lord.

11 Behold, we count those blessed who endured. You have heard of the endurance of Job and have seen the outcome of the Lord's dealings, that the Lord is full of compassion and *is* merciful.

12 But above all, my brethren, do not swear, either by heaven or by earth or with any other oath; but let your yes be yes, and your no, no; so that you may not fall under judgment.

13 Is anyone among you suffering? Let him pray. Is anyone cheerful? Let him sing praises.

14 Is anyone among you sick? Let him call for the elders of the church, and let them pray over him, anointing him with oil in the name of the Lord;

15 and the prayer offered in faith will ⁴restore the one who is sick, and the Lord will raise him up, and if he has committed sins, they will be forgiven him.

16 Therefore, confess your sins to one another, and pray for one

⁴ Or, *save*

another, so that you may be healed. The effective prayer of a righteous man can accomplish much.

17 Elijah was a man with a nature like ours, and he prayed earnestly that it might not rain; and it did not rain on the earth for three years and six months.

18 And he prayed again, and the sky poured rain, and the earth produced its fruit.

19 My brethren, if any among you strays from the truth, and one turns him back,

20 let him know that he who turns a sinner from the error of his way will save his soul from death, and will cover a multitude of sins.

THE FIRST EPISTLE OF

PETER

PETER, an apostle of Jesus Christ, to those who reside as aliens, scattered throughout Pontus, Galatia, Cappadocia, Asia, and Bithynia, who are chosen

2 according to the foreknowledge of God the Father, by the sanctifying work of the Spirit, that you may obey Jesus Christ and be sprinkled with His blood: May grace and peace be yours in fullest measure.

3 Blessed be the God and Father of our Lord Jesus Christ, who according to His great mercy has caused us to be born again to a living hope through the resurrection of Jesus Christ from the dead,

4 to *obtain* an inheritance *which is* imperishable and undefiled and will not fade away, reserved in heaven for you,

5 who are protected by the power of God through faith for a salvation ready to be revealed in the last time.

6 In this you greatly rejoice, even though now for a little while, if necessary, you have been distressed by various trials,

7 that the proof of your faith, *being* more precious than gold which is perishable, even though tested by fire, may be found to result in praise and glory and honor at the revelation of Jesus Christ;

8 and though you have not seen Him, you love Him, and though you do not see Him now, but believe in Him, you greatly rejoice with joy inexpressible and full of glory,

9 obtaining as the outcome of your faith the salvation of [1]your souls.

10 As to this salvation, the prophets who prophesied of the grace that *would come* to you made careful search and inquiry,

11 seeking to know what person or time the Spirit of Christ within them was indicating as He predicted the sufferings of Christ and the glories to follow.

12 It was revealed to them that they were not serving themselves, but you, in these things

[1] Some ancient mss. do not contain *your*

which now have been announced to you through those who preached the gospel to you by the Holy Spirit sent from heaven—things into which angels long to look.

13 Therefore, gird your minds for action, keep sober *in spirit*, fix your hope completely on the grace to be brought to you at the revelation of Jesus Christ.

14 As obedient children, do not be conformed to the former lusts *which were yours* in your ignorance,

15 but like the Holy One who called you, be holy yourselves also in all *your* behavior;

16 because it is written, "YOU SHALL BE HOLY, FOR I AM HOLY."

17 And if you address as Father the One who impartially judges according to each man's work, conduct yourselves in fear during the time of your stay *upon earth*;

18 knowing that you were not redeemed with perishable things like silver or gold from your futile way of life inherited from your forefathers,

19 but with precious blood, as of a lamb unblemished and spotless, *the blood* of Christ.

20 For He was foreknown before the foundation of the world, but has appeared in these last times for the sake of you

21 who through Him are believers in God, who raised Him from the dead and gave Him glory, so that your faith and hope are in God.

22 Since you have in obedience to the truth purified your souls for a sincere love of the brethren,

fervently love one another from [2]the heart,

23 for you have been born again not of seed which is perishable but imperishable, *that is,* through the living and abiding word of God.

24 For,

"ALL FLESH IS LIKE GRASS,
AND ALL ITS GLORY LIKE
THE FLOWER OF GRASS.
THE GRASS WITHERS,
AND THE FLOWER FALLS
OFF,

25 BUT THE WORD OF THE
LORD ABIDES FOREVER."

And this is the word which was preached to you.

CHAPTER 2

THEREFORE, putting aside all malice and all guile and hypocrisy and envy and all slander,

2 like newborn babes, long for the pure milk of the word, that by it you may grow in respect to salvation,

3 if you have tasted the kindness of the Lord.

4 And coming to Him as to a living stone, rejected by men, but choice and precious in the sight of God,

5 you also, as living stones, are being built up as a spiritual house for a holy priesthood, to offer up spiritual sacrifices acceptable to God through Jesus Christ.

6 For *this* is contained in Scripture:

"BEHOLD I LAY IN ZION A
CHOICE STONE, A PRECIOUS
CORNER *stone*,
AND HE WHO BELIEVES IN
HIM SHALL NOT BE DISAPPOINTED."

7 This precious value, then, is

---

[2] Some mss. read *a clean heart*

for you who believe. But for those who disbelieve,

"THE STONE WHICH THE BUILDERS REJECTED, THIS BECAME THE VERY CORNER *stone*,"

8 and,

"A STONE OF STUMBLING AND A ROCK OF OFFENSE"; for they stumble because they are disobedient to the word, and to this *doom* they were also appointed.

9 But you are A CHOSEN RACE, A royal PRIESTHOOD, A HOLY NATION, A PEOPLE FOR *God's* OWN POSSESSION, that you may proclaim the excellencies of Him who has called you out of darkness into His marvelous light;

10 for you once were NOT A PEOPLE, but now you are THE PEOPLE OF GOD; you had NOT RECEIVED MERCY, but now you have RECEIVED MERCY.

11 Beloved, I urge you as aliens and strangers to abstain from fleshly lusts, which wage war against the soul.

12 Keep your behavior excellent among the Gentiles, so that in the thing in which they slander you as evildoers, they may on account of your good deeds, which they observe *them*, glorify God in the day of ³visitation.

13 Submit yourselves for the Lord's sake to every human institution, whether to a king as the one in authority,

14 or to governors as sent by him for the punishment of evildoers and the praise of those who do right.

15 For such is the will of God that by doing right you may silence the ignorance of foolish men.

16 *Act* as free men, and do not use your freedom as a covering for evil, but *use it* as bondslaves of God.

17 Honor all men; love the brotherhood, fear God, honor the king.

18 Servants, be submissive to your masters with all respect, not only to those who are good and gentle, but also to those who are unreasonable.

19 For this *finds* favor, if for the sake of conscience toward God a man bears up under sorrows when suffering unjustly.

20 For what credit is there if, when you sin and are harshly treated, you endure it with patience? But if when you do what is right and suffer *for it* you patiently endure, this *finds* favor with God.

21 For you have been called for this purpose, since Christ also suffered for you, leaving you an example for you to follow in His steps,

22 WHO COMMITTED NO SIN, NOR WAS ANY DECEIT FOUND IN HIS MOUTH;

23 and while being reviled, He did not revile in return; while suffering, He uttered no threats, but kept entrusting *Himself* to Him who judges righteously;

24 and He Himself bore our sins in His body on the cross, that we might die to sin and live to righteousness; for by His wounds you were healed.

25 For you were continually straying like sheep, but now you have returned to the Shepherd and Guardian of your souls.

CHAPTER 3

IN the same way, you wives, be submissive to your own hus-

---

³ I.e., Christ's coming again in judgment

those who do not obey the gospel of God?

18 AND IF IT IS WITH DIFFI-CULTY THAT THE RIGHTEOUS IS SAVED, WHAT WILL BECOME OF THE GODLESS MAN AND THE SIN-NER?

19 Therefore, let those also who suffer according to the will of God entrust their souls to a faithful Creator in doing what is right.

CHAPTER 5

THEREFORE, I exhort the el-ders among you, as *your* fel-low elder and witness of the suf-ferings of Christ, and a partaker also of the glory that is to be re-vealed,

2 shepherd the flock of God among you, exercising oversight not under compulsion, but volun-tarily, according to *the will of* God; and not for sordid gain, but with eagerness;

3 nor yet as lording it over those allotted to your charge, but proving to be examples to the flock.

4 And when the Chief Shep-herd appears, you will receive the unfading crown of glory.

5 You younger men, likewise, be subject to your elders; and all of you, clothe yourselves with humility toward one another, for

GOD IS OPPOSED TO THE PROUD, BUT GIVES GRACE TO THE HUMBLE.

6 Humble yourselves, there-fore, under the mighty hand of God, that He may exalt you at the proper time,

7 casting all your anxiety upon Him, because He cares for you.

8 Be of sober *spirit*, be on the alert. Your adversary, the devil, prowls about like a roaring lion, seeking someone to devour.

9 But resist him, firm in *your* faith, knowing that the same ex-periences of suffering are being accomplished by your brethren who are in the world.

10 And after you have suffered for a little while, the God of all grace, who called you to His eter-nal glory in Christ, will Himself perfect, confirm, strengthen *and* establish you.

11 To Him *be* dominion forever and ever. Amen.

12 Through Silvanus, our faith-ful brother (for so I regard *him*), I have written to you briefly, ex-horting and testifying that this is the true grace of God. Stand firm in it!

13 [6]She who is in Babylon, cho-sen together with you, sends you greetings, and *so does* my son, Mark.

14 Greet one another with a kiss of love.

Peace be to you all who are in Christ.

6 Some mss. read *The church which*

PETER

SIMON PETER, a bond-servant and apostle of Jesus Christ, to those who have received a faith of the same kind as ours, by the righteousness of our God and Savior, Jesus Christ:

2 Grace and peace be multiplied to you in the knowledge of God and of Jesus our Lord;

3 seeing that His divine power has granted to us everything pertaining to life and godliness, through the true knowledge of Him who called us by His own glory and excellence.

4 For by these He has granted to us His precious and magnificent promises, in order that by them you might become partakers of *the* divine nature, having escaped the corruption that is in the world by lust.

5 Now for this very reason also, applying all diligence, in your faith supply moral excellence, and in *your* moral excellence, knowledge;

6 and in *your* knowledge, self-control, and in *your* self-control, perseverance, and in *your* perseverance, godliness;

7 and in *your* godliness, brotherly kindness, and in *your* brotherly kindness, love.

8 For if these *qualities* are yours and are increasing, they render you neither useless nor unfruitful in the true knowledge of our Lord Jesus Christ.

9 For he who lacks these *qualities* is blind *or* short-sighted, having forgotten *his* purification from his former sins.

10 Therefore, brethren, be all the more diligent to make certain about His calling and choosing you; for as long as you practice these things, you will never stumble;

11 for in this way the entrance into the eternal kingdom of our Lord and Savior Jesus Christ will be abundantly supplied to you.

12 Therefore, I shall always be ready to remind you of these things, even though you *already* know *them*, and have been established in the truth which is present with *you*.

13 And I consider it right, as long as I am in this *earthly* dwelling, to stir you up by way of reminder,

14 knowing that the laying aside of my *earthly* dwelling is imminent, as also our Lord Jesus Christ has made clear to me.

15 And I will also be diligent that at any time after my departure you may be able to call these things to mind.

16 For we did not follow cleverly devised tales when we made known to you the power and coming of our Lord Jesus Christ, but we were eyewitnesses of His majesty.

17 For when He received honor and glory from God the Father, such an utterance as this was made to Him by the Majestic Glory, "This is My beloved Son with whom I am well-pleased"—

18 and we ourselves heard this utterance made from heaven

---

[1] Most early mss. read *Simeon*

when we were with Him on the holy mountain.

19 And so we have the prophetic word made more sure, to which you do well to pay attention as to a lamp shining in a dark place, until the day dawns and the morning star arises in your hearts.

20 But know this first of all, that no prophecy of Scripture is a matter of one's own interpretation,

21 for no prophecy was ever made by an act of human will, but men moved by the Holy Spirit spoke from God.

CHAPTER 2

BUT false prophets also arose among the people, just as there will also be false teachers among you, who will secretly introduce destructive heresies, even denying the Master who bought them, bringing swift destruction upon themselves.

2 And many will follow their sensuality, and because of them the way of the truth will be maligned;

3 and in their greed they will exploit you with false words; their judgment from long ago is not idle, and their destruction is not asleep.

4 For if God did not spare angels when they sinned, but cast them into hell and committed them to pits of darkness, reserved for judgment;

5 and did not spare the ancient world, but preserved Noah, a preacher of righteousness, with seven others, when He brought a flood upon the world of the ungodly;

6 and if He condemned the cities of Sodom and Gomorrah to destruction by reducing them to ashes, having made them an example to those who would live ungodly thereafter;

7 and if He rescued righteous Lot, oppressed by the sensual conduct of unprincipled men

8 (for by what he saw and heard that righteous man, while living among them, felt his righteous soul tormented day after day with their lawless deeds),

9 then the Lord knows how to rescue the godly from temptation, and to keep the unrighteous under punishment for the day of judgment,

10 and especially those who indulge the flesh in its corrupt desires and despise authority. Daring, self-willed, they do not tremble when they revile angelic majesties,

11 whereas angels who are greater in might and power do not bring a reviling judgment against them before the Lord.

12 But these, like unreasoning animals, born as creatures of instinct to be captured and killed, reviling where they have no knowledge, will in the destruction of those creatures also be destroyed,

13 suffering wrong as the wages of doing wrong. They count it a pleasure to revel in the daytime. They are stains and blemishes, reveling in their [2]deceptions, as they carouse with you,

14 having eyes full of adultery and that never cease from sin, enticing unstable souls, having a

---

[2] Some ancient mss. read love feasts, (cf. Jude 12)

heart trained in greed, accursed children;

15 forsaking the right way they have gone astray, having followed the way of Balaam, the *son* of Beor, who loved the wages of unrighteousness,

16 but he received a rebuke for his own transgression; *for* a dumb donkey, speaking with a voice of a man, restrained the madness of the prophet.

17 These are springs without water, and mists driven by a storm, for whom the black darkness has been reserved.

18 For speaking out arrogant *words* of vanity they entice by fleshly desires, by sensuality, those who barely escape from the ones who live in error,

19 promising them freedom while they themselves are slaves of corruption; for by what a man is overcome, by this he is enslaved.

20 For if after they have escaped the defilements of the world by the knowledge of the Lord and Savior Jesus Christ, they are again entangled in them and are overcome, the last state has become worse for them than the first.

21 For it would be better for them not to have known the way of righteousness, than having known it, to turn away from the holy commandment delivered to them.

22 It has happened to them according to the true proverb, "A DOG RETURNS TO ITS OWN VOMIT," and, "A sow, after washing, *returns* to wallowing in the mire."

CHAPTER 3

THIS is now, beloved, the second letter I am writing to you in which I am stirring up your sincere mind by way of reminder,

2 that you should remember the words spoken beforehand by the holy prophets and the commandment of the Lord and Savior *spoken* by your apostles.

3 Know this first of all, that in the last days mockers will come with *their* mocking, following after their own lusts,

4 and saying, "Where is the promise of His coming? For *ever* since the fathers fell asleep, all continues just as it was from the beginning of creation."

5 For when they maintain this, it escapes their notice that by the word of God *the* heavens existed long ago and *the* earth was formed out of water and by water,

6 through which the world at that time was destroyed, being flooded with water.

7 But the present heavens and earth by His word are being reserved for fire, kept for the day of judgment and destruction of ungodly men.

8 But do not let this one *fact* escape your notice, beloved, that with the Lord one day is as a thousand years, and a thousand years as one day.

9 The Lord is not slow about His promise, as some count slowness, but is patient toward you, not wishing for any to perish but for all to come to repentance.

10 But the day of the Lord will come like a thief, in which the heavens will pass away with a roar and the elements will be destroyed with intense heat, and the earth and its works will be [3]burned up.

---

[3] Some ancient mss. read *discovered*

11 Since all these things are to be destroyed in this way, what sort of people ought you to be in holy conduct and godliness,

12 looking for and hastening the coming of the day of God, on account of which the heavens will be destroyed by burning, and the elements will melt with intense heat!

13 But according to His promise we are looking for new heavens and a new earth, in which righteousness dwells.

14 Therefore, beloved, since you look for these things, be diligent to be found by Him in peace, spotless and blameless,

15 and regard the patience of our Lord *to be* salvation; just as also our beloved brother Paul, according to the wisdom given him, wrote to you,

16 as also in all *his* letters, speaking in them of these things, in which are some things hard to understand, which the untaught and unstable distort, as *they do* also the rest of the Scriptures, to their own destruction.

17 You therefore, beloved, knowing this beforehand, be on your guard lest, being carried away by the error of unprincipled men, you fall from your own steadfastness,

18 but grow in the grace and knowledge of our Lord and Savior Jesus Christ. To Him *be* the glory, both now and to the day of eternity. Amen.

THE FIRST EPISTLE OF

JOHN

WHAT was from the beginning, what we have heard, what we have seen with our eyes, what we beheld and our hands handled, concerning the Word of Life—

2 and the life was manifested, and we have seen and bear witness and proclaim to you the eternal life, which was with the Father and was manifested to us—

3 what we have seen and heard we proclaim to you also, that you also may have fellowship with us; and indeed our fellowship is with the Father, and with His Son Jesus Christ.

4 And these things we write, so that our joy may be made complete.

5 And this is the message we have heard from Him and announce to you, that God is light, and in Him there is no darkness at all.

6 If we say that we have fellowship with Him and *yet* walk in the darkness, we lie and do not practice the truth;

7 but if we walk in the light as He Himself is in the light, we have fellowship with one another, and the blood of Jesus His Son cleanses us from all sin.

8 If we say that we have no sin, we are deceiving ourselves, and the truth is not in us.

9 If we confess our sins, He is faithful and righteous to forgive us our sins and to cleanse us from all unrighteousness.

10 If we say that we have not sinned, we make Him a liar, and His word is not in us.

CHAPTER 2

MY little children, I am writing these things to you that you may not sin. And if anyone sins, we have an ¹Advocate with the Father, Jesus Christ the righteous;

2 and He Himself is the propitiation for our sins; and not for ours only, but also for *those of* the whole world.

3 And by this we know that we have come to know Him, if we keep His commandments.

4 The one who says, "I have come to know Him," and does not keep His commandments, is a liar, and the truth is not in him;

5 but whoever keeps His word, in him the love of God has truly been perfected. By this we know that we are in Him:

6 the one who says he abides in Him ought himself to walk in the same manner as He walked.

7 Beloved, I am not writing a new commandment to you, but an old commandment which you have had from the beginning; the old commandment is the word which you have heard.

8 On the other hand, I am writing a new commandment to you, which is true in Him and in you, because the darkness is passing away, and the true light is already shining.

9 The one who says he is in the light and *yet* hates his brother is in the darkness until now.

10 The one who loves his brother abides in the light and there is no cause for stumbling in him.

11 But the one who hates his brother is in the darkness and walks in the darkness, and does not know where he is going because the darkness has blinded his eyes.

12 I am writing to you, little children, because your sins are forgiven you for His name's sake.

13 I am writing to you, fathers, because you know Him who has been from the beginning. I am writing to you, young men, because you have overcome the evil one. I have written to you, children, because you know the Father.

14 I have written to you, fathers, because you know Him who has been from the beginning. I have written to you, young men, because you are strong, and the word of God abides in you, and you have overcome the evil one.

15 Do not love the world, nor the things in the world. If anyone loves the world, the love of the Father is not in him.

16 For all that is in the world, the lust of the flesh and the lust of the eyes and the boastful pride of life, is not from the Father, but is from the world.

17 And the world is passing away, and *also* its lusts; but the one who does the will of God abides forever.

18 Children, it is the last hour; and just as you heard that antichrist is coming, even now many antichrists have arisen; from this we know that it is the last hour.

¹ Gr. *Parácletos*, one called alongside to help

19 They went out from us, but they were not *really* of us; for if they had been of us, they would have remained with us; but *they went out*, in order that it might be shown that they all are not of us.

20 But you have an anointing from the Holy One, and you all know.

21 I have not written to you because you do not know the truth, but because you do know it, and because no lie is of the truth.

22 Who is the liar but the one who denies that Jesus is the Christ? This is the antichrist, the one who denies the Father and the Son.

23 Whoever denies the Son does not have the Father; the one who confesses the Son has the Father also.

24 As for you, let that abide in you which you heard from the beginning. If what you heard from the beginning abides in you, you also will abide in the Son and in the Father.

25 And this is the promise which He Himself made to us: eternal life.

26 These things I have written to you concerning those who are trying to deceive you.

27 And as for you, the anointing which you received from Him abides in you, and you have no need for anyone to teach you; but as His anointing teaches you about all things, and is true and is not a lie, and just as it has taught you, you abide in Him.

28 And now, little children, abide in Him, so that when He appears, we may have confidence and not shrink away from Him in shame at His coming.

29 If you know that He is right-eous, you know that everyone also who practices righteousness is born of Him.

CHAPTER 3

SEE how great a love the Father has bestowed upon us, that we should be called children of God; and *such* we are. For this reason the world does not know us, because it did not know Him.

2 Beloved, now we are children of God, and it has not as yet appeared as yet what we shall be. We know that, when He appears, we shall be like Him, because we shall see Him just as He is.

3 And everyone who has this hope *fixed* on Him purifies himself, just as He is pure.

4 Everyone who practices sin also practices lawlessness; and sin is lawlessness.

5 And you know that He appeared in order to take away sins; and in Him there is no sin.

6 No one who abides in Him sins; no one who sins has seen Him or knows Him.

7 Little children, let no one deceive you; the one who practices righteousness is righteous, just as He is righteous;

8 the one who practices sin is of the devil; for the devil has sinned from the beginning. The Son of God appeared for this purpose, that He might destroy the works of the devil.

9 No one who is born of God practices sin, because His seed abides in him; and he cannot sin, because he is born of God.

10 By this the children of God and the children of the devil are obvious: anyone who does not practice righteousness is not of

God, nor the one who does not love his brother.

11 For this is the message which you have heard from the beginning, that we should love one another;

12 not as Cain, *who* was of the evil one, and slew his brother. And for what reason did he slay him? Because his deeds were evil, and his brother's were righteous.

13 Do not marvel, brethren, if the world hates you.

14 We know that we have passed out of death into life, because we love the brethren. He who does not love abides in death.

15 Everyone who hates his brother is a murderer; and you know that no murderer has eternal life abiding in him.

16 We know love by this, that He laid down His life for us; and we ought to lay down our lives for the brethren.

17 But whoever has the world's goods, and beholds his brother in need and closes his heart against him, how does the love of God abide in him?

18 Little children, let us not love with word or with tongue, but in deed and truth.

19 We shall know by this that we are of the truth, and shall assure our heart before Him,

20 in whatever our heart condemns us; for God is greater than our heart, and knows all things.

21 Beloved, if our heart does not condemn us, we have confidence before God;

22 and whatever we ask we receive from Him, because we keep His commandments and do the things that are pleasing in His sight.

23 And this is His commandment, that we believe in the name of His Son Jesus Christ, and love one another, just as He commanded us.

24 And the one who keeps His commandments abides in Him, and He in him. And we know by this that He abides in us, by the Spirit whom He has given us.

CHAPTER 4

BELOVED, do not believe every spirit, but test the spirits to see whether they are from God; because many false prophets have gone out into the world.

2 By this you know the Spirit of God: every spirit that confesses that Jesus Christ has come in the flesh is from God;

3 and every spirit that does not confess Jesus is not from God; and this is the *spirit* of the antichrist, of which you have heard that it is coming, and now it is already in the world.

4 You are from God, little children, and have overcome them; because greater is He who is in you than he who is in the world.

5 They are from the world; therefore they speak *as* from the world, and the world listens to them.

6 We are from God; he who knows God listens to us; he who is not from God does not listen to us. By this we know the spirit of truth and the spirit of error.

7 Beloved, let us love one another, for love is from God; and everyone who loves is born of God and knows God.

8 The one who does not love does not know God, for God is love.

9 By this the love of God was manifested in us, that God has sent His only begotten Son into the world so that we might live through Him.

10 In this is love, not that we loved God, but that He loved us and sent His Son *to be* the propitiation for our sins.

11 Beloved, if God so loved us, we also ought to love one another.

12 No one has beheld God at any time; if we love one another, God abides in us, and His love is perfected in us.

13 By this we know that we abide in Him and He in us, because He has given us of His Spirit.

14 And we have beheld and bear witness that the Father has sent the Son *to be* the Savior of the world.

15 Whoever confesses that Jesus is the Son of God, God abides in him, and he in God.

16 And we have come to know and have believed the love which God has for us. God is love, and the one who abides in love abides in God, and God abides in him.

17 By this, love is perfected with us, that we may have confidence in the day of judgment; because as He is, so also are we in this world.

18 There is no fear in love; but perfect love casts out fear, because fear involves punishment, and the one who fears is not perfected in love.

19 We love, because He first loved us.

20 If someone says, "I love God," and hates his brother, he is a liar; for the one who does not love his brother whom he has seen, cannot love God whom he has not seen.

21 And this commandment we have from Him, that the one who loves God should love his brother also.

CHAPTER 5

WHOEVER believes that Jesus is the [2]Christ is born of God; and whoever loves the Father loves the *child* born of Him.

2 By this we know that we love the children of God, when we love God and observe His commandments.

3 For this is the love of God, that we keep His commandments; and His commandments are not burdensome.

4 For whatever is born of God overcomes the world; and this is the victory that has overcome the world—our faith.

5 And who is the one who overcomes the world, but he who believes that Jesus is the Son of God?

6 This is the one who came by water and blood, Jesus Christ; not with the water only, but with the water and with the blood.

7 And it is the Spirit who bears witness, because the Spirit is the truth.

8 For there are three that bear witness, [3]the Spirit and the water and the blood; and the three are in agreement.

9 If we receive the witness of men, the witness of God is greater; for the witness of God is this, that He has borne witness concerning His Son.

[2] I.e., Messiah
[3] A few late mss. read *in heaven, the Father, the Word, and the Holy Spirit, and these three are one. And there are three that bear witness on earth, the Spirit*

10 The one who believes in the Son of God has the witness in himself; the one who does not believe God has made Him a liar, because he has not believed in the witness that God has borne concerning His Son.

11 And the witness is this, that God has given us eternal life, and this life is in His Son.

12 He who has the Son has the life; he who does not have the Son of God does not have the life.

13 These things I have written to you who believe in the name of the Son of God, in order that you may know that you have eternal life.

14 And this is the confidence which we have before Him, that, if we ask anything according to His will, He hears us.

15 And if we know that He hears us in whatever we ask, we know that we have the requests which we have asked from Him.

16 If anyone sees his brother committing a sin not *leading* to death, he shall ask and *God* will for him give life to those who commit sin not *leading* to death. There is a sin *leading* to death; I do not say that he should make request for this.

17 All unrighteousness is sin, and there is a sin not *leading* to death.

18 We know that no one who is born of God sins; but He who was born of God keeps him and the evil one does not touch him.

19 We know that we are of God, and the whole world lies in *the power of* the evil one.

20 And we know that the Son of God has come, and has given us understanding, in order that we might know Him who is true, and we are in Him who is true, in His Son Jesus Christ. This is the true God and eternal life.

21 Little children, guard yourselves from idols.

THE SECOND EPISTLE OF

JOHN

THE elder to the chosen lady and her children, whom I love in truth; and not only I, but also all who know the truth,

2 for the sake of the truth which abides in us and will be with us forever:

3 Grace, mercy *and* peace will be with us, from God the Father and from Jesus Christ, the Son of the Father, in truth and love.

4 I was very glad to find *some* of your children walking in truth,

just as we have received commandment *to* do from the Father.

5 And now I ask you, lady, not as writing to you a new commandment, but the one which we have had from the beginning, that we love one another.

6 And this is love, that we walk according to His commandments. This is the commandment, just as you have heard from the beginning, that you should walk in it.

7 For many deceivers have gone out into the world, those who do not acknowledge Jesus Christ *as* coming in the flesh. This is the deceiver and the antichrist.

8 Watch yourselves, that you might not lose what we have accomplished, but that you may receive a full reward.

9 Anyone who goes too far and does not abide in the teaching of Christ, does not have God; the one who abides in the teaching, he has both the Father and the Son.

10 If anyone comes to you and does not bring this teaching, do not receive him into *your* house, and do not give him a greeting;

11 for the one who gives him a greeting participates in his evil deeds.

12 Having many things to write to you, I do not want to *do* so with paper and ink; but I hope to come to you and speak face to face, that your joy may be made full.

13 The children of your chosen sister greet you.

THE THIRD EPISTLE OF

JOHN

THE elder to the beloved Gaius, whom I love in truth.

2 Beloved, I pray that in all respects you may prosper and be in good health, just as your soul prospers.

3 For I was very glad when brethren came and bore witness to your truth, *that is,* how you are walking in truth.

4 I have no greater joy than this, to hear of my children walking in the truth.

5 Beloved, you are acting faithfully in whatever you accomplish for the brethren, and especially *when they are* strangers;

6 and they bear witness to your love before the church; and you will do well to send them on their way in a manner worthy of God.

7 For they went out for the sake of the Name, accepting nothing from the Gentiles.

8 Therefore we ought to support such men, that we may be fellow workers with the truth.

9 I wrote something to the church; but Diotrephes, who loves to be first among them, does not accept what we say.

10 For this reason, if I come, I will call attention to his deeds which he does, unjustly accusing us with wicked words; and not satisfied with this, neither does he himself receive the brethren, and he forbids those who desire *to do so,* and puts *them* out of the church.

11 Beloved, do not imitate what is evil, but what is good. The one who does good is of God; the one who does evil has not seen God.

12 Demetrius has received a *good* testimony from everyone, and from the truth itself; and we also bear witness, and you know that our witness is true.

13 I had many things to write to you, but I am not willing to write *them* to you with pen and ink;

14 but I hope to see you shortly, and we shall speak face to face. Peace *be* to you. The friends greet you. Greet the friends by name.

THE EPISTLE OF

JUDE

JUDE, a bond-servant of Jesus Christ, and brother of James, to those who are the called, beloved in God the Father, and kept for Jesus Christ:

2 May mercy and peace and love be multiplied to you.

3 Beloved, while I was making every effort to write you about our common salvation, I felt the necessity to write to you appealing that you contend earnestly for the faith which was once for all delivered to the saints.

4 For certain persons have crept in unnoticed, those who were long beforehand marked out for this condemnation, ungodly persons who turn the grace of our God into licentiousness and deny our only Master and Lord, Jesus Christ.

5 Now I desire to remind you, though you know all things once for all, that ¹the Lord, after saving a people out of the land of Egypt, subsequently destroyed those who did not believe.

6 And angels who did not keep their own domain, but abandoned their proper abode, He has kept in eternal bonds under darkness for the judgment of the great day.

7 Just as Sodom and Gomorrah and the cities around them, since they in the same way as these indulged in gross immorality and went after strange flesh, are exhibited as an example, in undergoing the punishment of eternal fire.

8 Yet in the same manner these men, also by dreaming, defile the flesh, and reject authority, and revile angelic majesties.

9 But Michael the archangel, when he disputed with the devil and argued about the body of Moses, did not dare pronounce against him a railing judgment, but said, "The Lord rebuke you."

10 But these men revile the things which they do not understand; and the things which they know by instinct, like unreasoning animals, by these things they are destroyed.

11 Woe to them! For they have gone the way of Cain, and for pay they have rushed headlong into the error of Balaam, and perished in the rebellion of Korah.

12 These men are those who

¹ Some ancient mss. read *Jesus*

are hidden reefs in your love feasts when they feast with you without fear, caring for themselves; clouds without water, carried along by winds; autumn trees without fruit, doubly dead, uprooted;

13 wild waves of the sea, casting up their own shame like foam; wandering stars, for whom the black darkness has been reserved forever.

14 And about these also Enoch, *in* the seventh *generation* from Adam, prophesied, saying, "Behold, the Lord came with many thousands of His holy ones,

15 to execute judgment upon all, and to convict all the ungodly of all their ungodly deeds which they have done in an ungodly way, and of all the harsh things which ungodly sinners have spoken against Him."

16 These are grumblers, finding fault, following after their *own* lusts; they speak arrogantly, flattering people for the sake of *gaining an* advantage.

17 But you, beloved, ought to remember the words that were spoken beforehand by the apostles of our Lord Jesus Christ,

18 that they were saying to you, "In the last time there shall be mockers, following after their own ungodly lusts."

19 These are the ones who cause divisions, worldly-minded, devoid of the Spirit.

20 But you, beloved, building yourselves up on your most holy faith; praying in the Holy Spirit;

21 keep yourselves in the love of God, waiting anxiously for the mercy of our Lord Jesus Christ to eternal life.

22 And have mercy on some, who are doubting;

23 save others, snatching them out of the fire; and on some have mercy with fear, hating even the garment polluted by the flesh.

24 Now to Him who is able to keep you from stumbling, and to make you stand in the presence of His glory blameless with great joy,

25 to the only God our Savior, through Jesus Christ our Lord, *be* glory, majesty, dominion and authority, before all time and now and forever. Amen.

REVELATION TO JOHN

THE Revelation of Jesus Christ, which God gave Him to show to His bond-servants, the things which must shortly take place; and He sent and communicated *it* by His angel to His bond-servant John,

2 who bore witness to the word of God and to the testimony of Jesus Christ, *even* to all that he saw.

3 Blessed is he who reads and those who hear the words of the prophecy, and heed the things which are written in it; for the time is near.

4 John to the seven churches that are in Asia: Grace to you and peace, from Him who is and who was and who is to come; and from the seven Spirits who are before His throne;

5 and from Jesus Christ, the faithful witness, the first-born of the dead, and the ruler of the kings of the earth. To Him who loves us, and released us from our sins by His blood,

6 and He has made us *to be* a kingdom, priests to His God and Father; to Him *be* the glory and the dominion forever and ever. Amen.

7 BEHOLD, HE IS COMING WITH THE CLOUDS, and every eye will see Him, even those who pierced Him; and all the tribes of the earth will mourn over Him. Even so. Amen.

8 "I am the Alpha and the Omega," says the Lord God, "who is and who was and who is to come, the Almighty."

9 I, John, your brother and fellow partaker in the tribulation and kingdom and perseverance *which are* in Jesus, was on the island called Patmos, because of the word of God and the testimony of Jesus.

10 I was [1]in the Spirit on the Lord's day, and I heard behind me a loud voice like *the sound of* a trumpet,

11 saying, "Write in a book what you see, and send *it* to the seven churches: to Ephesus and to Smyrna and to Pergamum and to Thyatira and to Sardis and to Philadelphia and to Laodicea."

12 And I turned to see the voice that was speaking with me. And having turned I saw seven golden lampstands;

13 and in the middle of the lampstands one like [2]a son of man, clothed in a robe reaching to the feet, and girded across His breast with a golden girdle.

14 And His head and His hair were white like white wool, like snow; and His eyes were like a flame of fire;

15 and His feet *were* like burnished bronze, when it has been caused to glow in a furnace, and His voice *was* like the sound of many waters.

16 And in His right hand He held seven stars; and out of His mouth came a sharp two-edged sword; and His face was like the sun shining in its strength.

17 And when I saw Him, I fell

---

[1] Or, *in spirit* [2] Or, *the Son of Man*

at His feet as a dead man. And He laid His right hand upon me, saying, "Do not be afraid; I am the first and the last,

18 and the living One; and I was dead, and behold, I am alive forevermore, and I have the keys of death and of Hades.

19 "Write therefore the things which you have seen, and the things which are, and the things which shall take place after these things.

20 "As for the mystery of the seven stars which you saw in My right hand, and the seven golden lampstands: the seven stars are the angels of the seven churches, and the seven lampstands are the seven churches.

CHAPTER 2

"TO the angel of the church in Ephesus write:

The One who holds the seven stars in His right hand, the One who walks among the seven golden lampstands, says this:

2 'I know your deeds and your toil and perseverance, and that you cannot endure evil men, and you put to the test those who call themselves apostles, and they are not, and you found them to be false;

3 and you have perseverance and have endured for My name's sake, and have not grown weary.

4 'But I have this against you, that you have left your first love.

5 'Remember therefore from where you have fallen, and repent and do the deeds you did at first; or else I am coming to you, and will remove your lampstand out of its place—unless you repent.

6 'Yet this you do have, that you hate the deeds of the Nicolaitans, which I also hate.

7 'He who has an ear, let him hear what the Spirit says to the churches. To him who overcomes, I will grant to eat of the tree of life, which is in the Paradise of God.'

8 "And to the angel of the church in Smyrna write:

The first and the last, who was dead, and has come to life, says this:

9 'I know your tribulation and your poverty (but you are rich), and the blasphemy by those who say they are Jews and are not, but are a synagogue of Satan.

10 'Do not fear what you are about to suffer. Behold, the devil is about to cast some of you into prison, that you may be tested, and you will have tribulation ten days. Be faithful until death, and I will give you the crown of life.

11 'He who has an ear, let him hear what the Spirit says to the churches. He who overcomes shall not be hurt by the second death.'

12 "And to the angel of the church in Pergamum write:

The One who has the sharp two-edged sword says this:

13 'I know where you dwell, where Satan's throne is; and you hold fast My name, and did not deny My faith, even in the days of Antipas, My witness, My faithful one, who was killed among you, where Satan dwells.

14 'But I have a few things against you, because you have there some who hold the teaching of Balaam, who kept teaching Balak to put a stumbling block before the sons of Israel, to eat things sacrificed to idols, and to commit acts of immorality.

15 'Thus you also have some who in the same way hold the teaching of the Nicolaitans.

16 'Repent therefore; or else I am coming to you quickly, and I will make war against them with the sword of My mouth.

17 'He who has an ear, let him hear what the Spirit says to the churches. To him who overcomes, to him I will give *some* of the hidden manna, and I will give him a white stone, and a new name written on the stone which no one knows but he who receives it.'

18 "And to the angel of the church in Thyatira write:

The Son of God, who has eyes like a flame of fire, and His feet are like burnished bronze, says this:

19 'I know your deeds, and your love and faith and service and perseverance, and that your deeds of late are greater than at first.

20 'But I have *this* against you, that you tolerate the woman Jezebel, who calls herself a prophetess, and she teaches and leads My bond-servants astray, so that they commit *acts* of immorality and eat things sacrificed to idols.

21 'And I gave her time to repent; and she does not want to repent of her immorality.

22 'Behold, I will cast her upon a bed *of sickness*, and those who commit adultery with her into great tribulation, unless they repent of ³her deeds.

23 'And I will kill her children with pestilence; and all the churches will know that I am He who searches the minds and hearts; and I will give to each one of you according to your deeds.

24 'But I say to you, the rest who are in Thyatira, who do not hold this teaching, who have not known the deep things of Satan, as they call them —I place no other burden on you.

25 'Nevertheless what you have, hold fast until I come.

26 'And he who overcomes, and he who keeps My deeds until the end, TO HIM I WILL GIVE AUTHORITY OVER THE NATIONS;

27 AND HE SHALL RULE THEM WITH A ROD OF IRON, AS THE VESSELS OF THE POTTER ARE BROKEN TO PIECES, as I also have received *authority* from My Father;

28 and I will give him the morning star.

29 'He who has an ear, let him hear what the Spirit says to the churches.'

CHAPTER 3

"AND to the angel of the church in Sardis write:

He who has the seven Spirits of God, and the seven stars, says this: 'I know your deeds, that you have a name that you are alive, but you are dead.

2 'Wake up, and strengthen the things that remain, which were about to die; for I have not found your deeds completed in the sight of My God.

3 'Remember therefore what you have received and heard; and keep *it*, and repent. If therefore you will not wake up, I will come like a thief, and you will not know at what hour I will come upon you.

4 'But you have a few people in Sardis who have not soiled their garments; and they will

³ Some mss. read *their*

walk with Me in white; for they are worthy.

5 'He who overcomes shall thus be clothed in white garments; and I will not erase his name from the book of life, and I will confess his name before My Father, and before His angels.

6 'He who has an ear, let him hear what the Spirit says to the churches.'

7 "And to the angel of the church in Philadelphia write:

He who is holy, who is true, who has the key of David, who opens and no one will shut, and who shuts and no one opens, says this:

8 'I know your ⁴deeds. Behold, I have put before you an open door which no one can shut, because you have a little power, and have kept My word, and have not denied My name.

9 'Behold, I will cause those of the synagogue of Satan, who say that they are Jews, and are not, but lie—behold, I will make them to come and bow down at your feet, and to know that I have loved you.

10 'Because you have kept the word of My perseverance, I also will keep you from the hour of testing, that hour which is about to come upon the whole world, to test those who dwell upon the earth.

11 'I am coming quickly; hold fast what you have, in order that no one take your crown.

12 'He who overcomes, I will make him a pillar in the temple of My God, and he will not go out from it anymore; and I will write upon him the name of My God, and the name of the city of My God, the new Jerusalem, which comes down out of heaven from My God, and My new name.

13 'He who has an ear, let him hear what the Spirit says to the churches.'

14 "And to the angel of the church in Laodicea write:

The Amen, the faithful and true Witness, the ⁵Beginning of the creation of God, says this:

15 'I know your deeds, that you are neither cold nor hot; I would that you were cold or hot.

16 'So because you are lukewarm, and neither hot nor cold, I will spit you out of My mouth.

17 'Because you say, "I am rich, and have become wealthy, and have need of nothing," and you do not know that you are wretched and miserable and poor and blind and naked,

18 'I advise you to buy from Me gold refined by fire, that you may become rich, and white garments, that you may clothe yourself, and that the shame of your nakedness may not be revealed; and eyesalve to anoint your eyes, that you may see.

19 'Those whom I love, I reprove and discipline; be zealous therefore, and repent.

20 'Behold, I stand at the door and knock; if anyone hears My voice and opens the door, I will come in to him, and will dine with him, and he with Me.

21 'He who overcomes, I will grant to him to sit down with Me on My throne, as I also overcame and sat down with My Father on His throne.

22 'He who has an ear, let him hear what the Spirit says to the churches.'"

⁴ Or, deeds (behold . . . shut), that you
⁵ I.e., origin or source

CHAPTER 4

AFTER these things I looked, and behold, a door *standing* open in heaven, and the first voice which I had heard, like the *sound* of a trumpet speaking with me, said, "Come up here, and I will show you what must take place after these things."

2 Immediately I was [6]in the Spirit; and behold, a throne was standing in heaven, and One sitting on the throne.

3 And He who was sitting *was* like a jasper stone and a sardius in appearance; and *there was a* rainbow around the throne, like an emerald in appearance.

4 And around the throne *were* twenty-four thrones; and upon the thrones *I saw* twenty-four elders sitting, clothed in white garments, and golden crowns on their heads.

5 And from the throne proceed flashes of lightning and sounds and peals of thunder. And *there were* seven lamps of fire burning before the throne, which are the seven Spirits of God;

6 and before the throne *there was*, as it were, a sea of glass like crystal; and in the center and around the throne, four living creatures full of eyes in front and behind.

7 And the first creature *was* like a lion, and the second creature like a calf, and the third creature had a face like that of a man, and the fourth creature *was* like a flying eagle.

8 And the four living creatures, each one of them having six wings, are full of eyes around and within; and day and night they do not cease to say,

"HOLY, HOLY, HOLY, *is* THE LORD GOD, THE ALMIGHTY, who was and who is and who is to come."

9 And when the living creatures give glory and honor and thanks to Him who sits on the throne, to Him who lives forever and ever,

10 the twenty-four elders will fall down before Him who sits on the throne, and will worship Him who lives forever and ever, and will cast their crowns before the throne, saying,

11 "Worthy art Thou, our Lord and our God, to receive glory and honor and power; for Thou didst create all things, and because of Thy will they existed, and were created."

CHAPTER 5

AND I saw in the right hand of Him who sat on the throne a book written inside and on the back, sealed up with seven seals.

2 And I saw a strong angel proclaiming with a loud voice, "Who is worthy to open the book and to break its seals?"

3 And no one in heaven, or on the earth, or under the earth, was able to open the book, or to look into it.

4 And I *began* to weep greatly, because no one was found worthy to open the book, or to look into it;

5 and one of the elders *said to me, "Stop weeping; behold, the Lion that is from the tribe of Judah, the Root of David, has overcome so as to open the book and its seven seals."

6 Or, *in spirit*

6 And I saw [7]between the throne (with the four living creatures) and the elders a Lamb standing, as if slain, having seven horns and seven eyes, which are the seven Spirits of God, sent out into all the earth.

7 And He came, and He took *it* out of the right hand of Him who sat on the throne.

8 And when He had taken the book, the four living creatures and the twenty-four elders fell down before the Lamb, having each one a harp, and golden bowls full of incense, which are the prayers of the saints.

9 And they *sang a new song, saying,

"Worthy art Thou to take the book, and to break its seals; for Thou wast slain, and didst purchase for God with Thy blood *men* from every tribe and tongue and people and nation.

10 "And Thou hast made them *to be* a kingdom and priests to our God; and they will reign upon the earth."

11 And I looked, and I heard the voice of many angels around the throne and the living creatures and the elders; and the number of them was myriads of myriads, and thousands of thousands,

12 saying with a loud voice,

"Worthy is the Lamb that was slain to receive power and riches and wisdom

and might and honor and glory and blessing."

13 And every created thing which is in heaven and on the earth and under the earth and on the sea, and all things in them, I heard saying,

"To Him who sits on the throne, and to the Lamb, *be* blessing and honor and glory and dominion forever and ever."

14 And the four living creatures kept saying, "Amen." And the elders fell down and worshiped.

CHAPTER 6

AND I saw when the Lamb broke one of the seven seals, and I heard one of the four living creatures saying as with a voice of thunder, "Come."

2 And I looked, and behold, a white horse, and he who sat on it had a bow; and a crown was given to him; and he went out conquering, and to conquer.

3 And when He broke the second seal, I heard the second living creature saying, "Come."

4 And another, a red horse, went out; and to him who sat on it, it was granted to take peace from the earth, and that *men* should slay one another; and a great sword was given to him.

5 And when He broke the third seal, I heard the third living creature saying, "Come." And I looked, and behold, a black horse; and he who sat on it had a pair of scales in his hand.

6 And I heard as it were a voice in the center of the four living creatures saying, "A [8]quart of wheat for a [9]denarius, and three quarts of barley for a denarius;

---

[7] Lit., *in the middle of the throne and of the four living creatures, and in the middle of the elders*

[8] Gr., *choenix*; i.e., a dry measure almost equal to a quart

[9] The denarius was equivalent to one day's wage

and do not harm the oil and the wine."

7 And when He broke the fourth seal, I heard the voice of the fourth living creature saying, "Come."

8 And I looked, and behold, an ashen horse; and he who sat on it had the name Death; and Hades was following with him. And authority was given to them over a fourth of the earth, to kill with sword and with famine and with pestilence and by the wild beasts of the earth.

9 And when He broke the fifth seal, I saw underneath the altar the souls of those who had been slain because of the word of God, and because of the testimony which they had maintained;

10 and they cried out with a loud voice, saying, "How long, O Lord, holy and true, wilt Thou refrain from judging and avenging our blood on those who dwell on the earth?"

11 And there was given to each of them a white robe; and they were told that they should rest for a little while longer, until *the number of* their fellow servants and their brethren who were to be killed even as they had been, should be completed also.

12 And I looked when He broke the sixth seal, and there was a great earthquake; and the sun became black as sackcloth *made* of hair, and the whole moon became like blood;

13 and the stars of the sky fell to the earth, as a fig tree casts its unripe figs when shaken by a great wind.

14 And the sky was split apart like a scroll when it is rolled up; and every mountain and island

were moved out of their places.

15 And the kings of the earth and the great men and the [10]commanders and the rich and the strong and every slave and free man, hid themselves in the caves and among the rocks of the mountains;

16 and they *said to the mountains and to the rocks, "Fall on us and hide us from the presence of Him who sits on the throne, and from the wrath of the Lamb;

17 for the great day of their wrath has come; and who is able to stand?"

CHAPTER 7

AFTER this I saw four angels standing at the four corners of the earth, holding back the four winds of the earth, so that no wind should blow on the earth or on the sea or on any tree.

2 And I saw another angel ascending from the rising of the sun, having the seal of the living God; and he cried out with a loud voice to the four angels to whom it was granted to harm the earth and the sea,

3 saying, "Do not harm the earth or the sea or the trees, until we have sealed the bondservants of our God on their foreheads."

4 And I heard the number of those who were sealed, one hundred and forty-four thousand sealed from every tribe of the sons of Israel:

5 from the tribe of Judah, twelve thousand *were* sealed, from the tribe of Reuben twelve thousand, from the tribe of Gad twelve thousand,

[10] I.e., chiliarchs, in command of one thousand troops

6 from the tribe of Asher twelve thousand, from the tribe of Naphtali twelve thousand, from the tribe of Manasseh twelve thousand,

7 from the tribe of Simeon twelve thousand, from the tribe of Levi twelve thousand, from the tribe of Issachar twelve thousand,

8 from the tribe of Zebulun twelve thousand, from the tribe of Joseph twelve thousand, from the tribe of Benjamin, twelve thousand *were* sealed.

9 After these things I looked, and behold, a great multitude, which no one could count, from every nation and *all* tribes and peoples and tongues, standing before the throne and before the Lamb, clothed in white robes, and palm branches *were* in their hands;

10 and they cry out with a loud voice, saying,

"**S**alvation to our God who sits on the throne, and to the Lamb."

11 And all the angels were standing around the throne and *around* the elders and the four living creatures; and they fell on their faces before the throne and worshiped God,

12 saying,

"**A**men, blessing and glory and wisdom and thanksgiving and honor and power and might, *be* to our God forever and ever. Amen."

13 And one of the elders answered, saying to me, "These who are clothed in the white robes, who are they, and from where have they come?"

14 And I said to him, "My lord, you know." And he said to me, "These are the ones who come out of the great tribulation, and they have washed their robes and made them white in the blood of the Lamb.

15"For this reason, they are before the throne of God; and they serve Him day and night in His temple; and He who sits on the throne shall spread His tabernacle over them.

16"They shall hunger no more, neither thirst anymore; neither shall the sun beat down on them, nor any heat;

17 for the Lamb in the center of the throne shall be their shepherd, and shall guide them to springs of the water of life; and God shall wipe every tear from their eyes."

CHAPTER 8

AND when He broke the seventh seal, there was silence in heaven for about half an hour.

2 And I saw the seven angels who stand before God; and seven trumpets were given to them.

3 And another angel came and stood at the altar, holding a golden censer; and much incense was given to him, that he might add it to the prayers of all the saints upon the golden altar which was before the throne.

4 And the smoke of the incense, with the prayers of the saints, went up before God out of the angel's hand.

5 And the angel took the censer; and he filled it with the fire of the altar and threw it to the earth; and there followed peals of thunder and sounds and flashes of lightning and an earthquake.

6 And the seven angels who had the seven trumpets prepared themselves to sound them.

7 And the first sounded, and

there came hail and fire, mixed with blood, and they were thrown to the earth; and a third of the earth was burned up, and a third of the trees were burned up, and all the green grass was burned up.

8 And the second angel sounded, and *something* like a great mountain burning with fire was thrown into the sea; and a third of the sea became blood;

9 and a third of the creatures, which were in the sea and had life, died; and a third of the ships were destroyed.

10 And the third angel sounded, and a great star fell from heaven, burning like a torch, and it fell on a third of the rivers and on the springs of waters;

11 and the name of the star is called Wormwood; and a third of the waters became wormwood; and many men died from the waters, because they were made bitter.

12 And the fourth angel sounded, and a third of the sun and a third of the moon and a third of the stars were smitten, so that a third of them might be darkened and the day might not shine for a third of it, and the night in the same way.

13 And I looked, and I heard an eagle flying in midheaven, saying with a loud voice, "Woe, woe, woe, to those who dwell on the earth, because of the remaining blasts of the trumpet of the three angels who are about to sound!"

CHAPTER 9

AND the fifth angel sounded, and I saw a star from heaven which had fallen to the earth; and the key of the bottomless pit was given to him.

2 And he opened the bottomless pit; and smoke went up out of the pit, like the smoke of a great furnace; and the sun and the air were darkened by the smoke of the pit.

3 And out of the smoke came forth locusts upon the earth; and power was given them, as the scorpions of the earth have power.

4 And they were told that they should not hurt the grass of the earth, nor any green thing, nor any tree, but only the men who do not have the seal of God on their foreheads.

5 And they were not permitted to kill anyone, but to torment for five months; and their torment was like the torment of a scorpion when it stings a man.

6 And in those days men will seek death and will not find it; and they will long to die and death flees from them.

7 And the appearance of the locusts was like horses prepared for battle; and on their heads, as it were, crowns like gold, and their faces were like the faces of men.

8 And they had hair like the hair of women, and their teeth were like *the teeth* of lions.

9 And they had breastplates like breastplates of iron; and the sound of their wings was like the sound of chariots, of many horses rushing to battle.

10 And they have tails like scorpions, and stings; and in their tails is their power to hurt men for five months.

11 They have as king over them, the angel of the abyss; his

name in Hebrew is [11]Abaddon, and in the Greek he has the name Apollyon.

12 The first woe is past; behold, two woes are still coming after these things.

13 And the sixth angel sounded, and I heard a voice from the [12]four horns of the golden altar which is before God,

14 one saying to the sixth angel who had the trumpet, "Release the four angels who are bound at the great river Euphrates."

15 And the four angels, who had been prepared for the hour and day and month and year, were released, so that they might kill a third of mankind.

16 And the number of the armies of the horsemen was two hundred million; I heard the number of them.

17 And this is how I saw in the vision the horses and those who sat on them: *the riders* had breastplates *the color* of fire and of hyacinth and of brimstone; and the heads of the horses are like the heads of lions; and out of their mouths proceed fire and smoke and brimstone.

18 A third of mankind was killed by these three plagues, by the fire and the smoke and the brimstone, which proceeded out of their mouths.

19 For the power of the horses is in their mouths and in their tails; for their tails are like serpents and have heads; and with them they do harm.

20 And the rest of mankind, who were not killed by these plagues, did not repent of the works of their hands, so as not to worship demons, and the idols of

gold and of silver and of brass and of stone and of wood, which can neither see nor hear nor walk;

21 and they did not repent of their murders nor of their sorceries nor of their immorality nor of their thefts.

CHAPTER 10

AND I saw another strong angel coming down out of heaven, clothed with a cloud; and the rainbow was upon his head, and his face was like the sun, and his feet like pillars of fire;

2 and he had in his hand a little book which was open. And he placed his right foot on the sea and his left on the land;

3 and he cried out with a loud voice, as when a lion roars; and when he had cried out, the seven peals of thunder uttered their voices.

4 And when the seven peals of thunder had spoken, I was about to write; and I heard a voice from heaven saying, "Seal up the things which the seven peals of thunder have spoken, and do not write them."

5 And the angel whom I saw standing on the sea and on the land lifted up his right hand to heaven,

6 and swore by Him who lives forever and ever, WHO CREATED HEAVEN AND THE THINGS IN IT, AND THE EARTH AND THE THINGS IN IT, AND THE SEA AND THE THINGS IN IT, that there shall be delay no longer,

7 but in the days of the voice of the seventh angel, when he is about to sound, then the mystery of God is finished, as He preached to His servants the prophets.

[11] I.e., destruction
[12] Some ancient mss. do not contain *four*

8 And the voice which I heard from heaven, *I heard* again speaking with me, and saying, "Go, take the book which is open in the hand of the angel who stands on the sea and on the land."

9 And I went to the angel, telling him to give me the little book. And he *said to me, "Take it, and eat it; and it will make your stomach bitter, but in your mouth it will be sweet as honey."

10 And I took the little book out of the angel's hand and ate it, and it was in my mouth sweet as honey; and when I had eaten it, my stomach was made bitter.

11 And they *said to me, "You must prophesy again concerning many peoples and nations and tongues and kings."

CHAPTER 11

AND there was given me a measuring rod like a staff; and someone said, "Rise and measure the temple of God, and the altar, and those who worship in it.

2 "And leave out the court which is outside the temple, and do not measure it, for it has been given to the nations; and they will tread under foot the holy city for forty-two months.

3 "And I will grant *authority* to my two witnesses, and they will prophesy for twelve hundred and sixty days, clothed in sackcloth."

4 These are the two olive trees and the two lampstands that stand before the Lord of the earth.

5 And if anyone desires to harm them, fire proceeds out of their mouth and devours their enemies; and if anyone would de-sire to harm them, in this manner he must be killed.

6 These have the power to shut up the sky, in order that rain may not fall during the days of their prophesying; and they have power over the waters to turn them into blood, and to smite the earth with every plague, as often as they desire.

7 And when they have finished their testimony, the beast that comes up out of the abyss will make war with them, and overcome them and kill them.

8 And their dead [13]bodies *will lie* in the street of the great city which [14]mystically is called Sodom and Egypt, where also their Lord was crucified.

9 And those from the peoples and tribes and tongues and nations *will* look at their dead [13]bodies for three and a half days, and will not permit their dead bodies to be laid in a tomb.

10 And those who dwell on the earth *will* rejoice over them and make merry; and they will send gifts to one another, because these two prophets tormented those who dwell on the earth.

11 And after the three and a half days the breath of life from God came into them, and they stood on their feet; and great fear fell upon those who were beholding them.

12 And they heard a loud voice from heaven saying to them, "Come up here." And they went up into heaven in the cloud, and their enemies beheld them.

13 And in that hour there was a great earthquake, and a tenth of the city fell; and seven thousand people were killed in the earth-

---

[13] Some ancient mss. read body
[14] Lit., *spiritually*

quake, and the rest were terrified and gave glory to the God of heaven.

14 The second woe is past; behold, the third woe is coming quickly.

15 And the seventh angel sounded; and there arose loud voices in heaven, saying,

"The kingdom of the world has become *the kingdom* of our Lord, and of His [15]Christ; and He will reign forever and ever."

16 And the twenty-four elders, who sit on their thrones before God, fell on their faces and worshiped God,

17 saying,

"We give Thee thanks, O Lord God, the Almighty, who art and who wast, because Thou hast taken Thy great power and hast begun to reign.

18"And the nations were enraged, and Thy wrath came, and the time *came* for the dead to be judged, and *the time* to give their reward to Thy bond-servants the prophets and to the saints and to those who fear Thy name, the small and the great, and to destroy those who destroy the earth."

19 And the temple of God which is in heaven was opened; and the ark of His covenant appeared in His temple, and there were flashes of lightning and sounds and peals of thunder and an earthquake and a great hailstorm.

CHAPTER 12

AND a great sign appeared in heaven: a woman clothed with the sun, and the moon under her feet, and on her head a crown of twelve stars;

her feet, and on her head a crown of twelve stars;

2 and she was with child; and she *cried out, being in labor and in pain to give birth.

3 And another sign appeared in heaven: and behold, a great red dragon having seven heads and ten horns, and on his heads *were* seven diadems.

4 And his tail *swept away a third of the stars of heaven, and threw them to the earth. And the dragon stood before the woman who was about to give birth, so that when she gave birth he might devour her child.

5 And she gave birth to a son, a male *child*, who is to rule all the nations with a rod of iron; and her child was caught up to God and to His throne.

6 And the woman fled into the wilderness where she *had a place prepared by God, so that there she might be nourished for one thousand two hundred and sixty days.

7 And there was war in heaven, Michael and his angels waging war with the dragon. And the dragon and his angels waged war,

8 and they were not strong enough, and there was no longer a place found for them in heaven.

9 And the great dragon was thrown down, the serpent of old who is called the devil and Satan, who deceives the whole world; he was thrown down to the earth, and his angels were thrown down with him.

10 And I heard a loud voice in heaven, saying,

"Now the salvation, and the power, and the kingdom of our God and the authority of His Christ have come, for the accuser

[15] I.e., Messiah

of our brethren has been thrown down, who accuses them before our God day and night.

11 "And they overcame him because of the blood of the Lamb and because of the word of their testimony, and they did not love their life even to death.

12 "For this reason, rejoice, O heavens and you who dwell in them. Woe to the earth and the sea, because the devil has come down to you, having great wrath, knowing that he has *only* a short time."

13 And when the dragon saw that he was thrown down to the earth, he persecuted the woman who gave birth to the male *child*.

14 And the two wings of the great eagle were given to the woman, in order that she might fly into the wilderness to her place, where she *was nourished for a time and times and half a time, from the presence of the serpent.

15 And the serpent poured water like a river out of his mouth after the woman, so that he might cause her to be swept away with the flood.

16 And the earth helped the woman, and the earth opened its mouth and drank up the river which the dragon poured out of his mouth.

17 And the dragon was enraged with the woman, and went off to make war with the rest of her offspring, who keep the commandments of God and hold to the testimony of Jesus.

CHAPTER 13

AND he stood on the sand of the seashore.

And I saw a beast coming up out of the sea, having ten horns and seven heads, and on his horns *were* ten diadems, and on his heads *were* blasphemous names.

2 And the beast which I saw was like a leopard, and his feet were *like those* of a bear, and his mouth like the mouth of a lion. And the dragon gave him his power and his throne and great authority.

3 And *I saw* one of his heads as if it had been slain, and his fatal wound was healed. And the whole earth was amazed *and followed* after the beast;

4 and they worshiped the dragon, because he gave his authority to the beast; and they worshiped the beast, saying, "Who is like the beast, and who is able to wage war with him?"

5 And there was given to him a mouth speaking arrogant words and blasphemies; and authority to act for forty-two months was given to him.

6 And he opened his mouth in blasphemies against God, to blaspheme His name and His tabernacle, *that is,* those who dwell in heaven.

7 And it was given to him to make war with the saints and to overcome them; and authority over every tribe and people and tongue and nation was given to him.

8 And all who dwell on the earth will worship him, *everyone* whose name has not been [16]written from the foundation of the world in the book of life of the Lamb who has been slain.

9 If anyone has an ear, let him hear.

[16] Or, *written in the book … slain from the foundation of the world*

10 If anyone [17]*is destined* for captivity, to captivity he goes; if anyone kills with the sword, with the sword he must be killed. Here is the perseverance and the faith of the saints.

11 And I saw another beast coming up out of the earth; and he had two horns like a lamb, and he spoke as a dragon.

12 And he exercises all the authority of the first beast in his presence. And he makes the earth and those who dwell in it to worship the first beast, whose fatal wound was healed.

13 And he performs great signs, so that he even makes fire come down out of heaven to the earth in the presence of men.

14 And he deceives those who dwell on the earth because of the signs which it was given him to perform in the presence of the beast, telling those who dwell on the earth to make an image to the beast who *had the wound of the sword and has come to life.

15 And there was given to him to give breath to the image of the beast, that the image of the beast might even [18]speak and cause as many as do not worship the image of the beast to be killed.

16 And he causes all, the small and the great, and the rich and the poor, and the free men and the slaves, to be given a mark on their right hand, or on their forehead,

17 and *he provides* that no one should be able to buy or to sell, except the one who has the mark, *either* the name of the beast or the number of his name.

18 Here is wisdom. Let him who has understanding calculate the number of the beast, for the number is that of a man; and his number is [19]six hundred and sixty-six.

CHAPTER 14

AND I looked, and behold, the Lamb *was* standing on Mount Zion, and with Him one hundred and forty-four thousand, having His name and the name of His Father written on their foreheads.

2 And I heard a voice from heaven, like the sound of many waters and like the sound of loud thunder, and the voice which I heard *was* like *the sound* of harpists playing on their harps.

3 And they *sang a new song before the throne and before the four living creatures and the elders; and no one could learn the song except the one hundred and forty-four thousand who had been purchased from the earth.

4 These are the ones who have not been defiled with women, for they [20]have kept themselves chaste. These *are* the ones who follow the Lamb wherever He goes. These have been purchased from among men as first fruits to God and to the Lamb.

5 And no lie was found in their mouth; they are blameless.

6 And I saw another angel flying in midheaven, having an eternal gospel to preach to those who live on the earth, and to every nation and tribe and tongue and people;

7 and he said with a loud voice, "Fear God, and give Him glory, because the hour of His

---

[17] Or, leads *into captivity*
[18] Some ancient mss. read *speak, and he will cause*   [19] Some mss. read 616
[20] Lit., *are chaste men*

judgment has come; and worship Him who made the heaven and the earth and sea and springs of waters."

8 And another angel, a second one, followed, saying, "Fallen, fallen is Babylon the great, she who has made all the nations drink of the wine of the passion of her immorality."

9 And another angel, a third one, followed them, saying with a loud voice, "If anyone worships the beast and his image, and receives a mark on his forehead or upon his hand,

10 he also will drink of the wine of the wrath of God, which is mixed in full strength in the cup of His anger; and he will be tormented with fire and brimstone in the presence of the holy angels and in the presence of the Lamb.

11 "And the smoke of their torment goes up forever and ever; and they have no rest day and night, those who worship the beast and his image, and whoever receives the mark of his name."

12 Here is the perseverance of the saints who keep the commandments of God and their faith in Jesus.

13 And I heard a voice from heaven, saying, "Write, 'Blessed are the dead who die in the Lord from now on!'" "Yes," says the Spirit, "that they may rest from their labors, for their deeds follow with them."

14 And I looked, and behold, a white cloud, and sitting on the cloud was one like 21a son of man, having a golden crown on His head, and a sharp sickle in His hand.

15 And another angel came out of the temple, crying out with a loud voice to Him who sat on the cloud, "Put in your sickle and reap, because the hour to reap has come, because the harvest of the earth is ripe."

16 And He who sat on the cloud swung His sickle over the earth; and the earth was reaped.

17 And another angel came out of the temple which is in heaven, and he also had a sharp sickle.

18 And another angel, the one who has power over fire, came out from the altar; and he called with a loud voice to him who had the sharp sickle, saying, "Put in your sharp sickle, and gather the clusters from the vine of the earth, because her grapes are ripe."

19 And the angel swung his sickle to the earth, and gathered the clusters from the vine of the earth, and threw them into the great wine press of the wrath of God.

20 And the wine press was trodden outside the city, and blood came out from the wine press, up to the horses' bridles, for a distance of 22two hundred miles.

CHAPTER 15

AND I saw another sign in heaven, great and marvelous, seven angels who had seven plagues, which are the last, because in them the wrath of God is finished.

2 And I saw, as it were, a sea of glass mixed with fire, and those who had come off victorious from the beast and from his

---

21 Or, the Son of Man
22 Lit., sixteen hundred stadia. A stadion was about six hundred feet.

image and from the number of his name, standing on the sea of glass, holding harps of God.

3 And they *sang the song of Moses the bond-servant of God and the song of the Lamb, saying,

> "Great and marvelous are
>   Thy works,
> O Lord God, the Almighty;
> Righteous and true are Thy
>   ways,
> Thou King of the [23]nations.

4 "Who will not fear, O Lord, and glorify Thy name?
> For Thou alone art holy;
> For ALL THE NATIONS WILL
>   COME AND WORSHIP BE-
>   FORE THEE,
> For Thy righteous acts
>   have been revealed."

5 After these things I looked, and the temple of the tabernacle of testimony in heaven was opened,

6 and the seven angels who had the seven plagues came out of the temple, clothed in [24]linen, clean *and* bright, and girded around their breasts with golden girdles.

7 And one of the four living creatures gave to the seven angels seven golden bowls full of the wrath of God, who lives forever and ever.

8 And the temple was filled with smoke from the glory of God and from His power; and no one was able to enter the temple until the seven plagues of the seven angels were finished.

CHAPTER 16

AND I heard a loud voice from the temple, saying to the seven angels, "Go and pour out the seven bowls of the wrath of God into the earth."

2 And the first *angel* went and poured out his bowl into the earth; and it became a loathsome and malignant sore upon the men who had the mark of the beast and who worshiped his image.

3 And the second *angel* poured out his bowl into the sea, and it became blood like *that* of a dead man; and every living [25]thing in the sea died.

4 And the third *angel* poured out his bowl into the rivers and the springs of waters; and [26]they became blood.

5 And I heard the angel of the waters saying, "Righteous art Thou, who art and who wast, O Holy One, because Thou didst judge these things;

6 for they poured out the blood of saints and prophets, and Thou hast given them blood to drink. They deserve it."

7 And I heard the altar saying, "Yes, O Lord God, the Almighty, true and righteous are Thy judgments."

8 And the fourth *angel* poured out his bowl upon the sun; and it was given to it to scorch men with fire.

9 And men were scorched with fierce heat; and they blasphemed the name of God who has the power over these plagues; and they did not repent, so as to give Him glory.

10 And the fifth *angel* poured out his bowl upon the throne of the beast; and his kingdom

---

23 Some ancient mss. read *ages*
24 Some mss. read *stone*
25 Lit., *soul.* Some ancient mss. read *thing, the things in the sea.*
26 Some ancient mss. read *it became*

became darkened; and they gnawed their tongues because of pain,

11 and they blasphemed the God of heaven because of their pains and their sores; and they did not repent of their deeds.

12 And the sixth *angel* poured out his bowl upon the great river, the Euphrates; and its water was dried up, that the way might be prepared for the kings from the east.

13 And I saw *coming* out of the mouth of the dragon and out of the mouth of the beast and out of the mouth of the false prophet, three unclean spirits like frogs;

14 for they are spirits of demons, performing signs, which go out to the kings of the whole world, to gather them together for the war of the great day of God, the Almighty.

15 ("Behold, I am coming like a thief. Blessed is the one who stays awake and keeps his garments, lest he walk about naked and men see his shame.")

16 And they gathered them together to the place which in Hebrew is called [27]Har-Magedon.

17 And the seventh *angel* poured out his bowl upon the air; and a loud voice came out of the temple from the throne, saying, "It is done."

18 And there were flashes of lightning and sounds and peals of thunder; and there was a great earthquake, such as there had not been since man came to be upon the earth, so great an earthquake *was it, and* so mighty.

19 And the great city was split into three parts, and the cities of the nations fell. And Babylon the great was remembered before

God, to give her the cup of the wine of His fierce wrath.

20 And every island fled away, and the mountains were not found.

21 And huge hailstones, about [28]one hundred pounds each, *came down from heaven upon men; and men blasphemed God because of the plague of the hail, because its plague *was extremely severe.

CHAPTER 17

AND one of the seven angels who had the seven bowls came and spoke with me, saying, "Come here, I shall show you the judgment of the great harlot who sits on many waters,

2 with whom the kings of the earth committed *acts of* immorality, and those who dwell on the earth were made drunk with the wine of her immorality."

3 And he carried me away [29]in the Spirit into a wilderness; and I saw a woman sitting on a scarlet beast, full of blasphemous names, having seven heads and ten horns.

4 And the woman was clothed in purple and scarlet, and adorned with gold and precious stones and pearls, having in her hand a gold cup full of abominations and of the unclean things of her immorality,

5 and upon her forehead a name *was* written, a mystery, "BABYLON THE GREAT, THE MOTHER OF HARLOTS AND OF THE ABOMINATIONS OF THE EARTH."

6 And I saw the woman drunk

[27] Some authorities read *Armageddon*
[28] Lit., *the weight of a talent*
[29] Or, *in spirit*

with the blood of the saints, and with the blood of the witnesses of Jesus. And when I saw her, I wondered greatly.

7 And the angel said to me, "Why do you wonder? I shall tell you the mystery of the woman and of the beast that carries her, which has the seven heads and the ten horns.

8 "The beast that you saw was and is not, and is about to come up out of the abyss and 30 to go to destruction. And those who dwell on the earth will wonder, whose name has not been written in the book of life from the foundation of the world, when they see the beast, that he was and is not and will come.

9 "Here is the mind which has wisdom. The seven heads are seven mountains on which the woman sits,

10 and they are seven kings; five have fallen, one is, the other has not yet come; and when he comes, he must remain a little while.

11 "And the beast which was and is not, is himself also an eighth, and is one of the seven, and he goes to destruction.

12 "And the ten horns which you saw are ten kings, who have not yet received a kingdom, but they receive authority as kings with the beast for one hour.

13 "These have one purpose and they give their power and authority to the beast.

14 "These will wage war against the Lamb, and the Lamb will overcome them, because He is Lord of lords and King of kings, and those who are with Him are

the called and chosen and faithful."

15 And he *said to me, "The waters which you saw where the harlot sits, are peoples and multitudes and nations and tongues.

16 "And the ten horns which you saw, and the beast, these will hate the harlot and will make her desolate and naked, and will eat her flesh and will burn her up with fire.

17 "For God has put it in their hearts to execute His purpose by having a common purpose, and by giving their kingdom to the beast, until the words of God should be fulfilled.

18 "And the woman whom you saw is the great city, which reigns over the kings of the earth."

CHAPTER 18

AFTER these things I saw another angel coming down from heaven, having great authority, and the earth was illumined with his glory.

2 And he cried out with a mighty voice, saying, "Fallen, fallen is Babylon the great! And she has become a dwelling place of demons and a prison of every unclean spirit, and a prison of every unclean and hateful bird.

3 "For all the nations 31 have drunk of the wine of the passion of her immorality, and the kings of the earth have committed acts of immorality with her, and the merchants of the earth have become rich by the wealth of her sensuality."

4 And I heard another voice from heaven, saying, "Come out of her, my people, that you may not participate in her sins and

---

30 Some ancient mss. read he goes
31 Many ancient mss. read have fallen by

that you may not receive of her plagues;

5 for her sins have piled up as high as heaven, and God has remembered her iniquities.

6 "Pay her back even as she has paid, and give back *to her* double according to her deeds; in the cup which she has mixed, mix twice as much for her.

7 "To the degree that she glorified herself and lived sensuously, to the same degree give her torment and mourning; for she says in her heart, 'I SIT *as* A QUEEN AND I AM NOT A WIDOW,' and will never see mourning.'

8 "For this reason in one day her plagues will come, pestilence and mourning and famine, and she will be burned up with fire; for the Lord God who judges her is strong.

9 "And the kings of the earth, who committed *acts of* immorality and lived sensuously with her, will weep and lament over her when they see the smoke of her burning,

10 standing at a distance because of the fear of her torment, saying, 'Woe, woe, the great city, Babylon, the strong city! For in one hour your judgment has come.'

11 "And the merchants of the earth weep and mourn over her, because no one buys their cargoes any more;

12 cargoes of gold and silver and precious stones and pearls and fine linen and purple and silk and scarlet, and every *kind of* citron wood and every article of ivory and every article *made* from very costly wood and bronze and iron and marble,

13 and cinnamon and spice and incense and perfume and frankincense and wine and olive oil and fine flour and wheat and cattle and sheep, and *cargoes of* horses and chariots and slaves and human lives.

14 "And the fruit you long for has gone from you, and all things that were luxurious and splendid have passed away from you and *men* will no longer find them.

15 "The merchants of these things, who became rich from her, will stand at a distance because of the fear of her torment, weeping and mourning,

16 saying, 'Woe, woe, the great city, she who was clothed in fine linen and purple and scarlet, and adorned with gold and precious stones and pearls;

17 for in one hour such great wealth has been laid waste!' And every shipmaster and every passenger and sailor, and as many as make their living by the sea, stood at a distance,

18 and were crying out as they saw the smoke of her burning, saying, 'What *city* is like the great city?'

19 "And they threw dust on their heads and were crying out, weeping and mourning, saying, 'Woe, woe, the great city, in which all who had ships at sea became rich by her wealth, for in one hour she has been laid waste!'

20 "Rejoice over her, O heaven, and you saints and apostles and prophets, because God has pronounced judgment for you against her."

21 And a strong angel took up a stone like a great millstone and threw it into the sea, saying, "Thus will Babylon, the great city, be thrown down with vio-

lence, and will not be found any longer.

22 "And the sound of harpists and musicians and flute-players and trumpeters will not be heard in you any longer; and no craftsman of any craft will be found in you any longer; and the sound of a mill will not be heard in you any longer;

23 and the light of a lamp will not shine in you any longer; and the voice of the bridegroom and bride will not be heard in you any longer; for your merchants were the great men of the earth, because all the nations were deceived by your sorcery.

24 "And in her was found the blood of prophets and of saints and of all who have been slain on the earth."

CHAPTER 19

AFTER these things I heard, as it were, a loud voice of a great multitude in heaven, saying,

"Hallelujah! Salvation and glory and power belong to our God;

2 BECAUSE HIS JUDGMENTS ARE TRUE AND RIGHTEOUS; for He has judged the great harlot who was corrupting the earth with her immorality, and HE HAS AVENGED THE BLOOD OF HIS BOND-SERVANTS ON HER."

3 And a second time they said, "Hallelujah! HER SMOKE RISES UP FOREVER AND EVER."

4 And the twenty-four elders and the four living creatures fell down and worshiped God who sits on the throne saying, "Amen. Hallelujah!"

5 And a voice came from the throne, saying,

"Give praise to our God, all you His bond-servants, you who fear Him, the small and the great."

6 And I heard, as it were, the voice of a great multitude and as the sound of many waters and as the sound of mighty peals of thunder, saying,

"Hallelujah! For the Lord our God, the Almighty, reigns.

7 "Let us rejoice and be glad and give the glory to Him, for the marriage of the Lamb has come and His bride has made herself ready."

8 And it was given to her to clothe herself in fine linen, bright *and* clean; for the fine linen is the righteous acts of the saints.

9 And he *said to me, "Write, 'Blessed are those who are invited to the marriage supper of the Lamb.' " And he *said to me, "These are true words of God."

10 And I fell at his feet to worship him. And he *said to me, "Do not do that; I am a fellow servant of yours and your brethren who hold the testimony of Jesus; worship God. For the testimony of Jesus is the spirit of prophecy."

11 And I saw heaven opened; and behold, a white horse, and He who sat upon it *is* called Faithful and True; and in righteousness He judges and wages war.

12 And His eyes *are* a flame of fire, and upon His head *are* many diadems; and He has a name written *upon Him* which no one knows except Himself.

13 And *He is* clothed with a robe dipped in blood; and His name is called The Word of God.

14 And the armies which are in heaven, clothed in fine linen, white *and* clean, were following Him on white horses.

15 And from His mouth comes a sharp sword, so that with it He may smite the nations; and He will rule them with a rod of iron; and He treads the wine press of the fierce wrath of God, the Almighty.

16 And on His robe and on His thigh He has a name written, "KING OF KINGS, AND LORD OF LORDS."

17 And I saw an angel standing in the sun; and he cried out with a loud voice, saying to all the birds which fly in midheaven, "Come, assemble for the great supper of God;

18 in order that you may eat the flesh of kings and the flesh of [32]commanders and the flesh of mighty men and the flesh of horses and of those who sit on them and the flesh of all men, both free men and slaves, and small and great."

19 And I saw the beast and the kings of the earth and their armies, assembled to make war against Him who sat upon the horse, and against His army.

20 And the beast was seized, and with him the false prophet who performed the signs in his presence, by which he deceived those who had received the mark of the beast and those who worshiped his image; these two were thrown alive into the lake of fire which burns with brimstone.

21 And the rest were killed with the sword which came from the mouth of Him who sat upon the horse, and all the birds were filled with their flesh.

CHAPTER 20

AND I saw an angel coming down from heaven, having the key of the abyss and a great chain in his hand.

2 And he laid hold of the dragon, the serpent of old, who is the devil and Satan, and bound him for a thousand years,

3 and threw him into the abyss, and shut it and sealed it over him, so that he should not deceive the nations any longer, until the thousand years were completed; after these things he must be released for a short time.

4 And I saw thrones, and they sat upon them, and judgment was given to them. And I saw the souls of those who had been beheaded because of the testimony of Jesus and because of the word of God, and those who had not worshiped the beast or his image, and had not received the mark upon their forehead and upon their hand; and they came to life and reigned with Christ for a thousand years.

5 The rest of the dead did not come to life until the thousand years were completed. This is the first resurrection.

6 Blessed and holy is the one who has a part in the first resurrection; over these the second death has no power, but they will be priests of God and of Christ and will reign with Him for a thousand years.

7 And when the thousand years are completed, Satan will be released from his prison,

8 and will come out to deceive the nations which are in the four corners of the earth, Gog and Magog, to gather them together for the war; the number of them is like the sand of the seashore.

9 And they came up on the

[32] I.e., chiliarchs, in command of one thousand troops

broad plain of the earth and surrounded the camp of the saints and the beloved city, and fire came down from heaven and devoured them.

10 And the devil who deceived them was thrown into the lake of fire and brimstone, where the beast and the false prophet are also; and they will be tormented day and night forever and ever.

11 And I saw a great white throne and Him who sat upon it, from whose presence earth and heaven fled away, and no place was found for them.

12 And I saw the dead, the great and the small, standing before the throne, and books were opened; and another book was opened, which is *the book* of life; and the dead were judged from the things which were written in the books, according to their deeds.

13 And the sea gave up the dead which were in it, and death and Hades gave up the dead which were in them; and they were judged, every one *of them* according to their deeds.

14 And death and Hades were thrown into the lake of fire. This is the second death, the lake of fire.

15 And if anyone's name was not found written in the book of life, he was thrown into the lake of fire.

CHAPTER 21

AND I saw a new heaven and a new earth; for the first heaven and the first earth passed away, and there is no longer *any* sea.

2 And I saw the holy city, new Jerusalem, coming down out of heaven from God, made ready as a bride adorned for her husband.

3 And I heard a loud voice from the throne, saying, "Behold, the tabernacle of God is among men, and He shall dwell among them, and they shall be His people, and God Himself shall be among them,[33]

4 and He shall wipe away every tear from their eyes; and there shall no longer be *any* death; there shall no longer be *any* mourning, or crying, or pain; the first things have passed away."

5 And He who sits on the throne said, "Behold, I am making all things new." And He *said, "Write, for these words are faithful and true."

6 And He said to me, "It is done. I am the Alpha and the Omega, the beginning and the end. I will give to the one who thirsts from the spring of the water of life without cost.

7 "He who overcomes shall inherit these things, and I will be his God and he will be My son.

8 "But for the cowardly and unbelieving and abominable and murderers and immoral persons and sorcerers and idolaters and all liars, their part *will be* in the lake that burns with fire and brimstone, which is the second death."

9 And one of the seven angels who had the seven bowls full of the seven last plagues, came and spoke with me, saying, "Come here, I shall show you the bride, the wife of the Lamb."

10 And he carried me away [34]in the Spirit to a great and high

33 Some ancient mss. add, *and be their God*
34 Or, *in spirit*

mountain, and showed me the holy city, Jerusalem, coming down out of heaven from God,

11 having the glory of God. Her brilliance was like a very costly stone, as a stone of crystal-clear jasper.

12 It had a great and high wall, with twelve gates, and at the gates twelve angels; and names *were* written on them, which are *those* of the twelve tribes of the sons of Israel.

13 *There were* three gates on the east and three gates on the north and three gates on the south and three gates on the west.

14 And the wall of the city had twelve foundation stones, and on them *were* the twelve names of the twelve apostles of the Lamb.

15 And the one who spoke with me had a gold measuring rod to measure the city, and its gates and its wall.

16 And the city is laid out as a square, and its length is as great as the width; and he measured the city with the rod, [35]fifteen hundred miles; its length and width and height are equal.

17 And he measured its wall, [36]seventy-two yards, *according to human measurements, which are also angelic measurements.*

18 And the material of the wall was jasper; and the city was pure gold, like clear glass.

19 The foundation stones of the city wall were adorned with every kind of precious stone. The first foundation stone was jasper; the second, sapphire; the third, chalcedony; the fourth, emerald;

20 the fifth, sardonyx; the sixth, sardius; the seventh, chrysolite; the eighth, beryl; the ninth, topaz; the tenth, chrysoprase; the eleventh, jacinth; the twelfth, amethyst.

21 And the twelve gates were twelve pearls; each one of the gates was a single pearl. And the street of the city was pure gold, like transparent glass.

22 And I saw no temple in it, for the Lord God, the Almighty, and the Lamb, are its temple.

23 And the city has no need of the sun or of the moon to shine upon it, for the glory of God has illumined it, and its lamp *is* the Lamb.

24 And the nations shall walk by its light, and the kings of the earth shall bring their glory into it.

25 And in the daytime (for there shall be no night there) its gates shall never be closed;

26 and they shall bring the glory and the honor of the nations into it;

27 and nothing unclean and no one who practices abomination and lying, shall ever come into it, but only those whose names are written in the Lamb's book of life.

CHAPTER 22

AND he showed me a river of the water of life, clear as crystal, coming from the throne of God and of [37]the Lamb.

2 in the middle of its street. And on either side of the river was the tree of life, bearing twelve [38]*kinds of* fruit, yielding its fruit every month; and the leaves of the tree were for the healing of the nations.

---

[35] Lit., *twelve thousand stadia; a stadion* was about 600 ft.

[36] Lit., *one hundred forty-four cubits*

[37] Or, *the Lamb. In the middle of its street, and on either side of the river, was*

[38] Or, *crops of fruit*

3 And there shall no longer be any curse; and the throne of God and of the Lamb shall be in it, and His bond-servants shall serve Him;

4 and they shall see His face, and His name *shall be* on their foreheads.

5 And there shall no longer be *any* night; and they shall not have need of the light of a lamp nor the light of the sun, because the Lord God shall illumine them; and they shall reign forever and ever.

6 And he said to me, "These words are faithful and true"; and the Lord, the God of the spirits of the prophets, sent His angel to show to His bond-servants the things which must shortly take place.

7 "And behold, I am coming quickly. Blessed is he who heeds the words of the prophecy of this book."

8 And I, John, am the one who heard and saw these things. And when I heard and saw, I fell down to worship at the feet of the angel who showed me these things.

9 And he *said to me, "Do not do that; I am a fellow servant of yours and of your brethren the prophets and of those who heed the words of this book; worship God."

10 And he *said to me, "Do not seal up the words of the prophecy of this book, for the time is near.

11 "Let the one who does wrong, still do wrong; and let the one who is filthy, still be filthy; and let the one who is righteous, still practice righteousness; and

let the one who is holy, still keep himself holy."

12 "Behold, I am coming quickly, and My reward *is* with Me, to render to every man according to what he has done.

13 "I am the Alpha and the Omega, the first and the last, the beginning and the end."

14 Blessed are those who wash their robes, that they may have the right to the tree of life, and may enter by the gates into the city.

15 Outside are the dogs and the sorcerers and the immoral persons and the murderers and the idolaters, and everyone who loves and practices lying.

16 "I, Jesus, have sent My angel to testify to you these things for the churches. I am the root and the offspring of David, the bright morning star."

17 And the Spirit and the bride say, "Come." And let the one who hears say, "Come." And let the one who is thirsty come; let the one who wishes take the water of life without cost.

18 I testify to everyone who hears the words of the prophecy of this book: if anyone adds to them, God shall add to him the plagues which are written in this book;

19 and if anyone takes away from the words of the book of this prophecy, God shall take away his part from the tree of life and from the holy city, which are written in this book.

20 He who testifies to these things says, "Yes, I am coming quickly." Amen. Come, Lord Jesus.

21 The grace of the Lord Jesus be with **39**all. Amen.

39 Some ancient mss. read *the saints*

THE PSALMS

The following expressions occur often in the Psalms:

Selah   May mean *Pause, Crescendo* or *Musical Interlude*

Maskil   Possibly, *Contemplative,* or *Didactic,* or *Skillful Psalm*

Mikhtam Possibly, *Epigrammatic Poem,* or *Atonement Psalm*

Sheol   The nether world

BOOK 1

PSALM 1

The Righteous and the Wicked Contrasted.

HOW blessed is the man who does not walk in the counsel of the wicked,
Nor stand in the path of sinners,
Nor sit in the seat of scoffers!
2 But his delight is in the law of the LORD,
And in His law he meditates day and night.
3 And he will be like a tree *firmly* planted by streams of water,
Which yields its fruit in its season,
And its leaf does not wither;
And in whatever he does, he prospers.

4 The wicked are not so,
But they are like chaff which the wind drives away.
5 Therefore the wicked will not stand in the judgment,
Nor sinners in the assembly of the righteous.
6 For the LORD knows the way of the righteous,
But the way of the wicked will perish.

¹ Or, *Messiah*   ² Or, *is enthroned*

PSALM 2

The Reign of the LORD's Anointed.

WHY are the nations in an uproar,
And the peoples devising a vain thing?
2 The kings of the earth take their stand,
And the rulers take counsel together
Against the LORD and against His ¹Anointed:
3 "Let us tear their fetters apart,
And cast away their cords from us!"

4 He who ²sits in the heavens laughs,
The Lord scoffs at them.
5 Then He will speak to them in His anger
And terrify them in His fury:
6 "But as for Me, I have installed My King
Upon Zion, My holy mountain."

7 "I will surely tell of the decree of the LORD:
He said to Me, 'Thou art My Son,
Today I have begotten Thee.
8 'Ask of Me, and I will surely give the nations as Thine inheritance,
And the *very* ends of the earth as Thy possession.

9 'Thou shalt ³break them with a
   rod of iron,
   Thou shalt shatter them like
   earthenware.' "

10 Now therefore, O kings, show
   discernment;
   Take warning, O ⁴judges of
   the earth.

11 Worship the LORD with reverence,
   And rejoice with trembling.

12 Do homage to the Son, lest He
   become angry, and you
   perish in the way,
   For His wrath may ⁵soon be
   kindled.
   How blessed are all who take
   refuge in Him!

PSALM 3

Morning Prayer of Trust in God.

A Psalm of David, when he
fled from
Absalom his son.

O LORD, how my adversaries
   have increased!
   Many are rising up against
   me.

2 Many are saying of my soul,
   "There is no deliverance for
   him in God."   [⁶Selah.

3 But Thou, O LORD, art a shield
   about me,
   My glory, and the One who
   lifts my head.

4 I was crying to the LORD with
   my voice,
   And He answered me from
   His holy mountain. [Selah.

5 I lay down and slept;
   I awoke, for the LORD sustains
   me.

6 I will not be afraid of ten thousands of people
   Who have set themselves
   against me round about.

7 Arise, O LORD; save me, O my
   God!

For Thou hast smitten all my
   enemies on the cheek;
   Thou hast shattered the teeth
   of the wicked.

8 Salvation belongs to the LORD;
   Thy blessing be upon Thy
   people!   [Selah.

PSALM 4

Evening Prayer of Trust in God.

For the choir director; on
stringed instruments.
A Psalm of David.

A NSWER me when I call, O God
   of my righteousness!
   Thou hast relieved me in my
   distress;
   Be gracious to me and hear
   my prayer.

2 O sons of men, how long will
   my honor become a re-
   proach?
   How long will you love what
   is worthless and aim at deception?   [Selah.

3 But know that the LORD has
   set apart the godly man for
   Himself;
   The LORD hears when I call to
   Him.

4 Tremble, and do not sin;
   Meditate in your heart upon
   your bed, and be still.
                      [Selah.

5 Offer the sacrifices of righteousness,
   And trust in the LORD.

6 Many are saying, "Who will
   show us any good?"
   Lift up the light of Thy countenance upon us, O LORD!

7 Thou hast put gladness in my
   heart,
   More than when their grain
   and new wine abound.

³ Another reading is *rule* ⁴ Or, *leaders*
⁵ Or, *quickly, suddenly, easily*
⁶ *Selah* may mean: *Pause, Crescendo* or *Musical Interlude*

8 In peace I will both lie down
   and sleep,
   For Thou alone, O LORD, dost
     make me to dwell in safety.

PSALM 5

*Prayer for Protection from the
Wicked.*

For the choir director; for flute
   accompaniment.
    A Psalm of David.

GIVE ear to my words, O LORD,
   Consider my [7]groaning.
2 Heed the sound of my cry for
   help, my King and my God,
   For to Thee do I pray.
3 In the morning, O LORD, Thou
   wilt hear my voice;
   In the morning I will order *my
   prayer* to Thee and *eagerly*
   watch.

4 For Thou art not a God who
   takes pleasure in wickedness;
   No evil dwells with Thee.
5 The boastful shall not stand
   before Thine eyes;
   Thou dost hate all who do iniquity.
6 Thou dost destroy those who
   speak falsehood;
   The LORD abhors the man of
   bloodshed and deceit.
7 But as for me, by Thine abundant lovingkindness I will
   enter Thy house,
   At Thy holy temple I will bow
   in reverence for Thee.

8 O LORD, lead me in Thy righteousness because of my
   foes;
   Make Thy way straight before
   me.
9 There is nothing reliable in
   what they say;
   Their inward part is destruction *itself*;

   Their throat is an open grave;
   They flatter with their tongue.
10 Hold them guilty, O God;
   By their own devices let them
   fall!
   In the multitude of their trans-
   gressions thrust them out,
   For they are rebellious against
   Thee.

11 But let all who take refuge in
   Thee be glad,
   Let them ever sing for joy;
   And mayest Thou shelter
   them,
   That those who love Thy
   name may exult in Thee.
12 For it is Thou who dost bless
   the righteous man, O LORD,
   Thou dost surround him with
   favor as with a shield.

PSALM 6

*Prayer for Mercy in Time of
Trouble.*

For the choir director; with
   stringed instruments,
upon an eight-stringed lyre.
    A Psalm of David.

O LORD, do not rebuke me in
   Thine anger,
   Nor chasten me in Thy wrath.
2 Be gracious to me, O LORD, for
   I *am* pining away;
   Heal me, O LORD, for my
   bones are dismayed.
3 And my soul is greatly dis-
   mayed;
   But Thou, O LORD—how long?

4 Return, O LORD, rescue my
   [8]soul;
   Save me because of Thy
   lovingkindness.
5 For there is no [9]mention of
   Thee in death;
   In Sheol who will give Thee
   thanks?

6 I am weary with my sighing;
   Every night I make my bed
   swim,

[7] Or, *meditation*   [8] Or, *life*
[9] Or, *remembrance*

I dissolve my couch with my tears.
7 My eye has wasted away with grief;
It has become old because of all my adversaries.

8 Depart from me, all you who do iniquity,
For the LORD has heard the voice of my weeping.
9 The LORD has heard my supplication,
The LORD receives my prayer.
10 All my enemies shall be ashamed and greatly dismayed;
They shall turn back, they shall suddenly be ashamed.

PSALM 7

The LORD Implored to Defend the Psalmist against the Wicked.

A [10]Shiggaion of David, which he sang to the Lord concerning Cush, a Benjamite.

O LORD my God, in Thee I have taken refuge;
Save me from all those who pursue me, and deliver me,
2 Lest he tear my soul like a lion,
Dragging me away, while there is none to deliver.

3 O LORD my God, if I have done this,
If there is injustice in my hands,
4 If I have rewarded evil to my friend,
Or have plundered him who without cause was my adversary,
5 Let the enemy pursue my soul and overtake it;
And let him trample my life down to the ground,
And lay my glory in the dust.
[Selah.

6 Arise, O LORD, in Thine anger;
Lift up Thyself against the rage of my adversaries,
And arouse Thyself for me;
Thou hast appointed judgment.
7 And let the assembly of the peoples encompass Thee;
And over them return Thou on high.
8 The LORD judges the peoples;
Vindicate me, O LORD, according to my righteousness and my integrity that is in me.
9 O let the evil of the wicked come to an end, but establish the righteous;
For the righteous God tries the hearts and [11]minds.
10 My shield is with God,
Who saves the upright in heart.
11 God is a righteous judge,
And a God who has indignation every day.

12 If a man does not repent, He will sharpen His sword;
He has bent His bow and made it ready.
13 He has also prepared for Himself deadly weapons;
He makes His arrows fiery shafts.
14 Behold, he travails with wickedness,
And he conceives mischief, and brings forth falsehood.
15 He has dug a pit and hollowed it out,
And has fallen into the hole which he made.
16 His mischief will return upon his own head,
And his violence will descend upon [12]his own pate.

10 I.e., Dithyrambic rhythm, or, wild, passionate song
11 Lit., *kidneys*, figurative for inner man
12 I.e., the crown of his own head

17 I will give thanks to the LORD according to His righteousness,
And will sing praise to the name of the LORD Most High.

PSALM 8

The LORD's Glory and Man's Dignity.

For the choir director; on the Gittith. A Psalm of David.

O LORD, our Lord,
How majestic is Thy name in all the earth,
Who hast displayed Thy splendor above the heavens!

2 From the mouth of infants and nursing babes Thou hast established strength,
Because of Thine adversaries,
To make the enemy and the revengeful cease.

3 When I consider Thy heavens, the work of Thy fingers,
The moon and the stars, which Thou hast ordained;

4 What is man, that Thou dost take thought of him?
And the son of man, that Thou dost care for him?

5 Yet Thou hast made him a little lower than God,
And dost crown him with glory and majesty!

6 Thou dost make him to rule over the works of Thy hands;
Thou hast put all things under his feet,

7 All sheep and oxen,
And also the beasts of the field,

8 The birds of the heavens, and the fish of the sea,
Whatever passes through the paths of the seas.

9 O LORD, our Lord,
How majestic is Thy name in all the earth!

PSALM 9

A Psalm of Thanksgiving for God's Justice.

For the choir director; on [13]Muth-labben. A Psalm of David.

I WILL give thanks to the LORD with all my heart;
I will tell of all Thy wonders.

2 I will be glad and exult in Thee;
I will sing praise to Thy name, O Most High.

3 When my enemies turn back,
They stumble and perish before Thee.

4 For Thou hast maintained my just cause;
Thou dost sit on the throne judging righteously.

5 Thou hast rebuked the nations; Thou hast destroyed the wicked;
Thou hast blotted out their name forever and ever.

6 The enemy has come to an end in perpetual ruins,
And Thou hast uprooted the cities;
The very memory of them has perished.

7 But the LORD [14]abides forever;
He has established His throne for judgment;

8 And He will judge the world in righteousness;
He will execute judgment for the peoples with equity.

9 The LORD also will be a stronghold for the oppressed,
A stronghold in times of trouble;

10 And those who know Thy name will put their trust in Thee;

---

[13] I.e., "Death to the Son"
[14] Or, *sits as king*

For Thou, O LORD, hast not
forsaken those who seek
Thee.

11 Sing praises to the LORD, who
dwells in Zion;
Declare among the peoples
His deeds.

12 For He who [15]requires blood
remembers them;
He does not forget the cry of
the afflicted.

13 Be gracious to me, O LORD;
Behold my affliction from
those who hate me,
Thou who dost lift me up from
the gates of death;

14 That I may tell of all Thy
praises,
That in the gates of the daughter of Zion
I may rejoice in Thy salvation.

15 The nations have sunk down
in the pit which they have
made;
In the net which they hid,
their own foot has been
caught.

16 The LORD has made Himself
known;
He has executed judgment.
In the work of his own hands
the wicked is snared.
[Higgaion Selah.

17 The wicked will return to
Sheol,
Even all the nations who for-
get God.

18 For the needy will not always
be forgotten,
Nor the hope of the afflicted
perish forever.

19 Arise, O LORD, do not let man
prevail;
Let the nations be judged before Thee.

20 Put them in fear, O LORD;
Let the nations know that
they are but men.   [Selah.

PSALM 10

*A Prayer for the Overthrow of
the Wicked.*

WHY dost Thou stand afar off,
O LORD?
Why dost Thou hide *Thyself*
in times of trouble?

2 In pride the wicked hotly pursue the afflicted;
Let them be caught in the
plots which they have de-
vised.

3 For the wicked boasts of his
heart's desire,
And [16]the greedy man curses
and spurns the LORD.

4 The wicked, in the haughti-
ness of his countenance,
does not seek *Him.*
All his thoughts are, "There is
no God."

5 His ways prosper at all times;
Thy judgments are on high,
out of his sight;
As for all his adversaries, he
snorts at them.

6 He says to himself, "I shall not
be moved;
Throughout all generations I
shall not be in adversity."

7 His mouth is full of curses and
deceit and oppression;
Under his tongue is mischief
and wickedness.

8 He sits in the lurking places of
the villages;
In the hiding places he kills
the innocent;
His eyes stealthily watch for
the unfortunate.

9 He lurks in a hiding place as a
lion in his lair;
He lurks to catch the afflicted;
He catches the afflicted when
he draws him into his net.

10 He crouches, he bows down,

[15] I.e., avenges bloodshed
[16] Or, *blesses the greedy man*

And the unfortunate fall [17]by his mighty ones.

11 He says to himself, "God has forgotten;
He has hidden His face; He will never see it."

12 Arise, O LORD; O God, lift up Thy hand.
Do not forget the afflicted.

13 Why has the wicked spurned God?
He has said to himself, "Thou wilt not require it."

14 Thou hast seen it, for Thou hast beheld mischief and vexation to take it into Thy hand.
The unfortunate commits himself to Thee;
Thou hast been the helper of the orphan.

15 Break the arm of the wicked and the evildoer,
Seek out his wickedness until Thou dost find none.

16 The LORD is King forever and ever;
Nations have perished from His land.

17 O LORD, Thou hast heard the desire of the [18]humble;
Thou wilt strengthen their heart, Thou wilt incline Thine ear

18 To [19]vindicate the orphan and the oppressed,
That man who is of the earth may cause terror no more.

PSALM 11

The LORD a Refuge and Defense.

For the choir director. A Psalm of David.

IN the LORD I take refuge;
How can you say to my soul,
"Flee *as* a bird to your mountain;

2 For, behold, the wicked bend the bow,
They make ready their arrow upon the string,
To shoot in darkness at the upright in heart.

3 If the foundations are destroyed,
What can the righteous do?"

4 The LORD is in His holy temple; the LORD's throne is in heaven;
His eyes behold, His eyelids test the sons of men.

5 The LORD tests the righteous and the wicked,
And the one who loves violence His soul hates.

6 Upon the wicked He will rain [20]snares;
Fire and brimstone and burning wind will be the portion of their cup.

7 For the LORD is righteous; He loves righteousness;
The upright will behold His face.

PSALM 12

God, a Helper against the Treacherous.

For the choir director; upon an eight-stringed lyre.
A Psalm of David.

HELP, LORD, for the godly man ceases to be,
For the faithful disappear from among the sons of men.

2 They speak falsehood to one another;
With flattering lips and with a double heart they speak.

3 May the LORD cut off all flattering lips,
The tongue that speaks great things;

4 Who have said, "With our tongue we will prevail;

---

[17] Or, *into his claws*   [18] Or, *afflicted*
[19] Lit., *judge*   [20] Or, *coals of fire*

Our lips are our own; who is
lord over us?"

5 "Because of the devastation of
the afflicted, because of the
groaning of the needy,
Now I will arise," says the
LORD; "I will set him in the
safety for which he longs."

6 The words of the LORD are
pure words;
As silver tried in a furnace on
the earth, refined seven
times.

7 Thou, O LORD, wilt keep them;
Thou wilt preserve him from
this generation forever.

8 The wicked strut about on every side,
When 21vileness is exalted
among the sons of men.

PSALM 13

Prayer for Help in Trouble.

For the choir director. A
Psalm of David.

HOW long, O LORD? Wilt Thou
forget me forever?
How long wilt Thou hide Thy
face from me?

2 How long shall I take counsel
in my soul,
Having sorrow in my heart all
the day?
How long will my enemy be
exalted over me?

3 Consider *and* answer me, O
LORD, my God;
Enlighten my eyes, lest I sleep
the *sleep of* death,

4 Lest my enemy say, "I have
overcome him,"
Lest my adversaries rejoice
when I am shaken.

5 But I have trusted in Thy
lovingkindness;
My heart shall rejoice in Thy
salvation.

6 I will sing to the LORD,
Because He has dealt bountifully with me.

PSALM 14

Folly and Wickedness of Men.

For the choir director. A
Psalm of David.

THE fool has said in his heart,
"There is no God."
They are corrupt, they have
committed abominable
deeds;
There is no one who does
good.

2 The LORD has looked down
from heaven upon the sons
of men,
To see if there are any who
understand,
Who seek after God.

3 They have all turned aside; together they have become
corrupt;
There is no one who does
good, not even one.

4 Do all the workers of wicked-
ness not know,
Who eat up my people *as* they
eat bread,
And do not call upon the
LORD?

5 There they are in great dread,
For God is with the righteous
generation.

6 You would put to shame the
counsel of the afflicted,
But the LORD is his refuge.

7 Oh, that the salvation of Israel
would come out of Zion!
When the LORD 22restores His
captive people,
Jacob will rejoice, Israel will
be glad.

21 Or, *worthlessness*
22 Or, *restores the fortunes of His people*

PSALM 15

Description of a Citizen of Zion.

A Psalm of David.

O LORD, who may abide in Thy
tent?
Who may dwell on Thy holy
hill?
2 He who walks with integrity,
and works righteousness,
And speaks truth in his heart.
3 He does not slander with his
tongue,
Nor does evil to his neighbor,
Nor takes up a reproach
against his friend;
4 In whose eyes a reprobate is
despised,
But who honors those who
fear the LORD;
He swears to his own hurt,
and does not change;
5 He does not put out his money
[23]at interest,
Nor does he take a bribe
against the innocent.
He who does these things will
never be shaken.

PSALM 16

*The LORD the Psalmist's Portion
in Life and Deliverer in Death.*

A [24]Mikhtam of David.

PRESERVE me, O God, for I take
refuge in Thee.
2 I said to the LORD, "Thou art
my Lord;
I have no good besides Thee."
3 As for the saints who are in
the earth,
They are the majestic ones in
whom is all my delight.
4 The sorrows of those who
have bartered for another
god will be multiplied;

I shall not pour out their liba-
tions of blood,
Nor shall I take their names
upon my lips.
5 The LORD is the portion of my
inheritance and my cup;
Thou dost support my lot.
6 The lines have fallen to me in
pleasant places;
Indeed, my heritage is beautiful to me.

7 I will bless the LORD who has
counseled me;
Indeed, my mind instructs me
in the night.
8 I have set the LORD continually before me;
Because He is at my right
hand, I will not be shaken.
9 Therefore my heart is glad,
and my glory rejoices;
My flesh also will dwell securely.
10 For Thou wilt not abandon my
soul to Sheol;
Neither wilt Thou allow Thy
Holy One to [25]undergo decay.
11 Thou wilt make known to me
the path of life;
In Thy presence is fulness of
joy;
In Thy right hand there are
pleasures forever.

PSALM 17

*Prayer for Protection against
Oppressors.*

A Prayer of David.

HEAR a just cause, O LORD, give
heed to my cry;
Give ear to my prayer, which
is not from deceitful lips.
2 Let my judgment come forth
from Thy presence;
Let Thine eyes look with equity.
3 Thou hast tried my heart;
Thou hast visited *me* by night;

[23] I.e., to a fellow Israelite
[24] Possibly Epigrammatic Poem, or, Atonement
Psalm
[25] Or, *see* corruption *or* the pit

Thou hast tested me and dost
find [26]nothing;

I have purposed that my
mouth will not transgress.

4 As for the deeds of men, by
the word of Thy lips
I have kept from the paths of
the violent.

5 My steps have held fast to Thy
paths.

My feet have not slipped.

6 I have called upon Thee, for
Thou wilt answer me, O
God;

Incline Thine ear to me, hear
my speech.

7 Wondrously show Thy lovingkindness,

O Savior of those who take
refuge at Thy right hand
From those who rise up
against them.

8 Keep me as [27]the apple of the
eye;

Hide me in the shadow of Thy
wings,

9 From the wicked who despoil
me,

My deadly enemies, who surround me.

10 They have closed their unfeel-
ing *heart*;

With their mouth they speak
proudly.

11 They have now surrounded us
in our steps;

They set their eyes to cast *us*
down to the ground.

12 He is like a lion that is eager
to tear,

And as a young lion lurking in
hiding places.

13 Arise, O LORD, confront him,
bring him low;

Deliver my soul from the
wicked with Thy sword,

14 From men with Thy hand, O
LORD,

From men of the world,
whose portion is in *this* life;

And whose belly Thou dost fill
with Thy treasure;

They are satisfied with children,

And leave their abundance to
their babes.

15 As for me, I shall behold Thy
face in righteousness;

I will be satisfied with Thy
likeness when I awake.

PSALM 18

The LORD Praised for Giving
Deliverance.

For the choir director. *A Psalm
of David the servant of the
LORD, who spoke to the LORD
the words of this song in the
day that the LORD delivered
him from the hand of all his
enemies and from the hand of
Saul. And he said,*

"I LOVE Thee, O LORD, my
strength."

2 The LORD is my rock and my
fortress and my deliverer,

My God, my rock, in whom I
take refuge;

My shield and the horn of my
salvation, my stronghold.

3 I call upon the LORD, who is
worthy to be praised,

And I am saved from my enemies.

4 The cords of death encompassed me,

And the torrents of [28]ungodli-
ness terrified me.

5 The cords of Sheol sur-
rounded me;

The snares of death con-
fronted me.

6 In my distress I called upon
the LORD,

And cried to my God for help;

[26] Or, *no evil device in me*
[27] Lit., *the pupil, the daughter of the eye*
[28] Or, *destruction*

He heard my voice out of His temple,
And my cry for help before Him came into His ears.

7 Then the earth shook and quaked;
And the foundations of the mountains were trembling
And were shaken, because He was angry.

8 Smoke went up out of His nostrils,
And fire from His mouth devoured;
Coals were kindled by it.

9 He bowed the heavens also, and came down
With thick darkness under His feet.

10 And He rode upon a cherub and flew;
And He sped upon the wings of the wind.

11 He made darkness His hiding place, His canopy around Him,
Darkness of waters, thick clouds of the skies.

12 From the brightness before Him passed His thick clouds,
Hailstones and coals of fire.

13 The LORD also thundered in the heavens,
And the Most High uttered His voice,
Hailstones and coals of fire.

14 And He sent out His arrows, and scattered them,
And lightning flashes in abundance, and routed them.

15 Then the channels of water appeared,
And the foundations of the world were laid bare
At Thy rebuke, O LORD,
At the blast of the breath of Thy nostrils.

16 He sent from on high, He took me;
He drew me out of many waters.

17 He delivered me from my strong enemy,
And from those who hated me, for they were too mighty for me.

18 They confronted me in the day of my calamity,
But the LORD was my stay.

19 He brought me forth also into a broad place;
He rescued me, because He delighted in me.

20 The LORD has rewarded me according to my righteousness;
According to the cleanness of my hands He has recompensed me.

21 For I have kept the ways of the LORD,
And have not wickedly departed from my God.

22 For all His ordinances were before me,
And I did not put away His statutes from me.

23 I was also [29]blameless with Him,
And I kept myself from my iniquity.

24 Therefore the LORD has recompensed me according to my righteousness,
According to the cleanness of my hands in His eyes.

25 With the kind Thou dost show Thyself kind;
With the blameless Thou dost show Thyself blameless;

26 With the pure Thou dost show Thyself pure;
And with the crooked Thou dost show Thyself [30]astute.

27 For Thou dost save an afflicted people;
But haughty eyes Thou dost abase.

[29] Lit., *complete*; or, *having integrity*
[30] Lit., *twisted*

28 For Thou dost light my lamp;
   The LORD my God illumines
   my darkness.

29 For by Thee I can [31]run upon a
   troop;
   And by my God I can leap
   over a wall.

30 As for God, His way is blameless;
   The word of the LORD is tried;
   He is a shield to all who take
   refuge in Him.

31 For who is God, but the LORD?
   And who is a rock, except our
   God,

32 The God who girds me with
   strength,
   And makes my way blameless?

33 He makes my feet like hinds'
   feet,
   And sets me upon my high
   places.

34 He trains my hands for battle,
   So that my arms can bend a
   bow of bronze.

35 Thou hast also given me the
   shield of Thy salvation,
   And Thy right hand upholds
   me;
   And Thy gentleness makes me
   great.

36 Thou dost enlarge my steps
   under me,
   And my feet have not slipped.

37 I pursued my enemies and
   overtook them,
   And I did not turn back until
   they were consumed.

38 I shattered them, so that they
   were not able to rise;
   They fell under my feet.

39 For Thou hast girded me with
   strength for battle;
   Thou hast subdued under me
   those who rose up against
   me.

40 Thou hast also made my enemies turn their backs to
   me,

And I [32]destroyed those who
   hated me.

41 They cried for help, but there
   was none to save,
   Even to the LORD, but He did
   not answer them.

42 Then I beat them fine as the
   dust before the wind;
   I emptied them out as the
   mire of the streets.

43 Thou hast delivered me from
   the contentions of the people;
   Thou hast placed me as head
   of the nations;
   A people whom I have not
   known serve me.

44 As soon as they hear, they
   obey me;
   Foreigners [33]submit to me.

45 Foreigners fade away,
   And come trembling out of
   their fortresses.

46 The LORD lives, and blessed
   be my rock;
   And exalted be the God of my
   salvation,

47 The God who executes vengeance for me,
   And subdues peoples under
   me.

48 He delivers me from my enemies;
   Surely Thou dost lift me
   above those who rise up
   against me;
   Thou dost rescue me from the
   violent man.

49 Therefore I will give thanks to
   Thee among the nations, O
   LORD,
   And I will sing praises to Thy
   name.

50 He gives great [34]deliverance
   to His king,
   And shows lovingkindness to
   His anointed,

31 Or, *crush a troop*   32 Or, *silenced*
33 I.e., *give feigned obedience*
34 I.e., *victories*

To David and his descendants
forever.

PSALM 19

*The Works and the Word of
God.*

For the choir director. A
Psalm of David.

THE heavens are telling of the
glory of God;
And their expanse is declaring
the work of His hands.

2 Day to day pours forth
speech,
And night to night reveals
knowledge.

3 There is no speech, nor are
there words;
Their voice is not heard.

4 Their [35]line has gone out
through all the earth,
And their utterances to the
end of the world.
In them He has placed a tent
for the sun,

5 Which is as a bridegroom
coming out of his chamber;
It rejoices as a strong man to
run his course.

6 Its rising is from one end of
the heavens,
And its circuit to the other
end of them;
And there is nothing hidden
from its heat.

7 The law of the LORD is [36]per-
fect, restoring the soul;
The testimony of the LORD is
sure, making wise the simple.

8 The precepts of the LORD are
right, rejoicing the heart;
The commandment of the
LORD is pure, enlightening
the eyes.

9 The fear of the LORD is clean,
enduring forever;

The judgments of the LORD
are true; they are righteous
altogether.

10 They are more desirable than
gold, yes, than much fine
gold;
Sweeter also than honey and
the drippings of the honey-
comb.

11 Moreover, by them Thy servant is warned;
In keeping them there is great
reward.

12 Who can discern *his* errors?
Acquit me of hidden *faults.*

13 Also keep back Thy servant
from presumptuous *sins;*
Let them not rule over me;
Then I shall be [37]blameless,
And I shall be acquitted of
great transgression.

14 Let the words of my mouth
and the meditation of my
heart
Be acceptable in Thy sight,
O LORD, my rock and my Redeemer.

PSALM 20

Prayer for Victory over Enemies.

For the choir director. A
Psalm of David.

MAY the LORD answer you in
the day of trouble!
May the name of the God of
Jacob set you *securely* on
high!

2 May He send you help from
the sanctuary,
And support you from Zion!

3 May He remember all your
meal offerings,
And find your burnt offering
acceptable!   [Selah.

4 May He grant you your
heart's desire,
And fulfill all your [38]counsel!

5 We will sing for joy over your
victory,

---

[35] Another reading is *sound*
[36] I.e., blameless   [37] Lit., *complete*
[38] Or, *purpose*

And in the name of our God
we will set up our banners.
May the LORD fulfill all your
petitions.

6 Now I know that the LORD
saves His anointed;
He will answer him from His
holy heaven,
With the saving strength of
His right hand.

7 Some *boast* in chariots, and
some in horses;
But we will boast in the name
of the LORD, our God.

8 They have bowed down and
fallen;
But we have risen and stood
upright.

9 Save, O LORD;
May the King answer us in the
day we call.

PSALM 21

Praise for Deliverance.

For the choir director. A
Psalm of David.

O LORD, in Thy strength the
king will be glad,
And in Thy ³⁹salvation how
greatly he will rejoice!

2 Thou hast given him his
heart's desire,
And Thou hast not withheld
the request of his lips.
[Selah.

3 For Thou dost meet him with
the blessings of good
things;
Thou dost set a crown of fine
gold on his head.

4 He asked life of Thee,
Thou didst give it to him,
Length of days forever and
ever.

5 His glory is great through Thy
³⁹salvation,
Splendor and majesty Thou
dost place upon him.

6 For Thou dost make him most
blessed forever;

Thou dost make him joyful
with gladness in Thy presence.

7 For the king trusts in the
LORD,
And through the lovingkindness of the Most High he
will not be shaken.

8 Your hand will find out all
your enemies;
Your right hand will find out
those who hate you.

9 You will make them as a fiery
oven in the time of your anger;
The LORD will swallow them
up in His wrath,
And fire will devour them.

10 Their ⁴⁰offspring Thou wilt destroy from the earth,
And their ⁴¹descendants from
among the sons of men.

11 Though they intended evil
against Thee,
And devised a plot,
They will not succeed.

12 For Thou wilt make them turn
their back;
Thou wilt aim with Thy bow-
strings at their faces.

13 Be Thou exalted, O LORD, in
Thy strength;
We will sing and praise Thy
power.

PSALM 22

*A Cry of Anguish and a Song of
Praise.*

For the choir director; upon
⁴²Aijeleth Hashshahar. A Psalm
of David.

MY God, my God, why hast
Thou forsaken me?
Far from my deliverance are
the words of my groaning.

2 O my God, I cry by day, but
Thou dost not answer;

---

³⁹ Or, *victory*   ⁴⁰ Lit., *fruit*   ⁴¹ Lit., *seed*
⁴² Lit., *the hind of the morning*

And by night, but I have no rest.

3 Yet Thou art holy,
O Thou who art enthroned upon the praises of Israel.

4 In Thee our fathers trusted;
They trusted, and Thou didst deliver them.

5 To Thee they cried out, and were delivered;
In Thee they trusted, and were not disappointed.

6 But I am a worm, and not a man,
A reproach of men, and despised by the people.

7 All who see me sneer at me;
They [43]separate with the lip, they wag the head, *saying,*

8 "[44]Commit *yourself* to the LORD; let Him deliver him;
Let Him rescue him, because He delights in him."

9 Yet Thou art He who didst bring me forth from the womb;
Thou didst make me trust *when* upon my mother's breasts.

10 Upon Thee I was cast from birth;
Thou hast been my God from my mother's womb.

11 Be not far from me, for trouble is near;
For there is none to help.

12 Many bulls have surrounded me;
Strong *bulls* of Bashan have encircled me.

13 They open wide their mouth at me,
As a ravening and a roaring lion.

14 I am poured out like water,
And all my bones are out of joint;

My heart is like wax;
It is melted within me.

15 My strength is dried up like a potsherd,
And my tongue cleaves to my jaws;
And Thou dost lay me in the dust of death.

16 For dogs have surrounded me;
A band of evildoers has encompassed me;
They pierced my hands and my feet.

17 I can count all my bones.
They look, they stare at me;

18 They divide my garments among them,
And for my clothing they cast lots.

19 But Thou, O LORD, be not far off;
O Thou my help, hasten to my assistance.

20 Deliver my soul from the sword,
My only *life* from the power of the dog.

21 Save me from the lion's mouth;
And from the horns of the wild oxen Thou dost answer me.

22 I will tell of Thy name to my brethren;
In the midst of the assembly I will praise Thee.

23 You who fear the LORD, praise Him;
All you descendants of Jacob, glorify Him,
And stand in awe of Him, all you descendants of Israel.

24 For He has not despised nor abhorred the affliction of the afflicted;
Neither has He hidden His face from him;
But when he cried to Him for help, He heard.

[43] I.e., make mouths at me
[44] Another reading is *He committed himself*

25 From Thee *comes* my praise
  in the great assembly;
  I shall pay my vows before
  those who fear Him.
26 The 45afflicted shall eat and be
  satisfied;
  Those who seek Him will
  praise the LORD.
  Let your heart live forever!
27 All the ends of the earth will
  remember and turn to the
  LORD,
  And all the families of the nations will worship before
  Thee.
28 For the kingdom is the
  LORD's,
  And He rules over the nations.
29 All the prosperous of the earth
  will eat and worship,
  All those who go down to the
  dust will bow before Him,
  Even he who cannot keep his
  soul alive.
30 Posterity will serve Him;
  It will be told of the Lord to
  the *coming* generation.
31 They will come and will declare His righteousness
  To a people who will be born,
  that He has performed *it*.

PSALM 23

The LORD, the Psalmist's Shepherd.

A Psalm of David.

THE LORD is my shepherd,
  I shall not want.
2 He makes me lie down in
  green pastures;
  He leads me beside quiet waters.
3 He restores my soul;
  He guides me in the paths of
  righteousness
  For His name's sake.
4 Even though I walk through
  the 46valley of the shadow
  of death,

I fear no 47evil; for Thou art
  with me;
  Thy rod and Thy staff, they
  comfort me.
5 Thou dost prepare a table before me in the presence of
  my enemies;
  Thou hast anointed my head
  with oil;
  My cup overflows.
6 Surely goodness and lovingkindness will follow me all
  the days of my life,
  And I will 48dwell in the house
  of the LORD forever.

PSALM 24

The King of Glory Entering Zion.

A Psalm of David.

THE earth is the LORD's, and 49all
  it contains,
  The world, and those who
  dwell in it.
2 For He has founded it upon
  the seas,
  And established it upon the
  rivers.
3 Who may ascend into the hill
  of the LORD?
  And who may stand in His
  holy place?
4 He who has clean hands and a
  pure heart,
  Who has not lifted up his soul
  to falsehood,
  And has not sworn deceitfully.
5 He shall receive a blessing
  from the LORD
  And righteousness from the
  God of his salvation.
6 This is the generation of those
  who seek Him,
  Who seek Thy face—*even*
  Jacob.   [Selah.

45 Or, *poor* 46 Or, *valley of deep darkness*
47 Or, *harm* 48 Another reading is *return to*
49 Lit., *its fulness*

7 Lift up your heads, O gates,
   And be lifted up, O [50]ancient
      doors,
   That the King of glory may
      come in!
8 Who is the King of glory?
   The LORD strong and mighty,
   The LORD mighty in battle.
9 Lift up your heads, O gates,
   And lift *them* up, O [50]ancient
      doors,
   That the King of glory may
      come in!
10 Who is this King of glory?
   The LORD of hosts,
   He is the King of glory. [Selah.

PSALM 25

*Prayer for Protection, Guidance
and Pardon.*

A Psalm of David.

TO Thee, O LORD, I lift up my
      soul.
2 O my God, in Thee I trust,
   Do not let me be ashamed;
   Do not let my enemies exult
      over me.
3 Indeed, none of those who
      wait for Thee will be
      ashamed;
   Those who deal treacherously
      without cause will be
      ashamed.
4 Make me know Thy ways, O
      LORD;
   Teach me Thy paths.
5 Lead me in Thy truth and
      teach me,
   For Thou art the God of my
      salvation;
   For Thee I wait all the day.
6 Remember, O LORD, Thy com-
      passion and Thy loving-
      kindnesses,
   For they have been [50]from of
      old.
7 Do not remember the sins of

my youth or my transgres-
      sions;
   According to Thy lovingkind-
      ness remember Thou me,
   For Thy goodness' sake, O
      LORD.

8 Good and upright is the LORD;
   Therefore He instructs sinners
      in the way.
9 He leads the humble in jus-
      tice,
   And He teaches the humble
      His way.
10 All the paths of the LORD are
      lovingkindness and truth
   To those who keep His cov-
      enant and His testimonies.
11 For Thy name's sake, O LORD,
   Pardon my iniquity, for it is
      great.
12 Who is the man who fears the
      LORD?
   He will instruct him in the
      way he should choose.
13 His soul will abide in prosper-
      ity,
   And his [51]descendants will in-
      herit the land.
14 The secret of the LORD is for
      those who fear Him,
   And He will make them know
      His covenant.
15 My eyes are continually
      toward the LORD,
   For He will pluck my feet out
      of the net.
16 Turn to me and be gracious to
      me,
   For I am lonely and afflicted.
17 The troubles of my heart are
      enlarged;
   Bring me out of my distresses.
18 Look upon my affliction and
      my [52]trouble,
   And forgive all my sins.
19 Look upon my enemies, for
      they are many;
   And they hate me with violent
      hatred.

50 Lit., *everlasting* 51 Lit., *seed* 52 Lit., *toil*

20 Guard my soul and deliver
   me;
   Do not let me be ashamed, for
     I take refuge in Thee.
21 Let integrity and uprightness
     preserve me,
   For I wait for Thee.
22 Redeem Israel, O God,
   Out of all his troubles.

PSALM 26

*Protestation of Integrity and
   Prayer for Protection.*

A Psalm of David.

[53] VINDICATE me, O LORD, for I
   have walked in my integrity;
   And I have trusted in the
     LORD without wavering.
2 Examine me, O LORD, and try
   me;
   Test my [54]mind and my heart.
3 For Thy lovingkindness is be-
     fore my eyes,
   And I have walked in Thy
     truth.
4 I do not sit with [55]deceitful
   men,
   Nor will I go with pretenders.
5 I hate the assembly of evildoers,
   And I will not sit with the
     wicked.
6 I shall wash my hands in innocence,
   And I will go about Thine al-
     tar, O LORD,
7 That I may proclaim with the
     voice of thanksgiving,
   And declare all Thy wonders.

8 O LORD, I love the habitation
     of Thy house,
   And the place where Thy glo-
     ry dwells.
9 Do not take my soul away
     along with sinners,
   Nor my life with men of
     bloodshed,

10 In whose hands is a wicked
     scheme,
   And whose right hand is full
     of bribes.
11 But as for me, I shall walk in
     my integrity;
   Redeem me, and be gracious
     to me.
12 My foot stands on a level
     place;
   In the congregations I shall
     bless the LORD.

PSALM 27

*A Psalm of Fearless Trust in
   God.*

A Psalm of David.

THE LORD is my light and my
   salvation;
   Whom shall I fear?
   The LORD is the defense of my
     life;
   Whom shall I dread?
2 When evildoers came upon
     me to devour my flesh,
   My adversaries and my en-
     emies, they stumbled and
     fell.
3 Though a host encamp against
     me,
   My heart will not fear;
   Though war arise against me,
   In *spite of* this I shall be confi-
     dent.

4 One thing I have asked from
     the LORD, that I shall seek:
   That I may dwell in the house
     of the LORD all the days of
     my life,
   To behold the [56]beauty of the
     LORD,
   And to [57]meditate in His tem-
     ple.
5 For in the day of trouble He
     will conceal me in His tab-
     ernacle;

[53] Lit., *Judge*
[54] Lit., *kidneys*, figurative for inner man
[55] Or, *worthless*   [56] Lit., *delightfulness*
[57] Lit., *inquire*

In the secret place of His tent
    He will hide me;
He will lift me up on a rock.
6 And now my head will be
    lifted up above my enemies
    around me;
And I will offer in His tent
    sacrifices with shouts of
    joy;
I will sing, yes, I will sing
    praises to the LORD.

7 Hear, O LORD, when I cry with
    my voice,
And be gracious to me and an-
    swer me.
8 *When Thou didst say,* "Seek
    My face," my heart said to
    Thee,
    "Thy face, O LORD, I shall
    seek."
9 Do not hide Thy face from me,
    Do not turn Thy servant away
    in anger;
Thou hast been my help;
    Do not abandon me nor for-
    sake me,
O God of my salvation!
10 For my father and my mother
    have forsaken me,
But the LORD will take me up.
11 Teach me Thy way, O LORD,
    And lead me in a level path,
Because of my foes.
12 Do not deliver me over to the
    desire of my adversaries;
For false witnesses have risen
    against me,
And such as breathe out vio-
    lence.
13 *I would have despaired* unless
    I had believed that I would
    see the goodness of the
    LORD
In the land of the living.
14 Wait for the LORD;
Be strong, and let your heart
    take courage;
Yes, wait for the LORD.

PSALM 28

*A Prayer for Help, and Praise for
Its Answer.*

A Psalm of David.

To Thee, O LORD, I call;
    My rock, do not be deaf to me,
Lest, if Thou be silent to me,
    I become like those who go
    down to the pit.
2 Hear the voice of my supplica-
    tions when I cry to Thee for
    help,
When I lift up my hands
    toward [58] Thy holy sanctu-
    ary.
3 Do not drag me away with the
    wicked
And with those who work in-
    iquity;
Who speak peace with their
    neighbors,
While evil is in their hearts.
4 Requite them according to
    their work and according
    to the evil of their prac-
    tices;
Requite them according to the
    deeds of their hands;
Repay them their [59] recom-
    pense.
5 Because they do not regard
    the works of the LORD
Nor the deeds of His hands,
He will tear them down and
    not build them up.
6 Blessed be the LORD,
Because He has heard the
    voice of my supplication.
7 The LORD is my strength and
    my shield;
My heart trusts in Him, and I
    am helped;
Therefore my heart exults,
And with my song I shall
    thank Him.
8 The LORD is their strength,
And He is a saving defense to
    His anointed.
9 Save Thy people, and bless
    Thine inheritance;

[58] Lit., *the innermost place of Thy sanctuary*
[59] Or, *dealings*

Be their shepherd also, and carry them forever.

PSALM 29

The Voice of the LORD in the Storm.

A Psalm of David.

A SCRIBE to the LORD, O sons of the mighty,
Ascribe to the LORD glory and strength.

2 Ascribe to the LORD the glory due to His name;
Worship the LORD in holy array.

3 The voice of the LORD is upon the waters;
The God of glory thunders,
The LORD is over many waters.

4 The voice of the LORD is powerful,
The voice of the LORD is majestic.

5 The voice of the LORD breaks the cedars;
Yes, the LORD breaks in pieces the cedars of Lebanon.

6 And He makes Lebanon skip like a calf,
And Sirion like a young wild ox.

7 The voice of the LORD hews out flames of fire.

8 The voice of the LORD shakes the wilderness;
The LORD shakes the wilderness of Kadesh.

9 The voice of the LORD makes the deer to calve,
And strips the forests bare,
And in His temple everything says, "Glory!"

10 The LORD sat *as* King at the flood;
Yes, the LORD sits as King forever.

11 The LORD will give strength to His people;

The LORD will bless His people with peace.

PSALM 30

Thanksgiving for Deliverance from Death.

A Psalm; a Song at the Dedication of the House.
A Psalm of David.

I WILL extol Thee, O LORD, for Thou hast lifted me up,
And hast not let my enemies rejoice over me.

2 O LORD my God,
I cried to Thee for help, and Thou didst heal me.

3 O LORD, Thou hast brought up my soul from Sheol;
Thou hast kept me alive, that I should not go down to the pit.

4 Sing praise to the LORD, you His godly ones,
And give thanks to His holy name.

5 For His anger is but for a moment,
His favor is for a lifetime;
Weeping may last for the night,
But a shout of joy *comes* in the morning.

6 Now as for me, I said in my prosperity,
"I will never be moved."

7 O LORD, by Thy favor Thou hast made my mountain to stand strong;
Thou didst hide Thy face, I was dismayed.

8 To Thee, O LORD, I called,
And to the LORD I made supplication:

9 "What profit is there in my blood, if I go down to the pit?
Will the dust praise Thee?
Will it declare Thy faithfulness?

10 "Hear, O LORD, and be gracious
     to me;
   O LORD, be Thou my helper."
11 Thou hast turned for me my
     mourning into dancing;
   Thou hast loosed my sack-
     cloth and girded me with
     gladness;
12 That *my* soul may sing praise
     to Thee, and not be silent.
   O LORD my God, I will give
     thanks to Thee forever.

PSALM 31

*A Psalm of Complaint and of
Praise.*

For the choir director. A
     Psalm of David.

IN Thee, O LORD, I have taken ref-
     uge;
   Let me never be ashamed;
   In Thy righteousness deliver
     me.
2 Incline Thine ear to me, res-
     cue me quickly;
   Be Thou to me a rock of
     strength,
   A stronghold to save me.
3 For Thou art my rock and my
     fortress;
   For Thy name's sake Thou
     wilt lead me and guide me.
4 Thou wilt pull me out of the
     net which they have se-
     cretly laid for me;
   For Thou art my strength.
5 Into Thy hand I commit my
     spirit;
   Thou hast ransomed me, O
     LORD, God of truth.
6 I hate those who regard vain
     idols;
   But I trust in the LORD.
7 I will rejoice and be glad in
     Thy lovingkindness,
   Because Thou hast seen my
     affliction;
   Thou hast known the troubles
     of my soul,

8 And Thou hast not given me
     over into the hand of the
     enemy;
   Thou hast set my feet in a
     large place.
9 Be gracious to me, O LORD,
     for I am in distress;
   My eye is wasted away from
     grief, my soul and my body
     also.
10 For my life is spent with sor-
     row,
   And my years with sighing;
   My strength has failed be-
     cause of my iniquity,
   And my body has wasted
     away.
11 Because of all my adversaries,
     I have become a reproach,
   Especially to my neighbors,
   And an object of dread to my
     acquaintances;
   Those who see me in the
     street flee from me.
12 I am forgotten as a dead man,
     out of mind;
   I am like a broken vessel.
13 For I have heard the slander
     of many,
   Terror is on every side;
   While they took counsel to-
     gether against me,
   They schemed to take away
     my life.
14 But as for me, I trust in Thee,
     O LORD,
   I say, "Thou art my God."
15 My times are in Thy hand;
   Deliver me from the hand of
     my enemies, and from
     those who persecute me.
16 Make Thy face to shine upon
     Thy servant;
   Save me in Thy lovingkind-
     ness.
17 Let me not be put to shame, O
     LORD, for I call upon Thee;
   Let the wicked be put to
     shame, let them be silent in
     Sheol.

18 Let the lying lips be dumb,
   Which speak arrogantly
      against the righteous
   With pride and contempt.

19 How great is Thy goodness,
   Which Thou hast stored up for
      those who fear Thee,
   Which Thou hast wrought for
      those who take refuge in
      Thee,
   Before the sons of men!

20 Thou dost hide them in the se-
      cret place of Thy presence
      from the conspiracies of
      man;
   Thou dost keep them secretly
      in a shelter from the strife
      of tongues.

21 Blessed be the LORD,
   For He has made marvelous
      His lovingkindness to me
      in a besieged city.

22 As for me, I said in my alarm,
   "I am cut off from before Thine
      eyes";
   Nevertheless Thou didst hear
      the voice of my supplica-
      tions
   When I cried to Thee.

23 O love the LORD, all you His
      godly ones!
   The LORD preserves the faith-
      ful,
   And fully recompenses the
      proud doer.

24 Be strong, and let your heart
      take courage,
   All you who hope in the LORD.

PSALM 32

*Blessedness of Forgiveness and
of Trust in God.*

A Psalm of David. A [60]Maskil.

HOW blessed is he whose transgression is forgiven,
   Whose sin is covered!
2 How blessed is the man to
   whom the LORD does not
   impute iniquity,

And in whose spirit there is no
   deceit!

3 When I kept silent *about my
   sin*, my body wasted away
   Through my groaning all day
   long.

4 For day and night Thy hand
   was heavy upon me;
   My vitality was drained away
   as with the fever heat of
   summer.   [Selah.

5 I acknowledged my sin to
   Thee,
   And my iniquity I did not
   hide;
   I said, "I will confess my
   transgressions   to   the
   LORD";
   And Thou didst forgive the
   guilt of my sin.   [Selah.

6 Therefore, let everyone who is
   godly pray to Thee in a
   time when Thou mayest be
   found;
   Surely in a flood of great waters they shall not reach
   him.

7 Thou art my hiding place;
   Thou dost preserve me
   from trouble;
   Thou dost surround me with
   songs   of   deliverance.
                       [Selah.

8 I will instruct you and teach
   you in the way which you
   should go;
   I will counsel you with My eye
   upon you.

9 Do not be as the horse or as
   the mule which have no
   understanding,
   Whose trappings include bit
   and bridle to hold them in
   check,
   Otherwise they will not come
   near to you.

10 Many are the sorrows of the
   wicked;
   But he who trusts in the LORD,

[60] Possibly, *Contemplative* or *Didactic*, or
Skillful Psalm

lovingkindness shall surround him.

11 Be glad in the LORD and rejoice you righteous ones,
And shout for joy all you who are upright in heart.

PSALM 33

Praise to the Creator and Preserver.

SING for joy in the LORD, O you righteous ones;
Praise is becoming to the upright.

2 Give thanks to the LORD with the lyre;
Sing praises to Him with a harp of ten strings.

3 Sing to Him a new song;
Play skillfully with a shout of joy.

4 For the word of the LORD is upright;
And all His work is *done* in faithfulness.

5 He loves righteousness and justice;
The earth is full of the lovingkindness of the LORD.

6 By the word of the LORD the heavens were made,
And by the breath of His mouth all their host.

7 He gathers the waters of the sea together as a heap;
He lays up the deeps in storehouses.

8 Let all the earth fear the LORD;
Let all the inhabitants of the world stand in awe of Him.

9 For He spoke, and it was done;
He commanded, and it stood fast.

10 The LORD nullifies the counsel of the nations;
He frustrates the plans of the peoples.

11 The counsel of the LORD stands forever,

The plans of His heart from generation to generation.

12 Blessed is the nation whose God is the LORD,
The people whom He has chosen for His own inheritance.

13 The LORD looks from heaven;
He sees all the sons of men;

14 From His dwelling place He looks out
On all the inhabitants of the earth,

15 He who fashions the hearts of them all,
He who understands all their works.

16 The king is not saved by a mighty army;
A warrior is not delivered by great strength.

17 A horse is a false hope for victory;
Nor does it deliver anyone by its great strength.

18 Behold, the eye of the LORD is on those who fear Him,
On those who hope for His lovingkindness,

19 To deliver their soul from death,
And to keep them alive in famine.

20 Our soul waits for the LORD;
He is our help and our shield.

21 For our heart rejoices in Him,
Because we trust in His holy name.

22 Let Thy lovingkindness, O LORD, be upon us,
According as we have hoped in Thee.

PSALM 34

The LORD a Provider and Deliverer.

A Psalm of David when he feigned madness before Abimelech, who drove him away and he departed.

I WILL bless the LORD at all times;

His praise shall continually be
   in my mouth.
2 My soul shall make its boast
   in the LORD;
   The humble shall hear it and
    rejoice.
3 O magnify the LORD with me,
   And let us exalt His name to-
    gether.

4 I sought the LORD, and He answered me,
   And delivered me from all my
    fears.
5 They looked to Him and were
   radiant,
   And their faces shall never be
    ashamed.
6 This poor man cried and the
   LORD heard him,
   And saved him out of all his
    troubles.
7 The angel of the LORD en-
   camps around those who
   fear Him,
   And rescues them.

8 O taste and see that the LORD
   is good;
   How blessed is the man who
    takes refuge in Him!
9 O fear the LORD, you His
   saints;
   For to those who fear Him,
    there is no want.
10 The young lions do lack and
   suffer hunger;
   But they who seek the LORD
    shall not be in want of any
    good thing.
11 Come, you children, listen to
   me;
   I will teach you the fear of the
    LORD.
12 Who is the man who desires
   life,
   And loves *length of* days that
    he may see good?
13 Keep your tongue from evil,
   And your lips from speaking
    deceit.

14 Depart from evil, and do good;
   Seek peace, and pursue it.

15 The eyes of the LORD are
   toward the righteous,
   And His ears are *open* to their
    cry.
16 The face of the LORD is
   against evildoers,
   To cut off the memory of them
    from the earth.
17 *The righteous* cry and the
   LORD hears,
   And delivers them out of all
    their troubles.
18 The LORD is near to the brokenhearted,
   And saves those who are
    [61]crushed in spirit.

19 Many are the afflictions of the
   righteous;
   But the LORD delivers him out
    of them all.
20 He keeps all his bones;
   Not one of them is broken.
21 Evil shall slay the wicked;
   And those who hate the right-
    eous will be condemned.
22 The LORD redeems the soul of
   His servants;
   And none of those who take
    refuge in Him will be con-
    demned.

PSALM 35

Prayer for Rescue from Enemies.

A Psalm of David.

CONTEND, O LORD, with those
   who contend with me;
   Fight against those who fight
    against me.
2 Take hold of [62]buckler and
   shield,
   And rise up for my help.
3 Draw also the spear and the
   battle-axe to meet those
   who pursue me;

[61] Or, *contrite*   [62] I.e., small shield

Say to my soul, "I am your salvation."

4 Let those be ashamed and dishonored who seek my life;
Let those be turned back and humiliated who devise evil against me.

5 Let them be like chaff before the wind,
With the angel of the LORD driving *them* on.

6 Let their way be dark and slippery,
With the angel of the LORD pursuing them.

7 For without cause they hid their net for me;
Without cause they dug a pit for my soul.

8 Let destruction come upon him unawares;
And let the net which he hid catch himself;
Into that very destruction let him fall.

9 And my soul shall rejoice in the LORD;
It shall exult in His salvation.

10 All my bones will say, "LORD, who is like Thee,
Who delivers the afflicted from him who is too strong for him,
And the afflicted and the needy from him who robs him?"

11 Malicious witnesses rise up;
They ask me of things that I do not know.

12 They repay me evil for good,
To the bereavement of my soul.

13 But as for me, when they were sick, my clothing was sackcloth;
I humbled my soul with fasting;
And my prayer kept returning to my bosom.

14 I went about as though it were my friend or brother;
I bowed down mourning, as one who sorrows for a mother.

15 But at my [63]stumbling they rejoiced, and gathered themselves together;
The smiters whom I did not know gathered together against me,
They slandered me without ceasing.

16 Like godless jesters at a feast,
They gnashed at me with their teeth.

17 Lord, how long wilt Thou look on?
Rescue my soul from their ravages,
My only *life* from the lions.

18 I will give Thee thanks in the great congregation;
I will praise Thee among a mighty throng.

19 Do not let those who are wrongfully my enemies rejoice over me;
Neither let those who hate me without cause wink maliciously.

20 For they do not speak peace,
But they devise deceitful words against those who are quiet in the land.

21 And they opened their mouth wide against me;
They said, "Aha, aha, our eyes have seen it!"

22 Thou hast seen it, O LORD, do not keep silent;
O Lord, do not be far from me.

23 Stir up Thyself, and awake to my right,
And to my cause, my God and my Lord.

24 Judge me, O LORD my God, according to Thy righteousness;
And do not let them rejoice over me.

63 Or, limping

25 Do not let them say in their
   heart, "Aha, our desire!"
   Do not let them say, "We have
   swallowed him up!"

26 Let those be ashamed and humiliated altogether who rejoice at my distress;
   Let those be clothed with
   shame and dishonor who
   magnify themselves over
   me.

27 Let them shout for joy and rejoice, who favor my vindication;
   And let them say continually,
   "The LORD be magnified,
   Who delights in the prosperity
   of His servant."

28 And my tongue shall declare
   Thy righteousness
   And Thy praise all day long.

PSALM 36

*Wickedness of Men and
Lovingkindness of God.*

For the choir director. *A
Psalm* of David the servant of
   the LORD.

TRANSGRESSION speaks to the
   ungodly within his heart;
There is no fear of God before
   his eyes.

2 For it flatters him in his *own*
   eyes,
   Concerning the discovery of
   his iniquity *and* the hatred
   of it.

3 The words of his mouth are
   wickedness and deceit;
   He has ceased to be wise *and*
   to do good.

4 He plans wickedness upon his
   bed;
   He sets himself on a path that
   is not good;
   He does not despise evil.

5 Thy lovingkindness, O LORD,
   extends to the heavens,

Thy faithfulness *reaches* to
   the skies.

6 Thy righteousness is like the
   mountains of God;
   Thy judgments *are like* a great
   deep.
   O LORD, Thou preservest man
   and beast.

7 How precious is Thy lovingkindness, O God!
   And the children of men take
   refuge in the shadow of
   Thy wings.

8 They drink their fill of the
   abundance of Thy house;
   And Thou dost give them to
   drink of the river of Thy
   delights.

9 For with Thee is the fountain
   of life;
   In Thy light we see light.

10 O continue Thy lovingkindness to those who know
   Thee,
   And Thy righteousness to the
   upright in heart.

11 Let not the foot of pride come
   upon me,
   And let not the hand of the
   wicked drive me away.

12 There the doers of iniquity
   have fallen;
   They have been thrust down
   and cannot rise.

PSALM 37

*Security of Those Who Trust in
the LORD, and Insecurity of the
   Wicked.*

A Psalm of David.

DO not fret because of evildoers,
   Be not envious toward wrong-
   doers.

2 For they will wither quickly
   like the grass,
   And fade like the green herb.

3 Trust in the LORD, and do
   good;

Dwell in the land and [64]culti-
vate faithfulness.

4 Delight yourself in the LORD;
And He will give you the desires of your heart.

5 Commit your way to the
LORD,
Trust also in Him, and He will
do it.

6 And He will bring forth your
righteousness as the light,
And your judgment as the
noonday.

7 [65]Rest in the LORD and wait
[66]patiently for Him;
Do not fret because of him
who prospers in his way,
Because of the man who carries out wicked schemes.

8 Cease from anger, and forsake
wrath;
Do not fret, it leads only to
evildoing.

9 For evildoers will be cut off,
But those who wait for the
LORD, they will inherit the
land.

10 Yet a little while and the
wicked man will be no
more;
And you will look carefully for
his place, and he will not
be there.

11 But the humble will inherit the
land,
And will delight themselves in
abundant prosperity.

12 The wicked plots against the
righteous,
And gnashes at him with his
teeth.

13 The Lord laughs at him;
For He sees his day is coming.

14 The wicked have drawn the
sword and bent their bow,
To cast down the afflicted and
the needy,

To slay those who are upright
in conduct.

15 Their sword will enter their
own heart,
And their bows will be broken.

16 Better is the little of the righteous
Than the abundance of many
wicked.

17 For the arms of the wicked
will be broken;
But the LORD sustains the
righteous.

18 The LORD knows the days of
the blameless;
And their inheritance will be
forever.

19 They will not be ashamed in
the time of evil;
And in the days of famine
they will have abundance.

20 But the wicked will perish;
And the enemies of the LORD
will be like the [67]glory of
the pastures,
They vanish—like smoke they
vanish away.

21 The wicked borrows and does
not pay back,
But the righteous is gracious
and gives.

22 For those blessed by Him will
inherit the land;
But those cursed by Him will
be cut off.

23 The steps of a man are established by the LORD;
And He delights in his way.

24 When he falls, he shall not be
hurled headlong;
Because the LORD is the One
who holds his hand.

25 I have been young, and now I
am old;
Yet I have not seen the righteous forsaken,
Or his descendants begging
bread.

---

[64] Or, feed securely, or, feed on His faithfulness   [65] Or, Be still
[66] Or, longingly   [67] I.e., flowers

26 All day long he is gracious and
lends;
And his descendants are a
blessing.

27 Depart from evil, and do
good,
So you will abide forever.

28 For the LORD loves justice,
And does not forsake His god-
ly ones;
They are preserved forever;
But the descendants of the
wicked will be cut off.

29 The righteous will inherit the
land,
And dwell in it forever.

30 The mouth of the righteous utters wisdom,
And his tongue speaks justice.

31 The law of his God is in his
heart;
His steps do not slip.

32 The wicked spies upon the
righteous,
And seeks to kill him.

33 The LORD will not leave him in
his hand,
Or let him be condemned
when he is judged.

34 Wait for the LORD, and keep
His way,
And He will exalt you to in-
herit the land;
When the wicked are cut off,
you will see it.

35 I have seen a violent, wicked
man
Spreading himself like a lux-
uriant tree in its native soil.

36 Then he passed away, and lo,
he was no more;
I sought for him, but he could
not be found.

37 Mark the blameless man, and
behold the upright;
For the man of peace will
have a posterity.

38 But transgressors will be altogether destroyed;

The posterity of the wicked
will be cut off.

39 But the salvation of the righteous is from the LORD;
He is their strength in time of
trouble.

40 And the LORD helps them, and
delivers them;
He delivers them from the
wicked, and saves them,
Because they take refuge in
Him.

PSALM 38

Prayer of a Suffering Penitent.

A Psalm of David, for a
memorial.

O LORD, rebuke me not in Thy
wrath;
And chasten me not in Thy
burning anger.

2 For Thine arrows have sunk
deep into me,
And Thy hand has pressed
down on me.

3 There is no soundness in my
flesh because of Thine indignation;
There is no health in my bones
because of my sin.

4 For my iniquities are gone
over my head;
As a heavy burden they weigh
too much for me.

5 My wounds grow foul *and* fes-
ter.
Because of my folly,

6 I am bent over and greatly
bowed down;
I go mourning all day long.

7 For my loins are filled with
burning;
And there is no soundness in
my flesh.

8 I am benumbed and badly
crushed;
I groan because of the agita-
tion of my heart.

9 Lord, all my desire is before
Thee;

And my sighing is not hidden
from Thee.

10 My heart throbs, my strength
fails me;
And the light of my eyes, even
that has gone from me.

11 My loved ones and my friends
stand aloof from my
plague;
And my kinsmen stand afar
off.

12 Those who seek my life lay
snares *for me*;
And those who seek to injure
me have threatened de-
struction,
And they devise treachery all
day long.

13 But I, like a deaf man, do not
hear;
And I am like a dumb man
who does not open his
mouth.

14 Yes, I am like a man who does
not hear,
And in whose mouth are no
arguments.

15 For I hope in Thee, O LORD;
Thou wilt answer, O Lord my
God.

16 For I said, "May they not rejoice over me,
Who, when my foot slips,
would magnify themselves
against me."

17 For I am ready to fall,
And my [68]sorrow is continually before me.

18 For I confess my iniquity;
I am full of anxiety because of
my sin.

19 But my enemies are vigorous
and [69]strong;
And many are those who hate
me wrongfully.

20 And those who repay evil for
good,

They oppose me, because I
follow what is good.

21 Do not forsake me, O LORD;
O my God, do not be far from
me!

22 Make haste to help me,
O Lord, my salvation!

PSALM 39

The Vanity of Life.

For the choir director, for
Jeduthun.
A Psalm of David.

I SAID, "I will guard my ways,
That I may not sin with my
tongue;
I will guard my mouth as with
a muzzle,
While the wicked are in my
presence."

2 I was dumb and silent,
I [70]refrained *even* from good;
And my [68]sorrow grew worse.

3 My heart was hot within me;
While I was musing the fire
burned;
Then I spoke with my tongue:

4 "LORD, make me to know my
end,
And what is the extent of my
days,
Let me know how transient I
am.

5 "Behold, Thou hast made my
days *as* handbreadths,
And my lifetime as nothing in
Thy sight,
Surely every man at his best is
a mere breath.   [Selah.

6 "Surely every man walks about
as [71]a phantom;
Surely they make an uproar
for nothing;
He amasses *riches*, and does
not know who will gather
them.

7 "And now, Lord, for what do I
wait?
My hope is in Thee.

---

[68] Lit., *pain* [69] Or, *numerous*
[70] Lit., *kept silence* [71] Lit., *an image*

8"Deliver me from all my transgressions;
Make me not the reproach of
the foolish.

9"I have become dumb, I do not
open my mouth,
Because it is Thou who hast
done *it.*

10"Remove Thy plague from me;
Because of the opposition of
Thy hand, I am perishing.

11"With reproofs Thou dost chasten a man for iniquity;
Thou dost consume as a moth
what is precious to him;
Surely every man is a mere
breath.   [Selah.

12"Hear my prayer, O LORD, and
give ear to my cry;
Do not be silent at my tears;
For I am a stranger with Thee,
A sojourner like all my fa-
thers.

13"Turn Thy gaze away from me,
that I may [72]smile *again,*
Before I depart and am no
more."

PSALM 40

God Sustains His Servant.

For the choir director. A
Psalm of David.

I WAITED [73]patiently for the
LORD;
And He inclined to me, and
heard my cry.

2 He brought me up out of the
pit of destruction, out of
the miry clay;
And He set my feet upon a
rock making my footsteps
firm.

3 And He put a new song in my
mouth, a song of praise to
our God;
Many will see and fear,
And will trust in the LORD.

4 How blessed is the man who
has made the LORD his
trust,

And has not turned to the
proud, nor to those who
lapse into falsehood.

5 Many, O LORD my God, are
the wonders which Thou
hast done,
And Thy thoughts toward us;
There is none to compare with
Thee;
If I would declare and speak
of them,
They would be too numerous
to count.

6 Sacrifice and meal offering
Thou hast not desired;
My ears Thou hast [74]opened;
Burnt offering and sin offering
Thou hast not required.

7 Then I said, "Behold, I come;
In the scroll of the book it is
written of me;

8 I delight to do Thy will, O my
God;
Thy Law is within my heart."

9 I have proclaimed glad tidings
of righteousness in the
great congregation;
Behold, I will not restrain my
lips,
O LORD, Thou knowest.

10 I have not hidden Thy righteousness within my heart;
I have spoken of Thy faithfulness and Thy salvation;
I have not concealed Thy
lovingkindness and Thy
truth from the great con-
gregation.

11 Thou, O LORD, wilt not withhold Thy compassion from
me;
Thy lovingkindness and Thy
truth will continually preserve me.

12 For evils beyond number have
surrounded me;

[72] Or, *become cheerful*   [73] Or, *intently*
[74] Lit., *dug, or possibly, pierced*

My iniquities have overtaken
me, so that I am not able to
see;
They are more numerous than
the hairs of my head;
And my heart has failed me.

13 Be pleased, O LORD, to deliver
me;
Make haste, O LORD, to help
me.

14 Let those be ashamed and humiliated together
Who seek my [75]life to destroy
it;
Let those be turned back and
dishonored
Who delight [76]in my hurt.

15 Let those be appalled because
of their shame
Who say to me, "Aha, aha!"

16 Let all who seek Thee rejoice
and be glad in Thee;
Let those who love Thy salvation say continually,
"The LORD be magnified!"

17 Since I am afflicted and needy,
Let the Lord be mindful of me;
Thou art my help and my de-
liverer;
Do not delay, O my God.

PSALM 41

*The Psalmist in Sickness
Complains of
Enemies and False Friends.*

For the choir director. A
Psalm of David.

HOW blessed is he who considers the helpless;
The LORD will deliver him in a
day of trouble.

2 The LORD will protect him,
and keep him alive,
And he shall be called blessed
upon the earth;
And do not give him over to
the desire of his enemies.

3 The LORD will sustain him
upon his sickbed;
In his illness, Thou dost [77]re-
store him to health.

4 As for me, I said, "O LORD, be
gracious to me;
Heal my soul, for I have
sinned against Thee."

5 My enemies speak evil against
me,
"When will he die, and his
name perish?"

6 And when he comes to see
me, he speaks falsehood;
His heart gathers wickedness
to itself;
When he goes outside, he tells
it.

7 All who hate me whisper together against me;
Against me they devise my
hurt, *saying,*

8 "A wicked thing is poured out
upon him,
That when he lies down, he
will not rise up again."

9 Even my close friend, in
whom I trusted,
Who ate my bread,
Has lifted up his heel against
me.

10 But Thou, O LORD, be gracious to me, and raise me
up,
That I may repay them.

11 By this I know that Thou art
pleased with me,
Because my enemy does not
shout in triumph over me.

12 As for me, Thou dost uphold
me in my integrity,
And Thou dost set me in Thy
presence forever.

13 Blessed be the LORD, the God
of Israel,
From everlasting to ever-
lasting.
Amen, and Amen.

[75] Or, *soul* [76] Or, *to injure me*
[77] Lit., *turn all his bed*

BOOK 2

PSALM 42

Thirsting for God in Trouble and Exile.

For the choir director.
A Maskil of the sons of Korah.

AS the deer [78]pants for the water
brooks,
So my soul pants for Thee, O
God.

2 My soul thirsts for God, for
the living God;
When shall I come and appear
before God?

3 My tears have been my food
day and night,
While *they* say to me all day
long, "Where is your
God?"

4 These things I remember, and
I pour out my soul within
me.
For I used to go along with the
throng *and* lead them in
procession to the house of
God,
With the voice of joy and
thanksgiving, a multitude
keeping festival.

5 Why are you in despair, O my
soul?
And *why* have you become
disturbed within me?
Hope in God, for I shall again
praise Him
For the help of His presence.

6 O my God, my soul is in despair within me;
Therefore I remember Thee
from the land of the Jor-
dan,
And the peaks of Hermon,
from Mount Mizar.

7 Deep calls to deep at the
sound of Thy waterfalls;
All Thy breakers and Thy
waves have rolled over me.

8 The LORD will command His
lovingkindness in the daytime;
And His song will be with me
in the night,
A prayer to the God of my life.

9 I will say to God my rock,
"Why hast Thou forgotten
me?
Why do I go mourning be-
cause of the oppression of
the enemy?"

10 As a shattering of my bones,
my adversaries revile me,
While they say to me all day
long, "Where is your
God?"

11 Why are you in despair, O my
soul?
And why have you become
disturbed within me?
Hope in God, for I shall yet
praise Him,
The help of my countenance,
and my God.

PSALM 43

Prayer for Deliverance.

VINDICATE me, O God, and
plead my case against an
ungodly nation;
O deliver me from the deceitful and unjust man!

2 For Thou art the God of my
strength; why hast Thou
rejected me?
Why do I go mourning be-
cause of the oppression of
the enemy?

3 O send out Thy light and Thy
truth, let them lead me;
Let them bring me to Thy holy
hill,
And to Thy dwelling places.

4 Then I will go to the altar of
God,
To God my exceeding joy;

[78] Lit., *longs for*

And upon the lyre I shall
praise Thee, O God, my
God.

5 Why are you in despair, O my
soul?
And why are you disturbed
within me?
Hope in God, for I shall again
praise Him,
The help of my countenance,
and my God.

PSALM 44

*Former Deliverances and Present
Troubles.*

For the choir director.
A Maskil of the sons of Korah.

O GOD, we have heard with our
ears,
Our fathers have told us,
The work that Thou didst in
their days,
In the days of old.
2 Thou with Thine own hand
didst drive out the nations;
Then Thou didst plant them;
Thou didst afflict the peoples,
Then Thou didst spread them
abroad.
3 For by their own sword they
did not possess the land;
And their own arm did not
save them;
But Thy right hand, and Thine
arm, and the light of Thy
presence,
For Thou didst favor them.

4 Thou art my King, O God;
Command victories for Jacob.
5 Through Thee we will push
back our adversaries;
Through Thy name we will
trample down those who
rise up against us.
6 For I will not trust in my bow,
Nor will my sword save me.

7 But Thou hast saved us from
our adversaries,
And Thou hast put to shame
those who hate us.
8 In God we have boasted all
day long,
And we will give thanks to
Thy name forever. [Selah.

9 Yet Thou hast rejected *us* and
brought us to dishonor,
And dost not go out with our
armies.
10 Thou dost cause us to turn
back from the adversary;
And those who hate us have
taken spoil for themselves.
11 Thou dost give us as sheep to
be eaten,
And hast scattered us among
the nations.
12 Thou dost sell Thy people
cheaply,
And hast not [79]profited by
their sale.
13 Thou dost make us a reproach
to our neighbors,
A scoffing and a derision to
those around us.
14 Thou dost make us a byword
among the nations,
A laughingstock among the
peoples.
15 All day long my dishonor is
before me,
And my humiliation has overwhelmed me,
16 Because of the voice of him
who reproaches and re-
viles,
Because of the presence of the
enemy and the avenger.

17 All this has come upon us, but
we have not forgotten
Thee,
And we have not dealt falsely
with Thy covenant.
18 Our heart has not turned
back,
And our steps have not devi-
ated from Thy way,

[79] Or, *set a high price on them*

19 Yet Thou hast crushed us in a
   place of jackals,
   And covered us with the
   shadow of death.

20 If we had forgotten the name
   of our God,
   Or extended our hands to a
   strange god;

21 Would not God find this out?
   For He knows the secrets of
   the heart.

22 But for Thy sake we are killed
   all day long;
   We are considered as sheep to
   be slaughtered.

23 Arouse Thyself, why dost
   Thou sleep, O Lord?
   Awake, do not reject us for-
   ever.

24 Why dost Thou hide Thy face,
   And forget our affliction and
   our oppression?

25 For our soul has sunk down
   into the dust;
   Our body cleaves to the earth.

26 Rise up, be our help,
   And redeem us for the sake of
   Thy lovingkindness.

PSALM 45

*A Song Celebrating the King's
Marriage.*

For the choir director;
according to the [80]Shoshannim.
A Maskil of the sons of Korah.
A Song of Love.

MY heart [81]overflows with a
good theme;
I address my verses to the
King;
My tongue is the pen of a
ready writer.

2 Thou art fairer than the sons
of men;
Grace is poured upon Thy lips;
Therefore God has blessed
Thee forever.

3 Gird Thy sword on *Thy* thigh,
O Mighty One,

In Thy splendor and Thy majesty!

4 And in Thy majesty ride on
victoriously,
For the cause of truth and
meekness *and* righteous-
ness;
Let Thy right hand teach Thee
awesome things.

5 Thine arrows are sharp;
The peoples fall under Thee;
Thine arrows are in the heart
of the King's enemies.

6 Thy throne, O God, is forever
and ever;
A scepter of uprightness is the
scepter of Thy kingdom.

7 Thou hast loved righteousness, and hated wicked-
ness;
Therefore God, Thy God, has
anointed Thee
With the oil of joy above Thy
fellows.

8 All Thy garments are fragrant
with myrrh and aloes *and*
cassia;
Out of ivory palaces stringed
instruments have made
Thee glad.

9 Kings' daughters are among
Thy noble ladies;
At Thy right hand stands the
queen in gold from Ophir.

10 Listen, O daughter, give attention and incline your ear;
Forget your people and your
father's house;

11 Then the King will desire your
beauty;
Because He is your Lord, bow
down to Him.

12 And the daughter of Tyre *will
come* with a gift;
The rich among the people
will entreat your favor.

13 The King's daughter is all glorious within;

Her clothing is interwoven
with gold.

14 She will be led to the King in
embroidered work;
The virgins, her companions
who follow her,
Will be brought to Thee.

15 They will be led forth with
gladness and rejoicing;
They will enter into the King's
palace.

16 In place of your fathers will be
your sons;
You shall make them princes
in all the earth.

17 I will cause Thy name to be remembered in all genera-
tions;
Therefore the peoples will
give Thee thanks forever
and ever.

PSALM 46

God the Refuge of His People.

For the choir director. *A Psalm*
of the sons of Korah, [82]set to
Alamoth. A Song.

GOD is our refuge and strength,
[83]A very present help in trouble.

2 Therefore we will not fear,
though the earth should
change,
And though the mountains
slip into the heart of the
sea;

3 Though its waters roar *and*
foam,
Though the mountains quake
at its swelling pride. [Selah.

4 There is a river whose
streams make glad the city
of God,
The holy dwelling places of
the Most High.

5 God is in the midst of her, she
will not be moved;

God will help her when morning dawns.

6 The nations made an uproar,
the kingdoms tottered;
He raised His voice, the earth
melted.

7 The LORD of hosts is with us;
The God of Jacob is our
stronghold.   [Selah.

8 Come, behold the works of
the LORD,
Who has wrought desolations
in the earth.

9 He makes wars to cease to the
end of the earth;
He breaks the bow and cuts
the spear in two;
He burns the chariots with
fire.

10 "Cease *striving* and know that I
am God;
I will be exalted among the
nations, I will be exalted in
the earth."

11 The LORD of hosts is with us;
The God of Jacob is our
stronghold.   [Selah.

PSALM 47

God the King of the Earth.

For the choir director.
A Psalm of the sons of Korah.

O CLAP your hands, all peoples;
Shout to God with the voice of
joy.

2 For the LORD Most High is to
be feared,
A great King over all the
earth.

3 He subdues peoples under us,
And nations under our feet.

4 He chooses our inheritance
for us,
The glory of Jacob whom He
loves.   [Selah.

5 God has ascended with a
shout,
The LORD, with the sound of a
trumpet.

---

[82] Possibly, *for soprano voices*
[83] Or, *Abundantly available for help*

6 Sing praises to God, sing
   praises;
  Sing praises to our King, sing
   praises.
7 For God is the King of all the
   earth;
  Sing praises with a skillful
   psalm.
8 God reigns over the nations,
  God sits on His holy throne.
9 The princes of the people have
   assembled themselves *as*
   the people of the God of
   Abraham;
  For the shields of the earth belong to God;
  He is highly exalted.

PSALM 48

The Beauty and Glory of Zion.

A Song; a Psalm of the sons of
   Korah.

GREAT is the LORD, and greatly
   to be praised,
  In the city of our God, His
   holy mountain.
2 Beautiful in elevation, the joy
   of the whole earth,
  Is Mount Zion *in* the far north,
  The city of the great King.
3 God, in her palaces,
  Has made Himself known as a
   stronghold.

4 For, lo, the kings assembled
   themselves,
  They passed by together.
5 They saw *it*, then they were
   amazed;
  They were terrified, they fled
   in alarm.
6 Panic seized them there,
  Anguish, as of a woman in
   childbirth.
7 With the east wind
  Thou dost break the ships of
   Tarshish.
8 As we have heard, so have we
   seen

In the city of the LORD of
   hosts, in the city of our
   God;
  God will establish her forever.
                        [Selah.

9 We have thought on Thy
   lovingkindness, O God,
  In the midst of Thy temple.
10 As is Thy name, O God,
  So is Thy praise to the ends of
   the earth;
  Thy right hand is full of righteousness.
11 Let Mount Zion be glad,
  Let the daughters of Judah rejoice,
  Because of Thy judgments.
12 Walk about Zion, and go
   around her;
  Count her towers;
13 Consider her ramparts;
  Go through her palaces;
  That you may tell *it* to the
   next generation.
14 For such is God,
  Our God forever and ever;
  He will guide us [84]until death.

PSALM 49

The Folly of Trusting in Riches.

For the choir director.
A Psalm of the sons of Korah.

HEAR this, all peoples;
  Give ear, all inhabitants of the
   world,
2 Both low and high,
  Rich and poor together.
3 My mouth will speak wisdom;
  And the meditation of my
   heart *will be* understanding.
4 I will incline my ear to a proverb;
  I will express my riddle on the
   harp.

[84] Some mss. and the Gr. read *forever*

5 Why should I fear in days of adversity,
When the iniquity of my foes surrounds me,
6 Even those who trust in their wealth,
And boast in the abundance of their riches?
7 No man can by any means redeem *his* brother,
Or give to God a ransom for him—
8 For the redemption of his soul is costly,
And he should cease *trying* forever—
9 That he should live on eternally;
That he should not [85]undergo decay.

10 For he sees *that even* wise men die;
The stupid and the senseless alike perish,
And leave their wealth to others.
11 Their [86]inner thought is, *that* their houses are forever,
And their dwelling places to all generations;
They have called their lands after their own names.
12 But man in *his* pomp will not endure;
He is like the beasts that perish.

13 This is the way of those who are foolish,
And of those after them who approve their words.
[Selah.
14 As sheep they are appointed for Sheol;
Death shall be their shepherd;
And the upright shall rule over them in the morning;

And their form shall be for Sheol to consume,
So that they have no habitation.
15 But God will redeem my soul from the power of Sheol;
For He will receive me.
[Selah.

16 Do not be afraid when a man becomes rich,
When the [87]glory of his house is increased;
17 For when he dies he will carry nothing away;
His [87]glory will not descend after him.
18 Though while he lives he congratulates himself—
And though *men* praise you when you do well for yourself—
19 He shall go to the generation of his fathers;
They shall never see the light.
20 Man in *his* pomp, yet without understanding,
Is like the beasts that perish.

PSALM 50

God the Judge of the Righteous and the Wicked.

A Psalm of Asaph.

THE Mighty One, God, the LORD, has spoken,
And summoned the earth from the rising of the sun to its setting.
2 Out of Zion, the perfection of beauty,
God has shone forth.
3 May our God come and not keep silence;
Fire devours before Him,
And it is very tempestuous around Him.
4 He summons the heavens above,
And the earth, to judge His people:

[85] Or, *see corruption* or *the pit*
[86] Some versions read *graves are their houses* [87] Or, *wealth*

5 "Gather My godly ones to Me,
     Those who have made a cov-
       enant with Me by sacri-
       fice."
6 And the heavens declare His
     righteousness,
     For God Himself is judge.
                  [Selah.

7 "Hear, O My people, and I will
     speak;
     O Israel, I will testify against
     you;
     I am God, your God.
8 "I do not reprove you for your
     sacrifices,
     And your burnt offerings are
     continually before Me.
9 "I shall take no young bull out
     of your house,
     Nor male goats out of your
     folds.
10 "For every beast of the forest is
     Mine,
     The cattle on a thousand hills.
11 "I know every bird of the
     mountains,
     And everything that moves in
     the field is [88]Mine.
12 "If I were hungry, I would not
     tell you;
     For the world is Mine, and all
     it contains.
13 "Shall I eat the flesh of bulls,
     Or drink the blood of male
     goats?
14 "Offer to God a sacrifice of
     thanksgiving,
     And pay your vows to the
     Most High;
15 And call upon Me in the day
     of trouble;
     I shall rescue you, and you
     will honor Me."

16 But to the wicked God says,
     "What right have you to tell of
     My statutes,
     And to take My covenant in
     your mouth?
17 "For you hate discipline,

     And you cast My words be-
     hind you.
18 "When you see a thief, you are
     pleased with him,
     And you associate with adul-
     terers.
19 "You let your mouth loose in
     evil,
     And your tongue frames de-
     ceit.
20 "You sit and speak against
     your brother;
     You slander your own moth-
     er's son.
21 "These things you have done,
     and I kept silence;
     You thought that I was just
     like you;
     I will reprove you, and state
     the case in order before
     your eyes.
22 "Now consider this, you who
     forget God,
     Lest I tear you in pieces, and
     there be none to deliver.
23 "He who offers a sacrifice of
     thanksgiving honors Me;
     And to him who orders his
     way aright
     I shall show the salvation of
     God."

PSALM 51

*A Contrite Sinner's Prayer for
Pardon.*

For the choir director. A
Psalm of David, when Nathan
the prophet came to him, after
he had gone in to Bathsheba.

BE gracious to me, O God, ac-
     cording to Thy lovingkind-
     ness;
     According to the greatness of
     Thy compassion blot out
     my transgressions.
2 Wash me thoroughly from my
     iniquity,
     And cleanse me from my sin.

[88] Or, in My mind

3 For I know my transgressions,
And my sin is ever before me.

4 Against Thee, Thee only, I
have sinned,
And done what is evil in Thy
sight,
So that Thou [89]art justified
when Thou dost speak,
And blameless when Thou
dost judge.

5 Behold, I was brought forth in
iniquity,
And in sin my mother con-
ceived me.

6 Behold, Thou dost desire truth
in the innermost being,
And in the hidden part Thou
wilt make me know wis-
dom.

7 Purify me with hyssop, and I
shall be clean;
Wash me, and I shall be whit-
er than snow.

8 Make me to hear joy and gladness,
Let the bones which Thou
hast broken rejoice.

9 Hide Thy face from my sins,
And blot out all my iniquities.

10 Create in me a clean heart, O
God,
And renew a steadfast spirit
within me.

11 Do not cast me away from
Thy presence,
And do not take Thy Holy
Spirit from me.

12 Restore to me the joy of Thy
salvation,
And sustain me with a willing
spirit.

13 Then I will teach transgressors Thy ways,
And sinners will [90]be converted to Thee.

14 Deliver me from bloodguilti-
ness, O God, Thou God of
my salvation;

[89] Or, mayest be in the right
[90] Or, turn back

Then my tongue will joyfully
sing of Thy righteousness.

15 O LORD, open my lips,
That my mouth may declare
Thy praise.

16 For Thou dost not delight in
sacrifice, otherwise I would
give it;
Thou art not pleased with
burnt offering.

17 The sacrifices of God are a
broken spirit;
A broken and a contrite heart,
O God, Thou wilt not de-
spise.

18 By Thy favor do good to Zion;
Build the walls of Jerusalem.

19 Then Thou wilt delight in
righteous sacrifices,
In burnt offering and whole
burnt offering;
Then young bulls will be offered on Thine altar.

PSALM 52

Futility of Boastful Wickedness.

For the choir director. A Maskil
of David, when Doeg the
Edomite came and told Saul, and
said to him, "David has come to
the house of Ahimelech."

WHY do you boast in evil, O
mighty man?
The lovingkindness of God endures all day long.

2 Your tongue devises destruction,
Like a sharp razor, O worker
of deceit.

3 You love evil more than good,
Falsehood more than speaking what is right. [Selah.

4 You love all words that devour,
O deceitful tongue.

5 But God will break you down
forever;
He will snatch you up, and
tear you away from your
tent,

And uproot you from the land
of the living.   [Selah.

6 And the righteous will see and
fear,
And will laugh at him, *saying,*

7"Behold, the man who would
not make God his refuge,
But trusted in the abundance
of his riches,
And was strong in his *evil* desire."

8 But as for me, I am like a
green olive tree in the
house of God;
I trust in the lovingkindness of
God forever and ever.

9 I will give Thee thanks forever, because Thou hast
done *it,*
And I will wait on Thy name,
for *it is* good, in the presence of Thy godly ones.

PSALM 53

Folly and Wickedness of Men.

For the choir director; according
to [91]Mahalath. A Maskil of
David.

THE fool has said in his heart,
"There is no God,"
They are corrupt, and have
committed abominable in-
justice;
There is no one who does
good.

2 God has looked down from
heaven upon the sons of
men,
To see if there is anyone who
understands,
Who seeks after God.

3 Every one of them has turned
aside; together they have
become corrupt;
There is no one who does
good, not even one.

4 Have the workers of wickedness no knowledge,
Who eat up My people *as
though* they ate bread,

And have not called upon
God?

5 There they were in great fear
where no fear had been;
For God scattered the bones
of him who encamped
against you;
You put *them* to shame, because God had rejected
them.

6 Oh, that the salvation of Israel
would come out of Zion!
When God restores His captive people,
Let Jacob rejoice, let Israel be
glad.

PSALM 54

*Prayer for Defense against
Enemies.*

For the choir director; on
stringed instruments. A Maskil
of David, when the Ziphites
came and said to Saul, "Is not
David hiding himself among us?"

SAVE me, O God, by Thy name,
And [92]vindicate me by Thy
power.

2 Hear my prayer, O God;
Give ear to the words of my
mouth.

3 For strangers have risen
against me,
And violent men have sought
my life;
They have not set God before
them.   [Selah.

4 Behold, God is my helper;
The Lord is the sustainer of
my soul.

5 [93]He will recompense the evil
to my foes;
Destroy them in Thy faithfulness.

6 Willingly I will sacrifice to
Thee;

[91] I.e., sickness, a sad tone   [92] Lit., *judge*
[93] Lit., *The evil will return*

I will give thanks to Thy
name, O LORD, for it is
good.
7 For He has delivered me from
all trouble;
And my eye has looked *with
satisfaction* upon my en-
emies.

PSALM 55

*Prayer for the Destruction of the
Treacherous.*

For the choir director; on
stringed instruments.
A Maskil of David.

GIVE ear to my prayer, O God;
And do not hide Thyself from
my supplication.
2 Give heed to me, and answer
me;
I am restless in my complaint
and [94]am surely distracted,
3 Because of the voice of the
enemy,
Because of the pressure of the
wicked;
For they bring down trouble
upon me,
And in anger they bear a
grudge against me.

4 My heart is in anguish within
me,
And the terrors of death have
fallen upon me.
5 Fear and trembling come
upon me;
And horror has overwhelmed
me.
6 And I said, "Oh, that I had
wings like a dove!
I would fly away and [95]be at
rest.
7 "Behold, I would wander far
away,
I would lodge in the
wilderness.   [Selah.

8 "I would hasten to my place of
refuge
From the stormy wind *and*
tempest."

9 Confuse, O Lord, divide their
tongues,
For I have seen violence and
strife in the city.
10 Day and night they go around
her upon her walls;
And iniquity and mischief are
in her midst.
11 Destruction is in her midst;
Oppression and deceit do not
depart from her streets.

12 For it is not an enemy who reproaches me,
Then I could bear *it*;
Nor is it one who hates me
who has exalted himself
against me,
Then I could hide myself from
him.
13 But it is you, a man my equal,
My companion and my famil-
iar friend.
14 We who had sweet [96]fellow-
ship together,
Walked in the house of God in
the throng.
15 Let death come deceitfully
upon them;
Let them go down alive to
Sheol,
For evil is in their dwelling, in
their midst.

16 As for me, I shall call upon
God,
And the LORD will save me.
17 Evening and morning and at
noon, I will complain and
murmur,
And He will hear my voice.
18 He will redeem my soul in
peace from the battle
which is against me,
For they are many *who strive*
with me.
19 God will hear and answer
them—

---

[94] Or, *I must moan*   [95] Lit., *settle down*
[96] Lit., *counsel*

Even the one who sits en-
throned from of old—
[Selah.
With whom there is no
change,
And who do not fear God.

20 He has put forth his hands
against those who were at
peace with him;
He has [97]violated his covenant.

21 His speech was smoother than
butter,
But his heart was war;
His words were softer than
oil,
Yet they were drawn swords.

22 Cast your burden upon the
LORD, and He will sustain
you;
He will never allow the righteous to be shaken.

23 But Thou, O God, wilt bring
them down to the pit of destruction;
Men of bloodshed and deceit
will not live out half their
days.
But I will trust in Thee.

PSALM 56

*Supplication for Deliverance, and
Grateful Trust in God.*

For the choir director; according
to Jonath elem rehokim. A
Mikhtam of David, when the
Philistines seized him in Gath.

BE gracious, O God, for man has
trampled upon me;
Fighting all day long he oppresses me.

2 My foes have trampled upon
me all day long,
For they are many who fight
proudly against me.

3 When I am afraid,
I will put my trust in Thee.

4 In God, whose word I praise,
In God I have put my trust;
I shall not be afraid.
What can *mere* man do to me?

5 All day long they [98]distort my
words;
All their thoughts are against
me for evil.

6 They [99]attack, they lurk,
They watch my steps,
As they have waited *to take*
my life.

7 Because of wickedness, cast
them forth,
In anger put down the peoples, O God!

8 Thou hast taken account of
my wanderings;
Put my tears in Thy bottle;
Are *they* not in Thy book?

9 Then my enemies will turn
back in the day when I call;
This I know, [100]that God is for
me.

10 In God, *whose* word I praise,
In the LORD, *whose* word I
praise,

11 In God I have put my [101]trust,
I shall not be afraid.
What can man do to me?

12 Thy vows are *binding* upon
me, O God;
I will render thank offerings to
Thee.

13 For Thou hast delivered my
soul from death,
Indeed my feet from stum-
bling,
So that I may walk before God
In the light of the living.

PSALM 57

*Prayer for Rescue from
Persecutors.*

For the choir director; set to
[102]Al-tashheth. A Mikhtam of
David, when he fled from Saul,
in the cave.

BE gracious to me, O God, be
gracious to me,

---

[97] Lit., *profaned* [98] Or, *trouble my affairs*
[99] Or, *stir up strife* [100] Or, *because*
[101] Or, *trust without fear*
[102] Lit., *Do Not Destroy*

For my soul takes refuge in
  Thee;
And in the shadow of Thy
  wings I will take refuge,
Until destruction passes by.
2 I will cry to God Most High,
  To God who accomplishes *all
    things* for me.
3 He will send from heaven and
    save me;
  He reproaches him who tram-
    ples upon me.   [Selah.
  God will send forth His
    lovingkindness   and   His
    truth.

4 My soul is among lions;
  I must lie among those who
    breathe forth fire,
  Even the sons of men, whose
    teeth are spears and ar-
    rows,
  And their tongue a sharp
    sword.
5 Be exalted above the heavens,
    O God;
  Let Thy glory *be* above all the
    earth.
6 They have [103]prepared a net
    for my steps;
  My soul is bowed down;
  They dug a pit before me;
  They *themselves* have fallen
    into the midst of it. [Selah.

7 My heart is steadfast, O God,
    my heart is steadfast;
  I will sing, yes, I will sing
    praises!
8 Awake, my glory;
  Awake, harp and lyre,
  I will awaken the dawn!
9 I will give thanks to Thee, O
    Lord, among the peoples;
  I will sing praises to Thee
    among the nations.
10 For Thy lovingkindness is
    great to the heavens,
  And Thy truth to the clouds.

11 Be exalted above the heavens,
    O God;
  Let Thy glory *be* above all the
    earth.

PSALM 58

*Prayer for the Punishment of the
  Wicked.*

For the choir director; *set to
  Al-tashheth.*
A Mikhtam of David.

DO you indeed speak righteous-
    ness, O [104]gods?
  Do you judge [105]uprightly, O
    sons of men?
2 No, in heart you work unright-
    eousness;
  On earth you weigh out the
    violence of your hands.
3 The wicked are estranged
    from the womb;
  These who speak lies go
    astray from birth.
4 They have venom like the
    venom of a serpent;
  Like a deaf cobra that stops
    up its ear,
5 So that it does not hear the
    voice of charmers,
  Or a skillful caster of spells.

6 O God, shatter their teeth in
    their mouth;
  Break out the fangs of the
    young lions, O LORD.
7 Let them flow away like water
    that runs off;
  When he aims his arrows, let
    them be as headless shafts.
8 *Let* him be as a snail which
    melts away as it goes
    along,
  Like the miscarriages of a
    woman which never see
    the sun.
9 Before your pots can feel *the
    fire of* thorns,
  He will sweep them away
    with a whirlwind, the green
    and the burning alike.

---

[103] Or, *spread*   [104] Or, *judges*
[105] Or, *uprightly the sons of men?*

10 The righteous will rejoice
when he sees the ven-
geance;
He will wash his feet in the
blood of the wicked.

11 And men will say, "Surely
there is a reward for the
righteous;
Surely there is a God who
judges on earth!"

PSALM 59

*Prayer for Deliverance from
Enemies.*

For the choir director; *set to
Al-tashheth.*A Mikhtam of
David, when Saul sent *men,*
and they watched the house
in order to kill him.

DELIVER me from my enemies,
O my God;
Set me *securely* on high away
from those who rise up
against me.

2 Deliver me from those who do
iniquity,
And save me from men of
bloodshed.

3 For behold, they have set an
ambush for my life;
Fierce men [106]launch an attack against me,
Not for my transgression nor
for my sin, O LORD,

4 For no guilt of *mine,* they run
and set themselves against
me.
Arouse Thyself to help me,
and see!

5 And Thou, O LORD God of
hosts, the God of Israel,
Awake to punish all the nations;
Do not be gracious to any *who
are* treacherous in iniquity.
[Selah.

6 They return at evening, they
howl like a dog,
And go around the city.

7 Behold, they belch forth with
their mouth,

Swords are in their lips,
For, *they say,* "Who hears?"

8 But Thou, O LORD, dost laugh
at them;
Thou dost scoff at all the nations.

9 *Because of* [107]his strength I
will watch for Thee,
For God is my stronghold.

10 My God in His lovingkindness
will meet me;
God will let me look *trium-
phantly* upon my foes.

11 Do not slay them, lest my people forget;
Scatter them by Thy power,
and bring them down,
O Lord, our shield.

12 *On account of* the sin of their
mouth *and* the words of
their lips,
Let them even be caught in
their pride,
And on account of curses and
lies which they utter.

13 [108]Destroy *them* in wrath,
[108]destroy *them,* that they
may be no more;
That *men* may know that God
rules in Jacob,
To the ends of the earth.
[Selah.

14 And they return at evening,
they howl like a dog,
And go around the city.

15 They wander about [109]for
food,
And growl if they are not satisfied.

16 But as for me, I shall sing of
Thy strength;
Yes, I shall joyfully sing of
Thy lovingkindness in the
morning,
For Thou hast been my
stronghold,

---

106 Or, *stir up strife*
107 Many mss. and some ancient versions
read *My strength* 108 Lit., *Bring to an end*
109 Or, *to devour*

And a refuge in the day of my distress.

17 O my strength, I will sing praises to Thee;
For God is my stronghold, the God who shows me loving-kindness.

PSALM 60

Lament over Defeat in Battle, and Prayer for Help.

For the choir director;
according to
[110]Shushan Eduth. A Mikhtam of David, to teach; when he struggled with Aram-naharaim and with Aram-zobah, and Joab returned, and smote twelve thousand of Edom in the Valley of Salt.

O GOD, Thou hast rejected us. Thou hast broken us;
Thou hast been angry; O, restore us.

2 Thou hast made the land quake, Thou hast split it open;
Heal its breaches, for it totters.

3 Thou hast made Thy people experience hardship;
Thou hast given us wine to drink that makes us stagger.

4 Thou hast given a banner to those who fear Thee,
That it may be displayed because of the truth. [Selah.

5 That Thy beloved may be delivered,
Save with Thy right hand, and answer us!

6 God has spoken in His [111]holiness:
"I will exult, I will portion out Shechem and measure out the valley of Succoth.

7 "Gilead is Mine, and Manasseh is Mine;
Ephraim also is the helmet of My head;
Judah is My [112]scepter.

8 "Moab is My washbowl;
Over Edom I shall throw My shoe;
Shout loud, O Philistia, because of Me!"

9 Who will bring me into the besieged city?
Who will lead me to Edom?

10 Hast not Thou Thyself, O God, rejected us?
And wilt Thou not go forth with our armies, O God?

11 O give us help against the adversary,
For deliverance by man is in vain.

12 Through God we shall do valiantly,
And it is He who will tread down our adversaries.

PSALM 61

Confidence in God's Protection.

For the choir director; on a stringed instrument.
A Psalm of David.

HEAR my cry, O God;
Give heed to my prayer.

2 From the end of the earth I call to Thee, when my heart is faint;
Lead me to the rock that is higher than I.

3 For Thou hast been a refuge for me,
A tower of strength against the enemy.

4 Let me dwell in Thy tent forever;
Let me take refuge in the shelter of Thy wings. [Selah.

5 For Thou hast heard my vows, O God;

110 Lit., *The lily of testimony*
111 Or, *sanctuary*   112 Or, *lawgiver*

Thou hast given *me* the inheritance of those who fear Thy name.

6 Thou wilt prolong the king's life;
His years will be as many generations.

7 He will abide before God forever;
Appoint lovingkindness and truth, that they may preserve him.

8 So I will sing praise to Thy name forever,
That I may pay my vows day by day.

PSALM 62

God Alone a Refuge from Treachery and Oppression.

For the choir director; according to Jeduthun. A Psalm of David.

MY soul *waits* in silence for God only;
From Him is my salvation.

2 He only is my rock and my salvation,
My stronghold; I shall not be greatly shaken.

3 How long will you assail a man,
That you may murder *him*, all of you,
Like a leaning wall, like a tottering fence?

4 They have counseled only to thrust him down from his high position;
They delight in falsehood;
They bless with their mouth,
But inwardly they curse. [Selah.

5 My soul, wait in silence for God only,
For my hope is from Him.

6 He only is my rock and my salvation,

My stronghold; I shall not be shaken.

7 On God my salvation and my glory *rest*;
The rock of my strength, my refuge is in God.

8 Trust in Him at all times, O people;
Pour out your heart before Him;
God is a refuge for us. [Selah.

9 Men of low degree are only vanity, and men of rank are a lie;
In the balances they go up;
They are together lighter than breath.

10 Do not trust in oppression,
And do not vainly hope in robbery;
If riches increase, do not set *your* heart *upon* them.

11 [113]Once God has spoken;
[114]Twice I have heard this:
That power belongs to God;

12 And lovingkindness is Thine, O Lord,
For Thou dost recompense a man according to his work.

PSALM 63

The Thirsting Soul Satisfied in God.

A Psalm of David, when he was in the wilderness of Judah.

O GOD, Thou art my God; I shall seek Thee [115]earnestly;
My soul thirsts for Thee, my flesh yearns for Thee,
In a dry and weary land where there is no water.

2 Thus I have beheld Thee in the sanctuary,
To see Thy power and Thy glory.

---

113 Or, *One thing*
114 Or, *These two things I have heard*
115 Lit., *early*

3 Because Thy lovingkindness is
   better than life,
   My lips will praise Thee.
4 So I will bless Thee as long as
   I live;
   I will lift up my hands in Thy
   name.
5 My soul is satisfied as with
   [116]marrow and fatness,
   And my mouth offers praises
   with joyful lips.

6 When I remember Thee on my
   bed,
   I meditate on Thee in the
   night watches,
7 For Thou hast been my help,
   And in the shadow of Thy
   wings I sing for joy.
8 My soul clings to Thee;
   Thy right hand upholds me.

9 But those who seek my life, to
   destroy it,
   Will go into the depths of the
   earth.
10 They will be delivered over to
   the power of the sword;
   They will be a prey for foxes.
11 But the king will rejoice in
   God;
   Everyone who swears by Him
   will glory,
   For the mouths of those who
   speak lies will be stopped.

PSALM 64

*Prayer for Deliverance from
Secret Enemies.*

For the choir director. A
Psalm of David.

HEAR my voice, O God, in my
[117]complaint;
   Preserve my life from dread of
   the enemy.
2 Hide me from the secret counsel of evildoers,
   From the tumult of those who
   do iniquity,

3 Who have sharpened their
   tongue like a sword.
   They aimed bitter speech *as*
   their arrow,
4 To shoot from concealment at
   the blameless;
   Suddenly they shoot at him,
   and do not fear.
5 They hold fast to themselves
   an evil purpose;
   They talk of laying snares secretly;
   They say, "Who can see
   them?"
6 They [118]devise injustices, *saying,*
   "We are ready with a well-
   conceived plot";
   For the inward thought and the
   heart of a man are
   [119]deep.

7 But God will shoot at them
   with an arrow;
   Suddenly they will be
   wounded.
8 So they will make him stumble;
   Their own tongue is against
   them;
   All who see them will shake
   the head.
9 Then all men will fear,
   And will declare the work of
   God,
   And will consider what He
   has done.

10 The righteous man will be
   glad in the LORD, and will
   take refuge in Him;
   And all the upright in heart
   will glory.

PSALM 65

*God's Abundant Favor to Earth
and Man.*

For the choir director. A
Psalm of David. A Song.

THERE will be silence before
Thee, *and* praise in Zion, O
God;

[116] Lit., *fat*   [117] Or, *concern*
[118] Or, *search out*   [119] Or, *unsearchable*

And to Thee the vow will be
performed.

2 O Thou who dost hear prayer,
To Thee all men come.

3 Iniquities prevail against me;
As for our transgressions,
Thou dost forgive them.

4 How blessed is the one whom
Thou dost choose, and
bring near *to Thee,*
To dwell in Thy courts.
We will be satisfied with the
goodness of Thy house,
Thy holy temple.

5 By awesome *deeds* Thou dost
answer us in righteous-
ness, O God of our salva-
tion,
Thou who art the trust of all
the ends of the earth and of
the farthest sea;

6 Who dost establish the mountains by His strength,
Being girded with might;

7 Who dost still the roaring of
the seas,
The roaring of their waves,
And the tumult of the peoples.

8 And they who dwell in the
ends *of the earth* stand in
awe of Thy signs;
Thou dost make the dawn and
the sunset shout for joy.

9 Thou dost visit the earth, and
cause it to overflow;
Thou dost greatly enrich it;
The stream of God is full of
water;
Thou dost prepare their grain,
for thus Thou dost prepare
the earth.

10 Thou dost water its furrows
abundantly;
Thou dost settle its ridges;
Thou dost soften it with show-
ers;
Thou dost bless its growth.

11 Thou hast crowned the year
with Thy bounty,

And Thy paths drip *with* fatness.

12 The pastures of the wilderness
drip,
And the hills gird themselves
with rejoicing.

13 The meadows are clothed
with flocks,
And the valleys are covered
with grain;
They shout for joy, yes, they
sing.

PSALM 66

*Praise for God's Mighty Deeds
and for His Answer to Prayer.*

For the choir director. A Song.
A Psalm.

SHOUT joyfully to God, all the
earth;

2 Sing the glory of His name;
Make His praise glorious.

3 Say to God, "How awesome
are Thy works!
Because of the greatness of
Thy power Thine enemies
will give feigned obedience
to Thee.

4 "All the earth will worship
Thee,
And will sing praises to Thee;
They will sing praises to Thy
name."   [Selah.

5 Come and see the works of
God,
Who is awesome in *His* deeds
toward the sons of men.

6 He turned the sea into dry
land;
They passed through the river
on foot;
There let us rejoice in Him!

7 He rules by His might forever;
His eyes keep watch on the
nations;
Let not the rebellious exalt
themselves.   [Selah.

8 Bless our God, O peoples,
And sound His praise abroad,

9 Who keeps us in life,
And does not allow our feet to
slip.
10 For Thou hast tried us, O God;
Thou hast refined us as silver
is refined.
11 Thou didst bring us into the
net;
Thou didst lay an oppressive
burden upon our loins.
12 Thou didst make men ride
over our heads;
We went through fire and
through water;
Yet Thou didst bring us out
into *a place of* abundance.
13 I shall come into Thy house
with burnt offerings,
I shall pay Thee my vows,
14 Which my lips uttered
And my mouth spoke when I
was in distress.
15 I shall offer to Thee burnt offerings of fat beasts,
With the smoke of rams;
I shall make *an offering of*
bulls with male goats.
[Selah.

16 Come *and* hear, all who
120fear God,
And I will tell of what He has
done for my soul.
17 I cried to Him with my mouth,
And He was extolled with my
tongue.
18 If I 121regard wickedness in
my heart,
The Lord will not hear;
19 But certainly God has heard;
He has given heed to the voice
of my prayer.
20 Blessed be God,
Who has not turned away my
prayer,
Nor His lovingkindness from
me.

120 Or, *revere*
121 Or, *had regarded . . . would not have
heard*
122 Or, *And let all . . . earth fear Him*

PSALM 67

*The Nations Exhorted to Praise
God.*

For the choir director; with
stringed instruments.
A Psalm. A Song.

GOD be gracious to us and bless
us,
And cause His face to shine
upon us—   [Selah.
2 That Thy way may be known
on the earth,
Thy salvation among all nations.
3 Let the peoples praise Thee, O
God;
Let all the peoples praise
Thee.
4 Let the nations be glad and
sing for joy;
For Thou wilt judge the peoples with uprightness,
And guide the nations on the
earth.   [Selah.
5 Let the peoples praise Thee, O
God;
Let all the peoples praise
Thee.
6 The earth has yielded its produce;
God, our God, blesses us.
7 God blesses us,
122That all the ends of the
earth may fear Him.

PSALM 68

*The God of Sinai and of the
Sanctuary.*

For the choir director. A
Psalm of David. A Song.

LET God arise, let His enemies be
scattered;
And let those who hate Him
flee before Him.
2 As smoke is driven away, *so*
drive *them* away;
As wax melts before the fire,
So let the wicked perish before God.

3 But let the righteous be glad;
      let them exult before God;
   Yes, let them rejoice with
      gladness.
4 Sing to God, sing praises to
      His name;
   Cast up a highway for Him
      who rides through the des-
      erts,
   Whose name is the LORD, and
      exult before Him.

5 A father of the fatherless and
      a judge [123]for the widows,
   Is God in His holy habitation.
6 God makes a home for the
      lonely;
   He leads out the prisoners into
      prosperity,
   Only the rebellious dwell in a
      parched land.

7 O God, when Thou didst go
      forth before Thy people,
   When Thou didst march
      through the wilderness,
      [Selah.
8 The earth quaked;
   The heavens also dropped
      rain at the presence of
      God;
   Sinai itself quaked at the pres-
      ence of God, the God of Is-
      rael.

9 Thou didst shed abroad a
      plentiful rain, O God;
   Thou didst confirm Thine in-
      heritance, when it was
      parched.
10 Thy creatures settled in it;
   Thou didst provide in Thy
      goodness for the poor, O
      God.

11 The Lord gives the command;
   The women who proclaim the
      good tidings are a great
      host:
12 "Kings of armies flee, they flee,
   And she who remains at home
      will divide the spoil!"

13 [124]When you lie down among
      the [125]sheepfolds,

You are like the wings of a
      dove covered with silver,
   And its pinions with glistening
      gold.
14 When the Almighty scattered
      the kings there,
   It was snowing in Zalmon.

15 A mountain of God is the
      mountain of Bashan;
   A mountain of many peaks is
      the mountain of Bashan.
16 Why do you look with envy, O
      mountains with many
      peaks,
   At the mountain which God
      has desired for His abode?
   Surely, the LORD will dwell
      there forever.
17 The chariots of God are
      [126]myriads, thousands
      upon thousands;
   The Lord is among them as at
      Sinai, in holiness.
18 Thou hast ascended on high,
      Thou hast led captive Thy
      captives;
   Thou hast received gifts
      among men,
   Even among the rebellious
      also, that the LORD God
      may dwell there.

19 Blessed be the Lord, who dai-
      ly bears our burden,
   The God who is our salvation.
      [Selah.
20 God is to us a God of deliver-
      ances;
   And to GOD the Lord belong
      escapes from death.
21 Surely God will shatter the
      head of His enemies,
   The hairy crown of him who
      goes on in his guilty deeds.
22 The Lord said, "I will bring
      them back from Bashan,
   I will bring them back from
      the depths of the sea;

[123] Lit., of   [124] Lit., If
[125] Or, cooking stones, or, saddle bags
[126] Lit., twice ten thousand

23 That your foot may shatter
    them in blood,
    The tongue of your dogs *may
    have* its portion from *your*
    enemies."

24 They have seen Thy proces-
    sion, O God,
    The procession of my God, my
    King, into the sanctuary.

25 The singers went on, the musi-
    cians after *them*,
    In the midst of the maidens
    beating tambourines.

26 Bless God in the congrega-
    tions,
    Even the LORD, *you who are of*
    the fountain of Israel.

27 There is Benjamin, the youn-
    gest, ruling them,
    The princes of Judah *in* their
    throng,
    The princes of Zebulun, the
    princes of Naphtali.

28 Your God has commanded
    your strength;
    Show Thyself strong, O God,
    who hast acted on our be-
    half.

29 Because of Thy temple at Je-
    rusalem
    Kings will bring gifts to Thee.

30 Rebuke the beasts in the
    reeds,
    The herd of bulls with the
    calves of the peoples,
    Trampling under foot the
    pieces of silver;
    He has scattered the peoples
    who delight in war.

31 Envoys will come out of
    Egypt;
    Ethiopia will quickly stretch
    out her hands to God.

32 Sing to God, O kingdoms of
    the earth;
    Sing praises to the Lord,
    [Selah.

33 To Him who rides upon the
    highest heavens, which are
    from ancient times;
    Behold, He speaks forth with
    His voice, a mighty voice.

34 Ascribe strength to God;
    His majesty is over Israel,
    And His strength is in the
    skies.

35 O God, *Thou art* awesome
    from Thy sanctuary.
    The God of Israel Himself
    gives strength and power
    to the people.
    Blessed be God!

PSALM 69

*A Cry of Distress and
Imprecation on Adversaries.*

For the choir director;
according to
[127]Shoshannim. *A Psalm of*
David.

SAVE me, O God,
    For the waters have threat-
    ened my life.

2 I have sunk in deep mire, and
    there is no foothold;
    I have come into deep waters,
    and a flood overflows me.

3 I am weary with my crying;
    my throat is parched;
    My eyes fail while I wait for
    my God.

4 Those who hate me without a
    cause are more than the
    hairs of my head;
    Those who would destroy me
    are powerful,
    What I did not steal, I then
    have to restore.

5 O God, it is Thou who dost
    know my folly,
    And my wrongs are not hid-
    den from Thee.

6 May those who wait for Thee
    not be ashamed through
    me, O Lord GOD of hosts;

[127] Or possibly, *Lilies*

May those who seek Thee not
    be dishonored through me,
    O God of Israel,

7 Because for Thy sake I have
    borne reproach;
Dishonor has covered my
    face.

8 I have become estranged from
    my brothers,
And an alien to my mother's
    sons.

9 For zeal for Thy house has
    consumed me,
And the reproaches of those
    who reproach Thee have
    fallen on me.

10 When I wept in my soul with
    fasting,
It became my reproach.

11 When I made sackcloth my
    clothing,
I became a byword to them.

12 Those who sit in the gate talk
    about me,
And I *am* the song of the
    drunkards.

13 But as for me, my prayer is to
    Thee, O LORD, at an accept-
    able time;
O God, in the greatness of Thy
    lovingkindness,
Answer me with Thy saving
    truth.

14 Deliver me from the mire, and
    do not let me sink;
May I be delivered from my
    foes, and from the deep
    waters.

15 May the flood of water not
    overflow me,
And may the deep not swal-
    low me up,
And may the pit not shut its
    mouth on me.

16 Answer me, O LORD, for Thy
    lovingkindness is good;
According to the greatness of
    Thy compassion, turn to
    me,

17 And do not hide Thy face from
    Thy servant,
For I am in distress; answer
    me quickly.

18 Oh draw near to my soul *and*
    redeem it;
Ransom me because of my en-
    emies!

19 Thou dost know my reproach
    and my shame and my dis-
    honor;
All my adversaries are [128]be-
    fore Thee.

20 Reproach has broken my
    heart, and I am so sick.
And I looked for sympathy,
    but there was none,
And for comforters, but I
    found none.

21 They also gave me [129]gall for
    my food,
And for my thirst they gave
    me vinegar to drink.

22 May their table before them
    become a snare;
And when they are in peace,
    may it become a trap.

23 May their eyes grow dim so
    that they cannot see,
And make their loins shake
    continually.

24 Pour out Thine indignation on
    them,
And may Thy burning anger
    overtake them.

25 May their camp be desolate;
May none dwell in their tents.

26 For they have persecuted him
    whom Thou Thyself hast
    smitten,
And they tell of the pain of
    those whom Thou hast
    wounded.

27 Do Thou add iniquity to their
    iniquity,
And may they not come into
    Thy righteousness.

28 May they be blotted out of the
    book of life,

128 Or, known *to Thee* 129 Or, *poison*

And may they not be recorded
with the righteous.

29 But I am afflicted and in pain;
May Thy salvation, O God, set
me *securely* on high.

30 I will praise the name of God
with song,
And shall magnify Him with
thanksgiving.

31 And it will please the LORD
better than an ox
Or a young bull with horns
and hoofs.

32 The humble have seen *it and
are glad;
You who seek God, let your
heart revive.

33 For the LORD hears the needy,
And does not despise His *who
are* prisoners.

34 Let heaven and earth praise
Him,
The seas and everything that
moves in them.

35 For God will save Zion and
build the cities of Judah,
That they may dwell there and
possess it.

36 And the descendants of His
servants will inherit it,
And those who love His name
will dwell in it.

PSALM 70

*Prayer for Help against
Persecutors.*

For the choir director. *A
Psalm* of David; for a memorial.

O GOD, *hasten* to deliver me;
O LORD, hasten to my help!

2 Let those be ashamed and hu-
miliated
Who seek my life;
Let those be turned back and
dishonored
Who delight in my hurt.

3 Let those be turned back because of their shame
Who say, "Aha, aha!"

4 Let all who seek Thee rejoice
and be glad in Thee;
And let those who love Thy
salvation say continually,
"Let God be magnified."

5 But I am afflicted and needy;
Hasten to me, O God!
Thou art my help and my de-
liverer;
O LORD, do not delay.

PSALM 71

*Prayer of an Old Man for
Deliverance.*

IN Thee, O LORD, I have taken refuge;
Let me never be ashamed.

2 In Thy righteousness deliver
me, and rescue me;
Incline Thine ear to me, and
save me.

3 Be Thou to me a rock of habitation, to which I may continually come;
Thou hast given command-
ment to save me,
For Thou art my rock and my
fortress.

4 Rescue me, O my God, out of
the hand of the wicked,
Out of the grasp of the wrongdoer and ruthless man,

5 For Thou art my hope;
O Lord GOD, *Thou art* my confidence from my youth.

6 By Thee I have been sustained
from *my* birth;
Thou art He who took me
from my mother's womb;
My praise is continually of
Thee.

7 I have become a marvel to
many;
For Thou art my strong refuge.

8 My mouth is filled with Thy
praise,
And with Thy glory all day
long.

9 Do not cast me off in the time
of old age;

Do not forsake me when my
strength fails.

10 For my enemies have spoken
against me;
And those who watch for my
life have consulted to-
gether,

11 Saying, "God has forsaken
him;
Pursue and seize him, for
there is no one to deliver."

12 O God, do not be far from me;
O my God, hasten to my help!

13 Let those who are adversaries
of my soul be ashamed *and*
consumed;
Let them be covered with reproach and dishonor, who
seek to injure me.

14 But as for me, I will hope continually,
And will praise Thee yet more
and more.

15 My mouth shall tell of Thy
righteousness,
And of Thy salvation all day
long;
For I do not know the sum *of
them.*

16 I will come with the mighty
deeds of the Lord GOD;
I will make mention of Thy
righteousness, Thine alone.

17 O God, Thou hast taught me
from my youth;
And I still declare Thy wondrous deeds.

18 And even when *I am* old and
gray, O God, do not for-
sake me,
Until I declare Thy strength to
this generation,
Thy power to all who are to
come.

19 For Thy righteousness, O God,
reaches to the heavens,
Thou who hast done great
things;
O God, who is like Thee?

20 Thou, who hast shown [130]me
many troubles and dis-
tresses,
Wilt revive [130]me again,
And wilt bring [130]me up again
from the depths of the
earth.

21 Mayest Thou increase my
greatness,
And turn *to* comfort me.

22 I will also praise Thee with a
harp,
Even Thy truth, O my God;
To Thee I will sing praises
with the lyre,
O Thou Holy One of Israel.

23 My lips will shout for joy
when I sing praises to
Thee;
And my soul, which Thou hast
redeemed.

24 My tongue also will utter Thy
righteousness all day long;
For they are ashamed, for
they are humiliated who
seek my hurt.

PSALM 72

The Reign of the Righteous King.

A Psalm of Solomon.

GIVE the king Thy judgments, O
God,
And Thy righteousness to the
king's son.

2 May he judge Thy people with
righteousness,
And [131]Thine afflicted with
justice.

3 Let the mountains bring peace
to the people,
And the hills in righteousness.

4 May he vindicate the afflicted
of the people,
Save the children of the
needy,
And crush the oppressor.

130 Another reading is *us*
131 Or, Thy humble

5 Let them fear Thee while the
   sun endures,
   And as long as the moon,
      throughout all generations.
6 May he come down like rain
   upon the mown grass,
   Like showers that water the
      earth.
7 In his days may the righteous
   flourish,
   And abundance of peace till
      the moon is no more.

8 May he also rule from sea to
   sea,
   And from the River to the
      ends of the earth.
9 Let the nomads of the desert
   bow before him;
   And his enemies lick the dust.
10 Let the kings of Tarshish and
   of the islands bring presents;
   The kings of Sheba and Seba
      offer gifts.
11 And let all kings bow down
   before him,
   All nations serve him.

12 For he will deliver the needy
   when he cries for help,
   The afflicted also, and him
      who has no helper.
13 He will have compassion on
   the poor and needy,
   And the lives of the needy he
      will save.
14 He will rescue their life from
   oppression and violence;
   And their blood will be pre-
      cious in his sight;
15 So may he live; and may the
   gold of Sheba be given to
   him;
   And let them pray for him
      continually;
   Let them bless him all day
      long.

16 May there be abundance of
   grain in the earth on top of
   the mountains;

Its fruit will wave like *the ce-
      dars of* Lebanon;
   And may those from the city
      flourish like vegetation of
      the earth.
17 May his name endure forever;
   May his name increase as long
      as the sun *shines*;
   And let *men* bless themselves
      by him;
   Let all nations call him
      blessed.

18 Blessed be the LORD God, the
   God of Israel,
   Who alone works wonders.
19 And blessed be His glorious
   name forever;
   And may the whole earth be
      filled with His glory.
   Amen, and Amen.

20 The prayers of David the son
   of Jesse are ended.

BOOK 3

PSALM 73

*The End of the Wicked
Contrasted with That of the
Righteous.*

A Psalm of Asaph.

SURELY God is good to Israel,
   To those who are pure in
      heart!
2 But as for me, my feet came
   close to stumbling;
   My steps had almost slipped.
3 For I was envious of the arrogant,
   As I saw the prosperity of the
      wicked.
4 For there are no pains in their
   death;
   And their body is fat.
5 They are not in trouble *as other* men;
   Nor are they plagued like
      mankind.
6 Therefore pride is their neck-
   lace;

The garment of violence covers them.

7 Their eye bulges from fatness;
The imaginations of *their* heart run riot.

8 They mock, and wickedly speak of oppression;
They speak from on high.

9 They have set their mouth against the heavens,
And their tongue parades through the earth.

10 Therefore his people return to this place;
And waters of abundance are drunk by them.

11 And they say, "How does God know?
And is there knowledge with the Most High?"

12 Behold, these are the wicked;
And always at ease, they have increased *in* wealth.

13 Surely in vain I have kept my heart pure,
And washed my hands in innocence;

14 For I have been stricken all day long,
And chastened every morning.

15 If I had said, "I will speak thus,"
Behold, I should have betrayed the generation of Thy children.

16 When I pondered to understand this,
It was troublesome in my sight

17 Until I came into the sanctuary of God;
Then I perceived their end.

18 Surely Thou dost set them in slippery places;
Thou dost cast them down to destruction.

19 How they are destroyed in a moment!

They are utterly swept away by sudden terrors!

20 Like a dream when one awakes,
O Lord, when aroused, Thou wilt despise their form.

21 When my heart was embittered,
And I was pierced within,

22 Then I was senseless and ignorant;
I was *like* a beast before Thee.

23 Nevertheless I am continually with Thee;
Thou hast taken hold of my right hand.

24 With Thy counsel Thou wilt guide me,
And afterward receive me to glory.

25 Whom have I in heaven *but* Thee?
And besides Thee, I desire nothing on earth.

26 My flesh and my heart may fail,
But God is the strength of my heart and my portion forever.

27 For, behold, those who are far from Thee will perish;
Thou hast destroyed all those who are unfaithful to Thee.

28 But as for me, the nearness of God is my good;
I have made the Lord GOD my refuge,
That I may tell of all Thy works.

PSALM 74

An Appeal against the Devastation of the Land by the Enemy.

A Maskil of Asaph.

O GOD, why hast Thou rejected us forever?
Why does Thine anger smoke against the sheep of Thy pasture?

2 Remember Thy congregation,
which Thou hast pur-
chased of old,
Which Thou hast redeemed to
be the tribe of Thine inheritance;
And Mount Zion, where Thou
hast dwelt.

3 Turn Thy footsteps toward the
perpetual ruins;
The enemy has damaged
everything within the sanctuary.

4 Thine adversaries have roared
in the midst of Thy meeting
place;
They have set up their own
standards for signs.

5 It seems as if one had lifted up
His axe in a forest of trees.

6 And now all its carved work
They smash with hatchet and
hammers.

7 They have burned Thy sanctuary to the ground;
They have defiled the dwelling
place of Thy name.

8 They said in their heart, "Let
us completely subdue
them."
They have burned all the
meeting places of God in
the land.

9 We do not see our signs;
There is no longer any
prophet,
Nor is there any among us
who knows how long.

10 How long, O God, will the adversary revile,
And the enemy spurn Thy
name forever?

11 Why dost Thou withdraw Thy
hand, even Thy right hand?
From within Thy bosom, destroy *them!*

12 Yet God is my king from of
old,

Who works deeds of deliverance in the midst of the
earth.

13 [132]Thou didst divide the sea by
Thy strength;
Thou didst break the heads of
the sea monsters in the waters.

14 Thou didst crush the heads of
Leviathan;
Thou didst give him as food
for the creatures of the wilderness.

15 Thou didst break open springs
and torrents;
Thou didst dry up ever-flow-
ing streams.

16 Thine is the day, Thine is the
night;
Thou hast prepared the light
and the sun.

17 Thou hast established all the
boundaries of the earth;
Thou hast made summer and
winter.

18 Remember this, O Lord, that
the enemy has reviled;
And a foolish people has
spurned Thy name.

19 Do not deliver the soul of Thy
turtledove to the wild
beast;
Do not forget the life of Thine
afflicted forever.

20 Consider the covenant;
For the dark places of the land
are full of the habitations
of violence.

21 Let not the oppressed return
dishonored;
Let the afflicted and needy
praise Thy name.

22 Do arise, O God, *and* plead
Thine own cause;
Remember how the foolish
man reproaches Thee all
day long.

23 Do not forget the voice of
Thine adversaries,

132 Or, *Thou Thyself,* and so through v. 17

The uproar of those who rise
against Thee which as-
cends continually.

PSALM 75

*God Abases the Proud, but
Exalts the Righteous.*

For the choir director; *set to
Al-tashheth.*
A Psalm of Asaph, a Song.

WE give thanks to Thee, O God,
we give thanks,
For Thy name is near;
Men declare Thy wondrous
works.

2 "When I select an appointed
time,
It is I who judge with equity.

3 "The earth and all who dwell in
it [133]melt;
It is I who have firmly set its
pillars. [Selah.

4 "I said to the boastful, 'Do not
boast,'
And to the wicked, 'Do not lift
up the horn;

5 Do not lift up your horn on
high,
Do not speak with insolent
pride.' "

6 For not from the east, nor
from the west,
Nor from the desert *comes* ex-
altation;

7 But God is the Judge;
He puts down one, and exalts
another.

8 For a cup is in the hand of the
LORD, and the wine foams;
It is well mixed, and He pours
out of this;
Surely all the wicked of the
earth must drain *and* drink
down its dregs.

9 But as for me, I will declare *it*
forever;
I will sing praises to the God
of Jacob.

10 And all the horns of the
wicked He will cut off,
But the horns of the righteous
will be lifted up.

PSALM 76

*The Victorious Power of the God
of Jacob.*

For the choir director; on
stringed instruments.
A Psalm of Asaph, a Song.

GOD is known in Judah;
His name is great in Israel.

2 And His tabernacle is in Sa-
lem;
His dwelling place also is in
Zion.

3 There He broke the flaming
arrows,
The shield, and the sword, and
the weapons of war. [Selah.

4 Thou art resplendent,
More majestic than the mountains of prey.

5 The stouthearted were plundered;
They sank into sleep;
And none of the warriors
could use his hands.

6 At Thy rebuke, O God of Jacob,
Both rider and horse were
cast into a dead sleep.

7 Thou, even Thou, art to be
feared;
And who may stand in Thy
presence when once Thou
art angry?

8 Thou didst cause judgment to
be heard from heaven;
The earth feared, and was
still,

9 When God arose to judgment,
To save all the humble of the
earth. [Selah.

10 For the wrath of man shall
praise Thee;

---

[133] Or, *totter*

With a remnant of wrath Thou
shalt gird Thyself.

11 Make vows to the LORD your
God and fulfill *them*;
Let all who are around Him
bring gifts to Him who is to
be feared.

12 He will cut off the spirit of
princes;
He is feared by the kings of
the earth.

PSALM 77

*Comfort in Trouble from
Recalling God's Mighty Deeds.*

For the choir director;
according to Jeduthun.
A Psalm of Asaph.

MY voice *rises* to God, and I
will cry aloud;
My voice *rises* to God, and He
will hear me.

2 In the day of my trouble I
sought the Lord;
In the night my hand was
stretched out [134]without
weariness;
My soul refused to be comforted.

3 *When* I remember God, then I
am disturbed;
When I sigh, then my spirit
grows faint. [Selah.

4 Thou hast held my eyelids
open;
I am so troubled that I cannot
speak.

5 I have considered the days of
old,
The years of long ago.

6 I will remember my song in
the night;
I will meditate with my heart;
And my spirit ponders.

7 Will the Lord reject forever?
And will He never be favor-
able again?

8 Has His lovingkindness
ceased forever?
Has *His* promise come to an
end forever?

9 Has God forgotten to be gra-
cious?
Or has He in anger withdrawn
His compassion? [Selah.

10 Then I said, "It is my grief,
That the right hand of the
Most High has changed."

11 I shall remember the deeds of
the LORD;
Surely I will remember Thy
wonders of old.

12 I will meditate on all Thy
work,
And muse on Thy deeds.

13 Thy way, O God, is holy;
What god is great like our
God?

14 Thou art the God who workest
wonders;
Thou hast made known Thy
strength among the peo-
ples.

15 Thou hast by Thy power re-
deemed Thy people,
The sons of Jacob and Joseph.
[Selah.

16 The waters saw Thee, O God;
The waters saw Thee, they
were in anguish;
The deeps also trembled.

17 The clouds poured out water;
The skies gave forth a sound;
Thy arrows flashed here and
there.

18 The sound of Thy thunder was
in the whirlwind;
The lightnings lit up the
world;
The earth trembled and
shook.

19 Thy way was in the sea,
And Thy paths in the mighty
waters,
And Thy footprints may not
be known.

[134] Lit., *and did not grow numb*

20 Thou didst lead Thy people
like a flock,
By the hand of Moses and
Aaron.

PSALM 78

*God's Guidance of His People in
Spite of Their Unfaithfulness.*

A Maskil of Asaph.

LISTEN, O my people, to my instruction;
Incline your ears to the words
of my mouth.

2 I will open my mouth in a parable;
I will utter dark sayings of old,

3 Which we have heard and
known,
And our fathers have told us.

4 We will not conceal them
from their children,
But tell to the generation to
come the praises of the
LORD,
And His strength and His
wondrous works that He
has done.

5 For He established a testimony in Jacob,
And appointed a law in Israel,
Which He commanded our fathers,
That they should teach them
to their children,

6 That the generation to come
might know, *even* the children *yet* to be born,
That they may arise and tell
them to their children,

7 That they should put their
confidence in God,
And not forget the works of
God,
But keep His commandments,

8 And not be like their fathers,
A stubborn and rebellious
generation,
A generation that did not
[135]prepare its heart,

And whose spirit was not
faithful to God.

9 The sons of Ephraim were
archers equipped with
bows,
Yet they turned back in the
day of battle.

10 They did not keep the covenant of God,
And refused to walk in His
law;

11 And they forgot His deeds,
And His miracles that He had
shown them.

12 He wrought wonders before
their fathers,
In the land of Egypt, in the
field of Zoan.

13 He divided the sea, and
caused them to pass
through;
And He made the waters
stand up like a heap.

14 Then He led them with the
cloud by day,
And all the night with a light
of fire.

15 He split the rocks in the wilderness,
And gave *them* abundant
drink like the ocean
depths.

16 He brought forth streams also
from the rock,
And caused waters to run
down like rivers.

17 Yet they still continued to sin
against Him,
To rebel against the Most
High in the desert.

18 And in their heart they put
God to the test
By asking food according to
their desire.

19 Then they spoke against God;
They said, "Can God prepare
a table in the wilderness?

20 "Behold, He struck the rock, so
that waters gushed out,

135 Or, *put right*

And streams were overflowing;
Can He give bread also?
Will He provide meat for His people?"

21 Therefore the LORD heard and was full of wrath,
And a fire was kindled against Jacob,
And anger also mounted against Israel;

22 Because they did not believe in God,
And did not trust in His salvation.

23 Yet He commanded the clouds above,
And opened the doors of heaven;

24 And He rained down manna upon them to eat,
And gave them food from heaven.

25 Man did eat the bread of angels;
He sent them food in abundance.

26 He caused the east wind to blow in the heavens;
And by His power He directed the south wind.

27 When He rained meat upon them like the dust,
Even winged fowl like the sand of the seas,

28 Then He let them fall in the midst of their camp,
Round about their dwellings.

29 So they ate and were well filled;
And their desire He gave to them.

30 Before they had satisfied their desire,
While their food was in their mouths,

31 The anger of God rose against them,
And killed some of their stoutest ones,

And subdued the choice men of Israel.

32 In spite of all this they still sinned,
And did not believe in His wonderful works.

33 So He brought their days to an end in futility,
And their years in sudden terror.

34 When He killed them, then they sought Him,
And returned and searched diligently for God;

35 And they remembered that God was their rock,
And the Most High God their Redeemer.

36 But they deceived Him with their mouth,
And lied to Him with their tongue.

37 For their heart was not steadfast toward Him,
Nor were they faithful in His covenant.

38 But He, being compassionate, forgave their iniquity, and did not destroy them;
And often He restrained His anger,
And did not arouse all His wrath.

39 Thus He remembered that they were but flesh,
A wind that passes and does not return.

40 How often they rebelled against Him in the wilderness,
And grieved Him in the desert!

41 And again and again they [136]tempted God,
And pained the Holy One of Israel.

42 They did not remember His power,
The day when He redeemed them from the adversary,

[136] Or, put to the test

43 When He performed His signs in Egypt,
   And His marvels in the field of Zoan,

44 And turned their rivers to blood,
   And their streams, they could not drink.

45 He sent among them swarms of flies, which devoured them,
   And frogs which destroyed them.

46 He gave also their crops to the grasshopper,
   And the product of their labor to the locust.

47 He destroyed their vines with hailstones,
   And their sycamore trees with frost.

48 He gave over their cattle also to the hailstones,
   And their herds to bolts of lightning.

49 He sent upon them His burning anger,
   Fury, and indignation, and trouble,
   A band of destroying angels.

50 He leveled a path for His anger;
   He did not spare their soul from death,
   But gave over their life to the plague,

51 And smote all the first-born in Egypt,
   The first *issue* of their virility in the tents of Ham.

52 But He led forth His own people like sheep,
   And guided them in the wilderness like a flock;

53 And He led them safely, so that they did not fear;
   But the sea engulfed their enemies.

54 So He brought them to His holy land,

To this hill country which His right hand had gained.

55 He also drove out the nations before them,
   And He apportioned them for an inheritance by measurement,
   And made the tribes of Israel dwell in their tents.

56 Yet they [136]tempted and rebelled against the Most High God,
   And did not keep His testimonies,

57 But turned back and acted treacherously like their fathers;
   They turned aside like a treacherous bow.

58 For they provoked Him with their high places,
   And aroused His jealousy with their graven images.

59 When God heard, He was filled with wrath,
   And greatly abhorred Israel;

60 So that He abandoned the dwelling place at Shiloh,
   The tent which He had pitched among men,

61 And gave up His strength to captivity,
   And His glory into the hand of the adversary.

62 He also delivered His people to the sword,
   And was filled with wrath at His inheritance.

63 Fire devoured His young men;
   And His virgins had no wedding songs.

64 His priests fell by the sword;
   And His widows could not weep.

65 Then the Lord awoke as if *from* sleep,
   Like a warrior overcome by wine.

[136] Or, *put to the test*

66 And He drove His adversaries
   backward;
   He put on them an everlasting
   reproach.
67 He also rejected the tent of
   Joseph,
   And did not choose the tribe
   of Ephraim,
68 But chose the tribe of Judah,
   Mount Zion which He loved.
69 And He built His sanctuary
   like the heights,
   Like the earth which He has
   founded forever.
70 He also chose David His servant,
   And took him from the sheep-
   folds;
71 From the care of the ewes
   with suckling lambs He
   brought him,
   To shepherd Jacob His people,
   And Israel His inheritance.
72 So he shepherded them according to the integrity of
   his heart,
   And guided them with his
   skillful hands.

PSALM 79

*A Lament over the Destruction
of Jerusalem, and Prayer for
Help.*

A Psalm of Asaph.

O GOD, the nations have in-
   vaded Thine inheritance;
   They have defiled Thy holy
   temple;
   They have laid Jerusalem in
   ruins.
2 They have given the dead bodies of Thy servants for food
   to the birds of the heavens,
   The flesh of Thy godly ones to
   the beasts of the earth.
3 They have poured out their
   blood like water round
   about Jerusalem;
   And there was no one to bury
   them.

4 We have become a reproach
   to our neighbors,
   A scoffing and derision to
   those around us.
5 How long, O LORD? Wilt Thou
   be angry forever?
   Will Thy jealousy burn like
   fire?
6 Pour out Thy wrath upon the
   nations which do not know
   Thee,
   And upon the kingdoms
   which do not call upon Thy
   name.
7 For they have devoured Jacob,
   And laid waste his habitation.

8 Do not remember the iniquities of *our* forefathers
   against us;
   Let Thy compassion come
   quickly to meet us;
   For we are brought very low.
9 Help us, O God of our salvation, for the glory of Thy
   name;
   And deliver us, and forgive
   our sins, for Thy name's
   sake.
10 Why should the nations say,
   "Where is their God?"
   Let there be known among the
   nations in our sight,
   Vengeance for the blood of
   Thy servants, which has
   been shed.
11 Let the groaning of the prisoner come before Thee;
   According to the greatness of
   Thy power preserve those
   who are doomed to die.
12 And return to our neighbors
   sevenfold into their bosom
   The reproach with which they
   have reproached Thee, O
   Lord.
13 So we Thy people and the
   sheep of Thy pasture
   Will give thanks to Thee forever;

To all generations we will tell
of Thy praise.

PSALM 80

*God Implored to Rescue His
People from Their Calamities.*

For the choir director; *set to*
El Shoshannim; Eduth.
A Psalm of Asaph.

OH, give ear, Shepherd of Israel,
Thou who dost lead Joseph
like a flock;
Thou who art enthroned
above the cherubim, shine
forth!

2 Before Ephraim and Benjamin
and Manasseh, stir up Thy
power,
And come to save us!

3 O God, restore us,
And cause Thy face to shine
upon us, and we will be
saved.

4 O LORD God *of* hosts,
How long wilt Thou be angry
with the prayer of Thy people?

5 Thou hast fed them with the
bread of tears,
And Thou hast made them to
drink tears in large mea-
sure.

6 Thou dost make us [137]an object of contention to our
neighbors;
And our enemies laugh among
themselves.

7 O God *of* hosts, restore us,
And cause Thy face to shine
upon us, [138]and we will be
saved.

8 Thou didst remove a vine
from Egypt;
Thou didst drive out the nations, and didst plant it.

9 Thou didst clear *the ground*
before it,
And it took deep root and
filled the land.

10 The mountains were covered
with its shadow;
And the cedars of God with its
boughs.

11 It was sending out its
branches to the sea,
And its shoots to the River.

12 Why hast Thou broken down
its hedges,
So that all who pass *that* way
pick its *fruit?*

13 A boar from the forest eats it
away,
And whatever moves in the
field feeds on it.

14 O God *of* hosts, turn again
now, we beseech Thee;
Look down from heaven and
see, and take care of this
vine,

15 Even the shoot which Thy
right hand has planted,
And on the son whom Thou
hast strengthened for Thyself.

16 It is burned with fire, it is cut
down;
They perish at the rebuke of
Thy countenance.

17 Let Thy hand be upon the man
of Thy right hand,
Upon the son of man whom
Thou didst make strong for
Thyself.

18 Then we shall not turn back
from Thee;
Revive us, and we will call
upon Thy name.

19 O LORD God of hosts, restore
us;
Cause Thy face to shine *upon
us,* and we will be saved.

137 Lit., *a strife to*   138 Or, *that we may*

PSALM 81

God's Goodness and Israel's Waywardness.

For the choir director; on the Gittith.
A Psalm of Asaph.

SING for joy to God our strength;
Shout joyfully to the God of Jacob.

2 Raise a song, strike the timbrel,
The sweet sounding lyre with the harp.

3 Blow the trumpet at the new moon,
At the full moon, on our feast day.

4 For it is a statute for Israel,
An ordinance of the God of Jacob.

5 He established it for a testimony in Joseph,
When he went throughout the land of Egypt.
I heard a language that I did not know:

6 "I relieved his shoulder of the burden,
His hands were freed from the basket.

7 "You called in trouble, and I rescued you;
I answered you in the hiding place of thunder;
I proved you at the waters of Meribah.   [Selah.

8 "Hear, O My people, and I will admonish you;
O Israel, if you would listen to Me!

9 "Let there be no strange god among you;
Nor shall you worship any foreign god.

10 "I, the LORD, am your God,
Who brought you up from the land of Egypt;
Open your mouth wide and I will fill it.

11 "But My people did not listen to My voice;
And Israel did not obey Me.

12 "So I gave them over to the stubbornness of their heart,
To walk in their own devices.

13 "Oh that My people would listen to Me,
That Israel would walk in My ways!

14 "I would quickly subdue their enemies,
And turn My hand against their adversaries.

15 "Those who hate the LORD would pretend obedience to Him;
And their time *of punishment* would be forever.

16 "But I would feed you with the finest of the wheat;
And with honey from the rock I would satisfy you."

PSALM 82

Unjust Judgments Rebuked.

A Psalm of Asaph.

GOD takes His stand in His own congregation;
He judges in the midst of the rulers.

2 How long will you judge unjustly,
And show partiality to the wicked?   [Selah.

3 Vindicate the weak and fatherless;
Do justice to the afflicted and destitute.

4 Rescue the weak and needy;
Deliver *them* out of the hand of the wicked.

5 They do not know nor do they understand;
They walk about in darkness;
All the foundations of the earth are shaken.

6 I said, "You are gods,

And all of you are sons of the
Most High.
7 "Nevertheless you will die like
men,
And fall like *any* one of the
princes."
8 Arise, O God, judge the earth!
For it is Thou who dost possess all the nations.

PSALM 83

*God Implored to Confound His
Enemies.*

A Song, a Psalm of Asaph.

O GOD, do not remain quiet;
Do not be silent and, O God,
do not be still.
2 For, behold, Thine enemies
make an uproar;
And those who hate Thee
have exalted themselves.
3 They make shrewd plans
against Thy people,
And conspire together against
Thy treasured ones.
4 They have said, "Come, and
let us wipe them out as a
nation,
That the name of Israel be remembered no more."
5 For they have conspired together with one mind;
Against Thee do they make a
covenant:
6 The tents of Edom and the
Ishmaelites;
Moab, and the Hagrites;
7 Gebal, and Ammon, and Ama-
lek;
Philistia with the inhabitants
of Tyre;
8 Assyria also has joined with
them;
They have become a help to
the children of Lot. [Selah.
9 Deal with them as with Midian,
As with Sisera *and* Jabin, at
the torrent of Kishon,
10 Who were destroyed at En-
dor,
Who became as dung for the
ground.
11 Make their nobles like Oreb
and Zeeb,
And all their princes like Ze-
bah and Zalmunna,
12 Who said, "Let us possess for
ourselves
The pastures of God."

13 O my God, make them like the
139whirling dust;
Like chaff before the wind.
14 Like fire that burns the forest,
And like a flame that sets the
mountains on fire,
15 So pursue them with Thy tempest,
And terrify them with Thy
storm.
16 Fill their faces with dishonor,
That they may seek Thy
name, O LORD.
17 Let them be ashamed and dismayed forever;
And let them be humiliated
and perish,
18 That they may know that
Thou alone, whose name is
the LORD,
Art the Most High over all the
earth.

PSALM 84

Longing for the Temple Worship.

For the choir director; on the
Gittith.
A Psalm of the sons of Korah.

H OW lovely are Thy dwelling
places,
O LORD of hosts!
2 My soul longed and even
yearned for the courts of
the LORD;

139 Or, *tumbleweed*

My heart and my flesh sing for
joy to the living God.
3 The bird also has found a
house,
And the swallow a nest for
herself, where she may lay
her young,
Even Thine altars, O LORD of
hosts,
My King and my God.
4 How blessed are those who
dwell in Thy house!
They are ever praising Thee.
[Selah.

5 How blessed is the man
whose strength is in Thee;
In whose heart are the highways *to* Zion!
6 Passing through the valley of
140Baca, they make it a
spring,
The early rain also covers it
with blessings.
7 They go from strength to
strength,
Every one of them appears before God in Zion.

8 O LORD God of hosts, hear my
prayer;
Give ear, O God of Jacob!
[Selah.
9 Behold our shield, O God,
And look upon the face of
Thine anointed.
10 For a day in Thy courts is better than a thousand *out-
side*.
I would rather stand at the
threshold of the house of
my God,
Than dwell in the tents of
wickedness.
11 For the LORD God is a sun and
shield;
The LORD gives grace and glory;

No good thing does He withhold from those who walk
uprightly.
12 O LORD of hosts,
How blessed is the man who
trusts in Thee!

PSALM 85

*Prayer for God's Mercy upon the
Nation.*

For the choir director.
A Psalm of the sons of Korah.

O LORD, Thou didst show favor
to Thy land;
Thou didst 141restore the captivity of Jacob.
2 Thou didst forgive the iniquity
of Thy people;
Thou didst cover all their sin.
[Selah.
3 Thou didst withdraw all Thy
fury;
Thou didst turn away from
Thy burning anger.

4 Restore us, O God of our salvation,
And cause Thine indignation
toward us to cease.
5 Wilt Thou be angry with us
forever?
Wilt Thou prolong Thine anger to all generations?
6 Wilt Thou not Thyself revive
us again,
That Thy people may rejoice
in Thee?
7 Show us Thy lovingkindness,
O LORD,
And grant us Thy salvation.

8 I will hear what God the LORD
will say;
For He will speak peace to His
people, to His godly ones;
But let them not turn back to
folly.
9 Surely His salvation is near to
those who 142fear Him,
That glory may dwell in our
land.

140 Probably, *Weeping* or *Balsam trees*
141 Or, *restore the fortunes* 142 Or, *reverence*

10 Lovingkindness and truth
    have met together;
    Righteousness and peace have
      kissed each other.
11 Truth springs from the earth;
    And righteousness looks
      down from heaven.
12 Indeed, the LORD will give
    what is good;
    And our land will yield its pro-
      duce.
13 Righteousness will go before
    Him,
    And will make His footsteps
      into a way.

PSALM 86

*A Psalm of Supplication and
Trust.*

A Prayer of David.

INCLINE Thine ear, O LORD, *and*
    answer me;
    For I am afflicted and needy.
2 Do preserve my soul, for I am
    a godly man;
    O Thou my God, save Thy ser-
      vant who trusts in Thee.
3 Be gracious to me, O Lord,
    For to Thee I cry all day long.
4 Make glad the soul of Thy ser-
    vant,
    For to Thee, O Lord, I lift up
      my soul.
5 For Thou, Lord, art good, and
    ready to forgive,
    And abundant in lovingkind-
      ness to all who call upon
      Thee.
6 Give ear, O LORD, to my
    prayer;
    And give heed to the voice of
      my supplications!
7 In the day of my trouble I
    shall call upon Thee,
    For Thou wilt answer me.
8 There is no one like Thee
    among the gods, O Lord;

Nor are there any works like
    Thine.
9 All nations whom Thou hast
    made shall come and wor-
      ship before Thee, O Lord;
    And they shall glorify Thy
      name.
10 For Thou art great and doest
    wondrous deeds;
    Thou alone art God.

11 Teach me Thy way, O LORD;
    I will walk in Thy truth;
    Unite my heart to fear Thy
      name.
12 I will give thanks to Thee, O
    Lord my God, with all my
      heart,
    And will glorify Thy name for-
      ever.
13 For Thy lovingkindness
    toward me is great,
    And Thou hast delivered my
      soul from the depths of
      Sheol.

14 O God, arrogant men have ris-
    en up against me,
    And a band of violent men
      have sought my life,
    And they have not set Thee
      before them.
15 But Thou, O Lord, art a God
    merciful and gracious,
    Slow to anger and abundant
      in lovingkindness and
      truth.
16 Turn to me, and be gracious to
    me;
    Oh grant Thy strength to Thy
      servant,
    And save the son of Thy hand-
      maid.
17 Show me a sign for good,
    That those who hate me may
      see *it*, and be ashamed,
    Because Thou, O LORD, hast
      helped me and comforted
      me.

PSALM 87

The Privileges of Citizenship in Zion.

A Psalm of the sons of Korah.
A Song.

HIS foundation is in the holy mountains.
2 The LORD loves the gates of Zion
More than all the *other* dwelling places of Jacob.
3 Glorious things are spoken of you,
O city of God.   [Selah.
4 "I shall mention [143]Rahab and Babylon among those who know Me;
Behold, Philistia and Tyre with Ethiopia:
'This one was born there.' "
5 But of Zion it shall be said,
"This one and that one were born in her";
And the Most High Himself will establish her.
6 The LORD shall count when He registers the peoples,
"This one was born there."
                              [Selah.
7 Then those who sing as well as those who play the flutes *shall say,*
"All my springs *of joy* are in you."

PSALM 88

A Petition to Be Saved from Death.

A Song. A Psalm of the sons of Korah. For the choir director; according to Mahalath Leannoth. A Maskil of Heman the Ezrahite.

O LORD, the God of my salvation,
I have cried out by day and in the night before Thee.

2 Let my prayer come before Thee;
Incline Thine ear to my cry!
3 For my soul has had enough troubles,
And my life has drawn near to Sheol.
4 I am reckoned among those who go down to the pit;
I have become like a man without strength,
5 Forsaken among the dead,
Like the slain who lie in the grave,
Whom Thou dost remember no more,
And they are cut off from Thy hand.
6 Thou hast put me in the lowest pit,
In dark places, in the depths.
7 Thy wrath has rested upon me
And Thou hast afflicted me with all Thy waves. [Selah.
8 Thou hast removed my acquaintances far from me;
Thou hast made me an [144]object of loathing to them;
I am shut up and cannot go out.
9 My eye has wasted away because of affliction;
I have called upon Thee every day, O LORD;
I have spread out my hands to Thee.

10 Wilt Thou perform wonders for the dead?
Will the departed spirits rise *and* praise Thee? [Selah.
11 Will Thy lovingkindness be declared in the grave,
Thy faithfulness in Abaddon?
12 Will Thy wonders be made known in the darkness?
And Thy righteousness in the land of forgetfulness?
13 But I, O LORD, have cried out to Thee for help,

[143] I.e., Egypt   [144] Lit., *abomination to them*

And in the morning my prayer
comes before Thee.

14 O LORD, why dost Thou reject
my soul?
Why dost Thou hide Thy face
from me?

15 I was afflicted and about to
die from my youth on;
I suffer Thy terrors; I am overcome.

16 Thy burning anger has passed
over me;
Thy terrors have destroyed
me.

17 They have surrounded me like
water all day long;
They have encompassed me
altogether.

18 Thou hast removed lover and
friend far from me;
My acquaintances are in darkness.

PSALM 89

*The LORD's Covenant with David,
and Israel's Afflictions.*

A Maskil of Ethan the Ezrahite.

I WILL sing of the lovingkindness
of the LORD forever;
To all generations I will make
known Thy faithfulness
with my mouth.

2 For I have said, "Lovingkindness will be built up forever;
In the heavens Thou wilt establish Thy faithfulness."

3 "I have made a covenant with
My chosen;
I have sworn to David My ser-
vant,

4 I will establish your seed forever,
And build up your throne to
all generations." [Selah.

5 And the heavens will praise
Thy wonders, O LORD;
Thy faithfulness also in the as-
sembly of the holy ones.

6 For who in the skies is comparable to the LORD?
Who among the sons of the
mighty is like the LORD,

7 A God greatly feared in the
council of the holy ones,
And awesome above all those
who are around Him?

8 O LORD God of hosts, who is
like Thee, O mighty LORD?
Thy faithfulness also surrounds Thee.

9 Thou dost rule the swelling of
the sea;
When its waves rise, Thou
dost still them.

10 Thou Thyself didst crush Rahab like one who is slain;
Thou didst scatter Thine enemies with Thy mighty
arm.

11 The heavens are Thine, the
earth also is Thine;
The world and [145]all it contains, Thou hast founded
them.

12 The north and the south, Thou
hast created them;
Tabor and Hermon shout for
joy at Thy name.

13 Thou hast a strong arm;
Thy hand is mighty, Thy right
hand is exalted.

14 Righteousness and justice are
the foundation of Thy
throne;
Lovingkindness and truth go
before Thee.

15 How blessed are the people
who know the [146]joyful
sound!
O LORD, they walk in the light
of Thy countenance.

16 In Thy name they rejoice all
the day,
And by Thy righteousness
they are exalted.

17 For Thou art the glory of their
strength,

---

[145] Lit., *its fullness*
[146] Or, *blast of the trumpet, shout of joy*

And by Thy favor our horn is exalted.

18 For our shield belongs to the LORD,
[147]And our king to the Holy One of Israel.

19 Once Thou didst speak in vision to Thy godly ones,
And didst say, "I have given help to one who is mighty;
I have exalted one chosen from the people.

20"I have found David My servant;
With My holy oil I have anointed him,

21 With whom My hand will be established;
My arm also will strengthen him.

22"The enemy will not [148]deceive him,
Nor the son of wickedness afflict him.

23"But I shall crush his adversaries before him,
And strike those who hate him.

24"And My faithfulness and My lovingkindness will be with him,
And in My name his horn will be exalted.

25"I shall also set his hand on the sea,
And his right hand on the rivers.

26"He will cry to Me, 'Thou art my Father,
My God, and the rock of my salvation.'

27"I also shall make him My firstborn,
The highest of the kings of the earth.

28"My lovingkindness I will keep for him forever,
And My covenant shall be confirmed to him.

29"So I will establish his descendants forever,
And his throne as the days of heaven.

30"If his sons forsake My law,
And do not walk in My judgments,

31 If they [149]violate My statutes,
And do not keep My commandments,

32 Then I will visit their transgression with the rod,
And their iniquity with stripes.

33"But I will not break off My lovingkindness from him,
Nor deal falsely in My faithfulness.

34"My covenant I will not violate,
Nor will I alter the utterance of My lips.

35"[150]Once I have sworn by My holiness;
I will not lie to David.

36"His descendants shall endure forever,
And his throne as the sun before Me.

37"It shall be established forever like the moon,
And the witness in the sky is faithful."   [Selah.

38 But Thou hast cast off and rejected,
Thou hast been full of wrath against Thine anointed.

39 Thou hast spurned the covenant of Thy servant;
Thou hast profaned his crown in the dust.

40 Thou hast broken down all his walls;
Thou hast brought his strongholds to ruin.

41 All who pass along the way plunder him;

---

[147] Or, *Even to the Holy One of Israel our King* [148] Or, *exact usury from him* [149] Lit., *profane* [150] Or, *One thing*

He has become a reproach to his neighbors.

42 Thou hast exalted the right hand of his adversaries;
Thou hast made all his enemies rejoice.

43 Thou dost also turn back the edge of his sword,
And hast not made him stand in battle.

44 Thou hast made his splendor to cease,
And cast his throne to the ground.

45 Thou hast shortened the days of his youth;
Thou hast covered him with shame. [Selah.

46 How long, O Lord?
Wilt Thou hide Thyself forever?
Will Thy wrath burn like fire?

47 Remember what my span of life is;
For what vanity Thou hast created all the sons of men!

48 What man can live and not see death?
Can he deliver his soul from the power of Sheol? [Selah.

49 Where are Thy former lovingkindnesses, O Lord,
Which Thou didst swear to David in Thy faithfulness?

50 Remember, O Lord, the reproach of Thy servants;
How I do bear in my bosom *the reproach of* all the many peoples,

51 With which Thine enemies have reproached, O Lord,
With which they have reproached the footsteps of Thine anointed.

52 Blessed be the Lord forever!
Amen and Amen.

BOOK 4

PSALM 90

God's Eternity and Man's Transitoriness.

A Prayer of Moses the man of God.

LORD, Thou hast been our [151]dwelling place in all generations.

2 Before the mountains were born,
Or Thou didst give birth to the earth and the world,
Even from everlasting to everlasting, Thou art God.

3 Thou dost turn man back into dust,
And dost say, "Return, O children of men."

4 For a thousand years in Thy sight
Are like yesterday when it passes by,
Or *as* a watch in the night.

5 Thou hast swept them away like a flood, they fall asleep;
In the morning they are like grass which sprouts anew.

6 In the morning it flourishes, and sprouts anew;
Toward evening it fades, and withers away.

7 For we have been consumed by Thine anger,
And by Thy wrath we have been dismayed.

8 Thou hast placed our iniquities before Thee,
Our secret *sins* in the light of Thy presence.

9 For all our days have declined in Thy fury;
We have finished our years like a sigh.

151 Or, *hiding place*; some ancient mss. read *place of refuge*

10 As for the days of our life,
    they contain seventy years,
   Or if due to strength, eighty
    years,
   Yet their pride is *but* labor
    and sorrow;
   For soon it is gone and we fly
    away.

11 Who understands the power
    of Thine anger,
   And Thy fury, according to
    the fear that is due Thee?

12 So teach us to number our
    days,
   That we may present to Thee
    a heart of wisdom.

13 Do return, O LORD; how long
    will it be?
   And be sorry for Thy servants.

14 O satisfy us in the morning
    with Thy lovingkindness,
   That we may sing for joy and
    be glad all our days.

15 Make us glad according to the
    days Thou hast afflicted us,
   And the years we have seen
    [152]evil.

16 Let Thy work appear to Thy
    servants,
   And Thy majesty to their chil-
    dren.

17 And let the favor of the Lord
    our God be upon us;
   And do [153]confirm for us the
    work of our hands;
   Yes, [153]confirm the work of
    our hands.

PSALM 91

*Security of the One Who Trusts
in the LORD.*

HE who dwells in the shelter of
    the Most High
   Will abide in the shadow of
    the Almighty.

2 I will say to the LORD, "My
   refuge and my fortress,
   My God, in whom I trust!"

3 For it is He who delivers you
    from the snare of the trap-
    per,
   And from the deadly pesti-
    lence.

4 He will cover you with His
    pinions,
   And under His wings you may
    seek refuge;
   His faithfulness is a shield and
    bulwark.

5 You will not be afraid of the
    terror by night,
   Or of the arrow that flies by
    day;

6 Of the pestilence that stalks in
    darkness,
   Or of the destruction that lays
    waste at noon.

7 A thousand may fall at your
    side,
   And ten thousand at your
    right hand;
   But it shall not approach you.

8 You will only look on with
    your eyes,
   And see the recompense of
    the wicked.

9 For you have made the LORD,
    my refuge,
   Even the Most High, your
    dwelling place.

10 No evil will befall you,
   Nor will any plague come near
    your tent.

11 For He will give His angels
    charge concerning you,
   To guard you in all your ways.

12 They will bear you up in their
    hands,
   Lest you strike your foot
    against a stone.

13 You will tread upon the lion
    and cobra,
   The young lion and the ser-
    pent you will trample
    down.

14 "Because he has loved Me,
    therefore I will deliver him;

[152] Or, *trouble* [153] Or, *give permanence to*

I will set him *securely* on high,
    because he has known My
    name.
15 "He will call upon Me, and I
    will answer him;
    I will be with him in trouble;
    I will rescue him, and honor
    him.
16 "With a long life I will satisfy
    him,
    And let him behold My salva-
    tion."

PSALM 92

Praise for the LORD's Goodness.

A Psalm, a Song for the
    Sabbath day.

IT is good to give thanks to the
    LORD,
    And to sing praises to Thy
    name, O Most High;
2 To declare Thy lovingkindness
    in the morning,
    And Thy faithfulness by night,
3 With the ten-stringed lute,
    and with the harp;
    With resounding music upon
    the lyre.
4 For Thou, O LORD, hast made
    me glad by what Thou hast
    done,
    I will sing for joy at the works
    of Thy hands.

5 How great are Thy works, O
    LORD!
    Thy thoughts are very deep.
6 A senseless man has no
    knowledge;
    Nor does a stupid man under-
    stand this:
7 That when the wicked
    sprouted up like grass,
    And all who did iniquity flour-
    ished,
    It *was only* that they might be
    destroyed forevermore.
8 But Thou, O LORD, art on high
    forever.

9 For, behold, Thine enemies, O
    LORD,
    For, behold, Thine enemies
    will perish;
    All who do iniquity will be
    scattered.
10 But Thou hast exalted my
    horn like *that of* the wild
    ox;
    I have been anointed with
    fresh oil.
11 And my eye has looked *exul-
    tantly* upon my foes,
    My ears hear of the evildoers
    who rise up against me.
12 The righteous man will flour-
    ish like the palm tree,
    He will grow like a cedar in
    Lebanon.
13 Planted in the house of the
    LORD,
    They will flourish in the courts
    of our God.
14 They will still yield fruit in old
    age;
    They shall be [154]full of sap and
    very green,
15 To declare that the LORD is
    upright;
    He is my rock, and there is no
    unrighteousness in Him.

PSALM 93

The Majesty of the LORD.

THE LORD reigns, He is clothed
    with majesty;
    The LORD has clothed and
    girded   Himself   with
    strength;
    Indeed, the world is firmly es-
    tablished, it will not be
    moved.
2 Thy throne is established from
    of old;
    Thou art from everlasting.
3 The floods have lifted up, O
    LORD,
    The floods have lifted up their
    voice;

[154] Lit., *fat and*

The floods lift up their pounding waves.

4 More than the sounds of many waters,

Than the mighty breakers of the sea,

The LORD on high is mighty.

5 Thy testimonies are fully confirmed;

Holiness befits Thy house,

O LORD, forevermore.

PSALM 94

The LORD *Implored to Avenge His People.*

O LORD, God of vengeance;
God of vengeance, shine forth!

2 Rise up, O Judge of the earth;
Render recompense to the proud.

3 How long shall the wicked, O LORD,
How long shall the wicked exult?

4 They pour forth *words*, they speak arrogantly;
All who do wickedness vaunt themselves.

5 They crush Thy people, O LORD,
And afflict Thy heritage.

6 They slay the widow and the stranger,
And murder the orphans.

7 And they have said, "The LORD does not see,
Nor does the God of Jacob pay heed."

8 Pay heed, you senseless among the people;
And when will you understand, stupid ones?

9 He who planted the ear, does He not hear?
He who formed the eye, does He not see?

10 He who chastens the nations, will He not rebuke,
Even He who teaches man knowledge?

11 The LORD knows the thoughts of man,
That they are a *mere* breath.

12 Blessed is the man whom Thou dost chasten, O LORD,
And dost teach out of Thy law;

13 That Thou mayest grant him relief from the days of adversity,
Until a pit is dug for the wicked.

14 For the LORD will not abandon His people,
Nor will He forsake His inheritance.

15 For judgment will again be righteous;
And all the upright in heart will follow it.

16 Who will stand up for me against evildoers?
Who will take his stand for me against those who do wickedness?

17 If the LORD had not been my help,
My soul would soon have dwelt in *the abode of* silence.

18 If I should say, "My foot has slipped,"
Thy lovingkindness, O LORD, will hold me up.

19 When my anxious thoughts multiply within me,
Thy consolations delight my soul.

20 Can a throne of destruction be allied with Thee,
One which devises mischief by decree?

21 They band themselves together against the life of the righteous,
And condemn the innocent to death.

22 But the LORD has been my stronghold,
And my God the rock of my refuge.

23 And He has brought back
their wickedness upon
them,
And will destroy them in their
evil;
The Lord our God will de-
stroy them.

PSALM 95

*Praise to the Lord, and Warning
against Unbelief.*

O COME, let us sing for joy to
the Lord;
Let us shout joyfully to the
rock of our salvation.

2 Let us come before His presence with thanksgiving;
Let us shout joyfully to Him
with psalms.

3 For the Lord is a great God,
And a great King above all
gods,

4 In whose hand are the depths
of the earth;
The peaks of the mountains
are His also.

5 The sea is His, for it was He
who made it;
And His hands formed the dry
land.

6 Come, let us worship and bow
down;
Let us kneel before the Lord
our Maker.

7 For He is our God,
And we are the people of His
pasture, and the sheep of
His hand.
Today, if you would hear His
voice,

8 Do not harden your hearts, as
at [155]Meribah,
As in the day of [156]Massah in
the wilderness,

9 "When your fathers tested Me,
They tried Me, though they
had seen My work.

10 "For forty years I loathed *that*
generation,

And said they are a people
who err in their heart,
And they do not know My
ways.

11 "Therefore I swore in My an-
ger,
Truly they shall not enter into
My rest."

PSALM 96

*A Call to Worship the Lord the
Righteous Judge.*

S ING to the Lord a new song;
Sing to the Lord, all the earth.

2 Sing to the Lord, bless His
name;
Proclaim good tidings of His
salvation from day to day.

3 Tell of His glory among the
nations,
His wonderful deeds among
all the peoples.

4 For great is the Lord, and
greatly to be praised;
He is to be feared above all
gods.

5 For all the gods of the peoples
are idols,
But the Lord made the heavens.

6 Splendor and majesty are before Him,
Strength and beauty are in His
sanctuary.

7 [157]Ascribe to the Lord, O families of the peoples,
[157]Ascribe to the Lord glory
and strength.

8 [157]Ascribe to the Lord the glory of His name;
Bring an offering, and come
into His courts.

9 Worship the Lord in [158]holy
attire;
Tremble before Him, all the
earth.

10 Say among the nations, "The
Lord reigns;

---

155 Or, *place of strife*
156 Or, *temptation* 157 Lit., *Give*
158 Or, *the splendor of holiness*

Indeed, the world is firmly established, it will not be moved;
He will judge the peoples with [159]equity."

11 Let the heavens be glad, and let the earth rejoice;
Let the sea roar, and all it contains;

12 Let the field exult, and all that is in it.
Then all the trees of the forest will sing for joy

13 Before the LORD, for He is coming;
For He is coming to judge the earth.
He will judge the world in righteousness,
And the peoples in His faithfulness.

PSALM 97

The LORD's Power and Dominion.

THE LORD reigns; let the earth rejoice;
Let the many [160]islands be glad.

2 Clouds and thick darkness surround Him;
Righteousness and justice are the foundation of His throne.

3 Fire goes before Him,
And burns up His adversaries round about.

4 His lightnings lit up the world;
The earth saw and trembled.

5 The mountains melted like wax at the presence of the LORD,
At the presence of the Lord of the whole earth.

6 The heavens declare His righteousness,
And all the peoples have seen His glory.

7 Let all those be ashamed who serve graven images,
Who boast themselves of idols;
Worship Him, all you gods.

8 Zion heard *this* and was glad,
And the daughters of Judah have rejoiced
Because of Thy judgments, O LORD.

9 For Thou art the LORD Most High over all the earth;
Thou art exalted far above all gods.

10 Hate evil, you who love the LORD,
Who preserves the souls of His godly ones;
He delivers them from the hand of the wicked.

11 Light is sown *like seed* for the righteous,
And gladness for the upright in heart.

12 Be glad in the LORD, you righteous ones;
And give thanks to His holy name.

PSALM 98

A Call to Praise the LORD for His Righteousness.

A Psalm.

O SING to the LORD a new song,
For He has done wonderful things,
His right hand and His holy arm have [161]gained the victory for Him.

2 The LORD has made known His salvation;
He has revealed His righteousness in the sight of the nations.

3 He has remembered His lovingkindness and His faithfulness to the house of Israel;

[159] Or, *uprightness*   [160] Or, *coastlands*
[161] Or, *accomplished salvation*

All the ends of the earth have seen the salvation of our God.

4 Shout joyfully to the LORD, all the earth;
   Break forth and sing for joy and sing praises.
5 Sing praises to the LORD with the lyre;
   With the lyre and the sound of melody.
6 With trumpets and the sound of the horn
   Shout joyfully before the King, the LORD.

7 Let the sea roar and all it contains,
   The world and those who dwell in it.
8 Let the rivers clap their hands;
   Let the mountains sing together for joy
9 Before the LORD; for He is coming to judge the earth;
   He will judge the world with righteousness,
   And the peoples with equity.

PSALM 99

Praise to the LORD for His Fidelity to Israel.

THE LORD reigns, let the peoples tremble;
   He is enthroned *above* the cherubim, let the earth shake!
2 The LORD is great in Zion,
   And He is exalted above all the peoples.
3 Let them praise Thy great and awesome name;
   Holy is He.
4 And the strength of the King loves [162]justice;
   Thou hast established equity;
   Thou hast executed [162]justice and righteousness in Jacob.
5 Exalt the LORD our God,

And worship at His footstool;
   Holy is He.

6 Moses and Aaron were among His priests,
   And Samuel was among those who called on His name;
   They called upon the LORD, and He answered them.
7 He spoke to them in the pillar of cloud;
   They kept His testimonies,
   And the statute that He gave them.
8 O LORD our God, Thou didst answer them;
   Thou wast a forgiving God to them,
   And *yet* an avenger of their *evil* deeds.
9 Exalt the LORD our God,
   And worship at His holy hill;
   For holy is the LORD our God.

PSALM 100

All Men Exhorted to Praise God.

A Psalm for Thanksgiving.

SHOUT joyfully to the LORD, all the earth.
2 Serve the LORD with gladness;
   Come before Him with joyful singing.
3 Know that the LORD Himself is God;
   It is He who has made us, and [163]not we ourselves;
   We are His people and the sheep of His pasture.

4 Enter His gates with thanksgiving,
   And His courts with praise.
   Give thanks to Him; bless His name.
5 For the LORD is good;
   His lovingkindness is everlasting,

---

[162] Or, *judgment*
[163] Some mss. read *His we are*

And His faithfulness to all
generations.

PSALM 101

*The Psalmist's Profession of
Uprightness.*

A Psalm of David.

I WILL sing of lovingkindness
and justice,
To Thee, O LORD, I will sing
praises.
2 I will give heed to the
[164]blameless way.
When wilt Thou come to me?
I will walk within my house in
the integrity of my heart.
3 I will set no worthless thing
before my eyes;
I hate the work of those who
fall away;
It shall not fasten its grip on
me.
4 A perverse heart shall depart
from me;
I will know no evil.
5 Whoever secretly slanders his
neighbor, him I will de-
stroy;
No one who has a haughty
look and an arrogant heart
will I endure.

6 My eyes shall be upon the
faithful of the land, that
they may dwell with me;
He who walks in a [164]blame-
less way is the one who
will minister to me.
7 He who practices deceit shall
not dwell within my house;
He who speaks falsehood
shall not maintain his position before me.
8 Every morning I will [165]de-
stroy all the wicked of the
land,
So as to cut off from the city
of the LORD all those who
do iniquity.

[164] Or, *way of integrity*   [165] Or, *silence*

PSALM 102

*Prayer of an Afflicted Man for
Mercy on Himself and on Zion.*

A Prayer of the Afflicted, when
he is faint, and pours out his
complaint before the LORD.

HEAR my prayer, O LORD!
And let my cry for help come
to Thee.
2 Do not hide Thy face from me
in the day of my distress;
Incline Thine ear to me;
In the day when I call answer
me quickly.
3 For my days have been consumed in smoke,
And my bones have been
scorched like a hearth.
4 My heart has been smitten
like grass and has withered
away,
Indeed, I forget to eat my
bread.
5 Because of the loudness of my
groaning
My bones cling to my flesh.
6 I resemble a pelican of the
wilderness;
I have become like an owl of
the waste places.
7 I lie awake,
I have become like a lonely
bird on a housetop.

8 My enemies have reproached
me all day long;
Those who deride me have
used my *name* as a curse.
9 For I have eaten ashes like
bread,
And mingled my drink with
weeping,
10 Because of Thine indignation
and Thy wrath;
For Thou hast lifted me up
and cast me away.
11 My days are like a lengthened
shadow;
And I wither away like grass.

12 But Thou, O LORD, dost abide
forever;
   And Thy name to all generations.
13 Thou wilt arise *and* have compassion on Zion;
   For it is time to be gracious to
her,
   For the appointed time has
come.
14 Surely Thy servants find pleasure in her stones,
   And feel pity for her dust.
15 So the nations will fear the
name of the LORD,
   And all the kings of the earth
Thy glory.
16 For the LORD has built up
Zion;
   He has appeared in His glory.
17 He has regarded the prayer of
the destitute,
   And has not despised their
prayer.

18 This will be written for the
generation to come;
   That a people yet to be created may praise the LORD.
19 For He looked down from His
holy height;
   From heaven the LORD gazed
upon the earth,
20 To hear the groaning of the
prisoner;
   To set free those who were
doomed to death;
21 That *men* may tell of the name
of the LORD in Zion,
   And His praise in Jerusalem;
22 When the peoples are gathered together,
   And the kingdoms, to serve
the LORD.

23 He has weakened my strength
in the way;
   He has shortened my days.
24 I say, "O my God, do not take
me away in the midst of
my days,

Thy years are throughout all
generations.
25 "Of old Thou didst found the
earth;
   And the heavens are the work
of Thy hands.
26 "Even they will perish, but
Thou dost endure;
   And all of them will wear out
like a garment;
   Like clothing Thou wilt
change them, and they will
be changed.
27 "But Thou art the same,
   And Thy years will not come
to an end.
28 "The children of Thy servants
will continue,
   And their descendants will be
established before Thee."

PSALM 103

Praise for the LORD's Mercies.

A Psalm of David.

BLESS the LORD, O my soul;
   And all that is within me,
bless His holy name.
2 Bless the LORD, O my soul,
   And forget none of His benefits;
3 Who pardons all your iniquities;
   Who heals all your diseases;
4 Who redeems your life from
the pit;
   Who crowns you with lovingkindness and compassion;
5 Who satisfies your [166]years
with good things,
   So that your youth is renewed
like the eagle.

6 The LORD performs righteous
deeds,
   And judgments for all who are
oppressed.
7 He made known His ways to
Moses,
   His acts to the sons of Israel.

---
[166] Or, *desire*

8 The LORD is compassionate
   and gracious,
   Slow to anger and abounding
   in lovingkindness.
9 He will not always strive *with
   us*;
   Nor will He keep *His anger*
   forever.
10 He has not dealt with us according to our sins,
   Nor rewarded us according to
   our iniquities.
11 For as high as the heavens are
   above the earth,
   So great is His lovingkindness
   toward those who [167]fear
   Him.
12 As far as the east is from the
   west,
   So far has He removed our
   transgressions from us.
13 Just as a father has compassion on *his* children,
   So the LORD has compassion
   on those who fear Him.
14 For He Himself knows [168]our
   frame;
   He is mindful that we are *but*
   dust.

15 As for man, his days are like
   grass;
   As a flower of the field, so he
   flourishes.
16 When the wind has passed
   over it, it is no more;
   And its place acknowledges it
   no longer.
17 But the lovingkindness of the
   LORD is from everlasting to
   everlasting on those who
   [167]fear Him,
   And His righteousness to children's children,
18 To those who keep His covenant,

And who remember His pre-
cepts to do them.
19 The LORD has established His
   throne in the heavens;
   And His [169]sovereignty rules
   over all.
20 Bless the LORD, you His angels,
   Mighty in strength, who perform His word,
   Obeying the voice of His
   word!
21 Bless the LORD, all you His
   hosts,
   You who serve Him, doing His
   will.
22 Bless the LORD, all you works
   of His,
   In all places of His dominion;
   Bless the LORD, O my soul!

PSALM 104

*The LORD's Care over All His
Works.*

BLESS the LORD, O my soul!
   O LORD my God, Thou art
   very great;
   Thou art clothed with splendor and majesty,
2 Covering Thyself with light as
   with a cloak,
   Stretching out heaven like a
   tent curtain.
3 [170]He lays the beams of His
   upper chambers in the waters;
   He makes the clouds His
   chariot;
   He walks upon the wings of
   the wind;
4 He makes [171]the winds His
   messengers,
   [172]Flaming fire His ministers.
5 He established the earth upon
   its foundations,
   So that it will not [173]totter forever and ever.
6 Thou didst cover it with the
   deep as with a garment;

---

167 Or, *revere*   168 I.e., what we are made of
169 Or, *kingdom*
170 Lit., *Who*, so through v. 4, and vv. 13, 14
171 Or, *His angels, spirits*
172 Or, *His ministers flames of fire*
173 Or, *move out of place*

The waters were standing above the mountains.

7 At Thy rebuke they fled;
At the sound of Thy thunder they hurried away.

8 The mountains rose; the valleys sank down
To the place which Thou didst establish for them.

9 Thou didst set a boundary that they may not pass over;
That they may not return to cover the earth.

10 He sends forth springs in the valleys;
They flow between the mountains;

11 They give drink to every beast of the field;
The wild donkeys quench their thirst.

12 Beside them the birds of the heavens dwell;
They lift up *their* voices among the branches.

13 He waters the mountains from His upper chambers;
The earth is satisfied with the fruit of His works.

14 He causes the grass to grow for the cattle,
And vegetation for the labor of man,
So that he may bring forth food from the earth,

15 And wine which makes man's heart glad,
So that he may make *his* face glisten with oil,
And food which sustains man's heart.

16 The trees of the Lord drink their fill,
The cedars of Lebanon which He planted,

17 Where the birds build their nests,
And the stork, *whose* home is the fir trees.

18 The high mountains are for the wild goats;
The cliffs are a refuge for the rock badgers.

19 He made the moon for the seasons;
The sun knows the place of its setting.

20 Thou dost appoint darkness and it becomes night,
In which all the beasts of the forest prowl about.

21 The young lions roar after their prey,
And seek their food from God.

22 *When* the sun rises they withdraw,
And lie down in their dens.

23 Man goes forth to his work
And to his labor until evening.

24 O Lord, how many are Thy works!
In wisdom Thou hast made them all;
The earth is full of Thy [174]possessions.

25 There is the sea, great and broad,
In which are swarms without number,
Animals both small and great.

26 There the ships move along,
And [175]Leviathan, which Thou hast formed to sport in it.

27 They all wait for Thee,
To give them their food in [176]due season.

28 Thou dost give to them, they gather it up;
Thou dost open Thy hand, they are satisfied with good.

29 Thou dost hide Thy face, they are dismayed;
Thou dost take away their [177]spirit, they expire,
And return to their dust.

[174] Or, *creatures*   [175] Or, *a sea monster*
[176] Lit., *its appointed time*   [177] Or, *breath*

30 Thou dost send forth Thy
   [177]Spirit, they are created;
   And Thou dost renew the face
       of the ground.

31 Let the glory of the LORD en-
       dure forever;
   Let the LORD be glad in His
       works;

32 He looks at the earth, and it
       trembles;
   He touches the mountains,
       and they smoke.

33 I will sing to the LORD as long
       as I live;
   I will sing praise to my God
       while I have my being.

34 Let my meditation be pleasing
       to Him;
   As for me, I shall be glad in
       the LORD.

35 Let sinners be consumed from
       the earth,
   And let the wicked be no
       more.
   Bless the LORD, O my soul.
   Praise the LORD!

PSALM 105

*The LORD's Wonderful Works in
       Behalf of Israel.*

OH give thanks to the LORD, call
       upon His name;
   Make known His deeds
       among the peoples.

2 Sing to Him, sing praises to
       Him;
   [178]Speak of all His wonders.

3 Glory in His holy name;
   Let the heart of those who
       seek the LORD be glad.

4 Seek the LORD and His
       strength;
   Seek His face continually.

5 Remember His wonders
       which He has done,
   His marvels, and the judg-
       ments uttered by His
       mouth,

6 O seed of Abraham, His ser-
       vant,
   O sons of Jacob, His chosen
       ones!

7 He is the LORD our God;
   His judgments are in all the
       earth.

8 He has remembered His cov-
       enant forever,
   The word which He com-
       manded to a thousand gen-
       erations,

9 *The covenant* which He made
       with Abraham,
   And His oath to Isaac.

10 Then He confirmed it to Jacob
       for a statute,
   To Israel as an everlasting
       covenant,

11 Saying, "To you I will give the
       land of Canaan
   As the portion of your inheri-
       tance,"

12 When they were only a few
       men in number,
   Very few, and strangers in it.

13 And they wandered about
       from nation to nation,
   From *one* kingdom to another
       people.

14 He permitted no man to op-
       press them,
   And He reproved kings for
       their sakes:

15 "Do not touch My anointed
       ones,
   And do My prophets no
       harm."

16 And He called for a famine
       upon the land;
   He broke the whole staff of
       bread.

17 He sent a man before them,
   Joseph, *who* was sold as a
       slave.

18 They afflicted his feet with fet-
       ters,
   He himself was laid in irons;

19 Until the time that his word
       came to pass,

[177] Or, *breath*   [178] Or, *Meditate on*

The word of the LORD tested him.

20 The king sent and released him,
   The ruler of peoples, and set him free.

21 He made him lord of his house,
   And ruler over all his possessions,

22 To imprison his princes at will,
   That he might teach his elders wisdom.

23 Israel also came into Egypt;
   Thus Jacob sojourned in the land of Ham.

24 And He caused His people to be very fruitful,
   And made them stronger than their adversaries.

25 He turned their heart to hate His people,
   To deal craftily with His servants.

26 He sent Moses His servant,
   And Aaron whom He had chosen.

27 They performed His wondrous acts among them,
   And miracles in the land of Ham.

28 He sent darkness and made *it* dark;
   And they did not rebel against His words.

29 He turned their waters into blood,
   And caused their fish to die.

30 Their land swarmed with frogs
   Even in the chambers of their kings.

31 He spoke, and there came a swarm of flies
   And gnats in all their territory.

32 He gave them hail for rain,
   And flaming fire in their land.

33 He struck down their vines also and their fig trees,
   And shattered the trees of their territory.

34 He spoke, and locusts came,
   And young locusts, even without number,

35 And ate up all vegetation in their land,
   And ate up the fruit of their ground.

36 He also struck down all the first-born in their land,
   The first fruits of all their vigor.

37 Then He brought them out with silver and gold;
   And among His tribes there was not one who stumbled.

38 Egypt was glad when they departed;
   For the dread of them had fallen upon them.

39 He spread a cloud for a [179]covering,
   And fire to illumine by night.

40 They asked, and He brought quail,
   And satisfied them with the bread of heaven.

41 He opened the rock, and water flowed out;
   It ran in the dry places *like* a river.

42 For He remembered His holy word
   With Abraham His servant;

43 And He brought forth His people with joy,
   His chosen ones with a joyful shout.

44 He gave them also the lands of the nations,
   That they might take possession *of the fruit* of the peoples' labor.

45 So that they might keep His statutes,

[179] Or, *curtain*

And observe His laws,
Praise the Lord!

PSALM 106

*Israel's Rebelliousness and the
Lord's Deliverances.*

PRAISE the Lord!
Oh give thanks to the Lord,
for He is good;
For His lovingkindness is
everlasting.
2 Who can speak of the mighty
deeds of the Lord,
Or can show forth all His
praise?
3 How blessed are those who
keep justice,
Who practice righteousness at
all times!

4 Remember me, O Lord, in
Thy favor toward Thy peo-
ple;
Visit me with Thy salvation,
5 That I may see the prosperity
of Thy chosen ones,
That I may rejoice in the gladness of Thy nation,
That I may glory with Thine
[180]inheritance.

6 We have sinned like our fathers,
We have committed iniquity,
we have behaved wickedly.
7 Our fathers in Egypt did not
understand Thy wonders;
They did not remember Thine
abundant kindnesses,
But rebelled by the sea, at the
[181]Red Sea.
8 Nevertheless He saved them
for the sake of His name,
That He might make His
power known.
9 Thus He rebuked the [181]Red
Sea and it dried up;

And He led them through the
deeps, as through the wilderness.
10 So He saved them from the
hand of the one who hated
them,
And redeemed them from the
hand of the enemy.
11 And the waters covered their
adversaries;
Not one of them was left.
12 Then they believed His words;
They sang His praise.

13 They quickly forgot His
works;
They did not wait for His
counsel,
14 But craved intensely in the
wilderness,
And tempted God in the desert.
15 So He gave them their request,
But sent a wasting disease
among them.

16 When they became envious of
Moses in the camp,
And of Aaron, the holy one of
the Lord,
17 The earth opened and swallowed up Dathan,
And engulfed the company of
Abiram.
18 And a fire blazed up in their
company;
The flame consumed the
wicked.

19 They made a calf in Horeb,
And worshiped a molten
image.
20 Thus they exchanged their
glory
For the image of an ox that
eats grass.
21 They forgot God their Savior,
Who had great things in
Egypt,

[180] I.e., people   [181] Lit., *Sea of Reeds*

22 Wonders in the land of Ham,
And awesome things by the
[181]Red Sea.

23 Therefore He said that He
would destroy them,
Had not Moses His chosen
one stood in the breach before Him,
To turn away His wrath from
destroying *them.*

24 Then they despised the pleasant land;
They did not believe in His
word,

25 But grumbled in their tents;
They did not listen to the
voice of the LORD.

26 Therefore He swore to them,
That He would cast them
down in the wilderness,

27 And that He would cast their
seed among the nations,
And scatter them in the lands.

28 They joined themselves also
to Baal-peor,
And ate sacrifices offered to
the dead.

29 Thus they provoked *Him* to
anger with their deeds;
And the plague broke out
among them.

30 Then Phinehas stood up and
interposed;
And so the plague was stayed.

31 And it was reckoned to him
for righteousness,
To all generations forever.

32 They also provoked *Him* to
wrath at the waters of
[182]Meribah,
So that it went hard with
Moses on their account;

33 Because they were rebellious
against His Spirit,
He spoke rashly with his lips.

34 They did not destroy the peoples,
As the LORD commanded
them,

35 But they mingled with the nations,
And learned their practices,

36 And served their idols,
Which became a snare to
them.

37 They even sacrificed their
sons and their daughters to
the demons,

38 And shed innocent blood,
The blood of their sons and
their daughters,
Whom they sacrificed to the
idols of Canaan;
And the land was polluted
with the blood.

39 Thus they became unclean in
their practices,
And played the harlot in their
deeds.

40 Therefore the anger of the
LORD was kindled against
His people,
And He abhorred His inheri-
tance.

41 Then He gave them into the
hand of the nations;
And those who hated them
ruled over them.

42 Their enemies also oppressed
them,
And they were subdued under
their power.

43 Many times He would deliver
them;
They, however, were rebellious in their counsel,
And *so* sank down in their iniquity.

44 Nevertheless He looked upon
their distress,
When He heard their cry;

45 And He remembered His covenant for their sake,
And relented according to the
greatness of His loving-
kindness.

46 He also made them *objects* of
compassion

181 Lit., *Sea of Reeds* 182 Lit., *strife*

In the presence of all their captors.

47 Save us, O LORD our God,
And gather us from among the nations,
To give thanks to Thy holy name,
And glory in Thy praise.

48 Blessed be the LORD, the God of Israel,
From everlasting even to everlasting.
And let all the people say, "Amen."
Praise the LORD!

BOOK 5

PSALM 107

The LORD Delivers Men from Manifold Troubles.

OH give thanks to the LORD, for He is good;
For His lovingkindness is everlasting.

2 Let the redeemed of the LORD say *so*,
Whom He has redeemed from the hand of the adversary,

3 And gathered from the lands,
From the east and from the west,
From the north and from the south.

4 They wandered in the wilderness in a desert region;
They did not find a way to an inhabited city.

5 *They were* hungry and thirsty;
Their soul fainted within them.

6 Then they cried out to the LORD in their trouble;
He delivered them out of their distresses.

7 He led them also by a straight way,
To go to an inhabited city.

8 Let them give thanks to the LORD for His lovingkindness,
And for His wonders to the sons of men!

9 For He has satisfied the thirsty soul,
And the hungry soul He has filled with what is good.

10 There were those who dwelt in darkness and in the shadow of death,
Prisoners in misery and chains,

11 Because they had rebelled against the words of God,
And spurned the counsel of the Most High.

12 Therefore He humbled their heart with labor;
They stumbled and there was none to help.

13 Then they cried out to the LORD in their trouble;
He saved them out of their distresses.

14 He brought them out of darkness and the shadow of death,
And broke their bands apart.

15 Let them give thanks to the LORD for His lovingkindness,
And for His wonders to the sons of men!

16 For He has shattered gates of bronze,
And cut bars of iron asunder.

17 Fools, because of their rebellious way,
And because of their iniquities, were afflicted.

18 Their soul abhorred all kinds of food;
And they drew near to the gates of death.

19 Then they cried out to the LORD in their trouble;
He saved them out of their distresses.

20 He sent His word and healed them,
And delivered *them* from their [183]destructions.

21 Let them give thanks to the LORD for His lovingkindness,
And for His wonders to the sons of men!

22 Let them also offer sacrifices of thanksgiving,
And tell of His works with joyful singing.

23 Those who go down to the sea in ships,
Who do business on great waters;

24 They have seen the works of the LORD,
And His wonders in the deep.

25 For He spoke and raised up a stormy wind,
Which lifted up the waves of the sea.

26 They rose up to the heavens, they went down to the depths;
Their soul melted away in *their* misery.

27 They reeled and staggered like a drunken man,
And [184]were at their wits' end.

28 Then they cried to the LORD in their trouble,
And He brought them out of their distresses.

29 He caused the storm to be still,
So that the waves of the sea were hushed.

30 Then they were glad because they were quiet;
So He guided them to their desired haven.

31 Let them give thanks to the LORD for His lovingkindness,
And for His wonders to the sons of men!

32 Let them extol Him also in the congregation of the people,
And praise Him at the seat of the elders.

33 He [185]changes rivers into a wilderness,
And springs of water into a thirsty ground;

34 A fruitful land into a salt waste,
Because of the wickedness of those who dwell in it.

35 He changes a wilderness into a pool of water,
And a dry land into springs of water;

36 And there He makes the hungry to dwell,
So that they may establish an inhabited city,

37 And sow fields, and plant vineyards,
And gather a fruitful harvest.

38 Also He blesses them and they multiply greatly;
And He does not let their cattle decrease.

39 When they are diminished and bowed down
Through oppression, misery, and sorrow,

40 He pours contempt upon princes,
And makes them wander in a pathless waste.

41 But He sets the needy securely on high away from affliction,
And makes *his* families like a flock.

42 The upright see it, and are glad;
But all unrighteousness shuts its mouth.

43 Who is wise? Let him give heed to these things;
And consider the lovingkindnesses of the LORD.

[183] Or, *pits*
[184] Lit., *all their wisdom was swallowed up*
[185] Or, *turns rivers into a desert*

PSALM 108

God Praised and Supplicated to Give Victory.

A Song, a Psalm of David.

MY heart is steadfast, O God;
I will sing, I will sing praises,
even with my soul.

2 Awake, harp and lyre;
I will awaken the dawn!

3 I will give thanks to Thee, O
LORD, among the peoples;
And I will sing praises to Thee
among the nations.

4 For Thy lovingkindness is
great above the heavens;
And Thy truth *reaches* to the
skies.

5 Be exalted, O God, above the
heavens,
And Thy glory above all the
earth.

6 That Thy beloved may be delivered,
Save with Thy right hand, and
answer me!

7 God has spoken in His [186]holi-
ness:
"I will exult, I will portion out
Shechem,
And measure out the valley of
Succoth.

8 "Gilead is Mine, Manasseh is
Mine;
Ephraim also is the helmet of
My head;
Judah is My [187]scepter.

9 "Moab is My washbowl;
Over Edom I shall throw My
shoe;
Over Philistia I will shout
aloud."

10 Who will bring me into the besieged city?
Who will lead me to Edom?

11 Hast not Thou Thyself, O God,
rejected us?

And wilt Thou not go forth
with our armies, O God?

12 Oh give us help against the
adversary,
For deliverance by man is in
vain.

13 Through God we shall do valiantly;
And it is He who will tread
down our adversaries.

PSALM 109

*Vengeance Invoked upon
Adversaries.*

For the choir director. A
Psalm of David.

O GOD of my praise,
Do not be silent!

2 For they have opened the
wicked and deceitful
mouth against me;
They have spoken against me
with a lying tongue.

3 They have also surrounded
me with words of hatred,
And fought against me without cause.

4 In return for my love they act
as my accusers;
But I am *in* prayer.

5 Thus they have repaid me evil
for good,
And hatred for my love.

6 Appoint a wicked man over
him;
And let an accuser stand at
his right hand.

7 When he is judged, let him
come forth guilty;
And let his prayer become sin.

8 Let his days be few;
Let another take his office.

9 Let his children be fatherless,
And his wife a widow.

10 Let his children wander about
and beg;
And let them seek *sustenance*
far from their ruined
homes.

[186] Or, *sanctuary*   [187] Or, *lawgiver*

11 Let the creditor seize all that
he has;
And let strangers plunder the
product of his labor.

12 Let there be none to extend
lovingkindness to him,
Nor any to be gracious to his
fatherless children.

13 Let his posterity be cut off;
In a following generation let
their name be blotted out.

14 Let the iniquity of his fathers
be remembered before the
LORD,
And do not let the sin of his
mother be blotted out.

15 Let them be before the LORD
continually,
That He may cut off their
memory from the earth;

16 Because he did not remember
to show lovingkindness,
But persecuted the afflicted
and needy man,
And the despondent in heart,
to put *them* to death.

17 He also loved cursing, so it
came to him;
And he did not delight in
blessing, so it was far from
him.

18 But he clothed himself with
cursing as with his gar-
ment,
And it entered into his body
like water,
And like oil into his bones.

19 Let it be to him as a garment
with which he covers him-
self,
And for a belt with which he
constantly girds himself.

20 Let this be the reward of my
accusers from the LORD,
And of those who speak evil
against my soul.

21 But Thou, O GOD, the Lord,
deal *kindly* with me for
Thy name's sake;

Because Thy lovingkindness is
good, deliver me;

22 For I am afflicted and needy,
And my heart is wounded
within me.

23 I am passing like a shadow
when it lengthens;
I am shaken off like the locust.

24 My knees are weak from fasting;
And my flesh has grown lean,
without fatness.

25 I also have become a reproach
to them;
When they see me, they wag
their head.

26 Help me, O LORD my God;
Save me according to Thy
lovingkindness.

27 And let them know that this is
Thy hand;
Thou, LORD, hast done it.

28 Let them curse, but do Thou
bless;
When they arise, they shall be
ashamed,
But Thy servant shall be glad.

29 Let my accusers be clothed
with dishonor,
And let them cover them-
selves with their own
shame as with a robe.

30 With my mouth I will give
thanks abundantly to the
LORD;
And in the midst of many I
will praise Him.

31 For He stands at the right
hand of the needy,
To save him from those who
judge his soul.

PSALM 110

*The LORD Gives Dominion to the
King.*

A Psalm of David.

THE LORD says to my Lord:
"Sit at My right hand,

Until I make Thine enemies a
footstool for Thy feet."

2 The LORD will stretch forth
Thy strong scepter from
Zion, *saying,*
"Rule in the midst of Thine en-
emies."

3 Thy people will volunteer
freely in the day of Thy
power;
In holy array, from the womb
of the dawn,
Thy youth are to Thee *as* the
dew.

4 The LORD has sworn and will
not change His mind,
"Thou art a priest forever
According to the order of Melchizedek."

5 The Lord is at Thy right hand;
He will shatter kings in the
day of His wrath.

6 He will judge among the nations,
He will fill *them* with corpses,
He will shatter the chief men
over a broad country.

7 He will drink from the brook
by the wayside;
Therefore He will lift up *His*
head.

PSALM 111

*The LORD Praised for His
Goodness.*

PRAISE the LORD!
I will give thanks to the LORD
with all *my* heart,
In the company of the upright
and in the assembly.

2 Great are the works of the
LORD;
They are studied by all who
delight in them.

3 Splendid and majestic is His
work;
And His righteousness en-
dures forever.

4 He has made His wonders to
be remembered;
The LORD is gracious and
compassionate.

5 He has given food to those
who [188]fear Him;
He will remember His cov-
enant forever.

6 He has made known to His
people the power of His
works,
In giving them the heritage of
the nations.

7 The works of His hands are
truth and justice;
All His precepts are sure.

8 They are upheld forever and
ever;
They are performed in truth
and uprightness.

9 He has sent redemption to His
people;
He has ordained His covenant
forever;
Holy and awesome is His
name.

10 The [189]fear of the LORD is the
beginning of wisdom;
A good understanding have all
those who do *His* com-
mandments;
His praise endures forever.

PSALM 112

*Prosperity of the One Who Fears
the LORD.*

PRAISE the LORD!
How blessed is the man who
fears the LORD,
Who greatly delights in His
commandments.

2 His [190]descendants will be
mighty on earth;
The generation of the upright
will be blessed.

3 Wealth and riches are in his
house,
And his righteousness en-
dures forever.

188 Or, *revere*　　189 Or, *reverence for*
190 Lit., *seed*

4 Light arises in the darkness
    for the upright;
  He is gracious and compas-
    sionate and righteous.
5 It is well with the man who is
    gracious and lends;
  He will maintain his cause in
    judgment.
6 For he will never be shaken;
  The righteous will be remem-
    bered forever.

7 He will not fear evil tidings;
  His heart is steadfast, trusting
    in the LORD.
8 His heart is upheld, he will not
    fear,
  Until he looks *with satisfac-
    tion* on his adversaries.
9 He has given freely to the
    poor;
  His righteousness endures for-
    ever;
  His horn will be exalted in
    honor.

10 The wicked will see it and be
    vexed;
  He will gnash his teeth and
    melt away;
  The desire of the wicked will
    perish.

PSALM 113

The LORD Exalts the Humble.

PRAISE the LORD!
  Praise, O servants of the
    LORD.
  Praise the name of the LORD.
2 Blessed be the name of the
    LORD
  From this time forth and for-
    ever.
3 From the rising of the sun to
    its setting
  The name of the LORD is to be
    praised.
4 The LORD is high above all na-
    tions;
  His glory is above the heav-
    ens.

5 Who is like the LORD our God,
  Who is enthroned on high,
6 Who humbles Himself to be-
    hold
  The things that are in heaven
    and in the earth?
7 He raises the poor from the
    dust,
  And lifts the needy from the
    ash heap,
8 To make *them* sit with
    princes,
  With the princes of His peo-
    ple.
9 He makes the barren woman
    abide in the house
  As a joyful mother of children.
  Praise the LORD!

PSALM 114

*God's Deliverance of Israel from
    Egypt.*

WHEN Israel went forth from
    Egypt,
  The house of Jacob from a
    people of strange language,
2 Judah became His sanctuary,
  Israel, His dominion.

3 The sea looked and fled;
  The Jordan turned back.
4 The mountains skipped like
    rams,
  The hills, like lambs.
5 What ails you, O sea, that you
    flee?
  O Jordan, that you turn back?
6 O mountains, that you skip
    like rams?
  O hills, like lambs?

7 Tremble, O earth, before the
    Lord,
  Before the God of Jacob,
8 Who turned the rock into a
    pool of water,
  The flint into a fountain of wa-
    ter.

PSALM 115

Heathen Idols Contrasted with the LORD.

NOT to us, O LORD, not to us,
But to Thy name give glory
Because of Thy lovingkind-
ness, because of Thy truth.

2 Why should the nations say,
"Where, now, is their God?"

3 But our God is in the heavens;
He does whatever He pleases.

4 Their idols are silver and gold,
The work of man's hands.

5 They have mouths, but they
cannot speak;
They have eyes, but they cannot see;

6 They have ears, but they cannot hear;
They have noses, but they
cannot smell;

7 They have hands, but they
cannot feel;
They have feet, but they cannot walk;
They cannot make a sound
with their throat.

8 Those who make them will become like them,
Everyone who trusts in them.

9 O Israel, trust in the LORD;
He is their help and their
shield.

10 O house of Aaron, trust in the
LORD;
He is their help and their
shield.

11 You who [191]fear the LORD,
trust in the LORD;
He is their help and their
shield.

12 The LORD has been mindful of
us; He will bless *us;*
He will bless the house of Israel;

He will bless the house of Aaron.

13 He will bless those who [191]fear
the LORD,
The small together with the
great.

14 May the LORD give you increase,
You and your children.

15 May you be blessed of the
LORD,
Maker of heaven and earth.

16 The heavens are the heavens
of the LORD;
But the earth He has given to
the sons of men.

17 The dead do not praise the
LORD,
Nor *do* any who go down into
silence;

18 But as for us, we will bless the
LORD
From this time forth and for-
ever.
Praise the LORD!

PSALM 116

*Thanksgiving for Deliverance
from Death.*

I LOVE the LORD, because He
hears
My voice *and* my supplications.

2 Because He has inclined His
ear to me,
Therefore I shall call *upon
Him* as long as I live.

3 The cords of death encompassed me,
And the terrors of Sheol came
upon me;
I found distress and sorrow.

4 Then I called upon the name
of the LORD:
"O LORD, I beseech Thee, save
my life!"

5 Gracious is the LORD, and
righteous;

191 Or, revere

Yes, our God is compassionate.

6 The LORD preserves the simple;
I was brought low, and He saved me.

7 Return to your rest, O my soul,
For the LORD has dealt bountifully with you.

8 For Thou hast rescued my soul from death,
My eyes from tears,
My feet from stumbling.

9 I shall walk before the LORD
In the land of the living.

10 I believed when I said,
"I am greatly afflicted."

11 I said in my alarm,
"All men are liars."

12 What shall I render to the LORD
For all His benefits toward me?

13 I shall lift up the cup of salvation,
And call upon the name of the LORD.

14 I shall pay my vows to the LORD,
Oh *may it be* in the presence of all His people.

15 Precious in the sight of the LORD
Is the death of His godly ones.

16 O LORD, surely I am Thy servant,
I am Thy servant, the son of Thy handmaid,
Thou hast loosed my bonds.

17 To Thee I shall offer a sacrifice of thanksgiving,
And call upon the name of the LORD.

18 I shall pay my vows to the LORD,
Oh *may it be* in the presence of all His people,

19 In the courts of the LORD's house,
In the midst of you, O Jerusalem.
Praise the LORD!

PSALM 117

A Psalm of Praise.

PRAISE the LORD, all nations;
Laud Him, all peoples!

2 For His lovingkindness [192]is great toward us,
And the truth of the LORD is everlasting.
Praise the LORD!

PSALM 118

Thanksgiving for the LORD's Saving Goodness.

GIVE thanks to the LORD, for He is good;
For His lovingkindness is everlasting.

2 Oh let Israel say,
"His lovingkindness is everlasting."

3 Oh let the house of Aaron say,
"His lovingkindness is everlasting."

4 Oh let those who [193]fear the LORD say,
"His lovingkindness is everlasting."

5 From *my* distress I called upon the LORD;
The LORD answered me *and set me* in a large place.

6 The LORD is for me; I will not fear;
What can man do to me?

7 The LORD is for me among those who help me;
Therefore I shall look *with satisfaction* on those who hate me.

8 It is better to take refuge in the LORD
Than to trust in man.

9 It is better to take refuge in
the LORD
Than to trust in princes.

10 All nations surrounded me;
In the name of the LORD I will
surely cut them off.

11 They surrounded me, yes,
they surrounded me;
In the name of the LORD I will
surely cut them off.

12 They surrounded me like bees;
They were extinguished as a
fire of thorns;
In the name of the LORD I will
surely cut them off.

13 You pushed me violently so
that I was falling,
But the LORD helped me.

14 The LORD is my strength and
song,
And He has become my salvation.

15 The sound of joyful shouting
and salvation is in the tents
of the righteous;
The right hand of the LORD
does valiantly.

16 The right hand of the LORD is
exalted;
The right hand of the LORD
does valiantly.

17 I shall not die, but live,
And tell of the works of the
LORD.

18 The LORD has disciplined me
severely,
But He has not given me over
to death.

19 Open to me the gates of righteousness;
I shall enter through them, I
shall give thanks to the
LORD.

20 This is the gate of the LORD;
The righteous will enter
through it.

21 I shall give thanks to Thee, for
Thou hast answered me;

And Thou hast become my
salvation.

22 The stone which the builders
rejected
Has become the chief corner
stone.

23 This is [194]the LORD's doing;
It is marvelous in our eyes.

24 This is the day which the
LORD has made;
Let us rejoice and be glad in it.

25 O LORD, do save, we beseech
Thee;
O LORD, we beseech Thee, do
send prosperity!

26 Blessed is the one who comes
in the name of the LORD;
We have blessed you from the
house of the LORD.

27 The LORD is God, and He has
given us light;
Bind the festival sacrifice with
cords to the horns of the altar.

28 Thou art my God, and I give
thanks to Thee;
Thou art my God, I extol
Thee.

29 Give thanks to the LORD, for
He is good;
For His lovingkindness is
everlasting.

PSALM 119

*Meditations and Prayers Relating
to the Law of God.*

Aleph.

HOW blessed are those whose
way is [195]blameless,
Who walk in the law of the
LORD.

2 How blessed are those who
observe His testimonies,
Who seek Him with all *their*
heart.

3 They also do no unrighteousness;
They walk in His ways.

---

194 Lit., *from the LORD*
195 Lit., *complete,* or, *having integrity*

4 Thou hast ordained Thy precepts,
   That we should keep *them* diligently.
5 Oh that my ways may be established
   To keep Thy statutes!
6 Then I shall not be ashamed
   When I look upon all Thy commandments.
7 I shall give thanks to Thee with uprightness of heart,
   When I learn Thy righteous judgments.
8 I shall keep Thy statutes;
   Do not forsake me utterly!

Beth.

9 How can a young man keep his way pure?
   By keeping *it* according to Thy word.
10 With all my heart I have sought Thee;
   Do not let me wander from Thy commandments.
11 Thy word I have treasured in my heart,
   That I may not sin against Thee.
12 Blessed art Thou, O LORD;
   Teach me Thy statutes.
13 With my lips I have told of All the ordinances of Thy mouth.
14 I have rejoiced in the way of Thy testimonies,
   As much as in all riches.
15 I will meditate on Thy precepts,
   And regard Thy ways.
16 I shall delight in Thy statutes;
   I shall not forget Thy word.

Gimel.

17 Deal bountifully with Thy servant,
   That I may live and keep Thy word.
18 Open my eyes, that I may behold

Wonderful things from Thy law.
19 I am a stranger in the earth;
   Do not hide Thy commandments from me.
20 My soul is crushed with longing
   After Thine ordinances at all times.
21 Thou dost rebuke the arrogant, the cursed,
   Who wander from Thy commandments.
22 Take away reproach and contempt from me,
   For I observe Thy testimonies.
23 Even though princes sit and talk against me,
   Thy servant meditates on Thy statutes.
24 Thy testimonies also are my delight;
   They are my counselors.

Daleth.

25 My soul cleaves to the dust;
   Revive me according to Thy word.
26 I have told of my ways, and Thou hast answered me;
   Teach me Thy statutes.
27 Make me understand the way of Thy precepts,
   So I will meditate on Thy wonders.
28 My soul weeps because of grief;
   Strengthen me according to Thy word.
29 Remove the false way from me,
   And graciously grant me Thy law.
30 I have chosen the faithful way;
   I have placed Thine ordinances *before me.*
31 I cleave to Thy testimonies;
   O LORD, do not put me to shame!

32 I shall run the way of Thy
    commandments,
    For Thou wilt enlarge my
    heart.

He.

33 Teach me, O LORD, the way of
    Thy statutes,
    And I shall observe it to the
    end.
34 Give me understanding, that I
    may observe Thy law,
    And keep it with all *my* heart.
35 Make me walk in the path of
    Thy commandments,
    For I delight in it.
36 Incline my heart to Thy testi-
    monies,
    And not to *dishonest* gain.
37 Turn away my eyes from look-
    ing at vanity,
    And revive me in Thy ways.
38 Establish Thy word to Thy
    servant,
    As that which produces rever-
    ence for Thee.
39 Turn away my reproach
    which I dread,
    For Thine ordinances are
    good.
40 Behold, I long for Thy pre-
    cepts;
    Revive me through Thy right-
    eousness.

Vav.

41 May Thy lovingkindnesses
    also come to me, O LORD,
    Thy salvation according to
    Thy word;
42 So I shall have an answer for
    him who reproaches me,
    For I trust in Thy word.
43 And do not take the word of
    truth utterly out of my
    mouth,
    For I wait for Thine ordi-
    nances.
44 So I will keep Thy law con-
    tinually,
    Forever and ever.

45 And I will walk at liberty,
    For I seek Thy precepts.
46 I will also speak of Thy testi-
    monies before kings,
    And shall not be ashamed.
47 And I shall delight in Thy
    commandments,
    Which I love.
48 And I shall lift up my hands to
    Thy commandments,
    Which I love;
    And I will meditate on Thy
    statutes.

Zayin.

49 Remember the word to Thy
    servant,
    In which Thou hast made me
    hope.
50 This is my comfort in my af-
    fliction,
    That Thy word has revived
    me.
51 The arrogant utterly deride
    me,
    Yet I do not turn aside from
    Thy law.
52 I have remembered Thine or-
    dinances from [196]of old, O
    LORD,
    And comfort myself.
53 Burning indignation has
    seized me because of the
    wicked,
    Who forsake Thy law.
54 Thy statutes are my songs
    In the house of my pilgrimage.
55 O LORD, I remember Thy
    name in the night,
    And keep Thy law.
56 This has become mine,
    That I observe Thy precepts.

Heth.

57 The LORD is my portion;
    I have promised to keep Thy
    words.
58 I entreated Thy favor with all
    my heart;
    Be gracious to me according
    to Thy word.

[196] Or, *everlasting*

59 I considered my ways,
   And turned my feet to Thy
      testimonies.

60 I hastened and did not delay
   To keep Thy commandments.

61 The cords of the wicked have
      encircled me,
   But I have not forgotten Thy
      law.

62 At midnight I shall rise to give
      thanks to Thee
   Because of Thy righteous or-
      dinances.

63 I am a companion of all those
      who fear Thee,
   And of those who keep Thy
      precepts.

64 The earth is full of Thy loving-
      kindness, O LORD;
   Teach me Thy statutes.

Teth.

65 Thou hast dealt well with Thy
      servant,
   O LORD, according to Thy
      word.

66 Teach me good discernment
      and knowledge,
   For I believe in Thy com-
      mandments.

67 Before I was afflicted I went
      astray,
   But now I keep Thy word.

68 Thou art good and doest good;
   Teach me Thy statutes.

69 The arrogant [197]have forged a
      lie against me;
   With all *my* heart I will ob-
      serve Thy precepts.

70 Their heart is covered with
      fat,
   But I delight in Thy law.

71 It is good for me that I was af-
      flicted,
   That I may learn Thy statutes.

72 The law of Thy mouth is bet-
      ter to me
   Than thousands of gold and
      silver *pieces.*

Yodh.

73 Thy hands made me and
      [198]fashioned me;
   Give me understanding, that I
      may learn Thy command-
      ments.

74 May those who fear Thee see
      me and be glad,
   Because I wait for Thy word.

75 I know, O LORD, that Thy
      judgments are righteous,
   And that in faithfulness Thou
      hast afflicted me.

76 O may Thy lovingkindness
      comfort me,
   According to Thy word to Thy
      servant.

77 May Thy compassion come to
      me that I may live,
   For Thy law is my delight.

78 May the arrogant be ashamed,
      for they subvert me with a
      lie;
   But I shall meditate on Thy
      precepts.

79 May those who fear Thee turn
      to me,
   Even those who know Thy
      testimonies.

80 May my heart be blameless in
      Thy statutes,
   That I may not be ashamed.

Kaph.

81 My soul languishes for Thy
      salvation;
   I wait for Thy word.

82 My eyes fail *with longing* for
      Thy word,
   While I say, "When wilt Thou
      comfort me?"

83 Though I have become like a
      wineskin in the smoke,
   I do not forget Thy statutes.

84 How many are the days of
      Thy servant?
   When wilt Thou execute judg-
      ment on those who perse-
      cute me?

197 Lit., *besmear me with lies*
198 Lit., *established*

85 The arrogant have dug pits for
   me,
   Men who are not in accord
      with Thy law.
86 All Thy commandments are
   faithful;
   They have persecuted me with
      a lie; help me!
87 They almost destroyed me on
   earth,
   But as for me, I did not for-
      sake Thy precepts.
88 Revive me according to Thy
   lovingkindness,
   So that I may keep the testi-
      mony of Thy mouth.

Lamedh.

89 Forever, O LORD,
   Thy word [199]is settled in
      heaven.
90 Thy faithfulness *continues*
   throughout all generations;
   Thou didst establish the earth,
      and it stands.
91 They stand this day according
   to Thine ordinances,
   For all things are Thy ser-
      vants.
92 If Thy law had not been my
   delight,
   Then I would have perished in
      my affliction.
93 I will never forget Thy precepts,
   For by them Thou hast re-
      vived me.
94 I am Thine, save me;
   For I have sought Thy pre-
      cepts.
95 The wicked wait for me to destroy me;
   I shall diligently consider Thy
      testimonies.
96 I have seen a limit to all perfection;
   Thy commandment is exceed-
      ingly broad.

Mem.

97 O how I love Thy law!
   It is my meditation all the day.
98 Thy commandments make me
      wiser than my enemies,
   For they are ever mine.
99 I have more insight than all
      my teachers,
   For Thy testimonies are my
      meditation.
100 I understand more than the
       aged,
   Because I have observed Thy
      precepts.
101 I have restrained my feet from
      every evil way,
   That I may keep Thy word.
102 I have not turned aside from
      Thine ordinances,
   For Thou Thyself hast taught
      me.
103 How sweet are Thy words to
      my taste!
   Yes, sweeter than honey to my
      mouth!
104 From Thy precepts I get un-
      derstanding;
   Therefore I hate every false
      way.

Nun.

105 Thy word is a lamp to my feet,
   And a light to my path.
106 I have sworn, and I will con-
      firm it,
   That I will keep Thy righteous
      ordinances.
107 I am exceedingly afflicted;
   Revive me, O LORD, according
      to Thy word.
108 O accept the freewill offerings
      of my mouth, O LORD,
   And teach me Thine ordi-
      nances.
109 My life is continually [200]in my
      hand,
   Yet I do not forget Thy law.
110 The wicked have laid a snare
      for me,
   Yet I have not gone astray
      from Thy precepts.

[199] Lit., *stands firm*   [200] I.e., in danger

111 I have inherited Thy testimonies forever,

For they are the joy of my heart.

112 I have inclined my heart to perform Thy statutes

Forever, *even* to the end.

Samekh.

113 I hate those who are double-minded,

But I love Thy law.

114 Thou art my hiding place and my shield;

I wait for Thy word.

115 Depart from me, evildoers,

That I may observe the commandments of my God.

116 Sustain me according to Thy word, that I may live;

And do not let me be ashamed of my hope.

117 Uphold me that I may be safe,

That I may have regard for Thy statutes continually.

118 Thou hast rejected all those who wander from Thy statutes,

For their deceitfulness is useless.

119 Thou hast removed all the wicked of the earth *like* dross;

Therefore I love Thy testimonies.

120 My flesh trembles for fear of Thee,

And I am afraid of Thy judgments.

Ayin.

121 I have done justice and righteousness;

Do not leave me to my oppressors.

122 Be surety for Thy servant for good;

Do not let the arrogant oppress me.

123 My eyes fail *with longing* for Thy salvation,

And for Thy righteous word.

124 Deal with Thy servant according to Thy lovingkindness,

And teach me Thy statutes.

125 I am Thy servant; give me understanding,

That I may know Thy testimonies.

126 It is time for the LORD to act,

For they have broken Thy law.

127 Therefore I love Thy commandments

Above gold, yes, above fine gold.

128 Therefore I esteem right all *Thy* precepts concerning everything,

I hate every false way.

Pe.

129 Thy testimonies are wonderful;

Therefore my soul observes them.

130 The unfolding of Thy words gives light;

It gives understanding to the simple.

131 I opened my mouth wide and panted,

For I longed for Thy commandments.

132 Turn to me and be gracious to me,

After Thy manner with those who love Thy name.

133 Establish my footsteps in Thy word,

And do not let any iniquity have dominion over me.

134 Redeem me from the oppression of man,

That I may keep Thy precepts.

135 Make Thy face shine upon Thy servant,

And teach me Thy statutes.

136 My eyes shed streams of water,

Because they do not keep Thy law.

Tsadhe.

137 Righteous art Thou, O LORD,

And upright are Thy judgments.

138 Thou hast commanded Thy testimonies in righteousness
And exceeding faithfulness.

139 My zeal has consumed me,
Because my adversaries have forgotten Thy words.

140 Thy word is very pure,
Therefore Thy servant loves it.

141 I am small and despised,
Yet I do not forget Thy precepts.

142 Thy righteousness is an everlasting righteousness,
And Thy law is truth.

143 Trouble and anguish have come upon me;
Yet Thy commandments are my delight.

144 Thy testimonies are righteous forever;
Give me understanding that I may live.

Qoph.

145 I cried with all my heart; answer me, O LORD!
I will observe Thy statutes.

146 I cried to Thee; save me,
And I shall keep Thy testimonies.

147 I rise before dawn and cry for help;
I wait for Thy words.

148 My eyes anticipate the night watches,
That I may meditate on Thy word.

149 Hear my voice according to Thy lovingkindness;
Revive me, O LORD, according to Thine ordinances.

150 Those who follow after wickedness draw near;
They are far from Thy law.

151 Thou art near, O LORD,
And all Thy commandments are truth.

152 Of old I have known from Thy testimonies,
That Thou hast founded them forever.

Resh.

153 Look upon my affliction and rescue me,
For I do not forget Thy law.

154 Plead my cause and redeem me;
Revive me according to Thy word.

155 Salvation is far from the wicked,
For they do not seek Thy statutes.

156 Great are Thy mercies, O LORD;
Revive me according to Thine ordinances.

157 Many are my persecutors and my adversaries,
Yet I do not turn aside from Thy testimonies.

158 I behold the treacherous and loathe them,
Because they do not keep Thy word.

159 Consider how I love Thy precepts;
Revive me, O LORD, according to Thy lovingkindness.

160 The sum of Thy word is truth,
And every one of Thy righteous ordinances is everlasting.

Shin.

161 Princes persecute me without cause,
But my heart stands in awe of Thy words.

162 I rejoice at Thy word,
As one who finds great spoil.

163 I hate and despise falsehood,
But I love Thy law.

164 Seven times a day I praise Thee,
Because of Thy righteous ordinances.

165 Those who love Thy law have great peace,

And nothing causes them to stumble.

166 I hope for Thy salvation, O LORD,

And do Thy commandments.

167 My soul keeps Thy testimonies,

And I love them exceedingly.

168 I keep Thy precepts and Thy testimonies,

For all my ways are before Thee.

Tav.

169 Let my cry come before Thee, O LORD,

Give me understanding according to Thy word.

170 Let my supplication come before Thee;

Deliver me according to Thy word.

171 Let my lips utter praise,

For Thou dost teach me Thy statutes.

172 Let my tongue sing of Thy word,

For all Thy commandments are righteousness.

173 Let Thy hand be ready to help me,

For I have chosen Thy precepts.

174 I long for Thy salvation, O LORD,

And Thy law is my delight.

175 Let my soul live that it may praise Thee,

And let Thine ordinances help me.

176 I have gone astray like a lost sheep; seek Thy servant,

For I do not forget Thy commandments.

PSALM 120

Prayer for Deliverance from the Treacherous.

A Song of Ascents.

IN my trouble I cried to the LORD, And He answered me.

2 Deliver my soul, O LORD, from lying lips,

From a deceitful tongue.

3 What shall be given to you, and what more shall be done to you,

You deceitful tongue?

4 Sharp arrows of the warrior,

With the *burning* coals of the broom tree.

5 Woe is me, for I sojourn in Meshech,

For I dwell among the tents of Kedar!

6 Too long has my soul had its dwelling

With those who hate peace.

7 I am *for* peace, but when I speak,

They are for war.

PSALM 121

The LORD the Keeper of Israel.

A Song of Ascents.

I WILL lift up my eyes to the mountains;

From whence shall my help come?

2 My help *comes* from the LORD,

Who made heaven and earth.

3 He will not allow your foot to slip;

He who keeps you will not slumber.

4 Behold, He who keeps Israel

Will neither slumber nor sleep.

5 The LORD is your keeper;

The LORD is your shade on your right hand.

6 The sun will not smite you by day,

Nor the moon by night.

7 The LORD will [201]protect you from all evil;

He will keep your soul.

---

[201] Or, *keep*

8 The LORD will [201]guard your
   going out and your coming
   in
From this time forth and forever.

PSALM 122

Prayer for the Peace of Jerusalem.

A Song of Ascents, of David.

I WAS glad when they said to me,
   "Let us go to the house of the
   LORD."
2 Our feet are standing
   Within your gates, O Jerusalem,
3 Jerusalem, that is built
   As a city that is compact together;
4 To which the tribes go up,
   even the tribes of the
   LORD—
An ordinance for Israel—
To give thanks to the name of
   the LORD.
5 For there thrones were set for
   judgment,
The thrones of the house of
   David.

6 Pray for the peace of Jerusalem:
"May they prosper who love
   you.
7 "May peace be within your
   walls,
And prosperity within your
   palaces."
8 For the sake of my brothers
   and my friends,
I will now say, "May peace be
   within you."
9 For the sake of the house of
   the LORD our God
I will seek your good.

PSALM 123

Prayer for the LORD's Help.

A Song of Ascents.

TO Thee I lift up my eyes,
   O Thou who art enthroned in
   the heavens!
2 Behold, as the eyes of servants *look* to the hand of
   their master,
As the eyes of a maid to the
   hand of her mistress;
So our eyes *look* to the LORD
   our God,
Until He shall be gracious to
   us.

3 Be gracious to us, O LORD, be
   gracious to us;
For we are greatly filled with
   contempt.
4 Our soul is greatly filled
With the scoffing of those who
   are at ease,
And with the contempt of the
   proud.

PSALM 124

Praise for Rescue from Enemies.

A Song of Ascents, of David.

"HAD it not been the LORD
   who was on our side,"
Let Israel now say,
2 "Had it not been the LORD who
   was on our side,
When men rose up against us;
3 Then they would have swallowed us alive,
When their anger was kindled
   against us;
4 Then the waters would have
   engulfed us,
The stream would have swept
   over our soul;
5 Then the raging waters would
   have swept over our soul."

6 Blessed be the LORD,
Who has not given us to be
   torn by their teeth.

[201] Or, *keep*

7 Our soul has escaped as a bird
    out of the snare of the trap-
    per;
  The snare is broken and we
    have escaped.
8 Our help is in the name of the
    LORD,
  Who made heaven and earth.

PSALM 125

The LORD Surrounds His People.

A Song of Ascents.

THOSE who trust in the LORD
  Are as Mount Zion, which
    cannot be moved, but
    abides forever.
2 As the mountains surround
    Jerusalem,
  So the LORD surrounds His
    people
  From this time forth and for-
    ever.
3 For the scepter of wickedness
    shall not rest upon the land
    of the righteous;
  That the righteous may not
    put forth their hands to do
    wrong.

4 Do good, O LORD, to those
    who are good,
  And to those who are upright
    in their hearts.
5 But as for those who turn
    aside to their crooked
    ways,
  The LORD will lead them away
    with the doers of iniquity.
  Peace be upon Israel.

PSALM 126

*Thanksgiving for Return from
    Captivity.*

A Song of Ascents.

WHEN the LORD brought back
  the captive ones of Zion,

  We were like those who
    dream.
2 Then our mouth was filled
    with laughter,
  And our tongue with joyful
    shouting;
  Then they said among the na-
    tions,
  "The LORD has done great
    things for them."
3 The LORD has done great
    things for us;
  We are glad.

4 Restore our captivity, O LORD,
  As the streams in the South.
5 Those who sow in tears shall
    reap with joyful shouting.
6 He who goes to and fro weep-
    ing, carrying *his* bag of
    seed,
  Shall indeed come again with
    a shout of joy, bringing his
    sheaves *with him.*

PSALM 127

Prosperity Comes from the LORD.

A Song of Ascents, of Solomon.

UNLESS the LORD builds the
  house,
  They labor in vain who build
    it;
  Unless the LORD guards the
    city,
  The watchman keeps awake
    in vain.
2 It is vain for you to rise up
    early,
  To retire late,
  To eat the bread of painful la-
    bors;
  For He gives to His beloved
    even in his sleep.

3 Behold, children are a gift of
    the LORD;
  The fruit of the womb is a re-
    ward.
4 Like arrows in the hand of a
    warrior,

So are the children of one's
youth.
5 How blessed is the man
whose quiver is full of
them;
They shall not be ashamed,
When they speak with their
enemies in the gate.

PSALM 128

*Blessedness of the Fear of the
Lord.*

A Song of Ascents.

HOW blessed is everyone who
fears the Lord,
Who walks in His ways.
2 When you shall eat of the
[202]fruit of your hands,
You will be happy and it will
be well with you.
3 Your wife shall be like a fruitful vine,
Within your house,
Your children like olive plants
Around your table.
4 Behold, for thus shall the man
be blessed
Who fears the Lord.

5 The Lord bless you from
Zion,
And may you see the prosperity of Jerusalem all the
days of your life.
6 Indeed, may you see your children's children.
Peace be upon Israel!

PSALM 129

*Prayer for the Overthrow of
Zion's Enemies.*

A Song of Ascents.

"MANY times they have persecuted me from my youth
up,"
Let Israel now say,

2 "Many times they have persecuted me from my youth
up;
Yet they have not prevailed
against me.
3 "The plowers plowed upon my
back;
They lengthened their furrows."
4 The Lord is righteous;
He has cut in two the cords of
the wicked.

5 May all who hate Zion,
Be put to shame and turned
backward,
6 Let them be like grass upon
the housetops,
Which withers before it grows
up;
7 With which the reaper does
not fill his hand,
Or the binder of sheaves his
bosom;
8 Nor do those who pass by say,
"The blessing of the Lord be
upon you;
We bless you in the name of
the Lord."

PSALM 130

*Hope in the Lord's Forgiving
Love.*

A Song of Ascents.

OUT of the depths I have cried
to Thee, O Lord.
2 Lord, hear my voice!
Let Thine ears be attentive
To the voice of my supplications.
3 If Thou, Lord, shouldst mark
iniquities,
O Lord, who could stand?
4 But there is forgiveness with
Thee,
That Thou mayest be feared.

5 I wait for the Lord, my soul
does wait,
And in His word do I hope.

202 Lit., *labor*

6 My soul *waits* for the Lord
   More than the watchmen for
      the morning;
   Indeed, more than the watch-
      men for the morning.

7 O Israel, hope in the LORD;
   For with the LORD there is
      lovingkindness,
   And with Him is abundant re-
      demption.

8 And He will redeem Israel
   From all his iniquities.

PSALM 131

Childlike Trust in the LORD.

A Song of Ascents, of David.

O LORD, my heart is not proud,
   nor my eyes haughty;
   Nor do I involve myself in
      great matters,
   Or in things too difficult for
      me.

2 Surely I have composed and
   quieted my soul;
   Like a weaned child *rests*
      against his mother,
   My soul is like a weaned child
      within me.

3 O Israel, hope in the LORD
   From this time forth and for-
      ever.

PSALM 132

*Prayer for the LORD's Blessing
upon the Sanctuary.*

A Song of Ascents.

REMEMBER, O LORD, on David's
   behalf,
   All his affliction;

2 How he swore to the LORD,
   And vowed to the Mighty One
      of Jacob,

3 "Surely I will not enter my
   house,
   Nor lie on my bed;

4 I will not give sleep to my
   eyes,
   Or slumber to my eyelids;

5 Until I find a place for the
   LORD,
   A dwelling place for the
      Mighty One of Jacob."

6 Behold, we heard of it in Eph-
   rathah;
   We found it in the field of
      Jaar.

7 Let us go into His dwelling
   place;
   Let us worship at His foot-
      stool.

8 Arise, O LORD, to Thy resting
   place;
   Thou and the ark of Thy
      strength.

9 Let Thy priests be clothed
   with righteousness;
   And let Thy godly ones sing
      for joy.

10 For the sake of David Thy servant,
   Do not turn away the face of
      Thine anointed.

11 The LORD has sworn to David,
   A truth from which He will
      not turn back;
   "Of the fruit of your body I will
      set upon your throne.

12 "If your sons will keep My cov-
   enant,
   And My testimony which I
      will teach them,
   Their sons also shall sit upon
      your throne forever."

13 For the LORD has chosen Zion;
   He has desired it for His habi-
      tation.

14 "This is My resting place forever;
   Here I will dwell, for I have
      desired it.

15 "I will abundantly bless her
   provision;
   I will satisfy her needy with
      bread.

16 "Her priests also I will clothe
   with salvation;
   And her godly ones will sing
      aloud for joy.

17"There I will cause the horn of
David to spring forth;
I have prepared a lamp for
Mine anointed.

18"His enemies I will clothe with
shame;
But upon himself his crown
shall shine."

PSALM 133

*The Excellency of Brotherly
Unity.*

A Song of Ascents, of David.

BEHOLD, how good and how
pleasant it is
For brothers to dwell together
in unity!

2 It is like the precious oil upon
the head,
Coming down upon the beard,
Even Aaron's beard,
Coming down upon the edge
of his robes.

3 It is like the dew of Hermon,
Coming down upon the mountains of Zion;
For there the LORD com-
manded the blessing—life
forever.

PSALM 134

Greetings of Night Watchers.

A Song of Ascents.

BEHOLD, bless the LORD, all servants of the LORD,
Who serve by night in the
house of the LORD!

2 Lift up your hands to the sanctuary,
And bless the LORD.

3 May the LORD bless you from
Zion,
He who made heaven and
earth.

PSALM 135

*Praise the LORD's Wonderful
Works. Vanity of Idols.*

PRAISE the LORD!
Praise the name of the LORD;
Praise Him, O servants of the
LORD,

2 You who stand in the house of
the LORD,
In the courts of the house of
our God!

3 Praise the LORD, for the LORD
is good;
Sing praises to His name, for
it is lovely.

4 For the LORD has chosen Jacob for Himself,
Israel for His own possession.

5 For I know that the LORD is
great,
And that our Lord is above all
gods.

6 Whatever the LORD pleases,
He does,
In heaven and in earth, in the
seas and in all deeps.

7 He causes the vapors to ascend from the ends of the
earth;
Who makes lightnings for the
rain;
Who brings forth the wind
from His treasuries.

8 He smote the first-born of
Egypt,
Both of man and beast.

9 He sent signs and wonders
into your midst, O Egypt,
Upon Pharaoh and all his servants.

10 He smote many nations,
And slew mighty kings,

11 Sihon, king of the Amorites,
And Og, king of Bashan,
And all the kingdoms of Ca-
naan,

12 And He gave their land as a
heritage,

A heritage to Israel His people.

13 Thy name, O Lord, is everlasting,

Thy remembrance, O Lord, throughout all generations.

14 For the Lord will judge His people,

And will have compassion on His servants.

15 The idols of the nations are *but* silver and gold,

The work of man's hands.

16 They have mouths, but they do not speak;

They have eyes, but they do not see;

17 They have ears, but they do not hear;

Nor is there any breath at all in their mouths.

18 Those who make them will be like them,

Yes, everyone who trusts in them.

19 O house of Israel, bless the Lord;

O house of Aaron, bless the Lord;

20 O house of Levi, bless the Lord;

You who [203]revere the Lord, bless the Lord.

21 Blessed be the Lord from Zion,

Who dwells in Jerusalem.

Praise the Lord!

PSALM 136

Thanks for the Lord's Goodness to Israel.

GIVE thanks to the Lord, for He is good;

For His lovingkindness is everlasting.

2 Give thanks to the God of gods,

For His lovingkindness is everlasting.

3 Give thanks to the Lord of lords,

For His lovingkindness is everlasting.

4 To Him who alone does great wonders,

For His lovingkindness is everlasting;

5 To Him who made the heavens with skill,

For His lovingkindness is everlasting;

6 To Him who spread out the earth above the waters,

For His lovingkindness is everlasting;

7 To Him who made *the* great lights,

For His lovingkindness is everlasting:

8 The sun to rule by day,

For His lovingkindness is everlasting,

9 The moon and stars to rule by night,

For His lovingkindness is everlasting.

10 To Him who smote the Egyptians in their first-born,

For His lovingkindness is everlasting,

11 And brought Israel out from their midst,

For His lovingkindness is everlasting,

12 With a strong hand and an outstretched arm,

For His lovingkindness is everlasting;

13 To Him who divided the Red Sea asunder,

For His lovingkindness is everlasting,

14 And made Israel pass through the midst of it,

For His lovingkindness is everlasting;

15 But He overthrew Pharaoh and his army in the Red Sea,

[203] Or, *fear*

For His lovingkindness is everlasting.

16 To Him who led His people through the wilderness,
For His lovingkindness is everlasting;

17 To Him who smote great kings,
For His lovingkindness is everlasting,

18 And slew mighty kings,
For His lovingkindness is everlasting,

19 Sihon, king of the Amorites,
For His lovingkindness is everlasting,

20 And Og, king of Bashan,
For His lovingkindness is everlasting,

21 And gave their land as a heritage,
For His lovingkindness is everlasting,

22 Even a heritage to Israel His servant,
For His lovingkindness is everlasting.

23 Who remembered us in our low estate,
For His lovingkindness is everlasting,

24 And has rescued us from our adversaries,
For His lovingkindness is everlasting,

25 Who gives food to all flesh,
For His lovingkindness is everlasting.

26 Give thanks to the God of heaven,
For His lovingkindness is everlasting.

PSALM 137

An Experience of the Captivity.

BY the rivers of Babylon,
There we sat down and wept,
When we remembered Zion.

2 Upon the willows in the midst of it

We hung our harps.

3 For there our captors demanded of us songs,
And our tormentors mirth, *saying,*
"Sing us one of the songs of Zion."

4 How can we sing the LORD's song
In a foreign land?

5 If I forget you, O Jerusalem,
May my right hand forget *her skill.*

6 May my tongue cleave to the roof of my mouth,
If I do not remember you,
If I do not exalt Jerusalem
Above my chief joy.

7 Remember, O LORD, against the sons of Edom
The day of Jerusalem,
Who said, "Raze it, raze it,
To its very foundation."

8 O daughter of Babylon, you devastated one,
How blessed will be the one who repays you
With the recompense with which you have repaid us.

9 How blessed will be the one who seizes and dashes your little ones
Against the rock.

PSALM 138

Thanksgiving for the LORD's Favor.

A Psalm of David.

I WILL give Thee thanks with all my heart;
I will sing praises to Thee before the gods.

2 I will bow down toward Thy holy temple,
And give thanks to Thy name for Thy lovingkindness and Thy truth;

For Thou hast magnified Thy
   word according to all Thy
   name.
3 On the day I called Thou didst
   answer me;
   Thou didst make me bold with
   strength in my soul.

4 All the kings of the earth will
   give thanks to Thee, O
   LORD,
   When they have heard the
   words of Thy mouth.
5 And they will sing of the ways
   of the LORD,
   For great is the glory of the
   LORD.
6 For though the LORD is exalted,
   Yet He regards the lowly;
   But the haughty He knows
   from afar.

7 Though I walk in the midst of
   trouble, Thou wilt revive
   me;
   Thou wilt stretch forth Thy
   hand against the wrath of
   my enemies,
   And Thy right hand will save
   me.
8 The LORD will accomplish
   what concerns me;
   Thy lovingkindness, O LORD,
   is everlasting;
   Do not forsake the works of
   Thy hands.

PSALM 139

*God's Omnipresence and
Omniscience.*

For the choir director. A
Psalm of David.

O LORD, Thou hast searched me
   and known *me*.
2 Thou dost know when I sit
   down and when I rise up;
   Thou dost understand my
   thought from afar.
3 Thou dost scrutinize my path
   and my lying down,

And art intimately acquainted
   with all my ways.
4 Even before there is a word on
   my tongue,
   Behold, O LORD, Thou dost
   know it all.
5 Thou hast enclosed me behind
   and before,
   And laid Thy hand upon me.
6 *Such* knowledge is too wonderful for me;
   It is *too* high, I cannot attain
   to it.

7 Where can I go from Thy
   Spirit?
   Or where can I flee from Thy
   presence?
8 If I ascend to heaven, Thou art
   there;
   If I make my bed in Sheol, behold, Thou art there.
9 If I take the wings of the
   dawn,
   If I dwell in the remotest part
   of the sea,
10 Even there Thy hand will lead
   me,
   And Thy right hand will lay
   hold of me.
11 If I say, "Surely the darkness
   will overwhelm me,
   And the light around me will
   be night,"
12 Even the darkness is not dark
   to Thee,
   And the night is as bright as
   the day.
   Darkness and light are alike *to
   Thee.*

13 For Thou didst form my inward parts;
   Thou didst weave me in my
   mother's womb.
14 I will give thanks to Thee, for
   [204]I am fearfully and won-
   derfully made;
   Wonderful are Thy works,

---

[204] Some ancient versions read *Thou art
fearfully wonderful*

And my soul knows it very well.

15 My frame was not hidden from Thee,
When I was made in secret,
And skillfully wrought in the depths of the earth.

16 Thine eyes have seen my unformed substance;
And in Thy book they were all written,
The days that were ordained *for me,*
When as yet there was not one of them.

17 How precious also are Thy thoughts to me, O God!
How vast is the sum of them!

18 If I should count them, they would outnumber the sand.
When I awake, I am still with Thee.

19 O that Thou wouldst slay the wicked, O God;
Depart from me, therefore, men of bloodshed.

20 For they speak against Thee wickedly,
And Thine enemies take *Thy name* in vain.

21 Do I not hate those who hate Thee, O LORD?
And do I not loathe those who rise up against Thee?

22 I hate them with the utmost hatred;
They have become my enemies.

23 Search me, O God, and know my heart;
Try me and know my anxious thoughts;

24 And see if there be any hurtful way in me,
And lead me in the everlasting way.

205 Lit., *push violently*

PSALM 140

Prayer for Protection against the Wicked.

For the choir director. A
Psalm of David.

RESCUE me, O LORD, from evil men;
Preserve me from violent men,

2 Who devise evil things in *their* hearts;
They continually stir up wars.

3 They sharpen their tongues as a serpent;
Poison of a viper is under their lips.   [Selah.

4 Keep me, O LORD, from the hands of the wicked;
Preserve me from violent men,
Who have purposed to 205trip up my feet.

5 The proud have hidden a trap for me, and cords;
They have spread a net by the wayside;
They have set snares for me.   [Selah.

6 I said to the LORD, "Thou art my God;
Give ear, O LORD, to the voice of my supplications.

7 "O GOD the Lord, the strength of my salvation,
Thou hast covered my head in the day of battle.

8 "Do not grant, O LORD, the desires of the wicked;
Do not promote his *evil* device, *lest* they be exalted.   [Selah.

9 "As for the head of those who surround me,
May the mischief of their lips cover them.

10 "May burning coals fall upon them;

May they be cast into the fire,
Into deep pits from which
they cannot rise.
11 "May a slanderer not be established in the earth;
May evil hunt the violent man
[206]speedily."

12 I know that the LORD will
maintain the cause of the
afflicted,
And justice for the poor.
13 Surely the righteous will give
thanks to Thy name;
The upright will dwell in Thy
presence.

PSALM 141

*An Evening Prayer for
Sanctification and Protection.*

A Psalm of David.

O LORD, I call upon Thee; hasten to me!
Give ear to my voice when I
call to Thee!
2 May my prayer be counted as
incense before Thee;
The lifting up of my hands as
the evening offering.
3 Set a guard, O LORD, over my
mouth;
Keep watch over the door of
my lips.
4 Do not incline my heart to any
evil thing,
To practice deeds of wickedness
With men who do iniquity;
And do not let me eat of their
delicacies.

5 Let the righteous smite me in
kindness and reprove me;
It is oil upon the head;
Do not let my head refuse it,
For still my prayer is against
their wicked deeds.
6 Their judges are thrown down
by the sides of the rock,
And they hear my words, for
they are pleasant.

7 As when one plows and
breaks open the earth,
Our bones have been scat-
tered at the mouth of
Sheol.

8 For my eyes are toward Thee,
O GOD, the Lord;
In Thee I take refuge; do not
leave me defenseless.
9 Keep me from the jaws of the
trap which they have set
for me,
And from the snares of those
who do iniquity.
10 Let the wicked fall into their
own nets,
While I pass by safely.

PSALM 142

Prayer for Help in Trouble.

Maskil of David, when he was
in the cave. A Prayer.

I CRY aloud with my voice to the
LORD;
I make supplication with my
voice to the LORD.
2 I pour out my complaint be-
fore Him;
I declare my trouble before
Him.
3 When my spirit was over-
whelmed within me,
Thou didst know my path.
In the way where I walk
They have hidden a trap for
me.
4 Look to the right and see;
For there is no one who re-
gards me;
There is no escape for me;
No one cares for my soul.

5 I cried out to Thee, O LORD;
I said, "Thou art my refuge,
My portion in the land of the
living.
6 "Give heed to my cry,
For I am brought very low;

[206] Lit., *thrust upon thrust*

Deliver me from my persecutors,
For they are too strong for me.

7 "Bring my soul out of prison,
So that I may give thanks to Thy name;
The righteous will surround me,
For Thou wilt deal bountifully with me."

PSALM 143

Prayer for Deliverance and Guidance.

A Psalm of David.

HEAR my prayer, O Lord,
Give ear to my supplications!
Answer me in Thy faithfulness, in Thy righteousness!

2 And do not enter into judgment with Thy servant,
For in Thy sight no man living is righteous.

3 For the enemy has persecuted my soul;
He has crushed my life to the ground;
He has made me dwell in dark places, like those who have long been dead.

4 Therefore my spirit is overwhelmed within me;
My heart is [207]appalled within me.

5 I remember the days of old;
I meditate on all Thy doings;
I muse on the work of Thy hands.

6 I stretch out my hands to Thee;
My soul *longs* for Thee, as a parched land.   [Selah.

7 Answer me quickly, O Lord, my spirit fails;
Do not hide Thy face from me,

Lest I become like those who go down to the pit.

8 Let me hear Thy lovingkindness in the morning;
For I trust in Thee;
Teach me the way in which I should walk;
For to Thee I lift up my soul.

9 Deliver me, O Lord, from my enemies;
I take refuge in Thee.

10 Teach me to do Thy will,
For Thou art my God;
Let Thy good Spirit lead me on level ground.

11 For the sake of Thy name, O Lord, revive me.
In Thy righteousness bring my soul out of trouble.

12 And in Thy lovingkindness cut off my enemies,
And destroy all those who afflict my soul;
For I am Thy servant.

PSALM 144

Prayer for Rescue and Prosperity.

A Psalm of David.

BLESSED be the Lord, my rock,
Who trains my hands for war,
And my fingers for battle;

2 My lovingkindness and my fortress,
My stronghold and my deliverer;
My shield and He in whom I take refuge;
Who subdues my people under me.

3 O Lord, what is man, that Thou dost take knowledge of him?
Or the son of man, that Thou dost think of him?

4 Man is like a mere breath;
His days are like a passing shadow.

207 Or, desolate

5 Bow Thy heavens, O LORD,
    and come down;
  Touch the mountains, that
    they may smoke.
6 Flash forth lightning and scat-
    ter them;
  Send out Thine arrows and
    confuse them.
7 Stretch forth Thy hand from
    on high;
  Rescue me and deliver me out
    of great waters,
  Out of the hand of aliens
8 Whose mouths speak deceit,
  And whose right hand is a
    right hand of falsehood.

9 I will sing a new song to Thee,
    O God;
  Upon a harp of ten strings I
    will sing praises to Thee.
10 Who dost give salvation to
    kings;
  Who dost rescue David His
    servant from the evil
    sword.
11 Rescue me, and deliver me
    out of the hand of aliens,
  Whose mouth speaks deceit,
  And whose right hand is a
    right hand of falsehood.

12 Let our sons in their youth be
    as grown-up plants,
  And our daughters as corner
    pillars fashioned as for a
    palace;
13 Let our garners be full, fur-
    nishing every kind of pro-
    duce,
  And our flocks bring forth
    thousands and ten thou-
    sands in our fields;
14 Let our cattle bear,
  Without mishap and without
    loss,
  Let there be no outcry in our
    streets!
15 How blessed are the people
    who are so situated;
  How blessed are the people
    whose God is the LORD!

PSALM 145

*The LORD Extolled for His
    Goodness.*

A Psalm of Praise, of David.

I WILL extol Thee, my God, O
    King;
  And I will bless Thy name for-
    ever and ever.
2 Every day I will bless Thee,
  And I will praise Thy name
    forever and ever.
3 Great is the LORD, and highly
    to be praised;
  And His greatness is un-
    searchable.
4 One generation shall praise
    Thy works to another,
  And shall declare Thy mighty
    acts.
5 On the glorious splendor of
    Thy majesty,
  And on Thy wonderful works,
    I will meditate.
6 And men shall speak of the
    power of Thine awesome
    acts;
  And I will tell of Thy great-
    ness.
7 They shall eagerly utter the
    memory of Thine abundant
    goodness,
  And shall shout joyfully of
    Thy righteousness.

8 The LORD is gracious and mer-
    ciful;
  Slow to anger and great in
    lovingkindness.
9 The LORD is good to all,
  And His mercies are over all
    His works.
10 All Thy works shall give
    thanks to Thee, O LORD,
  And Thy godly ones shall
    bless Thee.
11 They shall speak of the glory
    of Thy kingdom,
  And talk of Thy power;
12 To make known to the sons of
    men Thy mighty acts,

And the glory of the majesty of Thy kingdom.

13 Thy kingdom is an everlasting kingdom,
And Thy dominion *endures* throughout all generations.

14 The LORD sustains all who fall,
And raises up all who are bowed down.

15 The eyes of all look to Thee,
And Thou dost give them their food in due time.

16 Thou dost open Thy hand,
And dost satisfy the desire of every living thing.

17 The LORD is righteous in all His ways,
And kind in all His deeds.

18 The LORD is near to all who call upon Him,
To all who call upon Him in truth.

19 He will fulfill the desire of those who fear Him;
He will also hear their cry and will save them.

20 The LORD keeps all who love Him;
But all the wicked, He will destroy.

21 My mouth will speak the praise of the LORD;
And all flesh will bless His holy name forever and ever.

PSALM 146

The LORD an Abundant Helper.

PRAISE the LORD!
Praise the LORD, O my soul!

2 I will praise the LORD while I live;
I will sing praises to my God while I have my being.

3 Do not trust in princes,
In mortal man, in whom there is no salvation.

4 His spirit departs, he returns to the earth;
In that very day his thoughts perish.

5 How blessed is he whose help is the God of Jacob,
Whose hope is in the LORD his God;

6 Who made heaven and earth,
The sea and all that is in them;
Who keeps faith forever;

7 Who executes justice for the oppressed;
Who gives food to the hungry.
The LORD sets the prisoners free.

8 The LORD opens *the eyes of* the blind;
The LORD raises up those who are bowed down;
The LORD loves the righteous;

9 The LORD protects the strangers;
He supports the fatherless and the widow;
But He thwarts the way of the wicked.

10 The LORD will reign forever,
Thy God, O Zion, to all generations.
Praise the LORD!

PSALM 147

Praise for Jerusalem's Restoration and Prosperity.

PRAISE the LORD!
For it is good to sing praises to our God;
For [208]it is pleasant *and* praise is becoming.

2 The LORD builds up Jerusalem;
He gathers the outcasts of Israel.

3 He heals the brokenhearted,
And binds up their [209]wounds.

4 He counts the number of the stars;
He gives names to all of them.

206 Or, *He is gracious*   209 Lit., *sorrows*

5 Great is our Lord, and abundant in strength;
His understanding is infinite.

6 The LORD [210]supports the afflicted;
He brings down the wicked to the ground.

7 Sing to the LORD with thanksgiving;
Sing praises to our God on the lyre,

8 Who covers the heavens with clouds,
Who provides rain for the earth,
Who makes grass to grow on the mountains.

9 He gives to the beast its food,
And to the young ravens which cry.

10 He does not delight in the strength of the horse;
He does not take pleasure in the legs of a man.

11 The LORD favors those who fear Him,
Those who wait for His lovingkindness.

12 Praise the LORD, O Jerusalem!
Praise your God, O Zion!

13 For He has strengthened the bars of your gates;
He has blessed your sons within you.

14 He makes peace in your borders;
He satisfies you with the finest of the wheat.

15 He sends forth His command to the earth;
His word runs very swiftly.

16 He gives snow like wool;
He scatters the frost like ashes.

17 He casts forth His ice as fragments;
Who can stand before His cold?

18 He sends forth His word and melts them;

He causes His wind to blow and the waters to flow.

19 He declares His words to Jacob,
His statutes and His ordinances to Israel.

20 He has not dealt thus with any nation;
And as for His ordinances, they have not known them.
Praise the LORD!

PSALM 148

The Whole Creation Invoked to Praise the LORD.

PRAISE the LORD!
Praise the LORD from the heavens;
Praise Him in the heights!

2 Praise Him, all His angels;
Praise Him, all His hosts!

3 Praise Him, sun and moon;
Praise Him, all stars of light!

4 Praise Him, highest heavens,
And the waters that are above the heavens!

5 Let them praise the name of the LORD,
For He commanded and they were created.

6 He has also established them forever and ever;
He has made a decree which will not pass away.

7 Praise the LORD from the earth,
Sea monsters and all deeps;

8 Fire and hail, snow and clouds;
Stormy wind, fulfilling His word;

9 Mountains and all hills;
Fruit trees and all cedars;

10 Beasts and all cattle;
Creeping things and winged fowl;

11 Kings of the earth and all peoples;

210 Or, *relieves*

Princes and all judges of the
earth;
12 Both young men and virgins;
Old men and children.

13 Let them praise the name of
the LORD,
For His name alone is exalted;
His glory is above earth and
heaven.

14 And He has lifted up a horn
for His people,
Praise for all His godly ones;
Even for the sons of Israel, a
people near to Him.
Praise the LORD!

PSALM 149

*Israel Invoked to Praise the
LORD.*

PRAISE the LORD!
Sing to the LORD a new song,
And His praise in the congregation of the godly ones.
2 Let Israel be glad in his Maker;
Let the sons of Zion rejoice in
their King.
3 Let them praise His name
with dancing;
Let them sing praises to Him
with timbrel and lyre.
4 For the LORD takes pleasure in
His people;
He will beautify the afflicted
ones with salvation.

5 Let the godly ones exult in
glory;
Let them sing for joy on their
beds.
6 *Let* the high praises of God *be*
in their mouth,

And a two-edged sword in
their hand,
7 To execute vengeance on the
nations,
And punishment on the peoples;
8 To bind their kings with
chains,
And their nobles with fetters
of iron;
9 To execute on them the judgment written;
This is an honor for all His
godly ones.
Praise the LORD!

PSALM 150

A Psalm of Praise.

PRAISE the LORD!
Praise God in His sanctuary;
Praise Him in His mighty expanse.
2 Praise Him for His mighty
deeds;
Praise Him according to His
excellent greatness.

3 Praise Him with trumpet
sound;
Praise Him with harp and
lyre.
4 Praise Him with timbrel and
dancing;
Praise Him with stringed instruments and pipe.
5 Praise Him with loud cymbals;
Praise Him with resounding
cymbals.
6 Let everything that has breath
praise the LORD.
Praise the LORD!

THE PROVERBS

CHAPTER 1

THE proverbs of Solomon the son of David, king of Israel:

2 To know wisdom and instruction,

To discern the sayings of understanding,

3 To receive instruction in wise behavior,

Righteousness, justice and equity;

4 To give prudence to the naive,

To the youth knowledge and discretion,

5 A wise man will hear and increase in learning,

And a man of understanding will acquire wise counsel,

6 To understand a proverb and a figure,

The words of the wise and their riddles.

7 The fear of the LORD is the beginning of knowledge;

Fools despise wisdom and instruction.

8 Hear, my son, your father's instruction,

And do not forsake your mother's teaching;

9 Indeed, they are a graceful wreath to your head,

And ornaments about your neck.

10 My son, if sinners entice you,

Do not consent.

11 If they say, "Come with us,

Let us lie in wait for blood,

Let us ambush the innocent without cause;

12 Let us swallow them alive like Sheol,

Even whole, as those who go down to the pit;

13 We shall find all *kinds* of precious wealth,

We shall fill our houses with spoil;

14 Throw in your lot with us,

We shall all have one purse,"

15 My son, do not walk in the way with them.

Keep your feet from their path;

16 For their feet run to evil,

And they hasten to shed blood.

17 Indeed, it is useless to spread the net

In the eyes of any bird;

18 But they lie in wait for their own blood;

They ambush their own lives.

19 So are the ways of everyone who gains by violence;

It takes away the life of its possessors.

20 Wisdom shouts in the street,

She lifts her voice in the square;

21 At the head of the noisy *streets* she cries out;

At the entrance of the gates in the city, she utters her sayings:

22 "How long, O naive ones, will you love simplicity?

And scoffers delight themselves in scoffing,

And fools hate knowledge?

23 "Turn to my reproof,

Behold, I will pour out my spirit on you;

I will make my words known to you.

24 Because I called, and you refused;

I stretched out my hand, and no one paid attention;

25 And you neglected all my
counsel,
And did not want my reproof;
26 I will even laugh at your calamity;
I will mock when your dread
comes,
27 When your dread comes like a
storm,
And your calamity comes on
like a whirlwind,
When distress *and* anguish
come on you,
28 "Then they will call on me, but
I will not answer;
They will seek me diligently,
but they shall not find me,
29 Because they hated knowledge,
And did not choose the fear of
the LORD.
30 "They would not accept my
counsel,
They spurned all my reproof.
31 "So they shall eat of the fruit
of their own way,
And be satiated with their
own devices.
32 "For the waywardness of the
naive shall kill them,
And the complacency of fools
shall destroy them.
33 "But he who listens to me shall
live securely,
And shall be at ease from the
dread of evil."

CHAPTER 2

M Y son, if you will receive my
sayings,
And treasure my command-
ments within you,
2 Make your ear attentive to
wisdom,
Incline your heart to understanding;
3 For if you cry for discernment,

Lift your voice for understanding;
4 If you seek her as silver,
And search for her as for
hidden treasures;
5 Then you will discern the fear
of the LORD,
And discover the knowledge
of God.
6 For the LORD gives wisdom;
From His mouth *come* knowledge and understanding.
7 He stores up sound wisdom
for the upright;
He is a shield to those who
walk in integrity,
8 Guarding the paths of justice,
And He preserves the way of
His godly ones.
9 Then you will discern righteousness and justice
And equity *and* every good
course.
10 For wisdom will enter your
heart,
And knowledge will be pleasant to your soul;
11 Discretion will guard you,
Understanding will watch
over you,
12 To deliver you from the way
of evil,
From the man who speaks
perverse things;
13 From those who leave the
paths of uprightness,
To walk in the ways of darkness;
14 Who delight in doing evil,
And rejoice in the perversity
of evil;
15 Whose paths are crooked,
And who are devious in their
ways;
16 To deliver you from the
strange woman,
From the adulteress who flatters with her words;

17 That leaves the companion of
    her youth,
    And forgets the covenant of
    her God;
18 For her house sinks down to
    death,
    And her tracks *lead* to the
    dead;
19 None who go to her return
    again,
    Nor do they reach the paths
    of life.
20 So you will walk in the way of
    good men,
    And keep to the paths of the
    righteous.
21 For the upright will live in
    the land,
    And the blameless will re-
    main in it;
22 But the wicked will be cut off
    from the land,
    And the treacherous will be
    uprooted from it.

CHAPTER 3

MY son, do not forget my
    teaching,
    But let your heart keep my
    commandments;
2 For length of days and years
    of life,
    And peace they will add to
    you.
3 Do not let kindness and truth
    leave you;
    Bind them around your neck,
    Write them on the tablet of
    your heart.
4 So you will find favor and
    good repute
    In the sight of God and man.
5 Trust in the LORD with all
    your heart,
    And do not lean on your own
    understanding.
6 In all your ways acknowledge
    Him,

And He will make your paths
    straight.
7 Do not be wise in your own
    eyes;
    Fear the LORD and turn away
    from evil.
8 It will be healing to your
    body,
    And refreshment to your
    bones.
9 Honor the LORD from your
    wealth,
    And from the first of all your
    produce;
10 So your barns will be filled
    with plenty,
    And your vats will overflow
    with new wine.
11 My son, do not reject the dis-
    cipline of the LORD,
    Or loathe His reproof,
12 For whom the LORD loves He
    reproves,
    Even as a father, the son in
    whom he delights.

13 How blessed is the man who
    finds wisdom,
    And the man who gains un-
    derstanding.
14 For its profit is better than
    the profit of silver,
    And its gain than fine gold.
15 She is more precious than
    jewels;
    And nothing you desire com-
    pares with her.
16 Long life is in her right hand;
    In her left hand are riches
    and honor.
17 Her ways are pleasant ways,
    And all her paths are peace.
18 She is a tree of life to those
    who take hold of her,
    And happy are all who hold
    her fast.
19 The LORD by wisdom founded
    the earth;
    By understanding He estab-
    lished the heavens.

20 By His knowledge the deeps were broken up,
And the skies drip with dew.

21 My son, let them not depart from your sight;
Keep sound wisdom and discretion,

22 So they will be life to your soul,
And adornment to your neck.

23 Then you will walk in your way securely,
And your foot will not stumble.

24 When you lie down, you will not be afraid;
When you lie down, your sleep will be sweet.

25 Do not be afraid of sudden fear,
Nor of the onslaught of the wicked when it comes;

26 For the LORD will be your confidence,
And will keep your foot from being caught.

27 Do not withhold good from those to whom it is due,
When it is in your power to do *it*.

28 Do not say to your neighbor, "Go, and come back,
And tomorrow I will give *it*," When you have it with you.

29 Do not devise harm against your neighbor,
While he lives in security beside you.

30 Do not contend with a man without cause,
If he has done you no harm.

31 Do not envy a man of violence,
And do not choose any of his ways.

32 For the crooked *man* is an abomination to the LORD;
But He is intimate with the upright.

33 The curse of the LORD is on the house of the wicked,
But He blesses the dwelling of the righteous.

34 Though He scoffs at the scoffers,
Yet He gives grace to the afflicted.

35 The wise will inherit honor,
But fools display dishonor.

CHAPTER 4

HEAR, O sons, the instruction of a father,
And give attention that you may gain understanding,

2 For I give you sound teaching;
Do not abandon my instruction.

3 When I was a son to my father,
Tender and the only son in the sight of my mother,

4 Then he taught me and said to me,
"Let your heart hold fast my words;
Keep my commandments and live;

5 Acquire wisdom! Acquire understanding!
Do not forget, nor turn away from the words of my mouth.

6 "Do not forsake her, and she will guard you;
Love her, and she will watch over you.

7 "The beginning of wisdom *is:* Acquire wisdom;
And with all your acquiring, get understanding.

8 "Prize her, and she will exalt you;
She will honor you if you embrace her.

9 "She will place on your head a garland of grace;

She will present you with a crown of beauty."

10 Hear, my son, and accept my sayings,
And the years of your life will be many.

11 I have directed you in the way of wisdom;
I have led you in upright paths.

12 When you walk, your steps will not be impeded;
And if you run, you will not stumble.

13 Take hold of instruction; do not let go.
Guard her, for she is your life.

14 Do not enter the path of the wicked,
And do not proceed in the way of evil men.

15 Avoid it, do not pass by it;
Turn away from it and pass on.

16 For they cannot sleep unless they do evil;
And they are robbed of sleep unless they make *someone* stumble.

17 For they eat the bread of wickedness,
And drink the wine of violence.

18 But the path of the righteous is like the light of dawn,
That shines brighter and brighter until the full day.

19 The way of the wicked is like darkness;
They do not know over what they stumble.

20 My son, give attention to my words;
Incline your ear to my sayings.

21 Do not let them depart from your sight;
Keep them in the midst of your heart.

22 For they are life to those who find them,
And health to all their whole body.

23 Watch over your heart with all diligence,
For from it *flow* the springs of life.

24 Put away from you a deceitful mouth,
And put devious lips far from you.

25 Let your eyes look directly ahead,
And let your gaze be fixed straight in front of you.

26 Watch the path of your feet,
And all your ways will be established.

27 Do not turn to the right nor to the left;
Turn your foot from evil.

CHAPTER 5

MY son, give attention to my wisdom,
Incline your ear to my understanding;

2 That you may observe discretion,
And your lips may reserve knowledge.

3 For the lips of an adulteress drip honey,
And smoother than oil is her speech;

4 But in the end she is bitter as wormwood,
Sharp as a two-edged sword.

5 Her feet go down to death,
Her steps lay hold of Sheol.

6 She does not ponder the path of life;
Her ways are unstable, she does not know *it.*

7 Now then, *my* sons, listen to me,
And do not depart from the words of my mouth.

8 Keep your way far from her,
   And do not go near the door of
      her house,
9 Lest you give your vigor to
      others,
   And your years to the cruel
      one;
10 Lest strangers be filled with
      your strength,
   And your hard-earned goods
      go to the house of an alien;
11 And you groan at your latter
      end,
   When your flesh and your
      body are consumed;
12 And you say, "How I have
      hated instruction!
   And my heart spurned re-
      proof!
13 "And I have not listened to the
      voice of my teachers,
   Nor inclined my ear to my
      instructors!
14 "I was almost in utter ruin
   In the midst of the assembly
      and congregation."

15 Drink water from your own
      cistern,
   And fresh water from your
      own well.
16 Should your springs be dis-
      persed abroad,
   Streams of water in the
      streets?
17 Let them be yours alone,
   And not for strangers with
      you.
18 Let your fountain be blessed,
   And rejoice in the wife of
      your youth.
19 *As* a loving hind and a grace-
      ful doe,
   Let her breasts satisfy you at
      all times;
   Be exhilarated always with
      her love.
20 For why should you, my son,
      be exhilarated with an
      adulteress,

   And embrace the bosom of a
      foreigner?
21 For the ways of a man are
      before the eyes of the
      LORD,
   And He watches all his paths.
22 His own iniquities will cap-
      ture the wicked,
   And he will be held with the
      cords of his sin.
23 He will die for lack of instruc-
      tion,
   And in the greatness of his
      folly he will go astray.

CHAPTER 6

MY son, if you have become
   surety for your neighbor,
   Have given a pledge for a
      stranger,
2 *If* you have been snared with
      the words of your mouth,
   Have been caught with the
      words of your mouth,
3 Do this then, my son, and
      deliver yourself;
   Since you have come into the
      hand of your neighbor,
   Go, humble yourself, and im-
      portune your neighbor.
4 Do not give sleep to your eyes,
   Nor slumber to your eyelids;
5 Deliver yourself like a gazelle
      from *the hunter's* hand,
   And like a bird from the hand
      of the fowler.

6 Go to the ant, O sluggard,
   Observe her ways and be wise,
7 Which, having no chief,
   Officer or ruler,
8 Prepares her food in the sum-
      mer,
   And gathers her provision in
      the harvest.
9 How long will you lie down, O
      sluggard?
   When will you arise from
      your sleep?

10 "A little sleep, a little slumber,
A little folding of the hands to
rest"—

11 And your poverty will come in
like a vagabond,
And your need like an armed
man.

12 A worthless person, a wicked
man,
Is the one who walks with a
false mouth,

13 Who winks with his eyes, who
signals with his feet,
Who points with his fingers;

14 Who *with* perversity in his
heart devises evil continually,
Who spreads strife.

15 Therefore his calamity will
come suddenly;
Instantly he will be broken,
and there will be no healing.

16 There are six things which
the LORD hates,
Yes, seven which are an
abomination to Him:

17 Haughty eyes, a lying tongue,
And hands that shed innocent
blood,

18 A heart that devises wicked
plans,
Feet that run rapidly to evil,

19 A false witness *who* utters
lies,
And one who spreads strife
among brothers.

20 My son, observe the commandment of your father,
And do not forsake the teaching of your mother;

21 Bind them continually on
your heart;
Tie them around your neck.

22 When you walk about, they
will guide you;

When you sleep, they will
watch over you;
And when you awake, they
will talk to you.

23 For the commandment is a
lamp, and the teaching is
light;
And reproofs for discipline
are the way of life,

24 To keep you from the evil
woman,
From the smooth tongue of
the adulteress.

25 Do not desire her beauty in
your heart,
Nor let her catch you with her
eyelids.

26 For on account of a harlot *one
is reduced* to a loaf of
bread,
And an adulteress hunts for
the precious life.

27 Can a man take fire in his
bosom,
And his clothes not be
burned?

28 Or can a man walk on hot
coals,
And his feet not be scorched?

29 So is the one who goes in to
his neighbor's wife;
Whoever touches her will not
go unpunished.

30 Men do not despise a thief if
he steals
To satisfy himself when he is
hungry;

31 But when he is found, he must
repay sevenfold;
He must give all the sub-
stance of his house.

32 The one who commits adultery with a woman is lacking sense;
He who would destroy him-
self does it.

33 Wounds and disgrace he will
find,
And his reproach will not be
blotted out.

34 For jealousy enrages a man,
   And he will not spare in the
      day of vengeance.
35 He will not accept any ran-
      som,
   Nor will he be content though
      you give many gifts.

CHAPTER 7

MY son, keep my words,
   And treasure my command-
      ments within you.
2 Keep my commandments and
      live,
   And my teaching as the apple
      of your eye.
3 Bind them on your fingers;
   Write them on the tablet of
      your heart.
4 Say to wisdom, "You are my
      sister,"
   And call understanding *your*
      intimate friend;
5 That they may keep you from
      an adulteress,
   From the foreigner who flat-
      ters with her words.

6 For at the window of my
      house
   I looked out through my lat-
      tice,
7 And I saw among the naive,
   I discerned among the youths,
   A young man lacking sense,
8 Passing through the street
      near her corner;
   And he takes the way to her
      house,
9 In the twilight, in the even-
      ing,
   In the middle of the night and
      in the darkness.
10 And behold, a woman *comes*
      to meet him,
   Dressed as a harlot and cun-
      ning of heart.

11 She is boisterous and rebel-
      lious;
   Her feet do not remain at
      home;
12 *She is* now in the streets, now
      in the squares,
   And lurks by every corner.
13 So she seizes him and kisses
      him,
   And with a brazen face she
      says to him:
14 "I was due to offer peace offer-
      ings;
   Today I have paid my vows.
15 "Therefore I have come out to
      meet you,
   To seek your presence ear-
      nestly, and I have found
      you.
16 "I have spread my couch with
      coverings,
   With colored linens of Egypt.
17 "I have sprinkled my bed
   With myrrh, aloes and cinna-
      mon.
18 "Come, let us drink our fill of
      love until morning;
   Let us delight ourselves with
      caresses.
19 "For the man is not at home,
   He has gone on a long jour-
      ney;
20 He has taken a bag of money
      with him,
   At full moon he will come
      home."
21 With her many persuasions
      she entices him;
   With her flattering lips she
      seduces him.
22 Suddenly he follows her,
   As an ox goes to the slaugh-
      ter,
   Or as *one in* fetters to the
      discipline of a fool,
23 Until an arrow pierces
      through his liver;
   As a bird hastens to the
      snare,

So he does not know that it
will cost him his life.

24 Now therefore, *my* sons, listen to me,
And pay attention to the
words of my mouth.
25 Do not let your heart turn
aside to her ways,
Do not stray into her paths.
26 For many are the victims she
has cast down,
And numerous are all her
slain.
27 Her house is the way to Sheol,
Descending to the chambers
of death.

CHAPTER 8

DOES not wisdom call,
And understanding lift up her
voice?
2 On top of the heights beside
the way,
Where the paths meet, she
takes her stand;
3 Beside the gates, at the opening to the city,
At the entrance of the doors,
she cries out:
4 "To you, O men, I call,
And my voice is to the sons of
men.
5 "O naive ones, discern prudence;
And, O fools, discern wisdom.
6 "Listen, for I shall speak noble
things;
And the opening of my lips
will produce right things.
7 "For my mouth will utter
truth;
And wickedness is an abomination to my lips.
8 "All the utterances of my
mouth are in right-
eousness;
There is nothing crooked or
perverted in them.

9 "They are all straightforward
to him who understands,
And right to those who find
knowledge.
10 "Take my instruction, and not
silver,
And knowledge rather than
choicest gold.
11 "For wisdom is better than
jewels;
And all desirable things can
not compare with her.
12 "I, wisdom, dwell with prudence,
And I find knowledge *and* discretion.
13 "The fear of the LORD is to hate
evil;
Pride and arrogance and the
evil way,
And the perverted mouth, I
hate.
14 "Counsel is mine and sound
wisdom;
I am understanding, power is
mine.
15 "By me kings reign,
And rulers decree justice.
16 "By me princes rule, and nobles,
All who judge rightly.
17 "I love those who love me;
And those who diligently seek
me will find me.
18 "Riches and honor are with
me,
Enduring wealth and righteousness.
19 "My fruit is better than gold,
even pure gold,
And my yield than choicest
silver.
20 "I walk in the way of righteousness,
In the midst of the paths of
justice,
21 To endow those who love me
with wealth,

That I may fill their treasuries.

22 "The LORD possessed me at the beginning of His way,
Before His works of old.

23 "From everlasting I was established,
From the beginning, from the earliest times of the earth.

24 "When there were no depths I was brought forth,
When there were no springs abounding with water.

25 "Before the mountains were settled,
Before the hills I was brought forth;

26 While He had not yet made the earth and the fields,
Nor the first dust of the world.

27 "When He established the heavens, I was there,
When He inscribed a circle on the face of the deep,

28 When He made firm the skies above,
When the springs of the deep became fixed,

29 When He set for the sea its boundary,
So that the water should not transgress His command,
When He marked out the foundations of the earth;

30 Then I was beside Him, *as* a master workman;
And I was daily *His* delight,
Rejoicing always before Him,

31 Rejoicing in the world, His earth,
And *having* my delight in the sons of men.

32 "Now therefore, *O* sons, listen to me,
For blessed are they who keep my ways.

33 "Heed instruction and be wise,
And do not neglect *it.*

34 "Blessed is the man who listens to me,
Watching daily at my gates,
Waiting at my doorposts.

35 "For he who finds me finds life,
And obtains favor from the LORD.

36 "But he who sins against me injures himself;
All those who hate me love death."

CHAPTER 9

WISDOM has built her house,
She has hewn out her seven pillars;

2 She has prepared her food,
she has mixed her wine;
She has also set her table;

3 She has sent out her maidens,
she calls
From the tops of the heights of the city:

4 "Whoever is naive, let him turn in here!"
To him who lacks understanding she says,

5 "Come, eat of my food,
And drink of the wine I have mixed.

6 "Forsake *your* folly and live,
And proceed in the way of understanding."

7 He who corrects a scoffer gets dishonor for himself,
And he who reproves a wicked man *gets* insults for himself.

8 Do not reprove a scoffer, lest he hate you,
Reprove a wise man, and he will love you.

9 Give *instruction* to a wise man, and he will be still wiser,
Teach a righteous man, and he will increase *his* learning.

10 The fear of the LORD is the
   beginning of wisdom,
   And the knowledge of the
   Holy One is understanding.
11 For by me your days will be
   multiplied,
   And years of life will be added
   to you.
12 If you are wise, you are wise
   for yourself,
   And if you scoff, you alone
   will bear it.

13 The woman of folly is boisterous,
   She is naive, and knows nothing.
14 And she sits at the doorway of
   her house,
   On a seat by the high places
   of the city,
15 Calling to those who pass by,
   Who are making their paths
   straight:
16 "Whoever is naive, let him
   turn in here,"
   And to him who lacks understanding she says,
17 "Stolen water is sweet;
   And bread *eaten* in secret is
   pleasant."
18 But he does not know that the
   dead are there,
   That her guests are in the
   depths of Sheol.

CHAPTER 10

THE proverbs of Solomon.
   A wise son makes a father
   glad,
   But a foolish son is a grief to
   his mother.
2 Ill-gotten gains do not profit,
   But righteousness delivers
   from death.
3 The LORD will not allow the
   righteous to hunger,
   But He will thrust *aside* the
   craving of the wicked.

4 Poor is he who works with a
   negligent hand,
   But the hand of the diligent
   makes rich.
5 He who gathers in summer is
   a son who acts wisely,
   But he who sleeps in harvest
   is a son who acts shamefully.
6 Blessings are on the head of
   the righteous,
   But the mouth of the wicked
   conceals violence.
7 The memory of the righteous
   is blessed,
   But the name of the wicked
   will rot.
8 The wise of heart will receive
   commands,
   But a babbling fool will be
   thrown down.
9 He who walks in integrity
   walks securely,
   But he who perverts his ways
   will be found out.
10 He who winks the eye causes
   trouble,
   And a babbling fool will be
   thrown down.
11 The mouth of the righteous is
   a fountain of life,
   But the mouth of the wicked
   conceals violence.
12 Hatred stirs up strife,
   But love covers all transgressions.
13 On the lips of the discerning,
   wisdom is found,
   But a rod is for the back of
   him who lacks understanding.
14 Wise men store up knowledge,
   But with the mouth of the
   foolish, ruin is at hand.
15 The rich man's wealth is his
   fortress,
   The ruin of the poor is their
   poverty.
16 The wages of the righteous is
   life,

The income of the wicked, punishment.

17 He is *on* the path of life who heeds instruction,
But he who forsakes reproof goes astray.

18 He who conceals hatred *has* lying lips,
And he who spreads slander is a fool.

19 When there are many words, transgression is unavoidable,
But he who restrains his lips is wise.

20 The tongue of the righteous is *as* choice silver,
The heart of the wicked is *worth* little.

21 The lips of the righteous feed many,
But fools die for lack of understanding.

22 It is the blessing of the LORD that makes rich,
And He adds no sorrow to it.

23 Doing wickedness is like sport to a fool;
And *so is* wisdom to a man of understanding.

24 What the wicked fears will come upon him,
And the desire of the righteous will be granted.

25 When the whirlwind passes, the wicked is no more,
But the righteous *has* an everlasting foundation.

26 Like vinegar to the teeth and smoke to the eyes,
So is the lazy one to those who send him.

27 The fear of the LORD prolongs life,
But the years of the wicked will be shortened.

28 The hope of the righteous is gladness,
But the expectation of the wicked perishes.

29 The way of the LORD is a stronghold to the upright,
But ruin to the workers of iniquity.

30 The righteous will never be shaken,
But the wicked will not dwell in the land.

31 The mouth of the righteous flows with wisdom,
But the perverted tongue will be cut out.

32 The lips of the righteous bring forth what is acceptable,
But the mouth of the wicked, what is perverted.

CHAPTER 11

A FALSE balance is an abomination to the LORD,
But a just weight is His delight.

2 When pride comes, then comes dishonor,
But with the humble is wisdom.

3 The integrity of the upright will guide them,
But the falseness of the treacherous will destroy them.

4 Riches do not profit in the day of wrath,
But righteousness delivers from death.

5 The righteousness of the blameless will smooth his way,
But the wicked will fall by his own wickedness.

6 The righteousness of the upright will deliver them,
But the treacherous will be caught by *their own* greed.

7 When a wicked man dies, *his* expectation will perish,
And the hope of strong men perishes.

8 The righteous is delivered from trouble,
But the wicked takes his place.

9 With *his* mouth the godless man destroys his neighbor,
But through knowledge the righteous will be delivered.

10 When it goes well with the righteous, the city rejoices,
And when the wicked perish, there is glad shouting.

11 By the blessing of the upright a city is exalted,
But by the mouth of the wicked it is torn down.

12 He who despises his neighbor lacks sense,
But a man of understanding keeps silent.

13 He who goes about as a talebearer reveals secrets,
But he who is trustworthy conceals a matter.

14 Where there is no guidance, the people fall,
But in abundance of counselors there is victory.

15 He who is surety for a stranger will surely suffer for it,
But he who hates going surety is safe.

16 A gracious woman attains honor,
And violent men attain riches.

17 The merciful man does himself good,
But the cruel man does himself harm.

18 The wicked earns deceptive wages,
But he who sows righteousness *gets* a true reward.

19 He who is steadfast in righteousness *will attain* to life,
And he who pursues evil *will bring about* his own death.

20 The perverse in heart are an abomination to the LORD,
But the blameless in *their* walk are His delight.

21 Assuredly, the evil man will not go unpunished,
But the descendants of the righteous will be delivered.

22 *As* a ring of gold in a swine's snout,
So is a beautiful woman who lacks ¹discretion.

23 The desire of the righteous is only good,
But the expectation of the wicked is wrath.

24 There is one who scatters, yet increases all the more,
And there is one who withholds what is justly due, but *it results* only in want.

25 The generous man will be prosperous,
And he who waters will himself be watered.

26 He who withholds grain, the people will curse him,
But blessing will be on the head of him who sells *it*.

27 He who diligently seeks good seeks favor,
But he who searches after evil, it will come to him.

28 He who trusts in his riches will fall,
But the righteous will flourish like the *green* leaf.

29 He who troubles his own house will inherit wind,
And the foolish will be servant to the wisehearted.

30 The fruit of the righteous is a tree of life,
And he who is wise wins souls.

31 If the righteous will be rewarded in the earth,
How much more the wicked and the sinner!

¹ Lit., *taste*

CHAPTER 12

WHOEVER loves discipline loves knowledge,
But he who hates reproof is stupid.

2 A good man will obtain favor from the LORD,
But He will condemn a man who devises evil.

3 A man will not be established by wickedness,
But the root of the righteous will not be moved.

4 An excellent wife is the crown of her husband,
But she who shames *him* is as rottenness in his bones.

5 The thoughts of the righteous are just,
But the counsels of the wicked are deceitful.

6 The words of the wicked lie in wait for blood,
But the mouth of the upright will deliver them.

7 The wicked are overthrown and are no more,
But the house of the righteous will stand.

8 A man will be praised according to his insight,
But one of perverse mind will be despised.

9 Better is he who is lightly esteemed and has a servant,
Than he who honors himself and lacks bread.

10 A righteous man has regard for the life of his beast,
But the compassion of the wicked is cruel.

11 He who tills his land will have plenty of bread,
But he who pursues vain *things* lacks sense.

12 The wicked desires the booty of evil men,
But the root of the righteous yields *fruit.*

13 An evil man is ensnared by the transgression of his lips,
But the righteous will escape from trouble.

14 A man will be satisfied with good by the fruit of his words,
And the deeds of a man's hands will return to him.

15 The way of a fool is right in his own eyes,
But a wise man is he who listens to counsel.

16 A fool's vexation is known at once,
But a prudent man conceals dishonor.

17 He who speaks truth tells what is right,
But a false witness, deceit.

18 There is one who speaks rashly like the thrusts of a sword,
But the tongue of the wise brings healing.

19 Truthful lips will be established forever,
But a lying tongue is only for a moment.

20 Deceit is in the heart of those who devise evil,
But counselors of peace have joy.

21 No harm befalls the righteous,
But the wicked are filled with trouble.

22 Lying lips are an abomination to the LORD,
But those who deal faithfully are His delight.

23 A prudent man conceals knowledge,
But the heart of fools proclaims folly.

24 The hand of the diligent will rule,

But the slack *hand* will be put
to forced labor.

25 Anxiety in the heart of a man
weighs it down,
But a good word makes it
glad.

26 The righteous is a guide to his
neighbor,
But the way of the wicked
leads them astray.

27 A slothful man does not roast
his prey,
But the precious possession of
a man *is* diligence.

28 In the way of righteousness is
life,
And in *its* pathway there is no
death.

CHAPTER 13

A WISE son *accepts his* father's
discipline,
But a scoffer does not listen to
rebuke.

2 From the fruit of a man's
mouth he enjoys good,
But the desire of the treacherous is violence.

3 The one who guards his
mouth preserves his life;
The one who opens wide his
lips comes to ruin.

4 The soul of the sluggard
craves and *gets* nothing,
But the soul of the diligent is
made fat.

5 A righteous man hates falsehood,
But a wicked man acts dis-
gustingly and shamefully.

6 Righteousness guards the one
whose way is blameless,
But wickedness subverts the
sinner.

7 There is one who pretends to
be rich, but has nothing;
Another pretends to be poor,
but has great wealth.

8 The ransom of a man's life is
his riches,
But the poor hears no rebuke.

9 The light of the righteous [2]re-
joices,
But the lamp of the wicked
goes out.

10 Through presumption comes
nothing but strife,
But with those who receive
counsel is wisdom.

11 Wealth *obtained* by fraud
dwindles,
But the one who gathers by
labor increases *it*.

12 Hope deferred makes the
heart sick,
But desire fulfilled is a tree of
life.

13 The one who despises the
word will be in debt to it,
But the one who fears the
commandment will be re-
warded.

14 The teaching of the wise is a
fountain of life,
To turn aside from the snares
of death.

15 Good understanding produces
favor,
But the way of the treacherous is hard.

16 Every prudent man acts with
knowledge,
But a fool displays folly.

17 A wicked messenger falls into
adversity,
But a faithful envoy *brings*
healing.

18 Poverty and shame *will come*
to him who neglects discipline,
But he who regards reproof
will be honored.

19 Desire realized is sweet to the
soul,
But it is an abomination to
fools to depart from evil.

[2] I.e., shines brightly

20 He who walks with wise men
   will be wise,
   But the companion of fools
   will suffer harm.
21 Adversity pursues sinners,
   But the righteous will be rewarded with prosperity.
22 A good man leaves an inheritance to his children's children,
   And the wealth of the sinner
   is stored up for the righteous.
23 Abundant food *is in* the fal-
   low ground of the poor,
   But it is swept away by injustice.
24 He who spares his rod hates
   his son,
   But he who loves him disciplines him diligently.
25 The righteous has enough to
   satisfy his appetite,
   But the stomach of the wicked
   is in want.

CHAPTER 14

THE wise woman builds her
   house,
   But the foolish tears it down
   with her own hands.
2 He who walks in his uprightness fears the LORD,
   But he who is crooked in his
   ways despises Him.
3 In the mouth of the foolish is
   a rod for *his* back,
   But the lips of the wise will
   preserve them.
4 Where no oxen are, the manger is clean,
   But much increase *comes* by
   the strength of the ox.
5 A faithful witness will not lie,
   But a false witness speaks
   lies.
6 A scoffer seeks wisdom, and
   finds none,
   But knowledge is easy to him
   who has understanding.

7 Leave the presence of a fool,
   Or you will not discern words
   of knowledge.
8 The wisdom of the prudent is
   to understand his way,
   But the folly of fools is deceit.
9 Fools mock at sin,
   But among the upright there
   is good will.
10 The heart knows its own bitterness,
   And a stranger does not share
   its joy.
11 The house of the wicked will
   be destroyed,
   But the tent of the upright
   will flourish.
12 There is a way *which seems*
   right to a man,
   But its end is the way of
   death.
13 Even in laughter the heart
   may be in pain,
   And the end of joy may be
   grief.
14 The backslider in heart will
   have his fill of his own
   ways,
   But a good man will *be satisfied* with his.
15 The naive believes everything,
   But the prudent man considers his steps.
16 A wise man is cautious and
   turns away from evil,
   But a fool is arrogant and
   careless.
17 A quick-tempered man acts
   foolishly,
   And a man of evil devices is
   hated.
18 The naive inherit folly,
   But the prudent are crowned
   with knowledge.
19 The evil will bow down before
   the good,
   And the wicked at the gates of
   the righteous.
20 The poor is hated even by his
   neighbor,

But those who love the rich
    are many.
21 He who despises his neighbor
    sins,
But happy is he who is gra-
    cious to the poor.
22 Will they not go astray who
    devise evil?
But kindness and truth *will
    be to* those who devise
    good.
23 In all labor there is profit,
But mere talk *leads* only to
    poverty.
24 The crown of the wise is their
    riches,
But the folly of fools is fool-
    ishness.
25 A truthful witness saves lives,
But he who speaks lies is
    treacherous.
26 In the [3]fear of the LORD there
    is strong confidence,
And his children will have
    refuge.
27 The [3]fear of the LORD is a
    fountain of life,
That one may avoid the
    snares of death.
28 In a multitude of people is a
    king's glory,
But in the dearth of people is
    a prince's ruin.
29 He who is slow to anger has
    great understanding,
But he who is quick-tempered
    exalts folly.
30 A tranquil heart is life to the
    body,
But passion is rottenness to
    the bones.
31 He who oppresses the poor
    reproaches his Maker,
But he who is gracious to the
    needy honors Him.
32 The wicked is thrust down by
    his wrongdoing,
But the righteous has a refuge
    when he dies.

33 Wisdom rests in the heart of
    one who has understand-
    ing,
But in the bosom of fools it is
    made known.
34 Righteousness exalts a na-
    tion,
But sin is a disgrace to *any*
    people.
35 The king's favor is toward a
    servant who acts wisely,
But his anger is toward him
    who acts shamefully.

CHAPTER 15

A GENTLE answer turns away
    wrath,
But a harsh word stirs up
    anger.
2 The tongue of the wise makes
    knowledge acceptable,
But the mouth of fools spouts
    folly.
3 The eyes of the LORD are in
    every place,
Watching the evil and the
    good.
4 A soothing tongue is a tree of
    life,
But perversion in it crushes
    the spirit.
5 A fool rejects his father's dis-
    cipline,
But he who regards reproof is
    prudent.
6 Much wealth is *in* the house of
    the righteous,
But trouble is in the income of
    the wicked.
7 The lips of the wise spread
    knowledge,
But the hearts of fools are not
    so.
8 The sacrifice of the wicked is
    an abomination to the
    LORD,
But the prayer of the upright
    is His delight.
9 The way of the wicked is an
    abomination to the LORD,

[3] Or, *reverence*

But He loves him who pursues righteousness.

10 Stern discipline is for him who forsakes the way;
He who hates reproof will die.

11 Sheol and Abaddon *lie open* before the LORD,
How much more the hearts of men!

12 A scoffer does not love one who reproves him,
He will not go to the wise.

13 A joyful heart makes a cheerful face,
But when the heart is sad, the spirit is broken.

14 The mind of the intelligent seeks knowledge,
But the mouth of fools feeds on folly.

15 All the days of the afflicted are bad,
But a cheerful heart *has* a continual feast.

16 Better is a little with the fear of the LORD,
Than great treasure and turmoil with it.

17 Better is a dish of vegetables where love is,
Than a fattened ox and hatred with it.

18 A hot-tempered man stirs up strife,
But the slow to anger pacifies contention.

19 The way of the sluggard is as a hedge of thorns,
But the path of the upright is a highway.

20 A wise son makes a father glad,
But a foolish man despises his mother.

21 Folly is joy to him who lacks sense,
But a man of understanding walks straight.

22 Without consultation, plans are frustrated,

But with many counselors they succeed.

23 A man has joy in an apt answer,
And how delightful is a timely word!

24 The path of life *leads* upward for the wise,
That he may keep away from Sheol below.

25 The LORD will tear down the house of the proud,
But He will establish the boundary of the widow.

26 Evil plans are an abomination to the LORD,
But pleasant words are pure.

27 He who profits illicitly troubles his own house,
But he who hates bribes will live.

28 The heart of the righteous ponders how to answer,
But the mouth of the wicked pours out evil things.

29 The LORD is far from the wicked,
But He hears the prayer of the righteous.

30 Bright eyes gladden the heart;
Good news puts fat on the bones.

31 He whose ear listens to the life-giving reproof
Will dwell among the wise.

32 He who neglects discipline despises himself,
But he who listens to reproof acquires understanding.

33 The fear of the LORD is the instruction for wisdom,
And before honor *comes* humility.

CHAPTER 16

THE plans of the heart belong to man,
But the answer of the tongue is from the LORD.

2 All the ways of a man are
   clean in his own sight,
   But the LORD weighs the motives.

3 Commit your works to the
   LORD,
   And your plans will be estab-
   lished.

4 The LORD has made everything for its own purpose,
   Even the wicked for the day
   of evil.

5 Everyone who is proud in
   heart is an abomination to
   the LORD;
   Assuredly, he will not be unpunished.

6 By lovingkindness and truth
   iniquity is atoned for,
   And by the fear of the LORD
   one keeps away from evil.

7 When a man's ways are pleasing to the LORD,
   He makes even his enemies to
   be at peace with him.

8 Better is a little with righteousness
   Than great income with injustice.

9 The mind of man plans his
   way,
   But the LORD directs his
   steps.

10 A divine decision is in the lips
   of the king;
   His mouth should not err in
   judgment.

11 A just balance and scales be-
   long to the LORD;
   All the weights of the bag are
   His concern.

12 It is an abomination for kings
   to commit wickedness,
   For a throne is established on
   righteousness.

13 Righteous lips are the delight
   of kings,
   And he who speaks right is
   loved.

14 The wrath of a king is *as*
   messengers of death,
   But a wise man will appease
   it.

15 In the light of a king's face is
   life,
   And his favor is like a cloud
   with the spring rain.

16 How much better it is to get
   wisdom than gold!
   And to get understanding is
   to be chosen above silver.

17 The highway of the upright is
   to depart from evil;
   He who watches his way preserves his life.

18 Pride *goes* before destruction,
   And a haughty spirit before
   stumbling.

19 It is better to be of a humble
   spirit with the lowly,
   Than to divide the spoil with
   the proud.

20 He who gives attention to the
   word shall find good,
   And blessed is he who trusts
   in the LORD.

21 The wise in heart will be
   called discerning,
   And sweetness of speech increases persuasiveness.

22 Understanding is a fountain
   of life to him who has it,
   But the discipline of fools is
   folly.

23 The heart of the wise teaches
   his mouth,
   And adds persuasiveness to
   his lips.

24 Pleasant words are a honey-
   comb,
   Sweet to the soul and healing
   to the bones.

25 There is a way *which seems*
   right to a man,
   But its end is the way of
   death.

26 A worker's appetite works for
   him,
   For his hunger urges him *on.*

27 A worthless man digs up evil,
   While his words are as a scorching fire.

28 A perverse man spreads strife,
   And a slanderer separates intimate friends.

29 A man of violence entices his neighbor,
   And leads him in a way that is not good.

30 He who winks his eyes *does so* to devise perverse things;
   He who compresses his lips brings evil to pass.

31 A gray head is a crown of glory;
   It is found in the way of righteousness.

32 He who is slow to anger is better than the mighty,
   And he who rules his spirit, than he who captures a city.

33 The lot is cast into the lap,
   But its every decision is from the LORD.

CHAPTER 17

BETTER is a dry morsel and quietness with it
Than a house full of feasting with strife.

2 A servant who acts wisely will rule over a son who acts shamefully,
   And will share in the inheritance among brothers.

3 The refining pot is for silver and the furnace for gold,
   But the LORD tests hearts.

4 An evildoer listens to wicked lips,
   A liar pays attention to a destructive tongue.

5 He who mocks the poor reproaches his Maker;
   He who rejoices at calamity will not go unpunished.

6 Grandchildren are the crown of old men,
   And the glory of sons is their fathers.

7 Excellent speech is not fitting for a fool;
   Much less are lying lips to a prince.

8 A bribe is a charm in the sight of its owner;
   Wherever he turns, he prospers.

9 He who covers a transgression seeks love,
   But he who repeats a matter separates intimate friends.

10 A rebuke goes deeper into one who has understanding
   Than a hundred blows into a fool.

11 A rebellious man seeks only evil,
   So a cruel messenger will be sent against him.

12 Let a man meet a bear robbed of her cubs,
   Rather than a fool in his folly.

13 He who returns evil for good,
   Evil will not depart from his house.

14 The beginning of strife is *like* letting out water,
   So abandon the quarrel before it breaks out.

15 He who justifies the wicked, and he who condemns the righteous,
   Both of them alike are an abomination to the LORD.

16 Why is there a price in the hand of a fool to buy wisdom,
   When he has no sense?

17 A friend loves at all times,
   And a brother is born for adversity.

18 A man lacking in sense pledges,
   And becomes surety in the presence of his neighbor.

19 He who loves transgression loves strife;
   He who raises his door seeks destruction.

20 He who has a crooked mind finds no good,
   And he who is perverted in his language falls into evil.

21 He who begets a fool *does so* to his sorrow,
   And the father of a fool has no joy.

22 A joyful heart is good medicine,
   But a broken spirit dries up the bones.

23 A wicked man receives a bribe from the bosom
   To pervert the ways of justice.

24 Wisdom is in the presence of the one who has understanding,
   But the eyes of a fool are on the ends of the earth.

25 A foolish son is a grief to his father,
   And bitterness to her who bore him.

26 It is also not good to fine the righteous,
   Nor to strike the noble for *their* uprightness.

27 He who restrains his words has knowledge,
   And he who has a cool spirit is a man of understanding.

28 Even a fool, when he keeps silent, is considered wise;
   When he closes his lips, he is *counted* prudent.

CHAPTER 18

HE who separates himself seeks *his own* desire,
   He quarrels against all sound wisdom.

2 A fool does not delight in understanding,
   But only in revealing his own mind.

3 When a wicked man comes, contempt also comes,
   And with dishonor *comes* reproach.

4 The words of a man's mouth are deep waters;
   The fountain of wisdom is a bubbling brook.

5 To show partiality to the wicked is not good,
   Nor to thrust aside the righteous in judgment.

6 A fool's lips bring strife,
   And his mouth calls for blows.

7 A fool's mouth is his ruin,
   And his lips are the snare of his soul.

8 The words of a whisperer are like dainty morsels,
   And they go down into the innermost parts of the body.

9 He also who is slack in his work
   Is brother to him who destroys.

10 The name of the LORD is a strong tower;
   The righteous runs into it and is safe.

11 A rich man's wealth is his strong city,
   And like a high wall in his own imagination.

12 Before destruction the heart of man is haughty,
   But humility *goes* before honor.

13 He who gives an answer before he hears,
   It is folly and shame to him.

14 The spirit of a man can endure his sickness,
   But a broken spirit who can bear?

15 The mind of the prudent acquires knowledge,
   And the ear of the wise seeks knowledge.

16 A man's gift makes room for
   him,
   And brings him before great
   men.
17 The first to plead his case
   seems just,
   Until another comes and examines him.
18 The lot puts an end to contentions,
   And decides between the
   mighty.
19 A brother offended *is harder
   to be won* than a strong
   city,
   And contentions are like the
   bars of a castle.
20 With the fruit of a man's
   mouth his stomach will be
   satisfied;
   He will be satisfied *with* the
   product of his lips.
21 Death and life are in the
   power of the tongue,
   And those who love it will eat
   its fruit.
22 He who finds a wife finds a
   good thing,
   And obtains favor from the
   LORD.
23 The poor man utters supplications,
   But the rich man answers
   roughly.
24 A man of *many* friends *comes*
   to ruin,
   But there is a friend who
   sticks closer than a brother.

CHAPTER 19

BETTER is a poor man who
   walks in his integrity
   Than he who is perverse in
   speech and is a fool.
2 Also it is not good for a person to be without knowledge,
   And he who makes haste with
   his feet errs.

3 The foolishness of man subverts his way,
   And his heart rages against
   the LORD.
4 Wealth adds many friends,
   But a poor man is separated
   from his friend.
5 A false witness will not go
   unpunished,
   And he who tells lies will not
   escape.
6 Many will entreat the favor of
   a generous man,
   And every man is a friend to
   him who gives gifts.
7 All the brothers of a poor
   man hate him;
   How much more do his
   friends go far from him!
   He pursues *them with* words,
   but they are gone.
8 He who gets wisdom loves his
   own soul;
   He who keeps understanding
   will find good.
9 A false witness will not go
   unpunished,
   And he who tells lies will
   perish.
10 Luxury is not fitting for a
   fool;
   Much less for a slave to rule
   over princes.
11 A man's discretion makes him
   slow to anger,
   And it is his glory to overlook
   a transgression.
12 The king's wrath is like the
   roaring of a lion,
   But his favor is like dew on
   the grass.
13 A foolish son is destruction to
   his father,
   And the contentions of a wife
   are a constant dripping.
14 House and wealth are an inheritance from fathers,
   But a prudent wife is from the
   LORD.
15 Laziness casts into a deep
   sleep,

And an idle man will suffer hunger.

16 He who keeps the commandment keeps his soul,
But he who is careless of his ways will die.

17 He who is gracious to a poor man lends to the LORD,
And He will repay him for his good deed.

18 Discipline your son while there is hope,
And do not desire his death.

19 A man of great anger shall bear the penalty,
For if you rescue him, you will only have to do it again.

20 Listen to counsel and accept discipline,
That you may be wise the rest of your days.

21 Many are the plans in a man's heart,
But the counsel of the LORD, it will stand.

22 What is desirable in a man is his ⁴kindness,
And it is better to be a poor man than a liar.

23 The fear of the LORD leads to life,
So that one may sleep satisfied, untouched by evil.

24 The sluggard buries his hand in the dish,
And will not even bring it back to his mouth.

25 Strike a scoffer and the naive may become shrewd,
But reprove one who has understanding and he will gain knowledge.

26 He who assaults his father and drives his mother away
Is a shameful and disgraceful son.

27 Cease listening, my son, to discipline,

And you will stray from the words of knowledge.

28 A rascally witness makes a mockery of justice,
And the mouth of the wicked spreads iniquity.

29 Judgments are prepared for scoffers,
And blows for the back of fools.

CHAPTER 20

WINE is a mocker, strong drink a brawler,
And whoever is intoxicated by it is not wise.

2 The terror of a king is like the growling of a lion;
He who provokes him to anger forfeits his own life.

3 Keeping away from strife is an honor for a man,
But any fool will quarrel.

4 The sluggard does not plow after the autumn,
So he begs during the harvest and has nothing.

5 A plan in the heart of a man is like deep water,
But a man of understanding draws it out.

6 Many a man proclaims his own loyalty,
But who can find a trustworthy man?

7 A righteous man who walks in his integrity—
How blessed are his sons after him.

8 A king who sits on the throne of justice
Disperses all evil with his eyes.

9 Who can say, "I have cleansed my heart,
I am pure from my sin"?

10 Differing weights and differing measures,
Both of them are abominable to the LORD.

⁴ Or, loyalty

11 It is by his deeds that a lad
distinguishes himself
  If his conduct is pure and
right.

12 The hearing ear and the seeing eye,
  The LORD has made both of
them.

13 Do not love sleep, lest you
become poor;
  Open your eyes, *and* you will
be satisfied with food.

14 "Bad, bad," says the buyer;
  But when he goes his way,
then he boasts.

15 There is gold, and an abundance of jewels;
  But the lips of knowledge are
a more precious thing.

16 Take his garment when he
becomes surety for a
stranger;
  And for foreigners, hold him
in pledge.

17 Bread obtained by falsehood
is sweet to a man,
  But afterward his mouth will
be filled with gravel.

18 Prepare plans by consultation,
  And make war by wise guidance.

19 He who goes about as a slanderer reveals secrets,
  Therefore do not associate
with a gossip.

20 He who curses his father or
his mother,
  His lamp will go out in time of
darkness.

21 An inheritance gained hur-
riedly at the beginning,
  Will not be blessed in the end.

22 Do not say, "I will repay evil";
  Wait for the LORD, and He
will save you.

23 Differing weights are an
abomination to the LORD,
  And a false scale is not good.

24 Man's steps are *ordained* by
the LORD,

  How then can man under-
stand his way?

25 It is a snare for a man to say
rashly, "It is holy!"
  And after the vows to make
inquiry.

26 A wise king winnows the
wicked,
  And drives the *threshing*
wheel over them.

27 The spirit of man is the lamp
of the LORD,
  Searching all the innermost
parts of his being.

28 Loyalty and truth preserve
the king,
  And he upholds his throne by
righteousness.

29 The glory of young men is
their strength,
  And the honor of old men is
their gray hair.

30 Stripes that wound scour
away evil,
  And strokes *reach* the innermost parts.

CHAPTER 21

THE king's heart is *like* channels of water in the hand
of the LORD;
  He turns it wherever He
wishes.

2 Every man's way is right in
his own eyes,
  But the LORD weighs the
hearts.

3 To do righteousness and justice
  Is desired by the LORD rather
than sacrifice.

4 Haughty eyes and a proud
heart,
  The lamp of the wicked, is sin.

5 The plans of the diligent *lead*
surely to advantage,
  But everyone who is hasty
comes surely to poverty.

6 The getting of treasures by a
lying tongue

Is a fleeting vapor, the pursuit of death.

7 The violence of the wicked will drag them away,
Because they refuse to act with justice.

8 The way of a guilty man is crooked,
But as for the pure, his conduct is upright.

9 It is better to live in a corner of a roof,
Than in a house shared with a contentious woman.

10 The soul of the wicked desires evil;
His neighbor finds no favor in his eyes.

11 When the scoffer is punished, the naive becomes wise;
But when the wise is instructed, he receives knowledge.

12 The righteous one considers the house of the wicked,
Turning the wicked to ruin.

13 He who shuts his ear to the cry of the poor
Will also cry himself and not be answered.

14 A gift in secret subdues anger,
And a bribe in the bosom, strong wrath.

15 The execution of justice is joy for the righteous,
But is terror to the workers of iniquity.

16 A man who wanders from the way of understanding
Will rest in the assembly of the dead.

17 He who loves pleasure *will become* a poor man;
He who loves wine and oil will not become rich.

18 The wicked is a ransom for the righteous,
And the treacherous is in the place of the upright.

19 It is better to live in a desert land,
Than with a contentious and vexing woman.

20 There is precious treasure and oil in the dwelling of the wise,
But a foolish man swallows it up.

21 He who pursues righteousness and loyalty
Finds life, righteousness and honor.

22 A wise man scales the city of the mighty,
And brings down the stronghold in which they trust.

23 He who guards his mouth and his tongue,
Guards his soul from troubles.

24 "Proud," "Haughty," "Scoffer," are his names,
Who acts with insolent pride.

25 The desire of the sluggard puts him to death,
For his hands refuse to work;

26 All day long he is craving,
While the righteous gives and does not hold back.

27 The sacrifice of the wicked is an abomination,
How much more when he brings it with evil intent!

28 A false witness will perish,
But the man who listens *to the truth* will speak forever.

29 A wicked man shows a bold face,
But as for the upright, he makes his way sure.

30 There is no wisdom and no understanding
And no counsel against the LORD.

31 The horse is prepared for the day of battle,
But victory belongs to the LORD.

CHAPTER 22

A GOOD name is to be more
desired than great riches,
Favor is better than silver
and gold.

2 The rich and the poor have a
common bond,
The LORD is the maker of
them all.

3 The prudent sees the evil and
hides himself,
But the naive go on, and are
punished for it.

4 The reward of humility and
the fear of the LORD
Are riches, honor and life.

5 Thorns and snares are in the
way of the perverse;
He who guards himself will be
far from them.

6 Train up a child in the way he
should go,
Even when he is old he will
not depart from it.

7 The rich rules over the poor,
And the borrower becomes
the lender's slave.

8 He who sows iniquity will
reap vanity,
And the rod of his fury will
perish.

9 He who is generous will be
blessed,
For he gives some of his food
to the poor.

10 Drive out the scoffer, and contention will go out,
Even strife and dishonor will
cease.

11 He who loves purity of heart
And whose speech is gracious,
the king is his friend.

12 The eyes of the LORD preserve
knowledge,
But He overthrows the words
of the treacherous man.

13 The sluggard says, "There is a
lion outside;
I shall be slain in the streets!"

14 The mouth of an adulteress is
a deep pit;
He who is cursed of the LORD
will fall into it.

15 Foolishness is bound up in the
heart of a child;
The rod of discipline will remove it far from him.

16 He who oppresses the poor to
make much for himself
Or who gives to the rich, will
only come to poverty.

17 Incline your ear and hear the
words of the wise,
And apply your mind to my
knowledge;

18 For it will be pleasant if you
keep them within you,
That they may be ready on
your lips.

19 So that your trust may be in
the LORD,
I have taught you today, even
you.

20 Have I not written to you
excellent things
Of counsels and knowledge,

21 To make you know the certainty of the words of
truth
That you may correctly answer to him who sent you?

22 Do not rob the poor because
he is poor,
Or crush the afflicted at the
gate;

23 For the LORD will plead their
case,
And take the life of those who
rob them.

24 Do not associate with a man
given to anger;
Or go with a hot-tempered
man,

25 Lest you learn his ways,
And find a snare for yourself.

26 Do not be among those who
    give pledges,
    Among those who become
      sureties for debts.
27 If you have nothing with
    which to pay,
    Why should he take your bed
      from under you?

28 Do not move the ancient
    boundary
    Which your fathers have set.
29 Do you see a man skilled in
    his work?
    He will stand before kings;
    He will not stand before ob-
      scure men.

CHAPTER 23

WHEN you sit down to dine
    with a ruler,
    Consider carefully what is be-
      fore you;
2 And put a knife to your
    throat,
    If you are a man of *great*
      appetite.
3 Do not desire his delicacies,
    For it is deceptive food.

4 Do not weary yourself to gain
    wealth,
    Cease from your consider-
      ation *of it.*
5 When you set your eyes on it,
    it is gone.
    For *wealth* certainly makes
      itself wings,
    Like an eagle that flies to-
      ward the heavens.

6 Do not eat the bread of a
    selfish man,
    Or desire his delicacies;
7 For as he thinks within him-
    self, so he is.
    He says to you, "Eat and
      drink!"
    But his heart is not with you.

8 You will vomit up the morsel
    you have eaten,
    And waste your compliments.

9 Do not speak in the hearing of
    a fool,
    For he will despise the wis-
      dom of your words.

10 Do not move the ancient
    boundary,
    Or go into the fields of the
      fatherless;
11 For their Redeemer is strong;
    He will plead their case
      against you.
12 Apply your heart to disci-
    pline,
    And your ears to words of
      knowledge.

13 Do not hold back discipline
    from the child,
    Although you beat him with
      the rod, he will not die.
14 You shall beat him with the
    rod,
    And deliver his soul from
      Sheol.

15 My son, if your heart is wise,
    My own heart also will be
      glad;
16 And my inmost being will re-
    joice,
    When your lips speak what is
      right.

17 Do not let your heart envy
    sinners,
    But *live* in the fear of the
      LORD always.
18 Surely there is a future,
    And your hope will not be cut
      off.
19 Listen, my son, and be wise,
    And direct your heart in the
      way.
20 Do not be with heavy drinkers
    of wine,

Or with gluttonous eaters of meat;

21 For the heavy drinker and the glutton will come to poverty,
And drowsiness will clothe *a man* with rags.

22 Listen to your father who begot you,
And do not despise your mother when she is old.

23 Buy truth, and do not sell *it*,
Get wisdom and instruction and understanding.

24 The father of the righteous will greatly rejoice,
And he who begets a wise son will be glad in him.

25 Let your father and your mother be glad,
And let her rejoice who gave birth to you.

26 Give me your heart, my son,
And let your eyes delight in my ways.

27 For a harlot is a deep pit,
And an adulterous woman is a narrow well.

28 Surely she lurks as a robber,
And increases the faithless among men.

29 Who has woe? Who has sorrow?
Who has contentions? Who has complaining?
Who has wounds without cause?
Who has redness of eyes?

30 Those who linger long over wine,
Those who go to taste mixed wine.

31 Do not look on the wine when it is red,
When it sparkles in the cup,
When it goes down smoothly;

32 At the last it bites like a serpent,
And stings like a viper.

33 Your eyes will see strange things,
And your mind will utter perverse things.

34 And you will be like one who lies down in the middle of the sea,
Or like one who lies down on the top of a [5]mast.

35 "They struck me, *but* I did not become ill;
They beat me, *but* I did not know *it*.
When shall I awake?
I will seek another drink."

CHAPTER 24

DO not be envious of evil men,
Nor desire to be with them;

2 For their minds devise violence,
And their lips talk of trouble.

3 By wisdom a house is built,
And by understanding it is established;

4 And by knowledge the rooms are filled
With all precious and pleasant riches.

5 A wise man is strong,
And a man of knowledge increases power.

6 For by wise guidance you will wage war,
And in abundance of counselors there is victory.

7 Wisdom is too high for a fool,
He does not open his mouth in the gate.

8 He who plans to do evil,
Men will call him a schemer.

[5] Or, *lookout*

9 The devising of folly is sin,
And the scoffer is an abomination to men.

10 If you are slack in the day of distress,
Your strength is limited.

11 Deliver those who are being taken away to death,
And those who are staggering to slaughter, O hold *them* back.

12 If you say, "See, we did not know this,"
Does He not consider *it* who weighs the hearts?
And does He not know *it* who keeps your soul?
And will He not render to man according to his work?

13 My son, eat honey, for it is good,
Yes, the honey from the comb is sweet to your taste;

14 Know *that* wisdom is thus for your soul;
If you find *it,* then there will be a future,
And your hope will not be cut off.

15 Do not lie in wait, O wicked man, against the dwelling of the righteous;
Do not destroy his resting place;

16 For a righteous man falls seven times, and rises again,
But the wicked stumble in *time of* calamity.

17 Do not rejoice when your enemy falls,
And do not let your heart be glad when he stumbles;

18 Lest the LORD see *it* and be displeased,
And He turn away His anger from him.

19 Do not fret because of evildoers,
Or be envious of the wicked;

20 For there will be no future for the evil man;
The lamp of the wicked will be put out.

21 My son, fear the LORD and the king;
Do not associate with those who are given to change;

22 For their calamity will rise suddenly,
And who knows the ruin *that comes* from both of them?

23 These also are sayings of the wise.
To show partiality in judgment is not good.

24 He who says to the wicked, "You are righteous,"
Peoples will curse him, nations will abhor him;

25 But to those who rebuke the *wicked* will be delight,
And a good blessing will come upon them.

26 He kisses the lips
Who gives a right answer.

27 Prepare your work outside,
And make it ready for yourself in the field;
Afterwards, then, build your house.

28 Do not be a witness against your neighbor without cause,
And do not deceive with your lips.

29 Do not say, "Thus I shall do to him as he has done to me;
I will render to the man according to his work."

30 I passed by the field of the
sluggard,
And by the vineyard of the
man lacking sense;

31 And behold, it was completely
overgrown with thistles,
Its surface was covered with
nettles,
And its stone wall was broken
down.

32 When I saw, I reflected upon
it;
I looked, *and* received instruction.

33 "A little sleep, a little slumber,
A little folding of the hands to
rest,"

34 Then your poverty will come
as a robber,
And your want like an armed
man.

CHAPTER 25

THESE also are proverbs of Solomon which the men of Hezekiah, king of Judah, transcribed.

2 It is the glory of God to conceal a matter,
But the glory of kings is to
search out a matter.

3 *As* the heavens for height and
the earth for depth,
So the heart of kings is unsearchable.

4 Take away the dross from the
silver,
And there comes out a vessel
for the smith;

5 Take away the wicked *from*
before the king,
And his throne will be established in righteousness.

6 Do not claim honor in the
presence of the king,
And do not stand in the place
of great men;

7 For it is better that it be said
to you, "Come up here,"

Than that you should be put
lower in the presence of
the prince,
Whom your eyes have seen.

8 Do not go out hastily to argue
your case;
Otherwise, what will you do
in the end,
When your neighbor puts you
to shame?

9 Argue your case with your
neighbor,
And do not reveal the secret
of another,

10 Lest he who hears *it* reproach
you,
And the evil report about you
not pass away.

11 *Like* apples of gold in settings
of silver
Is a word spoken in right
circumstances.

12 *Like* an earring of gold and an
ornament of fine gold
Is a wise reprover to a listening ear.

13 Like the cold of snow in the
time of harvest
Is a faithful messenger to
those who send him,
For he refreshes the soul of
his masters.

14 *Like* clouds and wind without
rain
Is a man who boasts of his
gifts falsely.

15 By forbearance a ruler may be
persuaded,
And a soft tongue breaks the
bone.

16 Have you found honey? Eat
only what you need,
Lest you have it in excess and
vomit it.

17 Let your foot rarely be in your
neighbor's house,
Lest he become weary of you
and hate you.

18 *Like* a club and a sword and a
sharp arrow
   Is a man who bears false witness against his neighbor.

19 *Like* a bad tooth and an un-
steady foot
   Is confidence in a faithless
man in time of trouble.

20 *Like* one who takes off a garment on a cold day, *or like*
vinegar on soda,
   Is he who sings songs to a
troubled heart.

21 If your enemy is hungry, give
him food to eat;
   And if he is thirsty, give him
water to drink;

22 For you will heap burning
coals on his head,
   And the LORD will reward
you.

23 The north wind brings forth
rain,
   And a backbiting tongue, an
angry countenance.

24 It is better to live in a corner
of the roof
   Than in a house shared with a
contentious woman.

25 *Like* cold water to a weary
soul,
   So is good news from a distant land.

26 *Like* a trampled spring and a
polluted well
   Is a righteous man who gives
way before the wicked.

27 It is not good to eat much
honey,
   Nor is it glory to search out
one's own glory.

28 *Like* a city that is broken into
and without walls
   Is a man who has no control
over his spirit.

CHAPTER 26

LIKE snow in summer and like
rain in harvest,

So honor is not fitting for a
fool.

2 *Like* a sparrow in *its* flitting,
like a swallow in *its* flying,
   So a curse without cause does
not alight.

3 A whip is for the horse, a
bridle for the donkey,
   And a rod for the back of
fools.

4 Do not answer a fool according to his folly,
   Lest you also be like him.

5 Answer a fool as his folly
deserves,
   Lest he be wise in his own
eyes.

6 He cuts off *his own* feet, *and*
drinks violence
   Who sends a message by the
hand of a fool.

7 *Like* the legs *which* hang
down from the lame,
   So is a proverb in the mouth
of fools.

8 Like one who binds a stone in
a sling,
   So is he who gives honor to a
fool.

9 *Like* a thorn *which* falls into
the hand of a drunkard,
   So is a proverb in the mouth
of fools.

10 *Like* an archer who wounds
everyone,
   So is he who hires a fool or
who hires those who pass
by.

11 Like a dog that returns to its
vomit
   Is a fool who repeats his folly.

12 Do you see a man wise in his
own eyes?
   There is more hope for a fool
than for him.

13 The sluggard says, "There is a
lion in the road!
   A lion is in the open square!"

14 *As* the door turns on its
hinges,

So *does* the sluggard on his bed.

15 The sluggard buries his hand in the dish;

He is weary of bringing it to his mouth again.

16 The sluggard is wiser in his own eyes

Than seven men who can give a discreet answer.

17 *Like* one who takes a dog by the ears

Is he who passes by *and* meddles with strife not belonging to him.

18 Like a madman who throws

Firebrands, arrows and death,

19 So is the man who deceives his neighbor,

And says, "Was I not joking?"

20 For lack of wood the fire goes out,

And where there is no whisperer, contention quiets down.

21 *Like* charcoal to hot embers and wood to fire,

So is a contentious man to kindle strife.

22 The words of a whisperer are like dainty morsels,

And they go down into the innermost parts of the body.

23 *Like* an earthen vessel overlaid with silver dross

Are burning lips and a wicked heart.

24 He who hates disguises *it* with his lips,

But he lays up deceit in his heart.

25 When he speaks graciously, do not believe him,

For there are seven abominations in his heart.

26 *Though his* hatred covers itself with guile,

His wickedness will be revealed before the assembly.

27 He who digs a pit will fall into it,

And he who rolls a stone, it will come back on him.

28 A lying tongue hates those it crushes,

And a flattering mouth works ruin.

CHAPTER 27

DO not boast about tomorrow,

For you do not know what a day may bring forth.

2 Let another praise you, and not your own mouth;

A stranger, and not your own lips.

3 A stone is heavy and the sand weighty,

But the provocation of a fool is heavier than both of them.

4 Wrath is fierce and anger is a flood,

But who can stand before jealousy?

5 Better is open rebuke

Than love that is concealed.

6 Faithful are the wounds of a friend,

But deceitful are the kisses of an enemy.

7 A sated man loathes honey,

But to a famished man any bitter thing is sweet.

8 Like a bird that wanders from her nest,

So is a man who wanders from his home.

9 Oil and perfume make the heart glad,

So a man's counsel is sweet to his friend.

10 Do not forsake your own friend or your father's friend,

And do not go to your brother's house in the day of your calamity;

Better is a neighbor who is near than a brother far away.

11 Be wise, my son, and make my heart glad,

That I may reply to him who reproaches me.

12 A prudent man sees evil *and* hides himself,

The naive proceed *and* pay the penalty.

13 Take his garment when he becomes surety for a stranger;

And for an adulterous woman hold him in pledge.

14 He who blesses his friend with a loud voice early in the morning,

It will be reckoned a curse to him.

15 A constant dripping on a day of steady rain

And a contentious woman are alike;

16 He who would restrain her restrains the wind,

And grasps oil with his right hand.

17 Iron sharpens iron,

So one man sharpens another.

18 He who tends the fig tree will eat its fruit;

And he who cares for his master will be honored.

19 As in water face *reflects* face,

So the heart of man *reflects* man.

20 Sheol and Abaddon are never satisfied,

Nor are the eyes of man ever satisfied.

21 The crucible is for silver and the furnace for gold,

And a man *is tested* by the praise accorded him.

22 Though you pound a fool in a mortar with a pestle along with crushed grain,

Yet his folly will not depart from him.

23 Know well the condition of your flocks,

And pay attention to your herds;

24 For riches are not forever,

Nor does a crown *endure* to all generations.

25 *When* the grass disappears, the new growth is seen,

And the herbs of the mountains are gathered in,

26 The lambs *will be* for your clothing,

And the goats *will bring* the price of a field,

27 And *there will be* goats' milk enough for your food,

For the food of your household,

And sustenance for your maidens.

CHAPTER 28

THE wicked flee when no one is pursuing,

But the righteous are bold as a lion.

2 By the transgression of a land many are its princes,

But by a man of understanding *and* knowledge, so it endures.

3 A poor man who oppresses the lowly

Is *like* a driving rain which leaves no food.

4 Those who forsake the law praise the wicked,

But those who keep the law strive with them.

5 Evil men do not understand justice,

But those who seek the LORD understand all things.

6 Better is the poor who walks
      in his integrity,
    Than he who is crooked
      though he be rich.
7 He who keeps the law is a
      discerning son,
    But he who is a companion of
      gluttons humiliates his fa-
      ther.
8 He who increases his wealth
      by interest and usury,
    Gathers it for him who is
      gracious to the poor.
9 He who turns away his ear
      from listening to the law,
    Even his prayer is an abomi-
      nation.
10 He who leads the upright
      astray in an evil way
    Will himself fall into his own
      pit,
    But the blameless will inherit
      good.
11 The rich man is wise in his
      own eyes,
    But the poor who has under-
      standing sees through him.
12 When the righteous triumph,
      there is great glory,
    But when the wicked rise,
      men hide themselves.
13 He who conceals his trans-
      gressions will not prosper,
    But he who confesses and for-
      sakes *them* will find com-
      passion.
14 How blessed is the man who
      fears always,
    But he who hardens his heart
      will fall into calamity.
15 *Like* a roaring lion and a
      rushing bear
    Is a wicked ruler over a poor
      people.
16 A leader who is a great op-
      pressor lacks understand-
      ing,
    But he who hates unjust gain
      will prolong *his* days.
17 A man who is laden with the
      guilt of human blood

Will be a fugitive until death;
      let no one support him.
18 He who walks blamelessly
      will be delivered,
    But he who is crooked will fall
      all at once.
19 He who tills his land will have
      plenty of food,
    But he who follows empty
      pursuits will have poverty
      in plenty.
20 A faithful man will abound
      with blessings,
    But he who makes haste to be
      rich will not go unpun-
      ished.
21 To show partiality is not good,
    Because for a piece of bread a
      man will transgress.
22 A man with an evil eye has-
      tens after wealth,
    And does not know that want
      will come upon him.
23 He who rebukes a man will
      afterward find *more* favor
    Than he who flatters with the
      tongue.
24 He who robs his father or his
      mother,
    And says, "It is not a trans-
      gression,"
    Is the companion of a man
      who destroys.
25 An arrogant man stirs up
      strife,
    But he who trusts in the LORD
      will prosper.
26 He who trusts in his own
      heart is a fool,
    But he who walks wisely will
      be delivered.
27 He who gives to the poor will
      never want,
    But he who shuts his eyes will
      have many curses.
28 When the wicked rise, men
      hide themselves;
    But when they perish, the
      righteous increase.

CHAPTER 29

A MAN who hardens *his* neck
after much reproof
Will suddenly be broken beyond remedy.

2 When the righteous increase,
the people rejoice,
But when a wicked man rules,
people groan.

3 A man who loves wisdom
makes his father glad,
But he who keeps company
with harlots wastes *his*
wealth.

4 The king gives stability to the
land by justice,
But a man who takes bribes
overthrows it.

5 A man who flatters his neighbor
Is spreading a net for his
steps.

6 By transgression an evil man
is ensnared,
But the righteous sings and
rejoices.

7 The righteous is concerned
for the rights of the poor,
The wicked does not understand *such* concern.

8 Scorners set a city aflame,
But wise men turn away anger.

9 When a wise man has a con-
troversy with a foolish
man,
The foolish man either rages
or laughs, and there is no
rest.

10 Men of bloodshed hate the
blameless,
But the upright are concerned
for his life.

11 A fool always loses his tem-
per,
But a wise man holds it back.

12 If a ruler pays attention to
falsehood,
All his ministers *become*
wicked.

13 The poor man and the oppressor have this in common:
The LORD gives light to the
eyes of both.

14 If a king judges the poor with
truth,
His throne will be established
forever.

15 The rod and reproof give wisdom,
But a child who gets his own
way brings shame to his
mother.

16 When the wicked increase,
transgression increases;
But the righteous will see
their fall.

17 Correct your son, and he will
give you comfort;
He will also delight your soul.

18 Where there is no vision, the
people are unrestrained,
But happy is he who keeps the
law.

19 A slave will not be instructed
by words *alone;*
For though he understands,
there will be no response.

20 Do you see a man who is hasty
in his words?
There is more hope for a fool
than for him.

21 He who pampers his slave
from childhood
Will in the end find him to be
a son.

22 An angry man stirs up strife,
And a hot-tempered man
abounds in transgression.

23 A man's pride will bring him
low,
But a humble spirit will obtain honor.

24 He who is a partner with a
thief hates his own life;
He hears the oath but tells
nothing.

25 The fear of man brings a
snare,
But he who trusts in the LORD
will be exalted.

26 Many seek the ruler's favor,
   But justice for man *comes*
      from the Lord.
27 An unjust man is abominable
      to the righteous,
   And he who is upright in the
      way is abominable to the
      wicked.

CHAPTER 30

THE words of Agur the son of
   Jakeh, the oracle.
The man declares to Ithiel, to
Ithiel and Ucal:
2 Surely I am more stupid than
      any man,
   And I do not have the under-
      standing of a man.
3 Neither have I learned wis-
      dom,
   Nor do I have the knowledge
      of the Holy One.
4 Who has ascended into heav-
      en and descended?
   Who has gathered the wind in
      His fists?
   Who has wrapped the waters
      in His garment?
   Who has established all the
      ends of the earth?
   What is His name or His son's
      name?
   Surely you know!

5 Every word of God is tested;
   He is a shield to those who
      take refuge in Him.
6 Do not add to His words
   Lest He reprove you, and you
      be proved a liar.

7 Two things I asked of Thee,
   Do not refuse me before I die:
8 Keep deception and lies far
      from me,
   Give me neither poverty nor
      riches;
   Feed me with the food that is
      my portion,

9 Lest I be full and deny *Thee*
      and say, "Who is the
      Lord?"
   Or lest I be in want and steal,
   And profane the name of my
      God.

10 Do not slander a slave to his
      master,
   Lest he curse you and you be
      found guilty.

11 There is a [6]kind of *man* who
      curses his father,
   And does not bless his moth-
      er.
12 There is a kind who is pure in
      his own eyes,
   Yet is not washed from his
      filthiness.
13 There is a kind—oh how lofty
      are his eyes!
   And his eyelids are raised *in
      arrogance.*
14 There is a kind of *man* whose
      teeth are *like* swords,
   And his jaw teeth *like* knives,
   To devour the afflicted from
      the earth,
   And the needy from among
      men.

15 The leech has two daughters,
   "Give," "Give."
   There are three things that
      will not be satisfied,
   Four that will not say,
      "Enough":
16 Sheol, and the barren womb,
   Earth that is never satisfied
      with water,
   And fire that never says,
      "Enough."
17 The eye that mocks a father,
   And scorns a mother,
   The ravens of the valley will
      pick it out,
   And the young eagles will eat
      it.

[6] Or, *generation;* so through v. 14

18 There are three things which
    are too wonderful for me,
    Four which I do not under-
    stand:

19 The way of an eagle in the
    sky,
    The way of a serpent on a
    rock,
    The way of a ship in the
    middle of the sea,
    And the way of a man with a
    maid.

20 This is the way of an adulter-
    ous woman:
    She eats and wipes her
    mouth,
    And says, "I have done no
    wrong."

21 Under three things the earth
    quakes,
    And under four, it cannot
    bear up:

22 Under a slave when he be-
    comes king,
    And a fool when he is satis-
    fied with food,

23 Under an unloved woman
    when she gets a husband,
    And a maidservant when she
    supplants her mistress.

24 Four things are small on the
    earth,
    But they are exceedingly wise:

25 The ants are not a strong folk,
    But they prepare their food in
    the summer;

26 The badgers are not mighty
    folk,
    Yet they make their houses in
    the rocks;

27 The locusts have no king,
    Yet all of them go out in
    ranks;

28 The lizard you may grasp
    with the hands,
    Yet it is in kings' palaces.

29 There are three things which
    are stately in *their* march,

    Even four which are stately
    when they walk:

30 The lion *which* is mighty
    among beasts
    And does not retreat before
    any,

31 The strutting cock, the male
    goat also,
    And a king *when his* army is
    with him.

32 If you have been foolish in
    exalting yourself
    Or if you have plotted *evil,*
    put your hand on your
    mouth.

33 For the churning of milk pro-
    duces butter,
    And pressing the nose brings
    forth blood;
    So the churning of anger pro-
    duces strife.

CHAPTER 31

THE words of King Lemuel, the
oracle which his mother taught
him.

2 What, O my son?
    And what, O son of my
    womb?
    And what, O son of my vows?

3 Do not give your strength to
    women,
    Or your ways to that which
    destroys kings.

4 It is not for kings, O Lemuel,
    It is not for kings to drink
    wine,
    Or for rulers to desire strong
    drink,

5 Lest they drink and forget
    what is decreed,
    And pervert the rights of all
    the afflicted.

6 Give strong drink to him who
    is perishing,
    And wine to him whose life is
    bitter.

7 Let him drink and forget his
    poverty,

And remember his trouble no more.

8 Open your mouth for the dumb,
For the rights of all the unfortunate.

9 Open your mouth, judge righteously,
And defend the rights of the afflicted and needy.

10 An excellent wife, who can find?
For her worth is far above jewels.

11 The heart of her husband trusts in her,
And he will have no lack of gain.

12 She does him good and not evil
All the days of her life.

13 She looks for wool and flax,
And works with her hands in delight.

14 She is like merchant ships;
She brings her food from afar.

15 She rises also while it is still night,
And gives food to her household,
And portions to her maidens.

16 She considers a field and buys it;
From her earnings she plants a vineyard.

17 She girds herself with strength,
And makes her arms strong.

18 She senses that her gain is good;
Her lamp does not go out at night.

19 She stretches out her hands to the distaff,
And her hands grasp the spindle.

20 She extends her hand to the poor;
And she stretches out her hands to the needy.

21 She is not afraid of the snow for her household,
For all her household are clothed with scarlet.

22 She makes coverings for herself;
Her clothing is fine linen and purple.

23 Her husband is known in the gates,
When he sits among the elders of the land.

24 She makes linen garments and sells *them,*
And supplies belts to the tradesmen.

25 Strength and dignity are her clothing,
And she smiles at the future.

26 She opens her mouth in wisdom,
And the teaching of kindness is on her tongue.

27 She looks well to the ways of her household,
And does not eat the bread of idleness.

28 Her children rise up and bless her;
Her husband *also,* and he praises her, *saying:*

29 "Many daughters have done nobly,
But you excel them all."

30 Charm is deceitful and beauty is vain,
But a woman who fears the LORD, she shall be praised.

31 Give her the product of her hands,
And let her works praise her in the gates.

God Loves You

For God so loved the world, that He gave His only begotten Son, that whoever believes in Him should not perish, but have eternal life.

—John 3:16 (page 139)

All Are Sinners

For all have sinned and fall short of the glory of God.

—Romans 3:23 (page 230)

As it is written, "There is none righteous, not even one."

—Romans 3:10 (page 230)

God's Remedy for Sin

For the wages of sin is death, but the free gift of God is eternal life in Christ Jesus our Lord.

—Romans 6:23 (page 234)

But as many as received Him, to them He gave the right to become children of God, even to those who believe in His name. *—John 1:12 (page 135)*

For I delivered to you as of first importance what I also received, that Christ died for our sins according to the Scriptures, and that He was buried, and that He was raised on the third day according to the Scriptures.

—1 Corinthians 15:3, 4 (page 263)

All May Be Saved Now

Behold, I stand at the door and knock; if anyone hears My voice and opens the door, I will come in to him, and will dine with him, and he with Me.

—Revelation 3:20 (page 365)

My Decision to Receive Christ As My Saviour

Confessing to God that I am a sinner, and believing that the Lord Jesus Christ died for my sins on the cross and was raised for my justification, I do now receive and confess Him as my personal Saviour.

NAME

DATE

Assurance As a Believer

That if you confess with your mouth Jesus as Lord, and believe in your heart that God raised Him from the dead, you shall be saved.

—Romans 10:9 (page 239)

Truly, truly, I say to you, he who hears My word, and believes Him who sent Me, has eternal life, and does not come into judgment, but has passed out of death into life. *—John 5:24 (page 143)*

These things I have written to you who believe in the name of the Son of God, in order that you may know that you have eternal life.

—1 John 5:13 (page 358)

But these have been written that you may believe that Jesus is the Christ, the Son of God; and that believing you may have life in His name.

—John 20:31 (page 172)